CIMA
STUDY TEXT

Stage 1 Paper 2

Cost Accounting and Quantitative Methods

First edition 1994
Fourth edition June 1997

ISBN 0 7517 3077 7 (previous edition 0 7517 3061 0)

British Library Cataloguing-in-Publication Data
A catalogue record for this book
is available from the British Library

Published by

BPP Publishing Limited
Aldine House, Aldine Place
London W12 8AW

Printed in Great Britain by
WM Print Ltd
Frederick Street
Walsall
West Midlands WS2 9NE

We are grateful to the Chartered Institute of Management Accountants for permission to reproduce past examination questions. The suggested solutions to the illustrative questions have been prepared by BPP Publishing Limited.

Contents

PREFACE

Professional exams are not easy. They demand your time and commitment over a period which can feel never-ending. You want to qualify and get on with your career - but you don't want to put your life on hold. You don't want to spend a moment longer studying than you have to ...

At BPP we believe strongly that the secret of success is effective study material which is focused and relevant to the exam *you* will be sitting. It needs to see you through the entire study process - from knowledge acquisition (the Study Text, your core study and reference book), through recap and practice (the Practice and Revision Kit, with exam-standard questions and plenty of revision features) to *final* exam revision (when Passcards are invaluable) - and success!

That's why we have designed and written this Study Text on *Cost Accounting and Quantitative Methods* to set you firmly on the first step - the acquisition of knowledge, skills and application techniques.

- We include the actual syllabus, so you know what you're up against, and we cover it comprehensively. We continually consult with the examiner to make sure we - and you - are right on track.
- We encourage you to study thoroughly and methodically, giving you plenty of opportunity to check that the topics are sinking in, whilst at the same time we help you to 'dip in' if you wish (see the *How to use this Study Text* section).
- We focus your mind on the examination, with recently-examined topics highlighted.
- All topics are up-to-date as at 1 June 1997 - the cut-off date for the November 1997 and May 1998 exams.

Cost Accounting and Quantitative Methods June 1997

Now in its fourth edition, this Study Text has been enhanced in the following ways:

- The new CIMA Syllabus Guidance Notes 1997-98 have been taken into account as the text has been updated
- The text has been fully updated to reflect the latest edition of CIMA's *Official Terminology*
- Full account has been taken of the topics in the May 1997 and November 1996 exams

Market leaders for 20 years in targeted study material for CIMA exams, at BPP we have the experience and the commitment to produce for our customers effective study material which is smart, focused and student-friendly. The rest is up to you. Good luck!

BPP Publishing
June 1997

For details of the other BPP titles relevant to your studies for this examination and for a full list of books in the BPP CIMA range, including our innovative CIMA PASSCARDS, please turn to the end of the text. If you send us your comments on this Study Text, you will automatically be entered in our FREE PRIZE DRAW.

HOW TO USE THIS STUDY TEXT

This Study Text has been designed to help students and lecturers to get to grips as effectively as possible with the content and scope of Paper 2 *Cost Accounting and Quantitative Methods*.

- The framework of this Study Text is structured so that many will find it to be the most coherent way of covering the syllabus. However we have also aimed to help those who choose to take a different path by indicating (in the Introduction section beginning each chapter) those areas which naturally precede the current chapter, and those chapters in which topics introduced can be further explored.

- Syllabus coverage in the text is indicated on pages (viii) to (x) by chapter references set against each syllabus topic. Syllabus topics are also identified within each chapter of the text. It is thus easy to trace your path through the syllabus.

- As a further guide - and a convenient means of monitoring your progress - we have included a study checklist on pages (xx) and (xxi) on which to chart your completion of chapters and their related illustrative questions.

Each chapter of the Study Text is divided into sections.

- An introduction places the subject of the chapter in its context in the syllabus and the examination.
- The text gives clear, concise topic-by-topic coverage.
- Examples and exercises reinforce learning, confirm understanding and stimulate thought.
- A 'roundup' at the end of the chapter pulls together the key points.
- A test your knowledge quiz helps you to check that you have absorbed the material in the chapter.

Some features of the Study Text are worth looking at in more detail.

Exercises

Exercises are provided throughout the text to enable you to check your progress as you work through the text. These come in a large variety of forms: some test your ability to do a calculation just described, others see whether you have taken in the full significance of a piece of information. Some are meant to be discussed with colleagues, friends or fellow students.

A suggested solution is usually given, but often in an abbreviated form to help you avoid the temptation of merely reading the exercise rather than actively engaging your brain. We think it is preferable on the whole to give the solution immediately after the exercise rather than making you hunt for it at the end of the chapter, losing your place and your concentration. Cover up the solution with a piece of paper if you find the temptation to cheat too great!

Examples can also often be used as exercises, if not the first time you read a passage, then certainly afterwards when you come to revise.

Chapter roundup and Test your knowledge quiz

At the end of each chapter you will find two boxes. The first is the *Chapter roundup* which summarises key points and arguments and sets out what you should know or be able to do having studied the chapter. The second box is a quiz that serves a number of purposes.

- It is an essential part of the chapter roundup and can be glanced over quickly to remind yourself of key issues covered by the chapter.

- It is a quiz pure and simple. Try doing it first thing in the morning to revise what you read the night before.

- It is a revision tool. Shortly before your examination sit down with pen and paper and try to answer all the questions fully. Many of the questions are typical of the four- or five-mark-earning opportunities that feature so regularly in examination questions.

Illustrative questions

Each chapter also has at least one illustrative question, in the bank at the end of the Study Text. Initially you might attempt such questions with reference to the chapter you have just covered. Later in your studies, it would be helpful to attempt some without support from the text. Only when you have attempted each question as fully as possible should you refer to the suggested solution to check and correct your performance.

Following the suggested solutions, there are several class questions, without solutions. These are intended to be used by lecturers. The solutions are given in a separate lecturers' pack, available only to bona fide lecturers.

A number of the illustrative questions and class questions are in the style of full exam questions. These questions are provided with mark and time allocations.

Glossary and index

Finally, we have included a glossary to define key terms and a comprehensive index to help you locate key topics.

A note on pronouns

On occasions in this Study Text, 'he' is used for 'he or she', 'him' for 'him or her' and so forth. Whilst we try to avoid this practice it is sometimes necessary for reasons of style. No prejudice or stereotyping according to sex is intended or assumed.

SYLLABUS

The syllabus contains a weighting for each syllabus area, and a ranking of the level of ability required in each topic. The Institute has published the following explanatory notes on these points.

Study weightings

A percentage weighting is shown against each topic in the syllabus; this is intended as a guide to the amount of study time each topic requires.

All topics in a syllabus must be studied, as a question may examine more than one topic, or carry a higher proportion of marks than the percentage study time suggested.

The weightings do not specify the number of marks which will be allocated to topics in the examination.

Abilities required in the examination

Each examination paper contains a number of topics. Each topic has been given a number to indicate the level of ability required of the candidate.

The numbers range from 1 to 4 and represent the following ability levels:

Appreciation (1)
To understand a knowledge area at an early stage of learning, or outside the core of management accounting, at a level which enables the accountant to communicate and work with other members of the management team.

Knowledge (2)
To have detailed knowledge of such matters as laws, standards, facts and techniques so as to advise at a level appropriate to a management accounting specialist.

Skill (3)
To apply theoretical knowledge, concepts and techniques to the solutions of problems where it is clear what technique has to be used and the information needed is clearly indicated.

Application (4)
To apply knowledge and skills where candidates have to determine from a number of techniques which is the most appropriate and select the information required from a fairly wide range of data, some of which might not be relevant; to exercise professional judgement and to communicate and work with members of the management team and other recipients of financial reports.

Syllabus overview

This syllabus contains the two complementary areas of cost accounting and quantitative methods. In each area great importance will be attached to fundamental numeracy, analytical techniques and computer literacy. Students will be expected to understand the basic methods and techniques of cost accounting, and when and why they are used in practice. They should also have the ability to understand and interpret statistical and mathematical information.

The syllabus as a whole provides the essential background techniques for Operational Cost Accounting and Management Science Applications at Stage 2.

Aims

To test the candidate's ability to

- understand how component elements of cost make up the total cost of an activity, service or product
- prepare cost accounting records and statements of profit for management from cost accounting records in particular operational environments
- explain the purpose of various cost accounting methods and activities; explain their relevance to management and decision making
- recognise when a quantitative approach is applicable
- use quantitative methods to obtain accurate and reliable management information; explain and present results

Content and ability required

	Ability required	Covered in Chapter
2(a) Elements of cost *(study weighting 15%)*		
How and why costs are classified	2	1
Cost behaviour	2	2
Materials: cost collection	3	3
Stock valuation methods; the effect on profit of the valuation method selected	3	3
Labour: cost allocation; payroll routine	3	4
Overhead cost: classification and analysis	3	1,5
Principles of apportionment and absorption into cost centres and units; departmental accounts	3	5
Application of marginal costing principles to management reporting and the preparation of profit and loss accounts	3	6
Relevant cost concepts	2	7
2(b) Cost accounting systems *(study weighting 20%)*		
Work in progress accounts for job costing and process costing	3	9,10
Profit and loss accounts for job costing and process costing systems	3	9,10
Cost accounting statements for services and service industries	3	11
Accounting entries for integrated and non-integrated accounting systems	3	8
2(c) Budgets and variance accounting *(study weighting 15%)*		
Budget preparation, including a master budget and simple cash budget	3	12
The use of computers for budgeting	2	13
Reconciliation of operational cash flow with operating profit	3	12
Cost estimation and estimating techniques	3	13
Principles of standard costs	2	14
Preparation of a standard product cost	3	14
Variances: materials - total, price and usage; labour - total, rate and efficiency; overheads - total	3	15
2(d) Basic mathematics *(study weighting 5%)*		
Handling formulae (the use of positive and negative numbers, brackets and powers)	3	16
Percentages; ratios; discounts	3	16
Formulae in spreadsheets	3	16

		Ability required	Covered in Chapter
2(e)	**Summarising and analysing data** *(study weighting 15%)*		
	Sources of data; collection and tabulation	3	18,19
	Accuracy and approximation	3	17
	Presentation: summarisation and interpretation of collected data	3	19
	Graphs and diagrams	2	19
	Averages and variation for grouped and ungrouped data	3	20,21
	Index numbers and their uses	3	22
2(f)	**Sampling and probability** *(study weighting 10%)*		
	Probability: simple addition and multiplication rules; expected values; payoff tables	3	23
	Random and non-random sampling methods	2	18
	Properties and characteristics of the normal distribution	3	24
	Standard errors and confidence intervals for means and percentages	3	24
	Problems of sample size	2	18,24
2(g)	**Introduction to financial mathematics** *(study weighting 10%)*		
	Simple interest; compound interest; Annual Percentage Rate (APR)	3	25
	Discounting	3	26
	Simple applications (eg annuities and perpetuities, investments, and depreciation)	3	25,26
2(h)	**Introduction to forecasting** *(study weighting 10%)*		
	Elementary time series analysis: trend, seasonality, random fluctuations	3	27
	Establishing a line of best fit, either by inspection or by regression	3	27, 28
	Correlation	3	28

CIMA SYLLABUS GUIDANCE NOTES 1997-98

The following Guidance Notes will be published by the CIMA in the August 1997 CIMA Student *as an aid to students and lecturers.*

'The following guidelines have been drafted by the chief examiner for each of the subjects. They are intended to inform candidates and lecturers about the scope of the syllabus, the emphasis which should be placed on various topics and the approach which the examination papers will adopt.

These guidance notes are applicable immediately, insofar as they provide a general guidance on each subject. Where any major changes are indicated, these will not be applicable until the May 1998 examination (and will be highlighted, where relevant, in the notes).

Introduction

For the convenience of study and presentation, this syllabus is divided into eight sections, (a) to (h). However, candidates must remember that real problems in management accounting do not come in watertight boxes and in order to reflect this, questions may be set which range across more than one area of the syllabus. This means that the divisions of the syllabus are to an extent arbitrary and the study weightings are an approximate guide only. For example, sections (a) and (b), elements of cost and cost accounting systems, are very closely inter-related.

The overall aim of the cost accounting section of the syllabus is to ensure that candidates have a sound grasp of the fundamentals of cost accounting. They must demonstrate not only a detailed understanding of how basic principles are used, but also why they are used and their advantages and shortcomings. The development of a questioning, critical attitude to traditional methods and techniques is important preparation for a would-be chartered management accountant. An awareness of recent developments is required, particularly in terms of their effects on cost accounting systems.

The major objective of the quantitative methods section of the syllabus is to develop the three areas of competence that are all vital to the successful training and education of a chartered management accountant.

• Knowledge of available quantitative methods

• Understanding of how and why the methods are used

• Understanding and appreciation of the significance of the solutions provided by such quantitative methods

The quantitative methods syllabus is not intended to produce mathematicians or statisticians. It sets out to develop numeracy and the confidence to use basic, but essential, quantitative tools.

The examination paper

The examination paper will be in two sections, Cost Accounting and Quantitative Methods. Each section will be worth 50 marks and each will have a compulsory question consisting of ten multiple-choice sub-questions. These will range over the whole of the respective syllabuses. The other questions in each section are worth 15 marks each and candidates will have the choice of two questions out of three within each section. Although the paper is in two sections, performance will be judged on the basis of the total mark for the paper as a whole.

In general, cost accounting questions and quantitative methods questions will be separated into the two respective sections of the examination. However, because cost accounting is a numerical subject, it is inevitable that some basic mathematical or quantitative techniques which are listed in the quantitative methods section of the syllabus may be used within a cost accounting question. Examples include: handling formulae, percentages, interest and discounting calculations, graphs and diagrams.

Questions in the cost accounting section may require either numerical or discursive answers, or a mixture of the two. Although much basic cost accounting is carried out nowadays by computers, chartered management accountants still need numerical ability and this will be tested from time to time.

Applications other than manufacturing may form the background to questions. These may include: service industries, not-for-profit organisations, public sector organisations etc. Specific knowledge of these areas is *not* required.

Elements of cost   *Syllabus reference 2(a)*

This section deals with the various classifications of costs, eg labour/material/overheads, direct/indirect, fixed/semi-fixed/variable and how material, labour and overhead costs are collected.

In the examination, candidates may be required to do the following.

- Demonstrate a knowledge of the documentation and procedures associated with materials and labour including: storage, reception and issue, issue pricing, wage payment systems, the treatment of waste and idle time and so on.

- Demonstrate a knowledge of stock control levels.

- Demonstrate a thorough knowledge of the analysis of cost and the build-up of product cost using a conventional absorption approach.

- Demonstrate an appreciation of activity based costing (ABC).

- Carry out the apportionment of service department costs to production or operating departments.

- Apply a knowledge of marginal costing principles in the presentation of reports and statements, in decision making and in stock valuation.

- Identify relevant costs and carry out basic decision analysis including make or buy, choice of product, special order acceptance and single limiting factor decisions. These decisions would be based on contribution analysis, but an appreciation of other possible relevant costs, eg differential costs and opportunity costs, is required.

The following items are *not* examinable.

- Numerical calculations using ABC
- Reciprocal servicing within overhead apportionment
- Derivation/calculation of the economic order quantity (EOQ)
- Breakeven analysis, breakeven charts and profit charts

Cost accounting systems   *Syllabus reference 2(b)*

Candidates must be able to deal with the detailed accounting entries for all the types of systems mentioned in the syllabus.

Profit and loss accounts and other accounts may be based on either marginal or absorption costing principles.

In the examination, candidates may be required to do the following.

- Prepare accounting entries for standard cost systems.

- Deal with process losses, process gains and closing work-in-progress in a system of process costing.

- Demonstrate an awareness of the distinction between joint products and by-products and of their accounting treatment.

The following items are *not* examinable.

- Opening work-in-progress in a system of process costing
- Standard process costing
- The apportionment of joint costs between joint products

Budgets and variance accounting   *Syllabus reference 2(c)*

In the examination, candidates may be required to do the following.

- Prepare budgets, including flexible budgets.

- Calculate budget variances by comparing actual results with an appropriate flexed budget.
- Calculate basic variances as detailed in the syllabus, using absorption costing principles.
- Demonstrate an awareness of the arguments regarding the appropriateness, or otherwise, of standard costing in the modern industrial environment.
- Reconcile the profit and cash flow for a period, demonstrating a thorough understanding of the difference between them.

The following items are *not* examinable.

- The behavioural aspects of budgeting
- Zero-base budgeting
- Detailed overhead variance analysis and materials mix and yield variances

Basic mathematics
Syllabus reference 2(d)

The skills required for this part of the syllabus are fundamental and underpin all other parts. It is unlikely that a whole question would be based on this single section, but questions from other sections will draw on these skills.

In the examination, candidates may be required to do the following.

- Use the four rules of number: addition, subtraction, multiplication and division.
- Handle formulae and equations including simultaneous and quadratic equations.

Summarising and analysing data
Syllabus reference 2(e)

In the examination, candidates may be required to do the following.

- Demonstrate a knowledge of the characteristics of various sampling methods used to collect data, such as simple random sampling, multi-stage sampling, stratified sampling, quota and cluster sampling, and when they are appropriate.
- Answer numeric questions on sampling, based on simple random samples.
- Demonstrate an awareness of the main characteristics of interviewing and questionnaires.
- Summarise a set of raw data into a frequency table and from this
  - draw up a histogram and cumulative frequency table
  - calculate the arithmetic mean, the variance and the standard deviation.
- Derive or identify the median, the mode, upper and lower quartiles and deciles.
- Plot and interpret a range of charts and diagrams, eg various forms of bar chart, pie charts, Z charts, time series, semi-logarithmic charts and so on.
- Demonstrate a familiarity with the basic structure of price and quantity indexes, both base and current weighted.
- Use an index number series to take into account the effects of inflation, ie time series deflation.

The following item is *not* examinable.

- Calculations involving either the harmonic mean or the geometric mean

Sampling and probability
Syllabus reference 2(f)

Managers have to cope with risk and uncertainty, and probability is a major tool to handle this. Furthermore, many decisions are made on the basis of sample information.

In the examination, candidates may be required to do the following.

- Make an inference about a population mean or proportion based on sample evidence and calculate the appropriate confidence interval, for simple random samples only.
- Apply a knowledge of the properties and characteristics of the Normal Distribution.
- Demonstrate an understanding of the factors that determine an appropriate sample size both from a statistical and administrative viewpoint.
- Demonstrate knowledge of permutations and combinations.

The following item is *not* examinable.

- Bayes Theorem

Introduction to financial mathematics   *Syllabus reference 2(g)*

In the examination, candidates may be required to do the following.

- Demonstrate a sound working knowledge of simple and compound interest and the progressions which underlie these concepts.

- Use and interpret introductory discounted cash flow techniques such as net present value and internal rate of return. The discount rate will always be supplied.

- Use discount tables to deal with various cash flow patterns, both irregular and regular, ie annuities.

- Calculate and use perpetuity factors.

The following items are *not* examinable.

- The calculation of the annual percentage rate (APR) on loans
- The measurement of the cost of capital

Introduction to forecasting   *Syllabus reference 2(h)*

In the examination, candidates may be required to do the following.

- Construct a short-term forecast by calculating the trend using moving averages, the seasonal factors and the random fluctuations using either the additive or multiplicative models. Questions will specify the approach to be used.

- Fit and extrapolate a linear least-squares line of best fit to a time series for longer term forecasts or make forecasts of movements in one variable based on movements in an associated variable, eg predictions of sales based on advertising expenditure.

- Calculate the co-efficient of linear correlation and co-efficient of determination between two sets of variables and comment on the quality of a forecast based on linear regression.

- In addition, although not a forecasting technique, be able to calculate and use Spearman's Rank Correlation Coefficient.

BPP MEETS THE EXAMINERS

BPP keeps in touch with the CIMA examiners and seeks to determine the precise limits of the syllabus. On this page, we summarise the key points in question and answer form.

Will the examination of cost behaviour require students to use both simple linear ($y = a + bx$) and non-linear ($y = a + bx + cx^2$) equations?

Yes.

Could students be required to use both graphical and arithmetic approaches in their solutions to cost behaviour questions?

Yes

Are Lorenz curves examinable?

No.

Do students need to be aware of, and be able to use, Spearman's Rank correlation coefficient?

Yes

Are students expected to be aware of the concept of permutations and combinations?

Yes

Do students need to know about Bessel's correction factor?

No.

Could investment appraisal questions incorporate the use of expected values to assess risk?

Yes.

Will students be provided with any formulae required which are not in the Mathematical Tables?

Yes.

 BPP Publishing

THE EXAMINATION PAPER

Assessment methods and format of the paper

		Number of marks
Section A:	one compulsory question composed of ten multiple-choice sub-questions	20
Section B:	two questions from three	30
Section C:	one compulsory question composed of ten multiple-choice sub-questions	20
Section D:	two questions from three	30
		100

Time allowed : 3 hours

The cost accounting content and the quantitative methods content will each count for 50% of the marks. Sections A and B will contain cost accounting questions and sections C and D will concentrate on quantitative methods.

Analysis of past papers

The analysis below shows the topics which have been examined in the five sittings of the exam and the CIMA specimen paper for *Cost Accounting and Quantitative Methods*.

May 1997

Section A
1   Ten multiple choice questions covering various cost accounting topics

Section B
2   Fixed and variable costs
3   Functional and flexed budgets, budgeted profits
4   Standard costing and variances

Section C
5   Ten multiple choice questions covering various quantitative methods topics

Section D
6   Expectation and decision making
7   Discounting
8   The Normal Distribution

November 1996

Section A
1   Ten multiple choice questions covering various cost accounting topics

Section B
2   Forecast profits
3   Overhead absorption
4   Service costing

Section C
5   Ten multiple choice questions covering various quantitative methods topics

Section D
6   Sampling
7   Accuracy and appropriation
8   Time series analysts

May 1996

Section A

1   Ten multiple choice questions covering various cost accounting topics

Section B

2   Marginal costing and absorption costing
3   Standard costing and variance analysis
4   Process costing

Section C

5   Ten multiple choice questions covering various quantitative methods topics

Section D

6   Data presentation, averages and dispersion
7   Discounting
8   Sampling theory

November 1995

Section A

1   Ten multiple choice questions covering various cost accounting topics

Section B

2   Absorption costing
3   Profitability
4   Decision making

Section C

5   Ten multiple choice questions covering various quantitative methods topics

Section D

6   Regression
7   Index numbers
8   Probability

May 1995

Section A

1   Ten multiple choice questions covering various cost accounting
     topics

Section B

2   Marginal costing
3   Budgeting
4   Cost bookkeeping

Section C

5   Ten multiple choice questions covering various quantitative methods topics

Section D

6   Discounting
7   Correlation and regression
8   Averages and dispersion, presentation of data

Specimen paper

Section A

1   Ten multiple choice questions covering various cost accounting topics

Section B

2   Standard costing and variance analysis
3   Process costing; joint products and by-products
4   Overhead allocation, apportionment and absorption; developing cost accounting systems

Section C

5   Ten multiple choice questions covering various quantitative methods topics

Section D

6   Time series analysis and forecasting
7   Compounding and discounting
8   Calculation of arithmetic mean and standard deviation; construction of histogram and estimation of mode; probability

THE MEANING OF EXAMINERS' INSTRUCTIONS

The examinations department of the CIMA has asked the Institute's examiners to be precise when drafting questions. In particular, examiners have been asked to use precise instruction words. It will probably help you to know what instruction words may be used, and what they mean. With the Institute's permission, their list of recommended requirement words, and their meaning, is shown below.

Recommended requirement words are:

Advise/recommend	Present information, opinions or recommendations to someone to enable that recipient to take action
Amplify	Expand or enlarge upon the meaning of (a statement or quotation)
Analyse	Determine and explain the constituent parts of
Appraise/assess/evaluate	Judge the importance or value of
Assess	See 'appraise'
Clarify	Explain more clearly the meaning of
Comment (critically)	Explain
Compare (with)	Explain similarities and differences between
Contrast	Place in opposition to bring out difference(s)
Criticise	Present the faults in a theory or policy or opinion
Demonstrate	Show by reasoning the truth of
Describe	Present the details and characteristics of
Discuss	Explain the opposing arguments
Distinguish	Specify the differences between
Evaluate	See 'appraise'
Explain/interpret	Set out in detail the meaning of
Illustrate	Use an example - chart, diagram, graph or figure as appropriate - to explain something
Interpret	See 'explain'
Justify	State adequate grounds for
List (and explain)	Itemise (and detail the meaning of)
Prove	Show by testing the accuracy of
Recommend	See 'advise'
Reconcile	Make compatible apparently conflicting statements or theories
Relate	Show connections between separate matters
State	Express
Summarise	State briefly the essential points (dispensing with examples and details)
Tabulate	Set out facts or figures in a table

Requirement words which will be avoided

Examiners have been asked to avoid instructions which are imprecise or which may not specifically elicit an answer. The following words will *not* be used.

Consider	as candidates could do this without writing a word
Define	in the sense of stating exactly what a thing is, as CIMA wishes to avoid requiring evidence of rote learning
Examine	as this is what the Examiner is doing, not the candidate
Enumerate	list is preferred
Identify	
Justify	when the requirement is not 'to state adequate grounds for' but 'to state the advantage of'
List	on its own, without an additional requirement such as 'list and explain'
Outline	as its meaning is imprecise. The addition of the word 'briefly' to any of the suggested action words is more satisfactory
Review	
Specify	
Trace	

STUDY CHECKLIST

This page is designed to help you chart your progress through the Study Text, including the illustrative questions at the back of it. You can tick off each topic as you study and try questions on it. Insert the dates you complete the chapters and questions in the relevant boxes. You will thus ensure that you are on track to complete your study before the exam.

	Text chapters Date completed	Illustrative questions Question numbers	Date completed

PART A: ELEMENTS OF COST

1	Cost accounting and cost classification	1	
2	Cost behaviour	2	
3	Material costs	3,4	
4	Labour costs	5	
5	Overhead apportionment and absorption	6	
6	Marginal costing and absorption costing	7	
7	Relevant costing and decision making	8	

PART B: COST ACCOUNTING SYSTEMS

8	Cost bookkeeping	9	
9	Job, batch and output costing	10	
10	Process costing	11	
11	Service costing	12	

PART C: BUDGETS AND VARIANCE ACCOUNTING

12	Preparing the master budget	13	
13	Further aspects of budgeting	14	
14	Introduction to standard costing	15	
15	Variance analysis	16	

PART D: BASIC MATHEMATICS

16	Basic mathematics	17	
17	Accuracy and approximation	18	

PART E: SUMMARISING AND ANALYSING DATA

18	The collection of data	19	
19	Data presentation	20	
20	Averages	21	
21	Dispersion	22	
22	Index numbers	23	

STUDY CHECKLIST (continued)

		Text chapters *Date completed*	Illustrative questions *Question number*	*Date completed*

PART F: SAMPLING AND PROBABILITY

23	Probability		24	
24	The normal distribution and sampling theory		25	

PART G: INTRODUCTION TO FINANCIAL MATHEMATICS

25	Interest		26	
26	Discounting		27	

PART H: INTRODUCTION TO FORECASTING

27	Time series analysis		28	
28	Correlation and regression		29	

Part A
Elements of cost

Chapter 1

COST ACCOUNTING AND COST CLASSIFICATION

<table>
<tr><td colspan="3">This chapter covers the following topics.</td></tr>
<tr><td></td><td>Syllabus reference</td><td>Ability required</td></tr>
<tr><td>1   What is cost accounting?</td><td>2(a)</td><td>Knowledge</td></tr>
<tr><td>2   The organisation, cost centres and cost units</td><td>2(a)</td><td>Knowledge</td></tr>
<tr><td>3   Cost classification</td><td>2(a)</td><td>Knowledge</td></tr>
<tr><td>4   Cost classification for stock valuation and profit measurement</td><td>2(a)</td><td>Knowledge</td></tr>
<tr><td>5   Cost classification for decision making</td><td>2(a)</td><td>Knowledge</td></tr>
<tr><td>6   Cost classification for control</td><td>2(a)</td><td>Knowledge</td></tr>
</table>

Introduction

Welcome to cost accounting and quantitative methods, two topics which may, or may not, be new to you. You are going to be tackling cost accounting first, moving on to quantitative methods in the second part of this Study Text. This chapter will introduce the subject of cost accounting and explain what cost accounting is and what a cost accountant does. We will briefly consider how an organisation is structured from the point of view of the cost accountant and we will then turn our attention to costs (because that is what cost accounting is all about) and look at the various ways in which they can be classified to assist the cost accountant in his work.

An understanding of the areas covered in this chapter is vital before you proceed with any other chapter in this half of the Study Text and you are strongly advised to work through it very carefully. Moreover, terms and concepts introduced in this chapter could well feature in the multiple choice section of the paper. The examiner commented in his report on the May 95 exam, that 'Somewhat surprisingly, some candidates did not know even basic terminology such as the meaning of prime cost'. Make sure that you do!

Your study of cost behaviour in Chapter 2 will use the knowledge gained from this chapter on how costs can be divided into fixed and variable components.

1 WHAT IS COST ACCOUNTING?

1.1 Who can provide the answers to the following questions?

(a) What has the cost of goods produced or services provided been?
(b) What has the cost of operating a department been?
(c) What have revenues been?

Yes, you've guessed it, the cost accountant.

1.2 Knowing about costs incurred or revenues earned enables management to do the following.

(a) Assess the profitability of a product, a service, a department, or the organisation in total.

(b) Perhaps, set selling prices with some regard for the costs of sale.

(c) Put a value to stocks of goods (raw materials, work in progress, finished goods) that are still held in store at the end of a period, for preparing a balance sheet of the company's assets and liabilities.

1.3 That was quite easy. But who could answer the following questions?

(a) What are the future costs of goods and services likely to be?

(b) How do actual costs compare with planned costs?

(c) What information does management need in order to make sensible decisions about profits and costs?

Well, you may be surprised, but again it is the cost accountant.

1.4 Originally cost accounting did deal with ways of accumulating historical costs and of charging these costs to units of output, or to departments, in order to establish stock valuations, profits and balance sheet items (and hence enable cost accountants to answer the first set of questions above). It has since been extended into planning, control and decision making, so that the cost accountant is now able to answer the second set of questions. In today's modern industrial environment, the role of cost accounting in the provision of management information is therefore almost indistinguishable from that of management accounting, which is basically concerned with the provision of information to assist management with planning, control and decision making.

1.5 The managers of a business have the responsibility of planning and controlling the resources used. To carry out this task effectively they must be provided with sufficiently accurate and detailed information, and the cost accounting system should provide this. Cost accounting is a management information system which analyses past, present and future data to provide the basis for managerial action.

1.6 It would be wrong to suppose that cost accounting systems are restricted to manufacturing operations, although they are probably more fully developed in this area of work. Service industries, government departments and welfare organisations are all examples of areas where use can be made of cost accounting information. Within a manufacturing organisation, the cost accounting system should be applied not only to manufacturing but also to administration, selling and distribution, research and development and so on.

1.7 So, cost accounting is concerned with the following.

(a) Establishing stock valuations, profits and balance sheet items
(b) Planning
(c) Control
(d) Decision making

The relationship with financial accounting

1.8 The financial accounting and cost accounting systems in a business both record the same basic data for income and expenditure, but each set of records may analyse the data in a different way. This is because each system has a different purpose.

1.9 Financial accounting is primarily a method of reporting the results and financial position of a business. Although the financial accounts may be of interest to management, their principal function is to satisfy the information needs of those not involved in the day-to-day running of the business. Shareholders, for instance, may use them to assess how well the directors have carried out their stewardship function. Other outsiders whose information needs are satisfied wholly or in part by the financial accounts are suppliers, customers, employees and the Inland Revenue. In addition, there is a legal requirement to prepare financial accounts and they must be prepared in accordance with strict guidelines which are laid down in company law and in accounting standards and statements.

1.10 Cost accounting is an internal reporting system for an organisation's own management, providing it with the information which it needs to manage the business. Outsiders will not see this information, and there are no strict rules which govern the way in which cost accounting information should be prepared and presented. Each organisation can develop a system best suited to its individual needs, but since there is no legal requirement to operate a costing system, one will only be operated if management believes that cost information will help it to plan and control the resources of the organisation more efficiently than if no formal costing system existed.

2   THE ORGANISATION, COST CENTRES AND COST UNITS

2.1 An organisation, whether it is a manufacturing company, a provider of services (such as a bank or a hotel) or a public sector organisation (such as a hospital), is divided into a number of different *functions* within which there are a number of *departments*. A manufacturing organisation might be structured as follows.

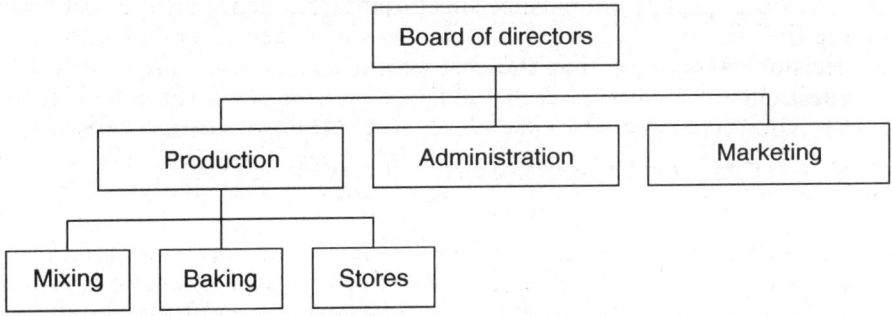

2.2 Suppose the organisation above produces chocolate cakes for a number of supermarket chains. The production function is involved with the making of the cakes, the administration department with the preparation of accounts and the employment of staff and the marketing department with the selling and distribution of the cakes.

2.3 Within the production function there are three departments, two of which are production departments (the mixing department and the baking department) which are actively involved in the production of the cakes and one of which is a service department (stores department) which provides a service or back-up to the production departments.

2.4 The administration function will be divided into a number of administration departments and the marketing function will be divided into a number of marketing, selling and distribution departments.

2.5 *In general*, for cost accounting purposes, departments are termed *cost centres* and the product produced by an organisation is termed the *cost unit*. In our example, the cost centres of the production function could be the mixing department, the baking department and the stores department and the organisation's cost unit could be one chocolate cake.

2.6 Different organisations use different cost units. Here are some suggestions.

Organisation	*Possible cost unit*
Steelworks	Tonne of steel produced
	Tonne of coke used
Hospital	Patient/day
	Operation
	Out-patient visit
Freight organisation	Tonne/kilometre (ton/mile)
Passenger transport organisation	Passenger/kilometre or mile
Accounting firm	Audit performed
	Chargeable hour
Restaurant	Meal served

2.7   One of the principal purposes of cost accounting is therefore to determine the cost of a single cost unit (for stock valuation and profit reporting purposes).

3   COST CLASSIFICATION

3.1   Before any attempt is made to establish stock valuations and measure profits, to plan, make decisions or exercise control (in other words, do any cost accounting), costs must be classified. Classification involves arranging costs into groupings of similar items in order to make stock valuation, profit measurement, planning, decision making and control easier.

4   COST CLASSIFICATION FOR STOCK VALUATION AND PROFIT MEASUREMENT

4.1   For the purposes of stock valuation and profit measurement, the cost accountant must calculate the cost of one unit of the product in question. The cost of a product (product cost) is made up of the following three elements of cost.

(a)   Materials
(b)   Labour
(c)   Other expenses (such as rent and rates, interest charges and so on)

Cost elements can be classified as direct costs or indirect costs.

Direct cost

4.2   A direct cost is a cost that can be traced in full to the product, service, or department that is being costed.

(a)   Direct materials costs are the costs of materials that are known to have been used in making and selling a product (or even providing a service).

(b)   Direct labour costs are the specific costs of the workforce used to make a product or provide a service. Direct labour costs are established by measuring the time taken for a job, or the time taken in 'direct production work'.

(c)   Other direct expenses are those expenses that have been incurred in full as a direct consequence of making a product, or providing a service, or running a department (depending on whether a product, a service or a department is being costed).

Indirect cost/overhead cost

4.3   An indirect cost /or overhead cost is a cost that is incurred in the course of making a product, providing a service or running a department, but which cannot be traced directly and in full to the product, service or department. Examples might be the cost of supervisors' wages, cleaning materials and buildings insurance.

4.4   Total expenditure may therefore be analysed as follows.

Materials cost	=	Direct materials cost	+	Indirect materials cost
+		+		+
Labour cost	=	Direct labour cost	+	Indirect labour cost
+		+		+
Expenses	=	Direct expenses		Indirect expenses
Total cost	=	Direct cost	+	Overhead cost

4.5   The CIMA *Official Terminology* restricts the term *prime cost* to direct materials and direct labour, but you will often find that questions also include direct expenses in prime cost.

4.6   You should be able to specify whether an item of expenditure is classed as a direct materials cost, a direct labour cost, a production overhead and so on. Further information on such cost items is given below.

Direct materials, labour and expenses

4.7 (a) All material becoming part of the product (unless used in negligible amounts and/or having negligible cost) is *direct material*, the cost of which is charged to the product as part of the prime cost. Materials used in negligible amounts and/or having negligible cost can be grouped under indirect materials as part of overhead. Examples of direct materials are as follows.

  (i)   Materials, including component parts, specially purchased for a particular job, order or process

  (ii)   Primary packing materials like cartons and boxes

(b) All wages paid for labour expended on work on the product itself are *direct wages*, the cost of which is charged to the product as part of the prime cost. Some indirect wages which can be accurately identified with the product (such as those paid to the foreman) may be considered a direct cost of the product and be included as direct wages. Examples of groups of labour receiving payment as direct wages are as follows.

  (i)   Workers engaged in altering the condition, conformation or composition of the product

  (ii)   Inspectors, analysts and testers *specifically required* for such production

  (iii) Foremen, chargehands, shop clerks and anyone else whose wages are *specifically identified* with production of the product

(c) If any expenses are incurred on a specific product other than the costs of direct materials and direct labour, these are *direct expenses*, the cost of which is charged to the product as part of the prime cost. Examples of direct expenses (chargeable expenses) are as follows.

  (i)   The cost of special designs, drawings or layouts
  (ii)   The hire of tools or equipment for a particular job
  (iii) Maintenance costs of tools, jigs, fixtures and so on

Overheads

4.8 (a) All indirect materials cost, indirect wages and indirect expenses incurred in the factory from receipt of the order until its completion are included in *production (or factory) overhead*. Examples are as follows.

  (i)   Indirect materials which cannot be traced to the finished product, such as minor items of material used either in negligible amounts or amounts which it is uneconomic to allocate to a particular product, like glue in box-making.

  (ii)   Indirect wages, meaning all wages not charged directly to a product, which generally includes salaries and wages of non-productive personnel in the production department, such as foremen, inspectors, general labourers, maintenance staff and stores staff.

  (iii) Indirect expenses (other than indirect materials and labour) not charged directly to production. Expenses included under this heading could include the rent, rates and insurance of a factory or depreciation, fuel, power, repairs and maintenance of plant, machinery and factory buildings.

(b) All indirect materials costs, wages and expenses incurred in the direction, control and administration of an undertaking are included in *administration overhead*. Examples are as follows.

  (i)   Depreciation of office machines

  (ii)   Office salaries, including salaries of secretaries and accountants

  (iii) Rent, rates, insurance, lighting, cleaning and heating of general offices, telephone and postal charges, bank charges, legal charges, audit fees and depreciation and repairs to office buildings and machinery

(c) All indirect materials costs, wages and expenses incurred in promoting sales and retaining customers are included in *selling overhead*. Examples are as follows.

  (i)   Salaries and commission of salesmen, representatives and sales department staff

      (ii)   Advertising and sales promotion, market research

      (iii)   Rent, rates and insurance of sales offices and showrooms, bad debts and collection charges, cash discounts allowed and after sales service

(d) *Distribution overhead* includes all indirect materials costs, wages and expenses incurred in making the packed product ready for despatch and delivering it to the customer. Examples of distribution overhead are as follows.

      (i)   Cost of packing cases and materials (for example oil and spare parts) used in the upkeep of delivery vehicles

      (ii)   Wages of packers, drivers and despatch clerks

      (iii)   Freight and insurance charges, rent, rates, insurance and depreciation of warehouses and depreciation and running expenses of delivery vehicles

---

Exercise 1

A direct labour employee's wage in week 5 consists of the following.

		£
(a)	Basic pay for normal hours worked, 36 hours at £4 per hour =	144
(b)	Pay at the basic rate for overtime, 6 hours at £4 per hour =	24
(c)	Overtime shift premium, with overtime paid at time-and-a-quarter ¼ × 6 hours × £4 per hour =	6
(d)	A bonus payment under a group bonus (or 'incentive') scheme =	30
	Total gross wages in week 5 for 42 hours of work	204

Required

Establish which costs are direct costs and which are indirect costs.

Solution

Items (a) and (b) are direct labour costs of the items produced in the 42 hours worked in week 5.

Overtime premium, item (c), is usually regarded as an overhead expense, because it is 'unfair' to charge the items produced in overtime hours with the premium. Why should an item made in overtime be more costly just because, by chance, it was made after the employee normally clocks off for the day?

Group bonus scheme payments, item (d), are usually overhead costs because they cannot normally be traced directly to individual products or jobs.

In this example, the direct labour employee costs were £168 in direct costs and £36 in indirect costs.

Product costs — identified with a product or service
Period costs — deducted as expenses

Product costs and period costs

4.9   When preparing financial statements (a profit and loss account and balance sheet), accountants frequently distinguish between product costs and period costs.

4.10   *Product costs* are costs identified with goods produced or purchased for resale. Such costs are initially identified as part of the value of stock. They become expenses (in the form of cost of goods sold) only when the stock is sold. In contrast, *period costs* are costs that are deducted as expenses during the current period without ever being included in the value of stock held.

4.11   Consider a retailer who acquires goods for resale without changing their basic form. The only product cost is therefore the purchase cost of the goods. Any unsold goods are held as stock, valued at the lower of purchase cost and net realisable value and included as an asset in the balance sheet. As the goods are sold, their cost becomes an expense in the form of 'cost of goods sold'. A retailer will also incur a variety of selling and administration expenses. Such costs are period costs because they are deducted from revenue without ever being regarded as part of the value of stock.

PRIME COST
=
Direct Materials
+
Direct wages
+
Direct Expenses

4.12 Now consider a manufacturing firm in which direct materials are transformed into saleable goods with the help of direct labour and factory overheads. All these costs are product costs because they are allocated to the value of stock until the goods are sold. As with the retailer, selling and administration expenses are regarded as period costs.

Functional costs

4.13 In a 'traditional' costing system for a manufacturing organisation, costs are classified as follows.

Manufacturing
Admin
Marketing

(a) Production or manufacturing costs
(b) Administration costs
(c) Marketing, or selling and distribution costs

Many expenses fall comfortably into one or other of these three broad classifications. Manufacturing costs are associated with the factory, selling and distribution costs with the sales, marketing, warehousing and transport departments and administration costs with general office departments (such as accounting and personnel). Classification in this way is known as classification by function. Other expenses that do not fall fully into one of these classifications might be categorised as 'general overheads' or even classified on their own (for example research and development costs).

4.14 In costing a small product made by a manufacturing organisation, direct costs are usually restricted to some of the production costs (although it is not uncommon to find a salesman's commission for selling the product as a direct selling cost). A commonly found build-up of costs is therefore as follows.

	£
Production costs	
Direct materials	A
Direct wages	B
Direct expenses	C
Prime cost	A+B+C
Production overheads	D
Full factory cost	A+B+C+D
Administration costs	E
Selling and distribution costs	F
Full cost of sales	A+B+C+D+E+F

Exercise 2

Within the costing system of a manufacturing company the following types of expense are incurred.

Reference number

q	1	Cost of oils used to lubricate production machinery
b	2	Motor vehicle licences for lorries
a	3	Depreciation of factory plant and equipment
d	4	Cost of chemicals used in the laboratory
b	5	Commission paid to sales representatives
c	6	Salary of the secretary to the finance director
b	7	Trade discount given to customers
d	8	Holiday pay of machine operatives
q	9	Salary of security guard in raw materials warehouse
b	10	Fees to advertising agency
b	11	Rent of finished goods warehouse
d	12	Salary of scientist in laboratory
c	13	Insurance of the company's premises
d	14	Salary of supervisor working in the factory
c	15	Cost of typewriter ribbons in the general office
d	16	Protective clothing for machine operatives

Required

Place each expense within the following classifications.

(a)   Production costs
(b)   Selling and distribution costs
(c)   Administration costs
(d)   Research and development costs

Each type of expense should appear only once in your answer. You may use the reference numbers in your answer.

Solution

The reference number for each expense can be classified as follows.

		Reference numbers
(a)	Production costs	1, 3, 8, 9, 14, 16
(b)	Selling and distribution costs	2, 5, 7, 10,11
(c)	Administration costs	6, 13, 15
(d)	Research and development costs	4, 12

5   COST CLASSIFICATION FOR DECISION MAKING

5.1   Decision making is based on the occurrence of future events and hence management require information on expected future costs and revenues. Cost accounting systems are designed to accumulate past costs and revenues for stock valuation and profit measurement and hence future costs and revenues play no part in such a system. Past costs and revenues may, however, provide a close approximation to future costs and revenues and it may therefore be possible to extract decision-making information from them.

Fixed costs and variable costs

5.2   A knowledge of how costs will vary at different levels of activity (or volume) is essential for decision making. The terms *fixed cost* and *variable cost* are generally used to describe how costs react to changes in activity level. A fixed cost is 'A cost which is incurred for an accounting period, and which, within certain output or turnover limits, tends to be unaffected by fluctuations in the levels of activity (output or turnover)' whereas a variable cost is 'Cost which varies with a measure of activity' (CIMA *Official Terminology).*

5.3   The distinction between fixed and variable costs lies in whether the amount of costs incurred will rise as the volume of activity increases, or whether the costs will remain the same, regardless of the volume of activity. Some examples are as follows.

(a)   Direct materials costs will rise as more units of a product are manufactured, and so they are variable costs that vary with the volume of production.

(b)   Sales commission is often a fixed percentage of sales turnover, and so is a variable cost that varies with the level of sales (but not with the level of production).

(c)   Telephone call charges are likely to increase if the volume of business expands, and so they are a variable cost, varying with the volume of production and sales.

(d)   The rental cost of business premises is a constant amount, at least within a stated time period, and so it is a fixed cost that does not vary with the level of activity conducted on the premises.

5.4   Note that costs can be classified as direct costs or indirect costs/overheads, or as fixed costs or variable costs. These alternative classifications are not, however, mutually exclusive, but are complementary to each other, so that we can find some direct costs that are fixed costs (although they are commonly variable costs) and some overhead costs that are fixed and some overhead costs that are variable.

6   COST CLASSIFICATION FOR CONTROL

Controllable and uncontrollable costs

6.1   One of the purposes of cost accounting is to provide control information to management who wish to know whether or not a particular cost item can be controlled by management action. A controllable cost can be influenced by management decisions and actions. An uncontrollable cost is any cost that cannot be affected by management within a given time span.

Chapter roundup

- This chapter began by explaining what cost accounting is (a method of establishing stock valuations, profits and balance sheet items as well as a system for planning, control and decision making).

- We considered the relationship of cost accounting with financial accounting. In general terms, financial accounting is for external reporting whereas cost accounting is for internal reporting. We then looked at how an organisation is structured for cost accounting purposes and at cost centres (basically, departments) and cost units (one unit of what an organisation produces).

- We then turned our attention to the different ways in which costs can be classified.

- A direct cost is a cost that can be traced in full to the product, service or department being costed. An indirect cost (or overhead cost) is a cost that is incurred in the course of making a product, providing a service or running a department, but which cannot be traced directly and in full to the product, service or department.

- For the preparation of financial statements, costs are often classified as either product costs or period costs. Product costs are costs identified with goods produced or purchased for resale. Period costs are costs deducted as expenses during the current period.

- Classification by function involves classifying costs as either production/manufacturing costs, administration costs or marketing/selling and distribution costs.

- A different way of analysing and classifying costs is into fixed costs and variable costs. Many items of expenditure are part-fixed and part-variable and hence are termed semi-fixed, semi-variable or mixed. We will look at such costs in more detail in Chapter 2.

- For control purposes, costs can be analysed as controllable or uncontrollable.

Test your knowledge

1   What are the main differences between cost accounting and financial accounting? (see paras 1.9, 1.10)

2   What are cost centres and cost units? (2.5)

3   Suggest a suitable cost unit for an accounting firm. (2.6)

4   What is a direct cost? (4.2)

5   What is an indirect cost? (4.3)

6   Give three examples of a direct expense. (4.7)

7   Give an example of an administration overhead, a selling overhead and a distribution overhead. (4.8)

8   What are product costs and period costs? (4.10)

9   What are functional costs? (4.13)

10   What is the distinction between fixed costs and variable costs? (5.2)

Now try illustrative question 1 at the end of the Study Text

Chapter 2

COST BEHAVIOUR

This chapter covers the following topics.

		Syllabus reference	Ability required
1	Cost behaviour and levels of activity	2(a)	Knowledge
2	Cost behaviour patterns	2(a)	Knowledge
3	Determining the fixed and variable elements of semi-variable costs	2(a)	Knowledge

Introduction

In Chapter 1 we introduced you to the subject of cost accounting and explained, in general terms, what it is and what it does. We then considered the principal methods of classifying costs. In particular we introduced the concept of the division of costs into those that vary directly with changes in activity levels (variable costs) and those that do not (fixed costs). This chapter examines further this particular two-way split of cost behaviour and explains two methods of splitting total costs into these two elements, the scattergraph method and the high-low method.

You will need to rely on concepts covered in this chapter and the previous chapter in the remainder of your cost accounting studies both at Stage 1 and at future examination levels. It is that important!

1 COST BEHAVIOUR AND LEVELS OF ACTIVITY

1.1 Cost behaviour is 'The variability of input costs with activity undertaken' (CIMA *Official Terminology*).

1.2 The level of activity (or capacity, output, volume or throughput) refers to the amount of work done, or the number of events that have occurred. Depending on circumstances, the level of activity may refer to the volume of production in a period, the number of items sold, the value of items sold, the number of invoices issued, the number of invoices received, the number of units of electricity consumed, the labour turnover and so on.

Basic principles of cost behaviour

1.3 The basic principle of cost behaviour is that as the level of activity rises, costs will usually rise. It will cost more to produce 2,000 units of output than it will cost to produce 1,000 units; it will usually cost more to make five telephone calls than to make one call and so on.

1.4 This principle is common sense. The problem for the accountant, however, is to determine, for each item of cost, the way in which costs rise and by how much as the level of activity increases.

For our purposes here, the level of activity cost will generally be taken to be the volume of production/output.

2   COST BEHAVIOUR PATTERNS

Fixed costs

2.1   A fixed cost is a cost which tends to be unaffected by increases or decreases in the volume of output. Fixed costs are a period charge, in that they relate to a span of time; as the time span increases, so too will the fixed costs (which are sometimes referred to as period costs for this reason).

2.2   A sketch graph of a fixed cost would look like this.

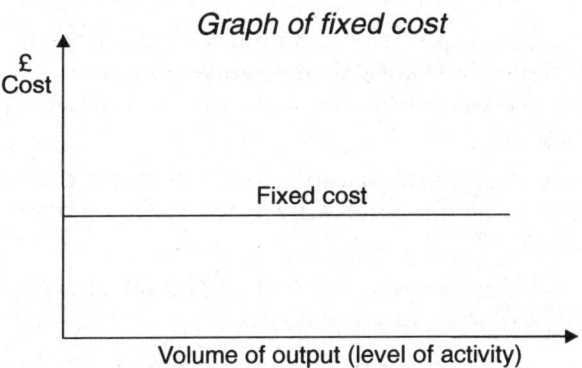

Examples of a fixed cost would be as follows.

(a)   The salary of the managing director (per month or per annum)
(b)   The rent of a single factory building (per month or per annum)
(c)   Straight line depreciation of a single machine (per month or per annum)

Step costs

2.3   Many items of cost are a fixed cost in nature within certain levels of activity. For example the depreciation of a machine may be fixed if production remains below 1,000 units per month, but if production exceeds 1,000 units, a second machine may be required, and the cost of depreciation (on two machines) would go up a step. A sketch graph of a step cost would look like this.

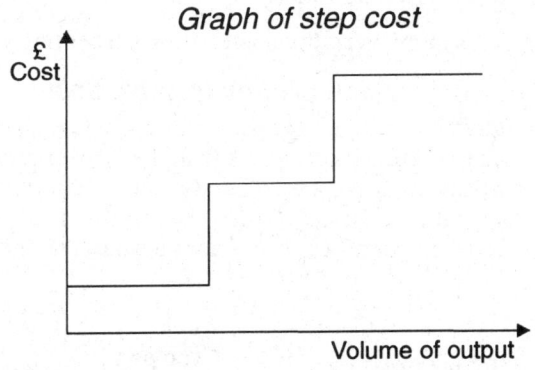

Other examples of step costs are as follows.

(a)   Rent is a step cost in situations where accommodation requirements increase as output levels get higher.

(b)   Basic pay of employees is nowadays usually fixed, but as output rises, more employees (direct workers, supervisors, managers and so on) are required.

Variable costs

2.4   A variable cost is a cost which tends to vary directly with the volume of output. The variable cost *per unit* is the same amount for each unit produced whereas *total* variable cost increases as volume of output increases. A sketch graph of a variable cost would look like this.

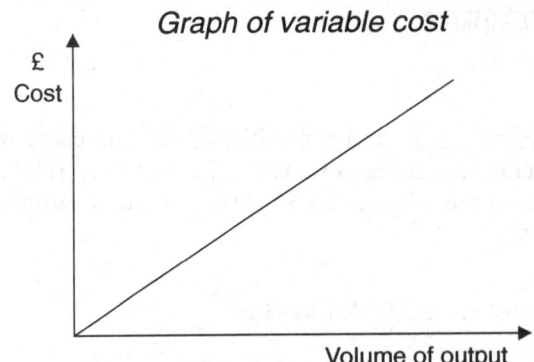

Graph of variable cost

2.5   A constant variable cost per unit implies that the price per unit of material purchased or cost per labour hour worked and so on is constant, and that the rate of material usage/labour productivity is also constant. In other words, constant rate and efficiency levels are implied.

(a)   The most important variable cost is the cost of raw materials (where there is no discount for bulk purchasing since bulk purchase discounts reduce the cost of purchases).

(b)   Direct labour costs are, for very important reasons, classed as a variable cost even though basic wages are usually fixed.

(c)   Sales commission is variable in relation to the volume or value of sales.

Semi-variable costs (or semi-fixed costs or mixed costs)

2.6   These are cost items which are part fixed and part variable.

Examples of these costs include the following.

(a)   *Electricity and gas bills*. There is a standing basic charge plus a charge per unit of consumption.

(b)   *Salesman's salary*. The salesman may earn a basic monthly amount of, say, £600 and then commission of 10% of the value of sales made.

(c)   *Costs of running a car*. The cost is made up of a fixed cost (which includes road tax and insurance) and variable costs (of petrol, oil, repairs and so on) which depend on the number of miles travelled.

The behaviour of a semi-variable cost can be presented graphically as follows.

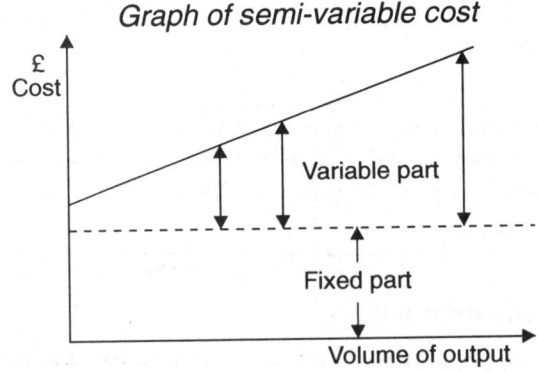

Graph of semi-variable cost

Cost behaviour and total and unit costs

2.7   If the variable cost of producing a widget is £5 per unit then it will remain at that cost per unit no matter how many widgets are produced. However if the business's fixed costs are £5,000 then the fixed cost *per unit* will decrease the more units are produced: one unit will have fixed costs of £5,000 per unit; if 2,500 are produced the fixed cost per unit will be £2; if 5,000 are produced the fixed cost per unit will be only £1. Thus as the level of activity increases the total costs *per unit* (fixed cost plus variable cost) will decrease.

In sketch graph form this may be illustrated as follows.

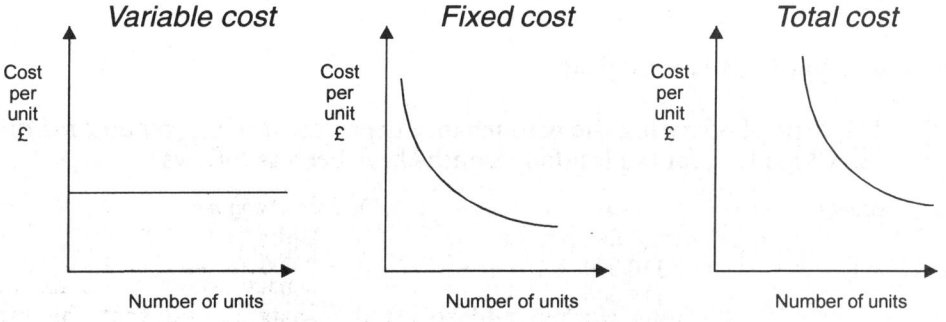

Exercise 1

Are the following likely to be fixed, variable or mixed costs?

- ᴹ (a) Telephone bill
- ꜰ (b) Annual salary of the chief accountant
- ꜰ (c) The management accountant's annual membership fee to CIMA (paid by the company)
- ᵥ (d) Cost of materials used to pack 20 units of product X into a box
- ╱ (e) Wages of warehousemen

Solution

- (a) Mixed
- (b) Fixed
- (c) Fixed
- (d) Variable
- (e) Variable

---

3 DETERMINING THE FIXED AND VARIABLE ELEMENTS OF SEMI-VARIABLE COSTS

5/97

3.1 It is often possible to assume that within the normal range of output, costs are either variable, fixed or semi-variable.

3.2 For this reason cost accountants usually treat all costs as fixed or variable, and semi-variable costs are divided into their variable and fixed elements.

3.3 There are several ways in which fixed cost elements and variable cost elements within semi-variable costs may be ascertained. Each method only gives an estimate, and can therefore give differing results from the other methods. The principal methods are as follows.

High-low method

3.4 (a) To estimate the fixed and variable elements of semi-variable costs, records of costs in previous periods are reviewed and the costs of the following two periods are selected.

   (i)   The period with the highest volume of output
   (ii) The period with the lowest volume of output

   (*Note.* The periods with the highest/lowest output may not be the periods with the highest/lowest cost.)

   (b) The difference between the total cost of the high output and the total cost of the low output will be the variable cost of the difference in output levels (since the same fixed cost is included in each total cost).

(c) The variable cost per unit may be calculated from this (difference in total costs ÷ difference in output levels), and the fixed cost may then also be determined (total cost at either output level – variable cost for output level chosen).

Example: the high-low method

3.5 The costs of operating the maintenance department of a computer manufacturer, Sillick and Chips Ltd, for the last four months have been as follows.

Month	Cost £	Production volume Units
1	110,000	7,000
2	115,000	8,000
3	111,000	7,700
4	97,000	6,000

Required

Calculate the costs that should be expected in month five when output is expected to be 7,500 units. Ignore inflation.

Solution

3.6 (a)

	Units		£
High output	8,000	total cost	115,000
Low output	6,000	total cost	97,000
Variable cost of	2,000		18,000
Variable cost per unit	£18,000/2,000 =		£9

(b) Substituting in either the high or low volume cost:

		High £		Low £
Total cost		115,000		97,000
Variable costs	(8,000 × £9)	72,000	(6,000 × £9)	54,000
Fixed costs		43,000		43,000

(c) Estimated costs of 7,500 units of output:

	£
Fixed costs	43,000
Variable costs (7,500 × £9)	67,500
Total costs	110,500

Exercise 2

Using the high-low method and the following information, determine the cost of electricity in July if 2,750 units of electricity are consumed.

Month	Cost £	Electricity consumed Units
January	204	2,600
February	212	2,800
March	200	2,500
April	220	3,000
May	184	2,100
June	188	2,200

Solution

	Units		£
High units	3,000	total cost =	220
Low units	2,100	total cost =	184
	900		36

Variable cost per unit = $\dfrac{£36}{900}$ = £0.04

Substituting:

	£
Total cost of 3,000 units	220
Variable costs (3,000 × £0.04)	120
Fixed cost	100

Total cost in July = £(100 + (2,750 × 0.04)) = £210

Scattergraph method

3.7   A scattergraph of costs in previous periods can be prepared (with cost on the vertical axis and volume of output on the horizontal axis). A *line of best fit*, which is a line drawn *by judgement* to pass through the middle of the points, thereby having as many points above the line as below it, can then be drawn and the fixed and variable costs determined.

3.8   A scattergraph of the cost and volume data in Paragraph 3.5 is shown below.

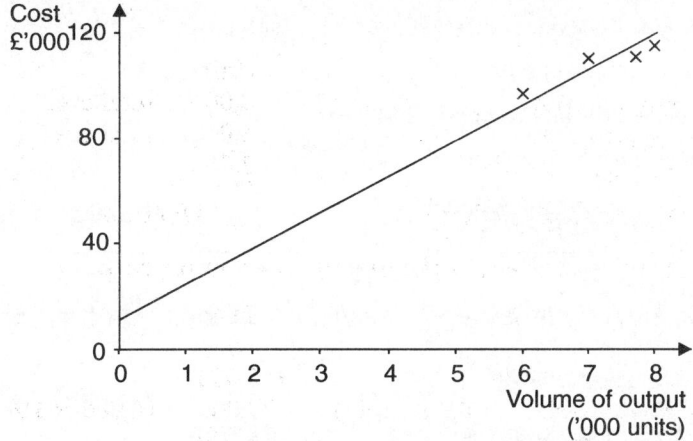

The point where the line cuts the vertical axis (approximately £12,000) is the fixed cost (the cost if there is no output). If we take the value of one of the plotted points which lies close to the line and deduct the fixed cost from the total cost, we can calculate the variable cost per unit.

Total cost for 8,000 units	= £115,000
Variable cost for 8,000 units	= £(115,000 − 12,000) = £103,000
Variable cost per unit	= £103,000/8,000 = £12.875

Least squares regression analysis

3.9   This statistical technique is described in Chapter 28. It involves calculating the equation of a line of best fit from past data.

Chapter roundup

- This chapter has considered the way in which costs are affected by changes in the level of activity.

- Costs which are not affected by the level of activity are fixed costs or period costs.

- Step costs are fixed within a certain range of activity.

- Variable costs increase or decrease with the level of activity

- Semi-fixed, semi-variable or mixed costs are costs which are part fixed and part variable.

- It is often possible to assume that, within the normal range of output, costs are either variable, fixed or semi-variable.

- The fixed and variable elements of semi-variable costs can be determined by the scattergraph method, least squares regression analysis or the high-low method.

Test your knowledge

1   Define cost behaviour and level of activity. (see paras 1.1, 1.2)

2   Give an example of a fixed cost and a step cost. (2.2, 2.3)

3   What is a semi-variable cost? (2.6)

4   Describe the high-low method. (3.4)

5   Describe the scattergraph method? (3.7, 3.8)

Now try illustrative question 2 at the end of the Study Text

Chapter 3

MATERIAL COSTS

This chapter covers the following topics.

		Syllabus reference	Ability required
1	The ordering, receipt and issue of raw materials	2(a)	Skill
2	The storage of raw materials	2(a)	Skill
3	Stock control levels	2(a)	Skill
4	Stock valuation	2(a)	Skill
5	FIFO (first in, first out)	2(a)	Skill
6	LIFO (last in, first out)	2(a)	Skill
7	Cumulative weighted average pricing	2(a)	Skill
8	Periodic weighted average pricing	2(a)	Skill
9	Other methods of pricing and valuation	2(a)	Skill
10	Stock valuation and profitability	2(a)	Skill

Introduction

In Chapter 1 we saw how the total of materials cost, labour cost, direct expenses and overhead costs resulted in the total cost of a product. The next four chapters will examine in detail each of these elements in turn, beginning, in this chapter, with materials.

The investment in stock is a very important one for most businesses, both in terms of monetary value and relationships with customers (no stock, no sale, loss of customer goodwill). It is therefore vital that management establish and maintain an effective stock control system *and* that they are aware of the major costing problem relating to materials, that of pricing materials issues and valuing stock at the end of each period.

The stock held by any organisation takes a variety of forms but generally can be classified as either raw materials, work in progress, spare parts/consumable or finished goods. Not all organisations will have stock of each of these four general kinds. For example, a retail or service organisation may only have stocks of consumables such as stationery. On the other hand, in a production situation it would be usual to find all the forms of stock mentioned above.

The first half of this chapter will concentrate on a stock control system for materials, but similar problems and considerations apply to all forms of stock. The scope of a stock control system is very wide. Controls should cover the ordering/purchasing of stock, the receipt of goods into store, storage and the issue of stock and its maintenance at an appropriate level. The stock control function may be quite an important position in some manufacturing operations: without efficient stock control, an organisation's manufacturing processes might be subject to sudden interruptions if raw materials are unavailable, and a great deal of expense can be incurred on stock with a short shelf life.

In the second half of the chapter we will consider the methods for pricing materials issues/valuing stock. We will look at the various methods, their advantages and disadvantages and their impact on profitability.

Chapter 4 will examine a similar range of topics to those covered in this chapter but in the context of labour.

1   THE ORDERING, RECEIPT AND ISSUE OF RAW MATERIALS

Ordering and receiving materials

1.1   Proper records must be kept of the physical procedures for ordering and receiving a consignment of materials for the following reasons.

(a)   To ensure that enough stock is held
(b)   To ensure that there is no duplication of ordering
(c)   To ensure that quality is maintained
(d)   To ensure that there is adequate record keeping for accounts purposes

A typical series of procedures might be as follows.

(a)   Current stocks run down to the level where a reorder is required. The stores department issues a purchase requisition which is sent to the purchasing department, authorising the department to order further stock.

An example of a purchase requisition is shown below.

PURCHASE REQUISITION Req. No.				
Department/job number: Suggested Supplier:		Date Requested by: Latest date required:		
Quantity	Code number	Description	Estimated Cost	
			Unit	£
Authorised signature:				

(b)   The purchasing department draws a purchase order which is sent to the supplier. (The supplier may be asked to return an acknowledgement copy as confirmation of his acceptance of the order.) Copies of the purchase order must be sent to the accounts department and the storekeeper (or receiving department).

Purchase Order/Confirmation					

Our Order Ref: Date
 To
 ⌐(Address)   ⌐ Please deliver to the above address
                                   Ordered by:
                                   Passed and checked by:
 L ⌐ Total Order Value £					

				Subtotal	
				VAT (@ 17.5%)	
				Total	

(c) The purchasing department may have to obtain a number of quotations if either a new stock line is required, the existing supplier's costs are too high or the existing supplier no longer stocks the goods needed. Trade discounts (reduction in the price per unit given to some customers) should be negotiated where possible.

(d) The supplier delivers the consignment of materials, and the storekeeper signs a delivery note for the carrier. The packages must then be checked against the copy of the purchase order, to ensure that the supplier has delivered the types and quantities of materials which were ordered. (Discrepancies would be referred to the purchasing department.)

(e) If the delivery is acceptable, the storekeeper prepares a goods received note (GRN), an example of which is shown below.

GOODS RECEIVED NOTE WAREHOUSE COPY
NO 5565
DATE: .... TIME: ....
OUR ORDER NO: ----------------------------------- WAREHOUSE A
SUPPLIER AND SUPPLIER'S ADVICE NOTE NO: -----------------------------

QUANTITY	CAT NO	DESCRIPTION

RECEIVED IN GOOD CONDITION:	(INITIALS)

(f) A copy of the GRN is sent to the accounts department, where it is matched with the copy of the purchase order. The supplier's invoice is checked against the purchase order and GRN, and the necessary steps are taken to pay the supplier. The invoice may contain details relating to discounts such as trade discounts, quantity discounts (order in excess of a specified amount) and settlement discounts (payment received within a specified number of days).

Exercise 1

What are the possible consequences of a failure of control over ordering and receipt of materials?

Solution

(a) Incorrect materials being delivered, disrupting operations
(b) Incorrect prices being paid
(c) Deliveries other than at the specified time (causing disruption)
(d) Insufficient control over quality
(e) Invoiced amounts differing from quantities of goods actually received or prices agreed

You may, of course, have thought of equally valid consequences.

Issue of materials

1.2 Materials can only be issued against a materials/stores requisition. This document must record not only the quantity of goods issued, but also the cost centre or the job number for which the requisition is being made. The materials requisition note may also have a column, to be filled in by the cost department, for recording the cost or value of the materials issued to the cost centre or job.

Materials requisition note			
Date required _ _ _ _ _ _ _ .		Cost centre No/ Job No _ _ _ _ _ _ _ _ _ _ .	
Quantity	Item code	Description	£
Signature of requisitioning Manager/ Foreman _ .		Date _ _ _ _ _ _	

We will be looking at methods of valuing issues in later sections of this chapter.

Materials transfers and returns

1.3 Where materials, having been issued to one job or cost centre, are later transferred to a different job or cost centre, a materials transfer note should be raised. Such a note must show not only the job receiving the transfer, but also the job from which it is transferred. This enables the appropriate charges to be made to jobs or cost centres.

1.4 Material returns must also be documented on a materials returned note. This document is the 'reverse' of a requisition note, and must contain similar information.

Impact of computerisation

1.5 You will have noticed that the system described above is a manual one. Many stock control systems these days are computerised, but remember that in both manual and computerised stock control systems similar information is required. Computerised stock control systems vary greatly, but most will have the features outlined below.

(a) Data must be input into the system. For example, details of goods received may simply be written on to a GRN for later entry into the computer system. Alternatively, this information may be keyed in directly to the computer: a GRN will be printed and then signed as evidence of the transaction, so that both the warehouse and the supplier can have a hard copy record in case of dispute. Some systems may incorporate the use of devices such as bar code readers.

Other types of transaction which will need to be recorded include the following.

(i) Transfers between different categories of stock (for example from work in progress to finished goods)

(ii) Despatch, resulting from a sale, of items of finished goods to customers

(iii) Adjustments to stock records if the amount of stock revealed in a physical stock count differs from the amount appearing on the stock records

Note that the input of data into the system may take place as the transaction is occurring, with hard copy records generated by the system as output, or after the transaction has happened, with data from manually prepared documents keyed in separately to the computer.

(b) A stock master file is maintained. This file will contain details for every category of stock and will be updated for new stock lines. A database file may be maintained.

Exercise 2

What type of information do you think should be held on a stock master file?

Solution

Here are some examples.

(a) Stock code number, for reference
(b) Brief description of stock item
(c) Reorder level
(d) Reorder quantity
(e) Cost per unit
(f) Selling price per unit (if finished goods)
(g) Amount in stock
(h) Frequency of usage

The file may also hold details of stock movements over a period, but this will depend on the type of system in operation. In a batch system, transactions will be grouped and input in one operation and details of the movements may be held in a separate transactions file, the master file updated in total only. In an on-line system, transactions may be input directly to the master file, where the record of movements is thus likely to be found. Such a system will mean that the stock records are constantly up to date, which will help in monitoring and controlling stock.

The system may generate orders automatically once the amount in stock has fallen to the reorder level.

(c) The system will generate outputs. These may include, depending on the type of system, any of the following.

  (i) Hard copy records, as described above, of transactions entered into the system

  (ii) Output on a VDU screen in response to an enquiry (for example the current level of a particular line of stock, or details of a particular transaction)

  (iii) Various printed reports, devised to fit in with the needs of the organisation. These may include stock movement reports, detailing over a period the movements on all stock lines, listings of GRNs, despatch notes and so forth, or listings of the physical amounts and values of stock lines at a particular time. The permutations are endless.

1.6 A computerised stock control system is usually able to give more up to date information and more flexible reporting than a manual system but remember that both manual and computer based stock control systems need the same types of data to function properly.

2 THE STORAGE OF RAW MATERIALS

2.1 Quite often organisations operate more controls and checks over a petty cash float of a couple of hundred pounds than they do over their store containing many thousands of pounds worth of stock.

2.2 The loss of a petty cash float is unlikely to signify the decline of an organisation. The loss of stock would, however, mean the end of trading for an organisation (unless the stock can be replaced very quickly). Storekeeping is therefore of the utmost importance to the smooth and efficient running of an organisation's activities.

2.3 Storekeeping involves storing materials to achieve the following objectives.

(a) Speedy issue and receipt of materials
(b) Full identification of all materials at all times
(c) Correct location of all materials at all times
(d) Protection of materials from damage and deterioration
(e) Provision of secure stores to avoid pilferage, theft and fire
(f) Efficient use of storage space
(g) Maintenance of correct stock levels
(h) Keeping correct and up-to-date records of receipts, issues and stock levels

Types of store

2.4   Materials may be kept in either a central (main) store or a departmental (sub) store The advantages of a central store are as follows.

(a)   Smaller stocks are required.

(b)   A smaller overall staff is required; staff can also specialise.

(c)   Control of stock levels is simplified; only one set of stores records needs to be kept instead of one for each sub-store.

(d)   Paperwork is therefore reduced.

(e)   Stocktaking is facilitated.

Exercise 3

What do you see as possible disadvantages to centralised storekeeping?

Solution

(a)   Handling and transportation costs are increased; stores must be sent out over longer distances.

(b)   There may be delays in issuing to departments.

(c)   Fire risk is increased.

(d)   If the centralised system breaks down, all other departments will suffer disruption.

You may have thought of others.

2.5   Sub-stores may be necessary for the storage of high value items, inflammable and corrosive materials, part-finished goods, raw materials or tools and fixtures.

Recording stock levels

2.6   One of the objectives of storekeeping is to maintain accurate records of current stock levels. This involves the accurate recording of stock movements (issues from and receipts into stores). The most frequently encountered system for recording stock movements is the use of bin cards and stores ledger accounts.

Bin cards

2.7   A bin card shows the level of stock of an item at a particular stores location. It is kept with the actual stock and is updated by the storekeeper as stocks are received and issued. A typical bin card is shown below.

Bin card

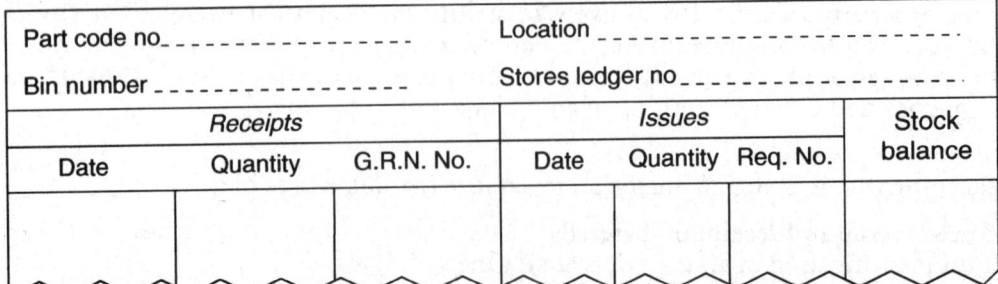

The use of bin cards is decreasing, partly due to the difficulty in keeping them updated and partly due to the merging of stock recording and control procedures, frequently using computers.

Stores ledger accounts

2.8 A typical stores ledger account is shown below. Note that it shows the value of stock whereas bin cards do not.

Stores ledger account

Material _ _ _ _ _ _ _ _ _ _ _ _ _ _ _ _ _ _ _				Maximum Quantity _ _ _ _ _ _ _ _ _ _ _ _ _ _						
Code _ _ _ _ _ _ _ _ _ _ _ _ _ _ _ _ _ _ _				Minimum Quantity _ _ _ _ _ _ _ _ _ _ _ _ _ _						
Date	Receipts				Issues				Stock		
	G.R.N. No.	Quantity	Unit Price £	Amount £	Stores Req. No.	Quantity	Unit Price £	Amount £	Quantity	Unit Price £	Amount £

2.9 The above illustration shows a card for a manual system, but even when the stock records are computerised, the same type of information is normally included in the computer file. The running balance on the stores ledger account allows stock levels and valuation to be monitored.

Free stock

2.10 As well as knowing the physical stock balance, knowledge of the free stock balance is also necessary in order to obtain a full picture of the current stock position of an item. Free stock represents what is really available for future use and is calculated as follows.

	Materials in stock	X
+	Materials on order from suppliers	X
−	Materials requisitioned, not yet issued	(X)
	Free stock balance	X

2.11 Knowledge of the level of physical stock assists stock issuing, stocktaking and controlling maximum and minimum stock levels: knowledge of the level of free stock assists ordering.

Identification of materials: stock codes (materials codes)

2.12 To assist in the achievement of the storekeeping objectives and to ensure that the stock control system runs smoothly, each item held in stores must be unambiguously identified. Materials are therefore coded and classified. Advantages of using code numbers to identify materials are as follows.

(a) Ambiguity is avoided. Different people may use different descriptions for materials. This is avoided if numbers are used.

(b) Time is saved. Descriptions can be lengthy and time-consuming, particularly when completing written forms.

(c) Production efficiency is improved. If the correct material can be accurately identified from a code number, production hold-ups caused by the issue of incorrect material can be avoided.

(d) Computerised processing is made easier.

(e) Numbered code systems can be designed to be flexible, and can be expanded to include more stock items as necessary.

The digits in a code can stand for the type of stock, supplier, department and so forth.

Stocktaking

2.13 Stocktaking involves counting the physical stock on hand at a certain date, and then checking this against the balance shown in the clerical records. There are two methods of carrying out this process, periodic stocktaking and continuous stocktaking.

Periodic stocktaking

2.14 Periodic stocktaking is a 'process whereby all stock items are physically counted and then valued' (CIMA *Official Terminology*). This is usually carried out annually and the objective is to count all items of stock on a specific date.

Continuous stocktaking

2.15 'Continuous stocktaking is the process of counting and valuing selected items at different times on a rotating basis' (CIMA *Official Terminology*). This involves a specialist team counting and checking a number of stock items each day, so that each item is checked at least once a year. Valuable items could be checked more frequently. The advantages of this system compared to periodic stocktaking are as follows.

(a) The annual stocktaking is unnecessary and the disruption it causes is avoided.

(b) Regular skilled stocktakers can be employed, reducing likely errors.

(c) More time is available, reducing errors and allowing investigation.

(d) Deficiencies and losses are revealed sooner than they would be if stocktaking were limited to an annual check.

(e) Production hold-ups are eliminated because the stores staff are at no time so busy as to be unable to deal with material issues to production departments.

(f) Staff morale is improved and standards raised.

(g) Control over stock levels is improved, and there is less likelihood of overstocking or running out of stock.

Stock discrepancies

2.16 There will be occasions when stock checks disclose discrepancies between the physical amount of an item in stock and the amount shown in the stock records. When this occurs, the cause of the discrepancy should be investigated, and appropriate action taken to ensure that it does not happen again.

Exercise 4

List as many possible causes of discrepancies between physical and book stock as you can think of.

Solution

Here are some ideas.

(a) Suppliers deliver a different quantity of goods than is shown on the goods received note. Since this note is used to update stock records, a discrepancy will arise. This can be avoided by ensuring that all stock is counted as it is received, and a responsible person should sign the document to verify the quantity.

(b) The quantity of stock issued to production is different from that shown on the materials requisition note. Careful counting of all issues will prevent this.

(c) Excess stock is returned from production without documentation. This can be avoided by ensuring that all movements of stock are accurately documented. In this case, a materials returned note should be raised.

(d) Clerical errors may occur in the stock records such as an entry made on the wrong bin card. Regular checks by independent staff should detect and correct mistakes.

(e) Breakages in stores may go unrecorded. All breakages should be documented and noted on the stock records.

(f) Employees may steal stock. Regular checks or continuous stocktaking will help to prevent this, and only authorised personnel should be allowed into the stores.

(g) Items may be placed in the wrong location.

(h) Arithmetical errors may have been made when calculating the balance on the bin card.

2.17 If the stock discrepancy is found to be caused by clerical error, then the records should be rectified immediately. If the discrepancy occurs because units of stock appear to be missing, the lost stock must be written off. The accounting transaction will be recorded by a stores credit note if items of stock have been lost, or a stores debit note if there is more physical stock than the amount recorded.

Perpetual inventory

2.18 A perpetual inventory system involves recording every receipt and issue of stock as it occurs on bin cards and stores ledger accounts. This means that there is a continuous clerical record of the balance of each item of stock. The balance on the stores ledger account therefore represents the stock on hand and this balance is used in the calculation of closing stock in monthly and annual accounts. In practice, physical stocks may not agree with recorded stocks and therefore continuous stocktaking is necessary to ensure that the perpetual inventory system is functioning correctly and that minor stock discrepancies are corrected.

Obsolete, deteriorating and slow-moving stocks and wastage

2.19 Obsolete stocks are those items which have become out-of-date and are no longer required. If stock records show that a particular item has not been used for a long time, an investigation should be made as to whether the item is still usable in production. If it is not, it should be regarded as obsolete and written off to the profit and loss account and disposed of.

2.20 Stock items may be wasted because, for example, they get broken or because of poor materials handling by production. All wastage should be noted on the stock records immediately so that physical stock equals book stock and the cost of the wastage written off to the profit and loss account.

2.21 Slow-moving stocks are those items of which the stockholding is likely to take a long time to be used up. For example, 5,000 units are in stock, and only 20 are being used each year. This is often caused by overstocking. Managers should investigate such stock items and, if it is felt that the usage rate is unlikely to increase, excess stock should be written off as for obsolete stock, leaving perhaps four or five years' supply in stock.

3   STOCK CONTROL LEVELS

Why hold stock?

3.1 The costs of purchasing stock are usually one of the largest costs faced by an organisation and, once obtained, stock has to be carefully controlled and checked. This involves significant manpower and resources. Why, then, do organisations hold stocks?

3.2 The main reasons for holding stocks can be summarised as follows.

(a) To ensure sufficient goods are available to meet expected demand
(b) To provide a buffer between processes
(c) To meet any future shortages
(d) To take advantage of bulk purchasing discounts
(e) To absorb seasonal fluctuations and any variations in usage and demand

(f) To allow production processes to flow smoothly and efficiently

(g) As a necessary part of the production process (such as when maturing cheese)

(h) As a deliberate investment policy, especially in times of inflation or possible shortages

Holding costs

3.3 These obvious advantages should not, however, provide free licence for huge stocks to be built up. If stocks are too high, holding costs will be incurred unnecessarily. Such costs occur for a number of reasons.

(a) *Costs of storage and stores operations.* Larger stocks require more storage space and possibly extra staff and equipment to control and handle them.

(b) *Interest charges.* Holding stocks involves the tying up of capital (cash) on which interest must be paid.

(c) *Insurance costs.* The larger the value of stocks held, the greater insurance premiums are likely to be.

(d) *Risk of obsolescence.* When materials or components become out-of-date and are no longer required, existing stocks must be thrown away and their cost written off to the profit and loss account.

(e) *Deterioration.* When materials in store deteriorate to the extent that they are unusable, they must be thrown away (with the likelihood that disposal costs would be incurred) and again, the value written off plus the disposal costs will be a charge to the profit and loss account.

(f) *Theft.*

Costs of obtaining stock

3.4 On the other hand, if stocks are kept low, small quantities of stock will have to be ordered more frequently, thereby increasing the following ordering or procurement costs.

(a) Clerical and administrative costs associated with purchasing, accounting for and receiving goods

(b) Transport costs

(c) Production run costs

Stockout costs

3.5 An additional type of cost which may arise if stocks are kept too low is the type associated with running out of stock, stockout costs. There are a number of causes of these costs.

(a) Lost contribution from lost sales
(b) Loss of future sales due to disgruntled customers
(c) Loss of customer goodwill
(d) Cost of production stoppages
(e) Labour frustration over stoppages
(f) Extra costs of urgent, small quantity, replenishment orders

Objective of stock control

3.6 The overall objective of stock control is, therefore, to maintain stock levels so that the combined costs mentioned in Paragraphs 3.3, 3.4 and 3.5 are minimised. This is done by establishing two things.

(a) When to order
(b) How many to order

Stock control levels

3.7   Based on an analysis of past stock usage and delivery times, a series of control levels can be calculated and used to maintain stocks at their optimum level (in other words, a level which minimises costs). These levels will determine 'when to order' and 'how many to order'.

(a)   *Reorder level.* When stocks reach this level, action should be taken to replenish stocks. The reorder level is determined by consideration of the following.

   (i)   The maximum rate of consumption

   (ii)   The maximum lead time, which is the time between placing an order with a supplier, and the stock becoming available for use

   Reorder level = maximum usage × maximum lead time

(b)   *Minimum level.* This is also a warning level to draw management attention to the fact that stocks are approaching a dangerously low level and that stockouts are possible. It is essentially a buffer stock and is set by consideration of the following.

   (i)   The reorder level
   (ii)   The average rate of consumption
   (iii) The average lead time

   Minimum level = reorder level − (average usage × average lead time)

(c)   *Maximum level.* Stock levels must not exceed this uppermost limit. It acts as a warning to management that stocks are reaching a potentially wasteful level. The maximum level is set by consideration of the following.

   (i)   The reorder level
   (ii)   The quantity ordered each time (the reorder quantity)
   (iii) The minimum rate of consumption
   (iv)   The minimum lead time

   Maximum level = reorder level + reorder quantity − (minimum usage × minimum lead time)

Exercise 5

A company uses a maximum of 1,000 units of component L each week. An order (which is always for 3,000 units) placed with the supplier of component L takes, at most, four weeks to arrive.

Required

At what level should the company reorder component L?

Solution

Reorder level   = maximum usage × maximum lead time
                = 1,000 × 4 = 4,000 units

(d)   *Reorder quantity.* This is the quantity of stock which is to be ordered when stock reaches the reorder level. If it is set so as to minimise the total costs associated with holding and ordering stock, then it is known as the economic order quantity.

Economic order quantity (EOQ)

3.8   Economic order theory assumes that the average stock held is equal to one half of the reorder quantity (although if an organisation maintains some sort of buffer or safety stock then average stock = buffer stock + half of the reorder quantity). We have seen that there are certain costs associated with holding stock. These costs tend to increase with the level of stocks, and so could be reduced by ordering smaller amounts from suppliers each time.

3.9 On the other hand, as we have seen, there are costs associated with ordering from suppliers: documentation, telephone calls, payment of invoices, receiving goods into stores and so on. These costs tend to increase if small orders are placed, because a larger number of orders would then be needed for a given annual demand.

3.10 Suppose that Jones Ltd purchases raw material from Beswetherick Ltd at a cost of £16 per unit. Jones Ltd's annual demand for the raw material is 25,000 units. The holding cost per unit is £6.40 and the cost of placing an order is £32.

3.11 We can tabulate the annual relevant costs for various order quantities as follows.

Order quantity (units)		100	200	300	400	500	600	800	1,000
Average stock (units)	(a)	50	100	150	200	250	300	400	500
Number of orders	(b)	250	125	83	63	50	42	31	25
		£	£	£	£	£	£	£	£
Annual holding cost	(c)	320	640	960	1,280	1,600	1,920	2,560	3,200
Annual order cost	(d)	8,000	4,000	2,656	2,016	1,600	1,344	992	800
Total relevant cost		8,320	4,640	3,616	3,296	3,200	3,264	3,552	4,000

Notes

(a) Average stock = Order quantity ÷ 2
(b) Number of orders = annual demand ÷ order quantity
(c) Annual holding cost = Average stock × £6.40
(d) Annual order cost = Number of orders × £32

3.12 You will see that the economic order quantity is 500 units. At this point the total annual relevant costs are at a minimum.

3.13 We can present the information tabulated in Paragraph 3.11 in graphical form. The vertical axis represents the relevant annual costs for the investment in stocks, and the horizontal axis can be used to represent either the various order quantities or the average stock levels; two scales are actually shown on the horizontal axis so that both items can be incorporated. The graph shows that, as the average stock level and order quantity increase, the holding cost increases. On the other hand, the ordering costs decline as stock levels and order quantities increase. The total cost line represents the sum of both the holding and the ordering costs.

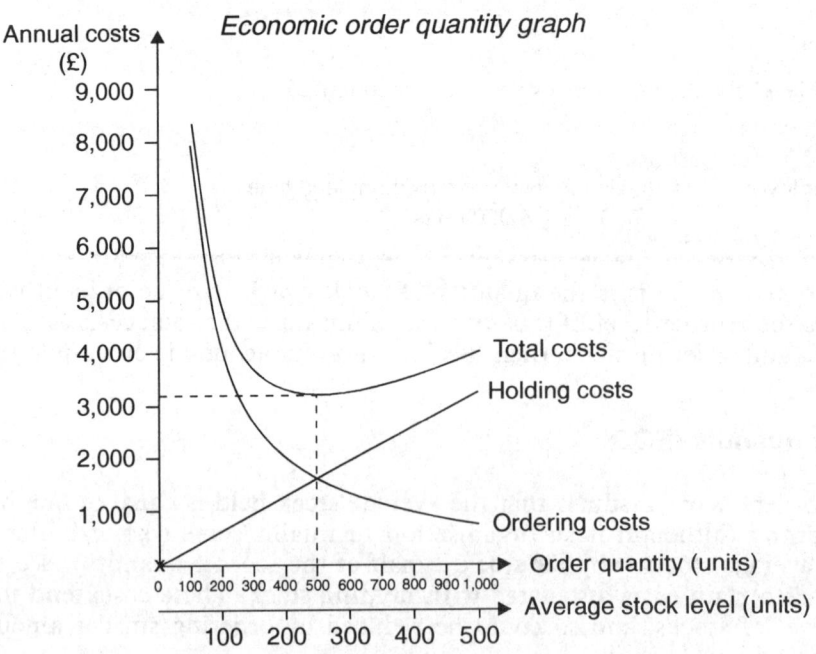

3.14 Note that the total cost line is at a minimum for an order quantity of 500 units and occurs at the point where the ordering cost curve and holding cost curve intersect. The EOQ is therefore found at the point where holding costs equal ordering costs.

3.15 There is also a formula for the EOQ.

$$EOQ = \sqrt{\frac{2C_0D}{Ch}}$$

$$= \frac{2 \times \overset{32}{6.40} \times 2500}{6.40} = 500$$

where   Ch = cost of holding one unit of stock for one time period
        C_0 = cost of ordering a consignment from a supplier
        D = demand during the time period

This formula is provided in the exam.

Exercise 6

Calculate the EOQ using the formula and the information in Paragraph 3.10.

Solution

$$EOQ = \sqrt{\frac{2 \times \pounds32 \times 25,000}{\pounds6.40}}$$

$$= \sqrt{250,000}$$

$$= 500$$

Other systems of stores control and reordering

3.16 (a) Under the *order cycling* method, quantities on hand of each stores item are reviewed periodically (every 1, 2 or 3 months). For low-cost items, a technique called the 90-60-30 day technique can be used, so that when stocks fall to 60 days' supply, a fresh order is placed for a 30 days' supply so as to boost stocks to 90 days' supply. For high-cost items, a more stringent stores control procedure is advisable so as to keep down the costs of stock holding.

      (b) The *two-bin system* of stores control (or *visual method* of control) is one whereby each stores item is kept in two storage bins. When the first bin is emptied, an order must be placed for re-supply; the second bin will contain sufficient quantities to last until the fresh delivery is received. This is a simple system which is not costly to operate but it is not based on any formal analysis of stock usage and may result in the holding of too much or too little stock.

      (c) Materials items may be classified as expensive, inexpensive or in a middle-cost range. Because of the practical advantages of simplifying stores control procedures without incurring unnecessary high costs, it may be possible to segregate materials for selective stores control.

            (i)   Expensive and medium-cost materials are subject to careful stores control procedures to minimise cost.

            (ii) Inexpensive materials can be stored in large quantities because the cost savings from careful stores control do not justify the administrative effort required to implement the control.

            This selective approach to stores control is sometimes called the *ABC method* whereby materials are classified A, B or C according to their expense - group A being the expensive, group B the medium-cost and group C the inexpensive materials.

      (d) A similar selective approach to stores control is the *Pareto (80/20) distribution* is based on the finding that in many stores, 80% of the value of stores is accounted for by only 20% of the stores items, and stocks of these more expensive items should be controlled more closely.

3.17 Note that control levels may prove unreliable for the control of stocks used to maintain vehicles, plant, machinery and other assets since maintenance is partly unpredictable:

past usage of stock cannot be used to predict future usage. Buffer stock (safety stock) can overcome this problem to a certain extent.

Just-in-time stock control techniques

3.18   A recent innovation in the way in which companies control stocks has been the introduction of just-in-time (JIT) techniques.

3.19   Briefly, an organisation using JIT seeks to minimise its holdings of stock by ensuring that an item of stock is only acquired from a supplying department (or company) when it is actually needed for input to a production process. JIT works on the principle that it is better not to produce at all than to produce unnecessarily: unnecessary production adds to costs rather than profitability (in other words, it is better to have machines idle than produce goods which sit in a warehouse, incurring holding costs for several weeks).

3.20   JIT has the following aims.

(a)   To minimise warehousing and storage costs.

(b)   To eliminate waste by maintaining control over the quality of stocks input to a production process.

(c)   To reduce the amount of raw materials, work in progress and finished goods stock carried as working capital, through more efficient production planning thus saving on financing costs.

4   STOCK VALUATION

4.1   You may be aware from your studies for Paper 1 that, for financial accounting purposes, stocks are valued at the lower of cost and net realisable value. In practice, stocks will probably be valued at cost in the stores records throughout the course of an accounting period. Only when the period ends will the value of the stock in hand be reconsidered so that items with a net realisable value below their original cost will be revalued downwards, and the stock records altered accordingly.

4.2   That seems fairly straightforward, doesn't it? In broad terms we simply value materials issues and stocks at cost. But let us think a bit more and consider what a storekeeper does when he issues materials to production (although exactly the same principles and arguments apply to issuing finished goods to customers).

4.3   A storekeeper may issue the oldest goods first, the last received first, his selection may be completely at random, or he may issue the stocks which are within easiest reach of the store's staff.

4.4   By comparison the cost of the goods issued must be determined on a consistently applied basis, and must ignore the likelihood that the materials issued will be costed at a price different to the amount paid for them.

4.5   This may seem a little confusing at first, and it may be helpful to explain the point further. Suppose that there are three units of a particular material in stock.

Units	Date received	Purchase cost
A	June 19X1	£100
B	July 19X1	£106
C	August 19X1	£109

In September, one unit is issued to production. As it happened, the physical unit actually issued was B. The accounting department must put a value or cost on the material issued, but the value would not be the cost of B, £106. The principles used to value the materials issued are not concerned with the actual unit issued, A, B, or C. Nevertheless, the accountant may choose to make one of the following assumptions.

(a) The unit issued is valued as though it were the earliest unit in stock, ie at the purchase cost of A, £100. This valuation principle is called FIFO, or first in, first out.

(b) The unit issued is valued as though it were the most recent unit received into stock, ie at the purchase cost of C, £109. This method of valuation is LIFO, or last in, first out.

(c) The unit issued is valued at an average price of A, B and C, ie £105.

4.6 In the following sections we will consider each of the pricing methods detailed above (and a few more), using the following transactions to illustrate the principles in each case.

TRANSACTIONS DURING MAY 19X3

	Quantity	Unit cost	Total cost	Market value per unit on date of transaction
	Units	£	£	£
Opening balance, 1 May	100	2.00	200	
Receipts, 3 May	400	2.10	840	2.11
Issues, 4 May	200			2.11
Receipts, 9 May	300	2.12	636	2.15
Issues, 11 May	400			2.20
Receipts, 18 May	100	2.40	240	2.35
Issues, 20 May	100			2.35
Closing balance, 31 May	200			2.38
			1,916	

5 FIFO (FIRST IN, FIRST OUT)

5.1 FIFO assumes that materials are issued out of stock in the order in which they were delivered into stock: issues are priced at the cost of the earliest delivery remaining in stock. The CIMA *Official Terminology* definition is 'The principle that the oldest items or costs are the first to be used.'

Using FIFO, the cost of issues and the closing stock value in the example would be as follows.

Date of issue	Quantity issued	Value		
	Units		£	£
4 May	200	100 o/s at £2	200	
		100 at £2.10	210	
				410
11 May	400	300 at £2.10	630	
		100 at £2.12	212	
				842
20 May	100	100 at £2.12		212
Cost of issues				1,464
Closing stock value	200	100 at £2.12	212	
		100 at £2.40	240	
				452
				1,916

Notes

(a) The cost of materials issued plus the value of closing stock equals the cost of purchases plus the value of opening stock (£1,916).

(b) The market price of purchased materials is rising dramatically. In a period of inflation, there is a tendency for materials to be issued at a cost lower than the current market value, although closing stocks tend to be valued at a cost approximating to current market value.

5.2   The advantages and disadvantages of the FIFO method are as follows.

(a) *Advantages*

   (i)   It is a logical pricing method which probably represents what is physically happening: in practice the oldest stock is likely to be used first.

  (ii)   It is easy to understand and explain to managers.

 (iii)   It can be near to a valuation based on replacement cost.

(b) *Disadvantages*

   (i)   FIFO can be cumbersome to operate because of the need to identify each batch of material separately.

  (ii)   Managers may find it difficult to compare costs and make decisions when they are charged with varying prices for the same materials.

Exercise 7

Complete the stores ledger account below as fully as possible, using the information in Paragraphs 4.6 and 5.1.

STORES LEDGER ACCOUNT

Material:_____   **Maximum Quantity:**_____

Code:_____   **Minimum Quantity:**_____

Date	Receipts				Issues				Stock		
	GRN No.	Quantity	Unit price £	Amount £	Stores Req. No.	Quantity	Unit price £	Amount £	Quantity	Unit price £	Amount £

Solution

			STORES LEDGER ACCOUNT								

Material:_____   **Maximum Quantity:**_____

Code:_____   **Minimum Quantity:**_____

Date	Receipts				Issues				Stock		
	GRN No.	Quantity	Unit price £	Amount £	Stores Req. No.	Quantity	Unit price £	Amount £	Quantity	Unit price £	Amount £
1.5.X3									100	2.00	200.00
3.5.X3		400	2.10	840.00					100	2.00	200.00
									400	2.10	840.00
									500		1,040.00
4.5.X3						100	2.00	200.00			
						100	2.10	210.00	300	2.10	630.00
9.5.X3		300	2.12	636.00					300	2.10	630.00
									300	2.12	636.00
									600		1,266.00
11.5.X3						300	2.10	630.00			
						100	2.12	212.00	200	2.12	424.00
18.5.X3		100	2.40	240.00					200	2.12	424.00
									100	2.40	240.00
									300		664.00
20.5.X3						100	2.12	212.00	100	2.12	212.00
									100	2.40	240.00
31.5.X3									200		452.00

6   LIFO (LAST IN, FIRST OUT)

6.1   LIFO assumes that materials are issued out of stock in the reverse order to which they were delivered: the most recent deliveries are issued before earlier ones, and are priced accordingly. The CIMA *Official Terminology* definition is 'A little used method of pricing the issue of material using the purchase price of the latest unit in stock'.

Using LIFO, the cost of issues and the closing stock value in the example above would be as follows.

Date of issue	*Quantity issued* Units	*Valuation*	£	£
4 May	200	200 at £2.10		420
11 May	400	300 at £2.12	636	
		100 at £2.10	210	
				846
20 May	100	100 at £2.40		240
Cost of issues				1,506
Closing stock value	200	100 at £2.10	210	
		100 at £2.00	200	
				410
				1,916

Notes

(a)   The cost of materials issued plus the value of closing stock equals the cost of purchases plus the value of opening stock (£1,916).

(b)   In a period of inflation there is a tendency with LIFO for the following to occur.

   (i)   Materials are issued at a price which approximates to current market value.

   (ii)   Closing stocks become undervalued when compared to market value.

6.2   The advantages and disadvantages of the LIFO method are as follows.

(a)   *Advantages*

   (i)   Stocks are issued at a price which is close to current market value. This is not the case with FIFO when there is a high rate of inflation.

   (ii)   Managers are continually aware of recent costs when making decisions, because the costs being charged to their department or products will be current costs.

(b)   *Disadvantages*

   (i)   The method can be cumbersome to operate because it sometimes results in several batches being only part-used in the stock records before another batch is received.

   (ii)   LIFO is often the opposite to what is physically happening and can therefore be difficult to explain to managers.

   (iii)   As with FIFO, decision making can be difficult because of the variations in prices.

7   CUMULATIVE WEIGHTED AVERAGE PRICING

7.1   The cumulative weighted average pricing method calculates a weighted average price for all units in stock. Issues are priced at this average cost, and the balance of stock remaining would have the same unit valuation. The average price is determined by dividing the total cost by the total number of units.

A new weighted average price is calculated whenever a new delivery of materials into store is received. This is the key feature of cumulative weighted average pricing.

7.2   In our example, issue costs and closing stock values would be as follows.

Date	Received Units	Issued Units	Balance Units	Total stock value £	Unit cost £	£
Opening stock			100	200	2.00	
3 May	400			840	2.10	
			* 500	1,040	2.08	
4 May		200		(416)	2.08	416
			300	624	2.08	
9 May	300			636	2.12	
			* 600	1,260	2.10	
11 May		400		(840)	2.10	840
			200	420	2.10	
18 May	100			240	2.40	
			* 300	660	2.20	
20 May		100		(220)	2.20	220
						1,476
Closing stock value			200	440	2.20	440
						1,916

* A new stock value per unit is calculated whenever a new receipt of materials occurs.

Notes

(a)   The cost of materials issued plus the value of closing stock equals the cost of purchases plus the value of opening stock (£1,916).

(b)   In a period of inflation, using the cumulative weighted average pricing system, the value of material issues will rise gradually, but will tend to lag a little behind the current market value at the date of issue. Closing stock values will also be a little below current market value.

7.3 The advantages and disadvantages of cumulative weighted average pricing are these.

(a) *Advantages*

    (i)   Fluctuations in prices are smoothed out, making it easier to use the data for decision making.

    (ii)   It is easier to administer than FIFO and LIFO, because there is no need to identify each batch separately.

(b) *Disadvantages*

    (i)   The resulting issue price is rarely an actual price that has been paid, and can run to several decimal places.

    (ii)   Prices tend to lag a little behind current market values when there is gradual inflation.

8 PERIODIC WEIGHTED AVERAGE PRICING

8.1 Under the periodic weighted average pricing method, a retrospective average price is calculated for *all* materials issued during the period. The average issue price is calculated as follows.

$$\frac{\text{Cost of all receipts in the period } + \text{ Cost of opening stock}}{\text{Number of units received in the period } + \text{ Number of units of opening stock}}$$

Closing stock values are a balancing figure.

8.2 In our example, issue costs and closing stock values would be as follows.

$$\frac{\text{Cost of receipts in period } + \text{ cost of opening stock}}{\text{Number of units received } + \text{ number of units of opening stock}} = \frac{£1,716 + £200}{800 + 100} = \frac{£1,916}{900}$$

Issue price = £2.129 per unit

Date of issue	*Quantity issued*	*Valuation*
	Units	£
4 May	200 × £2.129	426
11 May	400 × £2.129	852
20 May	100 × £2.129	213
Cost of issues		1,491
Value of opening stock plus purchases		1,916
Value of 200 units of closing stock (at £2.129)		425

(*Note*. The periodic weighted average pricing method is easier to calculate than the cumulative weighted average method, and therefore requires less effort, but it must be applied retrospectively since the costs of materials used cannot be calculated until the end of the period.)

Exercise 8

Receipts and issues of part number 6288 for the month of August are as follows.

	Receipts	*Total value*	*Issues*
	Units	£	Units
3 August	2,000	6,000	
7 August	3,000	9,900	
11 August	2,000	8,000	
16 August			4,000
24 August	3,000	10,500	
30 August			5,000

Opening stocks of part number 6288 were 1,000 units, valued at £2,800.

Required

Calculate the value of closing stock on 31 August using periodic weighted average pricing.

Solution

$$\frac{\text{Cost of receipts in period} + \text{cost of opening stock}}{\text{Number of units received} + \text{number of units in opening stock}} = \frac{£(34,400 + 2,800)}{10,000 + 1,000} = \frac{£37,200}{11,000}$$

Average issue price = £3.38 per unit

Closing stock of 2,000 (10,000 + 1,000 - 9,000) units = 2,000 × £3.38 = £6,760

9 OTHER METHODS OF PRICING AND VALUATION

Standard cost pricing

9.1 Under the standard cost pricing method, all issues are at predetermined standard price. Such a method is used with a system of standard costing, which will be covered later in this text.

Replacement cost pricing

9.2 In the preceding description of different methods for pricing materials, the problems of inflation have been repeatedly stressed. There is a strong body of accountancy opinion with the following argument.

(a) When materials are issued out of stores, they will be replaced with a new delivery; issues should therefore be priced at the current cost to the business of replacing them in stores.

(b) Closing stocks should be valued at current replacement cost in the balance sheet to show the true value of the assets of the business.

9.3 Replacement costing is a method of pricing material issues and stock values at the current replacement cost of material and is a method recommended for accounting for inflation. Unfortunately, in many instances, it may be difficult or impossible to maintain a record of material replacement market values, and replacement costing may therefore be impracticable.

9.4 The advantages and disadvantages of replacement costing are as follows.

(a) *Advantages*

(i) Issues are at up-to-date costs so that managers can take recent trends into account when making decisions based on their knowledge of the costs being incurred.

(ii) In a period of inflation, replacement costing will give a high (current) valuation to materials, thereby reducing 'true profit' in the profit and loss account, so as to preserve the assets of the business intact (in other words to allow for replacement of the materials used).

(iii) It is easy to operate once the replacement cost has been determined.

(b) *Disadvantages*

(i) The price may not be an actual price paid, and a difference will then arise on issues.

(ii) It can be difficult to determine the replacement cost.

(iii) The method is not acceptable to the Inland Revenue or for SSAP 9.

Exercise 9

Which pricing method can be used as a practical alternative to replacement cost pricing?

Solution

LIFO is a reasonably accurate method of accounting for inflation provided that closing stock values are periodically reviewed and revalued.

Highest in, first out (HIFO)

9.5   This method values issues at the highest price of the items in stock at the time of issue. Although prudent it is an approach which does not follow any particular chronological order.

Next in, first out (NIFO)

9.6   This method values issues at the price to be paid for the next delivery, which may or may not be the same as replacement cost. This method does value issues at the most up-to-date price but it is administratively difficult.

Specific price

9.7   This method values issues at their individual price and the stock balance is made up of individual items valued at individual prices. It is only really suitable for expensive stock lines where stock holdings and usage rates are low.

10   STOCK VALUATION AND PROFITABILITY

10.1 In the previous descriptions of FIFO, LIFO, average costing and so on, the example used raw materials as an illustration. Each method produced different figures for both the value of closing stocks and also the cost of material issues. Since raw materials costs affect the cost of production, and the cost of production works through eventually into the cost of sales, it follows that different methods of stock valuation will provide different profit figures. Attempt the following exercise which illustrates the point.

Exercise 10

On 1 November 19X2, Delilah's Dresses (Haute Couture Emporium) held 3 pink satin dresses with orange sashes, designed by Freda Swoggs. These were valued at £120 each. During November 19X2, 12 more of the dresses were delivered as follows.

Date	Units received	Purchase cost per dress
10 November	4	£125
20 November	4	£140
25 November	4	£150

A number of the pink satin dresses with orange sashes were sold during November as follows.

Date	Dresses sold	Sales price per dress
14 November	5	£200
21 November	5	£200
28 November	1	£200

Required

Calculate the profit (sales – (opening stock + purchases – closing stock) from selling the pink satin dresses with orange sashes in November 19X2, applying the following principles of stock valuation.

(a)   FIFO
(b)   LIFO
(c)   Cumulative weighted average pricing

Ignore administration, sales and distribution costs.

Solution

(a)   *FIFO*

Date	Cost of sales	Total £	Closing stock £
14 November	3 units × £120 + 2 units × £125	610	
21 November	2 units × £125 + 3 units × £140	670	
28 November	1 unit × £140	140	
Closing stock	4 units × £150		600
		1,420	600

(b)   *LIFO*

Date	Cost of sales	Total £	Closing stock £
14 November	4 units × £125 + 1 unit × £120	620	
21 November	4 units × £140 + 1 unit × £120	680	
28 November	1 unit × £150	150	
Closing stock	3 units × £150 + 1 unit × £120		570
		1,450	570

(c)   *Cumulative weighted average pricing*

		Unit cost £	Balance in stock £	Cost of sales £	Closing stock £
1 November	3	120.00	360		
10 November	4	125.00	500		
	7	122.86	860		
14 November	5	122.86	614	614	
	2		246		
20 November	4	140.00	560		
	6	134.33	806		
21 November	5	134.33	672	672	
	1		134		
25 November	4	150.00	600		
	5	146.80	734		
28 November	1	146.80	147	147	
30 November	4	146.80	587	1,433	587

Profitability

	FIFO £	LIFO £	Weighted average £
Opening stock	360	360	360
Purchases	1,660	1,660	1,660
	2,020	2,020	2,020
Closing stock	600	570	587
Cost of sales	1,420	1,450	1,433
Sales (11 × £200)	2,200	2,200	2,200
Profit	780	750	767

10.2   In the exercise above, different stock valuation methods produced different costs of sale and hence different profits. As opening stock values and purchase costs are the same for each method, the different costs of sale are due to different closing stock valuations. The differences in profits therefore equal the differences in closing stock valuations.

10.3   The profit differences are only temporary. In the exercise, the opening stock in December 19X2 will be £600, £570 or £587, depending on the stock valuation used. Different opening stock values will affect the cost of sales and profits in December, so that in the long run, inequalities in costs of sales each month will even themselves out.

Chapter roundup

- Stock control includes the functions of stock ordering and purchasing, receiving goods into store, storing and issuing stock and controlling the level of stocks.

- Every movement of material in a business should be documented using the following as appropriate: purchase requisition, purchase order, GRN, materials requisition note, materials transfer note and materials returned note.

- Perpetual inventory refers to a stock recording system whereby the records (bin cards and stores ledger accounts) are updated for each receipt and issue of stock as it occurs.

- Stocktaking can be carried out on a continuous or periodic basis.

- Free stock balance calculations take account of stock on order from suppliers, and of stock which has been requisitioned but not yet delivered.

- Stock costs include purchase costs, holding costs, ordering costs and stockout costs.

- Stock control levels can be calculated in order to maintain stocks at the optimum level. The three critical control levels are reorder level, minimum level and maximum level. The economic order quantity is the order quantity which minimises stock costs. The EOQ can be calculated using a table, graph or formula.

- The correct pricing of issues and valuation of stock are of the utmost importance because they have a direct effect on the calculation of profit.

- Several different methods can be used in practice. The method selected for each item of stock must be the most appropriate for management purposes and must be consistently applied.

- FIFO assumes that materials are issued out of stock in the order in which they were delivered into stock: issues are priced at the cost of the earliest delivery remaining in stock.

- LIFO assumes that materials are issued out of stock in the reverse order to which they were delivered: the most recent deliveries are issued before earlier ones and issues are priced accordingly.

- There are two weighted average methods of pricing: cumulative weighted average and periodic weighted average.

- Under the standard costing method, all issues are at a predetermined standard price.

- Although replacement costing is recommended as a method of accounting for inflation, in many instances it is impractical because of the difficulty of maintaining records of replacement market values.

- Remember that pricing methods have no connection with the choice of the items actually issued.

Test your knowledge

1   List five steps in the ordering and receipt of raw materials. (see para 1.1)

2   List six objectives of storekeeping. (2.3)

3   What is free stock? (2.10)

4   What are the differences between periodic stocktaking and continuous stocktaking? (2.14, 2.15)

5   List six elements in the cost of holding stock. (3.3)

6   What is the purpose of the minimum stock control level? (3.7)

7   In what three ways can the EOQ be calculated? (3.11, 3.13, 3.15)

8   List nine methods of charging materials issues to production. (5.1, 6.1, 7.1, 8.1, 9.1, 9.3, 9.5, 9.6, 9.7)

9   What are the advantages and disadvantages of using LIFO in materials issues pricing? (6.2)

10   How would you calculate a periodic weighted average price? (8.1)

Now try illustrative questions 3 and 4 at the end of the Study Text

Chapter 4

LABOUR COSTS

> ## This chapter covers the following topics.
>
> | | | Syllabus reference | Ability required |
> |---|---|---|---|
> | 1 | Remuneration methods | 2(a) | Skill |
> | 2 | Labour cost behaviour | 2(a) | Skill |
> | 3 | Recording labour costs | 2(a) | Skill |
> | 4 | Labour turnover | 2(a) | Skill |
> | 5 | Direct labour and indirect labour | 2(a) | Skill |
>
> ## Introduction
>
> In Chapter 3 we examined in detail one of the three major elements of cost, materials. That just leaves labour and overheads. This chapter is dedicated to labour.
>
> Just as management need to control stocks and operate an appropriate valuation policy in an attempt to control material costs, so too must they be aware of the most suitable remuneration policy for their organisation. We will be looking at a number of methods of remuneration and will consider the various types of incentive scheme that exist. We will also examine the procedures and documents required for the accurate recording of labour costs. Labour turnover, labour cost behaviour and the split of labour into direct and indirect labour will be studied too.
>
> Overheads, last but by no means least, is the topic of Chapter 4.

1 REMUNERATION METHODS

1.1 The correct choice of labour remuneration method in a business is very important for two main reasons.

    (a) The remuneration method may have a major effect on the cost of finished products or services, particularly in a labour intensive organisation.

    (b) The morale and efficiency of employees can be affected by the remuneration methods in operation, and serious consideration should therefore be given to the possible motivational impact of any scheme.

1.2 There are three basic methods of remuneration.

    (a) Time work
    (b) Piecework schemes
    (c) Bonus/incentive schemes

We will discuss each of these in the next few paragraphs.

Time work

1.3 The most common form of time work is a day-rate system. Wages are calculated by the following formula.

      Wages = Hours worked × rate of pay per hour

1.4   If an employee works for more hours than the basic daily requirement he may be entitled to an overtime payment. Hours of overtime are usually paid at a premium rate. For instance, if the basic day-rate is £4 per hour and overtime is paid at time-and-a-quarter, eight hours of overtime would be paid the following amount.

	£
Basic pay (8 × £4)	32
Overtime premium (8 × £1)	8
Total (8 × £5)	40

1.5   Notice that the overtime premium is the extra rate per hour which is paid, not the whole of the payment for the overtime hours. Overtime can be at any agreed rate; common examples are time-and-a-half or double time.

1.6   If employees work unsocial hours, for instance overnight, they may be entitled to a shift premium. This is similar to an overtime premium and means that the employee is paid an increased hourly rate. The extra amount paid per hour, above the basic hourly rate, is the shift premium.

1.7   Day-rate systems have the advantage of being easy to understand and they do not lead to very complex negotiations when they are being revised. They are most appropriate when the quality of output is more important than the quantity, or where there is no basis for payment by performance. There is, however, no incentive for employees who are paid on a day-rate basis to improve their performance.

Piecework schemes

1.8   In a piecework scheme, wages are calculated by the following formula.

Wages = units produced × rate of pay per unit

Suppose for example, an employee is paid £1 for each unit produced and works a 40 hour week. Production overhead is added at the rate of £2 per direct labour hour.

Weekly production Units	Pay (40 hours) £	Overhead £	Conversion cost £	Conversion cost per unit £
40	40	80	120	3.00
50	50	80	130	2.60
60	60	80	140	2.33
70	70	80	150	2.14

As his output increases, his wage increases and at the same time unit costs of output are reduced.

1.9   It is normal for pieceworkers to be offered a guaranteed minimum wage, so that they do not suffer loss of earnings when production is low through no fault of their own.

1.10   Sometimes an employee may make several different types of product, some of which take longer than others. In this case, it is not possible to add up the units for payment purposes; instead a standard time allowance is given for each unit to arrive at a total of piecework hours for payment.

Example: piecework

1.11   An employee is paid £3 per piecework hour produced. In a 40 hour week he produces the following output.

	Piecework time allowed per unit
15 units of product X	0.5 hours
20 units of product Y	2.0 hours

Required

Calculate the employee's pay for the week.

Solution

1.12 Piecework hours produced are as follows.

Product X 15 × 0.5 hours		7.5 hours
Product Y 20 × 2.0 hours		40.0 hours
Total piecework hours		47.5 hours

Therefore employee's pay = 47.5 × £3 = £142.50 for the week.

Differential piecework schemes

1.13 Differential piecework schemes offer an incentive to employees to increase their output by paying higher rates for increased levels of production. For example:

up to and including 80 units, rate of pay per unit in this band	=	£1.00
81 to 90 units, rate of pay per unit in this band	=	£1.20
above 90 units, rate of pay per unit in this band	=	£1.30

An employee producing 97 units would therefore receive (80 × £1.00) + (10 × £1.20) + (7 × £1.30) = £101.10.

Employers should obviously be careful to make it clear whether they intend to pay the increased rate on all units produced, or on the extra output only.

Piecework schemes generally

1.14 Piecework schemes enjoy fluctuating popularity. They are occasionally used by employers as a means of increasing pay levels when other means are not available to them, but they are frequently condemned as a means of driving employees to work too hard to earn a satisfactory wage.

Exercise 1

Can you think of another major disadvantage of piecework schemes?

Solution

A further disadvantage of piecework schemes is that careful inspection of output is necessary so that quality does not suffer as employees try to increase the quantity produced.

Bonus/incentive schemes

1.15 In general, bonus schemes were introduced to compensate workers paid under a time-based system for their inability to increase earnings by working more efficiently.

1.16 Various types of incentive and bonus schemes have been devised which encourage greater productivity. The characteristics of such schemes are as follows.

(a) A target is set and actual performance is compared with target.

(b) Employees are paid more for their efficiency.

(c) In spite of the extra labour cost, the unit cost of output is reduced and the profit earned per unit of sale is increased; in other words the profits arising from productivity improvements are shared between employer and employee.

(d) Morale of employees should be expected to improve since they are seen to receive extra reward for extra effort.

1.17 Whatever scheme is used, it must satisfy certain conditions to operate successfully.

(a) Its objectives should be clearly stated and attainable by the employees.

(b) The rules and conditions of the scheme should be easy to understand and not liable to be misinterpreted.

(c) It must win the full acceptance of everyone concerned including, of course, trade union negotiators and officials.

(d) It should be seen to be fair to employees and employers. Other groups of employees should not feel unjustly excluded from the scheme, as their work might be affected by their dissatisfaction.

(e) The bonus should ideally be paid soon after the extra effort has been made by the employees, to associate the ideas of effort and reward.

(f) Allowances should be made for external factors outside the employees' control which reduce their productivity such as machine breakdowns or raw materials shortages.

(g) Only those employees who make the extra effort should be rewarded. It would not be an incentive, for example, to institute a scheme in all factories in a country-wide organisation and to pay a productivity bonus to employees in London for work done by employees in a factory in the North of England (especially if these North of England employees fail to get an adequate bonus for their efforts as a result of this sharing).

(h) The scheme must be properly communicated to employees.

1.18 There are many possible types of incentive schemes. Some organisations employ a variety of incentive schemes. A scheme for a production labour force may not necessarily be appropriate for white-collar workers. An organisation's incentive schemes may be regularly reviewed, and altered as circumstances dictate.

(a) A *high day-rate system* is an incentive scheme where employees are paid a high wage rate so that they will work more efficiently than similar employees on a lower hourly rate.

(b) Under an *individual bonus scheme*, individual employees qualify for a bonus on top of their basic wage, with each person's bonus being calculated separately.

(c) Where individual effort cannot be measured, and employees work as a team, an individual incentive scheme is impractical but a *group bonus scheme* is feasible.

(d) In a *profit sharing scheme*, employees receive a certain proportion of their company's year-end profits (the size of their bonus being related to their position in the company and the length of their employment to date).

(e) Companies operating *incentive schemes involving shares* use their shares, or the right to acquire them, as a form of incentive.

1.19 Note that an employer may provide other bonuses and benefits (company cars, non-contributory pension schemes, subsidised canteen). Such benefits do not improve production so much as reduce labour turnover, which we will cover in Section 4.

Exercise 2

Swetton Tyres Ltd manufactures a single product. Its work force consists of 10 employees, who work a 36-hour week exclusive of lunch and tea breaks. The standard time required to make one unit of the product is two hours, but the current efficiency (or productivity) ratio being achieved is 80%. No overtime is worked, and the work force is paid £4 per attendance hour.

Because of agreements with the work force about work procedures, there is some unavoidable idle time due to bottlenecks in production, and about four hours per week per person are lost in this way.

The company can sell all the output it manufactures, and makes a 'cash profit' of £20 per unit sold, deducting currently achievable costs of production but *before* deducting labour costs.

An incentive scheme is proposed whereby the work force would be paid £5 per hour in exchange for agreeing to new work procedures that would reduce idle time per employee per week to two hours and also raise the efficiency ratio to 90%.

Evaluate the incentive scheme from the point of view of profitability.

Solution

The current situation

Hours in attendance	10×36	=	360 hours
Hours spent working	10×32	=	320 hours
Units produced, at 80% efficiency	$\dfrac{320}{2} \times \dfrac{80}{100}$	=	128 units

	£
Cash profits before deducting labour costs (128 × £20)	2,560
Less labour costs (£4 × 360 hours)	1,440
Net profit	1,120

The incentive scheme

Hours spent working	10×34	=	340 hours
Units produced, at 90% efficiency	$\dfrac{340}{2} \times \dfrac{90}{100}$	=	153 units

	£
Cash profits before deducting labour costs (153 × £20)	3,060
Less labour costs (£5 × 360)	1,800
Net profit	1,260

In spite of a 25% increase in labour costs, profits would rise by £140 per week. The company and the workforce would both benefit provided, of course, that management can hold the work force to their promise of work reorganisation and improved productivity.

2   LABOUR COST BEHAVIOUR

2.1   (a)   When employees are paid on a piecework basis their pay is a variable cost.

(b)   When employees are paid a basic day-rate wage, their pay per week is fixed, regardless of the volume of output. The high cost of redundancy payments and the scarcity of skilled labour will usually persuade a company to retain its employees at a basic wage even when output is low.

(c)   Because of productivity bonuses, overtime premium, commission and so on, labour costs are often mixed costs.

2.2   Labour costs tend to behave in a step cost fashion.

(a)   Where the steps are short (that is where extra labour is needed for small increases in output volumes), the labour costs tend to be more variable in nature.

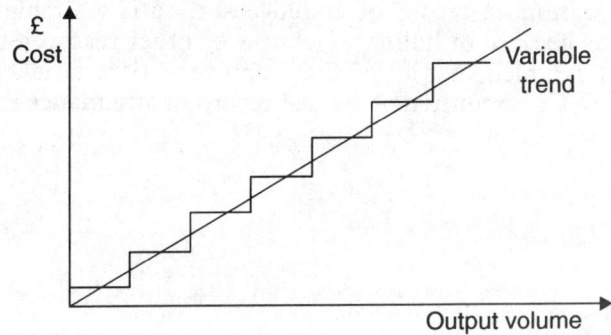

In this graph, the short steps approximate closely to a variable cost line, and for most purposes, it will be sufficiently accurate to treat labour as a purely variable cost.

(b)   If, on the other hand, the labour force is static for wide ranges of output, the cost tends to be fixed in nature.

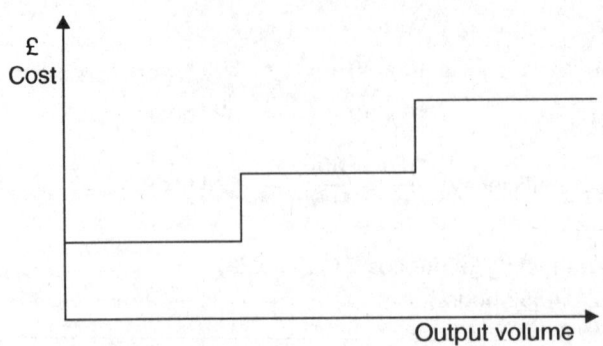

2.3   The cost accountant has to treat labour costs as fixed or variable.

(a)   Direct labour is usually regarded as being a variable cost in labour-intensive work. In highly automated industries it may be regarded as a fixed cost.

(b)   For control purposes, direct labour is regarded as a variable cost so that measures of efficiency or productivity can be obtained.

3   RECORDING LABOUR COSTS

3.1   We must now turn our attention to a different topic, and consider how a company records the time spent by a labour force on various aspects of work, and therefore how much the work has cost.

3.2   Several departments and management groups are involved in the collection, recording and costing of labour. These include personnel, time and motion study, production planning, time-keeping, wages, cost accounting and managers involved in labour budgeting.

3.3   From a cost accounting point of view, the timekeeping department provides the most important information to facilitate the recording of labour cost. The timekeeping department is responsible for accurately recording the time spent in the factory by each worker and time spent by each worker on each job or operation: attendance time and job time respectively. Such timekeeping provides basic data for statutory records, payroll preparation, labour costs of an operation or overhead distribution (where based on wages or labour hours) and statistical analysis of labour records for determining productivity and control of labour costs.

Attendance time

3.4   The bare minimum record of employees' time is a simple attendance record showing days absent because of holiday, sickness or other reason. Such a system is usually used when it is assumed that all of the employees' time is taken up doing one job and no further analysis is required. A typical record of attendance is shown below.

| NAME: A.N. OTHER | DEPT: 072 | NI REF: WD 4847 41C | LEAVE ENTITLEMENT: 20 |

	1	2	3	4	5	6	7	8	9	10	11	12	13	14	15	16	17	18	19	20	21	22	23	24	25	26	27	28	29	30	31
JAN																															
FEB																															
MAR																															
APR																															
MAY																															
JUNE																															
JULY																															
AUG																															
SEPT																															
OCT																															
NOV																															
DEC																															

Illness: I	Leave: L	Training: T	*Note overleaf:* (1) The reasons for special leave (eg bereavement).
Industrial Accident: IA	Unpaid Leave: UL	Jury Service: J	
Maternity: M	Special Leave: SL		(2) Ensure training is noted on personnel card.

RECORD OF ATTENDANCE

3.5 The next step up is to have some record of time of arrival, time of breaks and time of departure. The simplest form is a 'signing-in book' at the entrance to the building with, say, a page for each employee. Unless someone is watching constantly, however, this system is open to abuse and many employers use a time recording clock which stamps the time on a clock card inserted by the employee. A clock card is illustrated below. More modern systems involve the use of a plastic card like a credit card which is 'swiped' through a device which makes a computer record of the time of arrival and departure.

No			Ending	
Name				
HOURS	RATE	AMOUNT	DEDUCTIONS	
Basic			Income Tax	
O/T			NI	
Others			Other	
			Total deduction	
Total				
Less deductions				
Net due				
Time	Day		Basic time	Overtime
1230 T				
0803 T				
1700 M				
1305 M				
1234 M				
0750 M				
Signature _ _ _ _ _ _ _ _ _				

Job time

3.6 The next step is to analyse the hours spent at work according to what was done during those hours. The method adopted depends upon the size of the organisation, the nature of the work and the type of incentive scheme in operation.

3.7 *Continuous production.* Where routine, repetitive work is carried out it might not be practical to record the precise details. For example if a worker stands at a conveyor belt for seven hours his work can be measured by keeping a note of the number of units that pass through his part of the process during that time. If a group of employees all contribute to the same process, the total units processed per day (or week or whatever) can be divided by the total number of hours they collectively worked.

3.8   *Job costing.* When the work is not of a repetitive nature the records required might be one or several of the following.

(a)   *Daily time sheets.* A time sheet is filled in by the employee as a record of how his/her time has been spent. The total time on the time sheet should correspond with time shown on the attendance record. Times are recorded daily and so there is less risk that they will be forgotten or manipulated, but this system does produce considerable volumes of paperwork. It is most appropriate if the worker deals with a number of small jobs.

(b)   *Weekly time sheets.* These are similar to daily time sheets but are passed to the cost office at the end of the week, although entries must be made by employees on a daily basis to avoid error. Paperwork is reduced and weekly time sheets are particularly suitable where there are just a few job changes in a week. An example is shown below.

	Time Sheet No. _ _ _ _ _ _ _ _ _ _ _ _ _ _						
Employee Name _ _ _ _ _ _ _ _			Clock Code _ _ _ _ _ _ _ _		Dept _ _ _ _ _ _		
Date _ _ _ _ _ _ _ _ _ _ _ _ _ _			Week No. _ _ _ _ _ _ _ _ _ _ _				
Job No.	Start Time	Finish Time	Qty	Checker	Hrs	Rate	Extension

The time sheet will be filled in by the employee, for hours worked on each job (job code) or area of work (cost code). The cost of the hours worked will be entered at a later stage in the accounting department.

(c)   *Job cards.* Cards are prepared for each job or batch, unlike time sheets which are made out for each employee and which may contain bookings relating to numerous jobs. When an employee works on a job he or she records on the job card the time spent on that job and so job cards are likely to contain entries relating to numerous employees. On completion of the job it will contain a full record of the times involved in the job or batch. The problem of job cards, however, is that the reconciliation of job time and attendance time can be a difficult task, especially for jobs which stretch over several weeks. It is therefore difficult to incorporate them directly into wage calculation procedures. They do, however, reduce the amount of writing to be done by the employee and therefore the possibility of error. A typical job card is shown below.

JOB CARD			
Department _ _ _ _ _ _ _ _ _ _ _ _ _ _ Job no _ _ _ _ _ _ _ _ _ _ _ _ _ _ _ _			
Date _ _ _ _ _ _ _ _ _ _ _ _ _ _ _ Operation no _ _ _ _ _ _ _ _ _ _ _ _ _ _			
Time allowance _ _ _ _ _ _ _ _ _ _ _ Time started _ _ _ _ _ _ _ _ _ _ _ _ _			
	Time finished _ _ _ _ _ _ _ _ _ _ _ _ _		
	Hours on the job _ _ _ _ _ _ _ _ _ _ _		
Description of job	Hours	Rate	Cost
Employee no _ _ _ _ _ _ _ _ _ _ _ _ Certified by _ _ _ _ _ _ _ _ _ _ _ _ _ _			
Signature _ _ _ _ _ _ _ _ _ _ _ _ _			

3.9 *Piecework*. The wages of pieceworkers and the labour cost of work done by them is determined from what is known as a piecework ticket or an operation card. The card records the total number of items (or 'pieces') produced and the number of rejects. Payment is only made for 'good' production. A typical operation card is shown below.

Note that the attendance record of a pieceworker is required for calculations of holidays, sick pay and so on.

3.10 *Other types of work*. Casual workers are paid from job cards or time sheets. Time sheets are also used where outworkers are concerned.

3.11 Office work can be measured in a similar way, provided that the work can be divided into distinct jobs. Firms of accountants and advertising agencies, for example, book their staff time to individual clients and so make use of time sheets for salaried staff.

Salaried labour

3.12 You might think there is little point in salaried staff filling in a detailed timesheet about what they do every hour of the day, as their basic pay is a flat rate every month but, in fact, in many enterprises they are required to do so. There are a number of reasons for this.

(a) Such timesheets aid the creation of management information about product costs, and hence profitability.

(b) The timesheet information may have a direct impact on the revenue the enterprise receives (see below).

(c) Timesheets are used to record hours spent and so support claims for overtime payments by salaried staff. (This is just as true for hourly paid workers as it is for salaried staff.)

3.13 Below is shown the type of time sheet which can be found in large firms in the service sector of the economy: examples would be a firm of solicitors, a firm of accountants, or a firm of management consultants.

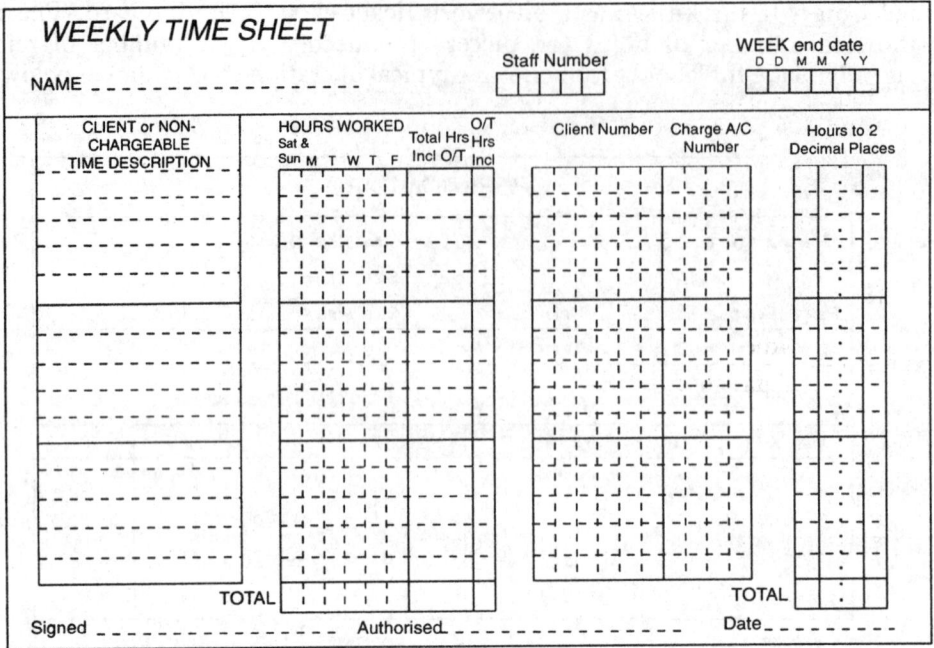

3.14 Service firms are chiefly in the business of selling the time and expertise of their employees to clients. This means that if an employee spends an hour at a particular client, the client will be billed for one hour of the employee's time. A time sheet is necessary so that clients are charged for the correct amount of time that has been spent doing their work.

Idle time

3.15 In many jobs there are times when, through no fault of their own, employees cannot get on with their work. They may be waiting for another department to finish its contribution to a job, or a machine may break down or there may simply be a temporary shortage of work.

3.16 Idle time has a cost because employees will still be paid their basic wage or salary for these unproductive hours and so there should be a record of idle time. This may simply comprise an entry on time sheets coded to 'idle time' generally, or separate idle time cards may be prepared. A supervisor might enter the time of a stoppage, its cause, its duration and the employees made idle on an idle time record card. Each stoppage should have a separate reference number which can be entered on time sheets or job cards as appropriate.

Cost accounting department

3.17 The cost accounting department will make use of clock cards, job cards, idle time cards and the payroll to produce a detailed analysis of all wages paid to enable the labour costs involved in products, operations, jobs, cost centres and departments to be established.

3.18 That proportion of the wages of production employees which is directly attributable to production (as ascertained from job cards and time sheets) is charged to the appropriate job or operation. At the end of a period the total of direct wages is charged to a departmental work in progress control account.

3.19 The wages of such employees as inspectors, store assistants and supervisors should be coded to the appropriate department to form part of the overheads of that department. That proportion of production workers' wages which cannot be classified as direct, such as idle time, should also be included in indirect costs and subsequently absorbed into production costs via the appropriate overhead absorption rate.

(*Note.* The last section of this chapter gives you some guidelines on distinguishing between direct and indirect labour.)

3.20 The cost accounting department may also produce an idle time report from the idle time cards at the end of each period. This report summarises the hours lost through idle time, analysed by cause. If possible the idle time should be separated into controllable causes, such as failure of material supply or shortage of skilled labour in an earlier process, and uncontrollable causes (such as power failure).

3.21 A useful ratio for the control of idle time is the 'idle time ratio'.

$$\text{Idle time ratio} = \frac{\text{Idle hours}}{\text{Total hours}} \times 100\%$$

The ratio is useful because it shows the proportion of available hours which were lost as a result of idle time.

4 LABOUR TURNOVER

The reasons for labour turnover

4.1 Some employees will leave their job and go to work for another company or organisation. Sometimes the reasons are unavoidable.

  (a) Illness or accidents
  (b) A family move away from the locality
  (c) Marriage, pregnancy or difficulties with child care provision
  (d) Retirement or death

4.2 Other causes of labour turnover are to some extent controllable.

  (a) Paying a lower wage rate than is available elsewhere
  (b) Requiring employees to work in unsafe or highly stressful conditions
  (c) Requiring employees to work uncongenial hours
  (d) Poor relationships between management and staff
  (e) Lack of opportunity for career enhancement
  (f) Requiring employees to work in inaccessible places (with no public transport, for example)
  (g) Discharging employees for misconduct, bad timekeeping or unsuitability

The costs of labour turnover

4.3 The costs of labour turnover can be large and management should attempt to keep labour turnover as low as possible so as to minimise these costs.

4.4 The cost of labour turnover may be divided into preventative costs and replacement costs.

  (a) *Preventative costs* are the costs incurred in trying to keep employees in their jobs. These comprise the following.

     (i) Cost of personnel administration incurred in maintaining good relationships

     (ii) Cost of medical services including check-ups, nursing staff and so on

     (iii) Cost of welfare services, including sports facilities, laundry services and canteen meals

     (iv) Pension schemes providing security to employees

  (b) *Replacement costs* are the costs incurred as a result of hiring new employees.

Exercise 3

What replacement costs can you think of?

Solution

Here are some ideas.

(a) Cost of selection and placement

(b) Inefficiency of new labour; productivity will be lower

(c) Costs of training; training costs will include formal training courses plus the costs of on-the-job instructors diverted from their own work to teach new recruits

(d) Loss of output due to delay in new labour becoming available

(e) Increased wastage and spoilage due to lack of expertise among new staff

(f) The possibility of more frequent accidents at work

(g) Cost of tool and machine breakages

The prevention of high labour turnover

4.5 Labour turnover will be reduced by the following actions.

(a) Paying satisfactory wages

(b) Offering satisfactory hours and conditions of work

(c) Creating a good informal relationship between fellow workers and between supervisors and subordinates

(d) Offering good training schemes and a well-understood career or promotion ladder

(e) Improving the content of jobs to create job satisfaction

(f) Proper planning so as to avoid redundancies

(g) Providing benefits such as company cars, staff discounts, subsidised canteen, health insurance, non-contributory pension schemes and so on

5   DIRECT LABOUR AND INDIRECT LABOUR

5.1 You should be aware of which items of labour cost constitute a direct cost and which constitute an indirect cost.

5.2 Labour costs include the following.

(a) The basic pay of direct workers (includes cash paid, PAYE and other deductions)
(b) The basic pay of indirect workers
(c) Overtime premium
(d) Bonus payments
(e) Employer's National Insurance contributions
(f) Idle time of direct workers
(g) Work on installation of equipment

5.3 The guidelines which help you to distinguish direct and indirect costs are as follows.

(a) The basic pay of direct workers is a direct cost to the unit, job or process.

(b) The basic pay of indirect workers is an indirect cost, unless a customer asks for an order to be carried out which involves the dedicated use of indirect workers' time, when the cost of this time would be a direct labour cost of the order.

(c) Overtime premium paid to both direct and indirect workers is an indirect cost, except in two particular circumstances.

(i)   If overtime is worked at the specific request of a customer to get his order completed, the overtime premium paid is a direct cost of the order.

(ii) If overtime is worked regularly by a production department in the normal course of operations, the overtime premium paid to direct workers could be incorporated into the (average) direct labour hourly rate.

(d)   Bonus payments are generally an indirect cost (unless they can be allocated to a specific job/task).

(e)   Employer's National Insurance contributions (which are added to employees' total pay as a wages cost) are normally treated as an indirect labour cost.

(f)   Idle time is an overhead cost, that is an indirect labour cost.

(g)   The cost of work on capital equipment is incorporated into the capital cost of the equipment.

(h)   The wages of support staff will automatically be an indirect cost.

Chapter roundup

- Labour is a major cost in many businesses and it is therefore vital that you have understood this chapter's topics, a summary of them being set out below.

- There are three basic groups of remuneration method - time work, piecework schemes and bonus/incentive schemes.

- Although labour costs tend to behave in a step cost fashion, cost accountants usually treat labour costs as fixed or variable.

- Labour attendance time is recorded on, for example, an attendance record or clock card. Job time may be recorded on daily time sheets, weekly time sheets or job cards depending on the circumstances. The manual recording of times on time sheets or job cards is, however, liable to error or even deliberate deception and may therefore be unreliable.

- The labour cost of pieceworkers is recorded on a piecework ticket/operation card.

- Idle time has a cost and must therefore be recorded.

- Labour turnover is the rate at which employees leave a company and this rate should be kept as low as possible. The cost of labour turnover can be divided into preventative and replacement costs.

- Ensure that you are able to distinguish between direct and indirect labour costs.

Test your knowledge

1   What is a differential piecework scheme? (see para 1.13)

2   List five types of incentive scheme. (1.18)

3   When might direct labour be regarded as a fixed cost? (2.3)

4   List four types of document used in recording job time. (3.7 - 3.11)

5   Define the idle time ratio. (3.21)

6   List six methods of reducing labour turnover. (4.5)

7   In what circumstances is overtime premium *not* an indirect cost? (5.3)

Now try illustrative question 5 at the end of the Study Text

Chapter 5

OVERHEAD APPORTIONMENT AND ABSORPTION

This chapter covers the following topics.

		Syllabus reference	Ability required
1	Overhead allocation	2(a)	Skill
2	Overhead apportionment	2(a)	Skill
3	Overhead absorption	2(a)	Skill
4	Blanket absorption rates and departmental absorption rates	2(a)	Skill
5	Over and under absorption of overheads	2(a)	Skill
6	Activity based costing	2(a)	Skill

Introduction

Finally, we come to the last of the cost elements, overheads.

The concept of overheads was introduced way back in Chapter 1 but will now be examined in much greater detail.

So, what are overheads? 'What a stupid question' you may be thinking to yourself. You would be surprised, however, by the number of students who are not 100% certain about overheads and what they are. Overhead is actually the total of indirect materials, indirect labour and indirect expenses. In other words, overheads are those costs which are not directly attributable to cost units, as opposed to direct costs which are. The total of these indirect costs is usually split into production overhead, administration overhead and selling and distribution overhead.

There are basically two schools of thought as to the correct method of dealing with overheads, marginal costing (which we will be looking at in the next chapter) and absorption costing, the topic of this chapter.

The objective of absorption costing is to include in the total cost of a product (unit, job, process and so on) an appropriate share of the organisation's total overhead. An appropriate share is generally taken to mean an amount which reflects the amount of time and effort that has gone into producing a unit or completing a job.

If an organisation had but one production department and produced identical units then the total overheads would be divided among the total units produced. Life is, of course, never that simple. Absorption costing is a method for sharing overheads between a number of different products on a fair basis.

The topic was examined in the November 95 exam. On the whole the question was reasonably well answered except for the part on over and under absorption of overheads. Over/under absorption is quite tricky so work through Section 5 very carefully.

In Section 6 we will look briefly at a recent development in the treatment of overheads, activity based costing.

1 OVERHEAD ALLOCATION

1.1 Allocation is the process by which whole cost items are charged direct to a cost unit (in the case of direct costs) or to a cost centre (in the case of overheads). Most overheads cannot be economically attributed to a cost unit but they can be attributed to a cost centre. Cost centres may be one of the following types.

(a)   A production department, to which production overheads are charged

(b)   A production area service department, to which production overheads are charged

(c)   An administrative department, to which administration overheads are charged

(d)   A selling or a distribution department, to which sales and distribution overheads are charged

(e)   An overhead cost centre, to which items of expense which are shared by a number of departments, such as rent and rates, heat and light and the canteen, are charged

1.2   The following costs would therefore be charged to the following cost centres via the process of allocation.

(a)   The cost of a warehouse security guard will be charged to the warehouse cost centre.

(b)   Paper on which computer output is recorded will be charged to the computer department.

(c)   Costs such as the canteen are charged direct to various overhead cost centres.

1.3   As an example of overhead allocation, consider the following costs of a company.

Wages of the foreman of department A	£200
Wages of the foreman of department B	£150
Indirect materials consumed in department A	£50
Rent of the premises shared by departments A and B	£300

The cost accounting system might include three cost centres.

Cost centre:	101	Department A
	102	Department B
	201	Rent

Overhead costs would be allocated directly to each cost centre, ie £200 + £50 to cost centre 101, £150 to cost centre 102 and £300 to cost centre 201. The rent of the factory will be subsequently shared between the two production departments, but for the purpose of day to day cost recording, the rent will first of all be charged in full to a separate cost centre.

2   OVERHEAD APPORTIONMENT   11/96

First stage: apportioning general overheads

2.1   Overhead apportionment follows on from *overhead* allocation (we are not interested in the *direct costs* allocated direct to cost units since they automatically become part of a product cost). The first stage of overhead apportionment is to identify all overhead costs as production department, production service department, administration or selling and distribution overhead. This means that the costs for heat and light, rent and rates, the canteen and so on (that is, costs which have been allocated to general overhead cost centres) must be shared out between the other cost centres.

Bases of apportionment

2.2   It is considered important that overhead costs should be shared out on a fair basis. You will appreciate that because of the complexity of items of cost it is rarely possible to use only one method of apportioning costs to the various departments of an organisation. The bases of apportionment for the most usual cases are given below.

Overhead to which the basis applies	*Basis*
Rent, rates, heating and light, repairs and depreciation of buildings	Floor area occupied by each cost centre
Depreciation, insurance of equipment	Cost or book value of equipment
Personnel office, canteen, welfare, wages and cost offices, first aid	Number of employees, or labour hours worked in each cost centre
Heating, lighting (see above)	Volume of space occupied by each cost centre
Carriage inwards (costs paid for the delivery of material supplies)	Value of material issues to each cost centre

An examination question may be set which calls for the apportionment of overhead items. In the majority of cases the basis to be used is obvious, but you may encounter one or two items for which two (or more) bases may appear to be equally acceptable. In such circumstances, do not waste time trying to weigh up the merits of each: use the method you prefer. Always indicate the basis of apportionment you have chosen, and in any case of doubt explain why you chose one basis in preference to another.

Example: overhead apportionment

2.3   Millie Ltd has incurred the following overhead costs.

	£'000
Depreciation of factory	100
Factory repairs and maintenance	60
Factory office costs (treat as production overhead)	150
Depreciation of equipment	80
Insurance of equipment	20
Heating	39
Lighting	10
Canteen	90
	549

Information relating to the production and service departments in the factory is as follows.

	Department			
	Production 1	*Production 2*	*Service 100*	*Service 101*
Floor space (square metres)	1,200	1,600	800	400
Volume (cubic metres)	3,000	6,000	2,400	1,600
Number of employees	30	30	15	15
Book value of equipment	£30,000	£20,000	£10,000	£20,000

Required

Determine how the overhead costs should be apportioned between the four departments.

Solution

2.4   Costs are apportioned using the following general formula.

$$\frac{\text{Total overhead cost}}{\text{Total value of apportionment base}} \times \text{value of apportionment base of cost centre}$$

For example, heating for department $1 = \dfrac{£39,000}{13,000} \times 3,000 = £9,000$

Item of cost	Basis of apportionment	Total cost	To Department			
			1	2	100	102
		£	£	£	£	£
Factory depreciation	(floor area)	100	30.0	40	20.0	10.0
Factory repairs	(floor area)	60	18.0	24	12.0	6.0
Factory office costs	(number of employees)	150	50.0	50	25.0	25.0
Equipment depreciation	(book value)	80	30.0	20	10.0	20.0
Equipment insurance	(book value)	20	7.5	5	2.5	5.0
Heating	(volume)	39	9.0	18	7.2	4.8
Lighting	(floor area)	10	3.0	4	2.0	1.0
Canteen	(number of employees)	90	30.0	30	15.0	15.0
Total		549	177.5	191	93.7	86.8

Exercise 1

Pippin Ltd has three production departments (forming, machines and assembly) and two service departments (maintenance and general).

The following is an analysis of budgeted overhead costs for a twelve-month period.

	£	£
Rent and rates		8,000
Power		750
Light, heat		5,000
Repairs, maintenance:		
Forming	800	
Machines	1,800	
Assembly	300	
Maintenance	200	
General	100	
		3,200
Departmental expenses:		
Forming	1,500	
Machines	2,300	
Assembly	1,100	
Maintenance	900	
General	1,500	
		7,300
Depreciation:		
Plant		10,000
Fixtures and fittings		250
Insurance:		
Plant		2,000
Buildings		500
Indirect labour:		
Forming	3,000	
Machines	5,000	
Assembly	1,500	
Maintenance	4,000	
General	2,000	
		15,500
		52,500

Other available data are as follows

	Floor area sq.ft	Plant value £	Fixtures & fittings £	Effective horse-power	Direct cost for year £	Labour hours worked	Machine hours worked
Forming	2,000	25,000	1,000	40	20,500	14,400	12,000
Machines	4,000	60,000	500	90	30,300	20,500	21,600
Assembly	3,000	7,500	2,000	15	24,200	20,200	2,000
Maintenance	500	7,500	1,000	5	-	-	-
General	500	-	500	-	-	-	-
	10,000	100,000	5,000	150	75,000	55,100	35,600

Required

Using the data provided apportion overheads to the five departments.

Solution

	Basis	Forming £	Machines £	Assembly £	Maint'nce £	General £	Total £
Directly allocated overheads:							
Repairs, maintenance		800	1,800	300	200	100	3,200
Departmental expenses		1,500	2,300	1,100	900	1,500	7,300
Indirect labour		3,000	5,000	1,500	4,000	2,000	15,500
Apportionment of other overheads:							
Rent, rates	1	1,600	3,200	2,400	400	400	8,000
Power	2	200	450	75	25	0	750
Light, heat	1	1,000	2,000	1,500	250	250	5,000
Dep'n of plant	3	2,500	6,000	750	750	0	10,000
Dep'n of F & F	4	50	25	100	50	25	250
Insurance of plant	3	500	1,200	150	150	0	2,000
Insurance of buildings	1	100	200	150	25	25	500
		11,250	22,175	8,025	6,750	4,300	52,500

Basis of apportionment:

1   floor area
2   effective horsepower
3   plant value
4   fixtures and fittings value

Second stage: service cost centre cost apportionment

2.5   The second stage of overhead apportionment concerns the treatment of service cost centres. A factory is divided into several production departments and also a number of service departments, but only the production departments are directly involved in the manufacture of the units. In order to be able to add production overheads to unit costs, it is necessary to have all the overheads charged to (or located in) the production departments. The next stage in absorption costing is, therefore, to apportion the costs of service cost centres to the production cost centres. Examples of possible apportionment bases are as follows.

Service cost centre	*Possible basis of apportionment*
Stores	Number or cost value of materials requisitions
Maintenance	Hours of maintenance and repair work done for each cost centre
Production planning	Direct labour hours worked for each production cost centre

Example: apportioning service cost centre costs direct to production cost centres

2.6   Mac Ltd incurred the following overhead costs.

	Production departments		*Stores department*	*Maintenance department*
	X	*Y*		
	£	£	£	£
Allocated costs	6,000	4,000	1,000	2,000
Apportioned costs	2,000	1,000	1,000	500
	8,000	5,000	2,000	2,500

The maintenance department worked 500 hours for department X and 750 hours for department Y. Production department X requisitioned materials to the value of £12,000. Department Y requisitioned £8,000 of materials.

Required

Calculate the total production overhead costs of departments X and Y.

Solution

2.7

Service department	*Basis of apportionment*	*Total cost*	*Dept A*	*Dept B*
		£	£	£
Stores	Value of requisitions	2,000	1,200	800
Maintenance	Hours	2,500	1,000	1,500
		4,500	2,200	2,300
Previously allocated and apportioned costs		13,000	8,000	5,000
Total overhead		17,500	10,200	7,300

Never forget to include the directly allocated costs when determining overheads to be apportioned.

Exercise 2

Using your solution to exercise 1 and the following information about the apportionment of service department costs, apportion the costs of the two service departments of Pippin Ltd to the three production departments and hence determine the total overhead for those departments.

	Maintenance	*General*
	%	%
Forming	20	30
Machines	50	60
Assembly	30	10
	100	100

Solution

Service department	*Basis of apportionment*	*Total cost*	*Forming*	*Machines*	*Assembly*
		£	£	£	£
Maintenance	2:5:3	6,750	1,350	3,375	2,025
General	3:6:1	4,300	1,290	2,580	430
		11,050	2,640	5,955	2,455
Previously allocated and apportioned costs		41,450	11,250	22,175	8,025
Total overhead		52,500	13,890	28,130	10,480

---

3   OVERHEAD ABSORPTION   *11/95, 11/96*

3.1   Having allocated and/or apportioned all overheads, the next stage in absorption costing is to add them to, or absorb them into, the cost of production or sales.

(a) Production costs are added to the prime cost (direct materials, labour and expenses), the total of the two being the factory cost, or full cost of production. Production overheads are therefore included in the value of stocks of finished goods.

(b) Administration and selling and distribution overheads are then added, the sum of the factory cost and these overheads being the total cost of sales. These overheads are therefore not included in the value of closing stock.

Use of a predetermined absorption rate

3.2 The figure for overheads included or absorbed into cost of sales is not the actual overheads incurred but rather a value based on estimated or budgeted figures (calculated prior to the beginning of the period). The rate at which overheads are included in cost of sales (absorption rate) is predetermined before the accounting period actually begins for a number of reasons.

(a) Goods are produced and sold throughout the year, but many actual overheads are not known until the end of the year. It would be inconvenient to wait until the year end in order to decide what overhead costs should be. Unacceptable delays in procedures such as invoicing and estimating, price setting and periodic stock and profit calculations would occur.

(b) An attempt to calculate overhead costs more regularly (such as each month) is possible, although estimated costs must be added for occasional expenditures such as rent and rates (incurred once or twice a year). The difficulty with this approach would be that actual overheads from month to month would fluctuate randomly; therefore, overhead costs charged to production would depend on a certain extent on random events and changes. A unit made in one week might be charged with £4 of overhead, in a subsequent week with £5, and in a third week with £4.50. Only units made in winter would be charged with the heating overhead. Such changes are considered misleading for costing purposes and administratively and clerically inconvenient to deal with.

An example may help to highlight these problems

3.3 Suppose that a company budgets to make 1,200 units of a product in the first half of 19X5. Budgeted production overhead costs, all fixed costs, are £12,000. Due to seasonal demand for the company's product, the volume of production varies from month to month. Actual overhead costs are £2,000 per month. Actual monthly production in the first half of 19X5 is listed below, and total actual production in the period is 1,080 units.

The table below shows the production overhead cost per unit using the following.

(a) A predetermined absorption rate of $\dfrac{£12,000}{1,200} = £10$ per unit

(b) An actual overhead cost per unit each month

(c) An actual overhead cost per unit based on actual six-monthly expenditure of £12,000 and actual six-monthly output of 1,080 units = £11.11 per unit

				Overhead cost per unit	
			(a)	*(b)*	*(c)*
			Predetermined	*Actual cost*	*Average actual cost*
Month	*Expenditure*	*Output*	*unit rate*	*each month*	*in the six months*
	(A)	*(B)*		*(A) ÷ (B)*	
	£	Units	£	£	£
Jan	2,000	100	10	20.00	11.11
Feb	2,000	120	10	16.67	11.11
Mar	2,000	140	10	14.29	11.11
April	2,000	160	10	12.50	11.11
May	2,000	320	10	6.25	11.11
June	2,000	240	10	8.33	11.11
	12,000	1,080			

3.4   *Points to note*

(a)   Methods (a) and (c) give a constant overhead cost per unit each month, regardless of seasonal variations in output. Method (b) gives variable unit overhead costs, depending on the season of the year. For this reason, it is argued that method (a) or (c) would provide more useful (long-term) costing information.

In addition, if prices are based on full cost with a percentage mark-up for profit, method (b) would give seasonal variations in selling prices, with high prices in low season and low prices in high season. Methods (a) and (c) would give a constant price based on 'cost plus'.

(b)   With method (a), overhead costs per unit are known throughout the period, and cost statements can be prepared at any time. This is because predetermined overhead rates are known in advance. With method (c), overhead costs cannot be established until after the end of an accounting period. For example, overhead costs of output in January 19X5 cannot be established until actual costs and output for the period are known, which will be not until after the end of June 19X5.

For the reasons given above, predetermined overhead rates are preferable to rates based on actual overhead costs, in spite of being based on cost and activity level estimates.

3.5   Overhead absorption rates are therefore calculated as follows.

(a)   The overhead likely to be incurred during the coming year is estimated.

(b)   The total hours, units, or direct costs on which the overhead absorption rates are to be based (activity level) are estimated.

(c)   The estimated overhead is divided by the budgeted activity level to arrive at an absorption rate.

Choosing the appropriate absorption base

3.6   There are a number of different bases of absorption which can be used. Examples are as follows.

(a)   A percentage of direct materials cost
(b)   A percentage of direct labour cost
(c)   A percentage of prime cost
(d)   A rate per machine hour
(e)   A rate per direct labour hour
(f)   A rate per unit

3.7   The choice of an absorption basis is a matter of judgement and common sense. There are no strict rules or formulae involved, although factors which should be taken into account are set out below. What is required is an absorption basis which realistically reflects the characteristics of a given cost centre and which avoids undue anomalies.

3.8   It is safe to assume, for example, that the indirect costs for producing brass screws are similar to those for producing steel screws. The cost of brass is, however, very much greater than that of steel. Consequently, the overhead charge for brass screws would be too high and that for steel screws too low, if a percentage of cost of materials rate were to be used.

3.9   Using prime cost as the absorption base would lead to anomalies because of the inclusion of the cost of material, as outlined above.

3.10 If the overhead actually attributable to units was incurred on, say a time basis, but one highly-paid employee was engaged on producing one item, while a lower-paid employee was producing another item, the overhead charged to the first item using a percentage of wages rate might be too high while the amount absorbed by the second item might be too low. This method should therefore only be used if similar wage rates are paid to all direct employees in a production department. A direct labour hour rate might be considered 'fairer'.

3.11 It is for this reason that many factories use a direct labour hour rate or machine hour rate in preference to a rate based on a percentage of direct materials cost, wages or prime cost. A direct labour hour basis is most appropriate in a labour intensive environment. A machine hour rate would be used in departments where production is controlled or dictated by machines. This basis is becoming more appropriate as factories become more heavily automated.

3.12 A rate per unit would be effective only if all units were identical.

Example: overhead absorption

3.13 The budgeted production overheads and other budget data of Calculator Ltd are as follows.

Budget	Production dept 1	Production dept 2
Overhead cost	£36,000	£5,000
Direct materials cost	£32,000	
Direct labour cost	£40,000	
Machine hours	10,000	
Direct labour hours	18,000	
Units of production		1,000

Required

Calculate the absorption rate using the various bases of apportionment.

Solution

3.14 (a) Department 1

(i) Percentage of direct materials cost $\dfrac{£36,000}{£32,000} \times 100\% = 112.5\%$

(ii) Percentage of direct labour cost $\dfrac{£36,000}{£40,000} \times 100\% = 90\%$

(iii) Percentage of prime cost $\dfrac{£36,000}{£72,000} \times 100\% = 50\%$

(iv) Rate per machine hour $\dfrac{£36,000}{10,000 \text{ hrs}} = £3.60$ per machine hour

(v) Rate per direct labour hour $\dfrac{£36,000}{18,000 \text{ hrs}} = £2$ per direct labour hour

(b) The department 2 absorption rate will be based on units of output.

$\dfrac{£5,000}{1,000 \text{ units}} = £5$ per unit produced

3.15 The choice of the basis of absorption is significant in determining the cost of individual units, or jobs, produced. Using the previous example, suppose that an individual product has a material cost of £80, a labour cost of £85, and requires 36 labour hours and 23 machine hours to complete. The overhead cost of the product would vary, depending on the basis of absorption used by the company for overhead recovery.

(a) As a percentage of direct materials cost, the overhead cost would be
112.5% × £80   = £90.00

(b) As a percentage of direct labour cost, the overhead cost would be
90% × £85   = £76.50

(c) As a percentage of prime cost, the overhead cost would be 50% × £165   = £82.50

(d) Using a machine hour basis of absorption, the overhead cost would be
23 hrs × £3.60   = £82.80

(e) Using a labour hour basis, the overhead cost would be 36 hrs × £2   = £72.00

3.16 In theory, each basis of absorption would be possible, but the company should choose a basis for its own costs which seems to be 'fairest'. In our example, this choice will be significant in determining the cost of individual products, as the following summary shows, but the *total cost* of production overheads is the budgeted overhead expenditure, no matter what basis of absorption is selected. It is the relative share of overhead costs borne by individual products and jobs which is affected by the choice of overhead absorption basis.

3.17 A summary of the product costs in the previous example is shown below.

Basis of overhead recovery

	Percentage of materials cost	*Percentage of labour cost*	*Percentage of prime cost*	*Machine hours*	*Direct labour hours*
	£	£	£	£	£
Direct material	80	80.00	80.00	80.00	80
Direct labour	85	85.00	85.00	85.00	85
Production overhead	90	76.50	82.50	82.80	72
Full factory cost	255	241.50	247.50	247.80	237

Exercise 3

Using your solution to Exercise 2 and the following information, determine suitable overhead absorption rates for Pippin Ltd's three production departments.

	Forming	Machines	Assembly
Budgeted direct labour hours per annum	5,556	790	5,240
Budgeted machine hours per annum	1,350	5,626	147

Solution

Forming (labour intensive) $\dfrac{£13,890}{5,556}$ = £2.50 per direct labour hour

Machines (machine intensive) $\dfrac{£28,130}{5,626}$ = £5 per machine hour

Assembly (labour intensive) $\dfrac{£10,480}{5,240}$ = £2 per direct labour hour

---

4   BLANKET ABSORPTION RATES AND DEPARTMENTAL ABSORPTION RATES

4.1 A blanket overhead absorption rate is an absorption rate used throughout a factory and for all jobs and units of output irrespective of the department in which they were produced. If, for example, total overheads were £500,000 and there were 250,000 direct machine hours during the period, the blanket overhead rate would be £2 per direct machine hour and all jobs passing through the factory would be charged at that rate.

4.2 Such a rate is not appropriate, however, if there are a number of departments and jobs do not spend an equal amount of time in each department.

4.3 It is argued that if a single factory overhead absorption rate is used, some products will receive a higher overhead charge than they ought 'fairly' to bear, whereas other products will be under-charged. By using a separate absorption rate for each department, charging of overheads will be equitable and the full cost of production of items will be more representative of the cost of the efforts and resources put into making them.

(Remember, however, that only *one* absorption base can be used for each department.) An example may help to illustrate this point.

Example: separate absorption rates

4.4 AB Ltd has two production departments, for which the following budgeted information is available.

	Department 1	Department 2	Total
Budgeted overheads	£360,000	£200,000	£560,000
Budgeted direct labour hours	200,000 hrs	40,000 hrs	240,000 hrs

If a single factory overhead absorption rate is applied, the rate of overhead recovery would be:

$$\frac{£560,000}{240,000 \text{ hours}} = £2.33 \text{ per direct labour hour}$$

4.5 If separate departmental rates are applied, these would be:

Department 1	Department 2
$\dfrac{£360,000}{200,000 \text{ hours}}$	$\dfrac{£200,000}{40,000 \text{ hours}}$
= £1.80 per direct labour hour	= £5 per direct labour hour

Department 2 has a higher overhead cost per hour worked than department 1.

Now let us consider two separate jobs.

(a) Job A has a prime cost of £100, takes 30 hours in department 2 and does not involve any work in department 1.

(b) Job B has a prime cost of £100, takes 28 hours in department 1 and 2 hours in department 2.

4.6 What would be the factory cost of each job, using the following rates of overhead recovery.

(a) A single factory rate of overhead recovery
(b) Separate departmental rates of overhead recovery

Solution

4.7

			Job A £		Job B £
(a)	*Single factory rate*				
	Prime cost		100		100
	Factory overhead (30 × £2.33)		70		70
	Factory cost		170		170

			£		£
(b)	*Separate departmental rates*				
	Prime cost		100		100.00
	Factory overhead: department 1		0	(28 × £1.80)	50.40
	department 2	(30 × £5)	150	(2 × £5)	10.00
	Factory cost		250		160.40

4.8 Using a single factory overhead absorption rate, both jobs would cost the same. However, since job A is done entirely within department 2 where overhead costs are relatively higher, whereas job B is done mostly within department 1, where overhead costs are relatively lower, it is arguable that job A should cost more than job B. This will occur if separate departmental overhead recovery rates are used to reflect the work done on each job in each department separately.

4.9   If all jobs do not spend approximately the same time in each department then, to ensure that all jobs are charged with their fair share of overheads, it is necessary to establish separate overhead rates for each department.

5   OVER AND UNDER ABSORPTION OF OVERHEADS   *11/95, 11/96*

5.1   Suppose that Normal Ltd budgeted to make 100 units of product Z at a cost of £3 per unit in direct materials and £4 per unit in direct labour. The sales price would be £12 per unit, and production overheads were budgeted to amount to £200. A unit basis of overhead recovery is in operation. During the period 120 units were actually produced and sold (for £12 each) and the actual cost of direct materials was £380 and of direct labour, £450. Overheads incurred came to £210.

Ignoring administration, selling and distribution overheads, the cost of sales of product Z and the company's profit would be calculated as follows.

	£
Direct materials	380
Direct labour	450
Overheads absorbed (120 units × £2*)	240
Full cost of sales, product Z	1,070
Sales of product Z (120 units × £12)	1,440
Profit, product Z	370

* (£200 ÷ 100 units)

5.2   You may already have noticed that the actual overhead cost incurred, £210, is not the same as the overhead absorbed into the cost of production, £240; nevertheless, in absorption costing £240 is the 'correct' cost. This discrepancy between actual overheads incurred and the overheads absorbed, which is an inevitable feature of absorption costing, is only reconciled at the end of an accounting period, as the 'under absorption' or 'over absorption' of overhead.

5.3   The rate of overhead absorption is based on estimates (of both numerator and denominator) and it is quite likely that either one or both of the estimates will not agree with what *actually* occurs. Actual overheads incurred will probably be either greater than or less than overheads absorbed into the cost of production. Over absorption means that the overheads charged to the cost of sales are greater then the overheads actually incurred. Under absorption means that insufficient overheads have been included in the cost of sales. It is almost inevitable that at the end of the accounting year there will have been an over absorption or under absorption of the overhead actually incurred, such as described in Paragraph 5.2.

5.4   Suppose that the budgeted overhead in a production department is £80,000 and the budgeted activity is 40,000 direct labour hours. The overhead recovery rate (using a direct labour hour basis) would be £2 per direct labour hour.

Actual overheads in the period are, say £84,000 and 45,000 direct labour hours are worked.

	£
Overhead incurred (actual)	84,000
Overhead absorbed (45,000 × £2)	90,000
Over-absorption of overhead	6,000

In this example, the cost of produced units or jobs has been charged with £6,000 more than was actually spent. An adjustment to reconcile the overheads charged to the actual overhead is necessary and the over-absorbed overhead will be written as an adjustment to the profit and loss account at the end of the accounting period.

The reasons for under-/over-absorbed overhead

5.5 The overhead absorption rate is predetermined from budget estimates of overhead cost and the expected volume of activity. Under or over recovery of overhead will occur in the following circumstances.

(a) Actual overhead costs are different from budgeted overheads.

(b) The actual activity level is different from the budgeted activity level.

(c) Both actual overhead costs and actual activity level are different from the budgeted costs and level.

Example: reasons for under/over absorption

5.6 Trevor Ltd has a budgeted production overhead of £50,000 and a budgeted activity of 25,000 direct labour hours and therefore a recovery rate of £2 per direct labour hour.

Required

Calculate the under-/over-absorbed overhead, and the reasons for the under/over absorption, in the following circumstances.

(a) Actual overheads cost £47,000 and 25,000 direct labour hours are worked.
(b) Actual overheads cost £50,000 and 21,500 direct labour hours are worked.
(c) Actual overheads cost £47,000 and 21,500 direct labour hours are worked.

Solution

5.7 (a)

	£
Actual overhead	47,000
Absorbed overhead (25,000 × £2)	50,000
Over-absorbed overhead	3,000

The reason for the over absorption is that although the actual and budgeted direct labour hours are the same, actual overheads cost less than expected.

(b)

	£
Actual overhead	50,000
Absorbed overhead (21,500 × £2)	43,000
Under-absorbed overhead	7,000

The reason for the under absorption is that although budgeted and actual overhead costs were the same, fewer direct labour hours were worked than expected.

(c)

	£
Actual overhead	47,000
Absorbed overhead (21,500 × £2)	43,000
Under-absorbed overhead	4,000

The reason for the under absorption is a combination of the reasons in (a) and (b).

Example: under and over absorption of overheads

5.8 Rioch Havery Ltd is a small company which manufactures two products, A and B, in two production departments, machining and assembly. A canteen is operated as a separate production service department.

The budgeted production and sales in the year to 31 March 19X3 are as follows.

	Product A	*Product B*
Sales price per unit	£50	£70
Sales (units)	2,200	1,400
Production (units)	2,000	1,500
Material cost per unit	£14	£12

	Product A Hours per unit	Product B Hours per unit
Direct labour:		
Machining department (£4 per hour)	2	3
Assembly department (£3 per hour)	1	2
Machine hours per unit:		
Machining department	3	4
Assembly department	$^{1}/_{2}$	

Budgeted production overheads are as follows.

	Machining department £	Assembly department £	Canteen £	Total £
Allocated costs	10,000	25,000	12,000	47,000
Apportionment of other general production overheads	26,000	12,000	8,000	46,000
	36,000	37,000	20,000	93,000
Number of employees	30	20	1	51
Floor area (square metres)	5,000	2,000	500	7,500

Required

(a) Calculate an absorption rate for overheads in each production department for the year to 31 March 19X3.

(b) Suppose that in the year to 31 March 19X3, 2,200 units of Product A are produced and 1,500 units of Product B. Direct labour hours per unit and machine hours per unit in both departments were as budgeted.

Actual production overheads are as follows.

	Machining department £	Assembly department £	Canteen £	Total £
Allocated costs	30,700	27,600	10,000	68,300
Apportioned share of general production overheads	17,000	8,000	5,000	30,000
	47,700	35,600	15,000	98,300

Calculate the under- or over-absorbed overhead in each production department and in total.

Solution

5.9 (a) *Choose absorption rates*

Since machine time appears to be more significant than labour time in the machining department, a machine hour rate of absorption will be used for overhead recovery in this department. On the other hand, machining is insignificant in the assembly department, and a direct labour hour rate of absorption would seem to be the basis which will give the fairest method of overhead recovery.

Apportion budgeted overheads

Next we need to apportion *budgeted* overheads to the two production departments. Canteen costs will be apportioned on the basis of the number of employees in each department. (Direct labour hours in each department are an alternative basis of apportionment, but the number of employees seems to be more directly relevant to canteen costs.)

	Machining department £	Assembly department £	Total £
Budgeted allocated costs	10,000	25,000	35,000
Share of general overheads	26,000	12,000	38,000
Apportioned canteen costs (30:20)	12,000	8,000	20,000
	48,000	45,000	93,000

Calculate overhead absorption rates

The overhead absorption rates are predetermined, using budgeted estimates. Since the overheads are production overheads, the budgeted activity relates to the volume of production, in units (the production hours required for volume of sales being irrelevant).

	Product A	Product B	Total
Budgeted production (units)	2,000	1,500	
Machining department: machine hours	6,000 hrs	6,000 hrs	12,000 hrs
Assembly department: direct labour hours	2,000 hrs	3,000 hrs	5,000 hrs

The overhead absorption rates will be as follows.

	Machining department	Assembly department
Budgeted overheads	£48,000	£45,000
Budgeted activity	12,000 hrs	5,000 hrs
Absorption rate	£4 per machine hour	£9 per direct labour hour

(b) *Apportion actual service department overhead to production departments*

When the actual costs are analysed, the 'actual' overhead of the canteen department (£15,000) would be split between the machining and assembly departments.

	Machining department £	Assembly department £	Total £
Allocated cost	30,700	27,600	58,300
Apportioned general overhead	17,000	8,000	25,000
Canteen (30:20)	9,000	6,000	15,000
	56,700	41,600	98,300

Establish the over- or under-absorption of overheads

There would be an over- or under-absorption of overheads as follows.

		Machining department £		Assembly department £	Total £
Overheads absorbed					
Product A (2,200 units)	(× £4 × 3hrs)	26,400	(× £9 × 1hr)	19,800	46,200
Product B (1,500 units)	(× £4 × 4hrs)	24,000	(× £9 × 2hrs)	27,000	51,000
		50,400		46,800	97,200
Overheads incurred		56,700		41,600	98,300
Over-/(under)-absorbed overhead		(6,300)		5,200	(1,100)

The total under-absorbed overhead of £1,100 will be written off to the profit and loss account at the end of the year, to compensate for the fact that overheads charged to production (£97,200) were less than the overheads actually incurred (£98,300).

Exercise 4

Using your solution to Exercise 3 and the following information, determine the under-/over-absorbed overhead in each of the three production departments of Pippin Ltd for the twelve-month period.

	Forming	Machines	Assembly
Actual direct labour hours	5,370	950	5,400
Actual machine hours	1,300	6,370	100
Actual overhead	£13,900	£30,300	£8,500

Solution

Forming	£
Overhead absorbed (£2.50 × 5,370)	13,425
Overhead incurred	13,900
Under-absorbed overhead	475

Machines	£
Overhead absorbed (£5 × 6,370)	31,850
Overhead incurred	30,300
Over-absorbed overhead	1,550

Assembly	£
Overhead absorbed (£2 × 5,400)	10,800
Overhead incurred	8,500
Over-absorbed overhead	2,300

6   ACTIVITY BASED COSTING

6.1   Absorption costing appears to be a relatively straightforward way of adding overhead costs to units of production using, more often than not, a volume-related absorption basis (such as direct labour hours or direct machine hours). The assumption that all overheads are related primarily to production volume is implied in this system. Absorption costing was developed at a time when most organisations produced only a narrow range of products and when overhead costs were only a very small fraction of total costs, direct labour and direct material costs accounting for the largest proportion of the costs. Errors made in adding overheads to products were therefore not too significant.

6.2   Nowadays, however, with the advent of advanced manufacturing technology, overheads are likely to be far more important and in fact direct labour may account for as little as 5% of a product's cost. Moreover, there has been an increase in the costs of service support functions, such as setting-up, production scheduling, first item inspection and data processing, which assist the efficient manufacture of a wide range of products. These overheads are not, in general, affected by changes in production volume. They tend to vary in the long term according to the range and complexity of the products manufactured rather than the volume of output.

6.3   Because absorption costing tends to allocate too great a proportion of overheads to high volume products (which cause relatively little diversity), and too small a proportion of overheads to low volume products (which cause greater diversity and therefore use more support services), alternative methods of costing have been developed. Activity based costing (ABC) is one such development.

6.4   The major ideas behind activity based costing are as follows.

   (a)   Activities cause costs. Activities include ordering, materials handling, machining, assembly, production scheduling and despatching.

   (b)   Products create demand for the activities.

   (c)   Costs are assigned to products on the basis of a product's consumption of the activities.

Outline of an ABC system

6.5   An ABC costing system operates as follows.

   (a)   *Step 1*

      Identify an organisation's major activities.

   (b)   *Step 2*

      Identify the factors which determine the size of the costs of an activity/cause the costs of an activity. These are known as *cost drivers*. Look at the following examples.

Activity	*Cost driver*
Ordering	Number of orders
Materials handling	Number of production runs
Production scheduling	Number of production runs
Despatching	Number of despatches

For those costs that vary with production levels in the short term, ABC uses volume-related cost drivers such as labour or machine hours. The cost of oil used as a lubricant on the machines would therefore be added to products on the basis of the number of machine hours since oil would have to be used for each hour the machine ran.

(c) *Step 3*

Collect the costs associated with each activity into what are known as *cost pools* (equivalent to cost centres under more traditional costing methods).

(d) *Step 4*

Charge support overheads to products on the basis of their usage of the activity. A product's usage of an activity is measured by the number of the activity's cost driver it generates.

Suppose, for example, that the orders cost pool totalled £100,000 and that there were 10,000 orders. Each product would therefore be charged with £10 for each order it required. A batch requiring five orders would therefore be charged with £50.

6.6   Absorption costing and ABC are similar in many respects. In both systems, direct costs go straight to the product and overheads are allocated to production cost centres/cost pools. The difference lies in the manner in which overheads are absorbed into products. Absorption costing uses usually two absorption bases (labour hours and/or machine hours) to charge overheads to products whereas ABC uses many cost drivers as absorption bases (number of orders, number of dispatches and so on). Absorption rates under ABC should therefore be more closely linked to the causes of overhead costs and hence produce more realistic product costs, especially where support overheads are high.

Chapter roundup

- Absorption costing is a complex subject, but the main points can be summarised as follows.

- Product costs are built up using absorption costing by a process of allocation, apportionment and absorption.

- In absorption costing, it is usual to add overheads into product costs by applying a predetermined overhead absorption rate. The predetermined rate is set annually, in the budget.

- To work out the absorption rate, budgeted overheads are allocated to production cost centres, service department cost centres or general overhead cost centres. General overheads are then apportioned to production and service department cost centres using an appropriate basis (such as floor area occupied by each cost centre for the rent and rates overhead). The service department cost centre overheads are then apportioned to production cost centres. All production overhead is thus identified with cost centres engaged directly in production. Administration overhead and selling and distribution overhead are also separately identified.

- The absorption rate is calculated by dividing the budgeted overhead by the budgeted level of activity. For production overheads, the level of activity is often budgeted direct labour hours or budgeted machine hours.

- Management should try to establish an absorption rate that provides a reasonably 'accurate' estimate of overhead costs for jobs, products or services. This means that when a predetermined overhead rate is used the bases for apportioning overhead costs between departments should be 'fair', separate departmental absorption rates should be used and there should not be large fluctuations in unit overhead costs from period to period caused by variations in budgeted activity.

- The overhead absorption rate is predetermined using figures from the budget and so actual costs of production include overheads based on this predetermined recovery rate. As a consequence there will be a discrepancy between overheads incurred and overheads absorbed. If overheads absorbed exceed overheads incurred, the cost of production (or sales) will have been too high. The amount of over absorption will be written as a 'favourable' adjustment to the profit and loss account, to compensate for the excessive overhead charge in products. Similarly, if overheads absorbed are lower than the amount of overheads incurred, the cost of production (or sales) will have been too low. The amount of under absorption will be written as an 'adverse' adjustment to the profit and loss account, to compensate for the under charging of overheads in product costs.

- Under- or over-absorbed overhead is inevitable in absorption costing because the predetermined overhead absorption rates are based on forecasts (guesses) about overhead expenditure and the level, or volume, of activity. Both guesses are likely to be at least a bit wrong, and overhead under or over absorbed may be due to a combination of guessing the budgeted expenditure wrongly and guessing the volume of activity wrongly.

- Activity based costing (ABC) is an alternative to the more traditional absorption costing. ABC involves the identification of the factors (cost drivers) which cause the costs of an organisation's major activities. Support overheads are charged to products on the basis of their usage of an activity (measured by the number of the activity's cost driver the product generates).

Test your knowledge

1   What is overhead allocation? (see para 1.1)

2   What basis might be applied to apportion heat and light? (2.2)

3   What is service cost centre cost apportionment? (2.5)

4   Why is it common to use *predetermined* overhead absorption rates? (3.2, 3.4)

5   What is the problem with using a single factory overhead absorption rate? (4.3, 4.8, 4.9)

6   Why does under- or over-absorbed overhead occur? (5.5)

7   What are the basic ideas of activity based costing? (6.4)

Now try illustrative question 6 at the end of the Study Text

Chapter 6

MARGINAL COSTING AND ABSORPTION COSTING

> ## This chapter covers the following topics.
>
> | | | Syllabus reference | Ability required |
> |---|---|---|---|
> | 1 | Marginal costing | 2(a) | Skill |
> | 2 | Marginal costing and absorption costing compared | 2(a) | Skill |
>
> ### Introduction
>
> In Chapter 1 we introduced the idea of product costs and period costs. Product costs are costs identified with goods produced or purchased for resale. Such costs are initially identified as part of the value of stock and only become expenses when the stock is sold. In contrast, period costs are costs that are deducted as expenses during the current period without ever being included in the value of stock held. In the previous chapter we saw how product costs are absorbed into the cost of units of output.
>
> This chapter defines marginal costing and compares it with absorption costing. Whereas absorption costing recognises fixed costs (usually fixed production costs) as part of the cost of a unit of output and hence as product costs, marginal costing treats all fixed costs as period costs. Two such different costing methods obviously each have their supporters and we will be looking at the arguments both in favour of and against each method. Each costing method, because of the different stock valuation used, produces a different profit figure and we will be looking at this particular point in detail. According to the examiner, many candidates in the May 95 exam had little idea of marginal cost principles and so *you* should make sure that you work very carefully through the exercises and examples in this chapter so that you fully understand the concepts covered.
>
> On completion of this chapter you will have covered what you need to know to successfully determine the cost of a unit of production/service or whatever.
>
> So far we have been looking at costs with the aim of valuing stocks, measuring profitability and establishing balance sheet items. In the next chapter we are going to see which costs are used in decision making, another task of the cost accountant.

1   MARGINAL COSTING

5/95, 5/96, 5/97

1.1   Supporters of marginal costing believe that, since period fixed costs are the same, no matter what the volume of sales and production (provided the level of activity is within certain limits), it follows that by selling an extra product or service the following will happen.

(a)   Revenue will increase by the sales value of the item sold.

(b)   Costs will increase by the variable cost per unit.

(c)   The increase in profit will therefore equal the sales value minus variable costs, that is, the amount of *contribution* earned from the item.

Similarly, if the volume of sales falls by one item, the profit will fall by the amount of contribution earned from the item.

1.2   Profit measurement should therefore be based on an analysis of total contribution. Moreover, in their opinion, since fixed costs relate to a period of time, and do not change with increases or decreases in sales volume, it is misleading to charge products with a share of fixed costs. Absorption costing is therefore misleading, and it is more appropriate to deduct fixed costs from total contribution for the period to derive a profit figure.

1.3   And what about their views of stock valuation? They think that when a unit of a product is made, the extra costs incurred in its manufacture are the variable production costs. Fixed costs are unaffected, and no extra fixed costs are incurred when output is increased. It is therefore argued that the valuation of closing stocks should be at variable production cost or *marginal cost* (direct materials, direct labour, direct expenses (if any) and variable production overhead) because these are the only costs properly attributable to the product.

1.4   The practical implications of these beliefs are perhaps best explained by an example.

Example: marginal costing

1.5   Water Ltd makes a product, the Splash, which has a variable production cost of £6 per unit and a sales price of £10 per unit. At the beginning of September 19X0, there were no opening stocks and production during the month was 20,000 units. Fixed costs for the month were £45,000 (production, administration, sales and distribution). There were no variable marketing costs.

Required

Calculate the contribution and profit for September 19X0, using marginal costing principles, if sales were as follows.

(a)   10,000 Splashes
(b)   15,000 Splashes
(c)   20,000 Splashes

Solution

1.6   The first stage in the profit calculation must be to identify the variable costs, and then the contribution. Fixed costs are deducted from the total contribution to derive the profit. All closing stocks are valued at marginal production cost (£6 per unit).

	10,000 Splashes		15,000 Splashes		20,000 Splashes	
	£	£	£	£	£	£
Sales (at £10)		100,000		150,000		200,000
Opening stock	0		0		0	
Variable production cost	120,000		120,000		120,000	
	120,000		120,000		120,000	
Less value of closing stock (at marginal cost)	60,000		30,000		-	
Variable cost of sales		60,000		90,000		120,000
Contribution		40,000		60,000		80,000
Less fixed costs		45,000		45,000		45,000
Profit/(loss)		(5,000)		15,000		35,000
Profit/(loss) per unit		£(0.50)		£1		£1.75
Contribution per unit		£4		£4		£4

1.7   The conclusions which may be drawn from this example are as follows.

(a)   The profit per unit varies at differing levels of sales, because the average fixed overhead cost per unit changes with the volume of output and sales.

(b)   The contribution per unit is constant at all levels of output and sales. Total contribution, which is the contribution per unit multiplied by the number of units sold, increases in direct proportion to the volume of sales.

(c)   Since the contribution per unit does not change, the most effective way of calculating the expected profit at any level of output and sales would be as follows.

(i)   First calculate the total contribution.
(ii)   Then deduct fixed costs as a period charge in order to find the profit.

(d)   In our example the expected profit from the sale of 17,000 Splashes would be as follows.

	£
Total contribution (17,000 × £4)	68,000
Less fixed costs	45,000
Profit	23,000

1.8   (a)   If total contribution exceeds fixed costs, a profit is made.

(b)   If total contribution exactly equals fixed costs, no profit and no loss is made and breakeven point is reached.

(c)   If total contribution is less than fixed costs, there will be a loss.

Exercise 1

Plumber Ltd makes two products, the Loo and the Wash. Information relating to each of these products for April 19X1 is as follows.

	Loo	*Wash*
Opening stock	nil	nil
Production (units)	15,000	6,000
Sales (units)	10,000	5,000
	£	£
Sales price per unit	20	30
Unit costs		
Direct materials	8	14
Direct labour	4	2
Variable production overhead	2	1
Variable sales overhead	2	3

Fixed costs for the month	£
Production costs	40,000
Administration costs	15,000
Sales and distribution costs	25,000

Required

Using marginal costing principles, calculate the profit in April 19X1. Use the approach set out in Paragraph 2.4(d) above.

Solution

	£
Contribution from Loos (unit contribution = £20 − £16 = £4 × 10,000)	40,000
Contribution from Washes (unit contribution = £30 − £20 = £10 × 5,000)	50,000
Total contribution	90,000
Fixed costs for the period	80,000
Profit	10,000

---

2   MARGINAL COSTING AND ABSORPTION COSTING COMPARED   *5/96*

2.1   Marginal costing as a cost accounting system is significantly different from absorption costing. It is an *alternative* method of accounting for costs and profit, which rejects the principles of absorbing fixed overheads into unit costs.

(a) *In marginal costing*

   (i)   Closing stocks are valued at marginal production cost.

   (ii) Fixed costs are charged in full against the profit of the period in which they are incurred.

(b) *In absorption costing* (sometimes referred to as *full costing*)

   (i)   Closing stocks are valued at full production cost, and include a share of fixed production costs.

   (ii) This means that the cost of sales in a period will include some fixed overhead incurred in a previous period (in opening stock values) and will exclude some fixed overhead incurred in the current period but carried forward in closing stock values as a charge to a subsequent accounting period.

2.2   This distinction between marginal costing and absorption costing is very important and the contrast between the systems must be clearly understood. Work carefully through the following example to ensure that you are familiar with both methods.

Example: marginal and absorption costing compared

2.3   Two Left Feet Ltd manufactures a single product, the Claud. The following figures relate to the Claud for a one-year period.

Activity level	50%	100%
Sales and productions (units)	400	800
	£	£
Sales	8,000	16,000
Production costs: variable	3,200	6,400
fixed	1,600	1,600
Sales and distribution costs:		
variable	1,600	3,200
fixed	2,400	2,400

The normal level of activity for the year is 800 units. Fixed costs are incurred evenly throughout the year, and actual fixed costs are the same as budgeted.

There were no stocks of Claud at the beginning of the year.

In the first quarter, 220 units were produced and 160 units sold.

Required

(a) Calculate the fixed production costs absorbed by Clauds in the first quarter if absorption costing is used.

(b) Calculate the under/over recovery of overheads during the quarter.

(c) Calculate the profit using absorption costing.

(d) Calculate the profit using marginal costing.

(e) Explain why there is a difference between the answers to (c) and (d).

Solution

2.4   (a) $$\frac{\text{Budgeted fixed production costs}}{\text{Budgeted output (normal level of activity)}} = \frac{£1,600}{800 \text{ units}}$$

Absorption rate = £2 per unit produced.

During the quarter, the fixed production overhead absorbed was 220 units × £2 = £440.

(b)

	£
Actual fixed production overhead	400 (¼ of £1,600)
Absorbed fixed production overhead	440
Over absorption of overhead	40

(c) *Profit for the quarter, absorption costing*

	£	£
Sales (160 × £20)		3,200
Production costs		
Variable (220 × £8)	1,760	
Fixed (absorbed overhead (220 × £2))	440	
Total (220 × £10)	2,200	
Less closing stocks (60 × £10)	600	
Production cost of sales	1,600	
Adjustment for over-absorbed overhead	40	
Total production costs		1,560
Gross profit		1,640
Less: sales and distribution costs		
variable (160 × £4)	640	
fixed (1/4 of £2,400)	600	
		1,240
Net profit		400

(d) *Profit for the quarter, marginal costing*

	£	£
Sales		3,200
Variable production costs	1,760	
Less closing stocks (60 × £8)	480	
Variable production cost of sales	1,280	
Variable sales and distribution costs	640	
Total variable costs of sales		1,920
Total contribution		1,280
Less:		
Fixed production costs incurred	400	
Fixed sales and distribution costs	600	
		1,000
Actual profit		280

(e) The difference in profit is due to the different valuations of closing stock. In absorption costing, the 60 units of closing stock include absorbed fixed overheads of £120 (60 × £2), which are therefore costs carried over to the next quarter and not charged against the profit of the current quarter. In marginal costing, all fixed costs incurred in the period are charged against profit.

	£
Absorption costing profit	400
Fixed production costs carried forward in stock values	120
Marginal costing profit	280

2.5 We can draw a number of conclusions from this example.

(a) Marginal costing and absorption costing are different techniques for assessing profit in a period.

(b) If there are changes in stocks during a period, so that opening stock or closing stock values are different, marginal costing and absorption costing give different results for profit obtained.

(i) If stock levels increase between the beginning and end of a period, absorption costing will report the higher profit because some of the fixed production overhead incurred during the period will be carried forward in closing stock (which reduces cost of sales) to be set against sales revenue in the following period instead of being written off in full against profit in the period concerned (as in the case in the example above).

(ii) If stock levels decrease, absorption costing will report the lower profit because as well as the fixed overhead incurred, fixed production overhead which had been carried forward in opening stock is released and is also included in cost of sales.

(c)   If the opening and closing stock volumes and values are the same, marginal costing and absorption costing will give the same profit figure. This is because the total cost of sales during the period would be the same, no matter how calculated.

(d)   In the long run, total profit for a company will be the same whether marginal costing or absorption costing is used because in the long run, total costs will be the same by either method of accounting. Different accounting conventions merely affect the profit of individual accounting periods.

Exercise 2

The overhead absorption rate for product X is £10 per machine hour. Each unit of product X requires five machine hours. Stock of product X on 1.1.X1 was 100 units and on 31.12.X1 it was 50 units. What is the difference in profit between results reported using absorption costing and results reported using marginal costing?

Solution

Difference = change in stock levels × fixed overhead absorbed per unit = $(100 - 50) \times £10 \times 5$ = £2,500, with marginal costing reporting the higher profit because stock levels decreased.

Example: comparison of total profits

2.6   To illustrate the point in Paragraph 3.5(d), let us suppose that a company makes and sells a single product. At the beginning of period 1, there are no opening stocks of the product, for which the variable production cost is £4 and the sales price £6 per unit. Fixed costs are £2,000 per period, of which £1,500 are fixed production costs.

	Period 1	Period 2
Sales	1,200 units	1,800 units
Production	1,500 units	1,500 units

What would the profit be in each period using the following methods of costing?

(a)   Absorption costing. Assume normal output is 1,500 units per period.
(b)   Marginal costing.

Solution

2.7   It is important to notice that although production and sales volumes in each period are different (and therefore the profit for each period by absorption costing will be different from the profit by marginal costing), over the full period, total production equals sales volume, the total cost of sales is the same, and therefore the profit is the same by either method of accounting.

(a)   *Absorption costing:* the absorption rate for fixed production overhead is

$$\frac{£1,500}{1,500 \text{ units}} = £1 \text{ per unit}$$

	Period 1 £	Period 1 £	Period 2 £	Period 2 £	Total £	Total £
Sales		7,200		10,800		18,000
Production costs						
Variable	6,000		6,000		12,000	
Fixed	1,500		1,500		3,000	
	7,500		7,500		15,000	
Add opening stock b/f	-		1,500			
	7,500		9,000		15,000	
Less closing stock c/f	1,500		-		-	
Production cost of sales	6,000		9,000		15,000	
(Under-)/over-absorbed overhead	-		-		-	
Total production costs		6,000		9,000		15,000
Gross profit		1,200		1,800		3,000
Other costs		500		500		1,000
Net profit		700		1,300		2,000

(b) *Marginal costing*

	Period 1		Period 2		Total	
	£	£	£	£	£	£
Sales		7,200		10,800		18,000
Variable production cost	6,000		6,000		12,000	
Add opening stock b/f	-		1,200		-	
	6,000		7,200		12,000	
Less closing stock c/f	1,200		-		-	
Variable production cost						
of sales		4,800		7,200		12,000
Contribution		2,400		3,600		6,000
Fixed costs		2,000		2,000		4,000
Profit		400		1,600		2,000

Note that the total profit over the two periods is the same for each method of costing, but the profit in each period is different.

Exercise 3

Reconcile the absorption costing and marginal costing profits for each period in the example above.

Solution

			£
Period 1	Absorption costing profit		700
	minus increase in stock levels over period × fixed overhead		
	absorbed per unit (300 × £1)		(300)
	Marginal costing profit		400

			£
Period 2	Absorption costing profit		1,300
	plus decrease in stock levels over period × fixed overhead		
	absorbed per unit (300 × £1)		300
	Marginal costing profit		1,600

Marginal costing and absorption costing compared: which is better?

2.8   There are accountants who favour each costing method.

(a) Arguments in favour of absorption costing are as follows.

   (i)   Fixed production costs are incurred in order to make output; it is therefore 'fair' to charge all output with a share of these costs.

   (ii) Closing stock values, by including a share of fixed production overhead, will be valued on the principle required for the financial accounting valuation of stocks by statement of standard accounting practice on stocks and long term contracts (SSAP 9).

   (iii) A problem with calculating the contribution of various products made by a company is that it may not be clear whether the contribution earned by each product is enough to cover fixed costs, whereas by charging fixed overhead to a product it is possible to ascertain whether it is profitable or not.

(b) Arguments in favour of marginal costing are as follows.

   (i)   It is simple to operate.

   (ii) There are no apportionments, which are frequently done on an arbitrary basis, of fixed costs. Many costs, such as the managing director's salary, are indivisible by nature.

   (iii) Fixed costs will be the same regardless of the volume of output, because they are period costs. It makes sense, therefore, to charge them in full as a cost to the period.

(iv)   The cost to produce an extra unit is the variable production cost. It is realistic to value closing stock items at this directly attributable cost.

(v)   Under or over absorption of overheads is avoided.

(vi)   Marginal costing information can be used for decision making but (as we will see is Chapter 7) absorption costing information is not suitable for decision making.

(vii)   Fixed costs (such as depreciation, rent and salaries) relate to a period of time and should be charged against the revenues of the period in which they are incurred.

Exercise 4

Discuss the effect of absorption costing and marginal costing on short-term results where sales and production are not equal.

Solution

Each costing method will have a different effect on short-term reported profits when sales and production are not equal.

(a)   *When sales exceed production*

Stocks are being reduced and with absorption costing some fixed overheads will be released from stock and charged against sales for the period. Reported profits will therefore be lower with absorption costing than with marginal costing.

(b)   *When production exceeds sales*

Stocks are being increased and with absorption costing some fixed overheads will be carried forward in stock to be matched against the sales revenues of future periods. Reported profits will therefore be higher with absorption costing than with marginal costing.

2.9   Of course, the choice of method does not have to be between absorption costing and marginal costing. In Chapter 5 we looked at ABC as an alternative to absorption costing. *Attributable contribution costing* is another alternative. This involves attributing certain fixed costs to the activities which cause them and then using marginal costing to calculate a contribution for each activity, the surplus of contribution over attributable fixed costs being known as attributable contribution.

Chapter roundup

- In your examination you may be asked to calculate the profit for an accounting period using either of the two methods of accounting. Absorption costing is most often used for routine profit reporting and must be used for financial accounting purposes. Marginal costing provides better management information for planning and decision making.

- Marginal cost is the variable cost of one unit of product or service (the cost which would be avoided if that unit were not produced).

- Contribution is an important measure in marginal costing, and it is calculated as the difference between sales value and marginal or variable cost.

- In marginal costing, fixed production costs are treated as period costs and are written off as they are incurred. In absorption costing, fixed production costs are absorbed into the cost of units and are carried forward in stock to be charged against sales for the next period. Stock values using absorption costing are therefore greater than those calculated using marginal costing.

- Reported profit figures using marginal costing or absorption costing will differ if there is any change in the level of stocks in the period. If production is equal to sales, there will be no difference in calculated profits using these costing methods.

- SSAP 9 recommends the use of absorption costing for the valuation of stocks in financial accounts.

- There are a number of arguments both for and against each of the costing systems.

- The distinction between marginal costing and absorption costing is very important and it is vital that you now understand the contrast between the two systems.

- If you are confused over any points, you may find it useful to attempt the examples in this chapter yourself, without looking at our solutions.

Test your knowledge

1   Define contribution. (see para 1.1)

2   How are fixed costs dealt with in marginal costing? (1.1)

3   How are stocks valued in marginal costing? (2.1)

4   If opening and closing stock volumes and values are the same, does absorption costing or marginal costing give the higher profit? (2.5)

5   Describe three arguments in favour of absorption costing. (2.8)

6   Should absorption costing be used in short-term decision making? (2.8)

7   What are the arguments for and against the use of marginal costing? (2.8)

Now try illustrative question 7 at the end of the Study Text

Chapter 7

RELEVANT COSTING AND DECISION MAKING

This chapter covers the following topics.

		Syllabus reference	Ability required
1	Relevant and non-relevant costs	2(a)	Knowledge
2	Choice of product (product mix) decisions	2(a)	Knowledge
3	Make or buy decisions	2(a)	Knowledge
4	Discontinuing a product	2(a)	Knowledge
5	Acceptance of a special order	2(a)	Knowledge

Introduction

Cost accounting was defined in Chapter 1 and so far we have been looking at it as a means of establishing profits, balance sheet items and stock valuations but there is more to cost accounting than that. One of the other reasons for the existence of cost accounting is to assist management in decision making.

Management at all levels within an organisation take decisions. The overriding requirement of the information that should be supplied by you as the cost accountant to aid decision making is that of relevance. This chapter therefore begins by looking at the costing technique required in decision-making situations, that of relevant costing, and explains how to decide which costs need taking into account when a decision is being made and which costs do not. Exam questions (such as question 3 of the November 95 exam) often focus on the relevance or otherwise of fixed costs . We cover this area in Paragraphs 1.6 to 1.9.

We then go on to see how to apply relevant costing to some specific decision-making scenarios: product mix decisions, whether or not to discontinue a product, whether or not to accept a special order and whether to make a product in-house or buy it from a subcontractor. A make or buy decision formed the basis of a November 95 exam question. According to the examiner it was an unpopular question. The technique for solving such problems is very straightforward, however, as you will see in Section 3.

This chapter ends Part A of the Study Text. In the next part we look at how to deal with costs within various cost accounting systems. To do this you need to learn cost bookkeeping. Guess what? It's the topic of Chapter 8.

1 RELEVANT AND NON-RELEVANT COSTS

5/95

Relevant costs

1.1 The costs which should be used for decision making are often referred to as relevant costs.

1.2 A relevant cost is a future cash flow arising as a direct consequence of a decision.

(a) Relevant costs are *future costs*.

(i)   A decision is about the future; it cannot alter what has been done already. A cost that has been incurred in the past is totally irrelevant to any decision that is being made 'now'.

(ii)   Costs that have been incurred include not only costs that have already been paid, but also committed costs (a future cash flow that will be incurred anyway, regardless of the decision taken now).

(b)   Relevant costs are *cash flows*

(i)   The assumption in relevant costing is that the decision maker wishes to maximise profits and that, in the long run, a profit that is earned will eventually produce a net inflow of an equal amount of cash. Hence when accounting for decision making we look at cash flow as a means of measuring profits.

(ii)   Only cash flow information is required. This means that costs or charges which do not reflect additional cash spending (such as depreciation and notional costs) should be ignored for the purpose of decision making.

(c)   Relevant costs are *incremental costs*.

A relevant cost is one which arises as a direct consequence of a decision. Thus, only costs which will change as a result of the decision should be considered; relevant costs are therefore sometimes referred to as incremental costs. For example, if an employee is expected to have no other work to do during the next week, but will be paid his basic wage (of, say, £100 per week) for attending work and doing nothing, his manager might decide to give him a job which earns the organisation £40. The net gain is £40 and the £100 is irrelevant to the decision because although it is a future cash flow, it will be incurred anyway whether the employee is given work or not.

Relevant costs are therefore *future, incremental cash flows*.

1.3   Other terms are sometimes used to describe relevant costs.

(a)   *Differential cost*

(i)   This is the difference in total cost between alternatives. If decision option A costs £300 and decision option B costs £360, the differential cost is £60, with decision option B being more expensive. A differential cost is the difference between the relevant costs of each option.

(ii)   The differential cost of an extra unit of production is the extra cost required to make that unit: it is the difference in cost between making the unit and not making it. This type of cost is sometimes referred to as an incremental cost.

(b)   *Opportunity cost*

This is the benefit which could have been earned, but which has been given up, by choosing one option instead of another. Suppose for example that there are three options, A, B and C, only one of which can be chosen. The net profit from each would be £80, £100 and £70 respectively.

Since only one option can be selected option B would be chosen because it offers the biggest benefit.

	£
Profit from option B	100
Less opportunity cost (ie the benefit from the most profitable alternative, A)	80
Differential benefit of option B	20

The decision to choose option B would not be taken simply because it offers a profit of £100, but because it offers a differential profit of £20 in excess of the next best alternative. The CIMA *Official Terminology* defines an opportunity cost simply as 'The value of the benefit sacrificed when one course of action is chosen, in preference to an alternative'.

Opportunity costs will never appear in a set of double entry cost accounts.

Sunk costs

1.4   The principle underlying decision accounting is that 'bygones are bygones'. What has happened in the past is done, and cannot be undone. Management decisions can only affect the future. In decision making, managers therefore require information about future costs and revenues which would be affected by the decision under review, and they must not be misled by events, costs and revenues in the past, about which they can do nothing. Therefore sunk costs, which have been charged already as a cost of sales in a previous accounting period or will be charged in a future accounting period although the expenditure has already been incurred (or the expenditure decision irrevocably taken), are irrelevant to decision making.

An example of this type of cost is depreciation. If a fixed asset has been purchased, depreciation may be charged for several years but the cost is a sunk cost, about which nothing can now be done.

1.5   Another example of sunk costs are development costs which have already been incurred. Suppose that a company has spent £250,000 in developing a new service for customers, but the marketing department's most recent findings are that the service might not gain customer acceptance and could be a commercial failure. The decision whether or not to abandon the development of the new service would have to be taken, but the £250,000 spent so far should be ignored by the decision makers because they are sunk costs.

Fixed and variable costs

1.6   Unless you are given an indication to the contrary, you should assume the following.

(a)   Variable costs will be relevant costs.
(b)   Fixed costs are irrelevant to a decision.

This need not be the case, however, and you should analyse variable and fixed cost data carefully. Do not forget that 'fixed' costs may only be fixed in the short term.

Non-relevant variable costs

1.7   There might be occasions when a variable cost is in fact a sunk cost. For example, suppose that a company has some units of raw material in stock. They have been paid for already, and originally cost £2,000. They are now obsolete and are no longer used in regular production, and they have no scrap value. However, they could be used in a special job which the company is trying to decide whether to undertake. The special job is a 'one-off' customer order, and would use up all these materials in stock.

In deciding whether the job should be undertaken, the relevant cost of the materials to the special job is nil. Their original cost of £2,000 is a sunk cost, and should be ignored in the decision.

However, if the materials did have a scrap value of, say, £300, then their relevant cost to the job would be the opportunity cost of being unable to sell them for scrap, ie £300.

Attributable fixed costs

1.8   There might be occasions when a fixed cost is a relevant cost, and you must be aware of the distinction between 'specific' or 'directly attributable' fixed costs, and general fixed overheads.

(a)   Directly attributable fixed costs are those costs which, although fixed within a relevant range of activity level, or regarded as fixed because management has set a budgeted expenditure level (for example advertising costs are often treated as fixed), would, in fact, do one of two things.

(i)   Increase if certain extra activities were undertaken

(ii)   Decrease/be eliminated entirely if a decision were taken either to reduce the scale of operations or shut down entirely

(b) General fixed overheads are those fixed overheads which will be unaffected by decisions to increase or decrease the scale of operations, perhaps because they are an apportioned share of the fixed costs of items which would be completely unaffected by the decisions. An apportioned share of head office charges is an example of general fixed overheads for a local office or department.

1.9 You should appreciate that whereas directly attributable fixed costs will be relevant to a decision in hand, general fixed overheads will not be.

Absorbed overhead

1.10 Absorbed overhead is a notional accounting cost and hence should be ignored for decision-making purposes. It is overhead *incurred* which *may* be relevant to a decision.

The relevant cost of materials

1.11 The relevant cost of raw materials is generally their current replacement cost, *unless* the materials have already been purchased and would not be replaced once used.

If materials have already been purchased but will not be replaced, then the relevant cost of using them is the higher of the following.

(a) Their current resale value
(b) The value they would obtain if they were put to an alternative use

If the materials have no resale value and no other possible use, then the relevant cost of using them for the opportunity under consideration would be nil.

You should test your knowledge of the relevant cost of materials by attempting the following exercise.

Exercise 1

O'Reilly Ltd has been approached by a customer who would like a special job to be done for him, and who is willing to pay £22,000 for it. The job would require the following materials.

Material	Total units required	Units already in stock	Book value of units in stock £/unit	Realisable value £/unit	Replacement cost £/unit
A	1,000	0	-	-	6
B	1,000	600	2	2.50	5
C	1,000	700	3	2.50	4
D	200	200	4	6.00	9

(a) Material B is used regularly by O'Reilly Ltd, and if units of B are required for this job, they would need to be replaced to meet other production demand.

(b) Materials C and D are in stock as the result of previous over-buying, and they have a restricted use. No other use could be found for material C, but the units of material D could be used in another job as substitute for 300 units of material E, which currently costs £5 per unit (of which the company has no units in stock at the moment).

Required

Calculate the relevant costs of material for deciding whether or not to accept the contract.

Solution

(a) *Material A* is not yet owned. It would have to be bought in full at the replacement cost of £6 per unit.

(b) *Material B* is used regularly by the company. There are existing stocks (600 units) but if these are used on the contract under review a further 600 units would be bought to replace them. Relevant costs are therefore 1,000 units at the replacement cost of £5 per unit.

(c) 1,000 units of *material C* are needed and 700 are already in stock. If used for the contract, a further 300 units must be bought at £4 each. The existing stocks of 700 will not be replaced. If they are used for the contract, they could not be sold at £2.50 each. The realisable value of these 700 units is an opportunity cost of sales revenue forgone.

(d) The required units of *material D* are already in stock and will not be replaced. There is an opportunity cost of using D in the contract because there are alternative opportunities either to sell the existing stocks for £6 per unit (£1,200 in total) or avoid other purchases (of material E), which would cost 300 x £5 = £1,500. Since substitution for E is more beneficial, £1,500 is the opportunity cost.

(e) *Summary of relevant costs*

	£
Material A (1,000 × £6)	6,000
Material B (1,000 × £5)	5,000
Material C (300 × £4) plus (700 × £2.50)	2,950
Material D	1,500
Total	15,450

1.12 It is important that you should be able to identify the relevant costs which are appropriate to a decision. In many cases, this is a fairly straightforward problem, but there are cases where great care should be taken. Attempt the following exercise.

Exercise 2

A company has been making a machine to order for a customer, but the customer has since gone into liquidation, and there is no prospect that any money will be obtained from the winding up of the company.

Costs incurred to date in manufacturing the machine are £50,000 and progress payments of £15,000 had been received from the customer prior to the liquidation.

The sales department has found another company willing to buy the machine for £34,000 once it has been completed.

To complete the work, the following costs would be incurred.

(a) Materials: these have been bought at a cost of £6,000. They have no other use, and if the machine is not finished, they would be sold for scrap for £2,000.

(b) Further labour costs would be £8,000. Labour is in short supply, and if the machine is not finished, the work force would be switched to another job, which would earn £30,000 in revenue, and incur direct costs of £12,000 and absorbed (fixed) overhead of £8,000.

(c) Consultancy fees £4,000. If the work is not completed, the consultant's contract would be cancelled at a cost of £1,500.

(d) General overheads of £8,000 would be added to the cost of the additional work.

Required

Assess whether the new customer's offer should be accepted.

Solution

(a) Costs incurred in the past, or revenue received in the past are not relevant because they cannot affect a decision about what is best for the future. Costs incurred to date of £50,000 and revenue received of £15,000 are 'water under the bridge' and should be ignored.

(b) Similarly, the price paid in the past for the materials is irrelevant. The only relevant cost of materials affecting the decision is the opportunity cost of the revenue from scrap which would be forgone - £2,000.

(c) *Labour costs*

	£
Labour costs required to complete work	8,000
Opportunity costs: contribution forgone by losing	
other work £(30,000 – 12,000)	18,000
Relevant cost of labour	26,000

(d) The incremental cost of consultancy from completing the work is £2,500.

	£
Cost of completing work	4,000
Cost of cancelling contract	1,500
Incremental cost of completing work	2,500

(e) Absorbed overhead is a notional accounting cost and should be ignored. Actual overhead incurred is the only overhead cost to consider. General overhead costs (and the absorbed overhead of the alternative work for the labour force) should be ignored.

(f) Relevant costs may be summarised as follows.

	£	£
Revenue from completing work		34,000
Relevant costs		
Materials: opportunity cost	2,000	
Labour: basic pay	8,000	
opportunity cost	18,000	
Incremental cost of consultant	2,500	
		30,500
Extra profit to be earned by accepting the order		3,500

2 CHOICE OF PRODUCT (PRODUCT MIX) DECISIONS   11/95

2.1 One of the more common decision-making problems is a situation where there are not enough resources to meet the potential sales demand, and so a decision has to be made about what mix of products to produce, using what resources there are as effectively as possible. The *scarce resource* is known as a *limiting factor* or a *key factor* since it limits the organisation's activities. There might be just one limiting factor (other than maximum sales demand) but there might also be several scarce resources, with two or more of them acting as limiting factors by putting an effective limit on the level of activity that can be achieved. We will be concentrating on single limiting factor problems and a technique for resolving these, however.

2.2 A limiting factor could be sales if there is a limit to sales demand but any one of the organisation's resources (labour, materials, manufacturing capacity, financial resources and so on) may be insufficient to meet the level of production demanded. If sales demand is the factor which restricts greater production output, profit will be maximised by making exactly the amount required for sales (and no more) provided that each product sold earns a positive contribution. If labour supply, materials availability, machine capacity or cash availability limits production to less than the volume which could be sold, management is faced with the problem of deciding what products to produce because there are insufficient resources to make everything.

2.3 It is assumed in limiting factor accounting that management wishes to maximise profit and that profit will be maximised when contribution is maximised (given no change in fixed cost expenditure incurred). In other words, marginal costing ideas are applied.

Contribution will be maximised by earning the biggest possible contribution from each unit of limiting factor. Thus if grade A labour is the limiting factor, contribution will be maximised by earning the biggest contribution from each hour of grade A labour worked. Similarly, if machine time is in short supply, profit will be maximised by earning the biggest contribution from each machine hour worked.

The limiting factor decision therefore involves the determination of the contribution earned by each different product from each unit of the limiting factor. In limiting factor decisions, we generally assume that fixed costs are the same whatever production mix is selected, so that the only relevant costs are variable costs.

Example: limiting factor

2.4 AB Ltd makes two products, the Ay and the Be. Unit variable costs are as follows.

	Ay	*Be*
	£	£
Direct materials	1	3
Direct labour (£3 per hour)	6	3
Variable overhead	1	1
	8	7

The sales price per unit is £14 per Ay and £11 per Be. During July 19X2 the available direct labour is limited to 8,000 hours. Sales demand in July is expected to be 3,000 units for Ays and 5,000 units for Bes.

Required

Determine the profit-maximising production mix, assuming that monthly fixed costs are £20,000, and that opening stocks of finished goods and work in progress are nil.

Solution

2.5   (a)   The first step in the solution is to confirm that the limiting factor is something other than sales demand.

	Ays	*Bes*	*Total*
Labour hours per unit	2 hrs	1 hr	
Sales demand	3,000 units	5,000 units	
Labour hours needed	6,000 hrs	5,000 hrs	11,000 hrs
Labour hours available			8,000 hrs
Shortfall			3,000 hrs

Labour is the limiting factor on production.

(b)   The second step is to identify the contribution earned by each product per unit of limiting factor, that is per labour hour worked.

	Ays	*Bes*
	£	£
Sales price	14	11
Variable cost	8	7
Unit contribution	6	4
Labour hours per unit	2 hrs	1 hr
Contribution per labour hour (= unit of limiting factor)	£3	£4

Although Ays have a higher unit contribution than Bes, two Bes can be made in the time it takes to make one Ay. Because labour is in short supply it is more profitable to make Bes than Ays.

2.6   The final stage in the solution is to work out the budgeted production and sales mix. Sufficient Bes will be made to meet the full sales demand, and the remaining labour hours available will then be used to make Ays.

(a)

Product	*Demand*	*Hours required*	*Hours available*	*Priority of manufacture*
Bes	5,000	5,000	5,000	1st
Ays	3,000	6,000	3,000 (bal)	2nd
		11,000	8,000	

(b)

Product	*Units*	*Hours needed*	*Contribution per unit*	*Total*
			£	£
Bes	5,000	5,000	4	20,000
Ays	1,500	3,000	6	9,000
		8,000		29,000
Less fixed costs				20,000
Profit				9,000

Note that it is *not* more profitable to begin by making as many units as possible with the bigger unit contribution. We could make 3,000 units of Ay in 6,000 hours and 2,000 units of Be in the remaining 2,000 hours but profit would be only £6,000. Unit contribution is not the correct way to decide priorities, because it takes two hours to earn £6 from a Ay and one hour to earn £4 from a Be. Bes make more profitable use of the scarce resource, labour hours.

Other considerations regarding limiting factors

2.7   The following points should also be borne in mind when making a decision which involves limiting factors.

(a)   In the long run management should seek to remove the limiting factor.

(b)   In the short term management may be able to find ways around the limiting factors (such as overtime working and sub-contracting).

(c)   It may not be easy to identify the limiting factor.

3   MAKE OR BUY DECISIONS   *11/95*

3.1   A make or buy problem involves a decision by an organisation about whether it should make a product/carry out an activity with its own internal resources, or whether it should pay another organisation to make the product/carry out the activity. Examples of make or buy decisions would be as follows.

(a)   Whether a company should manufacture its own components, or else buy the components from an outside supplier.

(b)   Whether a construction company should do some work with its own employees, or whether it should subcontract the work to another company.

(c)   Whether the design and development of a new computer system should be entrusted to in-house data processing staff or whether an external software house should be hired to do the work.

3.2   The 'make' option should give management more direct control over the work, but the 'buy' option often has the benefit that the external organisation has a specialist skill and expertise in the work. Make or buy decisions should certainly not be based exclusively on cost considerations.

3.3   If an organisation has the freedom of choice about whether to make internally or buy externally and has no scarce resources that put a restriction on what it can do itself, the relevant costs for the decision will be the differential costs between the two options.

Example: make or buy

3.4   Buster Ltd makes four components, W, X, Y and Z, for which costs in the forthcoming year are expected to be as follows.

	W	*X*	*Y*	*Z*
Production (units)	1,000	2,000	4,000	3,000
Unit marginal costs	£	£	£	£
Direct materials	4	5	2	4
Direct labour	8	9	4	6
Variable production overheads	2	3	1	2
	14	17	7	12

Directly attributable fixed costs per annum and committed fixed costs are as follows.

	£
Incurred as a direct consequence of making W	1,000
Incurred as a direct consequence of making X	5,000
Incurred as a direct consequence of making Y	6,000
Incurred as a direct consequence of making Z	8,000
Other fixed costs (committed)	30,000
	50,000

A subcontractor has offered to supply units of W, X, Y and Z for £12, £21, £10 and £14 respectively.

Required

Decide whether Buster Ltd should make or buy the components.

Solution and discussion

3.5 (a)   The relevant costs are the differential costs between making and buying, and they consist of differences in unit variable costs plus differences in directly attributable fixed costs. Subcontracting will result in some fixed cost savings.

	W	X	Y	Z
	£	£	£	£
Unit variable cost of making	14	17	7	12
Unit variable cost of buying	12	21	10	14
	£(2)	£4	£3	£2
Annual requirements (units)	1,000	2,000	4,000	3,000
	£	£	£	£
Extra variable cost of buying (per annum)	(2,000)	8,000	12,000	6,000
Fixed costs saved by buying	1,000	5,000	6,000	8,000
Extra total cost of buying	(3,000)	3,000	6,000	(2,000)

(b)   The company would save £3,000 pa by subcontracting component W (where the purchase cost would be less than the marginal cost per unit to make internally) and would save £2,000 pa by subcontracting component Z (because of the saving in fixed costs of £8,000).

(c)   In this example, relevant costs are the variable costs of in-house manufacture, the variable costs of subcontracted units, and the saving in fixed costs.

(d)   Important further considerations would be as follows.

(i)   If components W and Z are subcontracted, the company will have spare capacity. How should that spare capacity be profitably used? Are there hidden benefits to be obtained from subcontracting? Would the company's workforce resent the loss of work to an outside subcontractor, and might such a decision cause an industrial dispute?

(ii)   Would the subcontractor be reliable with delivery times, and would he supply components of the same quality as those manufactured internally?

(iii)   Does the company wish to be flexible and maintain better control over operations by making everything itself?

(iv)   Are the estimates of fixed cost savings reliable? In the case of Product W, buying is clearly cheaper than making in-house. In the case of product Z, the decision to buy rather than make would only be financially beneficial if the fixed cost savings of £8,000 could really be 'delivered' by management. All too often in practice, promised savings fail to materialise!

Make or buy decisions and limiting factors

3.6   Where there are limiting factors on production other than sales one way of overcoming the limitation on production is to subcontract work. Where this problem arises, profit is maximised by producing or buying all the components or products at the cheapest cost. The cost of bought in components supplied by subcontractors normally exceeds the marginal cost of making products internally because the supplier's cost includes a contribution/profit margin on his costs. A company would then prefer to make all its own products, but the limiting factor makes this impossible.

3.7   In a situation where a company must subcontract work to make up a shortfall in its own production capability, its total costs are minimised if those components/products subcontracted are those with the lowest extra variable cost of buying per unit of limiting factor saved by buying.

Example: make or buy and limiting factors

3.8   Green Ltd manufactures two components, the alpha and the beta, using the same machines for each. The budget for the next year calls for the production and assembly of 4,000 of each component. The variable production cost per unit of the final product, the gamma, is as follows.

	Machine hours	*Variable cost*
		£
1 unit of alpha	3	20
1 unit of beta	2	36
Assembly		20
		76

Only 16,000 hours of machine time will be available during the year, and a subcontractor has quoted the following unit prices for supplying components: Alpha £29; Beta £40. Advise Green Ltd.

Solution

3.9   (a)   There is a shortfall in machine hours available, and some products must be sub-contracted.

Product	*Units*		*Machine hours*
Alpha	4,000		12,000
Beta	4,000		8,000
		Required	20,000
		Available	16,000
		Shortfall	4,000

(b)   The assembly costs are not relevant costs because they are unaffected by the make or buy decision. The units subcontracted should be those which will add least to the costs of Green Ltd. Since 4,000 hours of work must be sub-contracted, the cheapest policy is to subcontract work which adds the least extra costs (the least extra variable costs) per hour of own-time saved.

(c)

	Alpha	*Beta*
	£	£
Variable cost of making	20	36
Variable cost of buying	29	40
Extra variable cost of buying	9	4
Machine hours saved by buying	3 hrs	2 hrs
Extra variable cost of buying, per hour saved	£3	£2

It is cheaper to buy Betas than to buy Alphas and so the priority for making the components in-house will be in the reverse order to the preference for buying them from a subcontractor.

(d)

Component	*Hrs per unit to make in-house*	*Hrs required in total*	*Cumulative hours*
Alpha	3 hrs	12,000	12,000
Beta	2 hrs	8,000	20,000
		20,000	
Hours available		16,000	
Shortfall		4,000	

There are enough machine hours to make all 4,000 units of Alpha and 2,000 units of Beta. 4,000 hours production of Beta must be sub-contracted. This will be the cheapest production policy available

(e)

Component	Machine hours	Number of units	Unit variable cost	Total variable cost
Make			£	£
Alpha	12,000	4,000	20	80,000
Beta (balance)	4,000	2,000	36	72,000
	16,000			152,000
Buy	*Hours saved*			
Beta (balance)	4,000	2,000	40	80,000

Total variable costs of components	232,000
Assembly costs (4,000 × £20)	80,000
Total variable costs	312,000

4 DISCONTINUING A PRODUCT

11/95

4.1 Suppose that a company manufactures three products, Corfus, Cretes and Zantes. The present net profit from these is as follows.

	Corfus	Cretes	Zantes	Total
	£	£	£	£
Sales	50,000	40,000	60,000	150,000
Variable costs	30,000	25,000	35,000	90,000
Contribution	20,000	15,000	25,000	60,000
Fixed costs	17,000	18,000	20,000	55,000
Profit/loss	3,000	(3,000)	5,000	5,000

The company is concerned about its poor profit performance, and is considering whether or not to cease selling Cretes. It is felt that selling prices cannot be raised or lowered without adversely affecting net income. £5,000 of the fixed costs of Cretes are direct fixed costs which would be saved if production ceased (that is, there are some attributable fixed costs). All other fixed costs, it is considered, would remain the same.

4.2 By stopping production of Cretes, the consequences would be a £10,000 fall in profits.

	£
Loss of contribution	(15,000)
Savings in fixed costs	5,000
Incremental loss	(10,000)

4.3 Suppose, however, it were possible to use the resources realised by stopping production of Cretes and switch to producing a new item, Rhodes, which would sell for £50,000 and incur variable costs of £30,000 and extra direct fixed costs of £6,000. A new decision is now required.

	Cretes	Rhodes
	£	£
Sales	40,000	50,000
Less variable costs	25,000	30,000
Contribution	15,000	20,000
Less direct fixed costs	5,000	6,000
Contribution to shared fixed costs and profit	10,000	14,000

It would be more profitable to shut down production of Cretes and switch resources to making Rhodes, in order to boost profits to £9,000.

5 ACCEPTANCE OF A SPECIAL ORDER

11/96

5.1 This type of decision-making situation will concern an order which would utilise an organisation's spare capacity but which would have to be accepted at a price lower than that normally required by the organisation. In general you can assume that an order will probably be accepted if it increases contribution and hence profit, and rejected if it reduces profit. Let us consider an example.

Example: accept or reject

5.2   Belt and Braces Ltd makes a single product which sells for £20. It has a full cost of £15 which is made up as follows.

	£
Direct material	4
Direct labour (2 hours)	6
Variable overhead	2
General fixed overhead	3
	15

The labour force is currently working at 90% of capacity and so there is a spare capacity for 2,000 units. A customer has approached the company with a request for the manufacture of a special order of 2,000 units for which he is willing to pay £25,000. Assess whether the order should be accepted.

Solution

5.3

	£	£
Value of order		25,000
Cost of order		
Direct materials (£4 × 2,000)	8,000	
Direct labour (£6 × 2,000)	12,000	
Variable overhead (£2 × 2,000)	4,000	
Relevant cost of order		24,000
Profit from order acceptance		1,000

Fixed costs will be incurred regardless of whether the order is accepted and so are not relevant to the decision. The order should be accepted since it increases contribution to profit by £1,000.

5.4   There are, however, several other factors which would need to be considered before a final decision is taken: the acceptance of the order at a lower price may lead other customers to demand lower prices as well; there may be more profitable ways of using the spare capacity; accepting the order may lock up capacity that could be used for future full-price business; fixed costs may, in fact, alter if the order is accepted.

Chapter roundup

- In making decisions, the only costs which are relevant are those which will be affected by the decision. Such costs will be future, incremental cash flows.

- Other terms used to describe relevant costs are differential cost, incremental cost and opportunity cost. An opportunity cost is the benefit which could have been earned, but which has been given up, by choosing one option instead of another.

- Sunk costs are non-relevant costs.

- Fixed costs which are affected by a decision are called directly attributable fixed costs.

- In a limiting factor situation, contribution will be maximised by earning the biggest possible contribution per unit of limiting factor.

- In a make or buy situation with no limiting factors, the relevant costs for the decision maker are the differential costs between the two options.

- If an organisation has to subcontract work to make up a shortfall in its own in-house capabilities, its total costs will be minimised if those products which have the least extra marginal cost of buying for each unit of limiting factor saved by buying are subcontracted.

- The decision to accept or reject an order should be made on the basis of whether or not the order increases contribution and profit.

Test your knowledge

1   What are relevant costs? (see paras 1.1, 1.2)

2   What is an opportunity cost? (1.3)

3   What are sunk costs? (1.4)

4   What is an attributable fixed cost? (1.8)

5   What is the relevant cost of materials that have already been purchased and will not be replaced. (1.11)

6   What is the general rule for maximising contribution in a limiting factor decision? (2.3)

7   What matters other than cost should be considered in a make or buy situation? (3.5)

8   How are total costs minimised in a make or buy situation with limiting factors? (3.7)

9   What is the general rule to follow on whether or not to accept a special order? (5.1)

Now try illustrative question 8 at the end of the Study Text

Part B
Cost accounting systems

Chapter 8

COST BOOKKEEPING

1 ACCOUNTING FOR COSTS

1.1 There are no statutory requirements to keep detailed cost records and so some small firms only keep traditional financial accounts and prepare cost information in an ad-hoc fashion. This approach is, however, unsatisfactory for all but the smallest organisations: most firms therefore maintain some form of cost accounting system.

1.2 Cost accounting systems range from simple analysis systems to computer based accounting systems incorporating standards, variance analysis and the automatic production of control and operating standards. Often systems are tailored to the users' requirements and therefore incorporate unique features. Despite this, all systems will incorporate a number of common aspects and all records will be maintained using the principles of double entry.

Control accounts

1.3 One common aspect of cost accounting systems is that information is kept, not only of the value of individual stock items, or the cost of individual products or jobs, but also of total costs. Total costs are recorded in control accounts. The CIMA definition of a control account is as follows. 'A ledger account which collects the sum of the postings into the individual accounts which it controls. The balance on the control account should equal the sum of the balances on the individual accounts, which are maintained as subsidiary records.' An account which records the total cost of materials in stock and material issues is called a stores control account. Similarly there is a wages control account, to show how total wage costs are charged as direct labour costs to work in progress, or as indirect costs to production, administration or selling and distribution overheads. A work in progress control account is a record of the total cost of production (direct materials, direct labour, direct expenses (if any) and production overheads), and the cost of finished output transferred to the finished goods control account.

Interlocking and integrated accounts

1.4 Recording cost transactions using the self-balancing double entry method of a debit and credit entry for each transaction may be achieved in either of the following ways.

(a) *Interlocking accounts.* Separate ledger accounts are kept for both the cost accounting function and the financial accounting function, which necessitates the reconciliation of the profits produced by the separate profit and loss accounts. The cost accounts use the same basic data (purchases, wages and so on) as the financial accounts, but frequently adopt different bases for matters such as depreciation and stock valuation.

(b) *Integrated accounts.* The cost accounting function and the financial accounting function are combined in one system of ledger accounts. The same basis for items such as stock valuation and depreciation will be used and there is no need for a reconciliation between cost profit and financial profit. Financial profit will simply be the cost profit adjusted by non-cost items such as income from investments and charitable donations.

1.5 The principles of double entry bookkeeping are not described in this chapter, but if you have not yet begun your studies of basic financial accounting, you may not be familiar with the concept of 'debits and credits'. Nevertheless you may still be able to follow the explanations below, provided that you remember the 'golden rule' of double entry bookkeeping, that for every entry made in one account, there must be a corresponding balancing entry in another account.

1.6 We shall begin with a description of a system of control accounts where the cost accounts are maintained separately from the financial accounting system.

2 INTERLOCKING SYSTEMS   5/95

2.1 *The principal accounts in a system of interlocking accounts*

(a) The resources accounts

(i) Materials control account or stores control account
(ii) Wages (and salaries) control account
(iii) Production overhead control account
(iv) Administration overhead control account
(v) Selling and distribution overhead control account

(b) Accounts which record the cost of production items from the start of production work through to cost of sales

(i) Work in progress control account
(ii) Finished goods control account
(iii) Cost of sales control account

(c) Sales account

(d) The costing profit and loss account

(e) The under-/over-absorbed overhead account

(f)   Cost ledger control account (in the cost ledger)

(g)   Financial ledger control account (in the financial ledger)

How an interlocking system works

2.2   It was mentioned that an interlocking system features two ledgers.

(a)   The financial ledger contains asset, liability, revenue, expense and appropriation (eg dividend) accounts. The trial balance of an enterprise is prepared from the financial ledger.

(b)   The cost ledger, on the other hand, is where cost information such as the build-up of work in progress is analysed in more detail.

The cost ledger control account

2.3   There are certain items of cost or revenue which are of no interest to the cost accountant because they are financial accounting items. These include the following.

(a)   Interest or dividends received

(b)   Dividends paid

(c)   Discounts allowed or received for prompt payment of invoices

2.4   There are, however, various financial accounting items which are related to costs and profits (and hence interest the cost accountant), although accounts for these items are not included in the separate cost accounting books. The most important of these items are cash, creditors, debtors and profit and loss reserves. To overcome the need to have accounts for cash, creditors and so on in the cost books, a cost ledger control account is used. It represents all the accounts in the financial accounting books which are not included in the corresponding cost accounting books.

2.5   The cost ledger control account is therefore a sort of 'dustbin' account which is used to keep the double entry system working. (Don't worry about the financial ledger control account at this stage of your studies.)

Accounting entries in a system of cost ledger accounts

2.6   The accounting entries in a system of cost ledger accounts can be confusing and it is important to keep in mind some general principles.

(a)   When expenditure is incurred on materials, wages or overheads, the actual amounts paid or payable are debited to the appropriate resources accounts. The credit entries (which in a financial accounting ledger would be in the cash or creditors accounts) are in the cost ledger control account.

(b)   When production begins, resources are allocated to work in progress. This is recorded by crediting the resources accounts and debiting the work in progress account. In the case of production overheads, the amount credited to the overhead account and debited to work in progress should be the amount of overhead absorbed. If this differs from the amount of overhead incurred, there will be a difference on the overhead control account; this should be written off to an under-/over-absorbed overhead account. (One other point to remember is that when *indirect* materials and labour are allocated to production, the entries are to credit the materials and wages accounts and debit production overhead account.)

(c)   As finished goods are produced, work in progress is reduced. This is recorded by debiting the finished goods control account and crediting the work in progress control account.

(d)   To establish the cost of goods sold, the balances on finished goods control account, administration overhead control account and selling and distribution overhead control account are transferred to cost of sales control account.

(e) Sales are debited to the financial ledger control account and credited to sales account.

(f) Profit is established by transferring to the cost profit and loss account the balances on the sales account, cost of sales account and under-/over-absorbed overhead account.

Accounting entries in absorption costing and marginal costing systems

2.7 Cost bookkeeping can appear quite daunting to begin with. You may find the diagrams on the pages 103 and 104, which illustrate the (simplified) operation of interlocking systems using absorption costing and marginal costing, useful. Follow the entries through the various control accounts and note the differences between the two diagrams. You will then be ready to attempt the following example.

Example: interlocking accounts

2.8 You are required to write up the cost ledger accounts of a manufacturing company for the latest accounting period. The following data is relevant.

(a) There is no stock on hand at the beginning of the period.

(b) Details of the transactions for the period received from the financial accounts department include the following.

	£
Sales	420,000
Indirect wages:	
production	25,000
administration	15,000
sales and distribution	20,000
Materials purchased	101,000
Direct factory wages	153,200
Production overheads	46,500
Selling and distribution expenses	39,500
Administration expenses	32,000

(c) Other cost data for the period include the following.

Raw materials issued to production as indirect materials	£15,000
Stores issued to production as direct materials	£77,000
Raw materials of finished production	£270,200
Cost of goods sold at finished goods stock valuation	£267,700
Standard rate of production overhead absorption	50p per operating hour
Rate of administration overhead absorption	20% of production cost of sales
Rate of sales and distribution overhead absorption	10% of sales revenue
Actual operating hours worked	160,000

Solution

2.9 The problem should be tackled methodically, in the order suggested by paragraph 2.6 above. The letters in brackets show the sequence in which the various entries are made.

Cost accounting using absorption costing

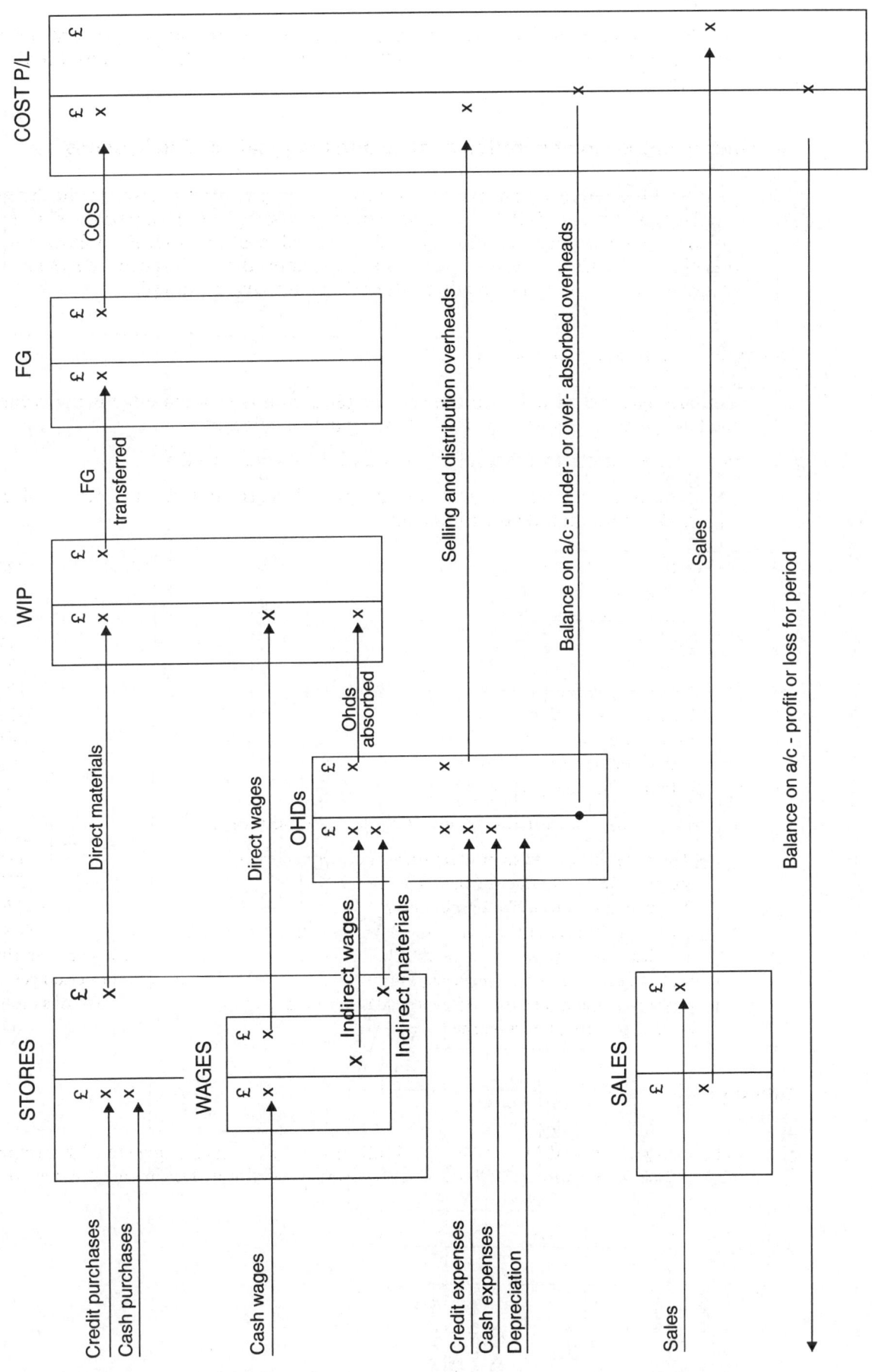

Cost accounting using marginal costing

COST P/L

3 x		Marginal COS x	3 x	Sales x
		Contribution x		
		Contribution c/d		Contribution b/d
			Fixed overheads x	

COS

FG
- 3 x
- 3 x
- FG transferred at marginal cost

WIP
- 3 x
- 3 x
- Valued at marginal cost

Direct materials
Direct wages
Direct expenses

VARIABLE OVERHEADS
- 3 x | 3 x
- V Ohds
- Variable

FIXED OVERHEADS
- 3 x | 3 x
- Fixed

Fixed overheads for current period

Balance on a/c - profit or loss for period

STORES
- 3 x | 3 x
- x

WAGES
- 3 x | 3 x

EXPENSES
- 3 x | 3 x
- x

Indirect materials
Indirect wages
Indirect expenses

SALES
- 3 x | 3 x
- x

Sales

Credit purchases
Cash purchases

Cash wages

Credit expenses
Cash expenses

Sales

COST LEDGER CONTROL (CLC)

	£		£
Sales (a)	420,000	Wages control (b)	213,200
Balance c/d	51,500	Materials control (c)	101,000
		Prod'n o'hd control (d)	46,500
		S & D o'hd control (e)	39,500
		Admin o'hd control (f)	32,000
		Cost profit and loss a/c	39,300
	471,500		471,500
		Balance b/d	51,500

MATERIALS CONTROL

	£		£
CLC (c) - purchases	101,000	Prod'n o'hd control (k)(indirect materials)	15,000
		WIP control (l)(issues to production)	77,000
		∴ Closing stock c/d (bal fig)	9,000
	101,000		101,000
Closing stock b/d	9,000		

WAGES CONTROL

	£		£
CLC (b)	213,200	Prod'n o'hd control (g)	25,000
		Admin o'hd control (h)	15,000
		S & D o'hd control (j)	20,000
		WIP control (m)(direct labour)	153,200
	213,200		213,200

PRODUCTION OVERHEAD CONTROL

	£		£
CLC (d)	46,500	WIP control (p)(160,000 × 50p)	
Wages control (g)	25,000	(overheads absorbed)	80,000
Materials control (k)	15,000	∴ O'hds under-absorbed (bal fig)	6,500
	86,500		86,500

ADMINISTRATION OVERHEAD CONTROL

	£		£
CLC (f)	32,000	Cost of sales control (o/hds absorbed)(q)	
Wages control (h)	15,000	(20% × £267,700)	53,540
∴ O'hds over-absorbed (bal fig)	6,540		
	53,540		53,540

SELLING AND DISTRIBUTION OVERHEAD CONTROL

	£		£
CLC (e)	39,500	Cost of sales control (r)(o/hds absorbed) (10% × £420,000)	42,000
Wages control (j)	20,000		
		∴ O'hds under-absorbed (bal fig)	17,500
	59,500		59,500

WORK IN PROGRESS CONTROL

	£		£
Materials control (l)	77,000	Finished goods control (n)	270,200
Wages control (m)	153,200	∴ Closing stock of WIP c/d (bal fig)	40,000
Prod'n o'hd control (p)	80,000		
	310,200		310,200
Balance b/d	40,000		

FINISHED GOODS CONTROL

	£		£
WIP control (n)	270,200	Cost of sales control (o)	267,700
		∴ Stock of finished goods c/d (bal fig)	2,500
	270,200		270,200
Balance b/d	2,500		

COST OF SALES CONTROL

	£		£
Finished goods control (o)	267,700	Cost profit and loss a/c	363,240
Admin o'hd control (q)	53,540		
S & D o'hd control (r)	42,000		
	363,240		363,240

SALES

	£		£
Cost profit and loss a/c	420,000	CLC (a)	420,000

UNDER-/OVER-ABSORBED OVERHEAD

	£		£
Prod'n o'hd control	6,500	Admin o'hd control	6,540
S & D o'hd control	17,500	∴ Cost profit and loss a/c	17,460
	24,000		24,000

COST PROFIT AND LOSS

	£		£
Cost of sales control	363,240	Sales	420,000
Under-/over-absorbed o'hd	17,460		
CLC (profit for period)	39,300		
	420,000		420,000

2.10 Note how the trial balance can be extracted from the accounts.

TRIAL BALANCE

	Debit £	Credit £
Cost ledger control		51,500
Materials stock	9,000	
Work in progress	40,000	
Finished goods stocks	2,500	
	51,500	51,500

2.11 Examination questions sometimes ask you to prepare just one or two control accounts. Here is an example about a wages control account.

Example: the wages control account

2.12 The following details were extracted from a weekly payroll for 750 employees at a factory.

	Direct workers £	Indirect workers £	Total £
Analysis of gross pay:			
Ordinary time	36,000	22,000	58,000
Overtime: basic wage	8,700	5,430	14,130
premium	4,350	2,715	7,065
Shift allowance	3,465	1,830	5,295
Sick pay	950	500	1,450
Idle time	3,200	-	3,200
	56,665	32,475	89,140
Net wages paid to employees	£45,605	£24,220	£69,825

Required

Prepare the wages control account for the week.

Solution

2.13 (a) The *wages control account* acts as a sort of 'collecting place' for net wages paid and deductions made from gross pay. The gross pay is then analysed between direct and indirect wages.

(b) The first step is to determine which wage costs are direct and which are indirect. The direct wages will be debited to the work in progress account and the indirect wages will be debited to the production overhead account.

(c) There are in fact only two items of direct wages cost in this example - the ordinary time (£36,000) and the basic overtime wage (£8,700) paid to direct workers. All other payments (including the overtime premium) are indirect wages.

(d) The net wages paid are debited to the control account, and the balance then represents the deductions which have been made for income tax, national insurance, and so on.

WAGES CONTROL ACCOUNT

	£		£
Bank: net wages paid	69,825	Work in progress - direct labour	44,700
Deductions control accounts*		Production overhead control:	
(£89,140 – £69,825)	19,315	Indirect labour	27,430
		Overtime premium	7,065
		Shift allowance	5,295
		Sick pay	1,450
		Idle time	3,200
	89,140		89,140

* In practice there would be a separate deductions control account for each type of deduction made (such as PAYE, National Insurance).

3 INTERLOCKING SYSTEMS: RECONCILIATION OF COST ACCOUNTING AND FINANCIAL ACCOUNTING PROFITS   *5/95*

3.1 When an organisation maintains separate cost accounts and financial accounts, the cost profit will differ from the financial profit because of differences in the revenue and costs that are included in the respective profit and loss accounts. It is an essential accounting function that the cost profit and financial profit are reconciled, and this is effected through a memorandum reconciliation account.

3.2 A memorandum reconciliation account, being a memorandum account, is not a part of any double entry system of bookkeeping. It is simply a method by which a record can be made of the differences in the cost accounts and the financial accounts, in order to show why their respective profit figures are different. We are therefore not concerned, in this instance, with 'debits' and 'credits', only with a record of difference.

3.3 Some examples of items creating differences between the cost accounting and financial accounting profits are listed below.

(a) Items appearing in the financial accounts, but not in the cost accounts.

(i) Items of income which boost the financial accounts profit, but are excluded from the cost accounts.

(1) Interest or dividends received
(2) Discounts received (for early settlement of debts)
(3) Profits on disposal of fixed assets

(ii) Items of expenditure which reduce the financial accounts profit, but which are excluded from the cost accounts.

(1) Interest paid
(2) Discounts allowed (for early settlement of debt)
(3) Losses on disposal of fixed assets
(4) Losses on investments
(5) Fines and penalties

(iii) Items of expenditure which are capitalised as assets in the financial accounts, for example development costs.

(iv) Appropriations of profit in the financial profit and loss account.
   (1) Donations
   (2) Income tax
   (3) Dividends paid and proposed
   (4) Transfers to reserves
   (5) Write-offs of goodwill, investments and other assets

(b) Items appearing in the cost accounts, but not in the financial accounts are infrequent, but usually relate to *notional costs*. These are charges made in the cost accounts in order to give a more realistic picture of the cost of an activity. There are two main types of notional cost.

   (i) *Interest on capital*. This represents the nominal cost of capital tied up in production and accounts for the cost of using the capital internally rather than investing it outside the business. The cost accountant makes the charge so that managers are fully aware of the true cost, for example, of holding stocks in the production process. The charge can also help to make the cost of items made with expensive capital equipment more comparable to the cost of items which are not.

   (ii) *Nominal rent charge*. This is a nominal charge raised for the use of premises which are owned. This enables a comparison to be made between the cost of production in a factory which is owned and the costs in one which is rented. The nominal rent charge makes managers more aware of the true cost of occupying the premises.

Notional interest or nominal rent will not affect profit (except in so far as they may be included in stock values) because a counter-balancing adjustment will be made in the profit and loss account. For example, suppose that nominal rent is £8,000. The accounting entries in the cost ledger would be as follows.

NOMINAL RENT ACCOUNT

	£		£
Profit and loss a/c	8,000	Production overhead	8,000

It may be apparent that £8,000 is added to costs (as production overhead) and a counter-balancing £8,000 is added to costing profit and loss. Nominal rent and notional interest are self-cancelling items.

(c) Differences may arise between the financial and cost accounts in the calculation of actual overhead costs incurred. For example if the cost accounting books contain a provision for depreciation account, differences may arise in the choice of depreciation method (for example straight line method, reducing balance method, and so on) or in the expected life of the equipment.

(d) Valuation of stock on hand is likely to be made according to different bases for the respective accounts. For the financial accounts the basis of stock valuation will be the lower of FIFO and net realisable value. For the cost accounts, the basis of stock valuation might be any one of the following.

   (i) LIFO
   (ii) FIFO
   (iii) Weighted average cost
   (iv) Standard cost
   (v) Replacement cost

The calculation of the reconciling stock differences can be confusing. If you remember the following rule you should be able to determine all the combinations.

If the *closing* stock valuation is *higher* in the cost accounts than in the financial accounts, the cost accounting profit will be greater and so the difference between the two valuations should be deducted from the cost accounting profit to reach the financial accounting profit.

Example: reconciliation of cost and financial accounting profits

3.4 Jasper Ltd has separate financial and cost accounting systems. Extracts from both sets of accounts for the year ended 30 September 19X2 were as follows.

(a) FINANCIAL ACCOUNTS

	Opening stock £	Closing stock £
Stock valuations		
Raw materials	68,000	72,000
Work in progress	14,000	10,000
Finished goods	32,000	41,000

	£
Debenture interest	10,000
Interest received	1,500
Discounts allowed	4,000
Discounts received	2,000
Net profit (before taxation)	35,000

(b) COST ACCOUNTS

	Opening stock £	Closing stock £
Stock valuations		
Raw materials	66,000	69,000
Work in progress	16,000	14,000
Finished goods	34,000	40,000

Required

Reconcile the profit as reported in the financial accounts with the profit reported in the cost accounts, and calculate the cost accounting profit for the year.

3.5 MEMORANDUM RECONCILIATION ACCOUNT

	£	£	£
Financial accounting profit			35,000
Adjustments for items appearing in the financial accounts, but not in the cost accounts			
Debenture interest	10,000		
Discounts allowed	4,000		
		14,000	
Discounts received	(2,000)		
Interest received	(1,500)		
		(3,500)	
Net extra charges against financial accounting profit			10,500
			45,500
Stock differences		£	
Raw materials opening stock £(68,000 – 66,000)		2,000	
Raw materials closing stock £(72,000 – 69,000)		(3,000)	
Work in progress opening stock £(14,000 – 16,000)		(2,000)	
Work in progress closing stock £(10,000 – 14,000)		4,000	
Finished goods opening stock £(32,000 – 34,000)		(2,000)	
Finished goods closing stock £(41,000 – 40,000)		(1,000)	
Total stock adjustments			(2,000)
Cost accounting profit			43,500

Exercise 1

Use the information below to draw up the following accounts.

(a) Raw materials control account
(b) Work in progress control account
(c) Finished goods control account
(d) Cost of sales control account
(e) Profit and loss account

Raw materials	£
Opening stock	327,729
Purchases	1,455,389
Closing stock	299,408
Direct wages	608,130
Work in progress	
Opening stock	88,401
Closing stock	94,027
Finished goods	
Opening stock	211,088
Closing stock	198,103
Other costs	
Administration expenses	228,766
Sales expenses	89,858
Distribution expenses	58,697
Production expenses	676,795
Sales	3,498,179

Production overhead is absorbed at a rate of 120% of direct wages.

Solution

Absorbed production overhead = 120% of direct wages = 120% of £608,130 = £729,756. The over-absorbed overhead = £(729,756 – 676,795).

(a)   RAW MATERIALS CONTROL ACCOUNT

	£		£
Opening stock	327,729	Work in progress account	1,483,710
Purchases (CLC)	1,455,389	(balancing figure)	
		Closing stock	299,408
	1,783,118		1,783,118

(b)   WORK IN PROGRESS CONTROL ACCOUNT

	£		£
Opening stock	88,401	Finished goods account	2,815,970
Raw materials account	1,483,710	(balancing figure)	
Direct wages account	608,130	Closing stock	94,027
Production overhead control			
account	729,756		
	2,909,997		2,909,997

(c)   FINISHED GOODS CONTROL ACCOUNT

	£		£
Opening stock	211,088	Cost of sales account	2,828,955
Work in progress	2,815,970	(balancing figure)	
		Closing stock	198,103
	3,027,058		3,027,058

(d)   COST OF SALES ACCOUNT

	£		£
Finished goods account	2,828,955	Profit and loss account	2,828,955

It is assumed that overheads (other than production overhead) are taken straight to the profit and loss account.

(e)   PROFIT AND LOSS ACCOUNT

	£		£
Cost of sales account	2,828,955	Sales	3,498,179
Administration expenses	228,766	Over-absorbed production	
Sales expenses	89,858	overhead	52,961
Distribution expenses	58,697		
	3,206,276		
Net profit (bal fig)	344,864		
	3,551,140		3,551,140

4   INTEGRATED SYSTEMS

4.1   In a system of integrated accounts the financial and cost accounts are combined in one set of self-balancing ledger accounts. This eliminates the need to operate financial ledger control accounts and reconcile the respective cost and financial profits.

4.2   To facilitate the control of costs and assist with management information the same classification used in the cost ledger is also used in an integrated ledger. Furthermore, all transactions normally excluded from a cost ledger are included in an integrated ledger. Additional ledger accounts required by an integrated system would be as follows.

(a)   Debtors' and creditors' control accounts
(b)   Bank account
(c)   Fixed asset accounts
(d)   Other assets and liabilities accounts
(e)   Share capital account, retained profit account and other reserve accounts

There is no cost ledger control account, because this appears in a system of interlocking accounts only as a substitute for debtors, creditors, bank accounts and so on.

4.3   You should be able to refer back to the earlier example of interlocking accounts entries and identify the differences which would appear in a set of integrated accounts.

The advantage and disadvantage of integrated systems

4.4   The advantage of integrated systems over separate systems for cost and financial accounting is the saving in administrative effort. Only one set of accounts needs to be maintained instead of two and the possible confusion arising from having two sets of accounts with different figures (such as for stock values and profits) does not exist.

4.5   The disadvantage of integrated accounts is that one set of accounts is expected to fulfil two different purposes.

(a)   Stewardship of the business, and external reporting
(b)   Provision of internal management information

4.6   At times, these different purposes may conflict; for example, the valuation of stocks will conform to the requirements of SSAP 9, whereas the cost accountants might have preferred, given their own choice, to value closing stocks at, say, marginal cost or replacement cost. In addition, the cost coding of expenditures, to serve both financial accounting and cost accounting purposes, will be more complex and a double-purpose coding system (with longer numerical cost codes) will probably have to be used.

4.7   In practice, however, computers have swept away these objections and most modern cost accounting systems are integrated systems, incorporating coding systems which allow basic data to be analysed and presented in different ways for different purposes. The way in which integrated accounts actually work is perhaps best explained by an example.

Example: integrated accounts

4.8   KC Ltd manufactures a range of products which are sold through a network of wholesalers and dealers. A set of integrated accounts is kept, and for the year 19X0 the following information is relevant.

(a)   Production overhead is absorbed into the cost of products on the basis of a budgeted rate of 80% of direct labour cost.

(b)   Finished stocks are valued at factory cost.

(c)

	31 March 19X0	30 April 19X0
	£	£
Raw materials stock	17,200	15,160
Work in progress	5,600	4,750
Finished goods stock	10,500	12,090
Debtors for goods sold	9,200	11,140
Creditors for raw materials	7,600	9,420
Fixed assets at net book value	6,000	6,000

(d)   Bank transactions for the month of April 19X0 were as follows.

	£
Bank balance at 31 March	1,500
Receipts from debtors	27,560
Payments made	
Direct labour	6,400
Creditors for raw materials	8,960
Production overhead	5,400
Administration overhead	700
Selling and distribution overhead	2,300

Required

(a)   Use the information above to write up the following control accounts.

(i)   Raw materials stock
(ii)   Work in progress
(iii)   Finished goods
(iv)   Production overhead

(b)   Prepare the following statements.

(i)   A profit and loss account for the month of April 19X0
(ii)   A balance sheet as at 30 April 19X0

Solution

4.9   (a)   (i)

RAW MATERIALS STOCK

	£		£
Opening balance	17,200	Work in progress	
Creditors (W1)	10,780	(balancing figure)	12,820
		Balance c/d	15,160
	27,980		27,980
Balance b/d	15,160		

(ii)

WORK IN PROGRESS

	£		£
Opening balance	5,600	Finished goods	
Raw materials stock	12,820	(balancing figure)	25,190
Direct wages	6,400		
Production overhead (W2)	5,120	Balance c/d	4,750
	29,940		29,940
Balance b/d	4,750		

(iii)

FINISHED GOODS

	£		£
Opening balance	10,500	Profit and loss account	
Work in progress	25,190	(cost of sales) (bal fig)	23,600
		Balance c/d	12,090
	35,690		35,690
Balance b/d	12,090		

(iv)   PRODUCTION OVERHEAD

	£		£
Cash	5,400	Work in progress	5,120
		Profit and loss account	
		(under-absorbed)	280
	5,400		5,400

(b) (i) PROFIT AND LOSS ACCOUNT
     FOR THE MONTH OF APRIL 19X0

	£	£
Sales (W3)		29,500
Production cost of sales		23,600
Gross profit		5,900
Less: administration overhead	700	
sales and distribution overhead	2,300	
under-absorbed production overhead	280	
		3,280
Profit		2,620

(ii) BALANCE SHEET AS AT 30 APRIL 19X0

	£	£
Fixed assets (net book value)		6,000
Current assets		
Raw materials	15,160	
Work in progress	4,750	
Finished goods	12,090	
Debtors	11,140	
Cash (W4)	5,300	
	48,440	
Less current liabilities		
Creditors	9,420	
		39,020
		45,020
Long-term capital £(42,400 (balancing figure)+ 2,620)		45,020

Workings

1   CREDITORS FOR RAW MATERIALS

	£		£
Cash	8,960	Opening balance	7,600
Balance c/f	9,420	Raw materials purchases	
		(balancing figure)	10,780
	18,380		18,380

2 Direct labour   £6,400
   Production overhead absorbed (80%)   £5,120

3   DEBTORS

	£		£
Opening balance	9,200	Cash	27,560
Sales (balancing figure)	29,500	Balance c/f	11,140
	38,700		38,700

4   CASH

	£		£
Opening balance	1,500	Creditors for raw materials	8,960
Debtors	27,560	Direct labour	6,400
		Production overhead	5,400
		Administration overhead	700
		Sales and distribution o'hd	2,300
		Balance c/f	5,300
	29,060		29,060

5   JOURNAL ENTRIES

5.1   As well as being able to make entries in appropriate ledger accounts, you must be able to prepare journal entries to record transactions in either an integrated or non-integrated system.

Example: journal entries for materials

5.2   During July 19X0 the following transactions relating to an organisation's stores occurred.

	£
Materials purchased from suppliers on credit	120,000
Materials purchased for cash	8,000
Direct materials issued to the production department	110,000
Indirect materials issued as production overhead costs	25,000
Direct materials returned to stores from production	4,000

Required

Prepare journal entries to record the above information in the cost ledger of a set of interlocking accounts.

Solution

5.3

			£	£
DR	Stores ledger control a/c		120,000	
CR	CLCA			120,000
DR	Stores ledger control a/c		8,000	
CR	CLCA			8,000
DR	WIP a/c		110,000	
CR	Stores ledger control a/c			110,000
DR	Production overhead control a/c		25,000	
CR	Stores ledger control a/c			25,000
DR	Stores ledger control a/c		4,000	
CR	WIP a/c			4,000

Exercise 2

Prepare journal entries so as to record the following information in a set of integrated accounts.

	Gross wages £'000	PAYE and employees' NI £'000	Net £'000	Employer's NI £'000
Direct wages (£5.50 per hour)	33	8	25	2
Production indirect wages	7	1	6	-
Administrative staff wages and salaries	10	3	7	1
Selling staff wages and salaries	10	3	7	1
	60	15	45	4

Solution

		£'000	£'000
DR	Wages and salaries control account	45	
CR	Cash/bank account		45
DR	Wages and salaries control account	15	
CR	Creditor for PAYE and NI		15
DR	WIP control account	33	
CR	Wages and salaries control account		33
DR	Production overhead control account	7	
CR	Wages and salaries control account		7
DR	Administration overhead control account	10	
CR	Wages and salaries control account		10
DR	Selling overhead control account	10	
CR	Wages and salaries control account		10
DR	WIP control account	2	
CR	Creditor for PAYE and NI		2
DR	Administration overhead control account	1	
CR	Creditor for PAYE and NI		1
DR	Selling overhead control account	1	
CR	Creditor for PAYE and NI		1

Chapter roundup

- There are two types of cost accounting system - interlocking and integrated.

- Interlocking accounts contain separate ledgers for cost accounts and for financial accounts. A cost ledger control account is maintained in the cost ledger to complete the costing double entry. It represents the financial ledger accounts which are not maintained in the cost ledger (such as cash, debtors and creditors).

- When an organisation operates an interlocking accounts system, it is necessary to reconcile the cost accounting profit with the financial accounting profit. Items which create differences between the cost accounting and financial accounting profits include stock valuations, profits and losses on disposal of fixed assets, interest paid and received and appropriations of profit.

- Integrated systems combine both financial and cost accounts in one system of ledger accounts. A reconciliation between cost and financial profits is not necessary with an integrated system.

- This chapter covers a lot of ground and introduces a wide variety of techniques. Practice on bookkeeping questions is vital since it is not possible simply to read 'how to do it'. Make sure that you work through the illustrative question suggested at the end of the chapter.

Test your knowledge

1 List the principal accounts in a system of interlocking accounts. (see para 2.1)

2 What is the double entry for the following?

   (a) Production overhead absorbed in the cost of production (2.6(b))

   (b) Completed work transferred to finished goods store (2.6(c))

3 List ten items which might appear in a reconciliation of cost accounting profit and financial accounting profit. (3.3)

4 What are the advantages and disadvantages of integrated accounts? (4.4 - 4.6)

Now try illustrative question 9 at the end of the Study Text

Chapter 9

JOB, BATCH AND OUTPUT COSTING

This chapter covers the following topics.

		Syllabus reference	Ability required
1	Job costing	2(b)	Skill
2	Batch costing	2(b)	Skill
3	Output costing	2(b)	Skill

Introduction

Having learnt the basics of bookkeeping in the previous chapter, we will now apply these basics to particular cost accounting systems.

A cost accounting system is designed to suit the way goods are processed or manufactured or the way services are provided. Each organisation's cost accounting system will therefore have unique features but costing systems of firms in the same line of business will more than likely have common aspects. On the other hand, organisations involved in completely different activities, such as hospitals and car part manufacturers, will have very different systems.

This chapter will cover job, batch and output costing. We will see the circumstances in which job costing should be used and how the costs of jobs are calculated. We will then integrate our Chapter 8 knowledge to see how the costing of individual jobs fits in with the recording of total costs in control accounts. The chapter also considers batch costing, the procedure for which is similar to job costing, and output costing, used in organisations which produce just one product in a single process.

Process costing, a more complex form of output costing, is the subject of Chapter 10.

1 JOB COSTING

1.1 A job is a cost unit which consists of a single order or contract. Job costing is therefore 'A form of specific order costing in which costs are attributed to individual jobs' (CIMA *Official Terminology*) which applies where work is undertaken to customers' special requirements and each order is of comparatively short duration. The work is usually carried out within a factory or workshop and moves through processes and operations as a continuously identifiable unit. The CIMA *Official Terminology* definition of a job is 'A customer order or task of relatively short duration'. Note that job costing is one form of specific order costing (the other being contract costing, which you will meet in your Paper 6 studies).

1.2 With other methods of costing it is usual to produce for stock; this means that the management decide in advance how many units of each type, size, colour, quality and so on will be produced during the coming year regardless of the identity of the customers who will eventually buy the products. However, in job costing, production is usually carried out in accordance with the special requirements of each customer. It is therefore usual for each job to differ in one or more respects from every other job, which means that a separate record must be maintained to show the details of a particular job.

Procedure for the performance of jobs

1.3 The normal procedure which is adopted in jobbing concerns involves the following.

(a) The prospective customer approaches the supplier and indicates the requirements of the job.

(b) A responsible official sees the prospective customer and agrees with him the precise details of the items to be supplied, for example the quantity, quality, size and colour of the goods, the date of delivery and any special requirements.

(c) The estimating department of the organisation then prepares an estimate for the job. This will include the cost of the materials to be used, the wages expected to be paid, the appropriate amount for factory, administration, selling and distribution overhead, the cost where appropriate of additional equipment needed specially for the job, and finally the supplier's profit margin. The total of these items will represent the estimated selling price (often referred to as a quotation).

(d) At the appropriate time, the job will be 'loaded' on to the factory floor. This means that as soon as all materials, labour and equipment are available and subject to the scheduling of other orders, the job will be started. In an efficient organisation, the start of the job will be timed to ensure that while it will be ready for the customer by the promised date of delivery it will not be loaded too early, otherwise storage space will have to be found for the product until the date it is required by (and was promised to) the customer.

Collection of job costs

1.4 Materials requisitions are sent to stores. The material requisition note will be used to cost the materials issued to the job concerned, and this cost may then be recorded on a job cost sheet, which records all costs relating to a particular job. The cost may include items already in stock, at an appropriate valuation, and/or items specially purchased.

1.5 A job ticket is given to the worker who is to perform the first operation of the job. The times of his starting and finishing the operation are recorded on the ticket, which is then passed to the person who is to carry out the second operation, where a similar record of the times of starting and finishing is made. When the job is completed, the job ticket is sent to the cost office, where the time spent will be costed and recorded on the job cost sheet.

1.6 The job's share of the factory overhead, based on the absorption rate(s) in operation, is recorded as the job cost sheet.

1.7 The relevant costs of materials issued, direct labour performed and direct expenses incurred as recorded on the job cost sheet are charged to the job account in the work in progress ledger. The total value of the jobs in progress will represent the balance on the work in progress control account since each job is represented by an account in the WIP ledger.

1.8 *On completion of the job*, the job account is charged with the appropriate administration, selling and distribution overhead, after which the total cost of the job can be ascertained.

1.9 The difference between the agreed selling price and the total actual cost will be the supplier's profit (or loss).

Job cost sheet

1.10 An example of a job cost sheet (or job card) is shown below.

JOB COST SHEET

| | | Job No. | B641 |

Customer	Mr J White	Customer's Order No.		Vehicle make	Peugot 205 GTE
Job Description	Repair damage to offside front door			Vehicle reg. no.	G 614 SOX
Estimate Ref.	2599	Invoice No.			
Quoted price	£338.68	Invoice price	£355.05	Date to collect	14.6.93

Material

Date	Req. No.	Qty.	Price	Cost £	Cost p
12.6	36815	1	75.49	75	49
12.6	36816	1	33.19	33	19
12.6	36842	5	6.01	30	05
13.6	36881	5	3.99	19	95
Total C/F				**158**	**68**

Labour

Date	Employee	Cost Ctre	Hrs.	Rate	Bonus	Cost £	Cost p
12.6	018	B	1.98	6.50	-	12	87
13.6	018	B	5.92	6.50	-	38	48
					13.65	13	65
Total C/F						**65**	**00**

Overheads

Hrs	OAR	Cost £	Cost p
7.9	2.50	19	75
Total C/F		**19**	**75**

Expenses

Date	Ref.	Description	Cost £	Cost p
12.6	-	N. Jolley Panel-beating	50	-
Total C/F			**50**	**-**

Job Cost Summary

	Actual £	Actual p	Estimate £	Estimate p
Direct Materials B/F	158	68	158	68
Direct Expenses B/F	50	00		
Direct Labour B/F	65	00	180	00
Direct Cost	273	68		
Overheads B/F	19	75		
	293	43		
Admin overhead (add 10%)	29	34		
= Total Cost	322	77	338	68
Invoice Price	355	05		
Job Profit/Loss	32	28		

Comments

Job Cost Card Completed by _____

Job cost sheets show the detail of relatively small jobs or are used to summarise direct materials, direct labour and so on for larger jobs.

Work in progress at the end of an accounting period

1.11 At the end of an accounting period any jobs which are still in progress are regarded as work in progress, which is a form of stock. Stock and work in progress need to be valued at the lower of cost and net realisable value for financial accounting purposes. Job cost sheets will provide details of the costs incurred in bringing a job to its present condition. Provided this cost is less than the price to be charged to the customer, this will be the cost attributed to the job at the end of the accounting period.

Completed jobs

1.12 When jobs are completed, job cost sheets are transferred from the work in progress category to finished goods. When delivery is made to the customer, the costs become a cost of sale. If the completed job was carried out in order to build up finished goods stocks (rather than to meet a specific order) the quantity of items produced and their value are recorded in finished goods stores ledger accounts.

Rectification costs

1.13 Sometimes when finished output is inspected it is found to be sub-standard. It may be possible to rectify the fault, and the sub-standard output will then be returned to the department or cost centre where the fault arose. The costs arising from this are called rectification costs and can be treated in two ways, depending on the circumstances in which the costs have arisen.

(a) If rectification work is not a frequent occurrence, but arises on occasions with specific jobs to which it can be traced directly, then the rectification costs should be charged as a direct cost to the jobs concerned.

(b) If rectification is regarded as a normal part of the work carried out generally in the department, then the rectification costs should be treated as production overheads. This means that they would be included in the total of production overheads for the department and absorbed into the cost of all jobs for the period, using the overhead absorption rate.

Job costing and computerisation

1.14 Job cost sheets exist in manual systems, but it is increasingly likely that in large organisations the job costing system will be computerised, using accounting software specifically designed to deal with job costing requirements. A computerised job accounting system is likely to contain the following features.

(a) Every job will be given a job code number, which will determine how the data relating to the job is stored.

(b) A separate set of codes will be given for the type of costs that any job is likely to incur. Thus, 'direct wages', say, will have the same code whichever job they are allocated to.

(c) In a sophisticated system, costs can be analysed both by job (for example all costs related to Job 456), but also by type (for example direct wages incurred on all jobs). It is thus easy to perform control analysis and to make comparisons between jobs.

(d) A job costing system might have facilities built into it which incorporate other factors relating to the performance of the job. In complex jobs, sophisticated planning techniques might be employed to ensure that the job is performed in the minimum time possible: time management features may be incorporated into job costing software.

Cost plus pricing

1.15 In this chapter we have described the usual method of fixing selling prices within a jobbing concern. It is known as 'cost plus' pricing because a desired profit margin (say, 33%) is added to total costs to arrive at the selling price. It has a number of weaknesses. It offers no incentive to control costs as a profit is guaranteed and there is no motive to tackle inefficiencies or waste. It takes no account of the demand curve for a product (the way in which the selling price affects the demand) and the total cost (and hence the price) is dependent upon the arbitrary nature of the basis of apportionment of overhead costs.

1.16 Nevertheless, the cost plus system is often adopted where one-off jobs are carried out to customers' specifications.

Exercise 1

Frisbee Ltd is a company that carries out jobbing work. One of the jobs carried out in February was job 1357, to which the following information relates.

Direct material Y:	400 kilos were issued from stores at a cost of £5 per kilo.
Direct material Z:	800 kilos were issued from stores at a cost of £6 per kilo. 60 kilos were returned.
Department P:	300 labour hours were worked, of which 100 hours were done in overtime.
Department Q:	200 labour hours were worked, of which 100 hours were done in overtime.

Overtime work is not normal in Department P, where basic pay is £4 per hour plus an overtime premium of £1 per hour. Overtime work was done in Department Q in February because of a request by the customer of another job to complete his job quickly. Basic pay in Department Q is £5 per hour and overtime premium is £1.50 per hour.

Department P had to carry out rectification work which took 20 hours in normal time. These 20 hours are additional to the 300 hours above. This rectification work is normal for a job such as job 1357, and since it was expected, it is included in the direct cost of the job.

Overhead is absorbed at the rate of £3 per direct labour hour in both departments.

The organisation adds 30% to full production cost to arrive at a price for a job.

Required

Calculate the following.

(a) The direct materials cost of job 1357
(b) The direct labour cost of job 1357
(c) The full production cost of job 1357
(d) The price of job 1357

Solution

(a)

	£
Direct material Y (400 kilos × £5)	2,000
Direct material Z (800 – 60 kilos × £6)	4,440
Total direct material cost	6,440

(b)

	£
Department P (320 hours × £4)	1,280
Department Q (200 hours × £5)	1,000
Total direct labour cost	2,280

Rectification work, being normal and expected, is included in the direct labour cost of Department P. Overtime premium will be charged to overhead in the case of Department P, and to the job of the customer who asked for overtime to be worked in the case of Department Q.

(c)

	£
Direct material cost	6,440
Direct labour cost	2,280
Production overhead (520 hours × £3)	1,560
	10,280

(d)   Price = £10,280 × 130% = £13,364

1.17   An example may help to illustrate the principles of job costing, and the way in which the costing of individual jobs fits in with the recording of total costs in control accounts. Study the following example very carefully and make sure that you understand the solution.

Example: job costing

1.18   Pistachio Ltd is a jobbing company. On 1 June 19X2, there was one uncompleted job in the factory. The job cost sheet for this work is summarised as follows.

Job Cost Sheet, Job No 6832

Costs to date	£
Direct materials	630
Direct labour (120 hours)	350
Factory overhead (£2 per direct labour hour)	240
Factory cost to date	1,220

During June, three new jobs were started in the factory, and costs of production were as follows.

Direct materials	£
Issued to: job 6832	2,390
job 6833	1,680
job 6834	3,950
job 6835	4,420

Material transfers	£
Job 6834 to job 6833	250
Job 6832 to 6834	620

Materials returned to store	£
From job 6832	870
From job 6835	170

Direct labour hours recorded	
Job 6832	430 hrs
Job 6833	650 hrs
Job 6834	280 hrs
Job 6835	410 hrs

The cost of labour hours during June 19X2 was £3 per hour, and production overhead is absorbed at the rate of £2 per direct labour hour. Production overheads incurred during the month amounted to £3,800. Completed jobs were delivered to customers as soon as they were completed, and the invoiced amounts were as follows.

Job 6832	£5,500
Job 6834	£8,000
Job 6835	£7,500

Administration and marketing overheads are added to the cost of sales at the rate of 20% of factory cost on completion of jobs. Actual costs incurred during June 19X2 amounted to £3,200.

Required

(a)   Prepare the job accounts for each individual job during June 19X2. (The accounts should only show the cost of production, and not the full cost of sale.)

(b) Prepare summaries of the costs of each job, and calculate the profit on each completed job.

(c) Show how the costs would be shown in the company's cost control accounts. Note that you will be unable to complete the stores ledger control account. The company operates an integrated system.

Solution

1.19 (a) *Job accounts*

JOB 6832

	£		£
Balance b/f	1,220	Job 6834 a/c	620
Materials (stores a/c)	2,390	(materials transfer)	
Labour (wages a/c)	1,290	Stores a/c (materials returned)	870
Production overhead (o'hd a/c)	860	Cost of sales a/c (balance)	4,270
	5,760		5,760

JOB 6833

	£		£
Materials (stores a/c)	1,680	Balance c/f	5,180
Labour (wages a/c)	1,950		
Production overhead (o'hd a/c)	1,300		
Job 6834 a/c (materials transfer)	250		
	5,180		5,180

JOB 6834

	£		£
Materials (stores a/c)	3,950	Job 6833 a/c (materials transfer)	250
Labour (wages a/c)	840	Cost of sales a/c (balance)	5,720
Production overhead (o'hd a/c)	560		
Job 6832 a/c (materials transfer)	620		
	5,970		5,970

JOB 6835

	£		£
Materials (stores a/c)	4,420	Stores a/c (materials returned)	170
Labour (wages a/c)	1,230	Cost of sales a/c (balance)	6,300
Production overhead (o'hd a/c)	820		
	6,470		6,470

(b) *Job costs, summarised*

	Job 6832	Job 6833	Job 6834	Job 6835
	£	£	£	
Materials	*1,530	1,930	**4,320	4,250
Labour	1,640	1,950	840	1,230
Production overhead	1,100	1,300	560	820
Factory cost	4,270	5,180(c/f)	5,720	6,300
Admin & marketing o'hd (20%)	854		1,144	1,260
Cost of sale	5,124		6,864	7,560
Invoice value	5,500		8,000	7,500
Profit/(loss) on job	376		1,136	(60)

* £(630 + 2,390 − 620 − 870)   ** £(3,950 + 620 − 250)

(c) *Control accounts*

STORES CONTROL (incomplete)

	£		£
WIP a/c (returns)	1,040	WIP a/c	
		(2,390 + 1,680 + 3,950 + 4,420)	12,440

WORK IN PROGRESS CONTROL

	£		£
Balance b/f	1,220	Stores control a/c (returns)	1,040
Stores control a/c	12,440	Cost of sales a/c	
Wages control a/c	*5,310	(4,270 + 5,720 + 6,300)	16,290
Production o'hd control a/c	3,540	Balance c/f (Job No 6833)	5,180
	22,510		22,510

* 1,770 hours at £3 per hour

COST OF SALES CONTROL

	£		£
WIP control a/c	16,290	Profit and loss	19,548
Admin & marketing o'hd a/c			
(854 + 1,144 + 1,260)	3,258		
	19,548		19,548

SALES

	£		£
Profit and loss	21,000	Debtors/cash	21,000
		(5,500 + 8,000 + 7,500)	
	21,000		21,000

PRODUCTION OVERHEAD CONTROL

	£		£
Creditors/cash	3,800	WIP a/c	3,540
(overhead incurred)		Under-absorbed o'hd a/c	260
	3,800		3,800

UNDER-/OVER-ABSORBED O'HD

	£		£
Production o'hd control a/c	260	Admin & marketing o'hd a/c	58
		Profit and loss a/c	202
	260		260

ADMIN & MARKETING OVERHEAD CONTROL

	£		£
Creditors/cash	3,200	Cost of sales a/c	3,258
(overhead incurred)			
Over absorbed o'hd a/c	58		
	3,258		3,258

PROFIT AND LOSS

	£		£
Cost of sales a/c	19,548	Sales a/c	21,000
Under-absorbed overhead a/c	202		
Profit	1,250		
	21,000		21,000

2   BATCH COSTING

2.1   In general, the procedures for costing batches are very similar to those for costing jobs. The batch is treated as a job during production and the costs are collected in the manner already described in this chapter. Once the batch has been completed, the cost per unit can be calculated as the total batch cost divided by the number of units in the batch.

Example: batch costing

2.2   A company manufactures widgets to order and has the following budgeted overheads for the year, based on normal activity levels.

	Budgeted Overheads £	Budgeted activity
Department		
Welding	6,000	1,500 labour hours
Assembly	10,000	1,000 labour hours

Selling and administrative overheads are 20% of factory cost. An order for 250 widgets type X128, made as Batch 5997, incurred the following costs.

Materials	£12,000
Labour	100 hours welding shop at £2.50/hour
	200 hours assembly shop at £1/hour

£500 was paid for the hire of special X-ray equipment for testing the welds.

Required

Calculate the cost per unit for Batch 5997.

Solution

2.3   The first step is to calculate the overhead absorption rates for the production departments.

$$\text{Welding} \quad = \quad \frac{£6,000}{1,500} \quad = \quad £4 \text{ per labour hour}$$

$$\text{Assembly} \quad = \quad \frac{£10,000}{1,000} \quad = \quad £10 \text{ per labour hour}$$

Total cost - Batch no 5997

		£	£
Direct material			12,000
Direct expense			500
Direct labour	100 × £2.50 =	250	
	200 × £1.00 =	200	
			450
Prime cost			12,950
Overheads	100 × £4 =	400	
	200 × £10 =	2,000	
			2,400
Factory cost			15,350
Selling and administrative cost (20% of factory cost)			3,070
Total cost			18,420

$$\text{Cost per unit} = \frac{£18,420}{250} = £73.68$$

3   OUTPUT COSTING

3.1   This method of costing is used by organisations who produce just one product in a single process. An example of such a process is a quarry from which just one product (chalk, slate and so on) is extracted.

3.2   It is a very simple method of costing. Since there is only one product and one cost centre there is no point in making complex calculations and the cost of a unit of production (perhaps a tonne of chalk) is therefore ascertained by collecting and analysing all the relevant costs and then dividing each of the total costs by the total production to find the unit cost.

Exercise 2

If the cost of mining 100,000 kgs of a particular mineral during a control period is £3,750,000, what is the cost per kg?

Solution

$$\text{Cost per kg} = \frac{£3,750,000}{100,000} = £37.50$$

Chapter roundup

- Job costing is the costing method used where each cost unit is separately identifiable.

- Each job is given a number to distinguish it from other jobs.

- Costs for each job are collected on a job cost sheet.

- Material costs for each job are determined from material requisition notes.

- Labour times on each job are recorded on a job ticket, which is then costed and recorded on the job cost sheet. Some labour costs, such as overtime premium or the cost of rectifying sub-standard output, might be charged either directly to a job or else as an overhead cost, depending on the circumstances in which the costs have arisen.

- Overhead is absorbed into the cost of jobs using the predetermined overhead absorption rates.

- The usual method of fixing prices within a jobbing concern is cost plus pricing.

- Batch costing is similar to job costing in that each batch of similar articles is separately identifiable. The cost per unit manufactured in a batch is the total batch cost divided by the number of units in the batch.

- Output costing is typically used by organisations operating in industries such as mining and quarrying.

Test your knowledge

1 Describe the procedures by which job costs are collected. (see paras 1.4-1.6)

2 How is a job valued at the end of an accounting period if it is incomplete? (1.11)

3 Describe two ways of accounting for rectification costs. (1.13)

4 What is cost plus pricing? (1.15)

5 What is output costing? (3.1, 3.2)

Now try illustrative question 10 at the end of the Study Text

Chapter 10

PROCESS COSTING

This chapter covers the following topics.

		Syllabus reference	Ability required
1	The distinguishing features of process costing	2(b)	Skill
2	Simple process costing	2(b)	Skill
3	Normal loss and abnormal loss or gain	2(b)	Skill
4	Accounting for scrap	2(b)	Skill
5	Closing work in progress	2(b)	Skill
6	Closing work in progress and losses	2(b)	Skill
7	Identification of losses/gains at different stages in the process	2(b)	Skill
8	Joint products and by-products	2(b)	Skill

Introduction

We looked at three types of cost accounting system, job, batch and output costing, in the previous chapter. In this chapter we will consider another, process costing. We will begin from basics and look at how to account for the most simple of processes. We will then move on to how to account for any losses which might occur, as well as what to do with any scrapped units which are sold. Next we will consider how to deal with closing work in progress before examining situations involving closing work in progress *and* losses. Throughout the chapter we will be looking at how to record process costs in process accounts which are simply WIP ledger accounts.

We will end the chapter by looking at a particular feature of the process industry, joint products and by-products.

Chapter 11 is the last in the series of chapters which look at cost accounting systems. It considers the systems used by service industries and internal service departments.

1 THE DISTINGUISHING FEATURES OF PROCESS COSTING

1.1 Process costing is used where it is not possible to identify separate units of production, or individual jobs, usually because of the continuous nature of the production processes involved. It is common (but not essential) to identify process costing with continuous production such as oil refining, or the manufacture of soap, paint, textiles, paper, foods and drinks, many chemicals and so on. Process costing may also be associated with the continuous production of large volumes of low-cost items, such as cans or tins.

1.2 The features of process costing which make it different from job or batch costing are as follows.

(a) The continuous nature of production in many processes means that there will usually be closing work in progress which must be valued. In process costing it is not possible to build up cost records of the cost per unit of output or the cost per unit of closing stock because production in progress is an indistinguishable homogeneous mass.

(b) There is often a *loss in process* due to spoilage, wastage, evaporation and so on.

(c) Output from production may be a single product, but there may also be a by-product (or by-products) and/or joint products.

1.3 The aim of this chapter is to describe how cost accountants record the costs of production in a processing industry in process accounts. The aim of the set of accounts is to derive a cost, or valuation, for output and closing stock.

1.4 Finally, what you must not forget as you work through this chapter is that a process account is the same as a job account in that it is nothing more than a work in progress ledger account.

2 SIMPLE PROCESS COSTING

2.1 Before tackling the more complex areas of process costing, we will begin by looking at a very simple process costing example which will illustrate the basic techniques which we will build upon in the remainder of this chapter.

2.2 Suppose that Purr and Miaow Ltd make squeaky toys for cats. Production of the toys involves two processes, shaping and colouring. During the year to 31 March 19X3, 1,000,000 units of material worth £500,000 were input to the first process, shaping. Direct labour costs of £200,000 and production overhead costs of £200,000 were also incurred in connection with the shaping process. There were no opening or closing stocks in the shaping department. The process account for shaping for the year ended 31 March 19X3 is as follows.

PROCESS 1 (SHAPING) ACCOUNT

	Units	£		Units	£
Direct materials	1,000,000	500,000	Output to Process 2	1,000,000	900,000
Direct labour		200,000			
Production overheads		200,000			
	1,000,000	900,000		1,000,000	900,000

2.3 As we mentioned above, a process account is nothing more than a ledger account with debit and credit entries although it does have an additional column on both the debit and credit sides showing quantity. When preparing process accounts you are advised to include these memorandum quantity columns and to balance them off (ie ensure they total to the same amount on both sides) before attempting to complete the monetary value columns since they will help you to check that you have missed nothing out. This becomes increasingly important as more complications are introduced into questions.

2.4 Because process accounts are simply ledger accounts, the double entry works as it does for any other ledger account. For example, the corresponding credit entry of £200,000 for labour in the process 1 account above will be in the wages and salaries control account. Students often think process costing is difficult but if you bear in mind that you are simply completing a normal ledger account which is part of a system of double entry cost bookkeeping you will find this topic much more straightforward.

2.5 After that slight digression let us go back to Purr and Miaow Ltd. When using process costing, if a series of separate processes are needed to manufacture the finished product, the output of one process becomes the input to the next until the final output is made in the final process. In our example, all output from shaping was transferred to the second process, colouring, during the year to 31 March 19X3. An additional 500,000 units of material, costing £300,000, were input to the colouring process. Direct labour costs of £150,000 and production overhead costs of £150,000 were also incurred. There were no opening or closing stocks in the colouring department. The process account for colouring for the year ended 31 March 19X3 is as follows.

PROCESS 2 (COLOURING) ACCOUNT

	Units	£		Units	£
Materials from process 1	1,000,000	900,000	Output to finished		
Added materials	500,000	300,000	goods	1,500,000	1,500,000
Direct labour		150,000			
Production overhead		150,000			
	1,500,000	1,500,000		1,500,000	1,500,000

2.6 The cost per unit of output to finished goods is calculated as follows.

Output to finished goods = 1,500,000 units at total cost of £1,500,000

$$\text{Cost per unit of output} = £\left(\frac{1,500,000}{1,500,000}\right) = £1.00$$

2.7 Direct labour and production overhead may be treated together in an examination question as 'conversion cost'.

Added materials, labour and overhead in Process 2 are usually added gradually throughout the process. Materials from Process 1, in contrast, will often be introduced in full at the start of the second process.

2.8 Note that the costing system above is an absorption costing system since overheads have been absorbed into the cost of output to finished goods. In a marginal costing system, overheads would not have been included in the process accounts and therefore not included in the cost of output. They would simply have been written off in the period in which they were incurred.

3 NORMAL LOSS AND ABNORMAL LOSS OR GAIN   5/96

3.1 During a production process, a loss may occur due to wastage, spoilage, evaporation, and so on. Loss of this type may be one of the following.

(a) A loss expected during the normal course of operations, for unavoidable reasons. The average expected loss is known as normal loss.

(b) An unexpected loss, usually known as abnormal loss.

3.2 In the case of normal loss, it is argued that the cost of such losses is an inherent part of the production process. In other words, the cost of normal loss is as much a production cost as, say, the cost of materials or labour. The cost of normal loss is therefore spread across the *expected* units of good output (in the same way as are the costs of materials and labour) to arrive at a unit cost of production.

3.3 With abnormal loss the case is different. It would be unreasonable and contrary to SSAP 9 to include in the valuation of good units of output the costs arising from poor workmanship, poor quality materials, damage by accident and so on. Instead, the costs of abnormal loss should be written off to the profit and loss account so that they do not affect the valuation of expected units of output.

3.4 An example will make this distinction clearer.

Example: normal and abnormal loss

3.5 Gunner Ltd operates a manufacturing process, and during March 19X3 the following processing took place.

Opening stock	nil	Closing stock	nil
Units introduced	1,000 units	Output	900 units
Costs incurred	£4,500	Loss	100 units

Required

Determine the cost of output in the following circumstances.

(a) Expected or normal loss is 10% of input.
(b) There is no expected loss, so that the entire loss of 100 units was unexpected.

Solution

3.6 (a) *If loss is expected*, and is an unavoidable feature of processing, it is argued by cost accountants that there is no point in charging a cost to the loss. It is more sensible to accept that the loss will occur, and spread the costs of production over the expected units of output.

$$\frac{\text{Costs}}{\text{Expected output (90\% of 1,000)}} = \frac{£4,500}{900 \text{ units}}$$

$$\text{Cost per unit of output} = \frac{£4,500}{900} = £5$$

Normal loss is not given any cost, so that the process account would appear as follows.

PROCESS ACCOUNT

	Units	£		Units	£
Costs incurred	1,000	4,500	Normal loss	100	0
			Output units	900	4,500
	1,000	4,500		1,000	4,500

It helps to enter normal loss into the process 'T' account, just to make sure that your memorandum quantity columns for units are the same on the debit and the credit sides of the account.

(b) *If loss is unexpected* and occurred perhaps as a result of poor workmanship, poor quality materials, poor supervision, damage by accident, and so on, it is argued that it would be reasonable to charge a cost to the units of loss. The cost would then be transferred to an 'abnormal loss' account, and eventually written off to the profit and loss account as an item of loss in the period. Units of 'good output' are therefore not burdened with the cost of the units of abnormal loss. Units of abnormal loss are valued at the same rate per unit as the units of good output.

$$\frac{\text{Costs incurred}}{\text{Expected output}} = \frac{£4,500}{1,000 \text{ units}}$$

Costs per unit   £4.50

The process account and abnormal loss account would look like this.

PROCESS ACCOUNT

	Units	£		Units	£
Costs incurred	1,000	4,500	Abnormal loss	100	450
			Output units	900	4,050
	1,000	4,500		1,000	4,500

ABNORMAL LOSS ACCOUNT

	Units	£		Units	£
Process account	100	450	Profit and loss account	100	450

Abnormal losses and abnormal gains

3.7 It is almost inevitable that when there is an expected loss in a process, the actual loss which occurs will not be exactly the same amount as the average or normal loss. The difference between the normal loss and the actual loss is an abnormal loss or an abnormal gain.

(a) Where the actual loss is larger than the normal loss, the excess is known as *abnormal loss*.

(b) Where the actual loss is smaller than the normal loss, the difference (or 'saving') in loss is known as *abnormal gain*.

Provided that the estimated normal loss is an accurate 'average' figure, the abnormal losses and abnormal gains over a period of time should tend to cancel each other out.

Example: abnormal losses and gains

3.8   Suppose that input to a process is 1,000 units at a cost of £4,500. Normal loss is 10% and there are no opening or closing stocks. Determine the accounting entries for the cost of output and the cost of the loss if actual output were as follows.

(a) 860 units (so that actual loss is 140 units)
(b) 920 units (so that actual loss is 80 units)

Solution

3.9   The same principles described earlier for evaluating normal and abnormal loss may be applied to situations where normal loss and abnormal loss/gain occur together.

(a) Normal loss is given no share of cost.

(b) The cost of output is based on the *expected* units of output, which in our example amount to 90% of 1,000 = 900 units.

(c) Abnormal loss is given a cost, which is written off to the profit and loss account via an abnormal loss/gain account.

(d) Abnormal gain is treated in the same way, except that being a gain rather than a loss, it appears as a *debit* entry in the process account (whereas a loss appears as a *credit* entry in this account).

3.10   If actual output is 860 units and the actual loss is 140 units:

	Units
Actual loss	140
Normal loss (10% of 1,000)	100
Abnormal loss	40

The cost per unit of output and the cost per unit of abnormal loss are based on expected output.

$$\frac{\text{Costs incurred}}{\text{Expected output}} = \frac{£4,500}{900 \text{ units}}$$

Cost per unit   £5

Normal loss is not assigned any cost.

PROCESS ACCOUNT

	Units	£		Units	£
Cost incurred	1,000	4,500	Normal loss	100	0
			Output (finished goods a/c)	860	(× £5) 4,300
			Abnormal loss	40	(× £5) 200
	1,000	4,500		1,000	4,500

ABNORMAL LOSS ACCOUNT

	Units	£		Units	£
Process a/c	40	200	Profit and loss a/c	40	200

3.11   If actual output is 920 units and the actual loss is 80 units:

	Units
Actual loss	80
Normal loss (10% of 1,000)	100
Abnormal gain	20

The cost per unit of output and the cost per unit of abnormal gain are based on expected output.

$$\frac{\text{Costs incurred}}{\text{Expected output}} = \frac{\text{£4,500}}{\text{900 units}} = \text{£5 per unit}$$

(Whether there is abnormal loss or gain does not affect the valuation of units of output. The figure of £5 per unit is exactly the same as in the previous paragraph, when there were 40 units of abnormal loss.)

PROCESS ACCOUNT

	Units	£		Units	£
Cost incurred	1,000	4,500	Normal loss	100	0
Abnormal gain a/c	20	(× £5) 100	Output (finished goods a/c)	920	(× £5) 4,600
	1,020	4,600		1,020	4,600

ABNORMAL GAIN

	Units	£		Units	£
Profit and loss a/c	20	100	Process a/c	20	100

Example: abnormal losses and gains again

3.12   During a four-week period, period 3, costs of input to a process were £29,070. Input was 1,000 units, output was 850 units and normal loss is 10%.

During the next period, period 4, costs of input were again £29,070. Input was again 1,000 units, but output was 950 units.

There were no units of opening or closing stock.

Required

Prepare the process account and abnormal loss or gain account for each period.

Solution

3.13   For each period the cost per unit is based on expected output.

$$\frac{\text{Cost of input}}{\text{Expected units of output}} = \frac{\text{£29,070}}{900} = \text{£32.30 per unit}$$

During period 3, there was an abnormal loss of 50 units, and during period 4 there was an abnormal gain of 50 units. These are valued at £32.30 per unit.

PROCESS ACCOUNT

	Units	£		Units	£
Period 3					
Cost of input	1,000	29,070	Normal loss	100	0
			Finished goods a/c (× £32.30)	850	27,455
			Abnormal loss a/c (× £32.30)	50	1,615
	1,000	29,070		1,000	29,070
Period 4					
Cost of input	1,000	29,070	Normal loss	100	0
Abnormal gain a/c (× £32.30)	50	1,615	Finished goods a/c (× £32.30)	950	30,685
	1,050	30,685		1,050	30,685

ABNORMAL LOSS OR GAIN ACCOUNT

	£		£
Period 3		*Period 4*	
Abnormal loss in process a/c	1,615	Abnormal gain in process a/c	1,615

A nil balance on this account will be carried forward into period 5.

3.14   If there is a closing balance in the abnormal loss or gain account when the profit for the period is calculated, this balance is taken to the profit and loss account: an abnormal gain will adjust profit upwards and an abnormal loss will adjust profit downwards.

4   ACCOUNTING FOR SCRAP

4.1   Loss may have a scrap value. The accounting treatment of scrap in process costing is somewhat unusual and should be studied carefully. The following basic rules are applied.

(a)   Revenue from scrap is treated, not as an addition to sales revenue, but as a reduction in costs.

(b)   The scrap value of *normal loss* is therefore used to reduce the material costs of the process.

CREDIT   Process a/c (normal loss)
DEBIT   Scrap a/c

- with the scrap value of units of normal loss.

(c)   The scrap value of *abnormal loss* is used to reduce the cost of abnormal loss, and therefore to reduce the write-off of cost to the profit and loss account.

CREDIT   Abnormal loss a/c
DEBIT   Scrap a/c

- with the scrap value of units of abnormal loss.

Notice that the scrap value of abnormal loss is *not* credited to the process account.

(d)   The scrap value of *abnormal* gain arises because the actual units sold as scrap will be less than the scrap value of normal loss. Because there are fewer units of scrap than expected, there will be less revenue from scrap as a direct consequence of the abnormal gain. The accounting entry is therefore as follows.

CREDIT   Scrap a/c
DEBIT   Abnormal gain a/c

- with the scrap value of abnormal gain.

(e)   The scrap account is completed by recording the cash received from the sale of scrap.

CREDIT   Scrap a/c
DEBIT   Cash (or debtors or cost ledger control a/c)

- with the value of the actual number of units scrapped.

Example: scrap and normal loss

4.2   Suppose that input to a process costs £1,370, normal loss is 10% and units scrapped sell for £2 each. 100 units are input and 90 units output. The cost per unit of output would be calculated as follows.

	£
Cost of input	1,370
Less scrap value of normal loss (10 units × £2)	20
	1,350

Expected units of output	90 units
Cost per unit	£15 per unit

Required

Show the process account and the scrap account.

Solution

4.3   The accounting entries would be as follows.

PROCESS ACCOUNT

	Units	£		Units	£
Input costs	100	1,370	Normal loss (scrap a/c)	10	20
			Output (finished goods a/c)	90	1,350
	100	1,370		100	1,370

SCRAP ACCOUNT

	£		£
Scrap value of normal loss	20	Cash a/c (or CLC)	20
		= actual cash received for scrap	
	20		20

4.4 If there is abnormal loss or abnormal gain, the scrap value of actual loss will differ from the normal loss scrap value. This discrepancy is ignored in the process account and is dealt with instead in the abnormal loss or gain account and the scrap account. Study the next example closely.

Example: scrap and abnormal loss

4.5 A factory with two production processes. Normal loss in each process is 10% and scrapped units sell for £0.50 each from process 1 and £3 each from process 2. Relevant information for costing purposes relating to period 5 is as follows.

	Process 1	*Process 2*
Direct materials added:		
units	2,000	1,250
cost	£8,100	£1,900
Direct labour	£4,000	£10,000
Production overhead	150% of direct labour cost	120% of direct labour cost
Output to process 2/finished goods	1,750 units	2,800 units
Actual production overhead	£17,800	

Required

Prepare the accounts for process 1, process 2, scrap, abnormal loss or gain and production overhead.

Solution

4.6

PROCESS 1 ACCOUNT

	Units	£		Units	£
Direct material	2,000	8,100	Scrap a/c (normal loss)	200	100
Direct labour		4,000	Process 2 a/c	1,750	17,500
Production overhead a/c		6,000	Abnormal loss a/c	50	500
	2,000	18,100		2,000	18,100

$$\text{Cost per unit of output and abnormal loss} = \frac{£(18,100 - 100)}{90\% \text{ of } 2,000 \text{ units}} = £10 \text{ per unit}$$

PROCESS 2 ACCOUNT

	Units	£		Units	£
Direct materials					
From process 1	1,750	17,500	Scrap a/c (normal loss)	300	900
Added materials	1,250	1,900	Finished goods a/c	2,800	42,000
Direct labour		10,000			
Production overhead		12,000			
	3,000	41,400			
Abnormal gain	100	1,500			
	3,100	42,900		3,100	42,900

$$\text{Cost per unit of output and abnormal gain} = \frac{£(41,400 - 900)}{90\% \text{ of } 3,000 \text{ units}} = £15 \text{ per unit}$$

ABNORMAL LOSS ACCOUNT

	£		£
Process 1 (50 units)	500	Scrap a/c: sale of scrap of	
		extra loss (50 units)	25
		Profit and loss a/c	475
	500		500

ABNORMAL GAIN ACCOUNT

	£		£
Scrap a/c (loss of scrap revenue		Process 2 abnormal gain	
due to abnormal gain, 100 units		(100 units)	1,500
× £3)	300		
Profit and loss a/c	1,200		
	1,500		1,500

SCRAP ACCOUNT

	£		£
Scrap value of normal loss		Cash a/c - cash received	
Process 1 (200 units)	100	Loss in process 1 (250 units)	125
Process 2 (300 units)	900	Loss in process 2 (200 units)	600
Abnormal loss a/c (process 1)	25	Abnormal gain a/c (process 2)	300
	1,025		1,025

PRODUCTION OVERHEAD ACCOUNT

	£		£
Overhead incurred	17,800	Process 1 a/c	6,000
Over-absorbed overhead a/c		Process 2 a/c	12,000
(or P & L a/c)	200		
	18,000		18,000

Exercise 1

Parks Ltd operates a processing operation involving two stages, the output of process 1 being passed to process 2. The process costs for period 3 were as follows.

Process 1

Material	3,000 kg at £0.25 per kg
Labour	£120

Process 2

Material	2,000 kg at £0.40 per kg
Labour	£84

General overhead for period 3 amounted to £357 and is absorbed into process costs at a rate of 375% of direct labour costs in process 1 and 496% of direct labour costs in process 2.

The normal output of process 1 is 80% of input and of process 2, 90% of input. Waste matter from process 1 is sold for £0.20 per kg and that from process 2 for £0.30 per kg.

The output for period 3 was as follows.

Process 1	2,300 kgs
Process 2	4,000 kgs

There was no stock of work in progress at either the beginning or the end of the period and it may be assumed that all available waste matter had been sold at the prices indicated.

Required

Show how the foregoing data would be recorded in a system of cost accounts.

Solution

PROCESS 1 ACCOUNT

	kg	£		kg	£
Material	3,000	750	Normal loss to scrap a/c		
Labour		120	(20%)	600	120
General overhead		450	Production transferred to		
			process 2	2,300	1,150
			Abnormal loss a/c	100	50
	3,000	1,320		3,000	1,320

$$\text{Cost per unit of output} = \left(\frac{£1,320 - £120}{3,000 - 600} \right) = 50p$$

PROCESS 2 ACCOUNT

	kg	£		kg	£
Transferred from process 1	2,300	1,150	Normal loss to scrap a/c		
Material added	2,000	800	(10%)	430	129
Labour		84	Production transferred to		
General overhead		417	finished stock	4,000	2,400
	4,300	2,451			
Abnormal gain	130	78			
	4,430	2,529		4,430	2,529

$$\text{Cost per unit of output} = \left(\frac{£2,451 - £129}{4,300 - 430} \right) = 60p$$

FINISHED STOCK ACCOUNT

	kg	£
Process 2	4,000	2,400

SCRAP ACCOUNT

	kg	£		kg	£
Normal loss (process 1)	600	120	Abnormal gain (process 2)	130	39
Normal loss (process 2)	430	129	Cash	1,000	230
Abnormal loss (process 1)	100	20			
	1,130	269		1,130	269

ABNORMAL LOSS AND GAIN ACCOUNT

	kg	£		kg	£
Process 1 (loss)	100	50	Scrap value of		
Scrap value of abnormal			abnormal loss	100	20
gain	130	39	Process 2 (gain)	130	78
Profit and loss		9			
	230	98		230	98

(*Note.* In this solution, a single account has been prepared for abnormal loss/gain. Your solution will probably have separated this single account into two separate accounts, one for abnormal gain and one for abnormal loss.)

5 CLOSING WORK IN PROGRESS   *5/96*

5.1 In the examples we have looked at so far we have assumed that opening and closing stocks of work in process have been nil. We must now look at more realistic examples and consider how to allocate the costs incurred in a period between completed output (ie finished units) and partly completed closing stock.

5.2 Some examples will help to illustrate the problem, and the techniques used to share out (apportion) costs between finished output and closing stocks.

Example: valuation of closing stock

5.3 Trotter Ltd is a manufacturer of processed goods. In March 19X3, in one process, there was no opening stock, but 5,000 units of input were introduced to the process during the month, at the following cost.

	£
Direct materials	16,560
Direct labour	7,360
Production overhead	5,520
	29,440

Of the 5,000 units introduced, 4,000 were completely finished during the month and transferred to the next process. Closing stock of 1,000 units was only 60% complete with respect to materials and conversion costs.

5.4 The problem in this example is to divide the costs of production (£29,440) between the finished output of 4,000 units and the closing stock of 1,000 units. It is argued, with good reason, that a division of costs in proportion to the number of units of each (4,000:1,000) would not be 'fair' because closing stock has not been completed, and has not yet 'received' its full amount of materials and conversion costs, but only 60% of the full amount. The 1,000 units of closing stock, being only 60% complete, are the equivalent of 600 fully worked units.

5.5 To apportion costs fairly and proportionately, units of production must be converted into the equivalent of completed units, ie into *equivalent units of production*. Equivalent units, defined by the CIMA as 'Notional whole units representing uncompleted work', then provide a basis for apportioning costs.

	Total units	Completion	Equivalent units
Fully worked units	4,000	100%	4,000
Closing stock	1,000	60%	600
	5,000		4,600

5.6 Equivalent units are the basis for apportioning costs and so we need a 'cost per equivalent unit' as follows.

$$\frac{\text{Total cost}}{\text{Equivalent costs}} = \frac{£29,440}{4,600}$$

Cost per equivalent unit £6.40

5.7 A statement of evaluation may now be prepared, to show how the costs should be apportioned between finished output and closing stock.

Item	Equivalent units	Cost of equivalent unit	Valuation £
Fully worked units	4,000	£6.40	25,600
Closing stock	600	£6.40	3,840
	4,600		29,440

5.8 The process account (work in progress, or work in process account) would be shown as follows.

PROCESS ACCOUNT

		Units	£		Units	£
(Stores a/c)	Direct materials	5,000	16,560	Output to next process	4,000	25,600
(Wages a/c)	Direct labour		7,360	Closing stock c/f	1,000	3,840
(O'hd a/c)	Production o'hd		5,520			
		5,000	29,440		5,000	29,440

5.9 When preparing a process 'T' account, it might help to make the entries as follows.

(a) Enter the units first. The units columns are simply memorandum columns, but they help you to make sure that there are no units unaccounted for (for example as loss).

(b) Enter the costs of materials, labour and overheads next. These should be given to you.

(c) Enter your valuation of finished output and closing stock next. The value of the credit entries should, of course, equal the value of the debit entries.

Different rates of input

5.10 In many industries, materials, labour and overhead may be added at different rates during the course of production.

(a) Output from a previous process (for example the output from process 1 to process 2) may be introduced into the subsequent process all at once, so that closing stock is 100% complete in respect of these materials.

(b) Further materials may be added gradually during the process, so that closing stock is only partially complete in respect of these added materials.

(c) Labour and overhead may be 'added' at yet another different rate. When production overhead is absorbed on a labour hour basis, however, we should expect the degree of completion on overhead to be the same as the degree of completion on labour.

When this situation occurs, equivalent units, and a cost per equivalent unit, should be calculated separately for each type of material, and also for conversion costs.

Example: equivalent units and different degrees of completion

5.11 Suppose that Shaker Ltd is a manufacturer of processed goods, and that results in process 2 for April 19X3 were as follows.

Opening stock	nil
Material input from process 1	4,000 units
Costs of input:	£
material from process 1	6,000
added materials in process 2	1,080
conversion costs	1,720

Output is transferred into the next process, process 3.

Closing work in process amounted to 800 units, complete as to:

process 1 material	100%
added materials	50%
conversion costs	30%

Required

Prepare the account for process 2 for April 19X3.

Solution

5.12 (a) STATEMENT OF EQUIVALENT UNITS (OF PRODUCTION IN THE PERIOD)

			Process 1 material		*Equivalent units of production* *Added materials*		*Labour and overhead*	
Input	*Output*	*Total*						
Units		Units	Units	%	Units	%	Units	%
4,000	Completed production	3,200	3,200	100	3,200	100	3,200	100
	Closing stock	800	800	100	400	50	240	30
4,000		4,000	4,000		3,600		3,440	

(b)   STATEMENT OF COST (PER EQUIVALENT UNIT)

Input	Cost £	Equivalent production in units	Cost per unit £
Process 1 material	6,000	4,000	1.50
Added materials	1,080	3,600	0.30
Labour and overhead	1,720	3,440	0.50
	8,800		2.30

(c)   STATEMENT OF EVALUATION (OF FINISHED WORK AND CLOSING STOCKS)

Production	Cost element	Number of equivalent units	Cost per equivalent unit £	Total £	Cost £
Completed production		3,200	2.30		7,360
Closing stock:	process 1 material	800	1.50	1,200	
	added material	400	0.30	120	
	labour and overhead	240	0.50	120	
					1,440
					8,800

(d)   PROCESS ACCOUNT

	Units	£		Units	£
Process 1 material	4,000	6,000	Process 3 a/c	3,200	7,360
Added material		1,080	(finished output)		
Conversion costs		1,720	Closing stock c/f	800	1,440
	4,000	8,800		4,000	8,800

6   CLOSING WORK IN PROGRESS AND LOSSES   5/96

6.1   The previous paragraphs have dealt separately with the following.

(a)   The treatment of loss and scrap

(b)   The use of equivalent units as a basis for apportioning costs between units of output and units of closing stock

We must now look at a situation where both problems occur together, that is there is closing work in progress, and also losses occurring during the process. We shall begin with an example where loss has no scrap value.

6.2   The rules are as follows.

(a)   Costs should be divided between finished output, closing stock and abnormal loss/gain using equivalent units as a basis of apportionment.

(b)   Units of abnormal loss/gain are often taken to be one full equivalent unit each, and are valued on this basis.

(c)   Abnormal loss units are an addition to the total equivalent units produced but abnormal gain units are subtracted in arriving at the total number of equivalent units produced.

(d)   Units of normal loss are 'equivalent to' zero equivalent units.

Example: changes in stock level and losses

6.3   The following data has been collected.

Opening stock	none	Output to finished goods	2,000 units
Input units	2,800 units	Closing stock	450 units, 70% complete
Cost of input	£16,695	Total loss	350 units
Normal loss	10%; nil scrap value		

Required

Prepare the process account for the period.

Solution

6.4   (a)   STATEMENT OF EQUIVALENT UNITS

	Total units		Equivalent units of work done this period
Completely worked units	2,000	(× 100%)	2,000
Closing stock	450	(× 70%)	315
Normal loss	280		0
Abnormal loss	70	(× 100%)	70
	2,800		2,385

(b)   STATEMENT OF COST PER EQUIVALENT UNIT

$$\frac{\text{Costs incurred}}{\text{Equivalent units of work done}} = \frac{£16,695}{2,385}$$

Cost per equivalent unit   =   £7

(c)   STATEMENT OF EVALUATION

	Equivalent units	£
Completely worked units	2,000	14,000
Closing stock	315	2,205
Abnormal loss	70	490
	2,385	16,695

(d)   PROCESS ACCOUNT

	Units	£		Units	£
Input costs	2,800	16,695	Normal loss	280	0
			Finished goods a/c	2,000	14,000
			Abnormal loss a/c	70	490
			Closing stock c/d	450	2,205
	2,800	16,695		2,800	16,695

Closing work in progress, loss and scrap

6.5   When loss has a scrap value, the accounting procedures are the same as those previously described. However, if the equivalent units are a different percentage (of the total units) for materials, labour and overhead, it is a convention that the scrap value of normal loss is deducted from the cost of materials before a cost per equivalent unit is calculated.

Exercise 2

Prepare a process account from the following information.

Opening stock	Nil
Input units	10,000
Input costs	
Material	£5,150
Labour	£2,700
Normal loss	5% of input
Scrap value of units of loss	£1 per unit
Output to finished goods	8,000 units
Closing stock	1,000 units
Completion of closing stock	80% for material
	50% for labour

Solution

STATEMENT OF EQUIVALENT UNITS

| | | | Equivalent units | | |
| | Total | Material | | Labour | |
	Units	%	Units	%	Units
Completed production	8,000	100	8,000	100	8,000
Closing stock	1,000	80	800	50	500
Normal loss	500				
Abnormal loss	500	100	500	100	500
	10,000		9,300		9,000

STATEMENT OF COST PER EQUIVALENT UNIT

| | Cost | Equivalent units | Cost per equivalent unit |
	£		£
Material (£(5,150 – 500))	4,650	9,300	0.50
Labour	2,700	9,000	0.30
	7,350		0.80

STATEMENT OF EVALUATION

| | Equivalent units | Cost per equivalent unit | Total | |
			£	£
Completed production	8,000	0.80		6,400
Closing stock: material	800	0.50	400	
labour	500	0.30	150	
				550
Abnormal loss	500	0.80		400
				7,350

PROCESS ACCOUNT

	Units	£		Units	£
Material	10,000	5,150	Completed production	8,000	6,400
Labour		2,700	Closing stock	1,000	550
			Normal loss	500	500
			Abnormal loss	500	400
	10,000	7,850		10,000	7,850

7   IDENTIFICATION OF LOSSES/GAINS AT DIFFERENT STAGES IN THE PROCESS

7.1   In our previous examples, we have assumed that loss occurs at the completion of processing, so that units of abnormal loss or abnormal gain count as a full equivalent unit of production. It may be, however, that units are rejected as scrap or 'loss' at an inspection stage before the completion of processing. When this occurs, units of abnormal loss should count as a proportion of an equivalent unit, according to the volume of work done and materials added up to the point of inspection. An example may help as an illustration.

Example: incomplete rejected items

7.2   Coffee Ltd manufactures product X, and the following information relates to process 3 during September 19X2.

During the month 1,600 units of product X were transferred from process 2, at a valuation of £10,000. Other costs in process 3 were as follows.

Added materials	£4,650
Labour and overhead	£2,920

Units of product X are inspected in process 3 when added materials are 50% complete and conversion cost 30% complete. No losses are normally expected, but during September 19X2, actual loss at the inspection stage was 200 units of product X, which were sold as scrap for £2 each.

Required

Prepare the process 3 account and abnormal loss account for September 19X2.

Solution

7.3 (a)   The equivalent units of work done this period are as follows.

STATEMENT OF EQUIVALENT UNITS

Item	Total units	Process 2 material	Equivalent units Added material	Conversion costs
Units from process 2	1,600			
Abnormal loss	(200)	200	(50%) 100	(30%) 60
Fully worked units, Sept 19X2	1,400	1,400	1,400	1,400
		1,600	1,500	1,460

(b) STATEMENT OF COST PER EQUIVALENT UNIT

Costs incurred, Sept 19X2	£10,000	£4,650	£2,920
Equivalent units	1,600	1,500	1,460
Cost per equivalent unit	£6.25	£3.10	£2

(c) STATEMENT OF EVALUATION

	Process 2 material £	Added material £	Conversion cost £	Total £
Fully worked units	8,750	4,340	2,800	15,890
Abnormal loss	1,250	310	120	1,680
	10,000	4,650	2,920	17,570

The only difference between this example and earlier examples is that abnormal loss has been valued at less than one equivalent unit, for added materials and conversion costs.

(d)

PROCESS 3 ACCOUNT

	Units	£		Units	£
Process 2 output	1,600	10,000	*Output*		
Added materials	-	4,650	Good units	1,400	15,890
Labour and overhead	-	2,920	Abnormal loss	200	1,680
	1,600	17,570		1,600	17,570

(e)

ABNORMAL LOSS ACCOUNT

	Units	£		Units	£
Process 3 account	200	1,680	Cash (sale of scrap)	200	400
			Profit and loss a/c		1,280
	200	1,680		200	1,680

8   JOINT PRODUCTS AND BY-PRODUCTS

Definitions

8.1 (a)   *Joint products* are two or more products which are output from the same processing operation, but which are indistinguishable from each other (that is they are the same commonly processed materials) up to their point of separation. Often they require further processing before they are ready for sale. Joint products have a substantial sales value (or a substantial sales value after further, separate processing has been carried out to make them ready for sale). Joint products arise, for example, in the oil refining industry where diesel fuel, petrol, paraffin and lubricants are all produced from the same process. CIMA's definition is 'Two or more products separated in processing, each having a sufficiently high saleable value to merit recognition as a main product'

(b)   A *by-product* is a product which is similarly produced at the same time and from the same common process as the 'main product' or joint products. The distinguishing feature of a by-product is its relatively low sales value in comparison to the main product. Like joint products, a by-product may need further processing after the point of separation before it is saleable. In the timber industry, for example, by-products include sawdust, small offcuts and bark. The CIMA define by-product as 'Output of some value produced incidentally in manufacturing something else (main product)'.

Comparing joint and by-products

8.2   As indicated already, the difference between joint products and by-products is their relative sales value. But where is the dividing line? What exactly separates a joint product from a by-product?

The answer lies in management attitudes to the products, which in turn is reflected in the cost accounting system.

(a)   A joint product is regarded as an important saleable item, and so it should be separately costed. The profitability of each joint product should be assessed in the cost accounts.

(b)   A by-product is not important as a saleable item, and whatever revenue it earns is a 'bonus' for the organisation. It is not worth the trouble of measuring costs for by-products, because of their relative insignificance. It is therefore equally irrelevant to consider a by-product's profitability. The only question is how to account for the 'bonus' net revenue that a by-product earns.

Accounting for joint products

8.3   Joint products are not separately identifiable until a certain stage (the split-off point or point of separation) is reached in the processing operation. Costs incurred prior to this point of separation are common or joint costs, and these need to be allocated (apportioned) in some way to each of the joint products. (There are a number of ways of apportioning these joint costs but they are outside the scope of your syllabus.) Having shared the common costs, the joint products are accounted for separately (as far as is possible) in order to find their respective profits.

Accounting for by-products

8.4   A by-product is a supplementary or secondary product (arising as the result of a process) whose value is small relative to that of the principal product. Nevertheless the by-product has some commercial value and the usual accounting treatment is to deduct the net realisable value of the by-product from the cost of production of the main product. The net realisable value is the final saleable value of the by-product minus any post-separation costs. Any closing stock valuation of the main product or joint products would therefore be reduced.

Chapter roundup

- Many students find process costing daunting. It shouldn't be. It is based on a set of quite rigid rules which, once learnt, enable you to deal with any situation.

- Process costing is used where there is a continuous flow of identical units.

- The cost per unit in a process is calculated by dividing the total costs by the number of units produced.

- When units are partly complete at the end of a period, it is necessary to calculate the equivalent units of production in order to determine the cost of a complete unit.

- Losses may occur in process. If a certain level of loss is expected, this is known as normal loss. If losses are greater than expected, the extra loss is abnormal loss. If losses are less than expected, the difference is known as abnormal gain.

- The valuation of normal loss is either at scrap value or nil.

- It is conventional for the scrap value of normal loss to be deducted from the cost of materials before a cost per equivalent unit is calculated.

- Abnormal losses and gains never affect the cost of good units of production. The scrap value of abnormal losses is not credited to the process account, and abnormal loss and gain units carry the same full cost as a good unit of production.

- If units are rejected as scrap or loss before the completion of processing, units of loss should count as a proportion of an equivalent unit, according to the volume of work done and materials added up to the point of inspection.

- Joint products are two or more products separated in a process, each of which has a significant value compared to the other. A by-product is an incidental product from a process which has an insignificant value compared to the main product.

Test your knowledge

1   What are the distinguishing features of process costing? (see paras 1.1, 1.2)

2   Distinguish between normal loss and abnormal loss. (3.1)

3   Why are normal and abnormal losses accounted for in different ways? (3.6)

4   Is an abnormal gain a debt or credit entry in the process account? (3.9)

5   What are the different accounting treatments for the scrap value of normal loss and the scrap value of abnormal loss? (4.1)

6   What is an equivalent unit? (5.4 - 5.6)

7   What are the rules for situations involving closing work in progress and losses? (6.2)

8   What is the principal difference between a joint product and a by-product? (8.1, 8.2)

Now try illustrative question 11 at the end of the Study Text

Chapter 11

SERVICE COSTING

This chapter covers the following topics.

		Syllabus reference	Ability required
1	What is service costing?	2(b)	Skill
2	The application of basic cost accounting principles to service costing	2(b)	Skill
3	Service cost analysis in internal service situations	2(b)	Skill
4	The usefulness of costing services that do not earn revenue	2(b)	Skill
5	Service cost analysis in service industry situations	2(b)	Skill

Introduction

So far in this Study Text we have looked at different types of cost and different cost accounting systems and the inference has been that we have been discussing a manufacturing environment. However, the examiner has made the following comment in the syllabus guidance notes to this paper.

'Applications other than manufacturing may form the background to questions. These may include: service industries, not-for-profit organisations, public sector organisations and so on. Specific knowledge of these areas is not required.'

This is nowhere near as daunting as it sounds, however. Many of the cost accounting principles we have looked at so far can be applied to non-manufacturing organisations. In this chapter we will therefore look at the costing system used by the non-manufacturing organisations mentioned by the examiner which we will call, for simplicity, service costing. We will see how the knowledge you have built up can be easily applied to service organisations. All that you really need is a little common sense.

Service costing can also be applied when internal services are provided within an organisation, as we will see in Section 3.

Chapter 12 is the first in Part C of this Study Text, which looks at the planning and control aspects of cost accounting.

---

1 WHAT IS SERVICE COSTING?

1.1 Service costing (or function costing) is 'Cost accounting for services or functions, eg canteens, maintenance, personnel' (CIMA *Official Terminology*). It is concerned with establishing the costs, not of items of production, but of services rendered. Service costing is used in the following circumstances.

(a) A company operating in a service industry will cost its services, for which sales revenue will be earned; examples are electricians, car hire services, road, rail or air transport services and hotels.

(b) A company may wish to establish the cost of services carried out by some of its departments; for example the costs of the vans or lorries used in distribution, the costs of the computer department, or the staff canteen.

1.2 Service costing differs from product costing (such as job or process costing) in a number of ways.

(a) With many services, the cost of direct materials consumed will be relatively small compared to the costs of labour, direct expenses and overheads. In product costing the direct materials are often a greater proportion of the total cost.

(b) Although many services are revenue earning, others are not (such as the distribution facility or the staff canteen). This means that the purpose of service costing may not be to establish a profit or loss (nor to value closing stocks for the balance sheet) but may rather be to provide management information about the comparative costs or efficiency of the services, with a view to helping managers with budgeting and cost control.

(c) The procedures for recording material costs, labour hours and other expenses will vary according to the nature of the service.

2 THE APPLICATION OF BASIC COST ACCOUNTING PRINCIPLES TO SERVICE COSTING

Cost units

2.1 One particular problem with service costing is the difficulty in defining a realistic cost unit that represents a suitable measure of the service provided.

Exercise 1

Think back to Chapter 1 and our coverage of cost units. Can you suggest some cost units which could be used by organisations operating in service industries?

Solution

Organisation	*Possible cost unit*
Hospital	Patient/day
	Operation
	Out-patient visit
Freight organisation	Tonne/kilometre (ton/mile)
Passenger transport organisation	Passenger/kilometre or mile
Accounting firm	Audit performed
	Chargeable hour
Restaurant	Meal served
Hotel	Occupied bed/night
Education	Full-time student

2.2 Many of these cost units are what can be called composite cost units, which means that they are made up of two parts. A freight transport organisation, for example, carries goods over distance. The volume of goods carried can be measured in tonnes. However, a cost unit of cost per tonne carried does not take account of the distance the goods have been transported (which affects fuel costs and drivers' wages if paid on a time-rate basis). On the other hand, if the cost unit was based on kilometres travelled this would ignore whether the transport capacity was used efficiently, as the cost per kilometre would be the same for transporting a small item on an empty lorry or on a full one. So a composite cost unit, the cost taken to transport one tonne a distance of one kilometre, might be suitable.

2.3 Whatever the cost unit decided upon, the calculation of a cost per cost unit is as follows.

$$\text{Cost per cost unit} = \frac{\text{Total costs for period}}{\text{Number of service units in the period}}$$

2.4   Not all organisations which use service costing are profit making even in principle and so do not need to use cost units for measuring profitability. The National Health Service, for example, is not funded by and large by charging the public. Instead it is funded by government. But NHS cost units can be used as performance indicators. The cost per patient per day in two hospitals might be compared to see which is cheaper, although care should be taken when using such indicators as hospitals specialising in the treatment of different diseases might incur quite different costs. In general, however, if a number of organisations within an 'industry' use a common cost unit (especially hospitals, educational establishments and local authorities), valuable comparisons can be made between similar establishments.

2.5   Costs per unit of service can also be compared month by month, period by period, year by ear and so on and any unusual trends can be investigated.

2.6   The cost unit can be used to calculate the price for services sold to third parties. The procedure is similar to job costing. A mark-up is added to the cost per unit of service to arrive at a selling price.

2.7   It is therefore obvious that for service industries and not-for-profit organisations, the concept of cost units is just as relevant as for manufacturing organisations, both in assigning costs and as indicators and measures of performance.

Other measures of performance

2.8   Many organisations use other ratios and performance indicators in conjunction with or as well as costing information. For example, retail organisations use revenue per square foot or metre of selling space as a measurement of efficiency. British Rail publishes performance indicators (for example, percentage of trains cancelled or arriving more than five minutes late) on a regular basis so that its operating performance can be assessed.

Cost centres

2.9   It is not just manufacturing organisations that need to operate a system of cost centres. For control purposes it is equally important for service organisations. The structure of the organisation will usually determine which cost centres should be used. For example, each vehicle used in a distribution service may be a cost centre whereas cost centres in a hotel might include the restaurant, the leisure club, the bar and the bedrooms.

The collection, classification and ascertainment of costs

2.10   The type of service provided by an organisation will influence the headings under which costs should be classified, but whatever the headings used, a system of cost coding will be needed to ensure the correct collection and recording of costs. A school, for example, needs information about the cost of salaries and wages of teachers and support staff, costs of premises such as heating and lighting, costs of materials such as books and stationery, and costs of activities like sport, drama and educational visits.

2.11   Costs should be analysed into fixed, variable and semi-variable costs to help management with planning, control and decision making. Many services involve high levels of fixed costs. The variable cost per unit will indicate to management the additional cost involved in the provision of one unit of service.

3   SERVICE COST ANALYSIS IN INTERNAL SERVICE SITUATIONS

Transport costs

3.1   'Transport costs' is a term used here to refer to the costs of the transport services used by a company, rather than the costs of a transport organisation, such as British Rail.

3.2   If a company has a fleet of lorries or vans which it uses to distribute its goods, it is useful to know how much the department is costing for a number of reasons.

(a)   Management of the department should be able to budget for expected costs, and to control actual expenditure on transport by comparing actual costs with budgeted costs.

(b)   The company may charge customers for delivery or 'carriage outwards' costs, and a charge based on the cost of the transport service might be appropriate.

(c)   If management knows how much its own transport is costing, a comparison can be made with alternative forms of transport (independent transport companies, British Rail, security van services and so on) to decide whether a cheaper or better method of delivery can be found.

(d)   Similarly, if a company uses, say, a fleet of lorries, knowledge of the cost of transport by lorry should help management to decide whether another type of vehicle, say vans, would be cheaper to use.

3.3   Transport costs may be analysed to provide the cost of operating one van or lorry each year, but it is more informative to analyse costs as follows.

(a)   The cost per mile or kilometre travelled

(b)   The cost per ton/mile or tonne/kilometre (the cost of carrying one tonne of goods for one kilometre distance) or the cost per kilogram/metre

3.4   For example, suppose that a company lorry makes five deliveries in a week.

Delivery	Tonnes carried	Distance (one way) Kilometres	Tonne/kilometres carried
1	0.4	180	72
2	0.3	360	108
3	1.2	100	120
4	0.8	250	200
5	1.0	60	60
			560

If the costs of operating the lorry during the week are known to be £840, the cost per tonne/kilometre would be:

$$\frac{£840}{560 \text{ tonne / kilometre}} = £1.50 \text{ per tonne/kilometre}$$

3.5   Transport costs might be collected under five broad headings.

(a)   *Running costs* such as petrol, oil, drivers' wages
(b)   *Loading costs* (the labour costs of loading the lorries with goods for delivery)
(c)   *Servicing, repairs, spare parts and tyre usage*
(d)   *Annual direct expenses* such as road tax, insurance and depreciation
(e)   *Indirect costs of the distribution department* such as the wages of managers, office costs

3.6   The role of the cost accountant is to provide a system for recording and analysing costs. Just as production costs are recorded by means of material requisition notes, labour time sheets and so on, so too must transport costs be recorded by means of log sheets or time sheets, and material supply notes. A log sheet might be designed as follows.

Driver's log sheet

							Cost 123 code

Date _____

Vehicle number _____

Driver _____

Starting time _____ Finishing time _____

Starting km _____ Finishing km _____

Delivery No	Tonnes carried	From	To	Starting km	Finishing km	Km travelled	Time out	Time in

Supplies: Materials supply note No

Petrol _____

Other _____

_____

Notes: Delays, repairs, loading

Repairs reference No _____

Loading reference No _____

Other notes _____

The purpose of the log sheet is to record distance travelled, or the number of tonne/kilometres and the drivers' time (and assistants' time). There must be some cross referencing to costs of materials, loading and repairs, but these items will be recorded on a different document.

Canteen costs

3.7   Another example of service costing commonly referred to in texts is the cost of a company's canteen services. A feature of canteen costing is that some revenue is earned when employees pay for their meals, but the prices paid will be insufficient to cover the costs of the canteen service. The company will subsidise the canteen to the extent that costs exceed revenues and a major purpose of canteen costing is to establish the size of the subsidy.

3.8   If the costs of the canteen service are recorded by a system of service cost accounting, the likely headings of expense would be as follows.

(a)   *Food and drink*: separate canteen stores records may be kept, and the consumption of food and drink recorded by means of 'materials issues' notes.

(b)   *Labour costs of the canteen staff*: hourly paid staff will record their time at work on a time card or time sheet. Salaried staff will be an identifiable 'fixed' cost each month.

(c)   *Consumable stores* such as crockery, cutlery, glassware, table linen and cleaning materials will also be recorded in some form of stock control system.

(d)   *The cost of gas and electricity* may be separately metered; otherwise an apportionment of the total cost of such utilities for the building as a whole will be made to the canteen department.

(e)   Asset records will be kept and *depreciation charges* made for major items of equipment like ovens and furniture.

(f)   An apportionment of other *overhead costs* of the building (rent and rates, building insurance and maintenance and so on) may be charged against the canteen.

Cash income from canteen sales will also be recorded.

3.9 Suppose that a canteen recorded the following costs and revenue during the month.

	£
Food and drink	11,250
Labour	11,250
Heating and lighting	1,875
Repairs and consumable stores	1,125
Financing costs	1,000
Depreciation	750
Other apportioned costs	875
Revenue	22,500

The canteen served 37,500 meals in the month.

The size of the subsidy could be easily identified as follows:

	£
The total costs of the canteen	28,125
Revenue	22,500
Loss, to be covered by the company	5,625

The cost per meal averages 75p and the revenue per meal 60p. If the company decided that the canteen should pay its own way, without a subsidy, the average price of a meal would have to be raised by 15 pence.

4 THE USEFULNESS OF COSTING SERVICES THAT DO NOT EARN REVENUE

4.1 The costing of services that do not earn revenue will be a waste of time unless it has a purpose, and it has two basic purposes.

(a) *To control the costs in the service department.* If we establish a distribution cost per tonne kilometre, a canteen cost per employee, a maintenance cost per machine hour, or job costs of repairs, we can establish control measures in the following ways.

 (i) Comparing actual costs against a target or standard
 (ii) Comparing current actual costs against actual costs in previous periods

(b) *To control the costs of the user departments*, and prevent the unnecessary use of services. If the costs of services are charged to the user departments in such a way that the charges reflect the use actually made by each department of the service department's services then the following will occur.

 (i) The overhead costs of user departments will be established more accurately; indeed some service department variable costs might be identified as directly attributable costs of the user department.

 (ii) If the service department's charges for a user department are high, the user department might be encouraged to consider whether it is making an excessively costly and wasteful use of the service department's service.

 (iii) The user department might decide that it can obtain a similar service at a lower cost from an external service company.

Example: costing internal services

4.2 (a) If maintenance costs in a factory are costed as jobs (that is, if each bit of repair work is given a job number and costed accordingly) repair costs can be charged to the departments on the basis of repair jobs actually undertaken, instead of on a more generalised basis, such as apportionment according to machine hour capacity in each department. Departments with high repair costs could then consider their high incidence of repairs, the age and reliability of their machines, or the skills of the machine operatives.

(b) If mainframe computer costs are charged to a user department on the basis of a cost per hour, the user department would assess whether it was getting good value from its use of the mainframe computer and whether it might be better to hire the service of a computer bureau, or perhaps install a stand-alone microcomputer system in the department.

5   SERVICE COST ANALYSIS IN SERVICE INDUSTRY SITUATIONS   *11/96*

Distribution costs

5.1   The following example will show how a rate per tonne/kilometre can be calculated for a distribution service.

Example

5.2   Carry Ltd operates a small fleet of delivery vehicles. Expected costs are as follows.

Loading	1 hour per tonne loaded
Loading costs:	
Labour (casual)	£2 per hour
Equipment depreciation	£80 per week
Supervision	£80 per week
Drivers' wages (fixed)	£100 per man per week
Petrol	10p per kilometre
Repairs	5p per kilometre
Depreciation	£80 per week per vehicle
Supervision	£120 per week
Other general expenses (fixed)	£200 per week

There are two drivers and two vehicles in the fleet.

During a slack week, only six journeys were made.

Journey	Tonnes carried (one way)	One-way distance of journey Kilometres
1	5	100
2	8	20
3	2	60
4	4	50
5	6	200
6	5	300

Required

Calculate the expected average full cost per tonne/kilometre for the week.

Solution

5.3

Variable costs	*Journey*	*1*	*2*	*3*	*4*	*5*	*6*
		£	£	£	£	£	£
Loading labour		10	16	4	8	12	10
Petrol (both ways)		20	4	12	10	40	60
Repairs (both ways)		10	2	6	5	20	30
		40	22	22	23	72	100

Total costs

	£
Variable costs (total for journeys 1 to 6)	279
Loading equipment depreciation	80
Loading supervision	80
Drivers' wages	200
Vehicles depreciation	160
Drivers' supervision	120
Other costs	200
	1,119

Journey	Tonnes	One-way distance Kilometres	Tonne/kilometres
1	5	100	500
2	8	20	160
3	2	60	120
4	4	50	200
5	6	200	1,200
6	5	300	1,500
			3,680

Cost per tonne/kilometre $\dfrac{£1,119}{3,680} = £0.304$

Note that the large element of fixed costs may distort this measure but that a variable cost per tonne/kilometre of £279/3,680 = £0.076 may be useful for budgetary control.

Education

5.4 The techniques described in the preceding paragraphs can be applied, in general, to any service industry situation. Attempt the following exercise about education.

Exercise 2

A university with annual running costs of £3 million has the following students.

Classification	Number	Attendance weeks per annum	Hours per week
3 year	2,700	30	28
4 year	1,500	30	25
Sandwich	1,900	35	20

Calculate a cost per suitable cost unit for the university to the nearest penny.

Solution

We need to begin by establishing a cost unit for the university. Since there are three different categories of students we cannot use 'a student' as the cost unit. Attendance hours would seem to be the most appropriate cost unit.

The next step is to calculate the number of units.

Number of students	Weeks	Hours	Total hours per annum
2,700	× 30	× 28 =	2,268,000
1,500	× 30	× 25 =	1,125,000
1,900	× 35	× 20 =	1,330,000
			4,723,000

The cost per unit is calculated as follows.

$$\text{Cost per unit} = \frac{\text{Total cost}}{\text{Number of units}} = £(\frac{3,000,000}{4,723,000}) = £0.64$$

Chapter roundup

- Service costing can be used by companies operating in a service industry or by companies wishing to establish the cost of services carried out by some of their departments.

- A problem faced in both service costing situations is the selection of an appropriate cost unit. The unit will often be a two-part one, such as the tonne/kilometre. Whatever cost unit is decided upon, the calculation of a cost per unit will be the total costs for the period divided by the number of service units in the period.

- Service costing for internal services adds to the administrative burdens of an organisation because it costs time and money. The benefits of the system should therefore exceed the costs of its operation.

- Not all service departments can be costed using the approach laid out in this chapter. For example, it would be difficult to work out a job cost or service unit cost for the accounting department, personnel department or general administration work at head office. These service costs would be charged as general overheads and then apportioned between user departments on a suitable basis.

- Service costing differs from process costing in that it does not operate within rigid rules. You will therefore have to use your common sense in service costing situations.

Test your knowledge

1 Describe three differences between service costing and product costing. (see para 1.2)

2 What is a composite cost unit? Provide an example. (2.2)

3 Suggest five headings under which the costs of a transport department might be collected. (3.5)

4 Why is it useful to cost non-revenue-earning services? (4.1)

Now try illustrative question 12 at the end of the Study Text

Part C
Budgets and variance accounting

Chapter 12

PREPARING THE MASTER BUDGET

This chapter covers the following topics.

		Syllabus reference	Ability required
1	The purposes of a budget	2(c)	Skill
2	Steps in the preparation of a budget	2(c)	Skill
3	Preparing functional budgets	2(c)	Skill
4	Cash budgets	2(c)	Skill
5	Budgeted profit and loss account and balance sheet	2(c)	Skill
6	A comparison of profit and cash flows	2(c)	Skill

Introduction

This chapter is the first of two on a new topic, budgeting. It is a topic which you will meet at all stages of your examination studies so it is vital that you get a firm grasp of the basics now. The chapter begins by explaining the reasons why an organisation might prepare a budget and goes on to detail the steps in the preparation of a budget. The method of preparing and the relationship between the various functional budgets is then set out.

The chapter also considers the construction of cash budgets and budgeted profit and loss accounts and balance sheets, the budgeted profit and loss account and balance sheet making up what is known as a master budget. It concludes with an explanation of why budgeted profit/loss for a period will probably not be the same as the budgeted cash flow for the period.

To date, of the topics covered in this chapter, cash budgeting is the only one to have been examined as a Section B or D question. The examiner reported that the question was reasonably well answered but careless mistakes such as the inclusion of depreciation as a cash flow were common.

In Chapter 15 we will build on the general awareness of budgeting gained in this chapter and look at more specific budgeting issues.

1 THE PURPOSES OF A BUDGET

1.1 A budget is 'A quantitative statement, for a defined period of time, which may include planned revenues, expenses, assets, liabilities and cash flows'. (CIMA *Official Terminology*) for a forthcoming accounting period. A budget has four main purposes.

(a) To coordinate the activities of different departments towards a single plan

(b) To communicate targets to the managers responsible for achieving them

(c) To establish a system of control by having a plan against which actual results can be compared

(d) To compel planning

2 STEPS IN THE PREPARATION OF A BUDGET

2.1 Having seen why organisations prepare budgets we will turn our attention to the mechanics of budget preparation.

Budget committee

2.2   The coordination and administration of budgets is usually the responsibility of a budget committee (with the managing director as chairman). The budget committee is assisted by a budget officer who is usually an accountant. Every part of the organisation should be represented on the committee, so there should be a representative from sales, production, marketing and so on. Functions of the budget committee include the following.

(a)   Coordination and allocation of responsibility for the preparation of budgets

(b)   Issuing of the budget manual

(c)   Timetabling

(d)   Provision of information to assist in the preparation of budgets

(e)   Communication of final budgets to the appropriate managers

(f)   Monitoring the budgeting and planning process by comparing actual and budgeted results

Responsibility for budgets

2.3   The responsibility for preparing the budgets should, ideally, lie with the mangers who are responsible for implementing them. The preparation might therefore be allocated as follows.

(a)   The sales manager should draft the sales budget and the selling overhead cost centre budgets.

(b)   The purchasing manager should draft the material purchases budget.

(c)   The production manager should draft the direct production cost budgets.

The budget manual

2.4   The budget manual is a collection of instructions governing the responsibilities of persons and the procedures, forms and records relating to the preparation and use of budgetary data.

A budget manual may contain the following.

(a)   An explanation of the objectives of the budgetary process including the following.

(i)   The purpose of budgetary planning and control

(ii)   The objectives of the various stages of the budgetary process

(iii)   The importance of budgets in the long-term planning and administration of the enterprise

(b)   Organisational structures, including the following

(i)   An organisation chart
(ii)   A list of individuals holding budget responsibilities

(c)   An outline of the principal budgets and the relationship between them

(d)   Administrative details of budget preparation such as the following

(i)   Membership, and terms of reference of the budget committee
(ii)   The sequence in which budgets are to be prepared
(iii)   A timetable

(e)   Procedural matters such as the following

(i)   Specimen forms and instructions for completing them
(ii)   Specimen reports
(iii)   Account codes (or a chart of accounts)
(iv)   The name of the budget officer to whom enquiries must be sent

Steps in budget preparation

2.5   The procedures for preparing a budget will differ from organisation to organisation but the steps described below will be indicative of the steps followed by many organisations. The preparation of a budget may take weeks or months and the budget committee may meet several times before the master budget (budgeted profit and loss account and budgeted balance sheet) is finally agreed. Functional budgets (sales budgets, production budgets, direct labour budgets and so on), which are amalgamated into the master budget, may need to be amended many times over as a consequence of discussions between departments, changes in market conditions and so on during the course of budget preparation.

Identifying the principal budget factor

2.6   The first task in the budgetary process is to identify the principal budget factor. This is also known as the key budget factor or limiting budget factor.

2.7   For example, a company's sales department might estimate that it could sell 1,000 units of product X, which would require 5,000 hours of grade A labour to produce. If there are no units of product X already in stock, and only 4,000 hours of grade A labour available in the budget period, then the company would be unable to sell 1,000 units of X because of the shortage of labour hours. Grade A labour would be a limiting budget factor, and the company's management must choose one of the following options.

(a)   Reduce budgeted sales by 20%.

(b)   Try to increase the availability of grade A labour by 1,000 hours (25%) by recruitment or overtime working.

(c)   Try to sub-contract the production of 1,000 units to another manufacturer, but still profit on the transaction.

2.8   The principal budget factor is usually sales demand: a company is usually restricted from making and selling more of its products because there would be no sales demand for the increased output at a price which would be acceptable/profitable to the company. The principal budget factor may also be machine capacity, distribution and selling resources, the availability of key raw materials or the availability of cash. Once this factor is defined then the rest of the budget can be prepared. For example, if sales are the principal budget factor then the production manager can only prepare his budget after the sales budget is complete.

2.9   Management may not know what the limiting budget factor is until a draft budget has been attempted. The first draft budget will therefore usually begin with the preparation of a draft sales budget.

2.10   Once the principal budget factor has been identified, the stages involved in the preparation of a budget can be summarised as follows.

(a)   The sales budget is prepared in units of product and sales value. The finished goods stock budget can be prepared at the same time. This budget decides the planned increase or decrease in finished goods stock levels.

(b)   With the information from the sales and stock budgets, the production budget can be prepared. This is, in effect, the sales budget in units plus (or minus) the increase (or decrease) in finished goods stock. The production budget will be stated in terms of units.

(c)   This leads on logically to budgeting the resources for production. This involves preparing a materials usage budget, machine usage budget and a labour budget.

(d)   In addition to the materials usage budget, a materials stock budget will be prepared, to decide the planned increase or decrease in the level of stocks held. Once the raw materials usage requirements and the raw materials stock budget are known, the purchasing department can prepare a raw materials purchases budget in quantities and value for each type of material purchased.

(e) During the preparation of the sales and production budgets, the managers of the cost centres of the organisation will prepare their draft budgets for the department overhead costs. Such overheads will include maintenance, stores, administration, selling and research and development.

(f) From the above information a budgeted profit and loss account can be produced.

(g) In addition several other budgets must be prepared in order to arrive at the budgeted balance sheet. These are the capital expenditure budget (for fixed assets), the working capital budget (for budgeted increases or decreases in the level of debtors and creditors as well as stocks), and a cash budget.

3   PREPARING FUNCTIONAL BUDGETS   5/97

3.1   Having seen the theory of budget preparation, let us look at functional (or departmental) budget preparation.

Example: preparing a materials purchases budget

3.2   ECO Ltd manufactures two products, S and T, which use the same raw materials, D and E. One unit of S uses 3 litres of D and 4 kilograms of E. One unit of T uses 5 litres of D and 2 kilograms of E. A litre of D is expected to cost £3 and a kilogram of E £7.

Budgeted sales for 19X2 are 8,000 units of S and 6,000 units of T; finished goods in stock at 1 January 19X2 are 1,500 units of S and 300 units of T, and the company plans to hold stocks of 600 units of each product at 31 December 19X2.

Stocks of raw material are 6,000 litres of D and 2,800 kilograms of E at 1 January and the company plans to hold 5,000 litres and 3,500 kilograms respectively at 31 December 19X2.

The warehouse and stores managers have suggested that a provision should be made for damages and deterioration of items held in store, as follows.

Product S :	loss of 50 units
Product T :	loss of 100 units
Material D :	loss of 500 litres
Material E :	loss of 200 kilograms

Required

Prepare a material purchases budget for the year 19X2.

Solution

3.3   To calculate material purchases requirements it is first necessary to calculate the material usage requirements. That in turn depends on calculating the budgeted production volumes.

	Product S Units	*Product T* Units
Production required		
To meet sales demand	8,000	6,000
To provide for stock loss	50	100
For closing stock	600	600
	8,650	6,700
Less stock already in hand	1,500	300
Budgeted production volume	7,150	6,400

	Material D Litres	Material E Kgs
Usage requirements		
To produce 7,150 units of S	21,450	28,600
To produce 6,400 units of T	32,000	12,800
To provide for stock loss	500	200
For closing stock	5,000	3,500
	58,950	45,100
Less stock already in hand	6,000	2,800
Budgeted material purchases	52,950	42,300
Unit cost	£3	£7
Cost of material purchases	£158,850	£296,100
Total cost of material purchases	£454,950	

3.4 The basics of the preparation of each functional budget are similar to those above. Work carefully through the following exercise which covers the preparation of a number of different types of functional budget.

Exercise 1

XYZ company produces three products X, Y and Z. For the coming accounting period budgets are to be prepared based on the following information.

Budgeted sales

Product X	2,000 at £100 each
Product Y	4,000 at £130 each
Product Z	3,000 at £150 each

Budgeted usage of raw material

	RM11	RM22	RM33
Product X	5	2	-
Product Y	3	2	2
Product Z	2	1	3
Cost per unit of material	£5	£3	£4

Finished stocks budget

	Product X	Product Y	Product Z
Beginning	500	800	700
End	600	1,000	800

Raw materials stock

	RM11	RM22	RM33
Beginning	21,000	10,000	16,000
End	18,000	9,000	12,000

	Product X	Product Y	Product Z
Expected hours per unit	4	6	8
Expected hourly rate (labour)	£3	£3	£3

Required

Draw up the following functional budgets.

(a)   Sales budget in terms of both quantity and value
(b)   Production budget
(c)   Material usage budget
(d)   Material purchases budget
(e)   Labour budget

Solution

(a)

	Sales budget			
	Product X	*Product Y*	*Product Z*	*Total*
Sales quantity	2,000	4,000	3,000	
Sales price	£100	£130	£150	
Sales value	£200,000	£520,000	£450,000	£1,170,000

(b)

	Production budget		
	Product X	*Product Y*	*Product Z*
	Units	Units	Units
Sales quantity	2,000	4,000	3,000
Closing stocks	600	1,000	800
	2,600	5,000	3,800
Less opening stocks	500	800	700
Budgeted production	2,100	4,200	3,100

(c)

	Material usage budget			
	Production	*RM11*	*RM22*	*RM33*
	Units	Units	Units	Units
Product X	2,100	10,500	4,200	-
Product Y	4,200	12,600	8,400	8,400
Product Z	3,100	6,200	3,100	9,300
Budgeted material usage		29,300	15,700	17,700

(d)

	Material purchases budget		
	RM11	*RM22*	*RM33*
	Units	Units	Units
Budgeted material usage	29,300	15,700	17,700
Closing stocks	18,000	9,000	12,000
	47,300	24,700	29,700
Less opening stocks	21,000	10,000	16,000
Budgeted material purchases	26,300	14,700	13,700
Standard cost per unit	£5	£3	£4
Budgeted material purchases	£131,500	£44,100	£54,800

(e)

		Labour budget			
Product	*Production*	*Hours required per unit*	*Total hours*	*Rate per hour*	*Cost*
	Units			£	£
X	2,100	4	8,400	3	25,200
Y	4,200	6	25,200	3	75,600
Z	3,100	8	24,800	3	74,400
Budgeted total wages					175,200

---

4   CASH BUDGETS   5/95

4.1   A cash budget is a statement in which estimated future cash receipts and payments are tabulated in such a way as to show the forecast cash balance of a business at defined intervals. For example, in December 19X2 an accounts department might wish to estimate the cash position of the business during the three following months, January to March 19X3. A cash budget might be drawn up in the following format.

	Jan £	Feb £	Mar £
Estimated cash receipts			
From credit customers	14,000	16,500	17,000
From cash sales	3,000	4,000	4,500
Proceeds on disposal of fixed assets		2,200	
Total cash receipts	17,000	22,700	21,500
Estimated cash payments			
To suppliers of goods	8,000	7,800	10,500
To employees (wages)	3,000	3,500	3,500
Purchase of fixed assets		16,000	
Rent and rates			1,000
Other overheads	1,200	1,200	1,200
Repayment of loan	2,500		
	14,700	28,500	16,200
Net surplus/(deficit) for month	2,300	(5,800)	5,300
Opening cash balance	1,200	3,500	(2,300)
Closing cash balance	3,500	(2,300)	3,000

4.2   In the example above (where the figures are purely for illustration) the accounts department has calculated that the cash balance at the beginning of the budget period, 1 January, will be £1,200. Estimates have been made of the cash which is likely to be received by the business (from cash and credit sales, and from a planned disposal of fixed assets in February). Similar estimates have been made of cash due to be paid out by the business (payments to suppliers and employees, payments for rent, rates and other overheads, payment for a planned purchase of fixed assets in February and a loan repayment due in January).

4.3   From these estimates it is a simple step to calculate the excess of cash receipts over cash payments in each month. In some months cash payments may exceed cash receipts and there will be a deficit for the month; this occurs during February in the above example because of the large investment in fixed assets in that month.

4.4   The last part of the cash budget above shows how the business's estimated cash balance can then be rolled along from month to month. Starting with the opening balance of £1,200 at 1 January a cash surplus of £2,300 is generated in January. This leads to a closing January balance of £3,500 which becomes the opening balance for February. The deficit of £5,800 in February throws the business's cash position into overdraft and the overdrawn balance of £2,300 becomes the opening balance for March. Finally, the healthy cash surplus of £5,300 in March leaves the business with a favourable cash position of £3,000 at the end of the budget period.

The usefulness of cash budgets

4.5   The cash budget is one of the most important planning tools that an organisation can use. It shows the cash effect of all plans made within the budgetary process and hence its preparation can lead to a modification of budgets if it shows that there are insufficient cash resources to finance the planned operations.

4.6   It can also give management an indication of potential problems that could arise and allows them the opportunity to take action to avoid such problems. A cash budget can show four positions. Management will need to take appropriate action depending on the potential position.

Cash position	*Appropriate management action*	
Short-term surplus	(a)	Pay creditors early to obtain discount
	(b)	Attempt to increase sales by increasing debtors and stocks
	(c)	Make short-term investments
Short-term deficit	(a)	Increase creditors
	(b)	Reduce debtors
	(c)	Arrange an overdraft
Long-term surplus	(a)	Make long-term investments
	(b)	Expand
	(c)	Diversify
	(d)	Replace/update fixed assets
Long-term deficit	(a)	Raise long-term finance (such as via issue of share capital)
	(b)	Consider shutdown/disinvestment opportunities

4.7 A cash budgeting question in an examination could ask you to recommend appropriate action for management to take once you have prepared the cash budget. Ensure your advice takes account both of whether there is a surplus or deficit and whether the position is long or short term.

How are cash budgets constructed?

4.8 Constructing a cash budget in practice is a complex job because a great many forecasts need first to be formulated.

(a) The sales or marketing department might produce estimates of the level of sales.

(b) The credit control department might be able to supply information on how quickly debtors pay and what proportion of debts go bad.

(c) The production or purchasing department might estimate the level of purchases required and the credit period to be taken from suppliers.

(d) Other forecasts would need to be made about the dates and amounts of, for example, purchases and disposals of fixed assets.

4.9 In the examination, you will not be asked to formulate this kind of assumption. Instead you will be presented with a list of assumptions already made and you will be required to calculate the cash flows which follow from them.

Example: cash budget

4.10 Peter Blair has worked for some years as a sales representative, but has recently been made redundant. He intends to start up in business on his own account, using £15,000 which he currently has invested with a building society. Peter maintains a bank account showing a small credit balance, and he plans to approach his bank for the necessary additional finance. Peter asks you for advice and provides the following additional information.

(a) Arrangements have been made to purchase fixed assets costing £8,000. These will be paid for at the end of September and are expected to have a five-year life, at the end of which they will possess a nil residual value.

(b) Stocks costing £5,000 will be acquired on 28 September and subsequent monthly purchases will be at a level sufficient to replace forecast sales for the month.

(c) Forecast monthly sales are £3,000 for October, £6,000 for November and December, and £10,500 from January 19X4 onwards.

(d) Selling price is fixed at the cost of stock plus 50%.

(e) Two months' credit will be allowed to customers but only one month's credit will be received from suppliers of stock.

(f) Running expenses, including rent but excluding depreciation of fixed assets, are estimated at £1,600 per month.

(g) Blair intends to make monthly cash drawings of £1,000.

Required

Prepare a cash budget for the six months to 31 March 19X4.

Solution

4.11 The opening cash balance at 1 October will consist of Peter's initial £15,000 less the £8,000 expended on fixed assets purchased in September. In other words, the opening balance is £7,000. Cash receipts from credit customers arise two months after the relevant sales.

Payments to suppliers are a little more tricky. We are told that cost of sales is 100/150 × sales. Thus for October cost of sales is 100/150 × £3,000 = £2,000. These goods will be purchased in October but not paid for until November. Similar calculations can be made for later months. The initial stock of £5,000 is purchased in September and consequently paid for in October.

Depreciation is not a cash flow and so is *not* included in a cash budget.

4.12 The cash budget can now be constructed.

CASH BUDGET FOR THE SIX MONTHS ENDING 31 MARCH 19X4

	Oct £	*Nov* £	*Dec* £	*Jan* £	*Feb* £	*Mar* £
Payments						
Suppliers	5,000	2,000	4,000	4,000	7,000	7,000
Running expenses	1,600	1,600	1,600	1,600	1,600	1,600
Drawings	1,000	1,000	1,000	1,000	1,000	1,000
	7,600	4,600	6,600	6,600	9,600	9,600
Receipts						
Debtors	-	-	3,000	6,000	6,000	10,500
Surplus/(shortfall)	(7,600)	(4,600)	(3,600)	(600)	(3,600)	900
Opening balance	7,000	(600)	(5,200)	(8,800)	(9,400)	(13,000)
Closing balance	(600)	(5,200)	(8,800)	(9,400)	(13,000)	(12,100)

Exercise 2

(a) Accountants always stress the importance of budgeting for planning and control.

Required

Briefly explain how budgeting aids planning and control within an organisation over a budgetary cycle.

(b) A company that manufactures and sells a range of products, with sales potential limited by market share, is considering introducing a system of budgeting.

Required

(i) List the functional budgets that need to be prepared.

(ii) State which budgets the master budget will comprise of.

(iii) Consider how the work outlined in (i) and (ii) can be co-ordinated in order for the budgeting process to be successful.

(c) You are presented with the budgeted data shown in Annex A for the period November 19X1 to June 19X2 by your firm. It has been extracted from the other functional budgets that have been prepared.

You are also told the following.

(i) Sales are 40% cash, 60% credit. Credit sales are paid two months after the month of sale.

(ii)   Purchases are paid the month following purchase.

(iii) 75% of wages are paid in the current month and 25% the following month.

(iv)   Overheads are paid the month after they are incurred.

(v)   Dividends are paid three months after they are declared.

(vi)   Capital expenditure is paid two months after it is incurred.

(vii) The opening cash balance is £15,000.

The managing director is pleased with the above figures as they show sales will have increased by more than 100% in the period under review. In order to achieve this he has arranged a bank overdraft with a ceiling of £50,000 to accommodate the increased stock levels and wage bill for overtime worked.

Annex A

	Nov X1 £	Dec X1 £	Jan X2 £	Feb X2 £	Mar X2 £	Apr X2 £	May X2 £	June X2 £
Sales	80,000	100,000	110,000	130,000	140,000	150,000	160,000	180,000
Purchases	40,000	60,000	80,000	90,000	110,000	130,000	140,000	150,000
Wages	10,000	12,000	16,000	20,000	24,000	28,000	32,000	36,000
Overheads	10,000	10,000	15,000	15,000	15,000	20,000	20,000	20,000
Dividends		20,000						40,000
Capital expenditure			30,000			40,000		

Required

(i)   Prepare a cash budget for the 6 month period January to June 19X2.

(ii)   Comment upon your results in the light of your managing director's comments and offer advice.

Solution

(a)   A budget is a financial and/or quantitative plan of operations for a forthcoming accounting period. Budgetary control is the practice of establishing budgets which identify areas of responsibility for individual managers and of regularly comparing actual results against expected results. Budgets co-ordinate the activities of the various parts of an organisation, communicate senior management's plans to those responsible for carrying them out and motivate staff by setting them targets to achieve.

(b)   (i)   The sequence of budget preparation will be roughly as follows.

(1)   Sales budget (market share limits demand and so sales are the principal budget factor; all other activities will depend upon this forecast)

(2)   Finished goods stock budget (in units)

(3)   Production budget (in units)

(4)   Production resources budgets (materials, machine hours, labour)

(5)   Overhead budgets for production, administration, selling and distribution, research and development and so on.

Other budgets required will be the capital expenditure budget, the working capital budget (debtors and creditors) and, very importantly, the cash budget.

(ii)   The master budget is the summary of all the functional budgets. It includes a summary profit and loss account and balance sheet.

(iii) Procedures for preparing budgets can be contained in a budget manual which shows which budgets must be prepared when and by whom, what each functional budget should contain and detailed directions on how to prepare budgets including, for example, expected price increases, rates of interest, rates of depreciation and so on.

The formulation of budgets can be co-ordinated by a budget committee comprising the senior executives of the departments responsible for carrying out the budgets: sales, production, purchasing, personnel and so on.

(c)   (i)

	January £'000	February £'000	March £'000	April £'000	May £'000	June £'000
Receipts						
Sales revenue						
Cash	44	52	56	60	64	72
Credit	48	60	66	78	84	90
	92	112	122	138	148	162
Payments						
Purchases	60	80	90	110	130	140
Wages						
75%	12	15	18	21	24	27
25%	3	4	5	6	7	8
Overheads	10	15	15	15	20	20
Dividends			20			
Capital expenditure			30			40
	85	114	178	152	181	235
b/f	15	22	20	(36)	(50)	(83)
Net cash flow	7	(2)	(56)	(14)	(33)	(73)
c/f	22	20	(36)	(50)	(83)	(156)

(ii)   The overdraft arrangements are quite inadequate to service the cash needs of the business over the six month period. If the figures are realistic then action should be taken now to avoid difficulties in the near future. The following are possible courses of action.

(1)   Activities could be curtailed.

(2)   Other sources of cash could be explored, for example a long-term loan to finance the capital expenditure and a factoring arrangement to provide cash due from debtors more quickly.

(3)   Efforts to increase the speed of debt collection could be made.

(4)   Payments to creditors could be delayed.

(5)   The dividend payments could be postponed (the figures indicate that this is a small company, possibly owner-managed).

(6)   Staff might be persuaded to work at a lower rate in return for, say, an annual bonus or a profit-sharing agreement.

(7)   Extra staff might be taken on to reduce the amount of overtime paid.

(8)   The stockholding policy should be reviewed: it may be possible to meet demand from current production and minimise cash tied up in stocks.

5   BUDGETED PROFIT AND LOSS ACCOUNT AND BALANCE SHEET   S/97

5.1   As well as wishing to forecast its cash position, a business might want to estimate its profitability and its financial position for a coming period. This would involve the preparation of a budgeted profit and loss account and balance sheet, both of which form the master budget.

5.2   Just like historical financial statements, budgeted accounts are based on the accruals concept. If you keep this point in mind you will often be able to cut through the deliberately confusing detail of examination questions to prepare an answer very quickly. The example of Peter Blair in Paragraph 4.10 will be used to illustrate the procedure.

Example: preparing a budgeted profit and loss account and balance sheet

5.3   Using the information in Paragraph 4.10, you are required to prepare Peter Blair's budgeted profit and loss account for the six months ending on 31 March 19X4 and a budgeted balance sheet as at that date.

Solution

5.4   The profit and loss account is straightforward. The first figure is sales, which can be computed very easily from the information in Paragraph 4.10(c). It is sufficient to add up the monthly sales figures given there; for the profit and loss account there is no need to worry about any closing debtor. Similarly, cost of sales is calculated directly from the information on gross margin contained in Paragraph 4.10 (d).

FORECAST TRADING AND PROFIT AND LOSS ACCOUNT
FOR THE SIX MONTHS ENDING 31 MARCH 19X4

	£	£
Sales $(3,000 + (2 \times 6,000) + (3 \times 10,500))$		46,500
Cost of sales $(^2/_3 \times £46,500)$		31,000
Gross profit		15,500
Expenses		
Running expenses $(6 \times £1,600)$	9,600	
Depreciation $(£8,000 \times 20\% \times 6/12)$	800	
		10,400
Net profit		5,100

Items will be shown in the balance sheet as follows.

(a)   Stock will comprise the initial purchases of £5,000.

(b)   Debtors will comprise sales made in February and March (not paid until April and May respectively).

(c)   Creditors will comprise purchases made in March (not paid for until April).

(d)   The bank overdraft is the closing cash figure computed in the cash budget.

FORECAST BALANCE SHEET AT 31 MARCH 19X4

	£	£
Fixed assets £(8,000 – 800)		7,200
Current assets		
Stocks	5,000	
Debtors $(2 \times £10,500)$	21,000	
	26,000	
Current liabilities		
Bank overdraft	12,100	
Trade creditors (March purchases)	7,000	
	19,100	
Net current assets		6,900
		14,100
Proprietor's interest		
Capital introduced		15,000
Profit for the period	5,100	
Less drawings	6,000	
Deficit retained		(900)
		14,100

5.5   Budget questions are often accompanied by a large amount of sometimes confusing detail. This should not blind you to the fact that many figures can be entered very simply from the logic of the trading situation described. For example in the case of Blair you might feel tempted to begin a T-account to compute the closing debtors figure. This kind of working is rarely necessary, since you are told that debtors take two months to pay. Closing debtors will equal total credit sales in the last two months of the period.

5.6   Similarly, you may be given a simple statement that a business pays rates at £1,500 a year, followed by a lot of detail to enable you to calculate a prepayment at the beginning and end of the year. If you are preparing a budgeted profit and loss account for the year do not lose sight of the fact that the rates expense can be entered as £1,500 without any calculation at all.

6   A COMPARISON OF PROFIT AND CASH FLOWS

6.1   You might notice in the example about Peter Blair that the total profit of £5,100 differs from the total of receipts less payments (– £19,100). Profit and cash flows during a period need not be the same amount and, indeed, will not usually be the same.

(a)   Sales and cost of sales are recognised in a profit and loss account as soon as they are incurred; the cash budget does not show a figure for sales or cost of sales. It is concerned with cash actually received from customers or paid to suppliers.

(b)   A profit and loss account may include accrued amounts for rates, insurance and other expenses. In the cash budget such amounts will appear in full in the month in which they are paid. There is no attempt to apportion the payments to the period to which they relate.

(c)   Similarly a profit and loss account may show a charge for depreciation. This is not a cash expense and will never appear in a cash budget. The cash budget will show purchases of fixed assets as a payment in the month when the assets are paid for, and may also show the proceeds on disposal of a fixed asset as a receipt of cash. No attempt is made to allocate purchase cost over the life of the asset.

6.2   To reconcile the budgeted cash flow figure and the budgeted profit figure the method is to use the bank reconciliation statement approach. Commence with one of the figures and then add or subtract various balances until the other budgeted figure is reached.

Example: a reconciliation of cash flow and profit

6.3   Look back to the cash budget for Peter Blair in Paragraph 4.12 and the budgeted profit and loss account in Paragraph 5.4 and reconcile the budgeted cash flow to the budgeted profit for the six-month period.

6.4   RECONCILIATION OF BUDGETED CASH FLOW AND PROFIT

		£
Budgeted cashflow		(19,100)
Add:	payments appearing in the cash budget but never appearing in the profit and loss account Drawings	6,000
Add:	receipts appearing in the profit and loss account but never appearing in the cash budget	-
Less:	charges appearing in the profit and loss account but never appearing in the cash budget Depreciation	(800)
Less:	receipts appearing in the cash budget but never appearing in the profit and loss account	-
Add:	sales/receipts adjustment (£(46,500 – 25,500))	21,000
Less:	purchases/payments adjustment (£(31,000 – 29,000))	(2,000)
Less:	expenses/payment adjustment (£(9,600 – 9,600))	-
Budgeted profit		5,100

Chapter roundup

- The purposes of a budget are as follows.

  To coordinate activities
  To communicate targets
  To establish a system of control
  To compel planning

- A budget is a financial or quantitative plan of operations for a forthcoming accounting period.

- The budget committee is the coordinating body in the preparation and administration of budgets.

- The manager responsible for preparing each budget should ideally be the manager responsible for carrying out the budget.

- The budget manual is a collection of instructions governing the responsibilities of persons and the procedures, forms

and records relating to the preparation and use of budgetary data.

- The sales budget is usually the first functional budget prepared because sales is usually the principal budget factor. The order of preparation of the remaining budgets could be finished goods stock budget, production budget, budgets for resources of production, materials stock budget, raw materials purchases budget and overhead cost budgets.

- Cash budgets show the expected receipts and payments during a budget period. The usefulness of cash budgets is that they enable management to make any forward planning decisions that may be needed, such as advising their bank of estimated overdraft requirements or strengthening their credit control procedures to ensure that debtors pay more quickly.

- The master budget consists of a budgeted profit and loss account and a budgeted balance sheet.

- Budgeted profit and cash flow for a period are unlikely to be the same for a number of reasons.

Test your knowledge

1   What are the four main purposes of a budget? (see para 1.1)

2   List four functions of a budget committee (2.2)

3   Who, ideally, should prepare budgets? (2.3)

4   What does the materials stock budget show? (2.10)

5   Why are cash budgets useful? (4.5, 4.6)

6   What are the three principal reasons for budgeted profit and budgeted cash flow being different? (6.1)

Now try illustrative question 13 at the end of the Study Text

Chapter 13

FURTHER ASPECTS OF BUDGETING

	This chapter covers the following topics.	*Syllabus reference*	*Ability required*
1	Flexible budgets	2(c)	Skill
2	Flexible budgets and budgetary control	2(c)	Skill
3	Cost estimation	2(c)	Skill
4	Computers and budgeting	2(c)	Knowledge

Introduction

You should now be able to prepare functional budgets, a cash budget and a master budget and have some idea of the budgetary process. This chapter takes the budgeting theme further and looks at a number of specific issues.

We begin by looking at flexible budgets, a vital management planning and control tool. This part of the chapter relies on your understanding of cost behaviour covered in Chapter 2.

We then move on to methods of estimating the costs to be included in budgets and conclude with a look at how computers can assist the budgeting process.

This chapter ends our study of budgeting. You will, however, come across variances again, which are mentioned in this chapter in relation to flexible budgets, in Chapters 14 and 15, which look at a new topic and consider the use of standard costing and variance analysis.

1 FLEXIBLE BUDGETS

5/97

1.1 Master budgets are based on estimated volumes of production and sales but do not include any provision for the event that actual volumes may differ from the budget. In this sense they may be described as fixed budgets.

1.2 A flexible budget is 'A budget which, by recognising different cost behaviour patterns, is designed to change as volume of activity changes' (CIMA *Official Terminology*). This has two advantages.

(a) At the planning stage, it may be helpful to know what the effects would be if the actual outcome differs from the prediction. For example, a company may budget to sell 10,000 units of its product, but may prepare flexible budgets based on sales of, say, 8,000 and 12,000 units. This would enable contingency plans to be drawn up if necessary.

(b) At the end of each month or year, actual results may be compared with the flexible budget as a control procedure.

1.3 Flexible budgeting uses the principles of marginal costing. In estimating future costs it is often necessary to begin by looking at cost behaviour in the past. For costs which are wholly fixed or wholly variable no problem arises. But you may be presented with a cost which appears to have behaved in the past as a mixed cost (partly fixed and partly variable). A technique for estimating the level of the cost for the future is called the high/low method. We looked at this technique in Chapter 2: attempt the following exercise to ensure that you can remember what to do.

Exercise 1

The cost of factory power has behaved as follows in past years.

	Units of output produced	Cost of factory power £
19X1	7,900	38,700
19X2	7,700	38,100
19X3	9,800	44,400
19X4	9,100	42,300

Budgeted production for 19X5 is 10,200 units. Estimate the cost of factory power which will be incurred. Ignore inflation.

Solution

	Units	£
19X3 (highest output)	9,800	44,400
19X2 (lowest output)	7,700	38,100
	2,100	6,300

The variable cost per unit is therefore £6,300/2,100 = £3.

The level of fixed cost can be calculated by looking at any output level.

	£
Total cost of factory power in 19X3	44,400
Less variable cost of factory power (9,800 × £3)	29,400
Fixed cost of factory power	15,000

An estimate of costs is 19X5 is as follows.

	£
Fixed cost	15,000
Variable cost of budgeted production (10,200 × £3)	30,600
Total budgeted cost of factory power	45,600

1.4   We can now look at a full example of preparing a flexible budget.

Example: preparing a flexible budget

1.5   (a)   Prepare a budget for 19X6 for the direct labour costs and overhead expenses of a production department at the activity levels of 80%, 90% and 100%, using the information listed below.

　　　　(i)   The direct labour hourly rate is expected to be £3.75.

　　　　(ii)   100% activity represents 60,000 direct labour hours.

　　　　(iii)   Variable costs

　　　　　　　Indirect labour　　　　　　£0.75 per direct labour hour
　　　　　　　Consumable supplies　　　£0.375 per direct labour hour
　　　　　　　Canteen and other
　　　　　　　welfare services　　　　　6% of direct and indirect labour costs

　　　　(iv)   Semi-variable costs are expected to relate to the direct labour hours in the same manner as for the last five years.

Year	Direct labour hours	Semi-variable costs £	
19X1	64,000	20,800 —	*high*
19X2	59,000	19,800	
19X3	53,000	18,600	
19X4	49,000	17,800	
19X5	40,000 (estimate)	16,000 (estimate)	— Low

(v)   *Fixed costs*

	£
Depreciation	18,000
Maintenance	10,000
Insurance	4,000
Rates	15,000
Management salaries	25,000

(vi)   Inflation is to be ignored.

(b)   Calculate the budget cost allowance (ie expected expenditure) for 19X6 assuming that 57,000 direct labour hours are worked.

Solution

1.6   (a)

	80% level 48,000 hrs £'000	90% level 54,000 hrs £'000	100% level 60,000 hrs £'000
Direct labour	180.00	202.50	225.0
Other variable costs			
Indirect labour	36.00	40.50	45.0
Consumable supplies	18.00	20.25	22.5
Canteen etc	12.96	14.58	16.2
Total variable costs (£5.145 per hour)	246.96	277.83	308.7
Semi-variable costs (W)	17.60	18.80	20.0
Fixed costs			
Depreciation	18.00	18.00	18.0
Maintenance	10.00	10.00	10.0
Insurance	4.00	4.00	4.0
Rates	15.00	15.00	15.0
Management salaries	25.00	25.00	25.0
Budgeted costs	336.56	368.63	400.7

Working

Using the high/low method:

	£
Total cost of 64,000 hours	20,800
Total cost of 40,000 hours	16,000
Variable cost of 24,000 hours	4,800
Variable cost per hour (£4,800/24,000)	£0.20

	£
Total cost of 64,000 hours	20,800
Variable cost of 64,000 hours (× £0.20)	12,800
Fixed costs	8,000

Semi-variable costs are calculated as follows.

			£
60,000 hours	(60,000 × £0.20) + £8,000	=	20,000
54,000 hours	(54,000 × £0.20) + £8,000	=	18,800
48,000 hours	(48,000 × £0.20) + £8,000	=	17,600

(b)   The budget cost allowance for 57,000 direct labour hours of work would be as follows.

		£
Variable costs	(57,000 × £5.145)	293,265
Semi-variable costs	(£8,000 + (57,000 × £0.20))	19,400
Fixed costs		72,000
		384,665

2   FLEXIBLE BUDGETS AND BUDGETARY CONTROL

2.1   Budgetary control is the practice of establishing budgets which identify areas of responsibility for individual managers (for example production managers, purchasing managers and so on) and of regularly comparing actual results against expected results. The most important method of budgetary control, for the purpose of your examination, is variance analysis, which involves the comparison of actual results achieved during a control period (a month, or four weeks) with a flexible budget. The differences between actual results and expected results are called variances and these are used to provide a guideline for control action by individual managers. We will be looking at variances in some detail in Chapter 15.

2.2   The wrong approach to budgetary control is to compare actual results against a fixed budget. Consider the following example.

Windy Ltd manufactures a single product, the cloud. Budgeted results and actual results for June 19X2 are shown below.

	Budget	*Actual results*	*Variance*
Production and sales of the cloud (units)	2,000	3,000	
	£	£	£
Sales revenue (a)	20,000	30,000	10,000 (F)
Direct materials	6,000	8,500	2,500 (A)
Direct labour	4,000	4,500	500 (A)
Maintenance	1,000	1,400	400 (A)
Depreciation	2,000	2,200	200 (A)
Rent and rates	1,500	1,600	100 (A)
Other costs	3,600	5,000	1,400 (A)
Total costs (b)	18,100	23,200	5,100
Profit (a) – (b)	1,900	6,800	4,900 (F)

2.3   (a)   In this example, the variances are meaningless for purposes of control. Costs were higher than budget because the volume of output was also higher; variable costs would be expected to increase above the budgeted costs in the fixed budget. There is no information to show whether control action is needed for any aspect of costs or revenue.

(b)   For control purposes, it is necessary to know the answers to questions such as the following.

(i)   Were actual costs higher than they should have been to produce and sell 3,000 clouds?

(ii)   Was actual revenue satisfactory from the sale of 3,000 clouds?

2.4   The correct approach to budgetary control is as follows.

(a)   Identify fixed and variable costs.
(b)   Produce a flexible budget using marginal costing techniques.

2.5   In the previous example of Windy Ltd, let us suppose that we have the following estimates of cost behaviour.

(a)   Direct materials and maintenance costs are variable.

(b)   Although basic wages are a fixed cost, direct labour is regarded as variable in order to measure efficiency/productivity.

(c) Rent and rates and depreciation are fixed costs.

(d) Other costs consist of fixed costs of £1,600 plus a variable cost of £1 per unit made and sold.

2.6 The budgetary control analysis should be as follows.

	Fixed budget (a)	Flexible budget (b)	Actual results (c)	Budget variance (b) - (c)
Production & sales (units)	2,000	3,000	3,000	
	£	£	£	£
Sales revenue	20,000	30,000	30,000	0
Variable costs				
Direct materials	6,000	9,000	8,500	500 (F)
Direct labour	4,000	6,000	4,500	1,500 (F)
Maintenance	1,000	1,500	1,400	100 (F)
Semi-variable costs				
Other costs	3,600	4,600	5,000	400 (A)
Fixed costs				
Depreciation	2,000	2,000	2,200	200 (A)
Rent and rates	1,500	1,500	1,600	100 (A)
Total costs	18,100	24,600	23,200	1,400 (F)
Profit	1,900	5,400	6,800	1,400 (F)

Note. (F) denotes a favourable variance and (A) an adverse or unfavourable variance. Adverse variances are sometimes denoted as (U) for 'unfavourable'.

2.7 We can analyse the above as follows.

(a) In selling 3,000 units the expected profit should have been, not the fixed budget profit of £1,900, but the flexible budget profit of £5,400. Instead, actual profit was £6,800 ie £1,400 more than we should have expected. One of the reasons for the improvement is that, given output and sales of 3,000 units, costs were lower than expected (and sales revenue exactly as expected).

	£
Direct materials cost variance	500 (F)
Direct labour cost variance	1,500 (F)
Maintenance cost variance	100 (F)
Other costs variance	400 (A)
Fixed cost variances	
Depreciation	200 (A)
Rent and rates	100 (A)
	1,400 (F)

Profit was therefore increased by £1,400 because costs were lower than anticipated.

(b) Another reason for the improvement in profit above the fixed budget profit is the sales volume. Windy Ltd sold 3,000 clouds instead of 2,000 clouds, with the following result.

	£	£
Sales revenue increased by		10,000
Variable costs increased by:		
direct materials	3,000	
direct labour	2,000	
maintenance	500	
variable element of other costs	1,000	
Fixed costs are unchanged		6,500
Profit increased by		3,500

Profit was therefore increased by £3,500 because sales volumes increased.

(c) A full variance analysis statement would be as follows.

	£	£
Fixed budget profit		1,900
Variances		
Sales volume	3,500 (F)	*= profit*
Direct materials cost	500 (F)	
Direct labour cost	1,500 (F)	
Maintenance cost	100 (F)	
Other costs	400 (A)	
Depreciation	200 (A)	
Rent and rates	100 (A)	
		4,900 (F)
Actual profit		6,800

2.8 If management believes that any of these variances are large enough to justify it, they will investigate the reasons for them to see whether any corrective action is necessary.

Exercise 2

Explain what is meant by the terms 'fixed budget' and 'flexible budget' and state the main objective of preparing flexible budgets.

Solution

Fixed budgets are based on estimated volumes of production and sales but do not include any provision for the event that actual volumes may differ from budget.

A flexible budget is designed to change so as to relate to actual volumes achieved. This has two advantages.

(a) At the planning stage, it may be helpful to know what the effects would be if the actual outcome differs from the prediction. This would enable contingency plans to be drawn up if necessary.

(b) At the end of each month or year, actual results may be compared with the flexible budget as a control procedure.

---

3   COST ESTIMATION

3.1 It should be obvious that the production of a budget calls for the preparation of cost estimates and sales forecasts. In fact, budgeting could be said to be as much a test of estimating and forecasting skills than anything else. In this section we will consider various cost estimation techniques.

Cost estimation methods

3.2 Cost estimation involves the measurement of historical costs to predict future costs. Some estimation techniques are more sophisticated than others and are therefore likely to be more reliable but, in practice, the simple techniques are more commonly found and should give estimates that are accurate enough for their purpose. It is these simple techniques which we will be examining here.

3.3 Before looking at the techniques, however, it is important to understand the basic rule upon which such techniques are based: historical costs, as used in cost estimation techniques, are assumed to be mixed (in other words can be separated into their fixed and variable elements). Remember this when considering the following techniques (which are presented in order of complexity).

Account-classification method or engineering method

3.4 By this method, the manager responsible for estimating costs will go through a list of the individual expenditure items which make up the total costs. Each item will be classified as fixed, variable or semi-variable, and values will be assigned to these, probably by reference to the historical cost accounts with an adjustment for estimated cost inflation.

This, in rough terms, is how the direct cost items (materials and labour costs) might be built-up when a budgeted direct cost per unit of output is estimated. It is also commonly used by cost centre managers in budgeting overhead costs and is quick and inexpensive. The technique does, however, depend on the subjective judgement of each manager and his skill and realism in estimating costs, and so only an approximate accuracy can be expected from its use.

High/low method

3.5 We met the high/low method again earlier in this chapter. The major drawback to the high/low method is that only two historical cost records from previous periods are used in the cost estimation. Unless these two records are a reliable indicator of costs throughout the relevant range of output, which is unlikely, only a 'loose approximation' of fixed and variable costs will be obtained. The advantage of the method is its relative simplicity.

The scattergraph method

3.6 By this graphical method of cost estimation (which we have already looked at in Chapter 2), historical costs from previous periods are plotted, and from the resulting scatter diagram, a 'line-of-best-fit' can be drawn by visual estimation.

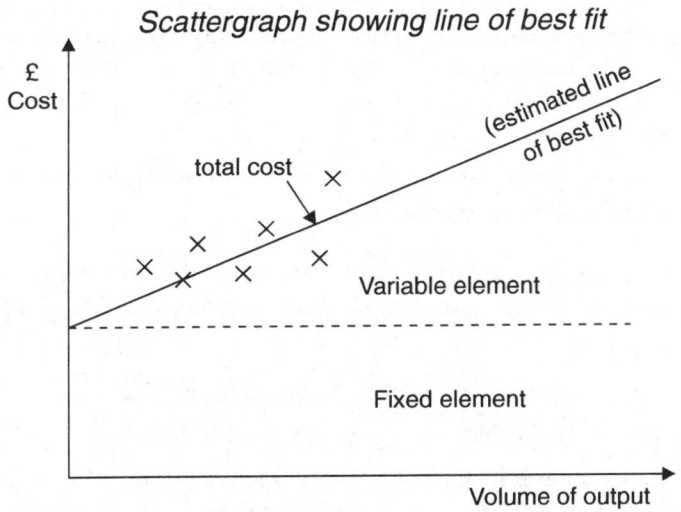

Scattergraph showing line of best fit

The fixed cost is the intercept of the line of best fit on the vertical axis. Suppose the fixed cost is £500 and that one of the plotted points (which is very close to the line or actually on it) represents output of 100 units and total cost of £1,000. The variable cost of 500 units is therefore calculated as £(1,000 − 500) = £500 and so the variable cost per unit is £5.

3.7 The advantage of the scattergraph over the high/low method is that a greater quantity of historical data is used in the estimation, but its disadvantage is that the cost line is drawn by visual judgement and so is a subjective approximation.

3.8 We will be looking at more sophisticated statistical techniques for estimating costs and forecasting sales in Chapters 27 and 28, which cover time series analysis and correlation and regression.

4   COMPUTERS AND BUDGETING

4.1   Budgeting used to be a dreaded task. The examples we have looked at so far have demonstrated the need for a great number of numerical manipulations to produce a budget, be it a cash budget or a master budget. Such examples are, however, far more simple than situations in the real world and so you can imagine the complexity of the budgetary process which even small organisations have to undergo. Remember, also, that it is highly unlikely that the execution of the steps in the process will be problem free. Functional budgets will be out of balance with each other and will require modification so that they are compatible. The revision of one budget may well lead to the revision of all of the budgets. The manual preparation of a master budget and a cash budget in the real world would therefore be daunting to say the very least.

4.2   Computers, however, can take the hard work out of budgeting: a computerised system will have four basic advantages over a manual system.

volume   (a)   A computer has the ability to process a larger volume of data.

speed   (b)   A computerised system can process data more rapidly than a manual system.

accuracy   (c)   Computerised systems tend to be more accurate than manual systems.

convenience   (d)   Computers have the ability to store large volumes of data in a readily accessible form.

4.3   Such advantages make computers ideal for taking over the manipulation of numbers, leaving staff to get involved in the real planning process.

4.4   Budgeting is usually computerised using either a computer program written specifically for the organisation or by a commercial spreadsheet package.

4.5   Both methods of computerisation of the budgeting process will involve a mathematical model which represents the real world in terms of financial values. The model will consist of several, or many, interrelated variables, a variable being an item in the model which has a value.

Example: a cash budgeting model

4.6   A cash budgeting model should include all the factors (variables) which have a significant influence on cash flow. For example, variables would include the following.

(a)   Total sales

(b)   Cash sales, perhaps as a percentage of total sales

(c)   Credit sales, perhaps as a percentage of total sales

(d)   Rate of growth in sales, or seasonal variation in sales

(e)   Time taken by debtors to pay what they owe

   (i)   Percentage paying one month after invoice
   (ii)   Percentage paying two months after invoice
   (iii)   Percentage paying three months after invoice
   (iv)   Percentage of bad debts

(f)   Purchases on credit

   (i)   Percentage paid within one month of receipt of invoice
   (ii)   Percentage paid within two months of receipt of invoice

(g)   Wages and salaries

(h)   Other cash expenses

(i)   Dividends

(j)   Taxation payments

(k)   Capital expenditure

4.7   Once the planning model has been constructed, the same model can be used week by week, month after month, or year after year, simply by changing the values of the variables to produce new results for cash inflows, cash outflows, net cash flows and cash/bank balance.

4.8   A major advantage of budget models is the ability to evaluate different options and carry out 'what if' analysis. By changing the value of certain variables (for example altering the ratio of cash sales to credit sales, increasing the amount of bad debts or capital expenditure, increasing the annual pay award to the workforce and so on) management are able to assess the effect of potential changes in their environment.

4.9   Computerised models can also incorporate actual results, period by period, and carry out the necessary calculations to produce budgetary control reports.

4.10   The use of a model also allows the budget for the remainder of the year to be adjusted once it is clear that the circumstances on which the budget was originally based have changed.

Spreadsheets

4.11   Most organisations do not have budgeting programs written for them but use standard spreadsheet packages.

4.12   'Spreadsheet' is defined in CIMA *Computing Terminology* as 'the term commonly used to describe many of the modelling packages available for microcomputers, being loosely derived from the likeness to a "spreadsheet of paper" divided into rows and columns'.

4.13   The idea behind a spreadsheet is that the model builder should construct a model in rows and columns format.

(a)   Variables are represented by a row or column of items, or even by just one 'cell' in the spreadsheet.

(b)   Numerical values for the variables are derived as follows.

(i)   They can be inserted into the model via keyboard input.

(ii)   They can be calculated from other data in the model using formulae specified within the construction of the model itself. In other words formulae can be included in the cells of the spreadsheet and referenced to other cells containing numerical information.

(iii)   They can be obtained from data held on disk file - in another spreadsheet, for example.

(c)   Text can also be entered and manipulated to some extent.

4.14   The more sophisticated modern packages can handle information in '3D' format (a 'pad' of paper, as it were, rather than a single sheet) and can present results as charts or graphs.

4.15   To assess the use of spreadsheets in budgeting let us consider a cash budget. A cash budget needs frequent updating to reflect current and forecast conditions, changes in credit behaviour and so on. Each period (week, month or whatever) up-to-date information is input and in combination with brought forward file data, the cash budget will be automatically projected forward by the spreadsheet program. Surpluses and deficiencies may well be highlighted.

4.16   Both abbreviated and detailed versions of the cash budget may be produced along with graphical representations of the same information.

	A	B	C	D	E	F	G	H
1								
2			Summary Cash Budget (Ref. Details Budgets A-L)					
3								
4			*Jan*	*Feb*	*Mar*	*Apr*	*May*	*June*
5			£'000	£'000	£'000	£'000	£'000	£'000
6	Opening balance		15	22	20	-36	-50	-83
7	add							
8	Total receipts		92	112	122	138	148	162
9	less							
10	Total payments		-85	-114	-178	-152	-181	-235
11	equals							
12	Closing balance		22	20	-36	-50	-83	-156
13								
14	Current overdraft limit		40	40	40	40	60	120
15								
16	Warning indicator					*	*	*
17						*	*	*
18							*	*
19								*

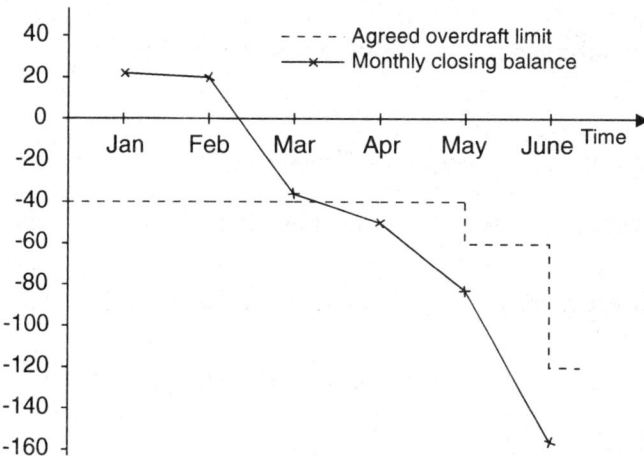

4.17 A example of spreadsheet preparation is given in Chapter 16 in the section dealing with formulae in spreadsheets.

4.18 Perhaps the greatest benefit that can be obtained from a spreadsheet package is its facility to perform 'what if' calculations at great speed. For example, the consequences throughout the organisation of sales growth per month of nil, $\frac{1}{2}$%, 1%, $1\frac{1}{2}$% and so on can be calculated at the touch of a button.

Chapter roundup

- Fixed budgets remain unchanged regardless of the level of activity; flexible budgets are designed to flex with the level of activity. Comparison of a fixed budget with the actual results for a different level of activity is of little use for control purposes. Flexible budgets should be used to show the cost and revenue allowances for the actual level of activity.

- A prerequisite of flexible budgeting is a knowledge of cost behaviour patterns.

- The differences between the components of the flexed budget and the actual results are budget variances.

- Simple cost estimation techniques include the account classification/engineering method, the high/low method and the scattergraph method.

- Computers can provide substantial assistance to the budgeting process. 'What if' analysis, budget versus actual comparisons and adjustments to the budget following pertinent changes to the circumstances on which the budget was based are all facilitated.

Test your knowledge

1   What are the advantages of a flexible budget over a fixed budget? (see para 1.2)

2   Flexible budgets are normally prepared on a marginal costing basis . True or false? (1.3)

3   Define budgetary control. (2.1)

4   What is the wrong approach to budgetary control? (2.2)

5   What is the correct approach to budgetary control? (2.4)

6   In what way is the scattergraph method more reliable than the high/low method of cost estimation? What is its main weakness? (3.7)

7   What are the advantages of a computerised system over a manual system? (4.2)

8   List eight possible variables in a cash budgeting model. (4.6)

9   What is a spreadsheet? (4.12)

Now try illustrative question 14 at the end of the Study Text

Chapter 14

INTRODUCTION TO STANDARD COSTING

This chapter covers the following topics.

		Syllabus reference	Ability required
1	What is standard costing?	2(c)	Knowledge
2	Setting standards	2(c)	Skill

Introduction

Just as there are standards for most things in our daily lives (cleanliness in hamburger restaurants, educational achievement of nine year olds, number of tubes on the Circle line running on time), there are standards for the costs of products and services. Moreover, just as the standards in our daily lives are not always met, the standards for the costs of products and services are not always met. We will not, however, be considering the standards of cleanliness of hamburger restaurants in this chapter but we will be looking at standards for costs, what they are used for and how they are set.

In the next chapter we will see how standard costing forms the basis of a process called variance analysis, a vital management control tool.

---

1 WHAT IS STANDARD COSTING?

1.1 The building blocks of standard costing are standard costs and so before we look at standard costing in any detail you really need to know what a standard cost is.

Standard cost   *5/96*

1.2 A standard cost is an estimated unit cost. The standard cost of product 1234 is set out below.

STANDARD COST CARD - PRODUCT 1234

	£	£
Direct materials		
Material X – 3 kg at £4 per kg	12	
Material Y – 9 litres at £2 per litre	18	
		30
Direct labour		
Grade A – 6 hours at £1.50 per hour	9	
Grade B – 8 hours at £2 per hour	16	
		25
Standard direct cost		55
Variable production overhead – 14 hours at £0.50 per hour		7
Standard variable cost of production		62
Fixed production overhead – 14 hours at £4.50 per hour		63
Standard full production cost		125
Administration and marketing overhead		15
Standard cost of sale		140
Standard profit		20
Standard sales price		160

1.3   Notice how it is built up from standards for each cost element: standard quantities of materials at standard prices, standard quantities of labour time at standard rates and so on. It is therefore determined by management's estimates of the following.

    (a)   The expected prices of materials, labour and expenses
    (b)   Efficiency levels in the use of materials and labour
    (c)   Budgeted overhead costs and budgeted volumes of activity

We will see how management arrives at these estimates in Section 2.

1.4   But why should management want to prepare standard costs? Obviously to assist with standard costing, but what is the point of standard costing?

The uses of standard costing

1.5   Standard costing has a variety of uses but its two principal ones are as follows.

    (a)   To value stocks and cost production for cost accounting purposes. It is an alternative method of valuation to methods like FIFO and LIFO which we looked at in Chapter 3.

    (b)   To act as a control device by establishing standards (expected costs), highlighting (via variance analysis which we will cover in the next chapter) activities that are not conforming to plan and thus alerting management to areas which may be out of control and in need of corrective action.

Exercise 1

Bloggs Ltd makes one product, the joe. Two types of labour are involved in the preparation of a joe, skilled and semi-skilled. Skilled labour is paid £10 per hour and semi-skilled £5 per hour. Twice as many skilled labour hours as semi-skilled labour hours are needed to produce a joe, four semi-skilled labour hours being needed.

A joe is made up of three different direct materials. Seven kilograms of direct material A, four litres of direct material B and three metres of direct material C are needed. Direct material A costs £1 per kilogram, direct material B £2 per litre and direct material C £3 per metre.

Variable production overheads are incurred at Bloggs Ltd at the rate of £2.50 per direct labour (skilled) hour.

A system of absorption costing is in operation at Bloggs Ltd. The basis of absorption is direct labour (skilled) hours. For the forthcoming accounting period, budgeted fixed production overheads are £250,000 and budgeted production of the joe is 5,000 units.

Administration, selling and distribution overheads are added to products at the rate of £10 per unit.

A mark-up of 25% is made on the joe.

Required

Using the above information draw up a standard cost card for the joe.

Solution

STANDARD COST CARD - PRODUCT JOE

	£	£
Direct materials		
A - 7 kgs × £1	7	
B - 4 litres × £2	8	
C - 3 m × £3	9	
		24
Direct labour		
Skilled - 8 × £10	80	
Semi-skilled - 4 × £5	20	
		100
Standard direct cost		124
Variable production overhead - 8 × £2.50		20
Standard variable cost of production		144
Fixed production overhead - 8 × £6.25 (W)		50
Standard full production cost		194
Administration, selling and distribution overhead		10
Standard cost of sale		204
Standard profit (25% × 204)		51
Standard sales price		255

Working

$$\text{Overhead absorption rate} = \frac{£250,000}{5,000 \times 8} = £6.25 \text{ per skilled labour hour}$$

1.6 Although the use of standard costs to simplify the keeping of cost accounting records should not be overlooked, we will be concentrating on the control and variance analysis aspect of standard costing. The CIMA *Official Terminology* definition highlights the control aspect, defining standard costing as 'A control technique which compares standard costs and revenues with actual results to obtain variances which are used to stimulate improved performance'.

Standard costing as a control technique

1.7 Standard costing therefore involves the establishment of predetermined estimates of the costs of products or services, the collection of actual costs and the comparison of the actual costs with the predetermined estimates. The predetermined costs are known as standard costs and the difference between standard and actual cost is known as a variance. The process by which the total difference between standard and actual results is analysed in known as variance analysis.

1.8 Although standard costing can be used in a variety of costing situations (batch and mass production, process manufacture, jobbing manufacture (where there is standardisation of parts) and service industries (if a realistic cost unit can be established)), the greatest benefit from its use can be gained if there is a degree of repetition in the production process. It is therefore most suited to mass production and repetitive assembly work.

2 SETTING STANDARDS

2.1 Standard costs may be used in both absorption costing and in marginal costing systems. We shall, however, confine our description to standard costs in absorption costing systems.

2.2 As we noted earlier, the standard cost of a product (or service) is made up of a number of different standards, one for each cost element, each of which has to be set by management. We have divided this section into two: the first part looks at setting the monetary part of each standard, whereas the second part looks at setting the resources requirement part of each standard.

Standard rates

Direct material prices

2.3   Direct material prices will be estimated by the purchasing department from their knowledge of the following.

(a)   Purchase contracts already agreed
(b)   Pricing discussions with regular suppliers
(c)   The forecast movement of prices in the market
(d)   The availability of bulk purchase discounts

2.4   Price inflation can cause difficulties in setting realistic standard prices. Suppose that a material costs £10 per kilogram at the moment and during the course of the next twelve months it is expected to go up in price by 20% to £12 per kilogram. What standard price should be selected?

(a)   The current price of £10 per kilogram
(b)   The average expected price for the year, say £11 per kilogram

2.5   Either would be possible, but neither would be entirely satisfactory.

(a)   If the current price were used in the standard, the reported price variance will become adverse as soon as prices go up, which might be very early in the year. If prices go up gradually rather than in one big jump, it would be difficult to select an appropriate time for revising the standard.

(b)   If an estimated mid-year price were used, price variances should be favourable in the first half of the year and adverse in the second half of the year, again assuming that prices go up gradually throughout the year. Management could only really check that in any month, the price variance did not become excessively adverse (or favourable) and that the price variance switched from being favourable to adverse around month six or seven and not sooner.

Direct labour rates

2.6   Direct labour rates per hour will be set by reference to the payroll and to any agreements on pay rises with trade union representatives of the employees.

(a)   A separate hourly rate or weekly wage will be set for each different labour grade/type of employee.

(b)   An average hourly rate will be applied for each grade (even though individual rates of pay may vary according to age and experience).

2.7   Similar problems when dealing with inflation to those set out in Paragraph 2.5 can be met when setting labour standards.

Overhead absorption rates

2.8   When standard costs are fully absorbed costs, the absorption rate of fixed production overheads will be predetermined, usually each year when the budget is prepared, and based in the usual manner on budgeted fixed production overhead expenditure and budgeted production.

For selling and distribution costs, standard costs might be absorbed as a percentage of the standard selling price.

Standard resource requirements

2.9 To estimate the materials required to make each product (material usage) and also the labour hours required (labour efficiency), technical specifications must be prepared for each product by production experts (either in the production department or the work study department).

(a) The 'standard product specification' for materials must list the quantities required per unit of each material in the product. These standard input quantities must be made known to the operators in the production department so that control action by management to deal with excess material wastage will be understood by them.

(b) The 'standard operation sheet' for labour will specify the expected hours required by each grade of labour in each department to make one unit of product. These standard times must be carefully set (for example by work study) and must be understood by the labour force. Where necessary, standard procedures or operating methods should be stated.

Performance standards

2.10 The quantity of material and labour time required will depend on the level of performance required by management. There are two types of performance standard which might be used. Standards may be set at 'attainable levels which assume efficient levels of operation, but which include allowances for normal loss, waste and machine downtime, or at ideal levels, which make no allowance for the above losses, and are only attainable under the most favourable conditions' (CIMA *Official Terminology*).

2.11 Ideal standards are sometimes thought to have a negative motivational impact, because employees will often feel that the goals are unattainable and not work so hard. When setting standards, managers must be aware of two requirements: the need to establish a useful control measure and the need to set a standard which will have the desired motivational effect. These two requirements are often conflicting, so that the final standard cost might be a compromise between the two.

Exercise 2

How can standards for direct material costs, direct labour costs and production overhead be set?

Solution

Direct material costs

It is necessary to establish a standard for material usage and a standard for material price. Standard material usage should take account of any allowances for breakages and losses and be based on careful monitoring and observation of the production processes used. Standard material price should take account of a number of factors including desired quality, the availability of bulk discounts and any anticipated price inflation.

Direct labour costs

Standards must be established for labour times and for hourly rates of pay. The former requires the assistance of a work study specialist, who investigates the method used and establishes an efficient standard time. Employees may be suspicious of the reasons for which they are being observed and timed as they are doing their work. This problem can be overcome by involving them fully in the task of establishing standard times. They should understand that the standard times are to be used for cost control purposes and not as a device to reduce or affect their remuneration or job security. The personnel department can assist in establishing standard rates of pay, taking account of the skill levels required and the likely results of any future negotiations with trade unions.

Production overhead

The cost centre structure can be used to allocate and apportion overheads to obtain cost centre totals for forecast overheads. There may be a problem in identifying the most appropriate basis for overhead absorption but it is likely to be some form of time-based method. An hourly rate can be determined for production overhead and this rate can be applied to the standard times identified in the work study exercise.

Problems in setting standards

Exercise 3

What sort of problems can you envisage arising when setting standards?

Solution

(a) Deciding how to incorporate inflation into planned unit costs

(b) Agreeing on a performance standard (attainable or ideal)

(c) Deciding on the quality of materials to be used (a better quality of material will cost more, but perhaps reduce material wastage)

(d) Estimating materials prices where seasonal price variations or bulk purchase discounts may be significant

(e) Finding sufficient time to construct accurate standards as standard setting can be a time-consuming process

(f) Incurring the cost of setting up and maintaining a system for establishing standards

(g) Dealing with possible behavioural problems, managers responsible for the achievement of standards possibly resisting the use of a standard costing control system for fear of being blamed for any adverse variances

2.12 Note that standard costing is most difficult in times of inflation but it is still worthwhile.

(a) Usage and efficiency variances will still be meaningful

(b) Inflation is measurable: there is no reason why its effects cannot be removed from the variances reported.

(c) Standard costs can be revised so long as this is not done too frequently.

The advantages of standard costing

Exercise 4

What do you think are the benefits to be gained from using standard costing?

Solution

The advantages for control in having a standard costing system in operation can be summarised as follows.

(a) Carefully planned standards are an aid to more accurate budgeting.

(b) Standard costs provide a yardstick against which actual costs can be measured.

(c) The setting of standards involves determining the best materials and methods which may lead to economies.

(d) A target of efficiency is set for employees to reach and cost consciousness is stimulated.

(e) Variances can be calculated which enable the principle of 'management by exception' to be operated. Only the variances which exceed acceptable tolerance limits need to be investigated by management with a view to control action.

(f) Standard costs simplify the process of bookkeeping in cost accounting, because they are easier to use than LIFO, FIFO and weighted average costs.

(g) Standard times simplify the process of production scheduling.

(h) Standard performance levels might provide an incentive for individuals to achieve targets for themselves at work.

Exercise 5

Before attempting to install a standard costing system, what aspect of an organisation and its products do you think you need to be familiar with?

Solution

Here are some suggestions

(a) A full understanding of the structure of the organisation: the cost centres in operation, the identity and ability of each cost centre manager, the reports and feedback information already available.

(b) The manufacturing processes in use: how operations are carried out, the extent to which they can be standardised and monitored, and so on.

(c) How other operations are carried out: the ordering and storage procedures for materials, any bonus schemes in operation for the payment of labour and so on.

Chapter roundup

- A standard cost is a predetermined estimated unit cost, used for stock valuation and control.

- A standard cost card shows full details of the standard cost of each product.

- Differences between actual and standard cost are called variances.

- Performance standards are used to set efficiency targets. There are basically two types: attainable and ideal.

- A standard cost is an average expected unit cost. The actual cost of individual items may fluctuate around this average.

- Management should only receive information of significant variances. This is known as 'management by exception'.

- There are a number of advantages and disadvantages associated with standard costing.

Test your knowledge

1   What is a standard cost? (see para 1.2)

2   What are the two principal uses of standard costing? (1.5)

3   What is a standard product specification? (2.9)

4   Name two types of performance standard. (2.10)

5   List six problems in setting standards. (Exercise 3)

6   List six advantages of using standard costs. (Exercise 4)

Now try illustrative question 15 at the end of the Study Text

Chapter 15

VARIANCE ANALYSIS

This chapter covers the following topics.

		Syllabus reference	Ability required
1	Variance analysis	2(c)	Skill
2	Direct material cost variances	2(c)	Skill
3	Direct labour cost variances	2(c)	Skill
4	Total variable overhead variance	2(c)	Skill
5	Total fixed overhead variance	2(c)	Skill
6	Deriving actual data from standard cost details and variances	2(c)	Skill
7	The reasons for cost variances	2(c)	Skill
8	Accounting entries for standard cost systems	2(c)	Skill
9	The appropriateness of standard costing in the modern industrial environment	2(c)	Skill

Introduction

The actual results achieved by an organisation during a reporting period (week, month, quarter, year) will, more than likely, be different from the expected results (the expected results being the standard costs). Such differences may occur between individual items, such as the cost of labour, and between the total expected profit and the total actual profit.

Management will have spent considerable time and trouble setting standards as we saw in Chapter 14. Actual results have differed from the standards. Have costs been controlled? What does the wise manager do? Ignore the difference and continue trying to attain the standards? Hopefully not. The wise manager will consider the differences that have occurred and use the results of his considerations to assist him in his attempts to attain the standards. The wise manager will use variance analysis as a control method.

This chapter examines variance analysis and sets out the method of calculating material cost variances, labour cost variances and total overhead variances. We will also see how to incorporate variances into cost bookkeeping (which you covered way back in Chapter 8). We will conclude our study of this topic by considering the appropriateness of standard costing, which has been around for a fair few years, in the modern industrial environment.

You will meet budgeting, standard costing and variance analysis in all future stages of your CIMA studies and so it is vital that you understand everything in Chapters 12 to 15.

Chapter 16 is the first chapter in the quantitative methods half of the Study Text and will go over the basic mathematical skills which you will need in the remainder of the text.

1 VARIANCE ANALYSIS

1.1 A variance is the 'Difference between a planned, budgeted, or standard cost and the actual cost incurred. The same comparisons may be made for revenues.' (CIMA *Official Terminology*). The process by which the *total* difference between standard and actual results is analysed is known as variance analysis. When actual results are better than expected results, we have a favourable variance (F). If, on the other hand, actual results are worse than expected results, we have an adverse variance (A).

1.2   The total profit variance (the difference between budgeted profit and actual profit) can be split into three: sales variances, production cost variances and non-production cost variances. In the remainder of this chapter we will consider production cost variances, both fixed and variable. You will cover the other types of variances later in your studies.

2   DIRECT MATERIAL COST VARIANCES   5/96

2.1   The total direct material cost variance (the difference between what the output actually cost and what it should have cost, in terms of material) can be divided into two sub-variances.

(a)   *The direct material price variance*

This is the difference between the standard cost and the actual cost for the *actual* quantity of material used or purchased. In other words, it is the difference between what the material did cost and what it should have cost.

(b)   *The direct material usage variance*

This is the difference between the standard quantity of materials that *should* have been used for the number of units *actually* produced, and the actual quantity of materials used, valued at the *standard* cost per unit of material. In other words, it is the difference between how much material should have been used and how much material was used, valued at standard cost.

Example: direct material cost variances

2.2   Product A has a standard direct material cost as follows.

5 kilograms of material M at £2 per kilogram = £10 per unit of A.

During April 19X3, 100 units of A were manufactured, using 520 kilograms of material M which cost £1,025.

Required

Calculate the following variances.

(a)   The total direct material cost variance
(b)   The direct material price variance
(c)   The direct material usage variance

Solution

2.3   (a)   *The total direct material cost variance*

This is the difference between what 100 units should have cost and what they did cost.

	£
100 units should have cost (× £10)	1,000
but did cost	1,025
Total direct material cost variance	25 (A)

The variance is adverse because the units cost more than they should have cost.

(b)   *The direct material price variance*

This is the difference between what 520 kgs should have cost and what 520 kgs did cost.

	£
520 kgs of M should have cost (× £2)	1,040
but did cost	1,025
Material M price variance	15 (F)

The variance is favourable because the material cost less than it should have.

(c) *The direct material usage variance*

This is the difference between how many kilograms of M should have been used to produce 100 units of A and how many kilograms were used, valued at the standard cost per kilogram.

100 units should have used (× 5 kgs)	500 kgs
but did use	520 kgs
Usage variance in kgs	20 kgs (A)
× standard cost per kilogram	× £2
Usage variance in £	£40 (A)

The variance is adverse because more material than should have been used was used.

(d) *Summary*

	£
Material price variance	15 (F)
Material usage variance	40 (A)
Total direct material cost variance	25 (A)

Material variances and opening and closing stock

2.4   Suppose that a company uses raw material P in production, and that this raw material has a standard price of £3 per metre. During one month 6,000 metres are bought for £18,600, and 5,000 metres are used in production. At the end of the month, stock will have been increased by 1,000 metres. In variance analysis, the problem is to decide whether the material price variance should be calculated on the basis of materials purchased (6,000 metres) or on the basis of materials used (5,000 metres).

2.5   The answer to this problem depends on how closing stocks of the raw materials will be valued.

(a) If they are valued at *standard cost* (1,000 units at £3 per unit) the price variance is calculated on material *purchases* in the period.

(b) If they are valued at *actual cost (FIFO)* (1,000 units at £3.10 per unit) the price variance is calculated on materials *used in production* in the period.

2.6   A full standard costing system is usually in operation and therefore the price variance is calculated on purchases in the period. The variance on the full 6,000 metres will be written off to the costing profit and loss account, even though only 5,000 metres are included in the cost of production.

2.7   There are two main advantages in extracting the material price variance at the time of receipt.

(a) If variances are extracted at the time of receipt they will be brought to the attention of managers earlier than if they are extracted as the material is used. If it is necessary to correct any variances then management action can be more timely.

(b) Since variances are extracted at the time of receipt, all stocks will be valued at standard price. This is administratively easier and it means that all issues from stocks can be made at standard price. If stocks are held at actual cost it is necessary to calculate a separate price variance on each batch as it is issued. Since issues are usually made in a number of small batches this can be a time consuming task, especially with a manual system.

2.8   The price variance would be calculated as follows.

	£
6,000 metres of material P purchased should cost (× £3)	18,000
but did cost	18,600
Price variance	600 (A)

3 DIRECT LABOUR COST VARIANCES

5/96

3.1 The calculation of direct labour variances is very similar to the calculation of direct material variances.

The total direct labour cost variance (the difference between what the output should have cost and what it did cost, in terms of labour) can be divided into two sub-variances.

(a) *The direct labour rate variance*

This is similar to the direct material price variance. It is the difference between the standard cost and the actual cost for the actual number of hours paid for.

In other words, it is the difference between what the labour did cost and what it should have cost.

(b) *The direct labour efficiency variance*

This is similar to the direct material usage variance. It is the difference between the hours that *should* have been worked for the number of units *actually* produced, and the actual number of hours worked, valued at the standard rate per hour.

In other words, it is the difference between how many hours should have been worked and how many hours were worked, valued at the standard rate per hour.

Example: direct labour cost variances

3.2 The standard direct labour cost of product B is as follows.

4 hours of grade S labour at £3 per hour = £12 per unit of product B.

During May 19X3, 200 units of product B were made, and the direct labour cost of grade S labour was £2,440 for 785 hours of work.

Required

Calculate the following variances.

(a) The total direct labour cost variance
(b) The direct labour rate variance
(c) The direct labour efficiency (productivity) variance

Solution

3.3 (a) *The total direct labour cost variance*

This is the difference between what 200 units should have cost and what they did cost.

	£
200 units should have cost (× £12)	2,400
but did cost	2,440
Total direct labour cost variance	40 (A)

The variance is adverse because the units cost more than they should have done.

(b) *The direct labour rate variance*

This is the difference between what 785 hours should have cost and what 785 hours did cost.

	£
785 hours of work should have cost (× £3 per hr)	2,355
but did cost	2,440
Direct labour rate variance	85 (A)

The variance is adverse because the labour cost more than it should have cost.

(c) *The direct labour efficiency variance*

This is the difference between how many hours should have been worked to produce 200 units, and how many hours were worked, valued at the standard rate per hour.

200 units of B should have taken (× 4hrs)	800 hrs
but did take	785 hrs
Efficiency variance in hours	15 hrs (F)
× standard rate per hour	× £3
Efficiency variance in £	£45 (F)

The variance is favourable because less hours were worked than should have been worked.

(d) *Summary*

	£
Labour rate variance	85 (A)
Labour efficiency variance	45 (F)
Total direct labour cost variance	40 (A)

Idle time variance

3.4 A company may operate a costing system in which any idle time is recorded. Idle time may be caused by machine breakdowns or not having work to give to employees, perhaps because of bottlenecks in production or a shortage of orders from customers. When idle time occurs, the labour force is still paid wages for time at work, but no actual work is done. Time paid for without any work being done is unproductive and therefore inefficient. In variance analysis, idle time is an adverse efficiency variance.

3.5 When idle time is recorded separately, it is helpful to provide control information which identifies the cost of idle time separately and in variance analysis there will be an idle time variance as a separate part of the labour efficiency variance. The remaining efficiency variance will then relate only to the productivity of the labour force during the hours spent *actively* working.

Example: labour variances with idle time

3.6 The direct labour cost of product C is as follows.

> 3 hours of grade T labour at £2.50 per hour = £7.50 per unit of product C.

During June 19X3, 300 units of product C were made, and the cost of grade T labour was £2,200 for 910 hours. During the month, there was a machine breakdown, and 40 hours were recorded as idle time.

Required

Calculate the following variances.

(a) The total direct labour cost variance
(b) The direct labour rate variance
(c) The idle time variance
(d) The direct labour efficiency variance

Solution

3.7 (a) *The total direct labour cost variance*

	£
300 units of product C should cost (× £7.50)	2,250
but did cost	2,200
Total direct labour cost variance	50 (F)

Actual cost is less than standard cost. The variance is therefore favourable.

(b) *The direct labour rate variance*

The rate variance is a comparison of what the hours paid should have cost and what they did cost.

		£
910 hours of grade T labour should cost (× £2.50)		2,275
but did cost		2,200
Direct labour rate variance		75 (F)

Actual cost is less than standard cost. The variance is therefore favourable.

(c) *The idle time variance*

The idle time variance is the hours of idle time, valued at the standard rate per hour.

Idle time variance = 40 hours (A) × £2.50 = £100 (A)

Idle time is always an adverse variance.

(d) *The direct labour efficiency variance*

The efficiency variance considers the hours actively worked (the difference between hours paid for and idle time hours). In our example, there were (910 – 40) = 870 hours when the labour force was not idle. The variance is calculated by taking the amount of output produced (300 units of product C) and comparing the time it should have taken to make them, with the actual time spent *actively* making them (870 hours). Once again, the variance in hours is valued at the standard rate per labour hour.

300 units of product C should take (× 3 hrs)	900 hrs
but did take (910 – 40)	870 hrs
Direct labour efficiency variance in hours	30 hrs (F)
× standard rate per hour	× £2.50
Direct labour efficiency variance in £	£75 (F)

(e) *Summary*

	£
Direct labour rate variance	75 (F)
Idle time variance	100 (A)
Direct labour efficiency variance	75 (F)
Total direct labour cost variance	50 (F)

3.8 Remember that, if idle time is recorded, the actual hours used in the efficiency variance calculation are the hours *worked* and not the hours paid for.

4   TOTAL VARIABLE OVERHEAD VARIANCE

4.1 The total variable overhead variance is the difference between what the output actually cost and what it should have cost, in terms of variable overhead.

Example: total variable overhead variance

4.2 The variable overhead cost of product D is £10 per direct labour hour. Two labour hours are required to make one unit of product D. In July 19X3 225 labour hours were worked to produce 120 units of product D. The total cost for variable overhead was £2,350.

Required

Calculate the total variable overhead variance

Solution

4.3

	£
120 units of product D should have cost (× £10 × 2 hrs)	2,400
but did cost	2,350
Total variable overhead variance	50 (F)

The variance is favourable because the actual cost was less than the standard cost.

4.4   Note that variable overheads are assumed to be incurred during *active* working hours only (and not during hours of idle time).

5   TOTAL FIXED OVERHEAD VARIANCE

5.1   The total fixed overhead variance is the difference between the overhead absorbed and the actual cost incurred (where the overhead absorbed is based on the standard number of hours for the units actually produced).

Example: total overhead variance

5.2   A company budgets to produce 1,000 units of product E during August 19X3. The expected time to produce a unit of E is five hours. The budgeted fixed overhead is £20,000 and fixed overheads are absorbed on a labour hours basis. Actual fixed overhead turns out to be £20,450. Actual productive hours during the period were 5,150 and 1,010 units were produced.

Required

Calculate the total fixed overhead variance.

Solution

5.3   We begin by calculating a predetermined overhead absorption rates.

$$\text{Fixed overhead absorption rate} = \frac{\text{Budgeted fixed overheads}}{\text{Budgeted activity level}}$$

$$= \frac{£20,000}{1,000 \text{ units} \times 5\text{hrs}}$$

$$= £4 \text{ per hour}$$

5.4   We can now turn our attention to calculating the variance.

	£
Actual overhead cost incurred	20,450
Standard overhead absorbed ($1,010 \times 5 \times £4$)	20,200
	250 (A)

The variance is adverse since actual overheads were greater than overheads absorbed.

5.5   Note how the overhead absorbed is based on the standard number of hours for actual production.

Exercise 1

Brain Ltd produces and sells one product only, the Blob, the standard cost for one unit being as follows.

	£
Direct material - 10 kilograms at £20 per kg	200
Direct wages - 5 hours at £6 per hour	30
Variable production overhead - 5 hours at £1 per hour	5
Fixed production overhead	50
Total standard cost	285

The fixed production overhead included in the standard cost is based on an expected monthly output of 900 units.

During April 19X3 the actual results were as follows.

Production	800 units
Direct material	7,800 kg used, costing £159,900
Direct wages	4,200 hours worked for £24,150
Variable production overhead	£4,900
Fixed production overhead	£47,000

Required

(a)   Calculate direct material price and usage variances.
(b)   Calculate direct labour rate and efficiency variances.
(c)   Calculate the total fixed and variable overhead variances.

Solution

(a)   *Price variance*

	£
7,800 kgs should have cost (× £20)	156,000
but did cost	159,900
Price variance	3,900 (A)

   Usage variance

800 units should have used (× 10 kgs)	8,000 kgs
but did use	7,800 kgs
Usage variance in kgs	200 kgs (F)
× standard cost per kilogram	× £20
Usage variance in £	£4,000 (F)

(b)   *Labour rate*

	£
4,200 hours should have cost (× £6)	25,200
but did cost	24,150
Rate variance	1,050 (F)

   Labour efficiency

800 units should have taken (× 5 hrs)	4,000 hrs
but did take	4,200 hrs
Efficiency variance in hours	200 hrs (A)
× standard rate per hour	× £6
Efficiency variance in £	£1,200 (A)

(c)   *Variable overhead*

	£
800 units should have cost (× £5)	4,000
but did cost	4,900
Variable overhead variance	900 (A)

   Fixed overhead
   Fixed overhead absorption rate per hour = £50/5 = £10 per hour

	£
Actual overhead	47,000
Standard overhead absorbed (800 × 5 × £10)	40,000
Fixed overhead variance	7,000 (A)

6   DERIVING ACTUAL DATA FROM STANDARD COST DETAILS AND VARIANCES

6.1   The majority of examination questions provide you with data about actual results and you have to calculate variances. One way in which the examiner can test your understanding of the topic, however, is to provide information about variances from which you have to 'work backwards' to determine the actual results. Let's have a look at an example.

Example: working backwards

6.2   The standard direct material cost of Product X is £96 (16 kgs × £6 per kg) and the standard direct labour cost is £72 (6 hours × £12 per hour).

The following variances were among those reported in control period 10 in relation to Product X.

Direct material price: £18,840 favourable
Direct material usage: £480 adverse
Direct labour rate: £10,598 adverse
Direct labour efficiency: £8,478 favourable

Actual direct wages cost £171,320 and £5.50 was paid for each kg of direct material. There was no opening or closing stocks of the material.

Required

Calculate the following.

(a) Actual output
(b) Actual hours worked
(c) Average actual wage rate per hour
(d) Actual number of kilograms purchased and used

Solution

6.3   (a)

	£
Total direct wages cost	171,320
Adjust for variances:	
labour rate	(10,598)
labour efficiency	8,478
Standard direct wages cost	169,200

∴ Actual output = Total standard cost ÷ unit standard cost
= £169,200 ÷ £72
= 2,350 units

(b)

	£
Total direct wages cost	171,320.0
Less rate variance	(10,598.0)
Standard rate for actual hours	160,722.0
÷ standard rate per hour	÷ £12.0
Actual hours worked	13,393.5 hrs

(c) Average actual wage rate per hour = actual wages/actual hours = £171,320/13,393.5 = £12.79 per hour.

(d) Number of kgs purchased and used = x

	£
x kgs should have cost (× £6)	6.0x
but did cost (× £5.50)	5.5x
Direct material price variance	0.5x

∴ £0.5x = £18,840
∴   x = 37,680 kgs

Exercise 2

XYZ Ltd uses standard costing. The following data relates to labour grade II.

Actual hours worked	10,400 hours
Standard allowance for actual production	9,800 hours
Standard rate per hour	£5
Rate variance (adverse)	£416

What was the actual rate of pay per hour?

Solution

Rate variance per hour worked = $\dfrac{£416}{10,400}$ = £0.04 (A)

Actual rate per hour = £(5.00 + 0.04) = £5.04.

---

7   THE REASONS FOR COST VARIANCES

7.1   There are many possible reasons for cost variances arising, including efficiencies and inefficiencies of operations, errors in standard setting and changes in exchange rates. There now follows a list of a few possible causes of cost variances. This is not an exhaustive list and in an examination question you should review the information given and use your imagination and common sense to suggest possible reasons for variances.

Variance	*Favourable*	*Adverse*
(a) Material price	Unforeseen discounts received More care taken in purchasing Change in material standard	Price increase Careless purchasing Change in material standard
(b) Material usage	Material used of higher quality than standard More effective use made of material Errors in allocating material to jobs	Defective material Excessive waste Theft Stricter quality control Errors in allocating material to jobs
(c) Labour rate of pay	Use of apprentices or other workers at a rate of pay lower than standard	Wage rate increase
(d) Idle time		Machine breakdown Non-availability of material Illness or injury to worker
(e) Labour efficiency	Output produced more quickly than expected, ie actual output in excess of standard output set for same number of hours because of work motivation, better quality of equipment or materials Errors in allocating time to jobs	Lost time in excess of standard allowed Output lower than standard set because of deliberate restriction, lack of training, or sub-standard material used Errors in allocating time to jobs
(f) Variable overhead	Savings in costs incurred More economical use of services	Increase in cost of services used Excessive use of services Change in type of services used
(g) Fixed overhead	Savings in costs incurred More economical use of services	Increase in cost of services used Excessive use of services Change in type of services used

Interdependence between variances

7.2   The cause of one variance may be wholly or partly explained by the cause of another variance. Examples could be as follows.

(a) If the purchasing department buys a cheaper material which is poorer in quality than the expected standard, the material price variance will be favourable, but this may cause material wastage and an adverse usage variance.

(b) Similarly, if employees used to do some work are highly experienced, they may be paid a higher rate than the standard wage per hour, but they should do the work more efficiently than employees of 'average' skill. In other words, an adverse rate variance may be compensated for by a favourable efficiency variance.

(c) An adverse efficiency variance may be reported following the purchase of cheaper material because operatives find difficulty in processing the cheaper material.

8 ACCOUNTING ENTRIES FOR STANDARD COST SYSTEMS   *5/97*

8.1 If an organisation operates a standard costing system, account will need to be taken of this in the double entry bookkeeping system. The basic rule is that all cost variances are recorded in the account where they arise (ie they are recognised as early as possible), with the appropriate double entry taken to a variance account.

(a) Material price variances are apparent when materials are purchased and they are therefore recorded in the stores account. If a price variance is adverse, we should credit the stores account and debit a variance account with the amount of the variance.

(b) Material usage variances do not occur until output is actually produced in the factory, and they are therefore recorded in the work in progress account. If a usage variance is favourable, we should debit the work in progress account and credit a variance account with the amount of the variance (in £).

8.2 There are some possible variations in accounting method between one organisation's system and another's but the following are the basic principles.

(a) The material price variance is recorded in the stores control account.

(b) The labour rate variance is recorded in the wages control account.

(c) The material usage variance, idle time variance and labour efficiency variance are recorded in the work in progress control account.

(d) The total overhead variances are recorded in the overhead control accounts.

Example: accounting entries

8.3 Piano Ltd manufactures one product and the entire product is sold as soon as it is produced. There are no opening or closing stocks and work in progress is negligible. The company operates a standard costing system and analysis of variances is made every month. The standard cost card for the product, a pitcher is as follows.

PITCHER

		£
Direct materials	0.5 kilos at £4 per kg	2.00
Direct wages	2 hours at £2.00 per hour	4.00
Fixed production overheads	2 hours at £4.00 per hour	8.00
Standard cost		14.00
Standard profit		6.00
Standing selling price		20.00

Selling and administration expenses are not included in the standard cost and are deducted from profit as a period charge.

Budgeted output for the month of June 19X7 was 5,100 units. Actual results for June 19X7 were as follows.

Production of 4,850 units was sold for £95,600.
Materials purchased and consumed in production amounted to 2,300 kgs at a total cost of £9,800.
Labour hours paid for amounted to 8,500 hours at a cost of £16,800.

Actual operating hours amounted to 8,000 hours.
Total fixed overheads amounted to £44,900.
Selling and production administration expenses amounted to £18,000.

Required

Prepare a set of integrated accounts which incorporate any necessary variances.

Solution

8.4 We will begin by calculating the variances.

		£	
(a)	2,300 kg of material should cost (× £4)	9,200	
	but did cost	9,800	
	Material price variance	600	(A)
(b)	4,850 pitchers should use (× 0.5kgs)	2,425	kgs
	but did use	2,300	kgs
	Materials usage variance in kgs	125	kgs (F)
	× standard cost per kg	× £4	
	Material usage variance	£500	(F)
		£	
(c)	8,500 hours of labour should cost (× £2)	17,000	
	but did cost	16,800	
	Labour rate variance	200	(F)
(d)	4,850 pitchers should take (× 2 hrs)	9,700	hrs
	but did take (active hours)	8,000	hrs
	Labour efficiency variance in hrs	1,700	hrs (F)
	× standard cost per hour	× £2	
	Labour efficiency variance in £	£3,400	(F)
(e)	Idle time variance = 500 hrs (A) × £2 =	£1,000	(A)
		£	
(f)	Actual overhead incurred	44,900	
	Standard overhead absorbed (4,850 × 2 × £4)	38,800	
		6,100	(A)

We can now insert the various variances into the integrated accounting system.

STORES LEDGER CONTROL ACCOUNT

	£		£
Purchases (Bank/creditors)	9,800	WIP (2,300 kg × £4)	9,200
		Material price variance	600
	9,800		9,800

Materials are costed to production at the standard rate per kg.

DIRECT WAGES CONTROL ACCOUNT

	£		£
Bank/creditors	16,800	WIP (8,500 hrs × £2)	17,000
Labour rate variance	200		
	17,000		17,000

Labour hours are costed to production at the standard rate per hour.

PRODUCTION OVERHEAD CONTROL ACCOUNT

	£		£
Bank/creditors	44,900	WIP (4,850 units × £8)	38,800
		Variance	6,100
	44,900		44,900

Production is charged with the standard cost for the units produced.

SALES AND ADMINISTRATION EXPENSES ACCOUNT

	£		£
Bank/creditors	18,000	Cost of sales a/c	18,000

WORK IN PROGRESS CONTROL ACCOUNT

	£		£
Stores account	9,200	Finished goods account	
Direct wages account	17,000	(4,850 × £14)	67,900
Production overhead account	38,800	Idle time variance	1,000
Labour efficiency variance	3,400		
Material usage variance	500		
	68,900		68,900

(a)   The labour efficiency variance appears in this account.
(b)   Output is valued at standard production cost.

FINISHED GOODS CONTROL ACCOUNT

	£		£
WIP a/c	67,900	Cost of sales a/c	67,900

COST OF SALES CONTROL ACCOUNT

	£		£
Finished goods a/c	67,900	P & L a/c	85,900
Sales and admin expenses a/c	18,000		
	85,900		85,900

SALES ACCOUNT

	£		£
P & L account	95,600	Bank/debtors	95,600

VARIANCES ACCOUNT

	£		£
Stores a/c (material price)	600	Direct wages a/c (labour rate)	200
Production overhead a/c	6,100	WIP a/c (labour efficiency)	3,400
WIP a/c (idle time)	1,000	WIP a/c (material usage)	500
		P & L a/c (balance)	3,600
	7,700		7,700

The variances are recorded in a variances account as part of the double entry system. The balance on the account at the end of the period is written off to the profit and loss account. Sometimes a separate account is used for each variance, but the double entry principles would be the same. In an examination you should prepare a separate account for each variance unless you are instructed otherwise.

PROFIT AND LOSS ACCOUNT

	£		£
Cost of sales	85,900	Sales account	95,600
Variances account	3,600		
Profit	6,100		
	95,600		95,600

Because there are no closing stocks there are no closing balances on any account.

Journal entries

8.5   Instead of ledger accounts, you may be required to prepare journal entries.

Exercise 3

Suppose that 10 kgs of material P are required to make one unit of Product P Plus, each kilogram costing £10. During the period just ended, 950 kgs of material P were purchased at a cost of £10,000, 950 kgs were issued to production and 98 units of Product P Plus were produced.

Required

Calculate materials price and materials usage variances and prepare journal transactions to show the purchase of material P, the issue of material P to production, and the material P variances.

Solution

	£
950 kgs should have cost (× £10)	9,500
but did cost	10,000
Materials price variance	500 (A)

98 units should have used (× 10 kgs)	980 kgs
but did use	950 kgs
Materials usage variance in kgs	30 kgs (F)
× standard rate per kg	× £10
Materials usage variance in £	£300 (F)

Journal transactions

	£	£
Stores ledger control account (950 kgs × £10)	9,500	
Materials price variance	500	
Creditors/cash		1,000

being the purchase of materials

	£	£
Work in progress control account (950 kgs × £10)	9,500	
Stores ledger control account		9,500

being the issue of material P to production

	£	£
Work in progress control account	300	
Materials usage variance		300

being the bookkeeping of material P usage variance

---

9 THE APPROPRIATENESS OF STANDARD COSTING IN THE MODERN INDUSTRIAL ENVIRONMENT

5/96

How appropriate is standard costing?

9.1 The birth of advanced manufacturing technology has brought higher levels of control and reliability. Such a move may make standard costing obsolete. For example, advanced manufacturing technology should produce high quality output and there should be little difference between standard and actual costs. In such circumstances there should be no need to analyse variances.

9.2 Increased automation in manufacturing processes means that direct labour is less significant in the production process. There is a growing tendency for labour to be viewed as a fixed cost, thereby making the idea of labour variances senseless.

9.3 In the past twenty years or so, the rate of inflation has varied a great deal, reaching a peak of 25%. Rapid inflation tends to decrease the usefulness of the comparison of actual costs against standards set some time in the past and hence throws doubt on the usefulness of standard costing in such an economic environment.

9.4 In addition to the current environment providing evidence for the inappropriateness of the use of standard costing, current literature provides evidence of a widespread dissatisfaction with the nature and quality of the information being supplied by management accounting information systems. The dissatisfaction centres around the inability of the systems to adapt in response to the changes in the nature and structure of organisations (high quality production, multi-product production, automation and the introduction of information technology) and to provide information appropriate for management control and decision making. In the current highly competitive environment, management require an information system which focuses on product quality rather than financial performance.

9.5   Given the changes that have occurred in the industrial environment and the dissatisfaction with current management accounting systems, one would expect standard costing to be less common than in the past. It would appear, however, that such an assumption is not true.

Standard costing in practice

9.6   In 1989 CIMA published a research study by Anthony Puxty and David Lyall entitled *Cost Control into the 1990s: A Survey of Standard Costing and Budgeting Practices in the UK.* They reported the results of a questionnaire completed by a broad spectrum of British industrial companies, prompted by suggestions that the use of 'traditional' management accounting techniques ought to adapt in response to changing conditions.

9.7   If the survey is representative of British industry as a whole it reveals that standard cost systems are still widespread: 76% of the companies responding to the questionnaire use them. Less than 3% of companies responding to the questionnaire had abandoned standard costing within the previous decade but over two thirds reported some change to the system (most to reflect changes in technology which allow an increased scope to the system).

Chapter roundup

- Variances explain the difference between actual results and expected results.

- The total direct material cost variance can be subdivided into the direct material price variance and the direct material usage variance.

- Direct material price variances are extracted at the time of receipt of the materials, *not* the time of usage

- The total direct labour cost variance can be subdivided into the direct labour rate variance and the direct labour efficiency variance.

- If idle time arises, it is usual to calculate a separate idle time variance, and to base the calculation of the efficiency variance on active hours (when labour actually worked) only.

- The total variable overhead variance is the difference between what the total variable overhead cost should have been and what the overhead cost was.

- The total fixed overhead variance is the difference between the actual fixed overhead incurred and the overhead absorbed (based on standard hours for actual production).

- Ensure that you can provide possible reasons for cost variances and that you are aware of the interdependence between variances.

- The basic rule for accounting entries for standard cost systems is that all cost variances are recorded in the account in which they arise.

- Despite what appears to be an inappropriate industrial environment for the use of standard costing, its use is still widespread.

Test your knowledge

1   Which two variances subdivide the total direct material cost variance? (see para 2.1)

2   What are the two main advantages in calculating the material price variance at the time of receipt? (2.7)

3   What does the direct labour rate variance mean? (3.1)

4   Why might idle time occur? (3.4)

5   What does the total fixed overhead variance measure? (5.1)

6   Give three possible causes of an adverse material usage variance. (7.1)

7   What is meant by interdependence between variances? (7.2)

8   In which bookkeeping account is the idle time variance usually recorded? (8.2)

Now try illustrative question 16 at the end of the Study Text

Part D
Basic mathematics

Chapter 16

BASIC MATHEMATICS

This chapter covers the following topics.

		Syllabus reference	Ability required
1	Integers, fractions and decimals	2(d)	Skill
2	Mathematical notation	2(d)	Skill
3	Addition, subtraction, multiplication and division	2(d)	Skill
4	Percentages and ratios	2(d)	Skill
5	Roots and powers	2(d)	Skill
6	Formulae and equations	2(d)	Skill
7	Linear equations	2(d)	Skill
8	Linear equations and graphs	2(d)	Skill
9	Simultaneous and non-linear equations	2(d)	Skill
10	Formulae for spreadsheets	2(d)	Skill
11	Geometric progressions	2(d)	Skill
12	Logarithms	2(d)	Skill

Introduction

The previous chapter concluded our study of cost accounting. We are now going to turn our attention to quantitative methods.

It is the role of the cost accountant to provide information to management, much of that information being quantitative. The cost accountant therefore requires knowledge of techniques used to analyse available numerical information so as to be able to produce useful management information. It is thus essential that all those working in a cost accounting environment understand mathematics, statistics and related procedures.

Many students do not have a mathematical background and so this chapter is intended to cover the basic mathematics that you will need for the Paper 2 exam. The examiner has stated that it is unlikely that a *whole* question would be based on the topics covered in this chapter, but questions will draw on these skills. A number of multiple choice questions have been specifically concerned with basic mathematics (roots and powers, percentages and so on), however.

Even if you have done mathematics in the past don't ignore this chapter. Skim through it to make sure that you are aware of all the concepts and techniques covered. Since it provides the foundation for much of what is to follow it is an extremely important chapter.

1 INTEGERS, FRACTIONS AND DECIMALS

1.1 An integer is a whole number and can be either positive or negative. The integers are therefore as follows.

$$...,-5, -4, -3, -2, -1, 0, 1, 2, 3, 4, 5,...$$

1.2   Fractions (such as $^1/_2$, $^1/_4$, $^{19}/_{35}$, $^{101}/_{377}$, ...) and decimals (0.1, 0.25, 0.3135 ...) are both ways of showing parts of a whole. Fractions can be turned into decimals by dividing the numerator by the denominator (in other words, the top line by the bottom line). To turn decimals into fractions, all you have to do is remember that places after the decimal point stand for tenths, hundredths, thousandths and so on.

Significant digits

1.3   Sometimes a decimal number has too many digits in it for practical use. This problem can be overcome by rounding the decimal number to a specific number of significant digits by discarding digits using the following rule.

If the first digit to be discarded is greater than or equal to five then add one to the previous digit. Otherwise the previous digit is unchanged.

Example: significant digits

1.4   (a)   187.392 correct to five significant digits is 187.39

Discarding a 2 causes nothing to be added to the 9.

(b)   187.392 correct to four significant digits is 187.4

Discarding the 9 causes one to be added to the 3.

(c)   187.392 correct to three significant digits is 187

Discarding a 3 causes nothing to be added to the 7.

Exercise 1

What is 17.385 correct to four significant digits?

Solution

17.39

---

2   MATHEMATICAL NOTATION

Brackets

2.1   Brackets are commonly used to indicate which parts of a mathematical expression should be grouped together, and calculated before other parts. In other words, brackets can indicate a priority, or an order in which calculations should be made. The rule is as follows.

(a)   Do things in brackets before doing things outside them.

(b)   Subject to rule (a), do things in this order.

(i)   Powers and roots
(ii)   Multiplications and divisions, working from left to right
(iii)   Additions and subtractions, working from left to right

2.2   Thus brackets are used for the sake of clarity. Here are some examples.

(a) $3 + 6 \times 8 = 51$. This is the same as writing $3 + (6 \times 8) = 51$.

(b) $(3 + 6) \times 8 = 72$. The brackets indicate that we wish to multiply the sum of 3 and 6 by 8.

(c) $12 - 4 \div 2 = 10$. This is the same as writing $12 - (4 \div 2) = 10$ or $12 - (4/2) = 10$.

(d) $(12 - 4) \div 2 = 4$. The brackets tell us to do the subtraction first.

2.3 A figure outside a bracket may be multiplied by two or more figures inside a bracket, linked by addition or subtraction signs. Here is an example.

$5(6 + 8) = 5 \times (6 + 8) = 5 \times 6 + 5 \times 8 = 70$

This is the same as $5(14) = 5 \times 14 = 70$

The multiplication sign after the 5 can be omitted, as shown here $(5(6 + 8))$, but there is no harm in putting it in $(5 \times (6 + 8))$ if you want to.

Similarly:

$5(8 - 6) = 5(2) = 10$; or
$5 \times 8 - 5 \times 6 = 10$

2.4 When two sets of figures linked by addition or subtraction signs within brackets are multiplied together, each figure in one bracket is multiplied in turn by every figure in the second bracket. Thus:

$(8 + 4)(7 + 2) = (12)(9) = 108$ or
$8 \times 7 + 8 \times 2 + 4 \times 7 + 4 \times 2 = 56 + 16 + 28 + 8 = 108$

Negative numbers

2.5 When a negative number $(-p)$ is *added* to another number (q), the net effect is to subtract p from q.

(a) $10 + (-6) = 10 - 6 = 4$ (b) $-10 + (-6) = -10 - 6 = -16$

2.6 When a negative number $(-p)$ is *subtracted* from another number (q), the net effect is to add p to q.

(a) $12 - (-8) = 12 + 8 = 20$ (b) $-12 - (-8) = -12 + 8 = -4$

2.7 When a negative number is multiplied or divided by another negative number, the result is a positive number.

(a) $-8 \times (-4) = +32$ (b) $-18/(-3) = +6$

2.8 If there is only one negative number in a multiplication or division, the result is negative.

(a) $-8 \times 4 = -32$ (b) $3 \times (-2) = -6$ (c) $12/(-4) = -3$ (d) $-20/5 = -4$

Exercise 2

Work out the following.

(a) $(72 - 8) - (-2 + 1)$

(b) $\dfrac{88 + 8}{12} + \dfrac{(29 - 11)}{-2}$

(c) $8(2 - 5) - (4 - (-8))$

(d) $\dfrac{-36}{9 - 3} - \dfrac{84}{3 - 10} - \dfrac{-81}{3}$

Solution

(a) $64 - (-1) = 64 + 1 = 65$

(b) $8 + (-9) = -1$

(c) $-24 - (12) = -36$

(d) $-6 - (-12) - (-27) = -6 + 12 + 27 = 33$

Reciprocals

2.9 The reciprocal of a number is just 1 divided by that number. For example, the reciprocal of 2 is 1 divided by 2, in other words $^1/_2$.

Extra symbols

2.10 We will come across several other mathematical signs in this book but there are five which you should learn right away.

(a) > means 'greater than'. So 46 > 29 is true, but 40 > 86 is false.
(b) ≥ means 'is greater than or equal to'. So 4 ≥ 3 and 4 ≥ 4.
(c) < means 'is less than'. So 29 < 46 is true, but 86 < 40 is false.
(d) ≤ means 'is less than or equal to'. So 7 ≤ 8 and 7 ≤ 7.
(e) ≠ means 'is not equal to'. So we could write 100.004 ≠ 100.

3 ADDITION, SUBTRACTION, MULTIPLICATION AND DIVISION

3.1 To ensure that you have understood how to deal with brackets and negative numbers and to check that you are able to use your calculator to perform addition, subtraction, multiplication and division, try the following exercise.

Exercise 3

Work out all answers to four decimal places, using a calculator.

(a) $(43 + 26.705) \times 9.3$

(b) $(844.2 \div 26) - 2.45$

(c) $\dfrac{45.6 - 13.92 + 823.1}{14.3 \times 112.5}$

(d) $\dfrac{303.3 + 7.06 \times 42.11}{1.03 \times 111.03}$

(e) $\dfrac{7.6 \times 1,010}{10.1 \times 76,000}$

(f) $(43.756 + 26.321) \div 171.036$

(g) $(43.756 + 26.321) \times 171.036$

(h) $171.45 + (-221.36) + 143.22$

(i) $66 - (-43.57) + (-212.36)$

(j) $\dfrac{10.1 \times 76,000}{7.6 \times 1,010}$

(k) $\dfrac{21.032 + (-31.476)}{3.27 \times 41.201}$

(l) $\dfrac{-33.33 - (-41.37)}{11.21 + (-24.32)}$

(m) $\dfrac{-10.75 \times (-15.44)}{-14.25 \times 17.15} + \left(\dfrac{16.23}{8.4 + 3.002}\right)$

(n) $\dfrac{-7.366 \times 921.3}{10,493 - 2,422.8} - \left(\dfrac{8.4 + 3.002}{16.23}\right)$

Solution

(a) 648.2565

(b) 30.0192

(c) 0.5313

(d) 5.2518

(e) 0.01

(f) 0.4097

(g) 11,985.898

(h) 93.31

(i) –102.79

(j) 100 (Note that this question is the reciprocal of part (e), and so the answer is the reciprocal of the answer to part (e).)

(k) –0.0775

(l) –0.6133

(m) 0.7443

(n) –1.5434

4 PERCENTAGES AND RATIOS   *S/95*

4.1 Percentages are used to indicate the *relative* size or proportion of items, rather than their absolute size. For example, if one office employs ten accountants, six secretaries and four supervisors, the *absolute* values of staff numbers and the *percentage* of the total work force in each type would be as follows.

	Accountants	*Secretaries*	*Supervisors*	*Total*
Absolute numbers	10	6	4	20
Percentages	50%	30%	20%	100%

4.2   The idea of percentages is that the whole of something can be thought of as 100%. The whole of a cake, for example, is 100%. If you share it out equally with a friend, you will get half each, or 100%/2 = 50% each.

4.3   To turn a percentage into a fraction or decimal you divide by 100%. To turn a fraction or decimal back into a percentage you multiply by 100%. Consider the following.

(a) $0.16 = 0.16 \times 100\% = 16\%$
(b) $^4/_5 = \% \times 100\% = {}^{400}/_5\% = 80\%$
(c) $40\% = {}^{40\%}/_{100\%} = {}^2/_5 = 0.4$

4.4   There are two main types of situations involving percentages.

(a)   You may be required to calculate a percentage of a figures, having been given the percentage.

Question: What is 40% of £64?

Answer: 40% of £64 = 0.4 × £64 = £25.60.

(b)   You may be required to state what percentage one figure is of another, so that you have to work out the percentage yourself.

Question: What is £16 as a percentage of £64?

Answer: £16 as a percentage of £64 $= \dfrac{16}{64} \times 100\% = \dfrac{1}{4} \times 100\% = 25\%$

In other words, put the £16 as a fraction of the £64, and then multiply by 100%.

Discounts

4.5   The calculation of discounts requires an ability to manipulate percentages. The example which follows will illustrate the technique.

Exercise 4

A travel agent is offering a 17% discount on the brochure price of a particular holiday to America. The brochure price of the holiday is £795.

Required

Calculate the price being offered by the travel agent.

Solution

Let 100%   = £795

∴ 1% $= \dfrac{100\%}{100} = \dfrac{£795}{100} = £7.95$

∴ 17%   = 17 × 1% = 17 × £7.95 = £135.15

∴ Price offered = £(795 – 135.15) = £659.85

Alternatively   Price offered = £795 × (100 – 17)% = £795 × 83%= £795 × 0.83= £659.85

Exercise 5

(a)   A television has been reduced from £490.99 to £340.99. What is the percentage reduction in price to three decimal places?

(b)   A stereo cost £757 in 19X3 and £892 one year later. What is the percentage increase in price to one decimal place?

Solution

(a)   Difference in price = £(490.99 – 340.99) = £150.00

Percentage reduction = $\dfrac{150}{490.99} \times 100\% = 30.551\%$

(b)   Difference in price = £(892 – 757) = £135

Percentage increase = $\dfrac{135}{757} \times 100\% = 17.8\%$

Profits

4.6   You may be required in your examination to calculate profit, selling price or cost of sale of an item or number of items from certain information. To do this you need to remember the following crucial formula.

	Example
	%
Cost of sales	100
Plus Profit	25
Equals Sales	$\overline{125}$

Profit may be expressed either as a percentage of cost of sales (such as 25% ($^{25}\!/_{100}$) mark-up) or as a percentage of sales (such as 20% ($^{25}\!/_{125}$) margin).

Example: profits and percentages

4.7   Delilah's Dresses sells a dress at a 10% margin. The dress cost the shop £100.

Required

Calculate the profit made by Delilah's Dresses.

Solutions

4.8   The margin is 10% (ie ($^{10}\!/_{100}$))

∴ Let selling price   = 100%
∴ Profit   = 10%
∴ Cost   = 90% = £100
∴ 1%   = (£100/90)
∴ 10% = profit = £100/90 × 10 = £11.11

Example: percentages and profits

4.9   Trevor's Trousers sells a pair of trousers for £80 at a 15% mark-up.

Required

Calculate the profit made by Trevor's Trousers.

Solution

4.10   The markup is 15%.

∴ Let cost of sales   = 100%
∴ Profit   = 15%
∴ Selling price   = 115% = £80
∴ 1% = ($^{£80}\!/_{115}$)
∴ 15% = profit = ($^{£80}\!/_{115}$) × 15 = £10.43

Proportions

4.11   A proportion means writing a percentage as a proportion of 1 (that is, as a decimal).

100% can be thought of as the whole, or 1. 50% is half of that, or 0.5. Consider the following.

Question: There are 14 women in an audience of 70. What proportion of the audience are men?

Answer: Number of men $= 70 - 14 = 56$

Proportion of men $= \dfrac{56}{70} = \dfrac{8}{10} = 80\% = 0.8$

(a) $^8/_{10}$ or $^4/_5$ is the *fraction* of the audience made up of men.
(b)   80% is the *percentage* of the audience made up of men.
(c)   0.8 is the *proportion* of the audience made up of men.

Exercise 6

There are 30 students in a class room, 17 of whom have blonde hair. What proportion of the students do not have blonde hair.

Solution

$(30 - 17)/30 \times 100\% = 43.33\% = 0.4333$

Ratios

4.12   Suppose Tom has £12 and Dick has £8. The *ratio* of Tom's cash to Dick's cash is 12:8. This can be cancelled down, just like a fraction, to 3:2.

4.13   Usually an examination question will pose the problem the other way around: Tom and Dick wish to share £20 out in the ratio 3:2. How much will each receive?

4.14   Because $3 + 2 = 5$, we must divide the whole up into five equal parts, then give Tom three parts and Dick two parts.

(a)   £20 ÷ 5 = £4 (so each part is £4)

(b)   Tom's share $= 3 \times £4 = £12$

(c)   Dick's share $= 2 \times £4 = £8$

(d)   *Check:* £12 + £8 = £20 (adding up the two shares in the answer gets us back to the £20 in the question)

4.15   This method of calculating ratios as amounts works no matter how many ratios are involved. Here is another example.

Question: A, B, C and D wish to share £600 in the ratio 6:1:2:3. How much will each receive?

Answer: (a)   Number of parts $=$ $6 + 1 + 2 + 3 = 12$

(b)   Value of each part $=$ £600 ÷ 12 = £50

(c)   A: $6 \times £50$ $=$ £300
B: $1 \times £50$ $=$ £50
C: $2 \times £50$ $=$ £100
D $3 \times £50$ $=$ £150

(d)   *Check:* £300 + £50 + £100 + £150 = £600

Exercise 7

(a) Tom, Dick and Harry wish to share out £800. Calculate how much each would receive if the ratio used was:

  (i)   3 : 2 : 5;
  (ii) 5 : 3 : 2;
  (iii) 3 : 1 : 1.

(b) Lynn and Laura share out a certain sum of money in the ratio 4 : 5, and Laura ends up with £6.

  (i)   How much was shared out in the first place?

  (ii) How much would have been shared out if Laura had got £6 and the ratio had been 5 : 4 instead of 4 : 5?

Solution

(a) (i)   Total parts = 10
        Each part is worth £800 ÷ 10 = £80
        Tom gets   3 × £80 = £240
        Dick gets   2 × £80 = £160
        Harry gets   5 × £80 = £400

  (ii) Same parts as (i) but in a different order.
        Tom gets   £400
        Dick gets   £240
        Harry gets   £160

  (iii) Total parts = 5
        Each part is worth £800 ÷ 5 = £160
        Therefore Tom gets £480
        Dick and Harry each get £160

(b) (i)   Laura's share = £6 = 5 parts
        Therefore one part is worth £6 ÷ 5 = £1.20
        Total of 9 parts shared out originally
        Therefore total was 9 × £1.20 = £10.80

  (ii) Laura's share = £6 = 4 parts
        Therefore one part is worth £6 ÷ 4 = £1.50
        Therefore original total was 9 × £1.50 = £13.50

5   ROOTS AND POWERS

5.1 The square root of a number is a value which, when multiplied by itself, equals the original number.

$\sqrt{9} = 3$, since $3 \times 3 = 9$

Similarly, the cube root of a number is the value which, when multiplied by itself twice, equals the original number.

$\sqrt[3]{64} = 4$, since $4 \times 4 \times 4 = 64$

5.2 The nth root of a number is a value which, when multiplied by itself $(n - 1)$ times, equals the original number.

5.3 Powers work the other way round.
Thus the 6th power of $2 = 2^6 = 2 \times 2 \times 2 \times 2 \times 2 \times 2 = 64$.

Similarly, $3^4 = 3 \times 3 \times 3 \times 3 = 81$.

Since $\sqrt{9} = 3$, it also follows that $3^2 = 9$, and since $\sqrt[3]{64} = 4$, $4^3 = 64$.

5.4 When a number with an index (a 'to the power of' value) is multiplied by the *same* number with the same or a different index, the result is that number to the power of the sum of the indices.

(a) $5^2 \times 5 = 5^2 \times 5^1 = 5^{(2+1)} = 5^3 = 125$
(b) $4^3 \times 4^3 = 4^{(3+3)} = 4^6 = 4{,}096$

5.5 Similarly, when a number with an index is divided by the *same* number with the same or a different index, the result is that number to the power of the first index minus the second index.

(a) $6^4 \div 6^3 = 6^{(4-3)} = 6^1 = 6$
(b) $7^8 \div 7^6 = 7^{(8-6)} = 7^2 = 49$

5.6 Any figure to the power of zero equals one. $1^0 = 1$, $2^0 = 1$, $3^0 = 1$, $4^0 = 1$ and so on.

5.7 An index can be a fraction, as in $16^{\frac{1}{2}}$. What $16^{\frac{1}{2}}$ means is the square root of 16 ($\sqrt{16}$ or 4). If we multiply $16^{\frac{1}{2}}$ by $16^{\frac{1}{2}}$ we get $16^{(\frac{1}{2}+\frac{1}{2})}$ which equals 16^1 and thus 16. Similarly, $216^{\frac{1}{3}}$ is the cube root of 216 (which is 6) because $216^{\frac{1}{3}} \times 216^{\frac{1}{3}} \times 216^{\frac{1}{3}} = 216^{(\frac{1}{3}+\frac{1}{3}+\frac{1}{3})} = 216^1 = 216$.

5.8 An index can be a negative value. The negative sign represents a reciprocal. Thus 2^{-1} is the reciprocal of, or one over, 2^1.

$$2^{-1} = \frac{1}{2^1} = \frac{1}{2}$$

Likewise $2^{-2} = \frac{1}{2^2} = \frac{1}{4}$; $2^{-3} = \frac{1}{2^3} = \frac{1}{8}$; $5^{-6} = \frac{1}{5^6} = \frac{1}{15{,}625}$

5.9 When we multiply or divide by a number with a negative index, the rules previously stated still apply.

(a) $9^2 \times 9^{-2} = 9^{(2+(-2))} = 9^0 = 1$ (That is, $9^2 \times \frac{1}{9^2} = 1$)

(b) $4^5 \div 4^{-2} = 4^{(5-(-2))} = 4^7 = 16{,}384$

(c) $3^8 \times 3^{-5} = 3^{(8-5)} = 3^3 = 27$

(d) $3^{-5} \div 3^{-2} = 3^{-5-(-2)} = 3^{-3} = \frac{1}{3^3} = \frac{1}{27}$. (This could be re-expressed as
$\frac{1}{3^5} \div \frac{1}{3^2} = \frac{1}{3^5} \times 3^2 = \frac{1}{3^3}$.)

Exercise 8

Work out the following, using your calculator as necessary.

(a) $(18.6)^{2.6}$

(b) $(18.6)^{-2.6}$

(c) $\sqrt[2.6]{18.6}$

(d) $(14.2)^4 \times (14.2)^{\frac{1}{4}}$

(e) $(14.2)^4 + (14.2)^{\frac{1}{4}}$

Solution

(a) $(18.6)^{2.6} = 1{,}998.64$

(b) $(18.6)^{-2.6} = \left(\dfrac{1}{18.6}\right)^{2.6} = 0.0005$

(c) $= \sqrt[2.6]{18.6} = 3.078$

(d) $(14.2)^4 \times (14.2)^{\frac{1}{4}} = (14.2)^{4.25} = 78{,}926.98$

(e) $(14.2)^4 + (14.2)^{\frac{1}{4}} = 40{,}658.69 + 1.9412 = 40{,}660.6312$

6   FORMULAE AND EQUATIONS

6.1   So far all our problems have been formulated entirely in terms of specific numbers. However, think back to when you were calculating powers with your calculator earlier in this chapter. You probably used the x^y key on your calculator. x and y stood for whichever numbers we happened to have in our problem, for example, 3 and 4 if we wanted to work out 3^4. When we use letters like this to stand for any numbers we call them variables. When we work out 3^4, x stands for 3. When we work out 7^2, x will stand for 7: its value can vary.

6.2   The use of variables enables us to state general truths about mathematics.

For example:

$x = x$
$x^2 = x \times x$

If $y = 0.5 \times x$, then $x = 2 \times y$

These will be true *whatever* values x and y have. For example, let $y = 0.5 \times x$

If $y = 3$, $x = 2 \times y = 6$
If $y = 7$, $x = 2 \times y = 14$
If $y = 1$, $x = 2 \times y = 2$, and so on for any other choice of a value for y.

6.3   We can use variables to build up useful formulae, we can then put in values for the variables, and get out a value for something we are interested in.

6.4   Let us consider an example. For a business, profit = revenue – costs. Since revenue = selling price × units sold, we can say that

profit = selling price × units sold – costs.

'Selling price × units sold – costs' is a formula for profit.

We can then use single letters to make the formula quicker to write.

Let x = profit
     p = selling price
     u = units sold
     c = cost

Then $x = p \times u - c$.

If we are then told that in a particular month, $p = £5$, $u = 30$ and $c = £118$, we can find out the month's profit.

Profit = $x = p \times u - c = £5 \times 30 - £118$
        = $£150 - £118 = £32$

6.5   It is usual when writing formulae to leave out multiplication signs between letters. Thus $p \times u - c$ can be written as $pu - c$. We will also write (for example) $2x$ instead of $2 \times x$.

Equations

6.6 In the above example, pu – c was a formula for profit. If we write x = pu – c, we have written an equation. It says that one thing (profit, x) is equal to another (pu – c).

6.7 Sometimes, we are given an equation with numbers filled in for all but one of the variables. The problem is then to find the number which should be filled in for the last variable. This is called solving the equation.

6.8 (a) Returning to x = pu – c, we could be told that for a particular month p = £4, u = 60 and c = £208. We would then have the *equation* x = £4 × 60 – £208. We can solve this easily by working out £4 × 60 – £208 = £240 – £208 = £32. Thus x = £32.

(b) On the other hand, we might have been told that in a month when profits were £172, 50 units were sold and the selling price was £7. The thing we have not been told is the month's costs, c. We can work out c by writing out the equation.

£172 = £7 × 50 – c

£172 = £350 – c

We need c to be such that when it is taken away from £350 we have £172 left. With a bit of trial and error, we can get to c = £178.

6.9 Trial and error takes far too long in more complicated cases, however, and we will now go on to look at a rule for solving equations, which will take us directly to the answers we want.

The rule for solving equations

6.10 To solve an equation, we need to get it into the form:

Unknown variable = something with just numbers in it, which we can work out.

We therefore want to get the unknown variable on one side of the = sign, and everything else on the other side.

6.11 The rule is that you can do what you like to one side of an equation, so long as you do the same thing to the other side straightaway. The two sides are equal, and they will stay equal so long as you treat them in the same way.

6.12 For example, you can do any of the following.

Add 37 to both sides.
Subtract 3x from both sides.
Multiply both sides by –4.329.
Divide both sides by (x + 2).
Take the reciprocal of both sides.
Square both sides.
Take the cube root of both sides.

6.13 We can do any of these things to an equation either before or after filling in numbers for the variables for which we have values.

6.14 (a) In Paragraph 6.8 above, we had

£172 = £350 – c.

We can then get

£172 + c = £350   (add c to each side)
c = £350 – £172   (subtract £172 from each side)
c = £178   (work out the right hand side)

(b) 450 = 3x + 72   (initial equation: x unknown)

$$450 - 72 = 3x \qquad \text{(subtract 72 from each side)}$$
$$\frac{450 - 72}{3} = x \qquad \text{(divide each side by 3)}$$
$$126 = x \qquad \text{(work out the left hand side)}$$

(c)
$$3y + 2 = 5y - 7 \qquad \text{(initial equation: y unknown)}$$
$$3y + 9 = 5y \qquad \text{(add 7 to each side)}$$
$$9 = 2y \qquad \text{(subtract 3y from each side)}$$
$$4.5 = y \qquad \text{(divide each side by 2)}$$

(d)
$$\frac{\sqrt{3x^2 + x}}{2\sqrt{x}} = 7 \qquad \text{(initial equation: x unknown)}$$

$$\frac{3x^2 + x}{4x} = 49 \qquad \text{(square each side)}$$

$$(3x + 1)/4 = 49 \qquad \text{(cancel x in the numerator and the denominator of the left hand side: this does not affect the value of the left hand side, so we do not need to change the right hand side)}$$

$$3x + 1 = 196 \qquad \text{(multiply each side by 4)}$$

$$3x = 195 \qquad \text{(subtract 1 from each side)}$$

$$x = 65 \qquad \text{(divide each side by 3)}$$

(e) Our example in Paragraph 6.6 was x = pu − c. We could change this, so as to give a formula for p.

$$x = pu - c$$

$$x + c = pu \qquad \text{(add c to each side)}$$

$$\frac{x + c}{u} = p \qquad \text{(divide each side by u)}$$

$$p = \frac{x + c}{u} \qquad \text{(swap the sides for ease of reading)}$$

Given values for x, c and u we can now find p. We have rearranged the equation to give p in terms of x, c and u.

(f) Given that $y = \sqrt{3x + 7}$, we can get an equation giving x in terms of y.

$$y = \sqrt{3x + 7}$$

$$y^2 = 3x + 7 \qquad \text{(square each side)}$$

$$y^2 - 7 = 3x \qquad \text{(subtract 7 from each side)}$$

$$x = \frac{y^2 - 7}{3} \qquad \text{(divide each side by 3, and swap the sides for ease of reading)}$$

6.15 In equations, you may come across expressions like 3(x + 4y − 2) (that is, 3 × (x + 4y − 2)). These can be re-written in separate bits without the brackets, simply by multiplying the number outside the brackets by each item inside them. Thus 3(x + 4y − 2) = 3x + 12y − 6.

Exercise 9

Question 1

Find the value of x in each of the following equations.

(a) $47x + 256 = 52x$

(b) $4\sqrt{x} + 32 = 40.6718$

(c) $\dfrac{1}{3x + 4} = \dfrac{5}{2.7x - 2}$

(d) $x^3 = 4.913$

(e) $34x - 7.6 = (17x - 3.8) \times (x + 12.5)$

Solution 1

(a)

$47x +$ 256	$=$	$52x$
256	$=$	$5x$	(subtract 47x from each side)
51.2	$=$	x	(divide each side by 5)

(b)

$4\sqrt{x} + 32$	$=$	40.6718	
$4\sqrt{x}$	$=$	8.6718	(subtract 32 from each side)
$\sqrt{x}$	$=$	2.16795	(divide each side by 4)
x	$=$	4.7	(square each side).

(c) $\dfrac{1}{3x+4} = \dfrac{5}{2.7x-2}$

$3x + 4 = \dfrac{2.7x-2}{5}$ (take the reciprocal of each side)

$15x + 20$	$=$	$2.7x - 2$	(multiply each side by 5)
$12.3x$	$=$	-22	(subtract 20 and subtract 2.7x from each side)
x	$=$	-1.789	(divide each side by 12.3).

(d)

x^3	$=$	4.913	
x	$=$	1.7	(take the cube root of each side).

(e) $34x - 7.6 = (17x - 3.8) \times (x + 12.5)$

This one is easy if you realise that $17 \times 2 = 34$ and $3.8 \times 2 = 7.6$, so $2(17x - 3.8) = 34x - 7.6$

We can then divide each side by $17x - 3.8$ to get

2	$=$	$x + 12.5$
-10.5	$=$	x	(subtract 12.5 from each side).

Question 2

(a)   Rearrange $x = (3y - 20)^2$ to get an expression for y in terms of x.

(b)   Rearrange $2(y - 4) - 4(x^2 + 3) = 0$ to get an expression for x in terms of y.

Solution 2

(a) $x = (3y - 20)^2$

$4\sqrt{x} = 3y - 20$ (take the square root of each side)

$20 + 4\sqrt{x} = 3y$ (add 20 to each side)

$y = \dfrac{20 + \sqrt{x}}{3}$ (divide each side by 3, and swap the sides for ease of reading)

(b) $2(y - 4) - 4(x^2 + 3) = 0$

$2(y - 4) = 4(x^2 + 3)$ (add $4(x^2 + 3)$ to each side)

$0.5(y - 4) = x^2 + 3$ (divide each side by 4)

$0.5(y - 4) - 3 = x^2$ (subtract 3 from each side)

$x = \sqrt{0.5(y-4)-3}$ (take the square root of each side, and swap the sides for ease of reading)

$x = \sqrt{0.5y - 5}$

7   LINEAR EQUATIONS

7.1   A linear equation has the general form $y = a + bx$

   where   y   is the dependent variable, depending for its value on the value of x;

   x   is the independent variable whose value helps to determine the corresponding value of y;

   a   is a constant, that is, a fixed amount;

   b   is also a constant, being the coefficient of x (that is, the number by which the value of x should be multiplied to derive the value of y).

7.2   Let us establish some basic linear equations. Suppose that it takes Joe Bloggs 15 minutes to walk one mile. How long does it take Joe to walk two miles? Obviously it takes him 30 minutes. How did you calculate the time? You probably thought that if the distance is doubled then the time must be doubled. How do you explain (in words) the relationships between the distance walked and the time taken? One explanation would be that every mile walked takes 15 minutes.

7.3   That is an explanation in words. Can you explain the relationship with an equation?

7.4   First you must decide which is the dependent variable and which is the independent variable. In other words, does the time taken depend on the number of miles walked or does the number of miles walked depend on the time it takes to walk a mile? Obviously the time depends on the distance. We can therefore let y be the dependent variable (time taken in minutes) and x be the independent variable (distance walked in miles).

7.5   We now need to determine the constants a and b. There is no fixed amount so $a = 0$. To ascertain b, we need to establish the number of times by which the value of x should be multiplied to derive the value of y. Obviously $y = 15x$ where y is in minutes. If y were in hours then $y = \frac{x}{4}$.

Example: deriving a linear equation

7.6   A salesman's weekly wage is made up of a basic weekly wage of £100 and commission of £5 for every item he sells.

   Required

   Derive an equation which describes this scenario.

Solution

7.7 x = number of items sold and y = weekly wage
   a = £100 and b = £5
   ∴ $y = 5x + 100$

7.8   Note that the letters used in an equation do not have to be x and y. It may be sensible to use other letters, for example we could use p and q if we are describing the relationship between the price of an item and the quantity demanded.

8   LINEAR EQUATIONS AND GRAPHS

8.1   One of the clearest ways of presenting the relationship between two variables is by plotting a linear equation as a straight line on a graph.

The rules for drawing graphs

8.2   A graph has a horizontal axis, the x axis and a vertical axis, the y axis. The x axis is used to represent the independent variable and the y axis is used to represent the dependent variable.

8.3   If calendar time is one variable, it is always treated as the independent variable. When time is represented on the x axis of a graph, we have the graph of a time series.

8.4   (a)   If the data to be plotted are derived from calculations, rather than given in the question, make sure that there is a neat table in your working papers.

   (b)   The scales on each axis should be selected so as to use as much of the graph paper as possible. Do not cramp a graph into one corner.

   (c)   In some cases it is best not to start a scale at zero so as to avoid having a large area of wasted paper. This is perfectly acceptable as long as the scale adopted is clearly shown on the axis. One way of avoiding confusion is to break the axis concerned, as follows.

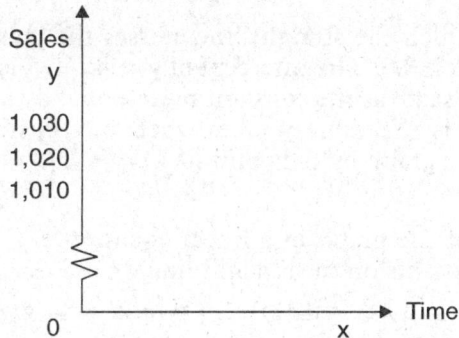

   (d)   The scales on the x axis and the y axis should be marked. For example, if the y axis relates to amounts of money, the axis should be marked at every £1, or £100 or £1,000 interval or at whatever other interval is appropriate. The axes must be marked with values to give the reader an idea of how big the values on the graph are.

   (e)   A graph should not be overcrowded with too many lines. Graphs should always give a clear, neat impression.

   (f)   A graph must always be given a title, and where appropriate, a reference should be made to the source of data.

Example: drawing graphs

8.5   Plot the graph for $y = 4x + 5$.
       Consider the range of values from $x = 0$ to $x = 10$.

Solution

8.6   The first step is to draw up a table for the equation. Although the problem mentions $x = 0$ to $x = 10$, it is not necessary to calculate values of y for $x = 1, 2, 3$ etc. A graph of a linear equation can actually be drawn from just two (x, y) values but it is always best to calculate a number of values in case you make an arithmetical error. We have calculated five values. You could settle for three or four.

x	y
0	5
2	13
4	21
6	29
8	37
10	45

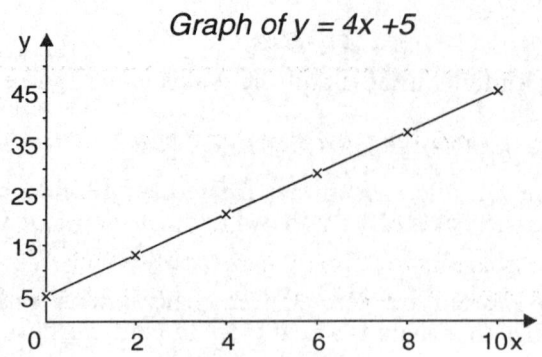

Graph of y = 4x +5

The intercept and the slope

8.7   The graph of a linear equation is determined by two things, the gradient (or slope) of the straight line and the point at which the straight line crosses the y axis.

8.8   The point at which the straight line crosses the y axis is known as the intercept. Look back at Paragraph 8.6. The intercept of $y = 4x + 5$ is $(0, 5)$. It is no coincidence that the intercept is the same as the constant represented by a in the general form of the equation $y = a + bx$. a is the value y takes when $x = 0$, in other words a constant, and so is represented on a graph by the point $(0, a)$.

8.9   The gradient of the graph of a linear equation is $(y_2 - y_1)/(x_2 - x_1)$ where (x_1, y_1) and (x_2, y_2) are two points on the straight line.

The slope of $y = 4x + 5 = (21 - 13)/(4 - 2) = 8/2 = 4$ where $(x_1, y_1) = (2, 13)$ and $(x_2, y_2) = (4, 21)$

Exercise 10

Find the gradient of $y = 10 - x$.

Solution

Gradient = –1

8.10   Note that the gradient of $y = 4x + 5$ is positive whereas the gradient of $y = 10 - x$ is negative. A positive gradient slopes upwards from left to right whereas a negative gradient slopes downwards from left to right. The greater the value of the gradient, the steeper the slope.

8.11   Just as the intercept can be found by inspection of the linear equation, so can the gradient. It is represented by the coefficient of x (b in the general form of the equation). The slope of the graph $y = 7x - 3$ is therefore 7 and the slope of the graph $y = 3,597 - 263x$ is –263.

Exercise 11

Find the intercept and slope of the graph of $4y = 16x - 12$.

Solution

$4y = 16x - 12$

Equation must be form $y = a + bx$

$y = -\dfrac{12}{4} + \dfrac{16}{4}x = -3 + 4x$

Intercept = a = –3 ie (0, –3)

Slope = 4

9   SIMULTANEOUS AND NON-LINEAR EQUATIONS

Simultaneous equations

9.1   Simultaneous equations are two or more equations which are satisfied by the same variable values. For example, we might have the following two linear equations.

$$y = 3x + 16$$
$$2y = x + 72$$

9.2   There are two unknown values, x and y, and there are two different equations which both involve x and y. There are as many equations as there are unknowns and so we can find the values of x and y.

Graphical solution

9.3   One way of finding a solution is by a graph. If both equations are satisfied together, the values of x and y must be those where the straight line graphs of the two equations intersect.

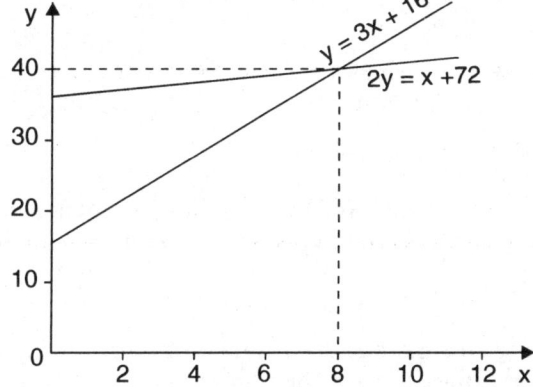

Since both equations are satisfied, the values of x and y must lie on both the lines. Since this happens only once, at the intersection of the lines, the value of x must be 8, and of y 40.

Algebraic solution

9.4   A more common method of solving simultaneous equations is by algebra.

(a)   Returning to the original equations, we have:

$$y = 3x + 16 \qquad (1)$$
$$2y = x + 72 \qquad (2)$$

(b)   Rearranging these, we have:

$$y - 3x = 16 \qquad (3)$$
$$2y - x = 72 \qquad (4)$$

(c)   If we now multiply equation (4) by 3, so that the coefficient for x becomes the same as in equation (3) we get:

$$6y - 3x \quad = 216 \qquad (5)$$
$$y - 3x \quad = 16 \qquad (3)$$

(d)   Subtracting (3) from (5) we get:

$$5y \quad = 200$$
$$y \quad = 40$$

(e)   Substituting 40 for y in any equation, we can derive a value for x. Thus substituting in equation (4) we get:

$$2(40) - x = 72$$
$$80 - 72 = x$$
$$8 = x$$

(f)   The solution is y = 40, x = 8.

Exercise 12

Solve the following simultaneous equations using algebra.

$$5x + 2y = 34$$
$$x + 3y = 25$$

Solution

5x + 2y	= 34	(1)
x + 3y	= 25	(2)
5x + 15y	= 125	(3) 5 × (2)
13y	= 91	(4) (3) – (1)
y	= 7	
x + 21	= 25	Substitute into (2)
x	= 25 – 21	
x	= 4	

The solution is x = 4, y = 7.

Non-linear equations

9.5   In the previous sections we have been looking at equations in which the highest power of the unknown variable(s) is one (that is, the equation contains x, y but not x^2, y^3 and so on).

9.6   We are now going to turn our attention to non-linear equations in which one variable varies with the nth power of another, where n > 1. The following are examples of non-linear equations.

$$y = x^2; \quad y = 3x^3 + 2; \quad 2y = 5x^4 - 6; \quad y = -x^{12} + 3$$

9.7   It is common for a non-linear equation to include a number of terms, all to different powers. Here are some examples.

$$y = x^2 + 6x + 10 \qquad\qquad y = -12x^9 + 3x^6 + 6x^3 + 3x^2 - 1$$
$$2y = 3x^3 - 4x^2 - 8x + 10 \qquad\qquad 3y = 22x^8 + 7x^7 + 3x^4 - 12$$

9.8   Non-linear equations can be expressed in the form

$$y = ax^n + bx^{n-1} + cx^{n-2} + dx^{n-3} + ... + \text{constant}.$$ Consider the following equation.

$$y = -12x^9 + 3x^6 + 6x^3 + 2x^2 - 1,$$

In this equation a = –12, b = 0, c = 0, d = 3, e = 0, f = 0, g = 6, h = 2, i = 0, constant = –1 and n = 9.

Graphing non-linear equations

9.9   The graph of a linear equation, as we saw earlier, is a straight line. The graph of a non-linear equation, on the other hand, is *not* a straight line. Let us consider an example.

Example: graphing non-linear equations

9.10   Graph the equation $y = -2x^3 + x^2 - 2x + 10$.

Solution

9.11   The graph of this equation can be plotted in the same way as the graph of a linear equation is plotted. Take a selection of values of x, calculate the corresponding values of y, plot the pairs of values and join the points together. The joining must be done using as smooth a curve as possible.

x	–3	–2	–1	0	1	2	3
$-2x$	6	4	2	0	–2	–4	–6
x^2	9	4	1	0	1	4	9
$-2x^3$	54	16	2	0	–2	–16	–54
10	10	10	10	10	10	10	10
y	79	34	15	10	7	–6	–41

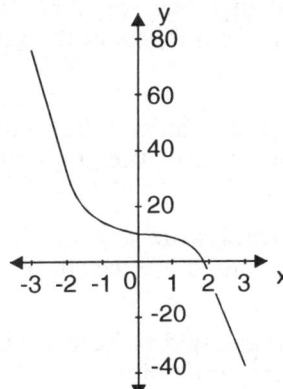

Quadratic equations

9.12   Quadratic equations are a type of non-linear equation in which one variable varies with the square (or second power) of the other variable. The following equations are all quadratic equations.

$$y = x^2 \qquad y = 5x^2 + 7 \qquad 2y = -2x^2 - 3 \qquad y = -x^2 + 3$$

9.13   A quadratic equation may include both a term involving the square and also a term involving the first power of a variable. Here are some examples.

$$y = x^2 + 6x + 10 \qquad 2y = 3x^2 - 4x - 8 \qquad y = 2x^2 + 3x + 6$$

9.14   All quadratic equations can be expressed in the form $y = ax^2 + bx + c$. For instance, in the equation $y = 3x^2 + 2x - 6$, a = 3, b = 2, c = –6.

Graphing a quadratic equation

9.15   The graph of a quadratic equation can be plotted using the same method as that illustrated in Paragraph 9.11.

Example: graphing a quadratic equation

9.16   Graph the equation $y = -2x^2 + x - 3$.

Solution

9.17

x	−3	−2	−1	0	1	2	3
−2x²	−18	−8	−2	0	−2	−8	−18
−3	−3	−3	−3	−3	−3	−3	−3
y	−24	−13	−6	−3	−4	−9	−18

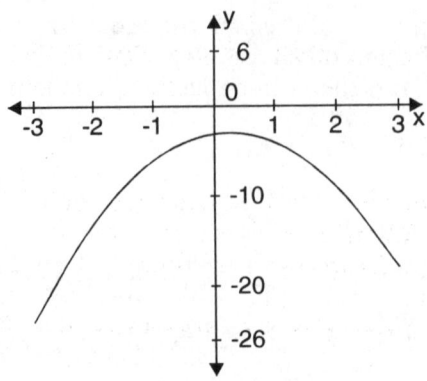

9.18   Graphs shaped like that in Paragraph 9.17 are sometimes referred to as parabolas and both illustrate a number of points about the graph of the equation

$$y = ax^2 + bx + c.$$

(a)   The constant term 'c' determines the value of y at the point where the curve crosses the y axis (the intercept). In the graph above, c = −3 and the curve crosses the y axis at y = −3.

(b)   The sign of 'a' determines the way up the curve appears. If a is positive, the curve is shaped like a ditch, but if a is negative, as in Paragraph 9.17, the curve is shaped like a bell.

A ditch-shaped curve is said to have a minimum point whereas a bell-shaped curve is said to have a maximum point.

(c)   The graph enables us to find the values of x when y = 0 (if there are any). In other words the graph allows us to solve the quadratic equation $0 = ax^2 + bx + c$.

For the curve in Paragraph 9.17 we see that there are no such values (that is, $0 = -2x^2 + x - 3$ cannot be solved).

Solving quadratic equations

9.19   The graphical method is not, in practice, the most efficient way to determine the solution of a quadratic equation. Many quadratic equations have two values of x (called 'solutions for x' or ' roots of the equation') which satisfy the equation for any particular value of y. These values can be found using the following formula.

$$\text{If } ax^2 + bx + c = 0 \text{ then } x = \frac{-b \pm \sqrt{(b^2 - 4ac)}}{2a}$$

Example: quadratic equations

9.20   Solve $x^2 + x - 2 = 0$.

Solution

9.21 $$x = \frac{-1 \pm \sqrt{\left(1^2 - \left(4 \times 1 \times (-2)\right)\right)}}{2 \times 1} = \frac{-1 \pm \sqrt{(1 + 8)}}{2} = \frac{-1 \pm 3}{2}$$

$$\therefore x = \frac{-4}{2} \text{ or } \frac{2}{2} \text{ ie } x = -2 \text{ or } x = 1$$

Quadratic equations with a single value for x

9.22   Sometimes, $b^2 - 4ac = 0$, and so there is only one solution to the quadratic equation. Let us solve $x^2 + 2x + 1 = 0$.

$$x = \frac{-2 \pm \sqrt{(2^2 - (4 \times 1 \times 1))}}{2} = \frac{-2 \pm 0}{2} = -1$$

This quadratic equation can only be solved by one value of x.

Cost behaviour, equations and graphs

9.23   You are expected to be able to deal with cost behaviour based on both linear and non-linear functions. Attempt the following exercises to ensure that you are able to apply the principles you learnt in Chapter 2 (on cost behaviour) to those in this chapter.

Exercise 13

A company manufactures a product. The total fixed costs are £75 and the variable cost per unit is £5.

Required

(a)   Find an expression for total costs in terms of q, the quantity produced.
(b)   Use your answer to (a) to determine the total costs if 100 units are produced.
(c)   Prepare a graph of the expression for total costs.
(d)   Use your graph to determine the total cost if 75 units are produced.

Solution

(a)   Let   C = total costs
              C = total variable costs + total fixed costs
              C = 5q + 75

(b)   If q = 100, C = (5 × 100) + 75 = £575

(c)   If q = 0,   C = £75
      If q = 100,   C = £575

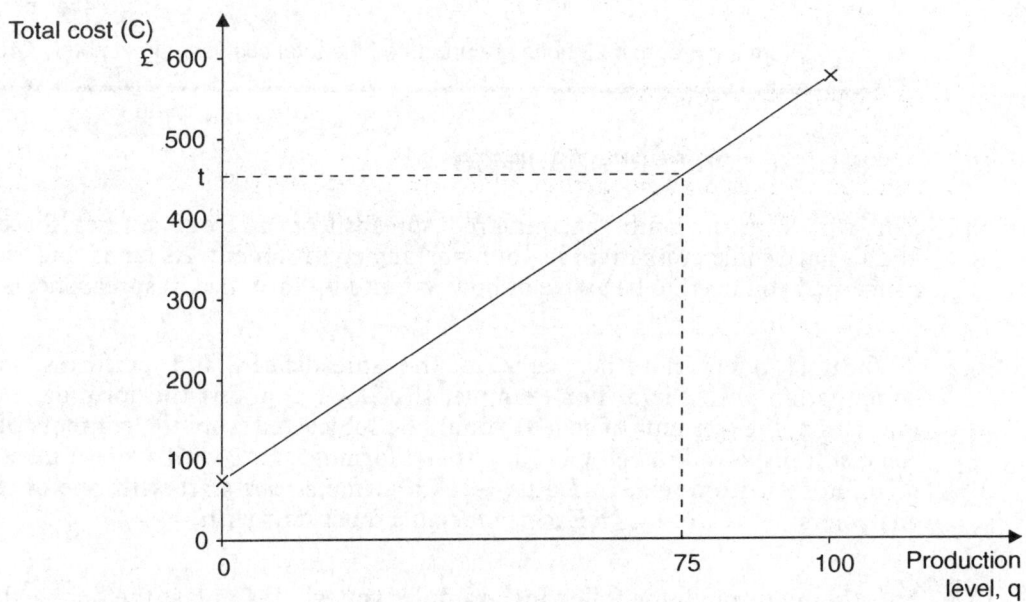

(d)   From graph above, if q = 75, C = £450

Exercise 14

A company manufactures a product, the total cost function for the product being given by C = (25 − q)q, where q is the quantity produced and C is in £.

Required

(a)   Calculate the total costs if 15 units are produced.

(b)   Draw a graph of the total cost function and use it to calculate the total cost if 23 units are produced.

Solution

(a) $C = (25 - q)q$

If $q = 15$, $C = (25 - 15) \times 15 = 10 \times 15 = £150$

(b)

q	C
0	0
5.0	100.00
10.0	150.00
12.5	156.25
15.0	150.00
20.0	100.00
25.0	0

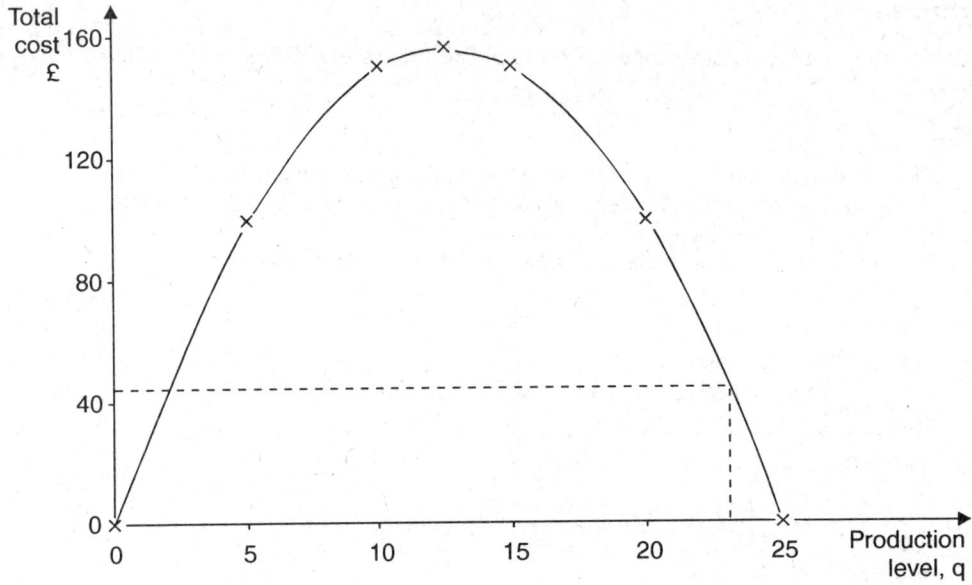

From the graph, if 23 units are produced the total cost is approximately £45.

10   FORMULAE FOR SPREADSHEETS

10.1   You will have no doubt encountered spreadsheets in your studies for other papers and/or have come cross them in your working environment. As far as this examination is concerned you need to be aware of how to build up formulae in spreadsheets.

10.2   A formula refers to other cells in the spreadsheet, and performs some sort of computation with them. For example, if cell C1 contains the formula +A1 –B1 this means that the contents of cell B1 should be subtracted from the contents of cell A1 and the result displayed in cell C1. Note that a formula starts with a '+' in most packages to distinguish it from text. In Lotus 1-2-3, a formula *must* start with one of the following characters: +, –, $ or @. In Excel, a formula must start with =.

10.3   By working through the following examples you will assimilate the knowledge required.

Example: easy spreadsheet formulae

10.4   Below is a spreadsheet processing budgeted sales figures for three geographic areas for the first quarter of the year.

	A	B	C	D	E
1		JAN	FEB	MARCH	TOTAL
2	NORTH	2,431	3,001	2,189	7,621
3	SOUTH	6,532	5,826	6,124	18,482
4	WEST	895	432	596	1,923
5	TOTAL	9,858	9,259	8,909	28,026
6					
7					
8					

Required

What formula would you put in the following cells.

(a)   Cell B5
(b)   Cell E4
(c)   Cell E5

Solution

10.5   (a)   + B2 + B3 + B4
     (b)   + B4 + C4 + D4
     (c)   Either + E2 + E3 + E4 or + B5 + C5 + D5

Example: formulae in a balance sheet model

10.6   Consider the balance sheet model shown below.

	A	B	C	D	E
1			£'000	£'000	
2					
3	Fixed assets: cost				
4	Accumulated depreciation				
5	Net book value				
6	*Current assets:*				
7	Stocks				
8	Debtors				
9	Cash				
10					
11	*Current liabilities:*				
12	Overdraft				
13	Creditors				
14	Taxation				
15					
16	Net current assets				
17					
18	Net assets				

Required

Note the formulae required for this balance sheet.

Solution

10.7   (a)   In cell C10:   + C7 + C8 + C9
     (b)   In cell C15:   + C12 + C13 + C14
     (c)   In cell D5:   + D3 – D4
     (d)   In cell D16:   + C10 – C15
     (e)   In cell D18:   +D5 + D16 (alternatively + D5 + C10 – C15)

More complicated formulae

10.8   So far we have used a formula to add and subtract. Formulae can be used to perform a variety of calculations. Here are some examples.

(a)   +C4*5. This formula multiplies the value in C4 by 5. The result will appear in the cell holding the formula.

(b)   +C4*B10. This multiplies the value in C4 by the value in B10.

(c)   +C4/E5. This divides the value in C4 by the value in E5. (Note that * means multiply and / means divide by.)

(d)   +C4*B10 – D1. This multiples the value in C4 by that in B10 and then deducts the value in D1 from the result. Note that generally the computer will perform multiplication before addition or subtraction.

(e)   +C4+17.5%. This adds 17.5% to the value in C4. It could be used to calculate a price including $17^1/_2$% VAT.

(f)   + (C4+C5+C6)/3. This, in effect, calculates the average of the values in C4, C5 and C6. Note that the brackets tell the computer to perform the addition first. Without the brackets the computer would first divide the value in C6 by 3 and then add the result to the total of the values in C4 and C5.

(g)   If may be quicker, when totalling a long row or column of figures, to use the formula @ SUM (B2..B12).

Example: more complicated formulae

10.9   The following four insurance salesmen earn a basic salary of £14,000 pa. They also earn a commission of 2% of sales. The following spreadsheet has been created to process their commission and total earnings.

	A	B	C	D	E
1	*Salesmen:*	*Salary and commission*			
2	*Name*	*Sales*	*Salary*	*Commission*	*Total earnings*
3					
4	*Ken*	284,000	14,000	5,680	19,680
5	*Mike*	193,000	14,000	3,860	17,860
6	*Alf*	12,000	14,000	240	14,240
7	*Jack*	152,000	14,000	3,040	17,040
8					
9	*Total*	641,000	56,000	12,820	68,820

Required

Give an appropriate formula for the following cells.

(a)   Cell D4
(b)   Cell E6
(c)   Cell D9
(d)   Cell E9

Solution

10.10 (a)   +B4*0.02

(b)   +C6+D6

(c)   +D4+D5+D6+D7; or @SUM(D4..D7)

(d)   One of the following would be suitable

(i)   +E4+E5+E6+E7
(ii)   @SUM(E4..E7)
(iii)   +B9+C9+D9
(iv)   @SUM(B9..D9)

10.11 Note that a formula which calculates a percentage of a value such as commission as a percentage of sales, could be used in preparing a payroll. For example, national insurance or pension contributions may be a set percentage of salary.

10.12 A business will often need to compare its results with budgets or targets to see how far it has exceeded, or fallen short of, its expectations. It is useful to express variations as a percentage of the original target, for example sales may be 10% higher than predicted.

Example: spreadsheet formulae involving percentage differences

10.13 Continuing the example of the insurance salesmen, a spreadsheet could be set up as follows showing differences between actual sales and target sales, and expressing the difference as a percentage of target sales.

	A	B	C	D	E	F
1	Salesmen:	Actual sales v target sales				
2	Name	Target sales	Actual sales	Difference	Difference as a % of target	
3						
4	Ken	275,000	284,000	9,000	3.27	
5	Mike	200,000	193,000	-7,000	-3.50	
6	Alf	10,000	12,000	2,000	20.00	
7	Jack	153,000	152,000	-1,000	-0.65	
8						
9	Total	638,000	641,000	3,000	0.47	
10						
11						

Required

Give a suitable formula for the following cells.

(a)   Cell D4
(b)   Cell E6
(c)   Cell E9

Solution

10.14 (a)   +C4 – B4

(b)   (D6/B6)*100. With some spreadsheets, for example Lotus 1-2-3, you do not need to use brackets because the formula automatically operates from left to right where you have both multiplication and division. The formula would thus be +D6/B6*100.

(c)   (D9/B9)*100 or +D9/B9*100. Note that in (c) you cannot simply add up the individual percentage differences. This is because the percentages are based on very different quantities. For example, Alf has exceeded his target by 20%, but this is only £2,000, while Ken's 3.27% difference is actually £9,000. You should always use common sense in thinking about any formula you choose to put in.

Spreadsheets and budgets

10.15 You need to have an awareness of a specific spreadsheet application, that of budgeting. Read through the following example to give you an idea of how to set up a spreadsheet which will assist in the budgeting process.

10.16 The cost accountant of a small company wishes to computerise his cash flow projections using a spreadsheet package. The cash flow projection is to provide a monthly cash flow analysis over a five-year period. The following data is relevant.

(a)   Initial cash held by company on 1 January 19X1 is expected to be £15,000.

(b) Sales in January are expected to be £25,000, and a growth rate of 2% per month in sales is predicted throughout the forecast period.

(c) The company buys stock one month in advance and pays in cash.

(d) On average, payment is received from customers as follows.

    (i)   60% one month in arrears
    (ii)   40% two months in arrears

    All sales are on credit. There are no bad debts.

(e) The cost of sales is 65% of sales value. Overhead costs (cash expenses) are expected to be £6,500 per month, rising by 5% at the start of each new calendar year.

(f) Purchases of capital equipment and payments of tax, interest charges and dividends must also be provided for within the model. The interest rate on bank overdrafts is expected to be 1% per month.

Inserting text

10.17 The first job is to put in the various headings that you want on the model. This is done by means of a facility within the program which enables you to specify the text for any column, combined columns or rows of data. (It is usually convenient to start the tabulation at row 1 and column A, although this is not essential).

10.18 The cost accountant might decide to label the spreadsheet rows and columns as follows.

	: A	: B	: C	: D	: E	: F	:
1:		19X1					
2:		Jan	Feb	March	April	May	
3:		£	£	£	£	£	
4:	Sales						
5:	Cash receipts						
6:	One month in arrears						
7:	Two months in arrears						
8:	Three months in arrears						
9:	Total receipts						
10:							
11:	Cash payments						
12:	Stock						
13:	Overheads						
14:	Interest						
15:	Tax						
16:	Dividends						
17:	Capital purchases						
18:	Total payments						
19:							
20:	Cash receipts less payments						
21:	Balance b/f						
22:	Balance c/f						

Inserting formulae

10.19 The next stage in constructing a model is to put in the calculations you want the computer to carry out, expressed as formulae. The formulae required can be constructed in a variety of ways. One way would be to insert some 'constant' values into cells of the spreadsheet.

	Column	
	A	*B*
Row		
23:	Sales growth factor per month	1.02
24:	Interest rate per month	0.01
25:	Debts paid within 1 month	0.6
26:	Debts paid within 2 months	0.4
27:	Debts paid within 3 months	0
28:	Bad debts	0
29:	Cost of sales as proportion of sales	0.65

Alternatively, these values could be specified in the formulae in the spreadsheet.

10.20 Unlike the text, these formulae will not be shown on the spreadsheet itself, but at the bottom of the screen. So at this stage, the spreadsheet looks just the same as it did after setting up the headings - but when the cursor is on a cell where a formula has been input, then that formula is shown at the bottom of the screen.

10.21 Examples of constructing formulae for the spreadsheet are as follows.

(a) The formulae for sales in February 19X1, in this example, would be (+B4*B23), in March 19X1 (+ C4*B23), in April 19X1 (+ D4*B23) and so on. Replication of the formula could be used to save input time.

(b) The formula for cash receipts in April 19X1 would be:

E6 = +D4*B25
E7 = +C4*B26
E8 = +B4*B27
E9 = +E6 + E7 + E8

(c) Cash payments for stock would be expressed as the cost of sales in the previous month; for February 19X1, this would be:

C12 = +B4*B29

(d) Total cash payments in May 19X1 would be the sum of cells F12 to F17.

F18 = @ SUM (F12..F17)

Inserting numerical data

10.22 The last stage in setting up a spreadsheet is to input data. Input data would include the opening cash balance on 1 January 19X1, dividend and tax payments, capital purchases, sales in January 19X1, the constant values (in our example in column B, rows 23 to 29) and the other data needed to establish cash receipts and payments in the first month or so of the forecast period (for example, receipts in January 19X1 will depend on sales in November and December 19X0, which the simplified model shown here has not provided for). With this input data, and the spreadsheet formulae, a full cash flow projection for the five-year period can be produced and, if required, printed out.

11 GEOMETRIC PROGRESSIONS

11.1 A geometric progression is a sequence of numbers in which there is a common or constant ratio between adjacent terms. Examples are as follows.

(a) 2, 4, 8, 16, 32, where there is a common ratio of 2.

(b) 121, 110, 100, 90.91, 82.64, where (allowing for rounding differences in the fourth and fifth terms) there is a common ratio of 1/1.1 = 0.9091.

11.2   An algebraic representation of a geometric progression is as follows.

A, AR, AR^2, AR^3, AR^4,..., AR^{n-1}

where A is the first term
   R is the common ratio
   n is the number of terms

Example: a geometric progression

11.3   A sales manager has reported that sales in the next year will amount to 5,000 units of product. He also estimates that sales will then increase in volume by 40% a year until year 6. What sales volume would be expected in year 6?

Solution

11.4   We require the sixth term in the geometric progression.

A = year 1 sales = 5,000
R = rate of growth = 140% (Note that R = 140% or 1.4, not 40% or 0.4.)
n = 6
T_6 = $5,000 \times 1.4^{(6-1)}$
   = $5,000 \times 5.37824$
   = 26,891.2 units (say 26,891 units)

The sum of a geometric progression

11.5   It is sometimes necessary to calculate the sum of the terms in a geometric progression. For example, suppose that a factory expects to produce 4,000 units in week 1 and to increase output by 20% each week for three more weeks.

Total output in the four weeks = 4,000 + 4,800 + 5,760 + 6,912 = 21,472 units

11.6   The calculation is relatively straightforward when the progression consists of a small number of terms. However, when we wish to calculate the sum of longer geometric progressions, it is easier to use a formula.

11.7   The formula for the sum (S) of a geometric progression is derived as follows.

$$S = A + AR + AR^2 + AR^3 + ... + AR^{n-1} \qquad (1)$$

Multiply both sides of the equation by R to give:

$$RS = AR + AR^2 + AR^3 + ... + AR^n \qquad (2)$$

Subtract (1) from (2).

$$RS - S = AR^n - A$$

$$\therefore S(R-1) = A(R^n - 1)$$

$$\therefore S = \frac{A(R^n - 1)}{R-1}$$

11.8   In the example in Paragraph 11.5, we have the following.

$$S = 4,000 + 4,000 \times 1.2 + 4,000 \times 1.2^2 + 4,000 \times 1.2^3$$

$$1.2S = 4,000 \times 1.2 + 4,000 \times 1.2^2 + 4,000 \times 1.2^3 + 4,000 \times 1.2^4$$

$$1.2S - S = (4,000 \times 1.2^4) - 4,000$$

$$S = \frac{4,000(1.2^4 - 1)}{(1.2 - 1)}$$

$$= +21,472 \text{ units}$$

11.9   You will need to know how to deal with geometric progressions when you study financial mathematics in Chapters 25 and 26.

12   LOGARITHMS

12.1   Your calculator might well enable you to work out complex values with little difficulty. For example, if you want the value of 1.12^{15} it could be a simple matter of entering two values into your calculator to obtain an answer.

12.2   However, when sophisticated calculators are unavailable, logarithms are one way of doing compounding arithmetic relatively easily. Furthermore, knowledge of logarithms enables us to ascertain the rate of change of a variable over time. Let us start by seeing what logarithms actually are.

12.3   The figure 10 can be expressed as 10^1. Similarly,

$$\begin{aligned}
100 \quad &\text{can be expressed as } 10^2 \\
1,000 \quad &\text{can be expressed as } 10^3 \\
10,000 \quad &\text{can be expressed as } 10^4 \\
1 \quad &\text{can be expressed as } 10^0
\end{aligned}$$

and so on.

To multiply 100 by 1,000, one way of expressing the calculation is

$$\begin{aligned}
100 \times 1,000 = 10^2 \times 10^3 \ &= 10^{(2+3)} \\
&= 10^5 \\
&= 10,000
\end{aligned}$$

12.4   Logarithms work on the same principle.

Every number can be converted into 10 to a certain power. For example:

$$\begin{aligned}
2 \ &= 10^{0.3010} \\
20 \ &= 10^{1.3010} \\
200 \ &= 10^{2.3010}
\end{aligned}$$

How do we know this?

(a)   Any value between 1 (10^0) and 10 (10^1) must have a 'to a certain power' value between 0 and 1.

(b)   Similarly, any value between 10 (10^1) and 100 (10^2) must have a 'to a certain power' value between 1 and 2.

(c)   Again, any value between 100 (10^2) and 1,000 (10^3) must have a 'to a certain power' value between 2 and 3.

This explains the figures to the left of the decimal points.

The value to the right of the decimal points, for 2, 20, 200 and indeed for 2,000, 20,000, 0.2, 0.02 and so on, is the same, and it is found by looking it up in logarithm tables. Tables are shown in the Appendix at the back of the Study Text. For 2, we look at row 20, column 0 and find .3010.

12.5   Here are some more examples to illustrate the use of logarithm tables.

(a)   (i)   The logarithm of 2.4 is 0.3802.

         The value to the left of the decimal point is 0 because we want the logarithm of a figure between 1 and 10.

         The value to the right of the decimal point is found from the tables, row 24, column 0.

   (ii)   The logarithm of 24 is 1.3802.

   (iii)   The logarithm of 240 is 2.3802.

(b)   The logarithm of 2.45 is 0.3892. The value to the right of the decimal point is found from the tables, row 24, column 5.

(c)   The logarithm of 24.8 is 1.3945. The value to the right of the decimal point is found from the tables, row 24, column 8.

(d)   What about the logarithm of 2.026? The value to the right of the decimal point is found from the tables by starting at row 20 column 2 (0.3054) and then looking at the columns 1-9 on the far right of the table for the value in column 6, which is 13. This is added to the 3054 to get 3067, and the logarithm of 2.026 is 0.3067.

12.6   To convert a logarithm answer back to a 'normal' number, we can again use tables.

(a)   There are antilogarithm tables, similar to logarithm tables, but which are used to convert logarithms back to normal numbers.

(b)   Alternatively, you can find the solution by looking for the logarithm within the logarithm tables.

Logarithms of values between 0 and 1

12.7   We know that $10^0 = 1$ and $10^{-1} = 0.1$.

It follows that numbers between 0.1 and 1 ought to have logarithms between 0 and –1.

Similarly, since $10^{-2} = 0.01$, it follows that numbers between 0.01 and 0.1 ought to have logarithms between –1 and –2.

12.8   This is so. The logarithm of 0.2 is written $\bar{1}.3010$, pronounced 'bar one point 3010'.

The bar means minus and so $\bar{1} = -1$, $\bar{2} = -2$ and so on. So the logarithm of 0.2, which is $\bar{1}.3010$, is minus 1 *plus* 0.3010.

(a)   Any figure from 0.1 up to just less than 1 has a logarithm with $\bar{1}$ to the left of the decimal point.

(b)   Any figure from 0.01 up to just less than 0.1 has a logarithm with $\bar{2}$ to the left of the decimal point.

(c)   Similarly, any figure from 0.001 up to just less than 0.01 has a logarithm with $\bar{3}$ to the left of the decimal point.

Logarithms and the examination

12.9   Logarithm tables will be provided in the examination and we have worked through this section using tables since this provides a greater understanding of how logarithms are devised.

In the examination you can, of course, use your calculator. Most calculators do not use the $\bar{1}$, $\bar{2}$ system but give you negative numbers where appropriate (–0.3979 for log 0.4).

Chapter roundup

- This chapter has covered the basic mathematics which you will need to understand before attempting the quantitative methods section of this Study Text.

- Brackets indicate a priority or an order in which calculations should be made.

- The negative number rules are as follows.

$$-p + q = q - p$$

$$q - (-p) = q + p$$

$$-p \times -q = pq \text{ and } \frac{-p}{-q} = \frac{p}{q}$$

$$-p \times q = -pq \text{ and } \frac{-p}{q} = \frac{-p}{q}$$

- The reciprocal of a number is 1 divided by that number.

- Percentages are used to indicate the relative size or proportion of items, rather than their absolute size. To turn a percentage into a fraction or decimal you divide by 100%. To turn a fraction or decimal back into a percentage you multiply by 100%

- A percentage increase or reduction is calculated as (difference ÷ initial value) × 100%.

- A proportion means writing a percentage as a proportion of 1 (that is, as a decimal).

- Ratios show relative shares of a whole.

- The nth root of a number is a value which, when multiplied by itself $(n-1)$ times, equals the original number. Powers work the other way round.

- When we use letters to stand for any numbers we call them variables. The use of variables enables us to state general truths about mathematics.

- The general rule for solving equations is that you can do what you like to one side of an equation, so long as you do the same thing to the other side straightaway.

- A linear equation has the general form $y = a + bx$, where x is the independent variable and y the dependent variable, and a and b are fixed amounts.

- Make sure that you are aware of the rules for drawing graphs.

- The graph of a linear equation is a straight line. The intercept of the line on the y axis is a in $y = a + bx$ and the slope of the line is b.

- Simultaneous equations are two or more equations which are satisfied by the same variable values. They can be solved graphically or algebraically.

- In non-linear equations, one variable varies with the nth power of another, where n> 1. The graph of a non-linear equation is *not* a straight line.

- Quadratic equations are non-linear equations in which one variable varies with the square of the other variable.

  Formulae for spreadsheets follow a particular format. Ensure that you are able to construct formulae which incorporate addition, subtraction, multiplication, division and percentage differences.

- A geometric progression is a sequence of numbers in which there is a common ratio between adjacent terms.

- The logarithm of a number is the power to which 10 has to be raised to get that number.

- Make sure that you have worked through all of the examples in this chapter since it provides the foundation for the remainder of the Study Text.

Test your knowledge

1   Is $3^3/_4$ an integer? (see para 1.1)

2   What is 1004.002955 to nine significant digits? (1.3, 1.4)

3   What is the product of a negative number and a negative number? (2.7)

4    $217 \leq 217$. True or false? (2.10)

5   How do you turn a fraction into a percentage? (4.3)

6   Define the nth root of a number. (5.2)

7   What is the difference between a formula and an equation? (6.6)

8   What is a linear equation? (7.1)

9   What are the rules for drawing graphs? (8.2 - 8.4)

10   What is the intercept? (8.8)

11   What are quadratic equations? (9.12)

12   What quick formula could you use to total the values in calls F15 to F27 in a spreadsheet? (10.8)

13   What is geometric progression? (11.1)

14   What is the formula for the sum of a geometric progression? (11.7)

15   What is the logarithm of 550.77? (Use your calculator.)

Now try illustrative question 17 at the end of the Study Text

Chapter 17

ACCURACY AND APPROXIMATION

This chapter covers the following topics.

		Syllabus reference	Ability required
1	Rounding	2(e)	Skill
2	Maximum errors	2(e)	Skill
3	Errors and calculations	2(e)	Skill

Introduction

Having covered basic mathematical ideas and techniques in the previous chapter, we are now going to turn our attention to a number of concepts which you must bear in mind when you read the remaining chapters in this Study Text. These concepts relate to approximation.

Approximation arises for two principal reasons. It is often not possible to obtain an accurate value for a large number (such as the population of a town) and some figures may only be easily measurable to the nearest whole number (for example the speed of a car). Sometimes, on the other hand, it may not be necessary or desirable to express data as accurately as they can be measured. In such circumstances numbers are rounded.

Obviously when calculations are made using rounded data, errors may be introduced into the results of the calculations and any subsequent conclusions drawn. Having looked at how numbers can be rounded we will turn our attention to the types of errors that can occur and look at how we can take account of such errors in calculations using rounded data.

Once you have completed this chapter we will be moving away from basic mathematics on to specific quantitative methods, beginning with ways of summarising and analysing data.

1   ROUNDING

1.1   There are three methods of rounding and these will be illustrated using the figure 18,600.

  (a) *Rounding up:* 18,600 would be expressed as 19,000 to the nearest thousand above.

  (b) *Rounding down:* 18,600 would be expressed as 18,000 to the nearest thousand below.

  (c) *Rounding to the nearest round amount:* 18,600 would be expressed as 19,000 to the nearest thousand.

Method (c) is the most commonly used.

In rounding to the nearest unit, a value ending in 0.5 is usually rounded up. Thus 3.5 rounded to the nearest unit would be 4.

1.2   Rounding can be specified to the nearest whole unit (as above), by the number of decimal places (3.94712 to 2 decimal places is 3.95), or by the number of significant digits (as covered in Chapter 16).

Exercise 1

(a) What is £482,365.15 to the nearest:

    (i)   £1

    (ii)   £100

    (iii)   £1,000

    (iv)   £10,000?

(b) What is 843.668 correct to:

    (i)   one decimal place

    (ii)   two decimal places?

(c) What is 628.0273 to:

    (i)   five significant figures

    (ii)   four significant figures?

Solution

(a) (i)   £482,365   (b) (i)   843.7   (c) (i)   628.03

    (ii)   £482,400   (ii)   843.67   (ii)   628.0

    (iii)   £482,000

    (iv)   £480,000

Spurious accuracy

1.3   Spurious accuracy arises when a statistic gives the impression that it is more accurate than it really is. For example we might see stated '24.68% of women over the age of 30 are smokers'. This result is probably based on a sample and so we know that it cannot be as accurate as it seems: the two decimal places have arisen simply because of the arithmetic of the calculations. It would be less misleading to state 'approximately 25% of women over the age of 30 are smokers'. This removes the spurious accuracy implied by the decimal places.

2   MAXIMUM ERRORS   *11/96*

Absolute errors

2.1   Suppose that the population of a country is stated as 40 million. It is quite likely that this figure has been rounded to the nearest million. We could therefore say that the country's population is

     40 million $\pm$ 500,000

where 40 million is the *estimate* of the population and 500,000 is the *maximum absolute error.*

2.2   In general terms an estimate with a maximum absolute error can be expressed as a $\pm$ b.

Relative errors

2.3   The error in the population of the country could also be expressed as

     40 million $\pm$ 1.25%

where 500,000 is 1.25% of 40 million. In this instance the maximum error is a *maximum relative error* and is calculated as $\dfrac{\text{maximum absolute error}}{\text{estimate}} \times 100\%$.

3   ERRORS AND CALCULATIONS   *11/96*

3.1   If calculations are made using values that have been rounded then the results of such calculations will only be approximate. However, provided that we are aware of the maximum errors that can occur, we can still draw conclusions from the results of the calculations.

3.2 There are two rules to remember when performing calculations involving rounded or approximate numbers.

(a) *Addition/subtraction*

When two or more rounded or approximate numbers are added or subtracted the *maximum absolute error* in the result equals the sum of the individual maximum absolute errors.

(b) *Multiplication/division*

When two or more rounded or approximate numbers are multiplied or divided, the *approximate maximum relative error* in the result is obtained by adding the individual maximum relative errors.

We will use an example to illustrate these rules.

Example: errors

3.3 A chemical producer plans to sell 50,000 litres (to the nearest 1,000 litres) of a particular chemical at a price of £10 (to the nearest pound) per litre.

The cost of materials used to produce the chemicals is expected to be £100,000 but depending on wastage levels this is subject to an error of ± 5%. Labour costs are estimated to be £300,000 ± 10%, depending on overtime working and pay negotiations.

Required

Calculate the maximum absolute error and the maximum relative error in revenue and costs of production.

Solution

3.4

	Estimate	Maximum absolute error	Maximum relative error %
Quantity sold	50,000 litres	500 litres	1
Price	£10	£0.50	5
Materials	£100,000	£5,000	5
Labour	£300,000	£30,000	10

(a) Revenue = quantity sold × price
= (50,000 ± 1%) × (£10 ± 5%)
= (50,000 × £10) ± (1% + 5%)
= £500,000 ± 6%
= £500,000 ± £30,000

∴ Approximate maximum absolute error = £30,000

Approximate maximum relative error = 6%

Note that we need to use relative errors when doing multiplication/division calculations.

(b) Costs of production = material + labour
= (£100,000 ± £5,000) + (£300,000 ± £30,000)
= (£100,000 + £300,000) ± (£5,000 + £30,000)
= £400,000 ± £35,000
= £400,000 ± 8.75 %

∴ Maximum absolute error = £35,000

Maximum relative error = 8.75%

Note that we need to use absolute errors when doing addition/subtraction calculations.

3.5   The rule in Paragraph 3.2(b) above only gives an approximate maximum relative error. Let's see what the actual error would have been in Paragraph 3.4(b) above.

Maximum revenue = maximum quantity × maximum price

$$= (50,000 + 1\%) \times (£10 + 5\%)$$

$$= 50,500 \times £10.50$$

$$= £530,250$$

∴ Our approximation of the maximum absolute error was correct to within £(530,250 − 530,000) = £250.

Exercise 2

Suppose that $A = \dfrac{J \times B}{M}$

where J and B are subject to a maximum relative error of 10% and M to a maximum relative error of 20%.

Required

(a)   Calculate the approximate maximum relative error in A (using the rule in Paragraph 3.2).
(b)   Calculate the actual maximum relative error.

Solution

(a)   Approximate maximum relative error   = 10% + 10% + 20%
                                                               = 40%

(b)   A is at a maximum when the numerator is big and the denominator small, that is when J and B are at a maximum and M at a minimum.

Maximum A = $\dfrac{1.1J \times 1.1B}{0.8M} = \dfrac{1.5125JB}{M}$

∴ Actual maximum positive relative error = 51.25%.

A is at a minimum when the numerator is small and the denominator big, that is when J and B are at a minimum and M at a maximum.

Minimum A = $\dfrac{0.9J \times 0.9B}{1.2M} = \dfrac{0.675JB}{M}$

∴ Actual maximum negative relative error = 32.5%

Chapter roundup

- Approximation arises if it is not possible to obtain an accurate figure or if a number has been rounded. Rounding can be specified to the nearest whole unit, by the number of decimal places or by the number of significant figures.

- Spurious accuracy arises when a statistic gives the impression that it is more accurate than it really is.

- Maximum errors can be absolute or relative.

- When two or more rounded or approximate numbers are added or subtracted, the maximum absolute error in the result equals the sum of the individual maximum absolute errors.

- When two or more rounded or approximate numbers are multiplied or divided, the *approximate* maximum relative error in the result is obtained by adding the individual relative errors.

- You can determine the actual error in calculations involving only a few values/variables without using the two rules.

Test your knowledge

1   What is a spurious accuracy? (see para 1.3)

2   How is a maximum relative error calculated? (2.3)

3   What are the two rules to remember when performing calculations using rounded or approximate numbers? (3.2)

Now try illustrative question 18 at the end of the Study Text

Part E
Summarising and analysing data

Chapter 18

THE COLLECTION OF DATA

This chapter covers the following topics.

		Syllabus reference	Ability required
1	Data	2(e)	Skill
2	Sources of secondary data	2(e)	Skill
3	Survey methods of collecting data	2(e)	Skill
4	Questionnaire design	2(e)	Skill
5	Interviews	2(e)	Skill
6	Postal questionnaires	2(e)	Skill
7	Sampling	2(f)	Knowledge
8	Random sampling	2(f)	Knowledge
9	Quasi-random sampling	2(f)	Knowledge
10	Non-random sampling	2(f)	Knowledge
11	The size of a sample	2(f)	Knowledge

Introduction

The words 'quantitative methods' often strike terror into the hearts of students. They conjure up images of complicated mathematical formulae, scientific analysis of reams of computer output and the drawing of strange graphs and diagrams. Such images are wrong. Quantitative methods simply involves collecting data, their presentation in a useful form and their interpretation.

A study of the subject will demonstrate that quantitative methods is nothing to be afraid of and that a knowledge of it is extremely advantageous in your working environment. The main advantage of quantitative techniques are that they offer methods which can be used to make sense of numbers. In a business environment, for example, a manager may collect all sorts of data on production levels, costs and sales, but on their own the numbers are unlikely to mean very much. By using quantitative techniques, a manager can try to make sense out of the numbers, which in turn should help in making sensible business decisions.

We will start our study of quantitative methods by looking at data collection. In Chapter 19 we will consider how to present data once they have been collected.

1 DATA

What are data?

1.1 'Data' is a term that you will come across time and time again in your study of quantitative methods but what does 'data' mean? 'Data' is simply a 'scientific' term for facts, figures, information and measurements. Data therefore include the number of people who pass their driving test each year with red hair, the number of goals scored by each football team in the second division in the current season to date, and the profit after tax for the past ten years of the four biggest supermarket chains.

Types of data

1.2   Data may be of several types, the first distinction being between attributes and variables.

Attributes and variables

1.3   An attribute is something an object has either got or not got. It cannot be measured. For example, an individual is either male or female. There is no measure of *how* male or *how* female somebody is: the sex of a person is an attribute.

1.4   A variable is something which can be measured. For example, the height of a person can be measured according to some scale (such as centimetres).

Discrete and continuous variables

1.5   Variables can be further classified as discrete or continuous.

(a)   Discrete variables can only take a finite or countable number of values within a given range. Examples of such variables include ' goals scored by Chachont United against Willford City', 'shoe size' and 'number of people entering SupaSave SupaMarket in Rutminster between 9.05am and 9.10am on a particular day'. If we arbitrarily chose a range of 0 - 10, 2 goals could be scored but not $2\frac{1}{2}$, a (British) shoe size could be $5\frac{1}{2}$ but not 5.193 and 9 people could enter the supermarket but not 9.999.

(b)   Continuous variables may take on any value. They are measured rather than counted. For example, it may be considered sufficient to measure the heights of a number of people to the nearest centimetre but there is no reason why the measurements should not be made to the nearest 1/100cm. Two people who are found to have the same height to the nearest cm could almost certainly be distinguished if more precise measurements were taken.

Exercise 1

Look through the following list of surveys and decide whether each is collecting data on attributes, discrete variables or continuous variables.

(a)   A survey of statistics text books, to determine how many diagrams they contain
(b)   A survey of cans in a shop, to determine whether or not each has a price sticker
(c)   A survey of athletes to find out how long they take to run a mile
(d)   A survey of the heights of telegraph poles in England

Solution

(a)   The number of diagrams in a textbook is a discrete variable, because it can only be counted in whole number steps. You cannot, for example, have 26½ diagrams or 47.32 diagrams in a book.

(b)   Whether or not a can possesses a sticker is an attribute. It is not something which can be measured. A can either possesses the attribute or it does not.

(c)   How long an athlete takes to run a mile is a continuous variable, because the time recorded can, in theory, take any value, for example 4 minutes 2.0643 seconds.

(d)   The height of a telegraph pole is a continuous variable.

Primary data and secondary data

1.6   The data used in a statistical survey, whether variables or attributes, can be either primary data or secondary data.

(a)   Primary data are data collected especially for the purpose of whatever survey is being conducted. Raw data are primary data which have not been processed at all, but are still just (for example) a list of numbers.

(b)   Secondary data are data which have already been collected elsewhere, for some other purpose, but which can be used or adapted for the survey being conducted.

1.7   An advantage of using primary data is that the investigator knows where the data came from, the circumstances under which they were collected, and any limitations or inadequacies in the data.

1.8   In contrast, note the following inadequacies of secondary data.

(a)   Any limitations in the data might not be known to the investigator, because he or she did not collect them.

(b)   The data might not be entirely suitable for the purpose they are being used for.

1.9   Secondary data are sometimes used despite their inadequacies, simply because they are available cheaply whereas the extra cost of collecting primary data would far outweigh their extra value.

1.10   Now that we have some idea of the different types of data, we can address ourselves to the problem of getting hold of them.

2   SOURCES OF SECONDARY DATA

2.1   Secondary data are data that were originally collected as primary data for a particular purpose or for general use, but are now being used for another purpose. The Government, for example, collects data to help with making decisions about running the country, and makes these data available to the public.

2.2   Examples of secondary data include the following.

(a)   *Published statistics.* For example, the Government publishes statistics through the Office for National Statistics (ONS) (following the merger of the Central Statistical Office and the Office of Population Censuses and Surveys in April 1996). The European Union and the United Nations also publish statistics. So do various newspapers and accountancy bodies.

(b)   *Historical records.* The type of historical record used for a survey obviously depends on what survey is being carried out. An accountant producing an estimate of future company sales might use historical records of past sales.

Sources of published statistics

2.3   You may be expected to identify the sources of certain published statistics. As you will probably be aware, the range of published economic, business and accounting data is very wide, and a comprehensive knowledge of sources is impracticable. In this chapter the better known sources will be described.

2.4   All published statistics are a source of secondary data. Great care must be taken in using them, since the data may not be obtained or classified in precisely the same way as primary data collected *specifically* for the purpose of the current statistical analysis would be.

2.5   Despite the general shortcomings of secondary data there are many circumstances in which published statistics can be of great value. Many Government statistics are compiled at least partly for the purpose of being used in further analysis and explanatory notes are given so that the user of the data knows to what extent they are relevant to his needs and what level of confidence he can have in the results of his analysis.

The Office for National Statistics (ONS) and other bodies

2.6   The ONS publishes the following.

(a)   The *Monthly Digest of Statistics* (which gives data for the recent past)
(b)   The *Annual Abstract of Statistics* (which gives data over a much longer period)
(c)   *Economic Trends* (published monthly)
(d)   *Financial Statistics* (published monthly)

2.7   The European Union has a Statistical Office of the European Community (SOEC) which gathers statistics from each of the member countries. The SOEC has several statistical publications, including *Basic Statistics of the Community.*

2.8   The United Nations also publishes some statistics on the world economy (for example the Statistical yearbook), and a Yearbook of labour statistics is published by the International Labour Organisation.

2.9   In the remainder of this section, we shall concentrate on statistical publications in the UK.

The Department of Employment Gazette

2.10 The Department of Employment publishes statistics monthly about employment and unemployment, and about retail prices. The statistics which are published monthly in the *Department of Employment Gazette* include, for example, statistics on the following.

(a)   Retail prices
(b)   Employment
(c)   Unemployment
(d)   Unfilled job vacancies
(e)   Wage rates
(f)   Overtime
(g)   Stoppages at work

2.11 Retail prices are very important to a wide variety of users.

(a)   For the Government, the Retail Prices Index (RPI) indicates the degree of success there has been in fighting inflation.

(b)   For employees, the RPI may give an indication of how much wages need to rise to keep pace with inflation.

(c)   For consumers, the RPI indicates the increases to be expected in the prices of goods in shops.

(d)   For businesses, the RPI may give a broad indication of how much costs should have been expected to rise over recent years and months.

(e)   For pensioners and social security recipients, the movement in the RPI is used to update benefit levels.

The Bank of England Quarterly Bulletin

2.12 The Bank of England issues a quarterly magazine which includes data on banks in the UK, the money supply and Government borrowing and financial transactions.

Population data

2.13 Data on the UK population, such as population numbers in total and by region, births, deaths and marriages, are produced monthly by ONS in a publication entitled *Population Trends.*

The ONS also produces an annual statistical review.

Every ten years, there is a full census of the whole population, and results of the census are published. The last census was in April 1991.

The Blue Book and the Pink Book

2.14 *The Blue Book on National Income and Expenditure* is published annually by the ONS, giving details of:

(a) gross national product (analysed into sections of the economy such as transport and communication, insurance, banking and finance, public administration and defence);

(b) gross national income (analysed into income from self-employment, income from employment, profits of companies, income from abroad and so on);

(c) gross national expenditure (analysed into expenditure on capital goods, expenditure by consumers and by public authorities, imports and so on).

2.15 This information is augmented by more detailed statistics, also provided in the Blue Book. There is also an annual *Pink Book, The UK Balance of Payments* which analyses the UK's external trade, external capital transactions (inflows and outflows of private capital) and official financing.

The Annual Abstract of Statistics

2.16 Most government statistics of economic and business data are brought together into a main reference book, the *Annual Abstract of Statistics*, which is published by the ONS. Notes about the data and definitions of the data provided are contained in the book.

The Monthly Digest of Statistics

2.17 The ONS's *Monthly Digest of Statistics* is an abbreviated version of the Annual Abstract, updated and published monthly. A January supplement provides definitions. The information included in the *Monthly Digest* covers a wide range of topics, such as industrial output, production costs, prices and wages, social services, law enforcement, national income, external trade, retailing, transport, construction, agriculture and food.

Financial Statistics

2.18 The ONS publishes a monthly compilation of financial data in *Financial Statistics*. This gives statistics on a variety of financial topics.

(a) Government income, expenditure and borrowing

(b) Assets and liabilities of banks and statistics on other financial institutions, such as building societies, unit trusts, investment trusts, insurance companies and pension funds

(c) Companies (profits, sources and uses of capital funds, acquisitions and mergers, share trading and so on)

(d) Personal sector finance (loans for home buying, consumer credit, personal income expenditure and saving and so on)

(e) The overseas sector

(f) The money supply

(g) Issues of capital and Stock Exchange transactions

(h) Exchange rates, interest rates and share prices

Economic Trends

2.19 Like the *Monthly Digest of Statistics* and *Financial Statistics*, *Economic Trends* is a monthly publication of the ONS. As its name implies, its main purpose is to indicate trends, and the publication includes graphs as well as numerical statistics.

The Financial Times

2.20 The *Financial Times* and other newspapers and investment journals provide statistics about the Stock Market. These include the following.

(a) The FT-Actuaries All-Share Index (compiled jointly by the *Financial Times*, the Institute of Actuaries in London and the Faculty of Actuaries in Edinburgh). This is an index of share prices quoted on the Stock Exchange.

(b) The FTSE 100 index. This is a stock market index of 100 leading shares, compiled by the *Financial Times* and the Stock Exchange.

The *Financial Times* also includes various other items of daily information on financial matters.

(a) Foreign exchange rates
(b) Interest rates
(c) Gilts and other stock prices

3   SURVEY METHODS OF COLLECTING DATA

3.1 There are two basic methods of collecting primary data from individuals: they can be asked questions or their behaviour can be observed. The latter method of collection is called observation and is outside the scope of this syllabus; the former involves the collection of data using surveys.

3.2 There are two main types of survey.

(a) Interviews
(b) Postal questionnaires

3.3 We will be looking at each type, and their respective advantages and disadvantages, in later sections.

3.4 Although surveys offer a quick, efficient and cost-effective way of obtaining the required data, they are not straightforward. Without skill, tact and expertise the results may easily become contaminated with bias and error and the conclusions subsequently drawn will be useless.

3.5 A famous example of this occurred years ago in the United States, when somebody was asked to conduct an opinion poll (which is a form of survey) on whether the next president was likely to be Democrat or Republican. The survey was carried out, but in a wrong way. The survey officer *telephoned* people, and far more Republicans than Democrats had telephones. The survey was useless, because it had not been planned properly.

3.6 The reason why the opinion poll turned out so badly was that the population for the survey had not been defined properly. In data collection, the word 'population' refers to the entire collection of items being considered. The opinion poll should have used the population 'all Americans of voting age', whereas it actually used the population 'all Americans with a telephone'.

Errors in survey methods of collecting data

3.7 There are three main types of error that can appear in survey methods of collecting data.

(a) *Sampling error* arises when the sample of the population surveyed (if the entire population is not being investigated) is not representative of the population from which it is drawn. For example, if a sample of the population of a city was composed entirely of babies less than three months old, the sample would obviously not be representative of the population of the city.

(b) *Response error* can occur even when all members of the population are surveyed and arises because respondents are either unable (through ignorance, forgetfulness or inarticulateness) or unwilling (due to time pressure, desire for privacy, guessing and so on) to respond.

(c) *Non-response error* can occur either if respondents refuse to take part in the survey or are 'not at home'.

3.8 Non-response in survey methods of data collection is a particular problem if those who refuse to take part in the survey are likely to be different in some way to those who do take part. The easiest way to reduce the effect of this situation is to try and increase the percentage of those taking part (responding).

(a) Reducing non-response for interviews

    (i)   The success of interviews relies on the quality of interaction between respondent and interviewer. Interviewers who appear/sound pleasant, interesting and interested in the respondent and who convincingly persuade the respondent that his/her views are important will produce lower rates of refusal.

    (ii)   If someone is 'not at home' the interviewer should call back.

    (iii) Respondents can be promised gifts/monetary reward.

(b) Reducing non-response for postal questionnaires

    (i)   Contact respondents prior to despatching the questionnaire to ask whether they would be prepared to aid the study by completing a questionnaire.

    (ii)   Include a covering letter to explain why the data are being collected and to put the respondent in the appropriate frame of mind.

    (iii) Include a freepost/stamped addressed envelope for ease of reply.

    (iv) Provide a gift or monetary incentive upon questionnaire completion.

    (v)   Address the respondent by name. This not only increases the response rate but will encourage the named person to complete the questionnaire personally.

    (vi) Use postal or telephone follow up reminders.

    (vii) Carefully select a target audience who have particular interest in the topic.

4   QUESTIONNAIRE DESIGN

Question content

4.1 When deciding on question content it is vital to think about the following.

(a) Is the question necessary?

(b) Will the respondent understand the question?

The language used should be that of the respondent group. Think about the different language used by managing directors and teenagers.

(c) Will the question elicit the required data?

A survey often fails to generate the required data because of badly-phrased questions or questions that are too ambiguous to elicit specific information. Double-barrelled questions ('Do you often go to pubs and restaurants?') should be split and words describing frequency ('often', 'slightly', 'somewhat') should be avoided as they have a wide range of interpretation.

Exercise 2

What might be a better way of asking 'Do you often go to the cinema?'

Solution

'Do you go to the cinema (a) once a week, (b) once a month, (c) twice a year?'

(d) Does the respondent have the necessary data to be able to answer the question?

The ability of the respondent to answer will depend on three factors.

(i)   If respondents do not know the answer to a question they may try to bluff their way out of, what is to them, an embarrassing situation by guessing. Such answers lead to errors in the conclusions drawn from the data collected. Questions should therefore be phrased so that is does *not* appear that the interviewer is suggesting that the respondent should know the answer.

(ii)   Questions relating to unimportant/ infrequent events or to events some time in the past, are likely to tempt respondents to guess. This may introduce error and so it is better to 'jog' respondents' memories in some way.

(iii)   Even the most articulate of respondents may find it difficult to be verbally adept about their feelings, beliefs, opinions and motivations.

(e) Is the respondent willing/able to answer the questions?

A respondent may refuse to answer one or more questions on a questionnaire (non-response) or many 'refuse' by providing a wrong or distorted answer. Certain techniques can be employed to eliminate distorted/wrong/inaccurate answers.

(i)   Assess whether the question is really necessary (especially if it will cause embarrassment, a loss of prestige).

(ii)   Reassure the respondent of the importance of the question and of the value of their response.

(iii)   Begin a 'difficult' question with a statement which implies the topic of the question is common/quite usual.

(iv)   Imply that the behaviour in which you are interested is an attribute of a third party.

(v)   Provide respondents with a card on which are listed possible responses, identified by a letter or a number, to potentially embarrassing questions. Respondents need only provide a letter/number as their answer.

(vi)   When analysing the data, replies to questions related to image/prestige should be upgraded or downgraded as necessary.

Exercise 3

How might the following question be rephrased?

'Do you visit the pub to get drunk?'

Solution

'Do you think that people go to the pub simply to get drunk?'

Question phrasing

4.2   Given below is a checklist of factors to consider when translating data requirements into words.

(a) Use a style of language appropriate to the target population.

(b) Avoid long questions.

(c) Avoid vague and ambiguous words.

(d) Avoid biased words and leading questions.

(e) Do not use double-barrelled questions.

(f) Avoid negative questions.

(g) Do not encourage respondents to guess.

(h) Avoid questions which assume respondents have possession of all the relevant factors pertaining to the question.

Types of response format

4.3 Questions can be open or closed. Open questions are difficult to analyse. An open question might be worded like this.

'How did you travel to work today?'

The responses may be so numerous that analysis becomes onerous and time consuming. The designer of the questionnaire should instead try to offer a full range of possible responses to the question, perhaps like this. 'Please indicate how you travelled to work today.

By bus

By train

By private car

On foot

By bicycle/motorcycle

I did not go to work today (illness, holidays etc)

I work at home

I do not work

Other (please give details)...................'

The responses from this closed question will be much easier to analyse. It is important, however, to avoid putting such lists of responses in order of supposed popularity.

Exercise 4

What types of problem can you envisage arising from the use of multiple choice questions? How can such problems be overcome?

Solution

Here are some ideas. You may have thought of others.

(a) Capturing a full range of possible responses to a question such as 'In which store do you buy the majority of your clothes?' can be impractical.

This problem can be overcome by listing the most popular stores and using an 'other (please specify)' option

(b) The position of the alternative responses may introduce bias.

This problem can be overcome (but not entirely) by producing different versions of the questionnaire.

(c) An unbalanced set of alternative responses could be provided such as the following.

Q: What do you think of TV programme 'XXX'?

A: 1   2   3

         Too boring   Very dull   Indifferent

Obviously such response sets should not be used.

Question sequence

4.4   (a)   Start with quota control questions so as to rapidly determine whether the interviewee is the right type of person. Quota control questions might identify whether the interviewee is employed or unemployed, under 40 or over 40 and so on. Such questions facilitate the termination of worthless interviews as early as possible.

        (b)   Move onto questions which will engage interest, reassure and give a foretaste of what is to follow.

        (c)   Questions should be in logical order as far as possible, but if difficult questions are necessary it may be more appropriate to put them at the end.

        (d)   Avoid questions which suggest the answers to later questions. This will cause bias.

Questionnaire layout

4.5   (a)   Use good quality paper.

        (b)   The questionnaire should be as short as possible. Questionnaires which are too long may discourage the respondent from even starting it.

        (c)   If respondents have to complete the questionnaire themselves, it must be as approachable as possible. Consider the use of lines, boxes, different type faces/print sizes and small pictures. Use plenty of space.

        (d)   Make sure that the instructions which guide the respondent through the questionnaire are as user friendly as possible and are kept to a minimum.

        (e)   Explain the purpose of the survey at the beginning of the questionnaire and where possible guarantee confidentiality. Emphasise the date by which it must be returned.

        (f)   At the end of the questionnaire, thank the respondent and make it clear what they should do with the completed questionnaire.

Pretest, revision and final version of the questionnaire

4.6   Pretesting the questionnaire will uncover faults in its design before it is too late and should therefore ensure that the final version of the questionnaire gathers the required data.

5   INTERVIEWS

5.1   There are basically two types of interview that can be used to collect data, the personal (face to face) interview and the telephone interview.

Advantages of personal interviews

5.2   (a)   The interviewer is able to reduce respondent anxiety and allay potential embarrassment, thereby increasing the response rate and decreasing the potential for error.

        (b)   The routing ('if yes go to question 7, if no go to question 10') of questions is made easier due to the experience of the interviewer.

        (c)   Interviewers can ask, within narrow limits, for a respondent's answer to be clarified.

        (d)   The questions can be given in a fixed order with a fixed wording and the answers can be recorded in a standard manner. If there is more than one interviewer involved in the survey this will reduce variability.

        (e)   Standardised questions and ways of recording the responses mean that less skilled interviewers may be used, thereby reducing the cost of the survey.

        (f)   Pictures, signs and objects can be used.

Disadvantages of personal interviews

5.3   (a)   They can be time consuming.

(b)   The cost per completed interview can be higher than with other survey methods.

(c)   Questionnaires can be difficult to design.

(d)   Fully-structured interviews have particular disadvantages.

(i)   Questions must be kept relatively simple, thus restricting the depth of data collected.

(ii)   Questions must normally be closed because of the difficulties of recording answers to open questions.

(iii)   Interviewers cannot probe vague or ambiguous replies.

Telephone interviews

5.4   Telephone interviews are a relatively fast and low-cost means of gathering data compared to personal interviews. They are most useful when only a small amount of information is required. They also benefit the respondent in terms of the short amount of time taken up by the interview.

5.5   CATI (computer-assisted telephone interviewing) has been used successfully by insurance services and banks as well as consumer research organisations. The telephone interviewer calls up a questionnaire on screen and reads questions to the respondent. Answers are then recorded instantly on computer. Complex questions with questionnaire routing may be handled in this way.

Advantages of telephone interviews

5.6   (a)   The response is rapid.

(b)   A wide geographical area can be covered fairly cheaply from a central location. There is no need for the interviewer to travel between respondents.

(c)   It may be easier to ask sensitive or embarrassing questions.

Disadvantages of telephone interviews

5.7   (a)   A biased sample may result from the fact that a proportion of people do not have telephones and many of those who do are ex-directory.

(b)   It is not possible to use 'showcards' or pictures.

(c)   The refusal rate is much higher than with face-to-face interviews.

(d)   It is not possible to see the interviewee's expression or to develop the rapport that is possible with personal interviews.

(e)   The interview must be short.

(f)   Respondents may be unwilling to participate for fear of being sold something.

6   POSTAL QUESTIONNAIRES

6.1   If the size of interviewer-induced error is likely to be large or its magnitude cannot be predicted with any degree of accuracy and if cost is an important factor when deciding on the data collection method, postal questionnaires should be given serious consideration.

6.2   As there is no one to clear up ambiguity in questions, their wording and sequence must be carefully thought out prior to use of the questionnaire.

Advantages of postal questionnaires

6.3 Postal questionnaires have the following advantages over personal interviews.

(a) The cost per person is likely to be less, so more people can be sampled.

(b) It is usually possible to ask more questions because the people completing the forms (the respondents) can do so in their own time.

(c) All respondents are presented with questions in the same way. There is no opportunity for an interviewer to influence responses (interviewer bias) or to misrecord them.

(d) It may be easier to ask personal or embarrassing questions in a postal questionnaire than in a personal interview.

(e) Respondents may need to look up information for the questionnaire. This will be easier if the questionnaire is sent to their home or place of work.

Disadvantages of postal questionnaires

6.4 On the other hand, the use of personal interviews does have certain advantages over the use of postal questionnaires.

(a) Large numbers of postal questionnaires may not be returned or may be returned only partly completed. This may lead to biased results if those replying are not representative of all people in the survey. Response rates are likely to be higher with personal interviews, and the interviewer can encourage people to answer all questions. Low response rates are a major problem with postal questionnaires.

(b) Misunderstanding is less likely with personal interviews because the interviewer can explain questions which the interviewee does not understand.

(c) Personal interviews are more suitable when deep or detailed questions are to be asked, since the interviewer can take the time required with each interviewee to explain the implications of the question. Also, the interviewer can probe for further information and encourage the respondent to think deeper.

7 SAMPLING

7.1 Sampling is one of the most important subjects in quantitative methods In most practical situations the population will be too large to carry out a complete survey and only a sample will be examined. A good example of this is a poll taken to try to predict the results of an election. It is not possible to ask everyone of voting age how they are going to vote: it would take too long and cost too much. So a sample of voters is taken, and the results from the sample are used to estimate the voting intentions of the whole population.

7.2 Occasionally a population is small enough that all of it can be examined: for example, the examination results of one class of students. When all of the population is examined, the survey is called a *census*. This type of survey is quite rare, however, and usually the investigator has to choose some sort of sample.

7.3 You may think that using a sample is very much a compromise, but you should consider the following points.

(a) In practice, a 100% survey (a census) never achieves the completeness required.

(b) A census may require the use of semi-skilled investigators, resulting in a loss of accuracy in the data collected.

(c) It can be shown mathematically that once a certain sample size has been reached, very little extra accuracy is gained by examining more items.

(d) It is possible to ask more questions with a sample.

(e) The higher cost of a census may exceed the value of results.

(f)   Things are always changing. Even if you took a census it could well be out of date by the time you completed it.

The choice of a sample

7.4   One of the most important requirements of sample data is that they should be complete. That is, the data should cover all areas of the population to be examined. If this requirement is not met, then the sample will be biased.

7.5   For example, suppose you wanted to survey the productivity of workers in a factory, and you went along every Monday and Tuesday for a few months to measure their output. Would these data be complete? The answer is no. You might have gathered very thorough data on what happens on Mondays and Tuesdays, but you would have missed out the rest of the week. It could be that the workers, keen and fresh after the weekend, work better at the start of the week than at the end. If this is the case, then your data will give you a misleadingly high productivity figure. Careful attention must therefore be given to the sampling method employed to produce a sample.

7.6   Sampling methods fall into three main groups.

(a)   Random sampling
(b)   Quasi-random sampling
(c)   Non-random sampling

8   RANDOM SAMPLING   *11/96*

8.1   To ensure that the sample selected is free from bias, random sampling must be used. Inferences about the population being sampled can then be made validly.

8.2   A simple random sample is a sample selected in such a way that every item in the population has an equal chance of being included.

8.3   For example, if you wanted to take a random sample of library books, it would not be good enough to pick them off the shelves, even if you picked them at random. This is because the books which were out on loan would stand no chance of being chosen. You would either have to make sure that all the books were on the shelves before taking your sample, or find some other way of sampling (for example, using the library index cards).

8.4   A random sample is not necessarily a perfect sample. For example, you might pick what you believe to be a completely random selection of library books, and find that every one of them is a detective thriller. It is a remote possibility, but it could happen. The only way to eliminate the possibility altogether is to take 100% survey (a census) of the books, which, unless it is a tiny library, is impractical.

Sampling frames

8.5   If random sampling is used then it is necessary to construct a sampling frame. A sampling frame is simply a numbered list of all the items in the population. Once such a list has been made, it is easy to select a random sample, simply by generating a list of random numbers. (You are provided with a set of random number tables in your examination.)

8.6   For instance, if you wanted to select a random sample of children from a school, it would be useful to have a list of names:

0   J Absolam
1   R Brown
2   S Brown
...

Now the numbers 0, 1, 2 and so on can be used to select the random sample. It is normal to start the numbering at 0, so that when 0 appears in a list of random numbers it can be used.

8.7   Sometimes it is not possible to draw up a sampling frame. For example, if you wanted to take a random sample of Americans, it would take too long to list all Americans.

8.8   A sampling frame should have the following characteristics.

(a)   *Completeness.* Are all members of the population included on the list?
(b)   *Accuracy.* Is the information correct?
(c)   *Adequacy.* Does it cover the entire population?
(d)   *Up to dateness.* Is the list up to date?
(e)   *Convenience.* Is the sampling frame readily accessible?
(f)   *Non-duplication.* Does each member of the population appear on the list only once?

8.9   Two readily available sampling frames for the human population of Great Britain are the council tax register (list of dwellings) and the electoral register (list of individuals).

Random number tables

8.10   Assuming that a sampling frame can be drawn up, then a random sample can be picked from it by one of the following methods.

(a)   The lottery method, which amounts to picking numbered pieces of paper out of a box

(b)   The use of random number tables

8.11   Set out below is part of a typical random number table.

93716	16894	98953	73231
32886	59780	09958	18065
92052	06831	19640	99413
39510	35905	85244	35159
27699	06494	03152	19121
92962	61773	22109	78508
10274	12202	94205	50380
75867	20717	82037	10268
85783	47619	87481	37220

You should note the following points.

(a)   The sample is found by selecting groups of random numbers with the number of digits depending on the total population size, as follows.

Total population size	Number of random digits
1 - 10	1
1 - 100	2
1 - 1,000	3

The items selected for the sample are those corresponding to the random numbers selected.

(b)   The starting point on the table should be selected at random. After that, however, numbers must be selected in a consistent manner. In other words, you should use the table row by row or column by column. By jumping around the table from place to place, personal bias may be introduced.

(c)   In many practical situations it is more convenient to use a computer to generate a list of random numbers, especially when a large sample is required.

Example: random number tables

8.12   An investigator wishes to select a random sample from a population of 800 people, who have been numbered 000, 001, ...799. As there are three digits in 799 the random numbers will be selected in groups of three. Working along the first line of the table given earlier, the first few groups are as follows.

937   161   689   498   953   732

Numbers over 799 are discarded. The first four people in the sample will therefore be those numbered 161, 689, 498 and 732.

Drawbacks of random sampling

8.13   (a)   The selected items are subject to the full range of variation inherent in the population.

   (b)   An unrepresentative sample may result.

   (c)   The members of the population selected may be scattered over a wide area, adding to the cost and difficulty of obtaining the data.

   (d)   An adequate sampling frame might not exist.

   (e)   The numbering of the population might be laborious.

Quasi- and non-random sampling

8.14   In many situations it might be too expensive to obtain a random sample, in which case quasi-random sampling is necessary, or else it may not be possible to draw up a sampling frame. In such cases, non-random sampling has to be used.

9   QUASI-RANDOM SAMPLING

9.1   Quasi-random sampling, which provides a good approximation to random sampling, necessitates the existence of a sampling frame.

The main methods of quasi-random sampling are as follows.

   (a)   Systematic sampling
   (b)   Stratified sampling
   (c)   Multistage sampling

Systematic sampling

9.2   Systematic sampling may provide a good approximation to random sampling. It works by selecting every nth item after a random start. For example, if it was decided to select a sample of 20 from a population of 800, then every 40th (800 ÷ 20) item after a random start in the first 40 should be selected. The starting point could be found using the lottery method or random number tables. If (say) 23 was chosen, then the sample would include the 23rd, 63rd, 103rd, 143rd ... 783rd items.

The gap of 40 is known as the sampling interval.

The investigator must ensure that there is no regular pattern to the population which, if it coincided with the sampling interval, might lead to a biased sample. In practice, this problem is often overcome by choosing multiple starting points and using varying sampling intervals whose size is selected at random.

9.3   If the sampling frame is in random order (such as an alphabetical list of students) a systematic sample is essentially the same as a simple random sample.

A systematic sample does not, however, fully meet the criterion of randomness since some samples of the given size have zero probability of being chosen. The method is, however, easy and cheap and hence is widely used.

Stratified sampling

9.4   In many situations stratified sampling is the best method of choosing a sample. The population must be divided into strata or categories.

If we took a random sample of all cost and management accountants in the country, it is conceivable that the entire sample might consist of members of the CIMA working in public companies. Stratified sampling removes this possibility as random samples could be taken from each type of employment, the number in each sample being proportional to the total number of cost and management accountants in each type (for example those in partnerships, those in public companies and those in private companies).

Example: stratified sampling

9.5   The number of cost and management accountants in each type of work in a particular country are as follows.

Partnerships	500
Public companies	500
Private companies	700
Public practice	800
	2,500

9.6   If a sample of 20 was required the sample would be made up as follows.

		Sample
Partnerships	$\dfrac{500}{2,500} \times 20$	4
Public companies	$\dfrac{500}{2,500} \times 20$	4
Private companies	$\dfrac{700}{2,500} \times 20$	6
Public practice	$\dfrac{800}{2,500} \times 20$	6
		20

9.7   The strata frequently involve multiple classifications. In social surveys, for example, there is usually stratification by age, sex and social class. This implies that the sampling frame must contain information on these three variables before the threefold stratification of the population can be made.

9.8   Advantages of stratification are as follows.

(a)   It ensures a representative sample since it guarantees that every important category will have elements in the final sample.

(b)   The structure of the sample will reflect that of the population if the same proportion of individuals is chosen from each stratum.

(c)   Each stratum is represented by a randomly chosen sample and therefore inferences can be made about each stratum.

(d)   Precision is increased. Sampling takes place within strata and, because the range of variation is less in each stratum than in the population as a whole and variation between strata does not enter as a chance effect, higher precision is obtainable. (For this to occur, the items in each stratum must be as similar as possible and the difference between the individual strata must be as great as possible.)

9.9   Note, however, that stratification requires prior knowledge of each item in the population. Sampling frames do not always contain this information. Stratification from the electoral register as to age structure would not be possible because the electoral register does not contain information about age.

Multistage sampling

9.10 Multistage sampling is normally used to cut down the number of investigators and the costs of obtaining a sample. An example will show how the method works.

Example: multistage sampling

9.11 A survey of spending habits is being planned to cover the whole of Britain. It is obviously impractical to draw up a sampling frame, so random sampling is not possible. Multi-stage sampling is to be used instead.

9.12 The country is divided into a number of areas and a small sample of these is selected at random. Each of the areas selected is subdivided into smaller units and again, a smaller number of these is selected at random. This process is repeated as many times as necessary and finally, a random sample of the relevant people living in each of the smallest units is taken. A fair approximation to a random sample can be obtained.

9.13 Thus, we might choose a random sample of eight areas, and from each of these areas, select a random sample of five towns. From each town, a random sample of 200 people might be selected so that the total sample size is $8 \times 5 \times 200 = 8,000$ people.

9.14 The main advantage of this method is one of cost saving but there are a number of disadvantages.

(a) There is the possibility of bias if, for example, only a small number of regions are selected.

(b) The method is not truly random as once the final sampling areas have been selected the rest of the population cannot be in the sample.

(c) If the population is heterogeneous, the areas chosen should reflect the full range of the diversity. Otherwise, choosing some areas and excluding others (even if it is done randomly) will result in a biased sample.

9.15 The sampling methods looked at so far have necessitated the existence of a sampling frame (or in multistage sampling, sampling frames of areas, sub-areas and items within selected sub-areas). It is often impossible to identify a satisfactory sampling frame and, in such instances, other sampling methods have to be employed.

10   NON-RANDOM SAMPLING

10.1 There are two main methods of non-random sampling, used when a sampling frame cannot be established.

(a) Quota sampling
(b) Cluster sampling

Quota sampling   *11/96*

10.2 In quota sampling, randomness is forfeited in the interests of cheapness and administrative simplicity. Investigators are told to interview all the people they meet up to a certain quota. A large degree of bias could be introduced accidentally. For example, an interviewer in a shopping centre may fill his quota by only meeting people who can go shopping during the week. In practice, this problem can be partly overcome by subdividing the quota into different types of people, for example on the basis of age, sex and income, to ensure that the sample mirrors the structure or stratification of the population. The interviewer is then told to interview, for example, 30 males between the ages of 30 and 40 from social class C 1. The actual choice of the individuals to be interviewed, within the limits of the *quota controls*, is left to the field worker.

Advantages of quota sampling

10.3 (a) It is cheap and administratively easy.

(b) A much larger sample can be studied, and hence more information can be gained at a faster speed for a given outlay than when compared with a fully randomised sampling method.

(c) Although a fairly detailed knowledge of the characteristics of a population is required, no sampling frame is necessary because the interviewer questions every person he meets up to the quota.

(d) Quota sampling may be the only possible approach in certain situations, such as television audience research.

(e) Given suitable, trained and properly briefed field workers, quota sampling yields enough accurate information for many forms of commercial market research.

Disadvantages of quota sampling

10.4 (a) The method can result in certain biases (although these can often be allowed for and/or may be unimportant for the purpose of the research).

(b) The non-random nature of the method rules out any valid estimate of the sampling error (a concept you will meet later in your studies) in estimates derived from the sample.

Conclusion

10.5 Quota sampling cannot be regarded as ultimately satisfactory in research where it is important that theoretically valid results should be obtained. It can be argued, however, that when other large sources of error, such as non response, exist, it is pointless to worry too much about sampling error.

Example: quota sampling

10.6 Consider the figures in Paragraph 9.5 above, but with the following additional information relating to the sex of the cost and management accountants.

	Male	*Female*
Partnerships	300	200
Public companies	400	100
Private companies	300	400
Public practice	300	500

10.7 An investigator's quotas might be as follows.

	Male	*Female*	*Total*
Partnerships	30	20	50
Public companies	40	10	50
Private companies	30	40	70
Public practice	30	50	80
			250

Using quota sampling, the investigator would interview the first 30 male cost and management accountants in partnerships that he met, the first 20 female cost and management accountants in partnerships that he met and so on.

Cluster sampling

10.8 Cluster sampling involves selecting one definable subsection of the population as the sample, that subsection taken to be representative of the population in question. The pupils of one school might be taken as a cluster sample of all children at school in one county.

Cluster sampling benefits from low costs in the same way as multistage sampling.

10.9 The advantages of cluster sampling are that it is a good alternative to multistage sampling if a satisfactory sampling frame does not exist and it is inexpensive to operate because little organisation or structure is involved. There is, however, the potential for considerable bias.

Exercise 5

Describe four methods a brewery could employ to test the market for a new canned beer. Discuss the relative advantages and disadvantages of each method chosen.

(a) The brewery could try to supply the beer to a random sample of beer drinkers, and then ask for their views. Such samples are taken in such a way that every member of the population (in this case, all beer drinkers and perhaps all potential beer drinkers) has an equal chance of being selected for the sample. The main advantage of random sampling is that it allows mathematical analysis of the data to be carried out. The main disadvantage is that a random sample can be difficult and expensive to collect. The brewery may well find that it is impossible to compile a list of all beer drinkers from which to select a sample.

(b) Stratified sampling may well be appropriate. The population would first be divided into groups, perhaps by age or by weekly beer consumption, and then samples would be selected from each group (reflecting the proportion of the population in the group). The main advantage of stratified sampling is that it ensures that each group is represented in the sample. The main disadvantage is that preliminary work is needed to determine which groupings are likely to be useful and the proportion of the population in each group.

(c) Cluster sampling may well be a practical alternative, giving some of the benefits of both random sampling and stratified sampling. The population could be divided geographically into beer drinkers at public houses in different regions of the country and beer purchasers at off licences within these regions. A sample of regions could be selected, and a sample of public houses and off licences in each selected region could be chosen. All consumers at the chosen public houses and off licences would then form the sample. The main advantage of cluster sampling is its relative cheapness. The main disadvantage is that the sample obtained will not be truly random, so some forms of statistical analysis will not be possible.

(d) Quota sampling has the advantage of being even cheaper than cluster sampling, but the disadvantage of producing a sample which is even further from being random. Researchers would simply visit a selection of public houses and off licences and interview the first beer drinkers they met until they had fulfilled some quota (say ten men and ten women).

---

11 THE SIZE OF A SAMPLE

11.1 As well as deciding on the appropriateness of a particular sampling method for a given situation, the size of the sample actually selected must also be given consideration.

11.2 Although, in certain circumstances, statistical processes can be used to calculate sample sizes, there is no universal law for determining the size of the sample. Two general considerations should, however, be borne in mind.

(a) The larger the size of the sample, the more accurate the results.

(b) There reaches a point after which there is little to be gained from increasing the size of the sample.

11.3 Despite these principles other, more administration-type factors, play a role in determining sample size.

(a) *Money and time available.*

(b) *Degree of precision required.* A survey may have the aim of discovering residents' reaction to a road widening scheme and hence a fairly small sample, producing imprecise results, would be acceptable. An enquiry into the safety of a new drug would, on the other hand, require an extremely large sample so that the information gained was as precise as possible.

(c) *Number of subsamples required.* If a complicated sampling method such as stratified sampling is to be used, the overall sample size will need to be large so as to ensure adequate representation of each subgroup (in this case, each stratum).

Chapter roundup

- This chapter has concentrated on the practical problems of collecting data.

- An attribute is something an object has either got or not got. It cannot be measured. A variable is something which can be measured.

- Variables can be discrete (may take specific values) or continuous (may take any value).

- Data may be primary (collected specifically for the current purpose) or secondary (collected already).

- Examples of secondary data include published statistics and historical records.

- Primary data can be collected using surveys. There are two main types of survey: interviews and postal questionnaires. Interviews can be face to face or performed over the telephone.

- questionnaire design involves considering question content, questions phrasing, types of response format, question required, layout. questionnaires should be pretested.

- Data are often collected from a sample rather than from a population. A sample can be selected using random sampling (using random number tables or the lottery method), quasi-random sampling (systematic, stratified and multistage sampling) or non-random sampling (quota and cluster sampling). Ensure that you know the characteristics, advantages and disadvantages of each sampling method.

- Once data have been collected they need to be presented and analysed. It is important to remember that if the data have not been collected properly, no amount of careful presentation or interpretation can remedy the defect.

Test your knowledge

1   What is a discrete variable? (see para 1.5)

2   What are secondary data? (1.6)

3   List some of the UK sources of published statistics. (2.6-2.20)

4   What types of error can appear in survey methods of collecting data? (3.8)

5   What factors relating to question sequence should be considered when designing a questionnaire? (4.4)

6   What are the advantages and disadvantages of personal interviews? (5.2, 5.3)

7   List the arguments in favour of using a sample. (7.3)

8   What is a simple random sample? (8.2)

9   What is stratified sampling? (9.4)

10   List three administrative factors which may affect the size of a sample. (11.3)

Now try illustrative question 19 at the end of the Study Text

Chapter 19

DATA PRESENTATION

This chapter covers the following topics.

		Syllabus reference	*Ability required*
1	Tables	2(e)	Skill
2	Charts	2(e)	Knowledge
3	Frequency distributions	2(e)	Skill
4	Histograms	2(e)	Knowledge
5	Ogives	2(e)	Knowledge
6	Time series graphs	2(e)	Knowledge
7	Z charts	2(e)	Knowledge
8	Semi-logarithmic graphs	2(e)	Knowledge

Introduction

You now know how to collect data. So what do we do now? We have to present the data we have collected so that they can be of use. This chapter begins by looking at how data can be presented in tables and charts. Such methods are helpful in presenting key data in a concise and easy to understand way. They are, however, purely descriptive and offer little opportunity for further detailed numerical analysis of a situation.

Data that are a mass of numbers can usefully be summarised into a frequency distribution (effectively a table which details the frequency with which a particular value occurs). Histograms and ogives are the pictorial representation of grouped and cumulative frequency distributions and provide the link between the purely descriptive approach to data analysis and the numerical approach covered in Chapters 20 and 21.

Data recorded over time can be presented as time series graphs. Z charts and semi-logarithmic graphs are special types of time series graph.

When facing exam questions on data presentation, read the question carefully and provide the correct diagram/chart/graph. The examiner was *not* impressed with those candidates in the May 95 exam who drew the incorrect diagram in Question 8.

1 TABLES

1.1 Raw data (the list of results from a survey) need to be summarised and analysed, to give them meaning. This chapter is concerned with several different ways of presenting data to convey their meaning. We will start with one of the most basic ways, the preparation of a table.

1.2 Tabulation means putting data into tables. A table is a matrix of data in rows and columns, with the rows and the columns having titles.

1.3 Since a table is two-dimensional, it can only show two variables. For example, the resources required to produce items in a factory could be tabulated, with one dimension (rows or columns) representing the items produced and the other dimension representing the resources.

Resources for production: all figures in pounds

		Product items			
	A	*B*	*C*	*D*	*Total*
Resources					
Direct material A	X	X	X	X	X
Direct material B	X	X	X	X	X
Direct labour grade 1	X	X	X	X	X
Direct labour grade 2	X	X	X	X	X
Supervision	X	X	X	X	X
Machine time	X	X	X	X	X
Total	X	X	X	X	X

1.4   To tabulate data, you need to recognise what the two dimensions should represent, prepare rows and columns accordingly with suitable titles, and then insert the data into the appropriate places in the table.

Guidelines for tabulation

1.5   The table in Paragraph 1.3 illustrates certain guidelines which you should apply when presenting data in tabular form. These are as follows.

(a)   The table should be given a clear title.

(b)   All columns should be clearly labelled.

(c)   Where appropriate, there should be clear sub-totals.

(d)   A total column may be presented; this would usually be the right-hand column.

(e)   A total figure is often advisable at the bottom of each column of figures.

(f)   Tables should not be packed with too much data so that reading the information is difficult.

(g)   Eliminate non-essential information, rounding large numbers to two or three significant figures.

(h)   Do not hide important figures in the middle of the table. Consider ordering columns/rows by order of importance/magnitude.

Example: tables

1.6   The total number of employees in a certain trading company is 1,000. They are employed in three departments: production, administration and sales. 600 people are employed in the production department and 300 in administration. There are 110 male juveniles in employment, 110 female juveniles, and 290 adult females. The remaining employees are adult males.

In the production department there are 350 adult males, 150 adult females and 50 male juveniles, whilst in the administration department there are 100 adult males, 110 adult females and 50 juvenile males.

Required

Draw up a table to show all the details of employment in the company and its departments and provide suitable secondary statistics to describe the distribution of people in departments.

Solution

1.7   The basic table required has the following two dimensions.

(a) Departments

(b) Age/sex analysis

1.8 Secondary statistics (not the same thing as secondary data) are supporting figures that are supplementary to the main items of data, and which clarify or amplify the main data. A major example of secondary statistics is percentages. In this example, we could show one of the following.

(a) The percentage of the total work force in each department belonging to each age/sex group

(b) The percentage of the total of each age/sex group employed in each department

In this example, (a) has been selected but you might consider that (b) would be more suitable. Either could be suitable, depending of course on what purposes the data are being collected and presented for.

1.9

Analysis of employees

	Production		Department Administration		Sales		Total	
	No	%	No	%	No	%	No	%
Adult males	350	58.4	100	33.3	**40	40	*490	49
Adult females	150	25.0	110	36.7	**30	30	290	29
Male juveniles	50	8.3	50	16.7	**10	10	110	11
Female juveniles	* 50	8.3	* 40	13.3	**20	20	110	11
Total	600	100.0	300	100.0	100	100	1,000	100

*   Balancing figure to make up the column total

**   Balancing figure then needed to make up the row total

Rounding errors

1.10 Rounding errors (which are looked at in Chapter 17) may become apparent when, for example, a percentages column does not add up to 100%. Any rounding should therefore be to the nearest unit and the potential size of errors should be kept to a tolerable level by rounding to a small enough unit (for example to the nearest £10, rather than to the nearest £1,000).

2   CHARTS   5/96

2.1 Instead of presenting data in a table, it might be preferable to give a visual display in the form of a chart.

2.2 The purpose of a chart is to convey the data in a way that will demonstrate its meaning or significance more clearly than a table of data would. Charts are not always more appropriate than tables, and the most suitable way of presenting data will depend on the following.

(a) What the data are intended to show. Visual displays usually make one or two points quite forcefully, whereas tables usually give more detailed information.

(b) Who is going to use the data. Some individuals might understand visual displays more readily than tabulated data.

Pie charts

2.3 A pie chart is used to show pictorially the relative sizes of component elements of a total. It is called a pie chart because it is circular, and so has the shape of a pie in a round pie dish and because the 'pie' is then cut into slices. Each slice represents a part of the total.

2.4   Pie charts have sectors of varying sizes, and you need to be able to draw sectors fairly accurately. To do this, you need a protractor. Working out sector sizes involves converting parts of the total into equivalent degrees of a circle.

Example: pie charts

2.5   The costs of production at Factory A and Factory B during March 19X2 were as follows.

	Factory A		Factory B	
	£'000	%	£'000	%
Direct materials	70	35	50	20
Direct labour	30	15	125	50
Production overhead	90	45	50	20
Office costs	10	5	25	10
	200	100	250	100

Required

Show the costs for the factories in pie charts.

Solution

2.6   To convert the components into degrees of a circle, we can use either the percentage figures or the actual cost figures.

(a)   Using the percentage figures, the total percentage is 100%, and the total number of degrees in a circle is 360°. To convert from one to the other, we multiply each percentage value by $360/100 = 3.6$.

	Factory A		Factory B	
	%	Degrees	%	Degrees
Direct materials	35	126	20	72
Direct labour	15	54	50	180
Production overhead	45	162	20	72
Office costs	5	18	10	36
	100	360	100	360

(b)   Using the actual cost figures, we would multiply each cost by

	Factory A	Factory B
$\dfrac{\text{Number of degrees}}{\text{Total cost}}$	$\dfrac{360}{200} = 1.8$	$\dfrac{360}{250} = 1.44$

	Factory A		Factory B	
	£'000	Degrees	£'000	Degrees
Direct materials	70	126	50	72
Direct labour	30	54	125	180
Production overhead	90	162	50	72
Office costs	10	18	25	36
	200	360	250	360

2.7   A pie chart could be drawn for each factory, as follows. A protractor is used to measure the degrees accurately to obtain the correct sector sizes.

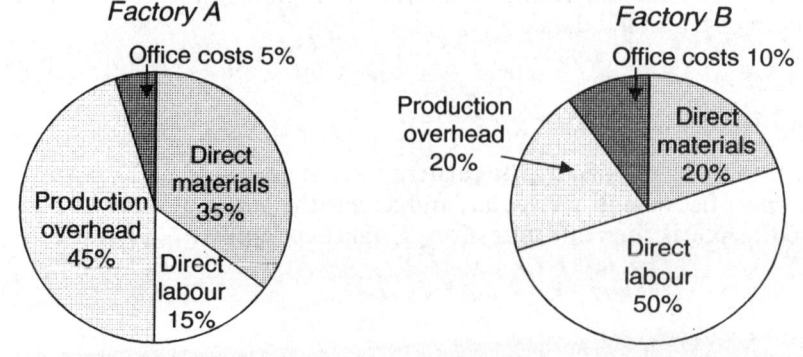

2.8   The advantages of pie charts are as follows.

(a)   They give a simple pictorial display of the relative sizes of elements of a total.

(b)   They show clearly when one element is much bigger than others.

(c)   They can sometimes clearly show differences in the elements of two different totals. In the example above, the pie charts for factories A and B show how factory A's costs mostly consist of production overhead and direct materials, whereas at factory B, direct labour is the largest cost element.

2.9   The disadvantages of pie charts are as follows.

(a)   They show only the relative sizes of elements. In the example of the two factories, for instance, the pie charts do not show that costs at Factory B were £50,000 higher in total than at Factory A.

(b)   They involve calculating degrees of a circle and drawing sectors accurately, and this can be time consuming.

(c)   It is sometimes difficult to compare sector sizes accurately by eye.

Bar charts

2.10   The bar chart is one of the most common methods of presenting data in a visual form. It is a chart in which quantities are shown in the form of bars.

2.11   There are three main types of bar chart.

(a)   Simple bar charts
(b)   Component bar charts, including percentage component bar charts
(c)   Multiple (or compound) bar charts

Simple bar charts

2.12   A simple bar chart is a chart consisting of one or more bars, in which the length of each bar indicates the magnitude of the corresponding data item.

Example: a simple bar chart

2.13   A company's total sales for the years from 19X1 to 19X6 are as follows.

Year	Sales
	£'000
19X1	800
19X2	1,200
19X3	1,100
19X4	1,400
19X5	1,600
19X6	1,700

The data could be shown on a simple bar chart as follows

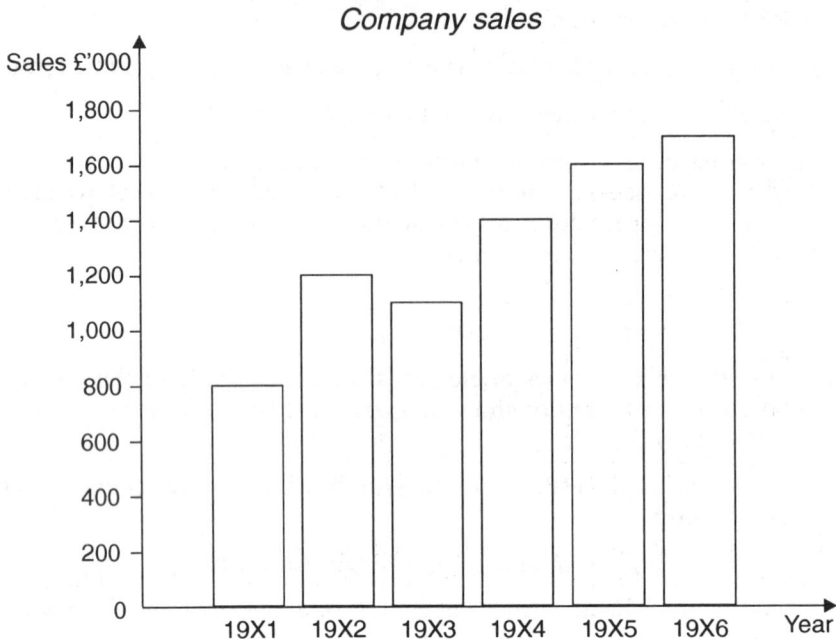

Company sales

2.14   Each axis of the chart must be clearly labelled, and there must be a scale to indicate the magnitude of the data. Here, the y axis includes a scale for the amount of sales, and so readers of the bar chart can see not only that sales have been rising year by year (with 19X3 being an exception) but also what the actual sales have been each year.

2.15   Simple bar charts serve two purposes.

   (a)   They show the actual magnitude of each item.

   (b)   They enable one to compare magnitudes, by comparing the lengths of bars on the chart.

Component bar charts

2.16   A component bar chart is a bar chart that gives a breakdown of each total into its components.

Example: a component bar chart

2.17   Charbart plc's sales for the years from 19X7 to 19X9 are as follows.

	19X7	*19X8*	*19X9*
	£'000	£'000	£'000
Product A	1,000	1,200	1,700
Product B	900	1,000	1,000
Product C	500	600	700
Total	2,400	2,800	3,400

2.18   A component bar chart would show the following.

   (a)   How total sales have changed from year to year
   (b)   The components of each year's total

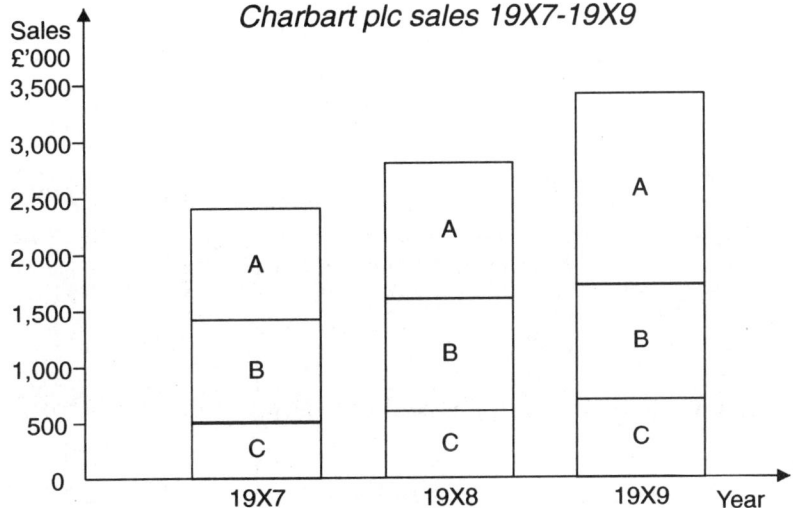

2.19 In this diagram the growth in sales is illustrated and the significance of growth in product A sales as the reason for the total sales growth is also fairly clear. The growth in product A sales would have been even clearer if product A had been drawn as the bottom element in each bar instead of the top one.

Percentage component bar charts

2.20 The difference between a component bar chart and a percentage component bar chart is that with a component bar chart, the total length of each bar (and the length of each component in it) indicates magnitude. A bigger amount is shown by a longer bar. With a percentage component bar chart, total magnitudes are not shown. If two or more bars are drawn on the chart, the total length of each bar is the same. The only varying lengths in a percentage component bar chart are the lengths of the sections of a bar, which vary according to the relative sizes of the components.

Example: a percentage component bar chart

2.21 The information in the previous example of sales of Charbart plc could have been shown in a percentage component bar chart as follows.

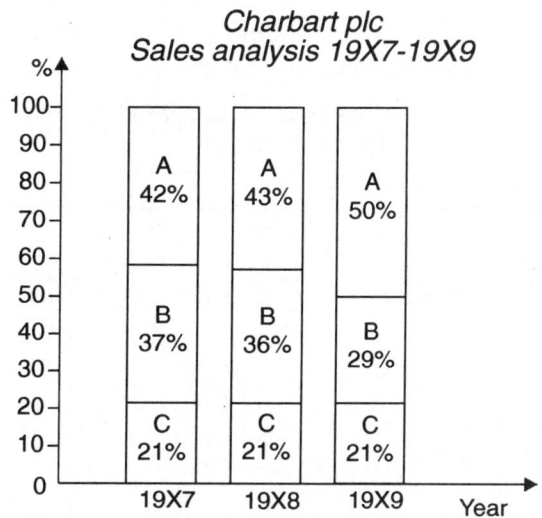

Working

	19X7		19X8		19X9	
	£'000	%	£'000	%	£'000	%
Product A	1,000	42	1,200	43	1,700	50
Product B	900	37	1,000	36	1,000	29
Product C	500	21	600	21	700	21
Total	2,400	100	2,800	100	3,400	100

2.22   This chart shows that sales of C have remained a steady proportion of total sales, but the proportion of A in total sales has gone up quite considerably, while the proportion of B has fallen correspondingly.

Multiple bar charts (compound bar charts)

2.23   A multiple bar chart (or compound bar chart) is a bar chart in which two or more separate bars are used to present sub-divisions of data.

Example: a multiple bar chart

2.24   The data on Charbart plc's sales could be shown in a multiple bar chart as follows.

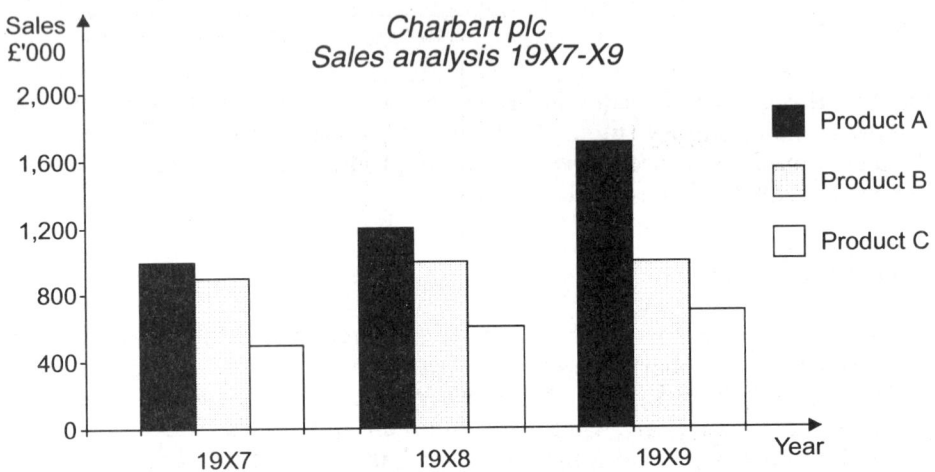

2.25   A multiple bar chart uses several bars for each total. In the above example, the sales in each year are shown as three separate bars, one for each product, A, B and C.

Multiple bar charts are sometimes drawn with the bars horizontal instead of vertical.

2.26   Multiple bar charts present similar information to component bar charts, except for the following.

(a)   Multiple bar charts do not show the grand total (in the above example, the total output each year) whereas component bar charts do.

(b)   Multiple bar charts illustrate the comparative magnitudes of the components more clearly than component bar charts.

Exercise 1

Income for Lemmi Bank in 19X0, 19X1 and 19X2 is made up as follows.

	19X0 £'000	19X1 £'000	19X2 £'000
Interest income	3,579	2,961	2,192
Commission income	857	893	917
Other income	62	59	70

Required

Using the above data, draw the following.

(a)   A simple bar chart
(b)   A component bar chart
(c)   A percentage component bar chart
(d)   A compound bar chart

Solution

(a)

	19X0 £'000	19X1 £'000	19X2 £'000
	3,579	2,961	2,192
	857	893	917
	62	59	70
	4,498	3,913	3,179

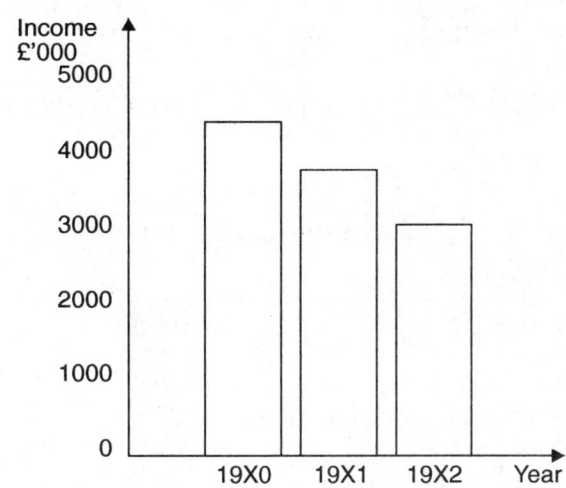

(b)

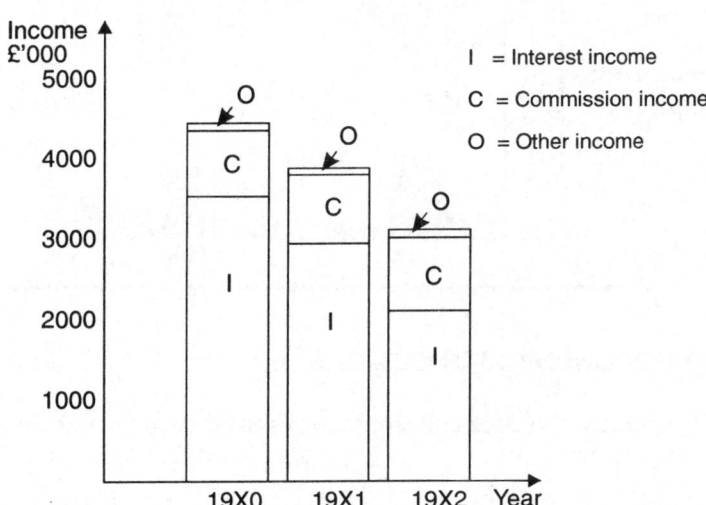

I = Interest income
C = Commission income
O = Other income

(c)

	19X0 £'000	%	19X1 £'000	%	19X2 £'000	%
	3,579	80	2,961	76	2,192	69
	857	19	893	23	917	29
	62	1	59	1	70	2
	4,498	100	3,913	100	3,179	100

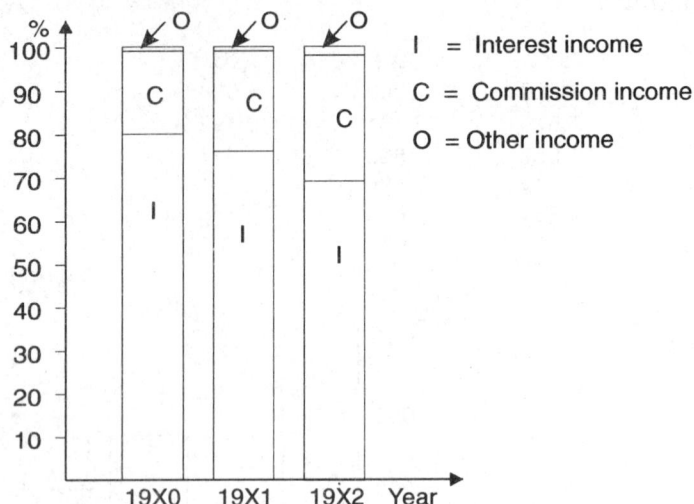

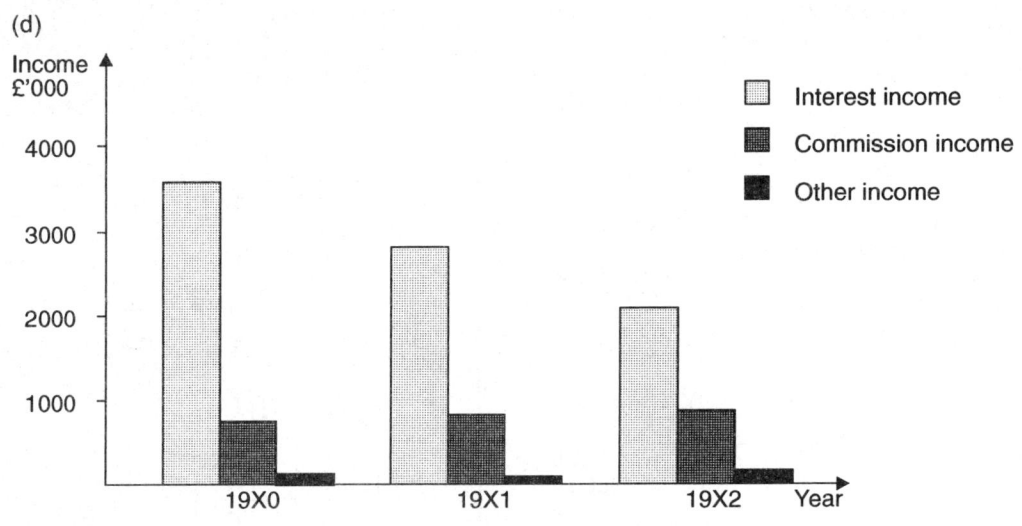

(d)

3   FREQUENCY DISTRIBUTIONS   S/95

3.1   Frequently the data collected from a statistical survey or investigation is simply a mass of numbers.

65	69	70	71	70	68	69	67	70	68
72	71	69	74	70	73	71	67	69	70

3.2   The raw data above yields little information as it stands; imagine how much more difficult it would be if there were hundreds or even thousands of data items. The data could, of course, be arranged in order size (an array) and the lowest and highest data items, as well as typical items, could be identified.

3.3   Many sets of data, however, contain a limited number of data values, even though there may be many occurrences of each value. It can therefore be useful to organise the data into what is known as a frequency distribution (or frequency table) which records the number of times each value occurs (the frequency). A frequency distribution for the data in Paragraph 3.1 (the output in units of 20 employees during one week) is as follows.

Output of employees in one week in units

Output Units	Number of employees (frequency)
65	1
66	0
67	2
68	2
69	4
70	5
71	3
72	1
73	1
74	1
	20

3.4 When the data are arranged in this way it is immediately obvious that 69 and 70 units are the most common volumes of output per employee per week.

Grouped frequency distributions

3.5 If there is a large set of data or if every (or nearly every) data item is different, it is often convenient to group frequencies together into bands or classes. For example, suppose that the output produced by another group of 20 employees during one week was as follows, in units.

1,087	850	1,084	792
924	1,226	1,012	1,205
1,265	1,028	1,230	1,182
1,086	1,130	989	1,155
1,134	1,166	1,129	1,160

3.6 The range of output from the lowest to the highest producer is 792 to 1,265, a range of 473 units. This range could be divided into classes of say, 100 units (the class width or class interval), and the number of employees producing output within each class could then be grouped into a single frequency, as follows.

Output Units	Number of employees (frequency)
700 - 799	1
800 - 899	1
900 - 999	2
1,000 - 1,099	5
1,100 - 1,199	7
1,200 - 1,299	4
	20

3.7 Note, however, that once items have been 'grouped' in this way their individual values are lost.

Grouped frequency distributions of continuous variables

3.8 As well as being used for discrete variables (as above), grouped frequency distributions (or grouped frequency tables) can be used to present data for continuous variables.

Example: a grouped frequency distribution for a continuous variable

3.9 Suppose we wish to record the heights of 50 different individuals. The information might be presented as a grouped frequency distribution, as follows.

Height cm	Number of individuals (frequency)
Up to and including 154	1
Over 154, up to and including 163	3
Over 163, up to and including 172	8
Over 172, up to and including 181	16
Over 181, up to and including 190	18
Over 190	4
	50

3.10   Note the following points.

(a)   It would be wrong to show the ranges as 0 - 154, 154 - 163, 163 - 172 and so on, because 154 cm and 163 cm would then be values in two classes, which is not permissible. Although each value should only be in one class, we have to make sure that each possible value can be included. Classes such as 154-162, 163-172 would not be suitable since a height of 162.5 cm would not belong in either class. Such classes could be used for discrete variables, however.

(b)   There is an *open ended* class at each end of the range. This is because heights up to 154 cm and over 190 cm are thought to be uncommon, so that a single 'open ended' class is used to group all the frequencies together.

Preparing grouped frequency distributions

3.11   To prepare a grouped frequency distribution, a decision must be made about how wide each class should be. In an examination, you might be told how many classes to use, or what the class interval should be. You should, however, generally observe the following guidelines.

(a)   The size of each class should be appropriate to the nature of the data being recorded, and the most appropriate class interval varies according to circumstances.

(b)   The upper and lower limits of each class interval should be suitable 'round' numbers for class intervals which are in multiples of 5, 10, 100, 1,000 and so on. For example, if the class interval is 10, and data items range in value from 23 to 62 (discrete values), the class intervals should be 20-29, 30-39, 40-49, 50-59 and 60-69, rather than 23-32, 33-42, 43-52 and 53-62.

(c)   With continuous variables, either:

(i)   the upper limit of a class should be 'up to and including ...' and the lower limit of the next class should be 'over ...'; or

(ii)   the upper limit of a class should be 'less than...', and the lower limit of the next class should be 'at least ...'.

Exercise 2

The commission earnings for May 19X3 of the assistants in a department store were as follows (in pounds).

60	35	53	47	25	44	55	58	47	71
63	67	57	44	61	48	50	56	61	42
43	38	41	39	61	51	27	56	57	50
55	68	55	50	25	48	44	43	49	73
53	35	36	41	45	71	56	40	69	52
36	47	66	52	32	46	44	32	52	58
49	41	45	45	48	36	46	42	52	33
31	36	40	66	53	58	60	52	66	51
51	44	59	53	51	57	35	45	46	54
46	54	51	39	64	43	54	47	60	45

Required

Prepare a grouped frequency distribution classifying the commission earnings into categories of £5 commencing with '£25 and under £30'.

Solution

We are told what classes to use, so the first step is to identify the lowest and highest values in the data. The lowest value is £25 (in the first row) and the highest value is £73 (in the fourth row). This means that the class intervals must go up to '£70 and under £75'.

We can now set out the classes in a column, and then count the number of items in each class using tally marks.

Class interval	Tally marks	Total
£25 and less than £30	///	3
£30 and less than £35	////	4
£35 and less than £40	HH HH	10
£40 and less than £45	HH HH HH	15
£45 and less than £50	HH HH HH ///	18
£50 and less than £55	HH HH HH HH	20
£55 and less than £60	HH HH ///	13
£60 and less than £65	HH ///	8
£65 and less than £70	HH /	6
£70 and less than £75	///	3
	Total	100

3.12 You should be able to interpret a grouped frequency distribution and express an interpretation in writing. In the example in Paragraph 3.9, an interpretation of the data is fairly straightforward.

(a) Most heights fell between 154 cm and 190 cm.

(b) Most heights were in the middle of this range, with few people having heights in the lower and upper ends of the range.

Cumulative frequency distributions

3.13 A cumulative frequency distribution (or cumulative frequency table) can be used to show the total number of times that a value above or below a certain amount occurs.

3.14 There are two possible cumulative frequency distributions for the grouped frequency distribution in Paragraph 3.6.

	Cumulative frequency		*Cumulative frequency*
≥ 700	20	< 800	1
≥ 800	19	< 900	2
≥ 900	18	<1,000	4
≥ 1,000	16	<1,100	9
≥ 1,100	11	<1,200	16
≥ 1,200	4	<1,300	20

Notes

(a) The symbol > means 'greater than' and ≥ means 'greater than or equal to'. The symbol < means 'less than' and ≤ means 'less than or equal to'. These symbols provide a convenient method of stating classes.

(b) The first cumulative frequency distribution shows that of the total of 20 employees, 19 produced 800 units or more, 18 produced 900 units or more, 16 produced 1,000 units or more and so on.

(c)   The second cumulative frequency distribution shows that, of the total of 20 employees, one produced under 800 units, two produced under 900 units, four produced under 1,000 units and so on.

4   HISTOGRAMS

4.1   It is often simpler to interpret data after they have been presented pictorially rather than as a table of figures. A frequency distribution can be represented pictorially by means of a histogram. Histograms look rather like bar charts except that the bars are joined together and whereas frequencies are represented by the height of bars on a bar chart, frequencies are represented by the *area* covered by bars on a histogram.

Histograms of frequency distributions with equal class intervals

4.2   If all the class intervals are the same, as in the frequency distribution in Paragraph 3.6, the bars of the histogram all have the same width and the heights will be proportional to the frequencies. The histogram looks almost identical to a bar chart except that the bars are joined together. Because the bars are joined together, when presenting discrete data the data must be treated as continuous so that there are no gaps between class intervals. For example, for a cricketer's scores in various games the classes would have to be ≥ 0 but < 10, ≥ 10 but < 20 and so on, instead of 0-9, 10-19 and so on.

4.3   A histogram of the distribution in Paragraph 3.6 would be drawn as follows.

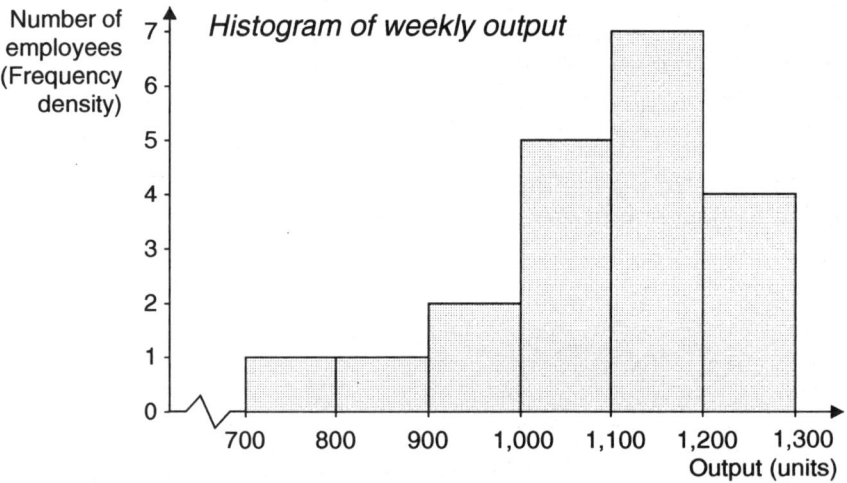

4.4   Note that the discrete data have been treated as continuous, the intervals being changed to >700 but ≤ 800, >800 but ≤ 900 and so on.

Histograms of frequency distributions with unequal class intervals

4.5   If a distribution has unequal class intervals, the heights of the bars have to be adjusted for the fact that the bars do not have the same width.

Example: a histogram with unequal class intervals

4.6   The weekly wages of employees of Salt Lake Ltd are as follows.

Wages per employee	*Number of employees*
Up to and including £60	4
> £60 ≤ £80	6
> £80 ≤ £90	6
> £90 ≤£120	6
More than £120	3

The class intervals for wages per employee are not all the same, and range from £10 to £30.

4.7 A histogram is drawn as follows.

(a) The width of each bar on the chart must be proportionate to the corresponding class interval. In other words, the bar representing wages of > £60 ≤ £80, a range of £20, will be oncewide as the bar representing wages of > £80 ≤ £90, a range of only £10.

(b) A standard width of bar must be selected. This should be the size of class interval which occurs most frequently. In our example, class intervals £10, £20 and £30 each occur once. An interval of £20 will be selected as the standard width.

(c) Open-ended classes must be closed off. It is usual for the width of such classes to be the same as that of the adjoining class. In this example, the class 'up to and including £60' will become >£40 ≤ £60 and the class 'more than £120' will become >£120 ≤ £150.

(d) Each frequency is then multiplied by (standard class width ÷ actual class width) to obtain the height of the bar in the histogram.

(e) The height of bars no longer corresponds to *frequency* but rather to *frequency density* and hence the vertical axis should be labelled frequency density.

(f) Note that the data is considered to be continuous since the gap between, for example, £79.99 and £80.00 is very, very small.

4.8

Class interval	Size of interval	Frequency	Adjustment	Height of bar
> £40 ≤ £60	20	4	× 20/20	4
> £60 ≤ £80	20	6	× 20/20	6
> £80 ≤ £90	10	6	× 20/10	12
> £90 ≤ £120	30	6	× 20/30	4
> £120 ≤ £150	30	3	× 20/30	2

(a) The first two bars will be of normal height.

(b) The third bar will be twice as high as the class frequency (6) would suggest, to compensate for the fact that the class interval, £10, is only half the standard size.

(c) The fourth and fifth bars will be two thirds as high as the class frequencies (6 and 3) would suggest, to compensate for the fact that the class interval, £30, is 150% of the standard size.

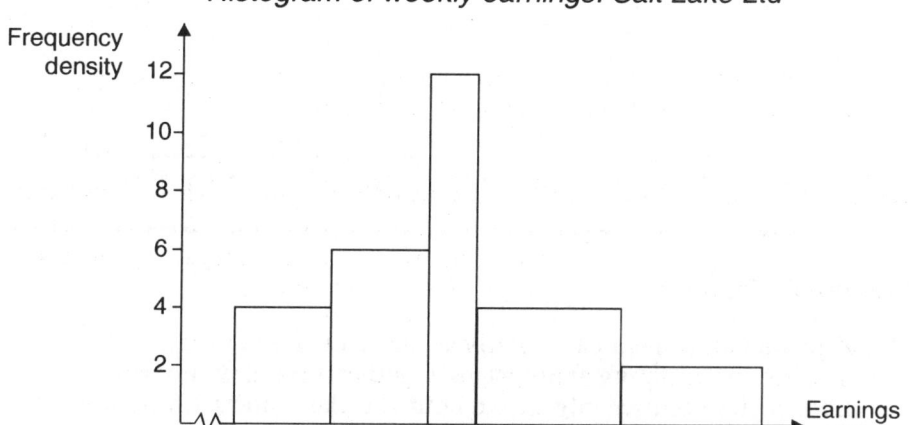

Histogram of weekly earnings: Salt Lake Ltd

Exercise 3

The sales force of a company have just completed a successful sales campaign. The performances of individual sales staff have been analysed as follows, into a grouped frequency distribution.

Sales	Number of sales staff
Up to £10,000	1
> £10,000 ≤ £12,000	10
> £12,000 ≤ £14,000	12
> £14,000 ≤ £18,000	8
> £18,000 ≤ £22,000	4
> £22,000	1

Required

Draw a histogram from this information.

Solution

Before drawing the histogram, we must decide on the following.

(a) A standard class width: £2,000 will be chosen.

(b) An open-ended class width. In this example, the open-ended class width will therefore be £2,000 for class 'up to £10,000' and £4,000 for the class '> £22,000'.

Class interval	Size of width £	Frequency	Adjustment	Height of block
Up to £10,000	2,000	1	× 2/2	1
> £10,000 ≤ £12,000	2,000	10	× 2/2	10
> £12,000 ≤ £14,000	2,000	12	× 2/2	12
> £14,000 ≤ £18,000	4,000	8	× 2/4	4
> £18,000 ≤ £22,000	4,000	4	× 2/4	2
> £22,000	4,000	1	× 2/4	$^1/_2$

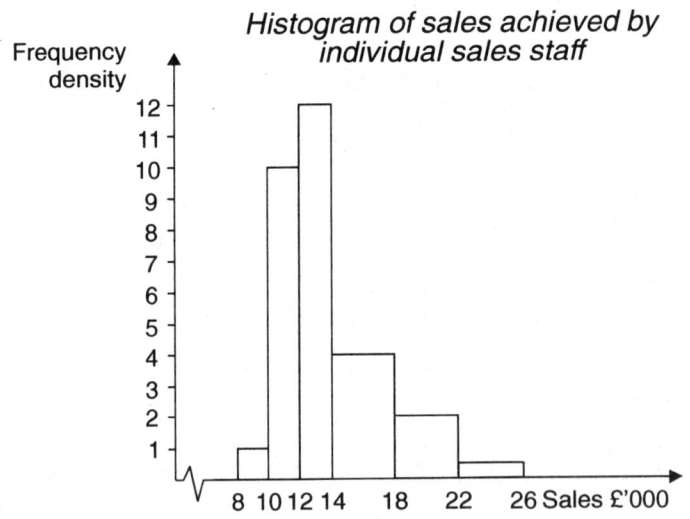

Histogram of sales achieved by individual sales staff

Frequency polygons

4.9 A histogram is not a particularly accurate method of presenting a frequency distribution because, in grouping frequencies together in a class interval, it is assumed that these frequencies occur evenly throughout the class interval, which is unlikely. To overcome this criticism, we can convert a histogram into a frequency polygon, which is drawn on the assumption that, within each class interval, the frequency of occurrence of data items is not evenly spread. There will be more values at the end of each class interval nearer the histogram's peak (if any), and so the flat top on a histogram bar should be converted into a rising or falling line.

4.10 A frequency polygon is drawn from a histogram, in the following way.

(a)   Mark the mid-point of the top of each bar in the histogram.
(b)   Join up all these points with straight lines.

4.11   The ends of the diagram (the mid-points of the two end bars) should be joined to the base line at the mid-points of the next class intervals outside the range of observed data. These intervals should be taken to be of the same size as the last class intervals for observed data.

Example: a frequency polygon

4.12   The following grouped frequency distribution relates to the number of occasions during the past 40 weeks that a particular cost has been a given amount.

Cost £	Number of occasions
> 800 ≤ 1,000	4
> 1,000 ≤ 1,200	10
> 1,200 ≤ 1,400	12
> 1,400 ≤ 1,600	10
> 1,600 ≤ 1,800	4
	40

Required

Prepare a frequency polygon.

Solution

4.13   A histogram is first drawn, in the way described earlier. All classes are of the same width.

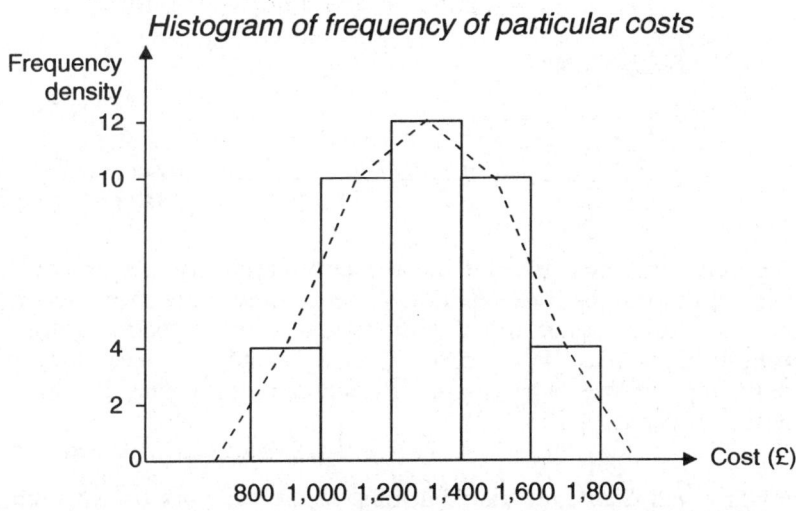

Histogram of frequency of particular costs

The mid-points of the class intervals outside the range of observed data are 700 and 1,900.

Frequency curves

4.14   Because a frequency polygon has straight lines between points, it too can be seen as an inaccurate way of presenting data. One method of obtaining greater accuracy would be to make the class intervals smaller. If the class intervals of a distribution were made small enough the frequency polygon would become very smooth. It would become a curve.

5   OGIVES   5/95

5.1   Just as a grouped frequency distribution can be graphed as a histogram, a cumulative frequency distribution can be graphed as an ogive. An ogive shows the cumulative number of items with a value less than or equal to, or alternatively greater than or equal to, a certain amount.

Example: ogives

5.2   Consider the following frequency distribution.

Number of faulty units rejected on inspection	Frequency	Cumulative frequency
> 0, ≤ 1	5	5
> 1, ≤ 2	5	10
> 2, ≤ 3	3	13
> 3, ≤ 4	1	14
	14	

An ogive would be drawn as follows.

Ogive of rejected items

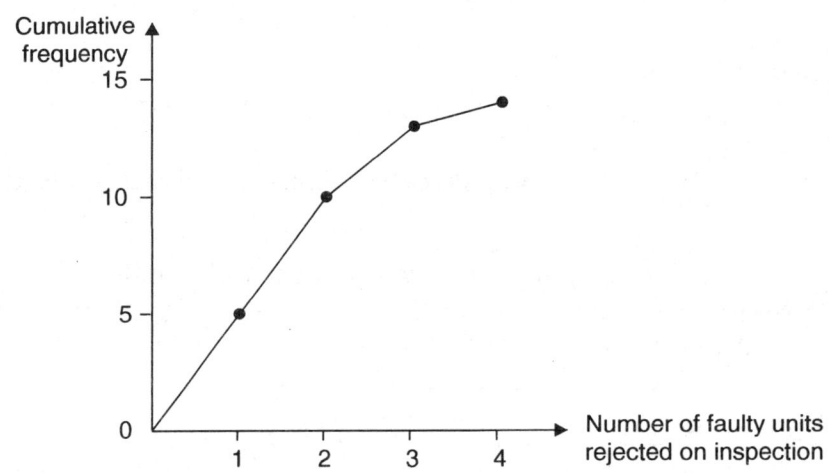

5.3   The ogive is drawn by plotting the cumulative frequencies on the graph, and joining them with straight lines. Although many ogives are more accurately curved lines, you can use straight lines in drawing an ogive in an examination. An ogive drawn with straight lines may be referred to as a cumulative frequency *polygon* (or cumulative frequency *diagram*) whereas one drawn as a curve may be referred to as a cumulative frequency *curve*.

5.4   For grouped frequency distributions, where we work up through values of the variable, the cumulative frequencies are plotted against the *upper* limits of the classes. For example, for the class 'over 2, up to and including 3', the cumulative frequency should be plotted against 3.

Exercise 4

A grouped frequency distribution for the volume of output produced at a factory over a period of 40 weeks is as follows.

Output (units)	Number of times output achieved
> 0 ≤ 200	4
>200 ≤ 400	8
>400 ≤ 600	12
>600 ≤ 800	10
>800 ≤1,000	6
	40

Required

Draw an appropriate ogive, and estimate the number of weeks in which output was 550 units or less.

Solution

Upper limit of interval	Frequency	Cumulative frequency
200	4	4
400	8	12
600	12	24
800	10	34
1,000	6	40

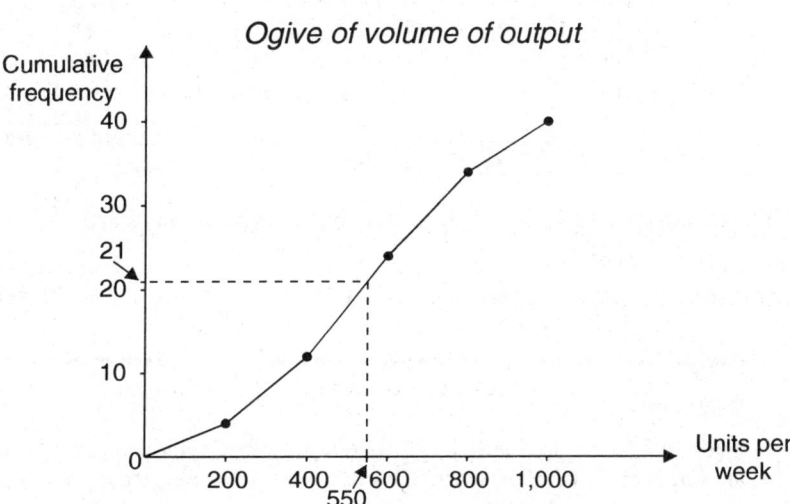

Ogive of volume of output

The dotted lines indicate that output of up to 550 units was achieved in 21 out of the 40 weeks.

5.5   We can also draw ogives to show the cumulative number of items with values greater than or equal to some given value.

Example: downward-sloping ogives

5.6   Output at a factory over a period of 80 weeks is shown by the following frequency distribution.

Output per week Units	Number of times output achieved
> 0 ≤ 100	10
> 100 ≤ 200	20
> 200 ≤ 300	25
> 300 ≤ 400	15
> 400 ≤ 500	10
	80

5.7   If we want to draw an ogive to show the number of weeks in which output exceeded a certain value, the cumulative total should begin at 80 and drop to 0. In drawing an ogive when we work down through values of the variable, the descending cumulative frequency should be plotted against the lower limit of each class interval.

Lower limit of interval	Frequency	Cumulative ('more than') frequency
0	10	80
100	20	70
200	25	50
300	15	25
400	10	10
500	0	0

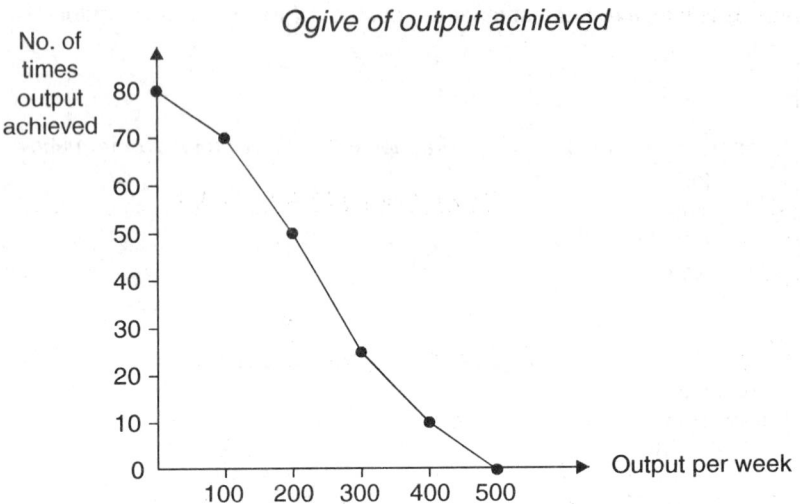

Make sure that you understand what this curve shows.

For example, 350 on the x axis corresponds with about 18 on the y axis. This means that output of 350 units or more was achieved 18 times out of the 80 weeks.

Exercise 5

If you wanted to produce an ogive showing the cumulative number of students in a class with an exam mark of 55% or more, would you need an upward-sloping or a downward-sloping ogive?

Solution

A downward-sloping ogive

---

6   TIME SERIES GRAPHS

6.1   A time series is a series of figures or values recorded over time such as monthly sales over the last two years.

6.2   A graph of a time series is called a historigram. (Note the 'ri'; this is not the same as a histogram). The horizontal axis of a historigram is always chosen to represent time and the vertical axis represents the values of the data recorded. The graph will give some indication of the trend in the data over time.

6.3   A *component time series* is data in which various classifications (for example sales in the four branches of a retail organisation each month) can be thought of as the components of a meaningful total (the total monthly sales of the retail organisation). A *multiple time series*, on the other hand, is data which have classifications for each time period which cannot be added to form meaningful totals. An example would be prices of selected food items (such as tea (per packet), bread (per loaf) and caviar (per jar)).

Example: time series

6.4   The following data show the sales of a product in the period 19X6-X8.

Year	Quarter 1 '000	Quarter 2 '000	Quarter 3 '000	Quarter 4 '000
19X6	86	42	57	112
19X7	81	39	55	107
19X8	77	35	52	99

Required

Plot a time series of the above data.

Solution

6.5

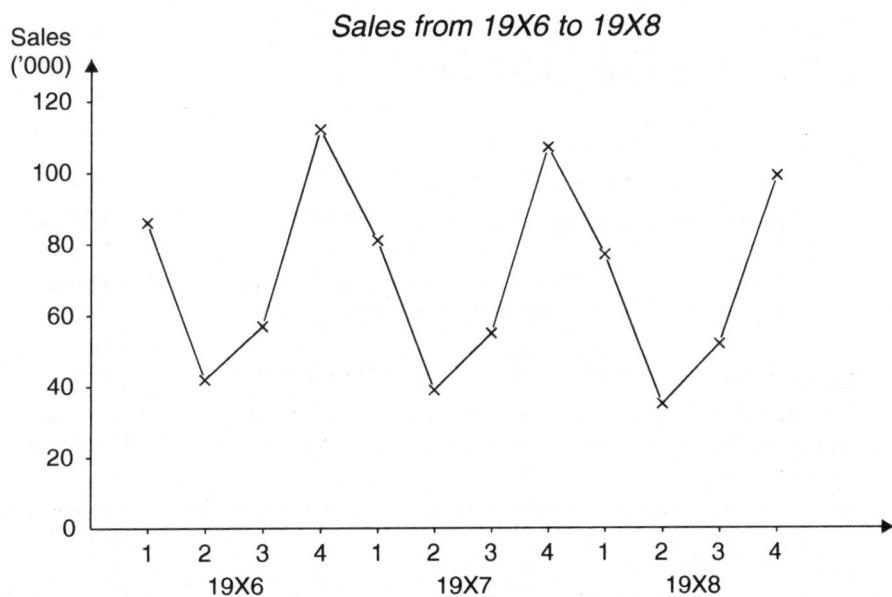

6.6   We will be looking at time series analysis in some detail in Chapter 27.

7   Z CHARTS

7.1   A Z chart is a time series graph which can be very useful for presenting business data. It shows the following.

(a)   The value of a variable plotted against time over the year
(b)   The cumulative sum of values for that variable over the year to date
(c)   The annual moving total for that variable

The annual moving total is the sum of values of the variable for the 12 month period up to the end of the month under consideration.

Example: Z charts

7.2   The sales figures for a company for 19X2 and 19X3 are as follows.

	19X2 sales	*19X3 sales*
	£m	£m
January	7	8
February	7	8
March	8	8
April	7	9
May	9	8
June	8	8
July	8	7
August	7	8
September	6	9
October	7	6
November	8	9
December	8	9
	90	97

Required

Draw a Z chart to represent these data.

Solution

7.3 The first thing to do is to calculate the cumulative sales for 19X3 and the annual moving total for the year.

	Sales 19X2	*Sales 19X3*	*Cumulative sales 19X3*	*Annual moving total*
	£m	£m	£m	£m
January	7	8	8	91
February	7	8	16	92
March	8	8	24	92
April	7	9	33	94
May	9	8	41	93
June	8	8	49	93
July	8	7	56	92
August	7	8	64	93
September	6	9	73	96
October	7	6	79	95
November	8	9	88	96
December	8	9	97	97

The first figure in the annual moving total is arrived at by taking the sales for the year ended December 19X2, adding those for January 19X3 and subtracting those for January 19X2. This gives the sales for a 12 month period to the end of January 19X3 as $90 + 8 - 7 = 91$.

A similar approach is used for the rest of the year, by adding on the new 19X3 month and deducting the corresponding 19X2 month.

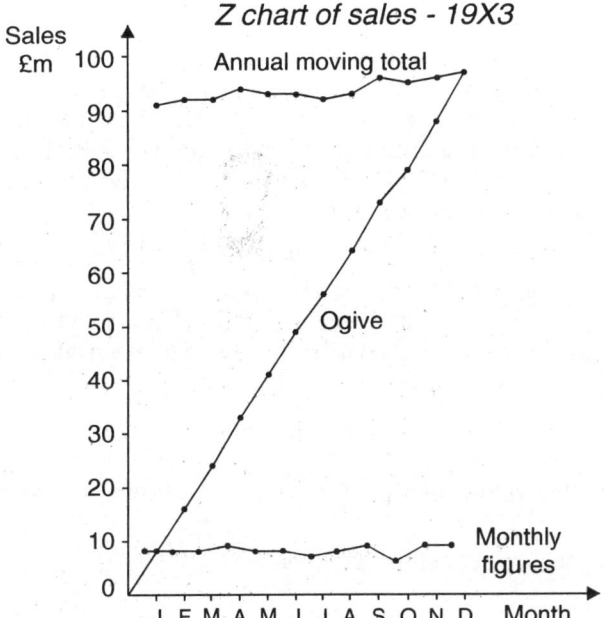

Z chart of sales - 19X3

7.4 You will notice that while the values of the annual moving total and the cumulative values are plotted on month-end positions, the values for the current monthly figures are plotted on mid-month positions. This is because the monthly figures represent achievement over a particular month whereas the annual moving totals and the cumulative values represent achievement up to a particular month end.

The interpretation of Z charts

7.5 The popularity of Z charts in practical applications derives from the wealth of information which they can contain.

(a) *Monthly totals* show the monthly results at a glance together with any seasonal variations.

(b) *Cumulative totals* show the performance to date, and can be easily compared with planned or budgeted performance by superimposing a budget line.

(c) *Annual moving totals* compare the current levels of performance with those of the previous year. If the line is rising then this year's monthly results are better than the results of the corresponding month last year. The opposite applies if the line is falling. The annual moving total line indicates the long-term trend in values of the variable, whether rising, falling or steady.

7.6 You should note that Z charts do not have to cover 12 months of a year. They could also be drawn for (for example) four quarters of a year, or seven days of a week. The method would be exactly the same.

Exercise 6

Why does the annual moving total line on a Z chart show the long-term trend, unaffected by seasonal effects such as sales being higher in summer than winter?

Solution

One example of each month is included in the annual moving total. Thus although July might be a very good month, but January a very bad month, there will be one July and one January in the total, balancing each other.

8   SEMI-LOGARITHMIC GRAPHS

8.1   A variation of the time series graph is the semi-logarithmic graph. A semi-logarithmic graph is plotted on special semi-logarithmic (log-linear) graph paper. This has a normal horizontal axis against which time is plotted but, on the vertical axis, equal intervals represent equal proportional changes in the variable. For example, the distance on the axis between y = 10 and y = 30 is the same as the distance between y = 30 and y = 90 (both represent a three-fold increase).

8.2   Sections of a graph having equal slope represent equal proportional changes in the variable. A straight line therefore indicates that a variable is increasing or decreasing at a constant rate whereas a curve indicates that a variable is increasing/decreasing at an increasing or decreasing rate. The steeper the line, the higher the rate of increase/decrease.

8.3   The principal relationships likely to be shown on semi-logarithmic graphs are as follows.

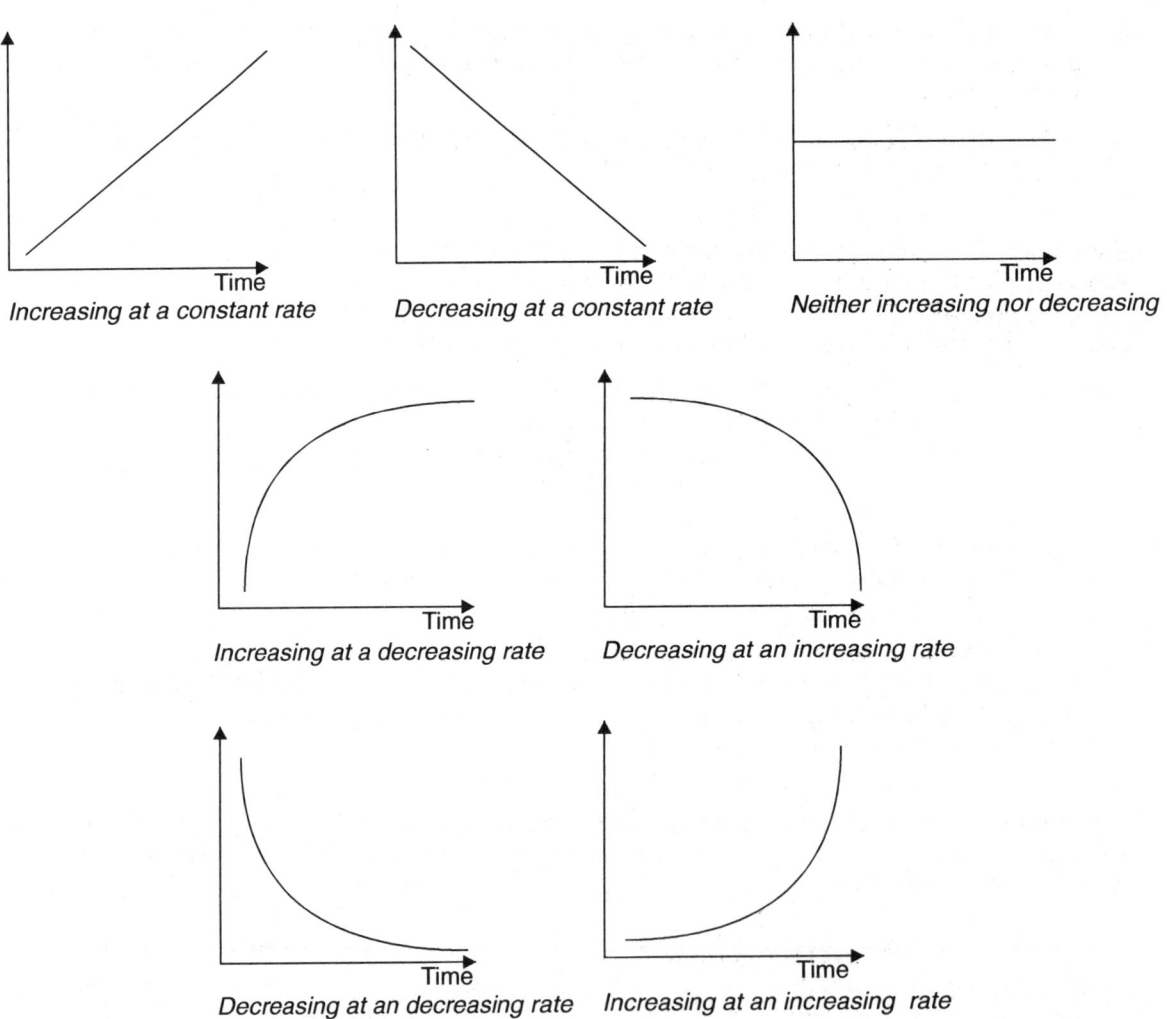

8.4   An alternative to using semi-logarithmic paper is to plot the logarithms of the values of the variable on the vertical axis against time on the horizontal axis.

8.5   Because only proportional changes are of interest, time series measured in different units can be compared on the same semi-logarithmic graph.

8.6   Such graphs are also useful in situations where the dependent variable covers a great range of values. In such a case, use of an ordinary graph would require such a small scale on the vertical axis that significant changes would be obscured.

8.7   Although semi-logarithmic graphs can be useful, they do have a number of disadvantages. Any variables having zero or negative values cannot be plotted. Perhaps more importantly, however, most people are used to interpreting normal graphs and may therefore misread semi-logarithmic graphs. It must therefore be clear if graphs have been drawn on a logarithmic basis. There is a case for not actually labelling the vertical axis since it is the slope of lines that are important, not values.

Example: semi-logarithmic graphs

8.8   The annual production volumes of a particular company over the last ten years are shown below.

Year	Production volume	Log	Year	Production volume	Log
1	1,014	3.0060	6	10,630	4.0265
2	1,622	3.2101	7	17,009	4.2307
3	2,595	3.4141	8	27,214	4.4348
4	4,152	3.6183	9	43,543	4.6389
5	6,644	3.8224	10	69,669	4.8430

(a)   The production volumes cover a very large range. To plot them on a conventional graph would require such a small scale as to make changes in early years impossible to decipher.

(b)   It is difficult to determine how production volumes have changed over the period simply by looking at the figures.

8.9   If we plot the logarithms of the production volumes against time (as in diagram (a) below) or plot the volumes against time on semi-logarithmic graph paper (as in diagram (b) below) we are able to view changes in volume across the entire ten-year period, and ascertain that the production volume has been increasing at a fairly constant rate.

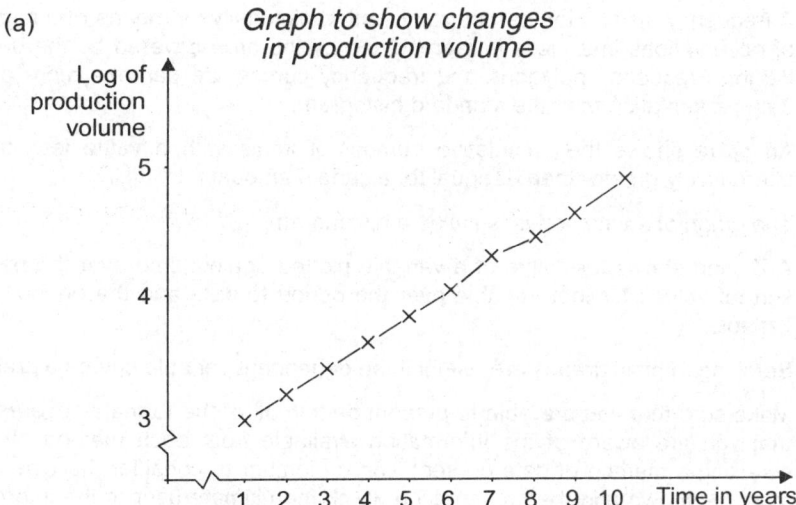

(a)   *Graph to show changes in production volume*

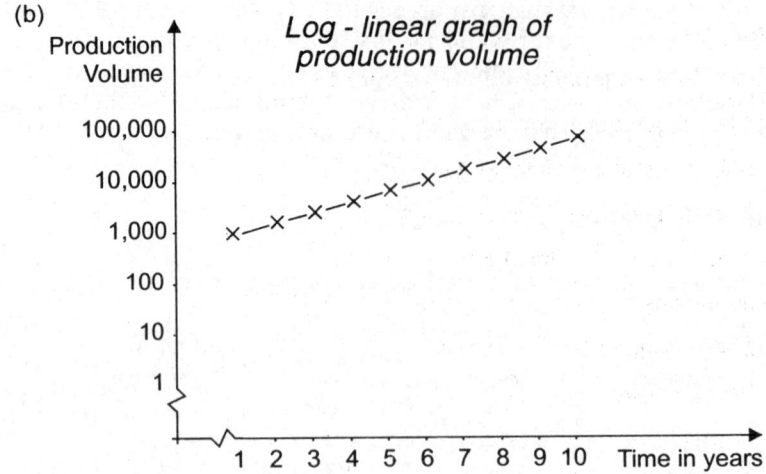

(b) Log - linear graph of production volume

Chapter roundup

- This chapter has considered a number of ways of presenting data.

- Tables are a simple way of presenting information about two variables.

- Charts often convey the meaning or significance of data more clearly than would a table.

- There are three main types of bar chart: simple, component (including percentage component) and multiple (or compound).

- Frequency distributions are used if values of particular variables occur more than once. Make sure that you know the difference between grouped frequency and cumulative frequency distributions.

- A frequency distribution can be represented pictorially by means of a histogram. The number of observations in a class is represented by the area covered by the bar, rather than by its height. Frequency polygons and frequency curves are perhaps more accurate methods of data presentation than the standard histogram.

- An ogive shows the cumulative number of items with a value less than or equal to, or alternatively greater than or equal to, a certain amount.

- The graph of a time series is called a historigram.

- A Z chart shows the value of a variable plotted against time over the period, the cumulative sum of values for that variable over the period to date and the period moving total for that variable.

- Semi-logarithmic graphs are useful if the dependent variable covers a great range of values.

- Make sure that you are able to present data in all of the formats covered in this chapter and that you are aware of the information available from each method of presentation. When selecting a method of data presentation remember to consider the type of information which must be shown and the presentation which the ultimate user of the information will find most helpful.

Test your knowledge

1   What are the main guidelines for tabulation? (see para 1.5)

2   What are the disadvantages of pie charts? (2.9)

3   Name the three main types of bar chart. (2.11)

4   How would you prepare a grouped frequency distribution? (3.11)

5   What is a cumulative frequency distribution? (3.13)

6   What are the computations needed to draw a histogram? (4.7)

7   How would you draw a frequency polygon from a histogram? (4.10)

8   How would you draw an ogive? (5.2 - 5.4)

9   What is a historigram? (6.2)

10   What three lines are drawn on a Z chart? (7.1)

11   What is log-linear paper? (8.1)

Now try illustrative question 20 at the end of the Study Text

Chapter 20

AVERAGES

This chapter covers the following topics.

		Syllabus reference	Ability required
1	The arithmetic mean	2(e)	Skill
2	The mode	2(e)	Skill
3	The median	2(e)	Skill

Introduction

In Chapter 19 we saw how data can be summarised and presented in tabular, chart and graphical formats. Such formats provide an overview of a situation and show the key features of the data. For example, a bar chart might show that very few CIMA students in Ruritania earn less then 100 Ruritanian dollars a month and that very few earn more than 700 Ruritanian dollars a month, the majority earning somewhere between the two extremes.

Sometimes you might need more information than that provided by diagrammatic representations of data. In such circumstances you may need to apply some sort of numerical analysis. A CIMA student in Ruritania, for example, might want some means of comparing her salary with those of other CIMA students.

There are two initial measures that we can take from a set of data: a measure of centrality and a measure of dispersion. In Chapter 21 we will look at measures of dispersion, in this chapter measures of centrality, or averages.

An average is a representative figure that is used to give some impression of the size of all the items in the population. The average salary of CIMA students in Ruritania will therefore be representative of all of the salaries. You may have thought that an average is simply 'an average' but there are in fact three main types of average.

(a) Arithmetic mean
(b) Mode
(c) Median

We will be looking at each of these averages in turn, their calculation, advantages and disadvantages. In the next chapter we will move on to the second type of numerical measure, measures of dispersion.

---

1 THE ARITHMETIC MEAN

S/95, S/96

1.1 This is the best known type of average. For ungrouped data, it is calculated by the formula

$$\text{Arithmetic mean} = \frac{\text{Sum of values of items}}{\text{Number of items}}$$

For example, the mean wage of a work force of ten men is the amount each worker would receive if all their earnings were pooled and then shared out equally among them.

Example: the arithmetic mean

1.2 The demand for a product on each of 20 days was as follows (in units).

3   12   7   17   3   14   9   6   11   10   1   4   19   7   15   6   9   12   12   8

The arithmetic mean of daily demand is

$$\frac{\text{Sum of demand}}{\text{Number of days}} = \frac{185}{20} = 9.25 \text{ units}$$

1.3   The arithmetic mean of a variable x is shown as $\overline{x}$ ('x bar').

Thus in the above example $\overline{x} = 9.25$ units.

1.4   In the above example, demand on any one day is never actually 9.25 units. The arithmetic mean is merely an average representation of demand on each of the 20 days.

Finding the arithmetic mean of data in a frequency distribution

1.5   It is more likely in an exam that you will be asked to calculate the arithmetic mean of a frequency distribution. In our previous example, the frequency distribution would be shown as follows.

Daily demand	Frequency	Demand × frequency
x	f	fx
1	1	1
3	2	6
4	1	4
6	2	12
7	2	14
8	1	8
9	2	18
10	1	10
11	1	11
12	3	36
14	1	14
15	1	15
17	1	17
19	1	19
	20	185

$$\overline{x} = \frac{185}{20} = 9.25$$

Sigma, Σ

1.6   The statistical notation for the arithmetic mean of a set of data uses the symbol Σ (sigma). Σ means 'the sum of' and is used as shorthand to mean 'the sum of a set of values'.

Thus, in the previous example:

(a) Σf would mean the sum of all the frequencies, which is 20;

(b) Σfx would mean the sum of all the values of 'frequency multiplied by daily demand', that is, all 14 values of fx, so $\Sigma fx = 185$.

The symbolic formula for the arithmetic mean of a frequency distribution

1.7   Using the Σ sign, the formula for the arithmetic mean of a frequency distribution is

$$\overline{x} = \frac{\Sigma fx}{n} \text{ or } \frac{\Sigma fx}{\Sigma f}$$

where n is the number of values recorded, or the number of items measured.

Finding the arithmetic mean of grouped data in class intervals

1.8   You might also be asked to calculate (or at least approximate) the arithmetic mean of a frequency distribution, where the frequencies are shown in class intervals.

Example: the arithmetic mean of grouped data

1.9   Using the example in Paragraph 1.5, the frequency distribution might have been shown as follows.

Daily demand	Frequency
> 0 ≤ 5	4
> 5 ≤ 10	8
> 10 ≤ 15	6
> 15 ≤ 20	2
	20

1.10   There is, of course, an extra difficulty with finding the average now; as the data have been collected into classes, a certain amount of detail has been lost and the values of the variables to be used in the calculation of the mean are not clearly specified.

To calculate the arithmetic mean of grouped data we therefore need to decide on a value which best represents all of the values in a particular class interval.

1.11   The mid-point of each class interval is conventionally taken, on the assumption that the frequencies occur evenly over the class interval range. In the example above, the variable is discrete, so the first class includes 1, 2, 3, 4 and 5, giving a mid-point of 3. With a continuous variable (such as quantities of fuel consumed in litres), the mid-points would have been 2.5, 7.5 and so on. Once the value of x has been decided, the mean is calculated in exactly the same way as in Paragraph 1.7.

Daily demand	Mid point x	Frequency f	fx
> 0 ≤ 5	3	4	12
> 5 ≤ 10	8	8	64
> 10 ≤ 15	13	6	78
> 15 ≤ 20	18	2	36
		$\Sigma f = 20$	$\Sigma fx = 190$

$$\text{Arithmetic mean } \bar{x} = \frac{\Sigma fx}{\Sigma f} = \frac{190}{20} = 9.5 \text{ units}$$

1.12   Because the assumption that frequencies occur evenly within each class interval is not quite correct in this example, our approximate mean of 9.5 is not exactly correct, and is in error by 0.25.

As the frequencies become larger, the size of this approximating error should become smaller.

Finding the arithmetic mean of combined data

1.13   Suppose that the mean age of a group of five people is 27 and the mean age of another group of eight people is 32. How would we find the mean age of the whole group of 13 people?

1.14   Remember that the arithmetic mean is calculated as

$$\frac{\text{Sum of values of items}}{\text{Number of items}}$$

The sum of the ages in the first group is $5 \times 27 \quad = 135$

The sum of the ages in the second group is $8 \times 32 = 256$

The sum of all 13 ages is $135 + 256 = 391$

The mean age is therefore $\dfrac{391}{13} = 30.07$ years.

Exercise 1

The mean weight of 10 units at 5 kgs, 10 units at 7 kgs and 20 units at X kgs is 8 kgs. What is the value of X?

Solution

$$\text{Mean} = \frac{\text{Sum of values of items}}{\text{Number of items}}$$

Sum of first 10 units = $5 \times 10 = 50$ kgs

Sum of second 10 units = $7 \times 10 = 70$ kgs

Sum of third 20 units = $20 \times X = 20X$

Sum of all 40 units = $50 + 70 + 20X = 120 + 20X$

$\therefore$ Arithmetic mean $= 8 = \dfrac{120 + 20X}{40}$

$\therefore$

$$8 \times 40 = 120 + 20X$$
$$320 - 120 = 20X$$
$$10 = X$$

The advantages and disadvantages of the arithmetic mean

1.15 The advantages of the arithmetic mean are as follows.

(a) It is easy to calculate.

(b) It is widely understood.

(c) The value of every item is included in the computation of the mean and so it can be determined with arithmetical precision and is representative of the whole set of data.

(d) It is supported by mathematical theory and is suited to further statistical analysis.

1.16 The disadvantages of the arithmetic mean are as follows.

(a) Its value may not correspond to any actual value. For example, the 'average' family might have 2.3 children, but no family has exactly 2.3 children.

(b) An arithmetic mean might be distorted by extremely high or low values. For example, the mean of 3, 4, 4 and 6 is 4.25, but the mean of 3, 4, 4, 6 and 15 is 6.4. The high value, 15, distorts the average and in some circumstances the mean would be a misleading and inappropriate figure. (Note that extreme values are not uncommon in economic data.)

Exercise 2

For the week ended 15 November, the wages earned by the 69 operators employed in the machine shop of Mermaid Ltd were as follows.

Wages	Number of Operatives
under £ 60	3
£60 and under £70	11
£70 and under £80	16
£80 and under £90	15
£90 and under £100	10
£100 and under £110	8
Over £110	6
	69

Required

Calculate the arithmetic mean wage of the machine operators of Mermaid Ltd for the week ended 15 November.

Solution

The mid point of the range 'under £60' is assumed to be £55 and that of the range over £110 to be £115, since all other class intervals are £10. This is obviously an approximation which might result in a loss of accuracy; nevertheless, there is no better alternative assumption to use. Because wages can vary in steps of 1p, they are virtually a continuous variable and hence the mid-points of the classes are halfway between their end points.

Mid-point of class	Frequency	
x	f	fx
£		
55	3	165
65	11	715
75	16	1,200
85	15	1,275
95	10	950
105	8	840
115	6	690
	69	5,835

Arithmetic mean = $\dfrac{£5,835}{69}$ = £84.57

2   THE MODE

2.1   The mode or modal value is an average which means 'the most frequently occurring value'.

Example: the mode

2.2   The daily demand for stock in a ten day period is as follows.

Demand Units	Number of days
6	3
7	6
8	1
	10

The mode is 7 units, because it is the value which occurs most frequently.

Finding the mode of a grouped frequency distribution

2.3   The mode of a grouped frequency distribution can be calculated from a histogram.

Example: finding the mode from a histogram

2.4   Consider the following grouped frequency distribution

Value		Frequency
At least	*Less than*	
0	10	0
10	20	50
20	30	150
30	40	100

2.5   The modal class (the one with the highest frequency) is 'at least 20, less than 30'. But how can we find a single value to represent the mode?

2.6   What we need to do is draw a histogram of the frequency distribution.

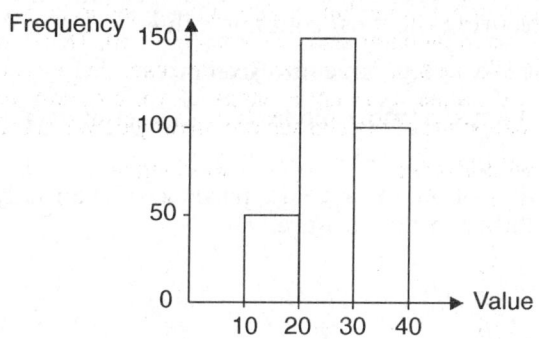

The modal class is always the class with the tallest bar. This which may not be the class with the highest frequency if the classes do not all have the same width.

2.7   We can estimate the mode graphically as follows.

   (a)   Join with a straight line the top left hand corner of the bar for the modal class and the top left hand corner of the next bar to the right.

   (b)   Join with a straight line the top right hand corner of the bar for the modal class and the top right hand corner of the next bar to the left.

2.8   Where these two lines intersect, we find the estimated modal value. In this example it is approximately 26.7.

Histogram showing mode

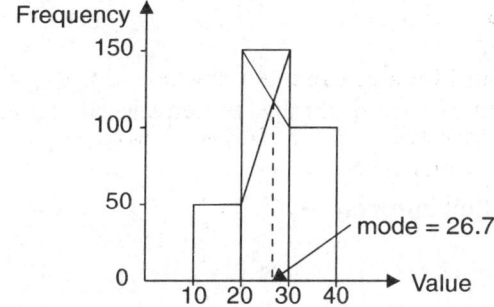

2.9   We are assuming that the frequencies occur evenly within each class interval but this may not always be correct. It is unlikely that the 150 values in the modal class occur evenly. Hence the mode in a grouped frequency distribution is only an estimate.

The advantages and disadvantages of the mode

2.10   The mode will be a more appropriate average to use than the mean in situations where it is useful to know the most common value. For example, if a manufacturer wishes to start production in a new industry, it might be helpful to know what sort of product made by the industry is most in demand with customers.

2.11   The advantages of the mode are as follows.

(a)   It is easy to find.
(b)   It is not influenced by a few extreme values.
(c)   It can be used for data which are not even numerical (unlike the mean and median).
(d)   It can be the value of an actual item in the distribution.

2.12   The mode does have a number of disadvantages.

(a)   It may be unrepresentative; it takes no account of a high proportion of the data, only representing the most common value.

(b)   It does not take every value into account

(c)   There can be two or more modes within a set of data.

(d)   If the modal class is only very slightly bigger than another class, just a few more items in this other class could mean a substantially different result, suggesting some instability in the measure.

3   THE MEDIAN   5/95

3.1   The third type of average is the median. The median is the value of the middle member of a distribution once all of the items have been arranged in order of magnitude.

3.2   The median of a set of ungrouped data is found by arranging the items in ascending or descending order of value, and selecting the item in the middle of the range. A list of items in order of value is called an array.

Example : the median

3.3   The median of the following nine values:

8   6   9   12   15   6   3   20   11

is found by taking the middle item (the fifth one) in the array:

3   6   6   8   9   11   12   15   20

The median is 9.

The middle item of an odd number of items is calculated as the $\dfrac{(n+1)^{\text{th}}}{2}$ item.

3.4   Consider the following array.

8   6   7   2   1   11   3   2   5   2

1   2   2   2   3   5   6   7   8   11

The median is 4 because, with an even number of items, we have to take the arithmetic mean of the two middle ones (in this example, (3 + 5)/2 = 4). When there are many items, however, it is not worth doing this.

Exercise 3

The following times taken to produce a batch of 100 units of Product X have been noted.

21 mins,	17 mins,	24 mins,	11 mins,	37 mins,	27 mins,
20 mins,	15 mins,	17 mins,	23 mins,	29 mins,	30 mins
24 mins,	18 mins,	17 mins,	21 mins,	24 mins,	20 mins

What is the median time?

Solution

The times can be arranged as follows.

11,   15,   17,   17,   17,   18,   20,   20,   21,   21,   23,   24,   24,
24,   27,   29   30,   37

The median = 21 mins. (We could have found the average of the 9th and 10th items if we had wanted to.)

Finding the median of an ungrouped frequency distribution

3.5   The median of an ungrouped frequency distribution is found in a similar way. Consider the following distribution.

Value x	Frequency f	Cumulative frequency
8	3	3
12	7	10
16	12	22
17	8	30
19	5	35
	35	

The median would be the $(35 + 1)/2 = 18$th item. The 18th item has a value of 16, as we can see from the cumulative frequencies in the right hand column of the above table.

Finding the median of a grouped frequency distribution

3.6   We can establish the median of a grouped frequency distribution from an ogive.

Example: the median from an ogive

3.7   Construct an ogive of the following frequency distribution and hence establish the median.

Class £	Frequency	Cumulative frequency
≥ 340, < 370	17	17
≥ 370, < 400	9	26
≥ 400, < 430	9	35
≥ 430, < 460	3	38
≥ 460, < 490	2	40
	40	

Solution

3.8

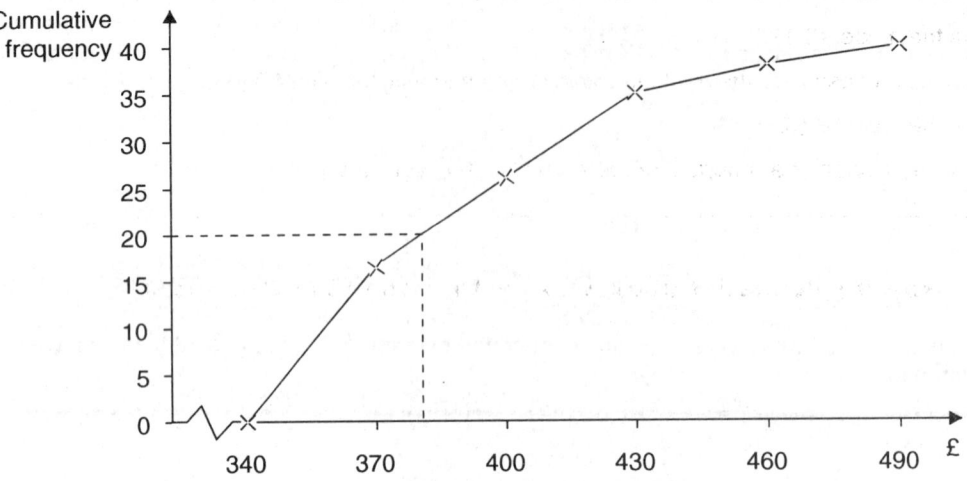

The median is at the $^1/_2 \times 40 = 20$th item. Reading off from the horizontal axis on the ogive, the value of the median is approximately £380.

3.9   Note that, because we are assuming that the values are spread evenly within each class, the median calculated is only approximate.

The advantages and disadvantages of the median

3.10   The median is only of interest where there is a range of values and the middle item is of some significance. Perhaps the most suitable application of the median is in comparing changes in a 'middle of the road' value over time.

   The median is easy to understand and (like the mode) is unaffected by extremely high or low values. It can be the value of an actual item in the distribution. On the other hand, it fails to reflect the full range of values, is unsuitable for further statistical analysis and the arrangement of the data in order of the size can be a tedious operation.

Chapter roundup

- This chapter has looked at the three main types of average.

- The arithmetic mean is the best known type of average and is widely understood. It is used for further statistical analysis.

- The mode is the most frequently occurring value.

- The median is the value of the middle member of an array.

- The arithmetic mean, mode and median of a grouped frequency distribution can only be estimated approximately.

- You should now be able to calculate any of the three averages for a basic set of values, an ungrouped frequency distribution and a grouped frequency distribution.

Test your knowledge

1   State a formula for the arithmetic mean of a frequency distribution. (see para 1.7)

2   Define the mode. (2.1)

3   Explain how to estimate the mode from a histogram of a distribution. (2.6- 2.8)

4   Define the median. (3.1)

5   How is the median of a grouped frequency distribution estimated? (3.6)

Now try illustrative question 21 at the end of the Study Text

Chapter 21

DISPERSION

This chapter covers the following topics.

		Syllabus reference	Ability required
1	The range	2(e)	Skill
2	Quartiles and other quantiles	2(e)	Skill
3	The mean deviation	2(e)	Skill
4	The standard deviation	2(e)	Skill
5	The coefficient of variation	2(e)	Skill
6	Skewness	2(e)	Skill

Introduction

In Chapter 20 we introduced the first type of statistic that can be used to describe certain aspects of a set of data - averages. Averages are a method of determining the 'location' or central point of a distribution, but they give no information about the dispersion of values in the distribution. For example, suppose CIMA students in North Ruritania wanted to compare their salary levels with those in South Ruritania.

Salary per month Ruritanian dollars	CIMA students - North Ruritania Frequency	CIMA students - South Ruritania Frequency
100	3	0
200	6	0
300	10	10
400	12	30
500	10	10
600	6	0
700	3	0
	50	50

Both distributions have the same mean, median and mode (400 dollars) but, although the distributions have the same averages, they are noticeably different. The salary range of CIMA students in North Ruritania is more spread out, and values range from 100 to 700 dollars; in South Ruritania, the range is restricted to 300, 400 and 500 dollars. The differences between the distributions are caused by their spread or dispersion.

Measures of dispersion give some idea of the spread of a variable about its average. The main measures are discussed in sections 1 to 5 of the chapter. Section 6 looks at a concept which affects the topics covered both in this chapter and Chapter 20, skewness.

---

1   THE RANGE

The range

1.1   The range is the difference between the highest observation and the lowest observation.

The main properties of the range as a measure of dispersion are as follows.

(a) It is easy to find and to understand.
(b) It is easily affected by one or two extreme values.
(c) It gives no indication of spread between the extremes.

(d) It is not suitable for further statistical analysis.

Exercise 1

Calculate the mean and the range of each of the following sets of data.

(a) x_1 =   4   8   7   3   5   16   24   5

(b) x_2 =   10   7   9   11   11   8   9   7

What do your calculations show about the dispersion of the data sets?

Solution

(a) $\bar{x}_1 = \dfrac{72}{8} = 9$

     The figures have a mean of 9 and a range of 24 -3 = 21.

(b) $\bar{x}_2 = \dfrac{72}{8} = 9$

     The figures have a mean of 9 and a range of 11 - 7 = 4.

The set of data x_1 is more widely dispersed than the set of data x_2.

---

2   QUARTILES AND OTHER QUANTILES   5/95

Quartiles

2.1   Quartiles are one means of identifying the range within which most of the values in the population occur. The lower quartile is the value below which 25% of the population fall and the upper quartile is the value above which 25% of the population fall. If there were 11 data items the lower quartile would be the third item and the upper quartile the ninth item. It follows that 50% of the total population fall between the lower and the upper quartiles. The quartiles and the median divide the population into four groups of equal size.

Deciles and percentiles

2.2   In a similar way, a population could be divided into ten equal groups, and the value of each dividing point is referred to, not as a quartile, but as a *decile*.

When a population is divided into 100 parts, the value of each dividing point is referred to as a *percentile*. For example, in a population of 200 values, the percentiles would be the second, fourth, sixth, eighth and so on, up to the 198th item, in rising order of values.

Quantiles

2.3   Quartiles, deciles and percentiles, and any other similar dividing points for analysing a frequency distribution, are referred to collectively as *quantiles*. The purpose of quantiles is to analyse the dispersion of data values. All quantiles can be found easily from an ogive.

The inter-quartile range

2.4   The lower and upper quartiles can be used to calculate a measure of dispersion called the inter-quartile range. The inter-quartile range is the difference between the values of the upper and lower quartiles and hence shows the range of values of the middle half of the population. The smaller the inter-quartile range, the less dispersed the population. Because values at the ends of the distribution are not taken into account, the inter-quartile range is not affected by extreme values.

2.5   For example, if the lower and upper quartiles of a frequency distribution were 6 and 11, the inter-quartile range would be 11 − 6 = 5. This shows that the range of values of the middle half of the population is 5 units.

Example: quartiles

2.6   The hours of overtime worked in a particular quarter by the 60 employees of ABC Ltd are shown below. The company has decided to give a bonus of £15 to the 10% of the workforce who worked the most overtime, a bonus of £5 to the 20% of the workforce who worked the least overtime and a £10 bonus to all other employees.

Hours		Frequency
More than	*Not more than*	
0	10	3
10	20	6
20	30	11
30	40	15
40	50	12
50	60	7
60	70	6
		60

Required

Calculate the range of overtime hours worked by those employees receiving a £10 bonus.

Solution

2.7

Hours	Cumulative frequency
> 0, ≤ 10	3
> 10, ≤ 20	9
> 20, ≤ 30	20
> 30, ≤ 40	35
> 40, ≤ 50	47
> 50, ≤ 60	54
> 60, ≤ 70	60

The 9th decile is at 60 − (10% of 60) = 54

The 2nd decile is at 20% of 60 = 12

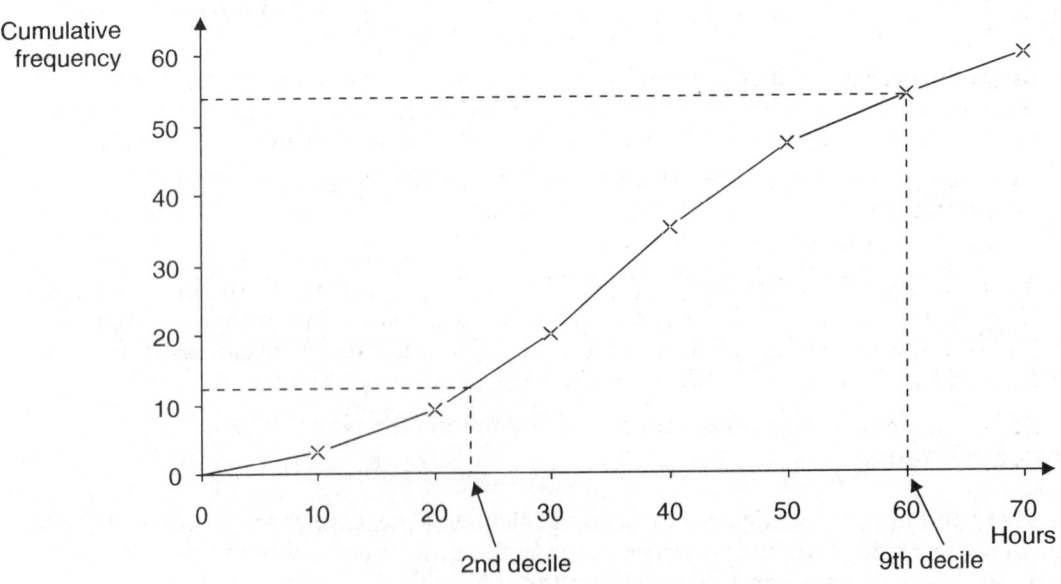

From the ogive the range of hours is approximately 23 to 60.

Exercise 2

Find the values of the upper and lower quartiles of the frequency distribution detailed in Paragraph 3.7 of Chapter 20.

Solution

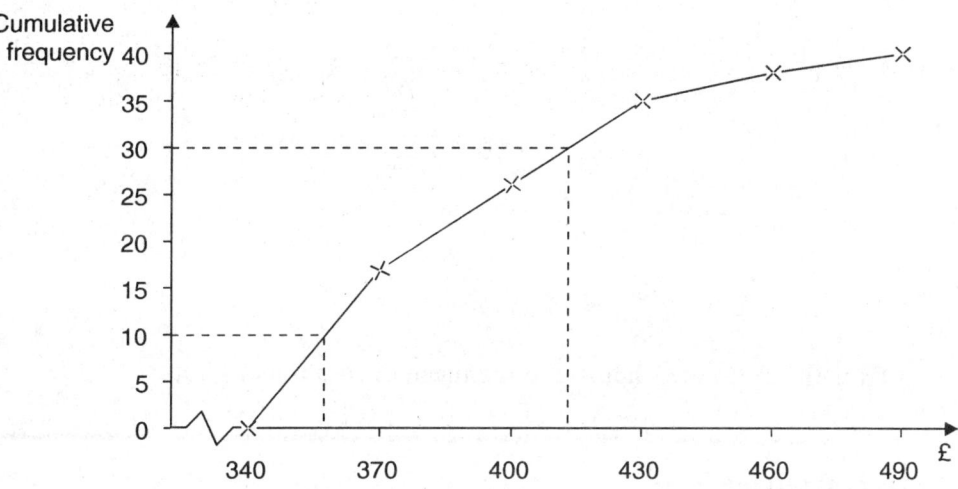

The upper quartile is the $^3/_4 \times 40 = 30$th value.

The lower quartile is the $^1/_4 \times 40 = 10$th value.

Reading off from the ogive these values are at approximately £358 and £412 respectively.

3   THE MEAN DEVIATION

3.1   Because it only uses the middle 50% of the population, the inter-quartile range is a useful measure of dispersion if there are extreme values in the distribution. If there are no extreme values which could potentially distort a measure of dispersion, however, it seems unreasonable to exclude 50% of the data. The mean deviation, which we will look at in this section, and the standard deviation (the topic of Section 4) are therefore often more useful measures.

3.2   The mean deviation is a measure of the *average* amount by which the values in a distribution differ from the arithmetic mean.

$$\text{Mean deviation} = \frac{\Sigma f |x - \bar{x}|}{n}$$

3.3   (a) $|x - \bar{x}|$ is the difference between each value (x) in the distribution and the arithmetic mean $\bar{x}$ of the distribution. When calculating the mean deviation for grouped data the deviations should be measured to the midpoint of each class: that is, x is the midpoint of the class interval. The vertical bars mean that all differences are taken as positive since the total of all of the differences, if this is not done, will always equal zero. Thus if x = 3 and $\bar{x}$ = 5, then $x - \bar{x}$ = –2 but $|x - \bar{x}|$ = 2.

(b) $f|x - \bar{x}|$ is the value in (a) above, multiplied by the frequency for the class.

(c) $\Sigma f |x - \bar{x}|$ is the sum of the results of all the calculations in (b) above.

(d)   n (which equals Σf) is the number of items in the distribution.

Example: the mean deviation

3.4   Calculate the mean deviation of the frequency distribution in Paragraph 2.6.

Solution

3.5

Midpoint x	f	fx	$\mid x - \bar{x} \mid$	$f \mid x - \bar{x} \mid$
5	3	15	32	96
15	6	90	22	132
25	11	275	12	132
35	15	525	2	30
45	12	540	8	96
55	7	385	18	126
65	6	390	28	168
	$\Sigma f = 60$	$\Sigma fx = 2,220$		780

$$\bar{x} = \frac{\Sigma fx}{\Sigma f} = \frac{2,220}{60} = 37$$

$$\text{Mean deviation} = \frac{780}{60} = 13 \text{ hours}$$

Thus the mean is 37 hours and the mean deviation is 13 hours.

Exercise 3

Calculate the mean deviation of the following frequency distribution.

Value	Frequency of occurrence
5	4
15	6
25	8
35	20
45	6
55	6
	50

Solution

x	f	fx	$\mid x - \bar{x} \mid$	$f \mid x - \bar{x} \mid$
5	4	20	27.2	108.8
15	6	90	17.2	103.2
25	8	200	7.2	57.6
35	20	700	2.8	56.0
45	6	270	12.8	76.8
55	6	330	22.8	136.8
	50	1,610		539.2

$$\text{Arithmetic mean } \bar{x} = \frac{1,610}{50} = 32.2$$

$$\text{Mean deviation} = \frac{539.2}{50} = 10.784, \text{ say } 10.8.$$

The usefulness of the mean deviation

3.6   The mean deviation is a measure of dispersion which shows by how much, on average, each item in the distribution differs in value from the arithmetic mean of the distribution.

Unlike quartiles, it uses all values in the distribution to measure the dispersion, but it is not greatly affected by a few extreme values because an average is taken.

The mean deviation is not, however, suitable for further statistical analysis.

4   THE STANDARD DEVIATION   5/96

4.1   Instead of taking the absolute value of the difference between the value and the mean to avoid the total of the differences summing to zero as we did with the mean deviation, we can square the differences. If we do this, we get the most important measure of dispersion in statistics, the standard deviation. It is denoted by σ, the lower case Greek letter sigma.

4.2   Difference between value and mean $x - \bar{x}$
      Square of the difference $(x - \bar{x})^2$
      Sum of the squares of the difference $\Sigma(x - \bar{x})^2$
      Average of the sum (= variance = σ^2) $\dfrac{\Sigma(x - \bar{x})^2}{n}$

The units of the variance are the square of those in the original data because we squared the differences. We therefore need to take the square root to get back to the units of the original data.

Square root of the variance = standard deviation = $\sqrt{\dfrac{\Sigma(x - \bar{x})^2}{n}}$

4.3   The same process can be applied to determine the standard deviation of data in a frequency distribution.

      Square of the difference between value and mean $(x - \bar{x})^2$
      Sum of the squares of the difference $\Sigma f(x - \bar{x})^2$
      Average of the sum (= variance) $\dfrac{\Sigma f(x - \bar{x})^2}{\Sigma f}$

Square root = standard deviation $\sqrt{\dfrac{\Sigma f(x - \bar{x})^2}{\Sigma f}}$

This formula can prove time consuming to use and so an alternative (which provides exactly the same answer) is provided in the examination.

Standard deviation = $\sqrt{\dfrac{\Sigma f x^2}{\Sigma f} - \bar{x}^2}$

Note that these formulae are appropriate if all the details are known of the whole population. You will meet a slightly modified version of the formulae when you come on to studying sampling theory in Chapter 24.

Example: the variance and the standard deviation

4.4   Calculate the variance and the standard deviation of the frequency distribution in Paragraph 2.6

Solution

4.5   Using the formula provided in the examination, the calculation is as follows.

Midpoint x	f	x^2	fx^2
5	3	25	75
15	6	225	1,350
25	11	625	6,875
35	15	1,225	18,375
45	12	2,025	24,300
55	7	3,025	21,175
65	6	4,225	25,350
	60		97,500

Part E: Summarising and analysing data

Mean = (from Paragraph 3.5) = 37

$$\text{Variance} = \frac{\Sigma fx^2}{\Sigma f} - \bar{x}^2 = \frac{97,500}{60} - (37)^2 = 256 \text{ hours}$$

Standard deviation = $\sqrt{256}$ = 16 hours

Exercise 4

Calculate the variance and the standard deviation of the frequency distribution in Exercise 3.

Solution

x	f	x^2	fx^2
5	4	25	100
15	6	225	1,350
25	8	625	5,000
35	20	1,225	24,500
45	6	2,025	12,150
55	6	3,025	18,150
	50		61,250

$\bar{x}$ = 32.2 (from Exercise 3)

$$\text{Variance} = \frac{61,250}{50} - (32.2)^2 = 188.16$$

Standard deviation = $\sqrt{188.16}$ = 13.72

The main properties of the standard deviation

4.6 The standard deviation's main properties are as follows.

(a) It is based on all the values in the distribution and so is more comprehensive than dispersion measures based on quantiles, such as the quartile deviation.

(b) It is suitable for further statistical analysis.

(c) It is more difficult to understand than some other measures of dispersion.

The importance of the standard deviation lies in its suitability for further statistical analysis.

5 THE COEFFICIENT OF VARIATION

5.1 It is sometimes useful to be able to compare the spreads of two distributions.

This comparison can be done using the coefficient of variation.

$$\text{Coefficient of variation} = \frac{\text{standard deviation}}{\text{mean}}$$

The coefficient of variation is sometimes known as the coefficient of relative dispersion.

5.2 The bigger the coefficient of variation, the wider the dispersion. For example, suppose that two sets of data, A and B, have the following means and standard deviations.

	A	B
Mean	120	125
Standard deviation	50	51
Coefficient of variation	0.417	0.408

Although B has a higher standard deviation in absolute terms (51 compared to 50) its relative dispersion is a bit less than A's since the coefficient of variation is a bit smaller.

Exercise 5

Calculate the coefficient of variation of the distribution in Exercises 3 and 4.

Solution

$$\text{Coefficient of variation} = \frac{\text{standard deviation}}{\text{mean}} = \frac{13.72}{32.2} = 0.426$$

---

6   SKEWNESS

6.1   As well as being able to calculate the average and spread of a frequency distribution, you should be aware of the skewness of a distribution. A frequency distribution must be either symmetrical or asymmetrical, that is, skewed.

6.2   A symmetrical frequency distribution is one which can be divided into two halves which are mirror images of each other. The arithmetic mean, the median and the mode will all have the same value.

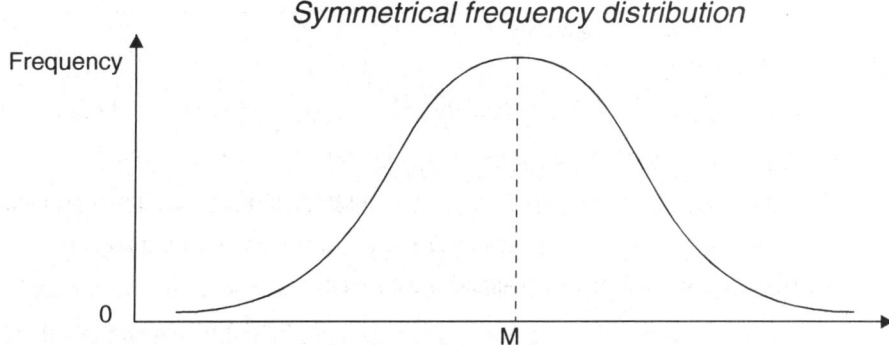

Symmetrical frequency distribution

The mean, the mode and the median will all have the same value, M.

6.3   A positively skewed distribution's graph will lean towards the left hand side, with a tail stretching out to the right. The mean, the median and the mode will have different values.

In a positively skewed distribution, the mode will be a lower value than the median and the mean will be a higher value than the median. The value of the mean is, in fact, higher than a great deal of the distribution.

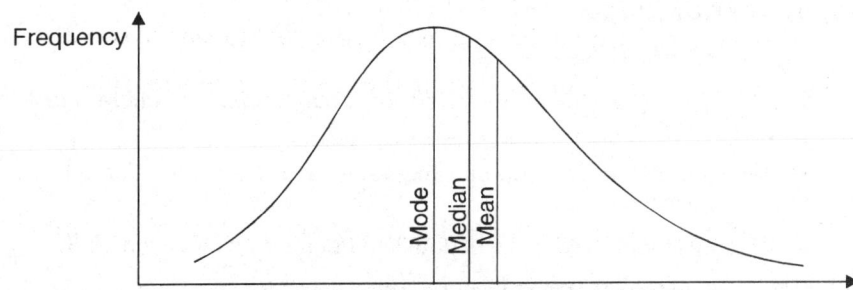

Positively skewed distribution graph

6.4   A negatively skewed distribution's graph will lean towards the right hand side, with a tail stretching out to the left. Once again, the mean, median and mode will have different values.

In a negatively skewed distribution, the mode will have a higher value than the median and the mean will have a lower value than the median. The value of the mean is lower than a great deal of the distribution.

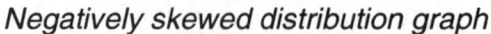

Negatively skewed distribution graph

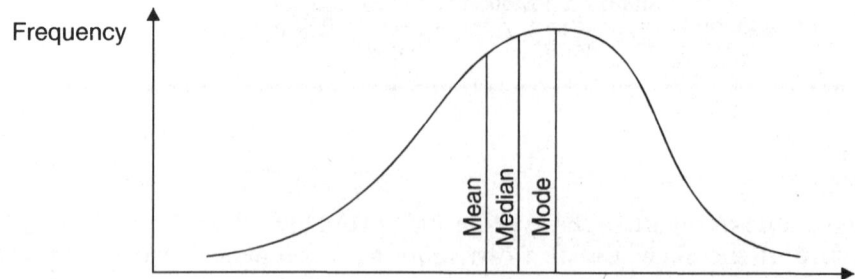

6.5   It is a criticism of the mean as an average that for very skewed distributions its value may not be representative of the majority of the items in the distribution since it is affected by extreme values.

Chapter roundup

- Measures of dispersion give some idea of the spread of variables about the average.

- The range is the difference between the highest and lowest observations.

- The quartiles and the median divide the population into four groups of equal size.

- Quartiles, deciles and percentiles are referred to collectively as quantiles.

- The inter-quartile range is the difference between the upper and lower quartiles.

- The mean deviation is a measure of the average amount by which the values in a distribution differ from the arithmetic mean.

- The standard deviation, which is the square root of the variance, is the most important measure of dispersion used in statistics. Make sure you understand how to calculate the standard deviation of a set of data.

- The spreads of two distributions can be compared using the coefficient of variation.

- Skewness is the asymmetry of a frequency distribution curve.

Test your knowledge

1   What are quantiles? (see para 2.3)

2   When calculating the mean deviation for grouped data, to where should the deviations be measured? (3.3)

3   Why are the differences between the value and the mean squared in the formula for the standard deviation? (4.1)

4   Give a formula for the variance of data in a frequency distribution. (4.3)

5   Define the coefficient of variation of a distribution. (5.1)

6   Distinguish between positive skewness and negative skewness. (6.3, 6.4)

Now try illustrative question 22 at the end of the Study Text

Chapter 22

INDEX NUMBERS

This chapter covers the following topics.

		Syllabus reference	Ability required
1	Basic terminology	2(e)	Skill
2	Simple indices	2(e)	Skill
3	Index relatives	2(e)	Skill
4	Composite index numbers	2(e)	Skill
5	Laspeyre and Paasche indices	2(e)	Skill
6	Practical issues	2(e)	Skill
7	The Retail Prices Index for the United Kingdom		

Introduction

A number of methods of data presentation looked at in Chapter 19 can be used to identify visually the trends in data over a period of time. It may also be useful, however, to identify trends using statistical rather than visual means. This is frequently achieved by constructing a set of index numbers.

Index numbers provide a standardised way of comparing the values, over time, of prices, wages, volume of output and so on. They are used extensively in business, government and commerce.

No doubt you will be aware of some index numbers - the RPI, the Financial Times All Share Index and so on. This chapter will explain to you how to construct indices and will look at associated issues such as their limitations.

Many exam questions on index numbers are based around indices for which the formulae are provided in the exam. In his report on the November 95 exam, the examiner commented that many candidates were unable to calculate indices even though formulae were provided. This highlights the fact that you must know how to use the formulae as well as how to find them in the Mathematical Tables.

1 BASIC TERMINOLOGY

1.1 An index is a measure, over time, of the average changes in the values (prices or quantities) of a group of items. An index comprises a series of index numbers. Although it is possible to prepare an index for a single item, for example the price of an ounce of gold, such an index would probably be unnecessary. It is only when there is a group of items that a simple list of changes in their values over time becomes rather hard to interpret, and an index provides a useful single measure of comparison.

Price indices and quantity indices

1.2 An index may be a price index or a quantity index.

(a) A price index measures the change in the money value of a group of items over time. Perhaps the best known price index in the UK is the Retail Prices Index (RPI) which measures changes in the costs of items of expenditure of the average household.

(b) A quantity index (also called a volume index) measures the change in the non-monetary values of a group of items over time. An example is a productivity index, which measures changes in the productivity of various departments or groups of workers.

Index points

1.3 The term 'points' refers to the difference between the index values in two years.

For example, suppose that the index of food prices in 19X1 – 19X6 was as follows.

19X1	180
19X2	200
19X3	230
19X4	250
19X5	300
19X6	336

The index has risen 156 points between 19X1 and 19X6. This is an increase of $(156/180) \times 100 = 86.7\%$.

Similarly, the index rose 36 points between 19X5 and 19X6, a rise of 12%.

The base period, or base year

1.4 Index numbers normally take the value for a base date, usually the starting point of the series though it could be part way through the series, as 100.

2   SIMPLE INDICES

2.1 When one commodity only is under consideration, we have the following formulae.

(a) Price index $= 100 \times \dfrac{P_1}{P_0}$

where P_1 is the price for the period under consideration and P_0 is the price for the base period.

(b) Quantity index $= 100 \times \dfrac{Q_1}{Q_0}$

where Q_1 is the quantity for the period under consideration and Q_0 is the quantity for the base period.

Example: single-item indices

2.2 If the price of a cup of coffee was 40p in 19X0, 50p in 19X1 and 76p in 19X2, then using 19X0 as a base year the price index numbers for 19X1 and 19X2 would be as follows.

19X1 price index $= 100 \times \dfrac{50}{40} = 125$

19X2 price index $= 100 \times \dfrac{76}{40} = 190$

2.3 If the number of cups of coffee sold in 19X0 was 500,000, in 19X1 700,000 and in 19X2 600,000, then using 19X0 as a base year, the quantity index numbers for 19X1 and 19X2 would be as follows.

$$19X1 \text{ quantity index} = 100 \times \frac{700,000}{500,000} = 140$$

$$19X2 \text{ quantity index} = 100 \times \frac{600,000}{500,000} = 120$$

3   INDEX RELATIVES   *11/95*

3.1   An index relative (sometimes just called a relative) is the name given to an index number which measures the change in a single distinct commodity.

3.2   A price relative is calculated as $100 \times P_1/P_0$. We calculated price relatives for a cup of coffee in Paragraph 2.2.

3.3   A quantity relative is calculated as $100 \times Q_1/Q_0$. We calculated quantity relatives for cups of coffee in Paragraph 2.3.

Time series of relatives

3.4   Given the values of some commodity over time (a time series), there are two ways in which index relatives can be calculated.

3.5   In the *fixed base method*, a base year is selected (index 100), and all subsequent changes are measured against this base. Such an approach should only be used if the basic nature of the commodity is unchanged over time.

3.6   In the *chain base method*, changes are calculated with respect to the value of the commodity in the period immediately before. This approach can be used for any set of commodity values but must be used if the basic nature of the commodity is changing over time.

Example: fixed base and chain base methods

3.7   The price of commodity was £2.70 in 19X0, £3.11 in 19X1, £3.42 in 19X2 and £3.83 in 19X3. Construct both a chain base index and a fixed base index for the years 19X0 to 19X3 using 19X0 as the base year.

Solution

3.8

Chain base index	19X0	2.70	100	
	19X1	3.11	115	$(3.11/2.70 \times 100)$
	19X2	3.42	110	$(3.42/3.11 \times 100)$
	19X3	3.83	112	$(3.83/3.42 \times 100)$
Fixed base index	19X0	2.70	100	
	19X1	3.11	115	
	19X2	3.42	127	$(3.42/2.70 \times 100)$
	19X3	3.83	142	$(3.83/2.70 \times 100)$

The chain base relatives show the rate of change in prices from year to year, whereas the fixed base relatives show changes relative to prices in the base year.

Changing the base of fixed base relatives

3.9   It is sometimes necessary to change the base of a time series of fixed base relatives, perhaps because the base time point is too far in the past. The following time series has a base date of 1970 which would probably be considered too out of date.

	1990	*1991*	*1992*	*1993*	*1994*	*1995*
Index (1970 = 100)	451	463	472	490	499	505

To change the base date (to *rebase*), divide each relative by the relative corresponding to the new base time point and multiply the result by 100.

Exercise 1

Rebase the index in Paragraph 3.9 to 1993.

	1990	*1991*	*1992*	*1993*	*1994*	*1995*
Index (1993 = 100)	92*	94	96	100**	102***	103

*   451/490 × 100
**   490/490 × 100
*** 499/490 × 100

Comparing sets of fixed base relatives

3.10   You may be required to compare two sets of time series relatives. For example, an index of the annual number of advertisements placed by an organisation in the press and the index of the number of the organisation's product sold per annum might be compared. If the base years of the two indices differ, however, comparison is extremely difficult (as the illustration below shows).

	19W8	*19W9*	*19X0*	*19X1*	*19X2*	*19X3*	*19X4*
Number of advertisements placed (19X0 = 100)	90	96	100	115	128	140	160
Volumes of sales (19W0 = 100)	340	347	355	420	472	515	572

3.11   From the figures above it is impossible to determine whether sales are increasing at a greater rate than the number of advertisements placed, or vice versa. This difficulty can be overcome by rebasing one set of relatives so that the base dates are the same. For example, we could rebase the index of volume of sales to 19X0.

	19W8	*19W9*	*19X0*	*19X1*	*19X2*	*19X3*	*19X4*
Number of advertisements placed (19X0 = 100)	90	96	100	115	128	140	160
Volumes of sales (19X0 = 100)	96	98*	100	118	133**	145	161

★   347/355 × 100
★★ 472/355 × 100

3.12   The two sets of relatives are now much easier to compare. They show that volume of sales is increasing at a slightly faster rate, in general, than the number of advertisements placed.

Time series deflation

3.13   The real value of a commodity can only be measured in terms of some 'indicator' such as the rate of inflation (normally represented by the Retail Prices Index) or the Index of Output of Production Industries. For example the cost of a commodity may have been £10 in 19X0 and £11 in 19X1, representing an increase of 10%. However, if we are told the prices in general (as measured by the RPI) increased by 12% between 19X0 and 19X1, we can argue that the *real* cost of the commodity has decreased.

Example: deflation

3.14   Mack Johnson works for Pound of Flesh Ltd. Over the last five years he has received an annual salary increase of £500. Despite his employer assuring him that £500 is a reasonable annual salary increase, Mack is unhappy because, although he agrees £500 is a lot of money, he finds it difficult to maintain the standard of living he had when he first joined the company.

Consider the figures below.

	(a)	*(b)*	*(c)*	*(d)*
Year	*Wages*	*RPI*	*Real wages*	*Real wages index*
	£		*£*	
1	12,000	250	12,000	100.0
2	12,500	260	12,019	100.2
3	13,000	275	11,818	98.5
4	13,500	295	11,441	95.3
5	14,000	315	11,111	92.6

(a) This column shows Mack's wages over the five-year period.

(b) This column shows the current RPI.

(c) This column shows what Mack's wages are worth taking prices, as represented by the RPI, into account. The wages have been deflated relative to the new base period (year 1). Economists call these deflated wage figures *real wages*. The real wages for years 2 and 4, for example, are calculated as follows.

Year 2:   £12,500 × 250/260 = £12,019
Year 4:   £13,500 × 250/295 = £11,441

(d) This column is calculated by dividing the entries in column (c) by £12,000:

$$\text{Real index} = \frac{\text{current value}}{\text{base value}} \times \frac{\text{base indicator}}{\text{current indicator}}$$

So, for example, the real wage index in year 4 $= \dfrac{13,500}{12,000} \times \dfrac{250}{295} \times 100 = 95.3$

3.15   The real wages index shows that the real value of Mack's wages has fallen by 7.4% over the five-year period. In real terms he is now earning £11,111 compared to £12,000 in year 1. He is probably justified, therefore, in being unhappy.

Exercise 2

The mean weekly take-home pay of the employees of Staples Ltd and a price index for the 11 years from 19X0 to 19Y0 are as follows.

Year	Weekly wage	Price index (19X0 = 100)
	£	
19X0	150	100
19X1	161	103
19X2	168	106
19X3	179	108
19X4	185	109
19X5	191	112
19X6	197	114
19X7	203	116
19X8	207	118
19X9	213	121
19Y0	231	123

Required

Construct a time series of real wages for 19X0 to 19Y0 using a price index with 19X6 as the base year.

Solution

The index number for each year with 19X6 as the base year will be the original index number divided by 1.14, and the real wages for each year will be (money wages × 100)/index number for the year.

Year	Index	Real wage £
19X0	88	170
19X1	90	179
19X2	93	181
19X3	95	188
19X4	96	193
19X5	98	195
19X6	100	197
19X7	102	199
19X8	104	199
19X9	106	201
19Y0	108	214

4 COMPOSITE INDEX NUMBERS

4.1 Most practical indices cover more than one item and are hence termed composite index numbers. The RPI, for example, considers components such as food, alcoholic drink, tobacco and housing. An index of motor car costs might consider components such as finance payments, service costs, repairs, insurance and so on.

4.2 Suppose that the cost of living index is calculated from only three commodities: bread, tea and caviar, and that the prices for 19X1 and 19X2 were as follows.

	19X1	19X2
Bread	20p a loaf	40p a loaf
Tea	25p a packet	30p a packet
Caviar	450p a jar	405p a jar

4.3 A simple index could be calculated by adding the prices for single items in 19X2 and dividing by the corresponding sum relating to 19X1 (if 19X1 is the base year). In general, if the sum of the prices in the base year is ΣP_0 and the sum of the prices in the new year is ΣP_1, the index is $100 \times \dfrac{\Sigma P_1}{\Sigma P_0}$. The index, known as a *simple aggregate price index*, would therefore be calculated as follows.

	P_0 19X1 £	P_1 19X2 £
Bread	0.20	0.40
Tea	0.25	0.30
Caviar	4.50	4.05
	$\Sigma P_0 = \overline{4.95}$	$\Sigma P_1 = \overline{4.75}$

Year	$\Sigma P_1 / \Sigma P_0$	*Simple aggregate price index*
19X1	4.95/4.95 = 1.00	100
19X2	4.75/4.95 = 0.96	96

4.4 This type of index has a number of disadvantages. It ignores the amounts of bread, tea and caviar consumed (and hence the importance of each item), and the units to which the prices refer. If, for example, we had been given the price of a cup of tea rather than a packet of tea, the index would have been different.

Average relatives indices

4.5 To overcome the problem of different units we consider the changes in prices as ratios rather than absolutes so that all price movements, whatever their absolute values, are treated as equally important.

4.6 Price changes are considered as ratios rather than absolutes by using the *average price relatives index* which is calculated as

$$100 \times \frac{1}{n} \times \Sigma(P_1/P_0)$$

where n is the number of goods. Here, the price relative P_1/P_0 (so called because it gives the new price level of each item relative to the base year price) for a particular commodity will have the same value whatever the unit for which the price is quoted.

4.7 Using the information in Paragraph 4.2, we can construct the average price relatives index as follows.

Commodity	P_0 £	P_1 £	P_1/P_0
Bread	0.20	0.40	2.00
Tea	0.25	0.30	1.20
Caviar	4.50	4.05	0.90
			4.10

Year	$\frac{1}{n}\Sigma(P_1/P_0)$	Average price relatives index
19X1	$^1/_3 \times 3.00 = 1.00$	100
19X2	$^1/_3 \times 4.10 = 1.37$	137

4.8 There has therefore been an average price increase of 37% between 19X1 and 19X2.

4.9 We could, of course, construct an average quantity relatives index if we had been given information on quantities purchased per time period.

4.10 No account has been taken of the relative importance of each item, however, in this index. Bread is probably more important than caviar. To overcome both the problem of quantities in different units and the need to attach importance to each item, we can use weighting which reflects the importance of each item. To decide the weightings of different items in an index, it is necessary to obtain information, perhaps by market research, about the relative importance of each item. Thus, in our example of a simple cost of living index, it would be necessary to find out how much the average person or household spends each week on each item to determine weightings.

4.11 There are two types of index which give different weights to different items, weighted means of relatives indices and weighted aggregate indices.

Weighted means of relatives indices

4.12 This method of weighting involves calculating index relatives for each of the components and using the weights given to obtain a weighted average of the relatives.

4.13 The general form of a weighted means of relatives index number is

$$\frac{\Sigma wI}{\Sigma w}$$

where   w is the weighting factor
and   I is the index relative

4.14 Values (price × quantity) relating to some point in time are usually used as weights.

4.15 Note that the weights may be from a year other than the base year. This is the method used for the index of wholesale prices. We could, for example, produce a weighted means of relatives index using 19X4 as base year, 19X6 as the given year and 19X5 values as weights.

4.16 Weighted means of relatives are very important in practice, the great majority of indices published in the UK being of this type.

Example: weighted means of relatives indices

4.17 Use both the information in Paragraph 4.2 and the following details about quantities purchased by each household in a week in 19X1 to determine a weighted means of price relatives index number for 19X2 using 19X1 as the base year.

	Quantity
Bread	6
Tea	2
Caviar	0.067

Solution

4.18 *Price relatives* (I)

Price relatives (I)	Bread	40/20 =	2.00
	Tea	30/25 =	1.20
	Caviar	405/450 =	0.90
Weightings (w)	Bread	$6 \times 0.20 =$	1.20
	Tea	$2 \times 0.25 =$	0.50
	Caviar	$0.067 \times 4.50 =$	0.30
	$\Sigma w =$		2.00
Index	Bread	$2 \times 1.2 =$	2.40
	Tea	$1.2 \times 0.5 =$	0.60
	Caviar	$0.9 \times 0.3 =$	0.27
	$\Sigma wI =$		3.27

$$\text{Index number} = \frac{3.27}{2} \times 100 = \quad 163.5$$

Weighted aggregate indices

4.19 This method of weighting involves multiplying each component value by its corresponding weight and adding these products to form an aggregate. This is done for both the base period and the period in question. The aggregate for the period under consideration is then divided by the base period aggregate.

4.20 The general form of a weighted aggregate index is

$$\frac{\Sigma wv_n}{\Sigma wv_o}$$

where w is the weighting factor
v_o is the value of the commodity in the base period
v_n is the value of the commodity in the period in question

4.21 Price indices are usually weighted by quantities and quantity indices are usually weighted by prices.

Exercise 3

What are the formulae for calculating price and quantity weighted aggregate indices if base year weights are used?

Solution

Price index: $100 \times \dfrac{\Sigma Q_0 P_1}{\Sigma Q_0 P_0}$

where P_0 represents the prices of items in the base year
         P_1 represents the prices of items in the new year
         Q_0 represents the quantities of the items consumed in the base year

Quantity index: $100 \times \dfrac{\Sigma P_0 Q_1}{\Sigma P_0 Q_0}$

where Q_0 represents the quantities consumed in the base year
         Q_1 represents the quantities consumed in the new year
         P_0 represents the prices in the base year

Example: a price index

4.22   In the previous example of the cost of living index (Paragraph 4.17), the 19X5 index value could have been calculated as follows.

Item	Quantity Q_0	Price in 19X1 P_0	$P_0 Q_0$	Price in 19X5 P_1	$P_1 Q_0$
Bread	6	20	120	40	240
Tea	2	25	50	30	60
Caviar	0.067	450	30	405	27
			200		327

Index in 19X5 $= \dfrac{327}{200} \times 100 = 163.5$

Example: a quantity index

4.23   The Falldown Construction Company uses four items of materials and components in a standard production job.

In 19X0 the quantities of each material or component used per job and their cost were as follows.

	Quantity Units	Price per unit £
Material A	20	2
Material B	5	10
Component C	40	3
Component D	15	6

In 19X2 the quantities of materials and components used per job were as follows.

	Quantity Units
Material A	15
Material B	6
Component C	36
Component D	25

Using 19X0 as a base year, calculate the quantity index value in 19X2 for the amount of materials used in a standard job.

Solution

4.24

	Price P_0	Quantity used in 19X0 Q_0	P_0Q_0	Quantity used in 19X2 Q_1	P_0Q_1
Material A	£2	20	40	15	30
Material B	£10	5	50	6	60
Component C	£3	40	120	36	108
Component D	£6	15	90	25	150
			300		348

$$\text{Quantity index} = \frac{348}{300} \times 100 = 116$$

This would suggest that the company is using 16% more materials in 19X2 than in 19X0 on a standard job.

5 LASPEYRE AND PAASCHE INDICES   *11/95*

5.1 Laspeyre and Paasche indices are special cases of weighted **aggregate** indices.

Laspeyre indices

5.2 Laspeyre indices use weights from the base period and are therefore sometimes called base weighted indices.

Laspeyre price index

5.3 A Laspeyre price index uses quantities consumed in the base period as weights. In the notation already used it can be expressed as follows.

$$\text{Laspeyre price index} = 100 \times \frac{\Sigma Q_0 P_1}{\Sigma Q_0 P_0}$$

Laspeyre quantity index

5.4 A Laspeyre quantity index uses prices from the base period as weights and can be expressed as follows.

$$\text{Laspeyre quantity index} = 100 \times \frac{\Sigma Q_1 P_0}{\Sigma Q_0 P_0}$$

Paasche indices

5.5 Paasche indices use current time period weights. In other words the weights are changed every time period.

Paasche price index

5.6 A Paasche price index uses quantities consumed in the current period as weights and can be expressed as follows.

$$\text{Paasche price index} = 100 \times \frac{\Sigma Q_1 P_1}{\Sigma Q_1 P_0}$$

Paasche quantity index

5.7 A Paasche quantity index uses prices from the current period as weights and can be expressed as follows.

Paasche quantity index $= 100 \times \dfrac{\Sigma Q_1 P_1}{\Sigma Q_0 P_1}$

5.8 You are provided with the formulae for Paasche and Laspeyre indices in your examination.

Example: Laspeyre and Paasche price indices

5.9 The wholesale price index in Ruritania is made up from the prices of five items. The price of each item, and the average quantities purchased by manufacturing and other companies each week were as follows, in 19X0 and 19X2.

Item	Quantity 19X0 '000 units	Price per unit 19X0 Roubles	Quantity 19X2 '000 units	Price per unit 19X2 Roubles
P	60	3	80	4
Q	30	6	40	5
R	40	5	20	8
S	100	2	150	2
T	20	7	10	10

Required

Calculate the price index in 19X2, if 19X0 is taken as the base year, using the following.

(a) A Laspeyre index
(b) A Paasche index

Solution

5.10 *Workings*

Item	Q_0	P_0	Q_1	P_1	Laspeyre $Q_0 P_0$	$Q_0 P_1$	Paasche $Q_1 P_1$	$Q_1 P_0$
P	60	3	80	4	180	240	320	240
Q	30	6	40	5	180	150	200	240
R	40	5	20	8	200	320	160	100
S	100	2	150	2	200	200	300	300
T	20	7	10	10	140	200	100	70
					900	1,110	1,080	950

19X2 index numbers are as follows.

(a) Laspeyre index $= 100 \times \dfrac{1,110}{900} = 123.3$

(b) Paasche index $= 100 \times \dfrac{1,080}{950} = 113.7$

The Paasche index for 19X2 reflects the decline in consumption of the relatively expensive items R and T since 19X0. The Laspeyre index for 19X2 fails to reflect this change.

Exercise 4

A baker has listed the ingredients he used and their prices, in 19X3 and 19X4, as follows.

	Kgs used 19X3 '000s	Price per kg 19X3 £	Kgs used 19X4 '000s	Price per kg 19X3 £
Milk	3	1.20	4	1.50
Eggs	6	0.95	5	0.98
Flour	1	1.40	2	1.30
Sugar	4	1.10	3	1.14

Required

Calculate the following quantity indices for 19X4 (with 19X3 as the base year).

(a) A Laspeyre index
(b) A Paasche index

Solution

Workings

| | Q_0 | P_0 | Q_1 | P_1 | Laspeyre | | Paasche | |
					Q_0P_0	Q_1P_0	Q_1P_1	Q_0P_1
Milk	3	1.20	4	1.50	3.60	4.80	6.00	4.50
Eggs	6	0.95	5	0.98	5.70	4.75	4.90	5.88
Flour	1	1.40	2	1.30	1.40	2.80	2.60	1.30
Sugar	4	1.10	3	1.14	4.40	3.30	3.42	4.56
					15.10	15.65	16.92	16.24

Quantity index numbers for 19X4 are as follows.

(a) Laspeyre method = $100 \times \dfrac{15.65}{15.10} = 103.64$

(b) Paasche method = $100 \times \dfrac{16.92}{16.24} = 104.19$

Which to use - Paasche or Laspeyre ?

5.11 Both patterns of consumption and prices change and a decision therefore has to be made as to whether a Paasche or a Laspeyre index should be used.

5.12 The following points should be considered when deciding which type of index to use.

(a) A Paasche index requires quantities to be ascertained each year. A Laspeyre index only requires them for the base year. Constructing a Paasche index may therefore be costly.

(b) For the Paasche index, the denominator has to be recalculated each year because the quantities/prices must be changed to current year consumption/price levels.

For the Laspeyre index, the denominator is fixed. The Laspeyre index can therefore be calculated as soon as current prices/quantities are known. The Paasche index, on the other hand, cannot be calculated until the end of a period, when information about current quantities/prices becomes available.

(c) The denominator of a Laspeyre index is fixed and therefore the Laspeyre index numbers for several different years can be directly compared. With the Paasche index, on the other hand, comparisons can only be drawn directly between the current year and the base year (although indirect comparisons can be made).

(d) The weights for a Laspeyre index become out of date, whereas those for the Paasche index are updated each year.

(e) A Laspeyre price index implicitly assumes that, whatever the price changes, the quantities purchased will remain the same. In terms of economic theory, no substitution of cheaper alternative goods and services is allowed to take place. Even if goods become relatively more expensive, it assumes that the same quantities are bought. As a result, the index tends to overstate inflation.

(f) The effect of current year weighting when using the Paasche price index means that greater importance is placed on goods that are relatively cheaper now than they were in the base year. As a consequence, the Paasche price index tends to understate inflation.

In practice, it is common to use a Laspeyre index and revise the weights every few years. (Where appropriate, a new base year may be created when the weights are changed.)

6   PRACTICAL ISSUES

What items to include

6.1   The purpose to which the index is to be put must be carefully considered. Once this has been done, the items selected must be as representative as possible, taking into account this purpose. Care must be taken to ensure that the items are unambiguously defined and that their values are readily ascertainable.

6.2   For some indices, the choice of items might be relatively straightforward. For example, the FT Actuaries All-Share Index, compiled jointly by the Financial Times, the Institute of Actuaries and the Faculty of Actuaries, is made up of the share prices of approximately 800 companies quoted on The Stock Exchange. The weights are based on the market capitalisations of the companies (the number of shares in issue multiplied by their market value).

6.3   For other indices, the choice of items will be more difficult. The Retail Prices Index is an excellent example of the problem. It would be impossible to include all items of domestic spending and a selective, representative basket of goods and services must be found, ranging from spending on mortgages and rents, to cars, public transport, food and drink, electricity, gas, telephone, clothing, leisure activities and so on.

Collecting the data

6.4   Data are required to determine the following.

(a)   The values for each item
(b)   The weight that will be attached to each item

Consider as an example a cost of living index. The prices of a particular commodity will vary from place to place, from shop to shop and from type to type. Also the price will vary during the period under consideration. The actual prices used must obviously be some sort of average. The way in which the average is to be obtained should be clearly defined at the outset.

6.5   When constructing a price index, it is common practice to use the quantities consumed as weights; similarly, when constructing a quantity index, the prices may be used as weights. Care must be taken in selecting the basis for the weighting. For example, in a cost of living index, it may be decided to use the consumption of a typical family as the weights, but some difficulty may be encountered in defining a typical family.

The choice of a base year

6.6   The choice of a base date, or base year is not significant, except that it should be representative. In the construction of a price index, the base year must not be one in which there were abnormally high or low prices for any items in the basket of goods making up the index. For example, a year in which there is a potato famine would be unsuitable as a base period for the Retail Prices Index.

The limitations and misinterpretation of index numbers

Limitations

6.7   Index numbers are usually only approximations of changes in price or quantity over time, and must be interpreted with care.

(a)   As we have seen, weightings become out of date over time. Unless a Paasche index is used, the weightings will gradually cease to reflect current reality.

(b)   New products or items may appear, and old ones may cease to be significant. For example, spending has changed in recent years, to include new items such as personal computers and video recorders, whereas the demand for twin tub washing machines has declined. These changes would make the weightings of a price index for such goods out of date.

(c)   The data used to calculate index numbers might be incomplete, out of date, or inaccurate. For example, the quantity indices of imports and exports are based on records supplied by traders which may be prone to error or even deliberate falsification.

(d)   The base year of an index should be a normal year, but there is probably no such thing as a perfectly normal year. Some error in the index will be caused by atypical values in the base period.

(e)   The 'basket of items' in an index is often selective. For example, the Retail Prices Index (RPI) is constructed from a sample of households and from a basket of less than 400 items.

(f)   A national index may not be very relevant to an individual town or region. For example, if the national index of wages and salaries rises from 100 to 115, we cannot conclude that the wages and salaries of people in, say, Glasgow, have gone up by 15%.

(g)   An index may exclude important items: for example, the RPI excludes payments of income tax out of gross wages.

Misinterpretation

6.8   You must be careful not to misinterpret index numbers. Several possible mistakes will be explained using the following example of a retail prices index.

19X0		*19X1*		*19X2*	
January	340.0	January	360.6	January	436.3
		February	362.5	February	437.1
		March	366.2	March	439.5
		April	370.0	April	442.1

(a)   It would be wrong to say that prices rose by 2.6% between March and April 19X2. It is correct to say that prices rose 2.6 points, or

$$\frac{2.6}{439.5} = 0.6\%$$

(b)   It would be correct to say that the annual rate of price increases (the rate of inflation) fell between March and April 19X2. It would be a mistake, however, to suppose that a fall in the rate of inflation means that prices are falling, therefore the price index is falling.

The rate of price increases has slowed down, but the trend of prices is still upwards.

(i)   The annual rate of inflation from March 19X1 to March 19X2 is

$$\left(\frac{439.5 - 366.2}{366.2}\right) = 20\%$$

(ii)   The annual rate of inflation from April 19X1 to April 19X2 is

$$\left(\frac{442.1 - 370.0}{370.0}\right) = 19.5\%$$

Thus the annual rate of inflation has dropped from 20% to 19.5% between March and April 19X2, even though prices went up in the month between March and April 19X2 by 0.6%. (The price increase between March and April 19X1 was over 1%. This is included in the calculation of the rate of inflation between March 19X1 and March 19X2, but is excluded in the comparison between April 19X1 and April 19X2 where it has been replaced by the lower price increase, 0.6%, between March and April 19X2.)

7   THE RETAIL PRICES INDEX FOR THE UNITED KINGDOM

7.1   We will conclude our study of index numbers by looking at the construction of the UK Retail Prices Index (RPI).

7.2   On one particular day of each month, data are collected about prices of the following groups of items.

   (a)   Food
   (b)   Alcoholic drink
   (c)   Tobacco
   (d)   Housing
   (e)   Fuel and light
   (f)   Durable household goods
   (g)   Clothing and footwear
   (h)   Transport and vehicles
   (i)   Miscellaneous goods
   (j)   Services
   (k)   Meals bought and consumed outside the home

7.3   Each group is sub-divided into sections: for example 'food' will be sub-divided into bread, butter, potatoes and so on. These sections may in turn be sub-divided into more specific items. The groups do not cover every item of expenditure (for example they exclude income tax, pension fund contributions and football pools).

7.4   The weightings given to each group, section and sub-section are based on information provided by the *Family Expenditure Survey* which is based on a survey of over 10,000 households, spread evenly over the year.

Each member of the selected households (aged 16 or over) is asked to keep a detailed record of their expenditure over a period of 14 days, and to provide information about longer-term payments (such as insurance premiums). Information is also obtained about their income.

7.5   The weightings used in the construction of the RPI are not revised every year, but are revised from time to time using information in the Family Expenditure Survey of the previous year.

Chapter roundup

- An index is a measure, over time, of the average changes in the value (price or quantity) of a group of items relative to the situation at some period in the past.

- An index relative is an index number which measures the change in a single distinct commodity.

- Index relatives can be calculated using the fixed base method or the chain base method.

- In order to compare two time series of relatives, each series should have the same base period and hence one (or both) may need rebasing.

- The real value of a commodity can only be measured in terms of some 'indicator' (such as the RPI).

- Time series deflation is a technique used to obtain a set of index relatives that measure the changes in the real value of some commodity with respect to some given indicator.

- Composite indices cover more than one item.

- Weighting is used to reflect the importance of each item in the index.

- Weighted means of relatives indices are found by calculating indices and then applying weights.

- Weighted aggregate indices are found by applying weights and then calculating the index.

- There are two types of weighted aggregate index, the Laspeyre (which uses quantities/prices from the base period as the weights) and the Paasche (which uses quantities/prices from the current period as weights).

- Index number are a very useful way of summarising a large amount of data in a single series of numbers. You should remember, however, that any summary hides some detail and that index numbers should therefore be interpreted with caution.

Test your knowledge

1   How are index relatives calculated using the chain base method? (see para 3.8)

2   How is a time series of relatives rebased? (3.9)

3   Why must the real value of a commodity be measured in terms of some indicator? (3.13)

4   What is the general form of

    (a)   a weighted means of relatives index (4.13)
    (b)   a weighted aggregate index? (4.20)

5   What do Laspeyre indices use as weights? (5.2)

6   What are the limitations of index numbers? (6.7)

7   Give some examples of how index numbers might be misinterpreted. (6.8)

Now try illustrative question 23 at the end of the Study Text

Part F
Sampling and probability

Chapter 23

PROBABILITY

This chapter covers the following topics.

		Syllabus reference	Ability required
1	The concept of probability	2(f)	Skill
2	The laws of probability	2(f)	Skill
3	Expected values	2(f)	Skill
4	Expectation and decision making	2(f)	Skill
5	Permutations and combinations	2(f)	Skill

Introduction

We are now going to move away from the summary and analysis of data and look at a new topic area, sampling and probability.

Let us begin by considering the case of Mrs Cracked, who is responsible for product development at Lovely Lips Ltd, a cosmetics company. She has recently been working hard to perfect 'Perky Pink', a copy of the lipstick that Luscious, the number one popstar of the moment, is rumoured to be going to wear on her forthcoming world tour. She is naturally very upset to read in the music press that Luscious may be cancelling her world tour.

Although she reckons that this rumour may only have a 40% chance of being true, it presents her with a difficult choice. Sales of Perky Pink are estimated to be 10,000 units, each earning a profit of £1. This projection was, however, based on the assumption of Luscious going on her world tour. If this is not the case, Mrs Cracked reckons sales might be as low as 1,000 units. She is therefore forced to consider abandoning the project now, although £3,000 has already been invested in it.

To make matters worse, the marketing director then rings to let her know that Lovely Lips Ltd's arch competitor, Kissable and Co, may be planning to launch a similar colour lipstick which would sell for less and would cut Lovely Lips Ltd's sales to 6,000 units. Admittedly the marketing director estimates that the chance of Kissable and Co launching their product is only 50-50 but the possibility must still be taken into account.

Mrs Cracked and Lovely Lips Ltd therefore have two alternatives: to abandon Perky Pink altogether or to go ahead and market the lipstick regardless of whether the tour goes ahead or not and take the risk that Kissable and Co will bring out its own product.

Such a scenario is typical of situations facing countless organisations everyday. Ideally the business community would know with certainty what was going to happen. The real world is, however, not normally helpful! The future is uncertain. Those running organisations must therefore be able to tackle and take account of this uncertainty. They must understand what '50-50' means, what 'a 40% chance means'. They must be able to evaluate choices by quantifying the 'expected' or 'most likely' future results and, in addition, be able to make some attempt to quantify the possible variations.

There are a number of ways of analysing uncertainty (which as specific methods are outside the scope of this syllabus). Underlying all of these methods is, however, one concept: probability. An understanding of the concept of probability is vital if you are to take account of uncertainty. Probability appeared in the November 95 exam. As the examiner reported, '... for the well prepared candidate high marks could be obtained with a few speedy calculations'.

This chapter will therefore explain various techniques for assessing probability and look at how it can be applied in business decision making. In Chapter 24, we will build upon the basics learnt in this chapter and look at probability distributions and sampling.

1 THE CONCEPT OF PROBABILITY

1.1 'The likelihood of rain this afternoon is fifty percent' warns the weather report from your radio alarm clock. 'There's no chance of you catching that bus' grunts the helpful soul as you puff up the hill. The headline on your newspaper screams 'Odds of Rainbow Party winning the election rise to one in four'.

1.2 'Likelihood' and 'chance' are expressions used in our everyday lives to denote a level of uncertainty. Probability, a word which often strikes fear into the hearts of students, is simply the mathematical term used when we need to imply a degree of uncertainty.

1.3 Probability is a measure of likelihood and can be stated as a percentage, a ratio, or more usually as a number from 0 to 1. Zero probability corresponds to impossibility, whereas a probability of one corresponds to certainty. A 50% chance of something happening is a probability of ½. A chance of 1 in 4 is equivalent to a probability of ¼ and we express 'there's no chance of catching the bus' as P(catching the bus) = 0.

1.4 In statistics, probabilities are more commonly expressed as proportions than as percentages: for example, if there are six possible different outcomes in a certain situation, the probabilities might be expressed as follows.

Possible outcome	Probability as a percentage	Probability as a proportion
A	15.0%	0.150
B	20.0%	0.200
C	32.5%	0.325
D	7.5%	0.075
E	12.5%	0.125
F	12.5%	0.125
	100.0%	1.000

1.5 It is useful to consider how probability can be quantified. A businessman might estimate that if the selling price of a product is raised by 20p, there would be a 90% probability that demand would fall by 30%, but how would he have reached his estimate of 90% probability?

1.6 There are several ways of assessing probabilities.

(a) They may be measurable with mathematical certainty.

(i) If a coin is tossed, there is a 0.5 probability that it will come down heads, and a 0.5 probability that it will come down tails.

(ii) If a die is thrown, there is a one-sixth probability that a 6 will turn up.

(b) They may be measurable from an analysis of past experience. For example, suppose that an analysis of the last 300 working days shows that on 180 days there were no machine breakdowns. Given no change in the average reliability of machinery, we would therefore be able to estimate that the probability of no machine breakdowns during a day is 180/300 = 0.6 (so the probability of at least one breakdown during the day must be 0.4).

(c) Probabilities can be estimated from research or surveys. For example, a new product might be test-marketed in selected trial areas, and from the results of the test it might be estimated that there is a 70% chance that demand would be sufficient to earn a satisfactory profit for the company if the product were sold nationally.

1.7 A final introductory point about probability is that it is a measure of the likelihood of an event happening *in the long run*, or over a large number of times. If we toss a coin eight times, we cannot predict that it will necessarily come down heads four times and tails four times. The coin may come down heads eight times, or not once in the eight throws; heads may occur any number of times between zero and eight. We can say, however, that in the long run heads will occur about 50% of the time if a coin is tossed a sufficiently large number of times.

2   THE LAWS OF PROBABILITY   *11/95*

2.1   It is the year 2020 and examiners are extinct. A mighty but completely fair computer churns out examinations that are equally likely to be easy or difficult. There is no link between the number of questions on each paper, which is arrived at on a fair basis by the computer, and the standard of the paper. You are about to take five examinations.

Simple probability

2.2   It is vital that the first examination is easy as it covers a subject which you have tried, but unfortunately failed, to understand. What is the probability that it will be an easy examination?

2.3   Obviously (let us hope), the probability of an easy paper is $^1/_2$ (or 50% or 0.5). This reveals a very important principle (which holds if each result is equally likely).

Probability of achieving the desired result

$$= \frac{\text{Number of ways of achieving desired result}}{\text{Total number of possible outcomes}}$$

Let us apply the principle to our example.

Total number of possible outcomes = 'easy' or 'difficult'   = 2
Total number of ways of achieving the desired result (which is 'easy')   = 1

The probability of an easy examination, or P(easy examination)   = $^1/_2$

Example: simple probability

2.4   Suppose that a coin is tossed in the air. What is the probability that it will come down heads?

Solution

2.5   P(heads)   = $\dfrac{\text{Number of ways of achieving desired result (heads)}}{\text{Total number of possible outcomes (heads or tails)}}$

= $^1/_2$ or 50% or 0.5.

Complementary outcomes

2.6   You are desperate to pass more of the examinations than your sworn enemy but, unlike you, he is more likely to pass the first examination if it is difficult. (He is very strange!!) What is the probability of the first examination being more suited to your enemy's requirements?

2.7   We know that the probability of certainty is one. The certainty in this scenario is that the examination will be easy or difficult.

P(easy or difficult examination)   =   1
From Paragraph 4.3, P(easy examination)   = $^1/_2$
P(not easy examination)   =   P(difficult examination)
                                                    =   1 − P(easy examination)
                                                    =   1 − $^1/_2$
                                                    = $^1/_2$

2.8 In general, $P(\overline{X}) = 1 - P(X)$, where $\overline{X}$ is 'not X'.

Example: complementary outcomes

2.9 If there is a 25 per cent chance of the Rainbow Party winning the next general election, use the law of complementary outcomes to calculate the probability of the Rainbow Party *not* winning the next election.

Solution

2.10 $P(\text{winning})$ $= 25\% = \frac{1}{4}$
$P(\text{not winning})$ $= 1 - P(\text{winning}) = 1 - \frac{1}{4} = \frac{3}{4}$

The simple addition or OR law

2.11 The time pressure in the second examination is enormous. The computer will produce a paper which will have between five and nine questions. You know that, easy or difficult, the examination must have six questions at the most for you to have any hope of passing it.

What is the probability of the computer producing an examination with six or fewer questions? In other words, what is the probability of an examination with five *or* six questions?

2.12 Don't panic. Let us start by using the basic principle.

$P(5 \text{ questions})$ $= \dfrac{\text{Total number of ways of achieving a five-question examination}}{\text{Total number of possible outcomes } (= 5,6,7,8 \text{ or } 9 \text{ questions})}$
$= \frac{1}{5}$
Likewise $P(6 \text{ questions}) = \frac{1}{5}$

Either five questions or six questions would be acceptable, so the probability of you passing the examination must be greater than if just five questions or just six questions (but not both) were acceptable. We therefore add the two probabilities together so that the probability of passing the examination has increased.

2.13 So $P(5 \text{ or } 6 \text{ questions})$ $= P(5 \text{ questions}) + P(6 \text{ questions})$
$= \frac{1}{5} + \frac{1}{5} = \frac{2}{5}$

In general, the simple addition or OR law is:

$$P(X \text{ or } Y \text{ or } Z) = P(X) + P(Y) + P(Z)$$

where X, Y and Z are *mutually exclusive outcomes*, which means that the occurrence of one of the outcomes excludes the possibility of any of the others happening. In the example the outcomes are mutually exclusive because it is impossible to have five questions *and* six questions in the same examination.

Example: mutually exclusive outcomes

2.14 The delivery of an item of raw material from a supplier may take up to six weeks from the time the order is placed. The probabilities of various delivery times are as follows.

Delivery time	Probability
≤ 1 week	0.10
$> 1, \leq 2$ weeks	0.25
$> 2, \leq 3$ weeks	0.20
$> 3, \leq 4$ weeks	0.20
$> 4, \leq 5$ weeks	0.15
$> 5, \leq 6$ weeks	0.10
	1.00

What is the probability that a delivery will take the following times?

(a) Two weeks or less

(b) More than three weeks

Solution

2.15 (a) P (≤ 1 or > 1, ≤ 2 weeks) =   P (≤ 1 week) + P (>1, ≤ 2 weeks)

                                =   0.10 + 0.25

                                =   0.35

    (b) P (> 3, ≤ 6 weeks)   =   P (> 3, ≤ 4 weeks) + P (> 4, ≤ 5 weeks) + P (> 5, ≤ 6 weeks)

                                =   0.20 + 0.15 + 0.10

                                =   0.45

The simple multiplication or AND law

2.16 You still have three examinations to sit: astrophysics, geography of the moon and computer art. Stupidly, you forgot to revise for the astrophysics examination, which will have between 15 and 20 questions. You think that you may scrape through this paper if it is easy *and* if there are only 15 questions.

What is the probability that the paper the computer produces will exactly match your needs? Do not forget that there is no link between the standard of the examination and the number of questions.

2.17 The best way to approach this question is diagrammatically, showing all the possible outcomes.

	Number of questions					
	15	*16*	*17*	*18*	*19*	*20*
Type of paper						
Easy (E)	E and 15⋆	E and 16	E and 17	E and 18	E and 19	E and 20
Difficult (D)	D and 15	D and 16	D and 17	D and 18	D and 19	D and 20

The diagram shows us that, of the twelve possible outcomes, there is only one 'desired result' (which is asterisked). We can therefore calculate the probability as follows.

P(easy paper *and* 15 questions) = $\frac{1}{12}$

2.18 The answer can be found more easily as follows.

P(easy paper *and* 15 questions) = P(easy paper) × P(15 questions) = $\frac{1}{2} \times \frac{1}{6} = \frac{1}{12}$

2.19 In general, the simple multiplication or AND law is:

P(X and Y) = P(X) P(Y)

where X and Y are *independent* events, which means that the occurrence of one event in no way affects the outcome of the other events: whether it is an easy or difficult paper has no effect on the number of questions.

Example: independent events

2.20 A die is thrown and a coin is tossed simultaneously. What is the probability of throwing a 5 and getting heads on the coin?

Solution

2.21   The probability of throwing a 5 on a die is $\frac{1}{6}$.

The probability of a tossed coin coming up heads is $\frac{1}{2}$.

The probability of throwing a 5 and getting heads on a coin is $\frac{1}{2} \times \frac{1}{6} = \frac{1}{12}$.

The general rule of addition

2.22   The three examinations you still have to sit are placed face down in a line in front of you at the final examination sitting. There is an easy astrophysics paper, a difficult geography of the moon paper and a difficult computer art paper. Without turning over any of the papers you are told to choose one of them. What is the probability that the first paper that you select is difficult or is the geography of the moon paper?

2.23   Let us think about this carefully.

There are two difficult papers, so P(difficult) = $\frac{2}{3}$.

There is one geography of the moon paper, so P(geography of the moon) = $\frac{1}{3}$.

2.24   If we use the OR law and add the two probabilities then we will have double counted the difficult geography of the moon paper. It is included in the set of difficult papers and in the set of geography of the moon papers. In other words, we are *not* faced with mutually exclusive outcomes because the occurrence of a geography of the moon paper does not exclude the possibility of the occurrence of a difficult paper. We therefore need to take account of this double counting.

P(difficult paper or geography of the moon paper) = P(difficult paper) + P(geography of the moon paper) – P(difficult paper and geography of the moon paper).

Using the AND law, P(difficult paper or geography of the moon paper) = $\frac{2}{3} + \frac{1}{3} - (\frac{1}{3})$ = $\frac{2}{3}$

2.25   In general, the general rule of addition is:

P(X or Y) = P(X) + P(Y) – P(X and Y)

where the word 'or' is used in an inclusive sense: either X or Y or both. X and Y are therefore *not* mutually exclusive: it is *not* impossible to have an examination which is difficult *and* about the geography of the moon.

Exercise 1

If one card is drawn from a normal pack of 52 playing cards, what is the probability of getting an ace or a spade?

Solution

P(ace) = 4/52

P (spade) = 13/52

P(ace of spades) = 1/52

$\therefore$ P(ace or spades) = $\dfrac{4}{52} + \dfrac{13}{52} - \dfrac{1}{52} = \dfrac{16}{52} = \dfrac{4}{13}$

The general rule of multiplication

2.26   Computer art is your last examination. Understandably you are very tired and you are uncertain whether you will be able to stay awake. You believe that there is a 70% chance of your falling asleep if it becomes too hot and stuffy in the examination hall. It is well known that the air conditioning system serving the examination hall was installed in the 1990s and is therefore extremely unreliable. There is a 1 in 4 chance of it breaking down during the examination, thereby causing the temperature in the hall to rise. What is the likelihood that you will drop off?

2.27   The scenario in Paragraph 2.26 has led us to face what is known as conditional probability. We can rephrase the information provided as 'the probability that you will fall asleep, given that it is too hot and stuffy, is equal to 70%' and we can write this as follows.

P(fall asleep/too hot and stuffy) = 70%

2.28   Whether you fall asleep is conditional upon whether the hall becomes too hot and stuffy. The events are not, therefore, independent and so we cannot use the simple multiplication law. So:

P(it becomes too hot and stuffy and you fall asleep)

$$= \text{P(too hot and stuffy)} \times \text{P(fall asleep/too hot and stuffy)}$$
$$= 25\% \times 70\% = 0.25 \times 0.7 = 0.175 = 17\frac{1}{2}\%$$

2.29   In general, if X and Y are two outcomes, then the probability that X and Y will occur is:

$$\text{P(X and Y)} = \text{P(X)} \times \text{P(Y/X)}$$
$$= \text{P(Y)} \times \text{P(X/Y)}$$

where X and Y are *dependent* events.

2.30   When X and Y are independent events, then P(Y/X) = P(Y) since, by definition, the occurrence of Y (and therefore P(Y)) does not depend upon the occurrence of X. Similarly P(X/Y) = P(X).

Example: conditional probability

2.31   The board of directors of Shuttem Ltd has warned that there is a 60% probability that a factory will be closed down unless its workforce improves its productivity. The factory's manager has estimated that the probability of success in agreeing a productivity deal with the workforce is only 30%. What is the likelihood that the factory will be closed?

Solution

2.32   If outcome A is the shutdown of the factory and outcome B is the failure to improve productivity:

$$\text{P (A and B)} = \text{P(B)} \times \text{P(A/B)}$$
$$= 0.7 \times 0.6$$
$$= 0.42$$

2.33   Another method of dealing with some conditional probabilities is by using contingency tables. Their use is best explained by an example.

Example: contingency tables

2.34   A cosmetics company has developed a new anti-dandruff shampoo which is being tested on volunteers. Seventy percent of the volunteers have used the shampoo whereas others have used a normal shampoo, believing it to be the new anti-dandruff shampoo. Two sevenths of those using the new shampoo showed no improvement whereas one third of those using the normal shampoo had less dandruff.

Required

A volunteer shows no improvement. What is the probability that he used the normal shampoo?

Solution

2.35 The problem is solved by drawing a contingency table, showing 'improvement' and 'no improvement', volunteers using normal shampoo and volunteers using the new shampoo.

Let us suppose that there were 1,000 volunteers (we could use any number). We could depict the results of the test on the 1,000 volunteers as follows.

	New shampoo	*Normal shampoo*	*Total*
Improvement	***500	****100	600
No improvement	**200	200	400
	*700	***300	1,000

* 70% × 1,000   ** $^2/_7$ × 700

*** Balancing figure   **** $^1/_3$ × 300

We can now calculate P(used normal shampoo/showed no improvement)

P(shows no improvement) = 400/1,000

P(used normal shampoo/shows no improvement) = 200/400 = $^1/_2$

Other probabilities are just as easy to calculate.

P(shows improvement/used new shampoo) = 500/700 = $^5/_7$

P(used new shampoo/shows improvement) = 500/600 = $^5/_6$

Exercise 2

The independent probabilities that the three sections of a management accounting department will encounter one computer error in a week are respectively 0.1, 0.2 and 0.3. There is never more than one computer error encountered by any one section in a week. Calculate the probability that there will be the following number of errors encountered by the management accounting department next week.

(a) At least one computer error
(b) One and only one computer error

Solution

(a) The probability of at least one computer error is 1 minus the probability of no error. The probability of no error is 0.9 × 0.8 × 0.7 = 0.504.

(Since the probability of an error is 0.1, 0.2 and 0.3 in each section, the probability of no error in each section must be 0.9, 0.8 and 0.7 respectively.)

The probability of at least one error is 1 − 0.504 = 0.496.

(b) Y = yes, N = no

	Section 1	*Section 2*	*Section 3*
(i) Error?	Y	N	N
(ii) Error?	N	Y	N
(iii) Error?	N	N	Y

			Probabilities
(i)	0.1 × 0.8 × 0.7	=	0.056
(ii)	0.9 × 0.2 × 0.7	=	0.126
(iii)	0.9 × 0.8 × 0.3	=	0.216
		Total	0.398

The probability of only one error only is 0.398.

---

3   EXPECTED VALUES

3.1   An expected value (or EV) is a weighted average value, based on probabilities.

3.2   If the probability of an outcome of an event is p, then the expected number of times that this outcome will occur in n events (the expected value) is equal to n × p.

For example, suppose that the probability that a transistor is defective is 0.02. How many defectives would we expect to find in a batch of 4,000 transistors?

EV   =   4,000 × 0.02
      =   80 defectives

Example: expected values

3.3   The daily sales of Product T may be as follows.

		Probability
Units		
1,000		0.2
2,000		0.3
3,000		0.4
4,000		0.1
		1.0

Required

Calculate the expected daily sales.

Solution

3.4   The EV of daily sales may be calculated by multiplying each possible outcome (volume of daily sales) by the probability that this outcome will occur.

	Probability	*Expected value*
Units		Units
1,000	0.2	200
2,000	0.3	600
3,000	0.4	1,200
4,000	0.1	400
	EV of daily sales	2,400

3.5   In the long run the expected value should be approximately the actual average, if the event occurs many times over. In the example above, we do not expect sales on any one day to equal 2,400 units, but in the long run, over a large number of days, average sales should equal 2,400 units a day.

Expected values and single events

3.6   The point made in the preceding paragraph is an important one. An expected value can be calculated when the event will only occur once or twice, but it will not be a true long-run average of what will actually happen, because there is no long run.

3.7   Suppose, for example, that a businessman is trying to decide whether to invest in a project. He estimates that there are three possible outcomes.

Outcome	*Profit/(loss)*	*Probability*
	£	
Success	10,000	0.2
Moderate success	2,000	0.7
Failure	(4,000)	0.1

The expected value of profit may be calculated as follows.

Profit/(loss) £	Probability	Expected value £
10,000	0.2	2,000
2,000	0.7	1,400
(4,000)	0.1	(400)
	Expected value of profit	3,000

3.8 In this example, the project is a one-off event, and as far as we are aware, it will not be repeated. The actual profit or loss will be £10,000, £2,000 or £(4,000), and the average value of £3,000 will not actually happen. There is no long-run average of a single event.

3.9 Nevertheless, the expected value can be used to help the manager decide whether or not to invest in the project. All other things being equal a project with a positive EV (an expected value which is a profit) should be accepted, and a project with a negative EV (an expected value which is a loss) should be rejected.

3.10 Provided that we understand the limitations of using expected values for single events, they can offer a helpful guide for management decisions, and suggest to managers whether any particular decision is worth the risk of taking (subject, of course, to reasonable accuracy in the estimates of the probabilities themselves).

Exercise 3

A company manufactures and sells product D. The selling price of the product is £6 per unit, and estimates of demand and variable costs of sales are as follows.

Probability	Demand Units	Probability	Variable cost per unit £
0.3	5,000	0.1	3.00
0.6	6,000	0.3	3.50
0.1	8,000	0.5	4.00
		0.1	4.50

The unit variable costs do not depend on the volume of sales.

Fixed costs will be £10,000.

Required

Calculate the expected profit.

Solution

The EV of demand is as follows.

Demand Units	Probability	Expected value Units
5,000	0.3	1,500
6,000	0.6	3,600
8,000	0.1	800
	EV of demand	5,900

The EV of the variable cost per unit is as follows.

Variable costs £	Probability	Expected value £
3.00	0.1	0.30
3.50	0.3	1.05
4.00	0.5	2.00
4.50	0.1	0.45
	EV of unit variable costs	3.80

		£
Sales	5,900 units × £6.00	35,400
Less variable costs	5,900 units × £3.80	22,420
Contribution		12,980
Less fixed costs		10,000
Expected profit		2,980

3.11 The expected value is summarised in equation form as follows.

$E(x) = \Sigma x P(x)$

This is read as 'the expected value of "x" is equal to the sum of the products of each value of x and the corresponding probability of that value of x occurring'.

4 EXPECTATION AND DECISION MAKING   5/97

4.1 The concepts of probability and expected value are vital in business decision making. The expected values for single events can offer a helpful guide for management decisions: a project with a positive EV should be accepted and a project with a negative EV should be rejected.

4.2 Another decision rule involving expected values that you are likely to come across is the choice of an option or alternative which has the highest EV of profit (or the lowest EV of cost).

4.3 Choosing the option with the highest EV of profit is a decision rule that has both merits and drawbacks, as the following simple example will show.

Example: the expected value criterion

4.4 Suppose that there are two mutually exclusive projects with the following possible profits.

Project A		*Project B*	
Probability	*Profit*	*Probability*	*Profit/(loss)*
	£		£
0.8	5,000	0.1	(2,000)
0.2	6,000	0.2	5,000
		0.6	7,000
		0.1	8,000

Required

Determine which project should be chosen.

Solution

4.5 The EV of profit for each project is as follows.   £

(a) Project A $(0.8 \times 5,000) + (0.2 \times 6,000)$ =   5,200
(b) Project B $(0.1 \times (2,000)) + (0.2 \times 5,000) + (0.6 \times 7,000) + (0.1 \times 8,000)$ = 5,800

4.6 (a) Project B has a higher EV of profit. This means that on the balance of probabilities, it could offer a better return than A, and so is arguably a better choice.

(b) On the other hand, the minimum return from project A would be £5,000 whereas with B there is a 0.1 chance of a loss of £2,000. So project A might be a safer choice.

Payoff tables

4.7   Decisions have to be taken about a wide variety of matters (capital investment, controls on production, project scheduling and so on) and under a wide variety of conditions from virtual certainty to complete uncertainty.

4.8   There are, however, certain common factors in many business decisions.

(a)   When a decision has to be made, there will be a range of possible *actions*.

(b)   Each action will have certain consequences, or payoffs (for example, profits or losses).

(c)   The payoff from any given action will depend on the *circumstances* (for example, high demand or low demand), which may or may not be known when the decision is taken. Frequently each circumstance will be assigned a probability of occurrence. The circumstances are *not* dependent on the action taken.

4.9   For a decision with these elements, a payoff table can be prepared. This is simply a table with rows for circumstances and columns for actions (or vice versa), and the payoffs in the cells of the table.

4.10   A payoff table may look something like this.

*Payoff table for decision on level of advertising expenditure:
payoffs in £'000 of profit after advertising expenditure*

		Actions: expenditure		
		High	*Medium*	*Low*
Circumstances:	Boom	+50	+30	+15
the state of the	Stable	+20	+25	+5
economy	Recession	0	–10	–35

Sometimes the circumstances will be another person's action, for example a competitor's level of advertising expenditure. Note that payoff tables can also show costs or losses instead of profits, in which case we would hope for low figures. A payoff table showing profits may be called a profit table.

Example: payoff table

4.11   A cinema has to decide how many programmes to print for a premiere of a film. From previous experience of similar events, it is expected that the probability of sales will be as follows.

Number of programmes demanded	*Probability of demand*
250	0.1
500	0.2
750	0.4
1,000	0.1
1,250	0.2

The best print quotation received is £2,000 plus 20 pence per copy. Advertising revenue from advertisements placed in the programme totals £2,500. Programmes are sold for £2 each. Unsold programmes are worthless.

Required

(a)   Construct a payoff table.
(b)   Find the most profitable number of programmes to have printed.

Solution

4.12 (a)

Actions: print levels

			250	500	750	1,000	1,250
	250	(p = 0.1)	950	900	850	800	750
Circumstances:	500	(p = 0.2)	950	1,400	1,350	1,300	1,250
demand levels	750	(p = 0.4)	950	1,400	1,850	1,800	1,750
	1,000	(p = 0.1)	950	1,400	1,850	2,300	2,250
	1,250	(p = 0.2)	950	1,400	1,850	2,300	2,750

These figures are calculated as the profit under each set of circumstances. For example, if the cinema produces 1,000 programmes and 1,000 are demanded, the profit is

$$£(2,500 + (1,000 \times 2) - 2,000 - (0.20 \times 1,000)) = £2,300$$

(b) The expected profits from each of the possible print levels are as follows.

Print 250

Expected profit $= £((950 \times 0.1) + (950 \times 0.2) + (950 \times 0.4) + (950 \times 0.1) + (950 \times 0.2)) = \underline{£950}$

Print 500

Expected profit $= £((900 \times 0.1) + (1,400 \times (0.2 + 0.4 + 0.1 + 0.2))) = \underline{£1,350}$

Print 750

Expected profit $= £((850 \times 0.1) + (1,350 \times 0.2) + (1,850 \times 0.7)) = \underline{£1,650}$

Print 1,000

Expected profit $= £((800 \times 0.1) + (1,300 \times 0.2) + (1,800 \times 0.4) + (2,300 \times 0.3)) = \underline{£1,750}$

Print 1,250

Expected profit $= £((750 \times 0.1) + (1,250 \times 0.2) + (1,750 \times 0.4) + (2,250 \times 0.1) + (2,750 \times 0.2)) = \underline{£1,800}$

1,250 programmes should therefore be printed in order to maximise expected profit.

Exercise 4

In a restaurant there is a 30% chance of five apple pies being ordered a day and a 70% chance of ten being ordered. Each apple pie sells for £2. It costs £1 to make an apple pie. Using a payoff table, decide how many apple pies the restaurant should prepare each day, bearing in mind that unsold apple pies must be thrown away at the end of each day.

Solution

		Prepared	
		5	10
Demand	5 (0.3)	5	0
	10 (0.7)	5	10

Prepare 5, profit = (£5 × 0.3) + (£5 × 0.7) = £5
Prepare 10, profit = (£0 × 0.3) + (£10 × 0.7) = £7

Ten pies should be prepared.

---

5 PERMUTATIONS AND COMBINATIONS

5.1 The theory of permutations and combinations is an important tool in probability theory.

5.2   A combination is a set of items, selected from a larger collection of items, regardless of the order in which they are selected. We refer to the number of possible combinations of r items from n items. For example, suppose that five people apply for two vacancies as junior administrators in Combo Ltd and these people are called A,B,C,D and E. The different possible combinations of people to fill the two posts from the five applicants would be AB, AC, AD, AE, BC, BD, BE, CD, CE and DE.

5.3   A permutation is a set of items, selected from a larger group of items, in which the order of selection or arrangement is significant. We refer to the number of possible permutations of x items from n items.

In the previous example, suppose that the two vacancies were for the post of senior administrator and junior administrator. The order of selection would be important and the possible permutations would be as follows.

Senior	Junior	Senior	Junior	Senior	Junior	Senior	Junior
A	B	B	C	C	D	D	E
A	C	B	D	C	E	E	A
A	D	B	E	D	A	E	B
A	E	C	A	D	B	E	C
B	A	C	B	D	C	E	D

Whereas there were ten combinations of two from five, there are 20 permutations of two from five.

The formula for the number of permutations

5.4   There is a formula to calculate the number of permutations of r items which are possible from a set of n items. The number is denoted by the term $_nP_x$ and the formula is

$$_nP_x = \frac{n!}{(n-x)!}$$

The notation here is as follows.

n!   is the factorial of n $(1 \times 2 \times 3 \times 4 \times 5 \times \ldots \times n)$, eg $3! = 1 \times 2 \times 3$
(n–x)! is the factorial of the difference between n and x, eg $(5-3)! = 2! = 1 \times 2$

Example: permutations

5.5   (a)   In the previous example of five candidates for two different jobs, as described in Paragraph 5.3, the number of different permutations would be

$$_5P_2 = \frac{5!}{(5-2)!} = \frac{5 \times 4 \times 3 \times 2 \times 1}{3 \times 2 \times 1} = 5 \times 4 = 20$$

(b)   0! is defined to equal 1.

For example, suppose that an investment manager must rank three projects, A, B and C in order of profitability. How many possible ways are there of ordering them 1st, 2nd and 3rd?

$$_3P_3 = \frac{3!}{0!} = 3 \times 2 \times 1 = 6$$

(The permutations are ABC, ACB, BCA, BAC, CBA and CAB.)

The formula for the number of combinations

5.6   There is also a formula to calculate the number of combinations of r items which are possible from a set of n items. This formula is

$$^nC_x = \frac{n!}{(n-x)!x!}$$

(The notation ^nC_x means 'the number of different combinations of x items from a set of n items'.)

Example: combinations

5.7 (a) In the example in Paragraph 5.2 of five candidates applying for two jobs of equal status, the number of possible combinations of two applicants would be

$$^5C_2 = \frac{5!}{3!2!} = \frac{5 \times 4 \times 3 \times 2 \times 1}{(3 \times 2 \times 1)(2 \times 1)} = \frac{5 \times 4}{2 \times 1} = 10$$

(b) The number of ways of choosing a work team of four people from a total number of only four people available would be

$$^4C_4 = \frac{4!}{0!4!} = 1$$

Example: combinations of one or two items

5.8 A hardware storekeeper sells paint which he mixes himself in pairs to get the right colours. If we assume that by mixing two of the basic paints he always gets a colour different to any of the other mixtures and different to any of the basic colours, how many different shades can he obtain by stocking n basic paints? (*Note.* Any one basic paint itself counts as one shade.)

Solution

5.9 The total number of mixtures (combinations) of two paints will be:

$$^nC_2 = \frac{n!}{(n-2)!2!} = \frac{n \times (n-1)}{2 \times 1} = \frac{n^2 - n}{2}$$

If we add to this the number of paints stocked, n, (which are themselves different shades) we get a total of

$$\frac{n^2 - n}{2} + n$$

Exercise 5

A class of 15 students is about to sit a statistics examination. They will subsequently be listed in descending order by reference to the marks scored. Assume that there are no tied positions with two or more students having the same mark.

Required

Calculate the following.

(a) The number of different possible orderings for the whole class

(b) The number of different possible results for the top three places

(c) The number of different possible ways of having three people taking the top three places (irrespective of order)

Solution

(a) The number of different possible orderings of the whole class is

$$_{15}P_{15} = \frac{15!}{(15-15)!} = \frac{15!}{0!} = 15! = 1{,}307{,}674{,}368{,}000$$

(b) The number of different possible results for the top three places is given by the number of permutations of three out of 15.

$$_{15}P_3 = \frac{15!}{(15-3)!} = \frac{15!}{12!} = 15 \times 14 \times 13 = 2{,}730$$

(c) The number of ways of having three people taking the top three places is given by the number of combinations of three out of 15.

$$^{15}C_3 = \frac{15!}{(15-3)!3!} = \frac{15 \times 14 \times 13}{3 \times 2 \times 1} = 455$$

Chapter roundup

- In this chapter we looked at the concept of probability. We introduced a number of terms and rules, which we have summarised below, and which you must be able to explain and use as appropriate.

- Mutually exclusive outcomes are outcomes where the occurrence of one of the outcomes excludes the possibility of any of the others happening.

- Independent events are events where the outcome of one event in no way affects the outcome of the other events.

- Dependent or conditional events are events where the outcome of one event depends on the outcome of the others.

- The addition laws for two events, X and Y, are as follows.

  P(X or Y) = P(X) + P(Y) when X and Y have mutually exclusive outcomes.
  P(X or Y) = P(X) + P(Y) – P(X and Y) when X and Y are independent probability.

- Contingency tables can be useful for dealing with conditional probability.

- The multiplication laws for two events, X and Y, are as follows.

  P(X and Y) = 0 when X and Y have mutually exclusive outcomes.
  P(X and Y) = P(X) P(Y) when X and Y are independent events.
  P(X and Y) = P(X) P(Y/X)
            = P(Y) P(X/Y) when X and Y are dependent/conditional events.

- An expected value (EV) is a weighted average, based on probabilities. The expected value for a single event can offer a helpful guide for management decisions: a project with a positive EV should be accepted and a project with a negative EV should be rejected.

- Probability and expectation should be seen as an *aid* to decision making.

  o Probabilities based on past experience have some degree of reliability.

  o Subjective estimates of probabilities may be open to question.

  o The use of the EV approach in one-off decisions may not be valid, although an EV based on repeated events may be more reliable.

  o Finally, probability and expectation take no account of the decision maker's attitude to risk.

- A combination is a set of items, selected from a larger collection of items, regardless of the order in which they are selected.

- A permutation is a set of items, selected from a larger group of items, in which the order of selection or arrangement is significant.

- This chapter has introduced some important topics that underpin a lot of your later studies. Make sure you are happy with all the concepts before moving on to the next chapter.

Test your knowledge

1   What is the probability of $\bar{x}$? (see para 2.8)

2   Define mutually exclusive outcomes, independent events and conditional events. (2.13, 2.19, 2.27)

3   What is the general rule of addition and when should it be used? (2.25)

4   How do you calculate an expected value? (3.4)

5   What is the decision rule for expected values for single events? (4.1)

6   Describe three common factors in many business decisions. (4.8)

7   What is the difference between a combination of items and a permutation of items? (5.2, 5.3)

Now try illustrative question 24 at the end of the Study Text

Chapter 24

THE NORMAL DISTRIBUTION AND SAMPLING THEORY

> **This chapter covers the following topics.**
>
> | | | Syllabus reference | Ability required |
> |---|---|---|---|
> | 1 | Probability distributions | 2(f) | Skill |
> | 2 | The normal distribution | 2(f) | Skill |
> | 3 | Sampling distribution of the mean | 2(f) | Skill |
> | 4 | Sampling distribution of a proportion | 2(f) | Skill |
> | 5 | The size of a sample | 2(f) | Knowledge |
>
> ## Introduction
>
> In Chapter 23 we looked at the calculation and interpretation of probability and uncertainty. This chapter begins by examining probability distributions. Probability distributions analyse the proportion of times a particular value occurs in a set of items. The importance of probability distributions is that they extend the areas to which probability can be applied and they provide a method of arriving at the probability of an event without having to go through all the probability rules examined in the previous chapter. We will then turn our attention to a particular probability distribution: the normal distribution.
>
> Having examined the normal distribution we will use it to study sampling theory, the final topic in this chapter. Sampling theory allows us to make estimates about values in a population using information from samples.
>
> Don't forget that we looked at methods for collecting samples in Chapter 18.

1 PROBABILITY DISTRIBUTIONS

1.1 A frequency distribution (considered in Chapter 19) gives an analysis of the number of times each particular value occurs in a set of items. A probability distribution simply replaces actual numbers (frequencies) with proportions of the total. For example, in a statistics test, the marks out of ten awarded to 50 students might be as follows.

Marks out of 10	*Number of students (frequency distribution)*	*Proportion or probability (probability distribution)*
0	0	0.00
1	0	0.00
2	1	0.02
3	2	0.04
4	4	0.08
5	10	0.20
6	15	0.30
7	10	0.20
8	6	0.12
9	2	0.04
10	0	0.00
	50	1.00

1.2   A graph of the probability distribution would be the same as the graph of the frequency distribution, but with the vertical axis marked in proportions rather than in numbers. In our example, this would be as follows.

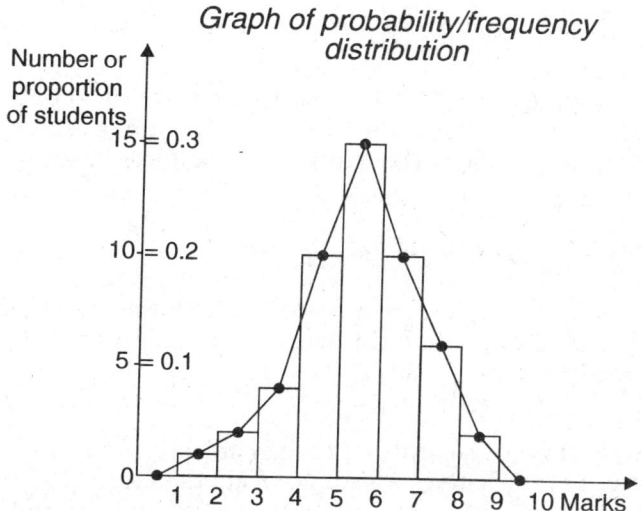

Graph of probability/frequency distribution

1.3   The area under the curve in the frequency distribution represents the total number of students whose marks have been recorded, 50 people. The area under the curve in a probability distribution is 100%, or 1 (the total of all the probabilities).

1.4   There are a number of different probability distributions but we shall confine our attention to just one.

2   THE NORMAL DISTRIBUTION   *S/97*

2.1   The normal distribution is an important probability distribution which is often applied to continuous variables. In other words, in calculating P(x), x can be any value, and does not have to be a whole number.

2.2   Examples of continuous variables include the following.

(a)   The heights of people. The height of a person need not be an exact number of centimetres, but can be anything within a range of possible figures.

(b)   The temperature of a room. It need not be an exact number of degrees, but can fall anywhere within a range of possible values.

2.3   The normal distribution can also apply to discrete variables which can take many possible values. For example, the volume of sales, in units, of a product might be any whole number in the range 100 – 5,000 units. There are so many possibilities within this range that the variable is for all practical purposes continuous.

2.4   The normal distribution can be drawn as a graph, and it would be a bell-shaped curve.

Normal distribution

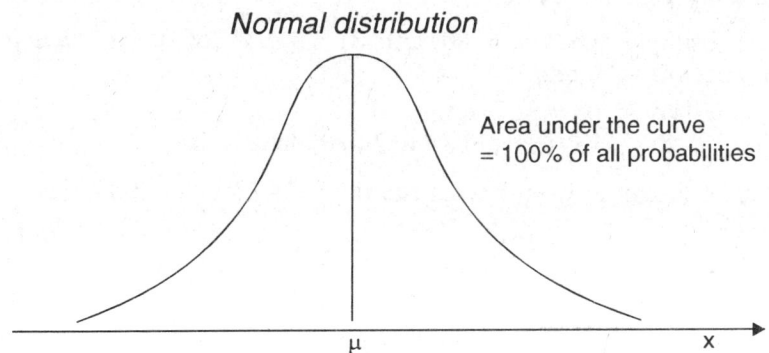

2.5   The normal curve is symmetrical. The left hand side of the area under the curve to the left of μ is the mirror image of the right hand side.

μ is the mean, or average of the distribution.

Because it is a probability distribution, the area under the curve totals exactly 1.

2.6   The normal distribution is important because in the practical application of statistics, it has been found that many probability distributions are close enough to a normal distribution to be treated as one without any significant loss of accuracy.

The standard deviation and the normal distribution

2.7   For any normal distribution, the dispersion around the mean of the frequency of occurrences can be measured exactly in terms of the standard deviation (a concept we covered in Chapter 21).

2.8   The entire frequency curve represents all the possible outcomes and their frequencies of occurrence and the normal curve is symmetrical; therefore 50% of outcomes have a value greater than the mean value, and 50% of outcomes have a value less than the mean value.

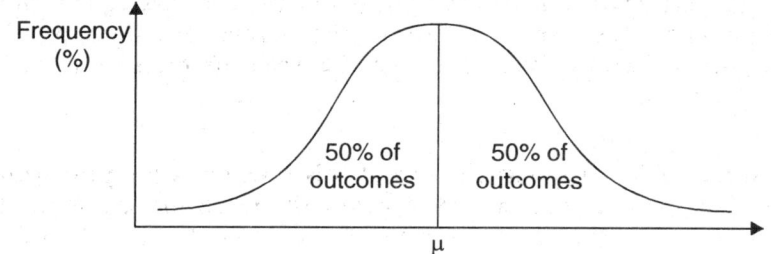

2.9   About 68% of frequencies have a value within one standard deviation either side of the mean. Thus if a normal distribution has a mean of 80 and a standard deviation of 3, 68% of the total outcomes would occur within the range ± one standard deviation from the mean, that is, within the range 77 – 83. Since the curve is symmetrical, 34% of the values must fall in the range 77 – 80 and 34% in the range 80 – 83.

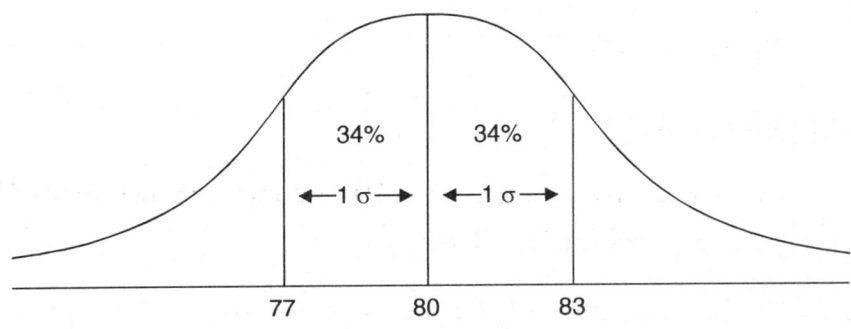

2.10   95% of the frequencies in a normal distribution occur in the range ± 1.96 standard deviations from the mean.

In our example, when μ = 80, and σ = 3, 95% of the frequencies in the distribution would occur in the range

$$80 \pm 1.96 \,(3)$$
$$= \quad 80 \pm 5.88 \text{ (the range 74.12 to 85.88)}$$

47½% of outcomes would be in the range 74.12 to 80 and 47½% would be in the range 80 to 85.88.

2.11   99% of the frequencies occur in the range ± 2.58 standard deviations from the mean.

In our example, 99% of frequencies in a normal distribution with μ = 80 and σ = 3 would lie in the range

$$80 \pm 2.58\,(3)$$
$$= \quad 80 \pm 7.74$$
$$= \quad 72.26 \text{ to } 87.74.$$

Exercise 1

What is the name of the point above which 25% of the frequencies occur?

Solution

The upper quartile

Normal distribution tables

2.12   Although there is an infinite number of normal distributions, depending on values of the mean μ and the standard deviation σ, the relative dispersion of frequencies around the mean, measured as proportions of the total population, is exactly the same for all normal distributions. In other words, whatever the normal distribution, $47\frac{1}{2}$% (for example) of outcomes will always be in the range between the mean and 1.96 standard deviations below the mean.

2.13   A normal distribution table, shown at the end of this text, gives the proportion of the total between the mean and a point above or below the mean for any multiple of the standard deviation.

2.14   Distances above or below the mean are expressed in numbers of standard deviations z.

$$z = \frac{x - \mu}{\sigma}$$

where   z   =   the number of standard deviations above or below the mean
        x   =   the value of the variable under consideration
        μ   =   the mean
        σ   =   the standard deviation

Example: the normal distribution

2.15   A frequency distribution is normal, with a mean of 100 and a standard deviation of 10.

What proportion of the total frequencies will be:

(a)   above 80;
(b)   above 90;
(c)   above 100;
(d)   above 115;
(e)   below 85;
(f)   below 95;
(g)   below 108;
(h)   in the range 80 - 110;
(i)   in the range 90 - 95?

Solution

2.16   To calculate the proportion of frequencies *above* a certain value (x):

(a)   if the value is below the mean (μ), the total proportion is:

0.5 plus proportion between the value and the mean (area (a));

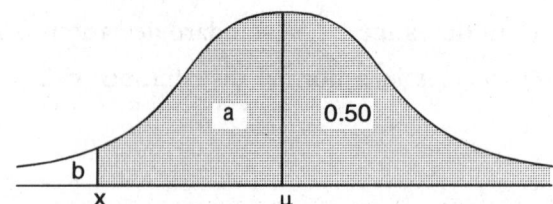

(b) if the value is above the mean, the proportion (b) is 0.5 – proportion between the value and the mean (area (a)).

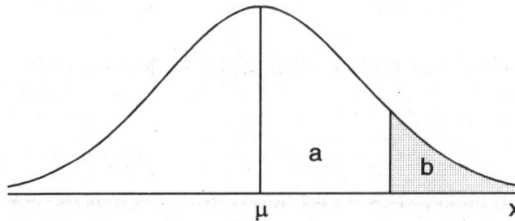

2.17 To calculate the proportion of frequencies *below* a certain value:

(a) if the value is below the mean, the proportion (b) is 0.5 – proportion between the value and the mean (area (a));

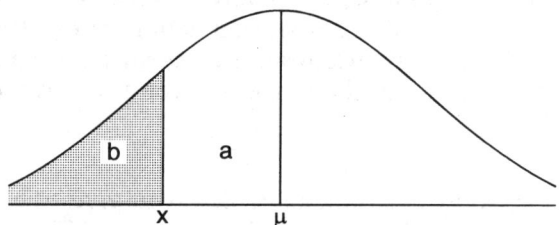

(b) if the value is above the mean, the proportion required (b) is 0.5 plus the proportion between the value and the mean (area (a)).

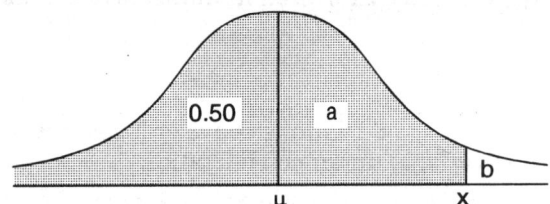

2.18 (a) 80 is $\dfrac{100-80}{10}$ = 2 standard deviations below the mean. From the tables, where $z = 2$ the proportion is 0.4772.

The proportion of frequencies above 80 is $0.5 + 0.4772 = 0.9772$.

(b) 90 is $\dfrac{100-90}{10}$ = 1 standard deviation below the mean. From the tables, when $z = 1$, the proportion is 0.3413.

The proportion of frequencies above 90 is $0.5 + 0.3413 = 0.8413$.

(c) 100 is the mean. The proportion above this is 0.5.

(d) 115 is $\dfrac{115-100}{10}$ = 1.5 standard deviations above the mean. From the tables, where $z = 1.5$, the proportion is 0.4332.

The proportion of frequencies above 115 is therefore $0.5 - 0.4332 = 0.0668$.

(e) 85 is 1.5 standard deviations below the mean. The proportion of frequencies below 85 is therefore the same as the proportion above 115, 0.0668.

(f)   95 is $\dfrac{100-95}{10}$ = 0.5 standard deviations below the mean. When z = 0.5, the proportion from the tables is 0.1915. The proportion of frequencies below 95 is therefore 0.5 – 0.1915 = 0.3085.

(g)   108 is $\dfrac{108-100}{10}$ = 0.8 standard deviations above the mean. From the tables for z = 0.8 the proportion is 0.2881.

The proportion of frequencies below 108 is 0.5 + 0.2881 = 0.7881.

(h)   The range 80 to 110 may be divided into two parts:

    (i)   80 to 100 (the mean);
    (ii)   100 to 110.

The proportion in the range 80 to 100 is (2 standard deviations) 0.4772

The proportion in the range 100 to 110 is (1 standard deviation) 0.3413

The proportion in the total range 80 to 110 is 0.4772 + 0.3413 = 0.8185.

(i)   The range 90 to 95 may be analysed as:

    (i)   the proportion above 90 and below the mean
    (ii)   minus the proportion above 95 and below the mean

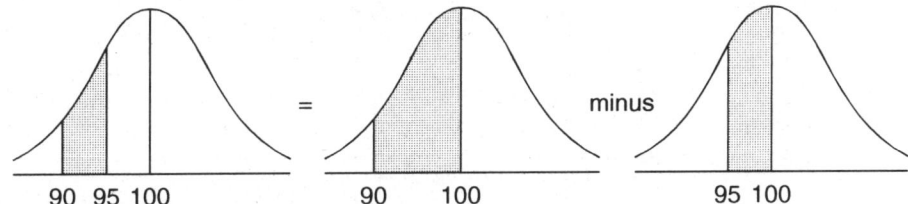

Proportion above 90 and below the mean (1 standard deviation)	0.3413
Proportion above 95 and below the mean (0.5 standard deviations)	0.1915
Proportion between 90 and 95	0.1498

Exercise 2

The salaries of employees in an industry are normally distributed, with a mean of £14,000 and a standard deviation of £2,700.

Required

(a)   Calculate the proportion of employees who earn less than £12,000.
(b)   Calculate the proportion of employees who earn between £11,000 and £19,000.

Solution

(a)   (12,000 – 14,000)/2,700 = –0.74

    From tables, the proportion of the normal distribution more than 0.74 standard deviations below the mean is 0.5 – 0.2704 = 0.2296.

(b)   (11,000 – 14,000)/2,700 = –1.11
    (19,000 – 14,000)/2,700 = 1.85

    The proportion with earnings between £11,000 and £14,000 is 0.3665.

    The proportion with earnings between £14,000 and £19,000 is 0.4678.

    The required proportion is 0.3665 + 0.4678 = 0.8343.

2.19   Note that the normal distribution is, in fact, a way of calculating probabilities. In the exercise above, for example, the *probability* that an employee earns less than £12,000 (part (a)) is 0.2296 and the probability that an employee earns between £11,000 and £19,000 is 0.8343.

3   SAMPLING DISTRIBUTION OF THE MEAN   5/96, 11/96, 5/97

3.1   Suppose that we wish to estimate the mean of a population, say the average weight of a product made in a factory. A sample of, say, 100 units of the product might be taken, and the mean weight per unit of the sample might be, say, 5.8 kg.

Another sample of 100 units might then be taken and the mean weight might be, say, 6.3 kg.

A large number of samples might be taken (over 30) and the mean of each sample calculated. These means will not all be the same and they can be plotted as a frequency distribution. This distribution is called a sampling distribution of the mean.

3.2   In our example, a frequency distribution of the mean weight per unit in each of 250 samples (of 100 units per sample) might be as follows.

Mean weight per unit kg	Mid-point of class interval	Frequency (No of samples)
5.45 and < 5.55	5.5	3
5.55 and < 5.65	5.6	7
5.65 and < 5.75	5.7	16
5.75 and < 5.85	5.8	30
5.85 and < 5.95	5.9	44
5.95 and < 6.05	6.0	50
6.05 and < 6.15	6.1	44
6.15 and < 6.25	6.2	30
6.25 and < 6.35	6.3	16
6.35 and < 6.45	6.4	7
6.45 and < 6.55	6.5	3
		$\overline{250}$ samples

The mean weight per unit of 100 units in a sample might thus range from 5.45 to 6.55 kg. The true mean of the population, that is, the true mean weight of all units produced, presumably lies somewhere within this range.

3.3   A sampling distribution of the mean has the following important properties.

(a)   It is very close to being normally distributed. This is true even if the distribution of the population from which the samples are drawn is fairly heavily skewed. The larger the sample the more closely will the sampling distribution approximate to a normal distribution. The statistical rule that a sampling distribution of sample means is normally distributed is known as the *central limit theorem*

(b)   The mean of the sampling distribution is the same as the population mean, μ.

(c)   The sampling distribution has a standard deviation which is called the standard error of the mean.

3.4   In our example, the 250 samples give an estimate of the population mean. This distribution of sample means would be (approximately) normally distributed, with a mean of about 6 kg (weight per unit of product).

This mean of 6 kg would be the same as the population mean, μ, so that we would be able to state that the true population mean is about 6 kg.

The standard deviation of the sampling distribution (which could be calculated as 0.2 kg: workings not shown) is the standard error (se).

The standard error

3.5   It can be shown that the standard error of the mean (se) is $\sigma/\sqrt{n}$, where n is the size of each sample and σ is the standard deviation *of the population*. σ is not normally known, however. To overcome this problem the standard deviation *of a sample* is taken as the best estimate of the standard deviation of the whole population, so that se $= s/\sqrt{n}$, where s is the standard deviation of a sample.

3.6   For reasons which will become apparent in later studies, if we need to calculate s we will use a formula for s which is slightly different from that used to find the standard deviation of a population when we have data on every member. The formula is

$$s = \sqrt{\Sigma(x - \bar{x})^2 / (n-1)}$$

This formula is provided in the examination.

The central limit theorem

3.7   The central limit theorem states that a sampling distribution of sample means is normally distributed. If we take a sample and calculate the mean of that sample we can therefore find the probability that the sample mean is within a given distance of the mean of the sampling distribution. But the mean of the sampling distribution is the same as the mean of the population (see Paragraph 3.3) and so, using sample data, we are able to make estimates about the mean of the population.

Confidence levels, limits and intervals

3.8   From our knowledge of the properties of a normal distribution, together with the rule that sample means are normally distributed around the true population mean, with a standard deviation equal to the standard error, we can predict (using normal distribution tables) the following.

(a)   68% of all sample means will be within one standard error of the population mean.
(b)   95% of all sample means will be within 1.96 standard errors of the population mean.
(c)   99% of all sample means will be within 2.58 standard errors of the population mean.

3.9   Let us look at it another way.

(a)   With 68% probability, the population mean lies within the range: sample mean ± one standard error.

(b)   With 95% probability, the population mean lies within the range: sample mean ± 1.96 standard errors.

(c)   With 99% probability, the population mean lies within the range: sample mean ± 2.58 standard errors.

These degrees of certainty (such as 95%) are known as *confidence levels*, and the ends of the ranges (such as sample mean + 2.58 standard errors) around the sample mean are called *confidence limits*. The ranges (such as sample mean ± one standard error) are called *confidence intervals*.

Example: confidence intervals

3.10   From a random sample of 576 of a company's 20,000 employees, it was found that the average number of days each person was absent from work due to illness was eight days a year, with a standard deviation (found using the formula with n–1 as the denominator) of 3.6 days.

What are the confidence limits for the average number of days absence a year through sickness per employee for the company as a whole at the following confidence levels?

(a)   95%
(b)   99%

Solution

3.11   We must first calculate the standard error, which is estimated as $s/\sqrt{n}$ (because we do not know the standard deviation of the entire population).

$$se = 3.6/\sqrt{576} = 0.15.$$

(a) At the 95% level of confidence z = 1.96 and therefore the true average number of days absence a year for the population is in the range $8 \pm (1.96 \times 0.15)$

   = 8 ± 0.294
   =   7.706 days to 8.294 days, say 7.7 days to 8.3 days.

(b) At the 99% level of confidence z = 2.58 and therefore the true average number of days absence a year for the population is in the range $8 \pm (2.58 \times 0.15)$

   $\coloneqq$ 8 ± 0.387
        7.613 days to 8.387 days, say 7.6 days to 8.4 days.

3.12 Why is it necessary to calculate confidence limits? If the sample mean was eight days would it not be sufficient to use eight days as a point estimate of the population mean?

3.13 In practice, a sample mean might indeed be used as a 'point estimate' of the population mean. However, we could not be sure how reliable the estimate might be, without first considering the size of the standard error. The sample mean might be above or below the true population mean, but we can say with 95% confidence that the sample mean is no more than 1.96 standard errors above or below the true population mean. We are therefore 95% confident that the average number of days absence a year through sickness per employee is in the range 7.7 days to 8.3 days.

3.14 If the confidence limits cover a wide range of values, a point estimate of the population mean from the sample would not be reliable. On the other hand, if the confidence limits cover a narrow range of values, a point estimate of the population mean, using the sample mean, would be reliable.

Exercise 3

The cost of assembling an item of equipment has been estimated by obtaining a sample of 144 jobs. The average cost of assembly derived from the sample was £4,000 with a standard deviation of £1,500.

Required

Estimate confidence limits for the true average cost of assembly. Use the 95% level of confidence.

Solution

The standard error is estimated as $1,500/\sqrt{144}$ = £125.

At the 95% level of confidence, the population mean is in the range £$(4,000 \pm (1.96 \times 125))$ = £$(4,000 \pm 245)$, that is, £3,755 to £4,245.

---

4   SAMPLING DISTRIBUTION OF A PROPORTION

4.1 The arithmetic mean is a very important statistic, and sampling is often concerned with estimating the mean of a population. Many surveys, however, especially those concerned with attitudes or opinions about an issue or the percentage of times an event occurs (for example, the proportion of faulty items out of the total number of items produced in a manufacturing department) attempt to estimate a proportion rather than an arithmetic mean.

Suppose for example, that we wished to know what proportion of an electorate intends to vote for the Jacobin party at the forthcoming general election. Several samples might be obtained, and the proportion of pro- Jacobin voters in a sample might vary, say from 37% to 45%. The central limit theorem would apply, and the proportion of pro-Jacobin voters in each sample could be arranged into a sampling distribution (the sampling distribution of a proportion) with the following features.

(a) It is normally distributed.
(b) It has a mean equal to the proportion of pro-Jacobin voters in the population.
(c) It has a standard deviation equal to the standard error of a proportion.

The formula for the standard error of a proportion is $\sqrt{[pq/n]}$

where   p is the proportion in the population
        q is $1 - p$
        n is the size of the sample.

We use the sample proportion p as an estimate of the population proportion.

Example: a confidence interval for a proportion

4.2   In a random sample of 500 out of 100,000 employees, 320 were members of a trade union. Estimate the proportion of trade union members in the entire organisation at the 95% confidence level.

Solution

4.3   The sample proportion is $320/500 = 0.64$.

$$\text{Standard error} = \sqrt{\frac{0.64 \times (1 - 0.64)}{500}} = = \sqrt{\frac{0.64 \times 0.36}{500}} = 0.0215$$

An estimate of the population proportion at the 95% confidence level (z = 1.96) is the sample proportion $\pm$ 1.96 standard errors.

The population proportion is $0.64 \pm (1.96 \times 0.0215) = 0.64 \pm 0.04$. The percentage of employees who are trade union members is between 60% and 68% at the 95% level of confidence.

Exercise 4

A researcher wishes to know the proportion of people who regularly travel by bus. Of a sample of 400 people, 285 said they did so. Estimate the population proportion with 99% confidence.

Solution

The sample proportion is $285/400 = 0.7125$.

The standard error is $\sqrt{\frac{0.7125 \times (1 - 0.7125)}{400}} = 0.0226$

The 99% confidence interval for the population proportion is

$$0.7125 \pm (2.58 \times 0.0226)$$
$$= \quad 0.7125 \pm 0.0583$$
$$= \quad 0.6542 \text{ to } 0.7708$$

---

5   THE SIZE OF A SAMPLE

5.1   Suppose that a trade association wants to find out the average salary to within £10 of all those working in the trade in question. A previous investigation estimated it to be £18,000, with a standard deviation of £50. How could the trade association decide on the size of the sample required to be able to estimate the true average salary to within £10?

5.2   We know that, at the 95% level of confidence, the population mean $= \bar{x} \pm 1.96$ se (where $\bar{x}$ is a sample mean).

If we require the estimate to be within $\pm$ £10 then 1.96 se $= 10$

$\therefore 1.96\, \sigma / \sqrt{n} = 10$

$\therefore \dfrac{1.96 \times £50}{\sqrt{n}} = 10$

$$\therefore \left(\frac{1.96 \times £50}{10}\right)^2 = n = 96.04, \text{ say } 97 \text{ (we have to round up)}$$

A sample size of 97 is therefore required to be able to estimate the true mean salary to within $\pm £10$.

5.3 In general terms the size of sample required to estimate a population mean with a sufficient degree of accuracy (r) at a given level of confidence $= n = (1.96\sigma/r)^2$. An estimate must be provided for σ even before the sample is collected. At the 99% confidence level, 1.96 is replaced by 2.58.

Example: sample sizes

5.4 The management of a company making a certain type of car component wish to ascertain the average number of components per hour produced by the workers. Based on a previous sample, it is estimated that the average number produced by each employee every hour is 100, with a standard deviation of 25. The management now wish to know the true average to within two units. Calculate the sample size at the 99% confidence level.

Solution

5.5 At a 99% level of confidence, $n = [2.58 \times 25/2]^2 = 32.25^2$

$= 1,040.06$ workers, say 1,041.

To have 99% confidence about the accuracy of the sample mean as an estimate of the population mean to within two units, the sample size would need to be 1,041 workers.

Selecting a sample size in order to estimate a proportion

5.6 The considerations relating to the size of sample required in order to calculate the arithmetic mean of a population with sufficient accuracy also apply to the problem of deciding a sample size to obtain the proportion of a population with sufficient accuracy.

5.7 Let r be the degree of accuracy required, expressed as units of the population proportion. Thus if we require an estimate of the proportion which is accurate to within $\pm 3\%$, r would be 0.03.

We know that, at the 95% level of confidence:

$r = 1.96 \text{ se} = 1.96 \sqrt{[pq/n]}$

$r^2 = \dfrac{1.96^2 \times pq}{n}$

$n = \dfrac{1.96^2 \times pq}{r^2}$

At the 99% confidence level, 1.96 is replaced by 2.58.

Example: sample sizes for estimating proportions

5.8 A manufacturer wishes to estimate the proportion of defective components. He would be satisfied if he obtained an estimate within 0.5% of the true proportion, and was 99% confident of his result. An initial (large) sample indicated that $p = 0.02$. What size of sample should he examine?

Solution

5.9   p   =   0.02, therefore q = 1 – p = 0.98
      r   =   0.5% = 0.005

At a 99% level of confidence

$$n \ = \ \frac{2.58^2 \times 0.02 \times 0.98}{0.005^2}$$

     =   5,218.6 units, say 5,219 units

The sample would need to consist of 5,219 units.

5.10   If we have no initial idea of the population proportion, we work out a required sample size using p = 0.5, as this gives the largest possible value for p(1 – p), and hence the largest possible value for n. We will thus at least achieve the required accuracy.

Sample sizes and the standard error

5.11   The standard error is given as $\sigma / \sqrt{n}$. As the sample size increases, the standard error therefore decreases (since σ remains the same whatever the sample size). In other words, the variability of the data around the mean decreases the larger the sample size taken.

Sample sizes from an administrative viewpoint

5.12   Remember that as well as calculating a sample size from a statistical point of view other, administrative-type factors may have to be taken into account. These factors are summarised below.

     (a)   Two basic statistical facts

          (i)   The larger the sample size, the more precise will be the information given about the population.

          (ii)   Above a certain size, little extra information is given by increasing the size.

         A sample therefore only need be large enough to be reasonably representative of the population.

     (b)   The amount of money and time available

     (c)   Aims of the survey

     (d)   Degree of precision required

     (e)   Number of sub-samples required

Chapter roundup

- The normal distribution is a probability distribution which usually applies to variables with a continuous range of possible values (continuous variables), such as distance and time. The distribution can be drawn as a bell-shaped curve, the area under the curve being exactly equal to one. The distance of a point above or below the mean is expressed in numbers of standard deviations, z, and 68%/95%/99% of outcomes are ±1/±1.96/±2.58 standard deviations from the mean. Make sure that you are able to calculate the proportion of outcomes/probability of an outcome being above/below a certain value. Drawing a sketch of a normal distribution curve often helps in normal distribution problems.

- According to the central limit theorem, if a large number of samples are taken from the population, their means calculated and the means plotted as a frequency distribution, this distribution (the sampling distribution of the mean) will be very close to being normally distributed.

- The mean of this sampling distribution is the same as the population mean, μ. The standard deviation of the distribution is called the standard error of the mean (se) and is estimated using the standard deviation, s, of a sample.

- Armed with knowledge of the central limit theorem and properties of the sampling distribution of the mean, we can say, with a certain level of confidence and using sample data, the range within which the true population mean falls.

- As well as being able to do this, you should also be able to calculate the size of the sample required to obtain a sufficient degree of accuracy at a given level of confidence in the estimation of the population mean.

- The chapter also looked at the sampling distribution of a proportion which is normally distributed, has a mean equal to the population proportion and has a standard deviation called the standard error of a proportion. Ensure that you are able to say, with a certain level of confidence and using sample data, the range within which the true population proportion falls.

- We encountered a number of symbols in the chapter. Students often get these symbols muddled up and consequently find the whole topic of sampling distributions confusing. Ensure that you know what all of the following symbols mean.

  $\bar{x}$ is the mean of a sample

  μ (mu) is the mean of a population

  s   is the standard deviation of a sample

  σ (sigma) is the standard deviation of a population

  se   the standard error of the mean, is the standard deviation of the sampling distribution of the mean.

Test your knowledge

1   What is the area under a curve in a probability distribution? (see para 1.3)

2   In what circumstances can the normal distribution be applied to discrete variables? (2.3)

3   What is the formula for the number of standard deviations, z? (2.14)

4   What is the sampling distribution of the mean? (3.1)

5   What is the statistical rule covered by the central limit theorem? (3.3)

6   What is the standard error of the mean? (3.3)

7   What is the formula for the standard error of the mean? (3.5)

8   What is used as the best estimate of the standard deviation of the whole population when calculating the standard error? (3.5)

9   Define confidence intervals, confidence levels and confidence limits. (3. 9)

10   What are the features of a sampling distribution of a proportion? (4.1)

11   What is the formula for the standard error of a proportion? (4.1)

12   What administrative-type factors need to be taken into account when deriving a sample size? (5.12)

Now try illustrative question 25 at the end of the Study Text

Part G
Introduction to financial mathematics

Chapter 25

INTEREST

This chapter covers the following topics.

		Syllabus reference	Ability required
1	Simple interest	2(g)	Skill
2	Compound interest	2(g)	Skill
3	Regular investments	2(g)	Skill
4	Effective and nominal rates of interest	2(g)	Skill
5	Simple applications	2(g)	Skill

Introduction

The previous chapters introduced a variety of quantitative methods relevant to business analysis. This chapter and the next extend the use of mathematics and look at aspects of financial analysis typically undertaken in a business organisation.

In general, financial mathematics deals with problems of investing money, or capital. If a company (or an individual investor) puts some capital into an investment, a financial return will be expected.

(a) If Arthur puts £1,000 into an account with a building society, he will expect a return in the form of interest, which will be added to the original investment in his account.

(b) If Newbegin Ltd invests £10,000 in an item of equipment, the company will expect to make a profit out of the item over its working life.

Investors may therefore wish to know the following.

(a) What return will be obtained by investing £X now for a given period, say n years?
(b) Do the returns over an investment's life make that investment worthwhile?

The two major techniques of financial mathematics are compounding and discounting. Compounding can be used to help provide an answer to the first question above and others like it. The second question (and, of course, others like it) can be answered by employing discounting. This chapter will describe compounding and the next will introduce discounting.

1 SIMPLE INTEREST

5/95

1.1 Interest is the amount of money which an investment earns over time.

Simple interest is interest which is earned in equal amounts every year (or month) and which is a given proportion of the original investment (the principal).

1.2 If a sum of money is invested for a period of time, then the amount of simple interest which accrues is equal to the number of periods × the interest rate × the amount invested.

$V = X + nrX$

where X = the original sum invested
       r = the interest rate (expressed as a proportion, so 10% = 0.1)
       n = the number of periods (normally years)
       V = the sum invested after n periods, consisting of the original capital (X) plus interest earned.

Example: simple interest

1.3   How much will an investor have after five years if he invests £1,000 at 10% simple interest per annum?

Solution

1.4   V = £1,000 + (5 × 0.1 × £1,000)
       = £1,500

1.5   If, for example, the sum of money is invested for 3 months and the interest rate is a rate per annum, then $n = ^3/_{12} = ^1/_4$. If the investment period is 197 days and the rate is an annual rate, then $n = ^{197}/_{365}$.

2   COMPOUND INTEREST

2.1   Interest is normally calculated by means of compounding.

If a sum of money, the principal, is invested at a fixed rate of interest such that the interest is added to the principal and no withdrawals are made, then the amount invested will grow by an increasing number of pounds in each successive time period, because interest earned in earlier periods will itself earn interest in later periods.

2.2   Suppose, for example, that £2,000 is invested to earn 10% interest. After one year, the original principal plus interest will amount to £2,200.

	£
Original investment	2,000
Interest in the first year (10%)	200
Total investment at the end of one year	2,200

(a)   After two years the total investment will be £2,420.

	£
Investment at end of one year	2,200
Interest in the second year (10%)	220
Total investment at the end of two years	2,420

The second year interest of £220 represents 10% of the original investment, and 10% of the interest earned in the first year.

(b)   Similarly, after three years, the total investment will be £2,662.

	£
Investment at the end of two years	2,420
Interest in the third year (10%)	242
Total investment at the end of three years	2,662

2.3   The basic formula for compound interest is $V = X(1 + r)^n$

where   X = the original sum invested
          r = the interest rate, expressed as a proportion (so 5% = 0.05)
          n = the number of periods
          V = the sum invested after n periods.

2.4   In the previous example, £2,000 invested at 10% per annum for three years would increase in value to

$$£2,000 × 1.10^3$$
$$= £2,000 × 1.331$$
$$= £2,662.$$

The interest earned over three years is £662.

Exercise 1

(a)   What would be the total value of £5,000 invested now:

    (i)   after three years, if the interest rate is 20% per annum;
    (ii)   after four years, if the interest rate is 15% per annum;
    (iii)   after three years, if the interest rate is 6% per annum?

(b)   At what annual rate of compound interest will £2,000 grow to £2,721 after four years?

Solution

(a)   (i) $£5,000 \times 1.20^3 = £8,640$
    (ii) $£5,000 \times 1.15^4 = £8,745.03$
    (iii) $£5,000 \times 1.06^3 = £5,955.08$

(b) $\begin{aligned} 2,721 &= 2,000 \times (1 + r)^4 \\ (1 + r)^4 &= 2,721/2,000 = 1.3605 \\ 1 + r &= \sqrt[4]{1.3605} = 1.08 \\ r &= 0.08 = 8\% \end{aligned}$

Inflation

2.5   The same compounding formula can be used to predict future prices after allowing for inflation. For example, if we wish to predict the salary of an employee in five years time, given that he earns £8,000 now and wage inflation is expected to be 10% per annum, the formula would be applied as follows.

$$\begin{aligned} V &= X(1 + r)^n \\ &= £8,000 \times 1.10^5 \\ &= £12,884.08 \end{aligned}$$

say,   £12,900.

Withdrawals of capital or interest

2.6   If an investor takes money out of an investment, it will cease to earn interest. Thus, if an investor puts £3,000 into a bank deposit account which pays interest at 8% per annum, and makes no withdrawals except at the end of year 2, when he takes out £1,000, what would be the balance in his account after four years?

	£
Original investment	3,000.00
Interest in year 1 (8%)	240.00
Investment at end of year 1	3,240.00
Interest in year 2 (8%)	259.20
Investment at end of year 2	3,499.20
Less withdrawal	1,000.00
Net investment at start of year 3	2,499.20
Interest in year 3 (8%)	199.94
Investment at end of year 3	2,699.14
Interest in year 4 (8%)	215.93
Investment at end of year 4	2,915.07

2.7   A quicker approach would be as follows.

	£
£3,000 invested for 2 years at 8% would increase in value to $£3,000 \times 1.08^2 =$	3,499.20
Less withdrawal	1,000.00
	2,499.20

£2,499.20 invested for a further two years at 8% would increase in value to

$£2,499.20 \times 1.08^2 = £2,915.07$

Changes in the rate of interest

2.8   If the rate of interest changes during the period of an investment, the compounding formula must be amended slightly, as follows.

$$V = X(1 + r_1)^y (1 + r_2)^{n-y}$$

where r_1 = the initial rate of interest
        y = the number of years in which the interest rate r_1 applies
        r_2 = the next rate of interest
        $n - y$ = the (balancing) number of years in which the interest rate r_2 applies.

Exercise 2

(a)   If £8,000 is invested now, to earn 10% interest for three years and 8% thereafter, what would be the size of the total investment at the end of five years?

(b)   An investor puts £10,000 into an investment for ten years. The annual rate of interest earned is 15% for the first four years, 12% for the next four years and 9% for the final two years. How much will the investment be worth at the end of ten years?

(c)   An item of equipment costs £6,000 now. The annual rates of inflation over the next four years are expected to be 16%, 20%, 15% and 10%. How much would the equipment cost after four years?

Solution

(a)   £8,000 × 1.10^3 × 1.08^2 = £12,419.83

(b)   £10,000 × 1.15^4 × 1.12^4 × 1.09^2 = £32,697.64

(c)   £6,000 × 1.16 × 1.20 × 1.15 × 1.10   = £10,565.28

---

3   REGULAR INVESTMENTS

3.1   An investor may decide to add to his investment from time to time, and you may be asked to calculate the final value (or terminal value) of an investment to which equal annual amounts will be added. An example might be an individual or a company making annual payments into a pension fund: we may wish to know the value of the fund after n years.

Example: regular investments

3.2   A person invests £400 now, and a further £400 each year for three more years. How much would the total investment be worth after four years, if interest is earned at the rate of 10% per annum?

Solution

3.3   In problems such as this, we call now 'Year 0', the time one year from now 'Year 1' and so on.

			£
(Year 0)	The first year's investment will grow to £400 $(1.10)^4$		585.64
(Year 1)	The second year's investment will grow to £400 $(1.10)^3$	=	532.40
(Year 2)	The third year's investment will grow to £400 $(1.10)^2$	=	484.00
(Year 3)	The fourth year's investment will grow to £400 (1.10)	=	440.00
			2,042.04

3.4   The solution can be written as $(400 \times 1.1) + (400 \times 1.1^2) + (400 \times 1.1^3) + (400 \times 1.1^4)$ with the values placed in reverse order for convenience. This is a *geometric progression* with A = (400×1.1), R = 1.1 and n = 4. (Look back to Chapter 16 if you need reminding about geometric progressions.)

The formula for the sum of a geometric progression is $S = \dfrac{A(R^n - 1)}{R - 1}$

In our example S $= \dfrac{(400 \times 1.1)(1.1^4 - 1)}{1.1 - 1} = £2{,}042.04$

Example: investments at the ends of years

3.5 If, in the previous example, the investments had been made at the end of each of the first, second, third and fourth years, so that the last £400 invested had no time to earn interest, the value of the fund after four years would have been

$$400 + 400 \times 1.1 + 400 \times 1.1^2 + 400 \times 1.1^3$$

$$= \quad 400 \, (1.1^4 - 1)/(1.1 - 1) = £1{,}856.40$$

3.6 If our investor made investments as in Paragraph 3.5, but also put in a £2,500 lump sum one year from now, the value of the fund after four years would be

$$£1{,}856.40 + £2{,}500 \times 1.1^3$$

$$= \quad £1{,}856.40 + £3{,}327.50 = £5{,}183.90$$

That is, we can compound parts of investments separately, and add up the results.

4   EFFECTIVE AND NOMINAL RATES OF INTEREST

Effective annual rate of interest

4.1 In the previous examples, interest has been calculated annually, but this need not be the case. Interest may be compounded daily, weekly, monthly or quarterly.

The equivalent annual rate of interest, when interest is compounded at shorter intervals, may be calculated as follows. This is known as an effective annual rate of interest.

$$\text{Effective Annual Rate} = [(1 + r)^{\frac{12}{n}} - 1] \text{ or } [(1 + r)^{\frac{365}{y}} - 1]$$

where   r is the rate of interest for each time period
n is the number of months in the time period
y is the number of days in the time period.

Example: the effective annual rate of interest

4.2 Calculate the effective annual rate of interest of:

(a)   1.5% per month, compound;
(b)   4.5% per quarter, compound;
(c)   9% per half year, compound.

Solution

4.3 (a) $(1.015)^{12} - 1 \;= 0.1956 = 19.56\%$
(b) $(1.045)^4 - 1 \;= 0.1925 = 19.25\%$
(c) $(1.09)^2 - 1 \;= 0.1881 = 18.81\%$

Nominal rates of interest and the annual percentage rate

4.4 Most interest rates are expressed as per annum figures even when the interest is compounded over periods of less than one year. In such cases, the given interest rate is called a nominal rate. We can, however, work out the effective rate. It is this effective rate (shortened to one decimal place) which is quoted in advertisements as the annual percentage rate (APR), sometimes called the *compound annual rate* (CAR).

Depending on whether the compounding is done daily, weekly, monthly, quarterly or six monthly, the APR will vary by differing amounts from the nominal rate.

Example: nominal and effective rates of interest

4.5 A building society may offer investors 10% per annum interest payable half-yearly. If the 10% is a nominal rate of interest, the building society would in fact pay 5% every six months, compounded so that the effective annual rate of interest would be

$$[(1.05)^2 - 1] = 0.1025 = 10.25\% \text{ per annum.}$$

4.6 Similarly, if a bank offers depositors a nominal 12% per annum, with interest payable quarterly, the effective rate of interest would be 3% compound every three months, which is

$$[(1.03)^4 - 1] = 0.1255 = 12.55\% \text{ per annum.}$$

Exercise 3

Calculate the effective annual rate of interest of:

(a) 15% nominal per annum compounded quarterly;

(b) 24% nominal per annum compounded monthly.

Solution

(a) 15% per annum (nominal rate) is 3.75% per quarter. The effective annual rate of interest is

$$[1.0375^4 - 1] = 0.1587 = 15.87\%$$

(b) 24% per annum (nominal rate) is 2% per month. The effective annual rate of interest is

$$[1.02^{12} - 1] = 0.2682 = 26.82\%$$

---

5   SIMPLE APPLICATIONS

5.1 The basic principles that we have covered in this chapter can be applied in a number of different situations.

Reducing balance depreciation

5.2 The basic compound interest formula can be used to deal with one method of depreciation (depreciation being an accounting technique whereby the cost of a capital asset is spread over a number of different accounting periods as a charge against profit in each of the periods).

5.3 The reducing balance method of depreciation is a kind of reverse compounding in which the value of the asset goes *down* at a certain rate. The rate of 'interest' is therefore negative.

Example: depreciation

5.4 An item of equipment is bought for £1,000 and is to be depreciated at a fixed rate of 40% per annum. What will be its value at the end of four years?

Solution

5.5 $X = £1,000, r = -0.4, n = 4$

$\therefore V = 1,000 (1 - 0.4)^4 = £129.60$

Other applications of 'reverse' compounding

5.6   As well as rising at a compound rate, perhaps because of inflation, costs can also *fall* at a compound rate. For example, suppose that the cost of product X is currently £10.80. It is estimated that over the next five years its cost will fall by 10% pa compound. The cost of product X at the end of five years is therefore given as

£10.80 $\times (1 - 0.1)^5$ = £6.38

Mortgages

5.7   As you are probably aware, when a mortgage is taken out on a property over a number of years, there are several ways in which the loan can be repaid. One such way is the repayment mortgage which has the following features.

(a)   A certain amount, S, is borrowed to be paid back over n years.
(b)   Interest, at a rate r, is added to the loan retrospectively at the end of each year.
(c)   A constant amount A is paid back each year.

Income tax relief affects repayments but, for simplicity, we will ignore it here.

5.8   Let us consider the repayments.

(a)   At the end of one year A has been repaid.

(b)   At the end of two years the initial repayment of A has earned interest and so has a value of $A(1 + r)$ and another A has been repaid. The value of the amount repaid is therefore $A(1 + r) + A$.

(c)   At the end of three years, the initial repayment will have a value of $A(1 + r)^2$, the second repayment a value of $A(1 + r)$ and a third repayment of A will have been made. The value of the amount repaid is therefore $A(1 + r)^2 + (1 + r) + A$.

(d)   At the end of n years the value of the repayments is therefore $A(1 + r)^{n-1} + A(1 + r)^{n-2} + ... + A(1 + r)^2 + A(1 + r) + A$.

This is a geometric progression with 'A' = A, 'R' = (1 + r) and 'n' = n and hence the

sum of the repayments = $\dfrac{A[(1+r)^n - 1]}{r}$

5.9   During the time the repayments have been made, the initial loan has accrued interest and hence has a value of $S(1 + r)^n$.

The repayments must, at the end of n years, repay the initial loan plus the accrued interest and hence, after n years

$\dfrac{A[(1+r)^n - 1]}{r} = S(1+r)^n$

$\therefore A = \dfrac{Sr(1+r)^n}{(1+r)^n - 1}$ = annual repayment

Example: mortgages

5.10   (a)   Sam has taken out a £30,000 mortgage over 25 years. Interest is to be charged at 12%. Calculate the monthly repayment.

(b)   After nine years, the interest rate changes to 10%. What is the new monthly repayment?

Solution

5.11   (a)   A = $\dfrac{Sr(1+r)^n}{(1+r)^n - 1}$ = $\dfrac{30,000 \times 0.12 \times (1.12)^{25}}{1.12^{25} - 1}$ = £3,825

$\therefore$ Monthly repayment = £3,825 ÷ 12 = £319

(b) We need to calculate the amount still owing after nine years.

The initial loan has increased to £30,000 × 1.12^9 = £83,192

The value of the repayments made is (using the formula in Paragraph 5.8)

£3,825 $\dfrac{\left(1.12^9 - 1\right)}{0.12}$ = £56,517

∴ The amount still owed = £(83,192 − 56,517) = £26,675

So, if £26,675 has to be repaid over 16 (25 − 9) years at 10%, the annual repayment is

$\dfrac{26,675 \times 0.1 \times (1.1)^{16}}{1.1^{16} - 1}$ = £3,410

∴ Monthly repayment = £3,410 ÷ 12 = £284.

Sinking funds

5.12 A sinking fund is an investment into which equal annual instalments are paid in order to earn interest, so that by the end of a given number of years, the investment is large enough to pay off a known commitment at that time.

5.13 Repayments against a repayment mortgage can of course be seen as payments into a sinking fund. The total of the constant annual payments (which are usually paid in equal monthly instalments) plus the interest they earn over the term of the mortgage must be sufficient to pay off the initial loan plus accrued interest.

5.14 Another common known future commitment is the need to replace an asset at the end of its life. To ensure that the money is available to buy a replacement a company might decide to invest cash in a sinking fund during the course of the life of the existing asset. Annual payments into the fund can be found in the same way as mortgage repayments in Paragraph 5.9 above.

Example: sinking funds

5.15 A company has just bought an asset with a life of four years. At the end of four years, a replacement asset will cost £12,000, and the company has decided to provide for this future commitment by setting up a sinking fund into which equal annual investments will be made, starting at year 1 (one year from now). The fund will earn interest at 12%.

Required

Calculate the annual repayment

Solution

5.16 The value for a sinking fund at the end of n years = $A\left[\dfrac{(1+r)^n - 1}{r}\right]$

Since the fund must equal £12,000 by year 4,

12,000 = $\dfrac{A(1.12^4 - 1)}{0.12}$

12,000 = $\dfrac{0.5735193A}{0.12}$

A = £2,510.81

Four investments, each of £2,510.81, should therefore be enough to allow the company to replace the asset.

Annuities

5.17 An annuity is a constant sum of money received or paid each year for a given number of years. An annuity might run until the recipient's death or for a guaranteed term of n years or it could be deferred until some time in the future (such as the recipient's retirement). The following example will show how the ideas which we have been looking at can be applied to annuities.

Example: annuities

5.18 Mrs Smith, aged 40, is planning for her retirement at age 60. She decides to set aside £1,800 a year (out of income) for 20 years. She has two possible investment alternatives.

She could buy a deferred annuity of £13,700 a year. She would receive annual payments of £13,700, the first on her 60th birthday, until death. There would be a guaranteed minimum payment of £68,500 if death occurs before her 64th birthday. The premiums for annuities can be considered 'gross', as they are chargeable against tax.

Alternatively she could invest her annual (net) savings in a Building Society for 19 years at 10% compound interest per annum. The first investment should be made just before her 41st birthday. (The savings are 'net' because tax has been deducted at 25% at source).

Required

(a) Find the value of the savings in the second option on Mrs Smith's 60th birthday.

(b) Assuming that Mrs Smith would withdraw £13,700 from the Building Society Account each birthday from age 60, consider what would happen to Mrs Smith under each option between the ages of 60 and 70 and hence compare the two alternatives to find their respective financial advantages.

Solution

5.19 (a) The annual investment would be £1,800 minus 25% tax, that is £1,350.

The first premium would be paid on her 41st birthday and on her 60th birthday its value is £1,350 × 1.1^{19}. The second premium would achieve a final value of £1,350 × 1.1^{18} and so on.

The total value of the investment at age 60 would be £1,350 × $[1.1^{19} + 1.1^{18} + ... + 1]$

The contents of the bracket are a geometric progression with A = 1, R = 1.1 and n = 20

∴ Total value = £1,350 × 1 × $\left(\dfrac{1.1^{20} - 1}{0.1} \right)$ = £77,321.

(b)

	Building society option			Annuity option	
	Cumulative	Value after	Value prior to	Cumulative	
Birthday	received	withdrawal	next birthday	received	Guaranteed
	£	£	£	£	£
60	13,700	*63,621	**69,983	13,700	***54,800
61	27,400	56,283	61,911	27,400	41,100
62	41,100	48,211	53,032	41,100	27,400
63	54,800	39,332	43,265	54,800	13,700
64	68,500	29,565	32,522	68,500	-
65	82,200	18,822	20,704	82,200	-
66	95,900	7,004	7,704	95,900	-
67	103,604	0	0	109,600	-
68	103,604	0	0	123,300	-
69	103,604	0	0	137,000	-

* £(77,321 – 13,700)
** £63,621 × 1.10
*** £(68,500 – 13,700)

Until the age of 67 Mrs Smith should choose the building society option since the income from both options is the same but the building society investment is greater than the guaranteed amount. After the age of 67, however, the annuity is clearly better since it continues to provide an income whereas the building society account has dried up. The age at which Mrs Smith dies will therefore determine the option which is the better of the two.

Chapter roundup

- Simple interest is interest which is earned in equal amounts every year (or month) and which is a given proportion of the principal. The simple interest formula is $V = X + nrX$.

- Compounding means that, as interest is earned, it is added to the original investment and starts to earn interest itself. The basic formula for compound interest is $V = X(1 + r)^n$.

- If the rate of interest changes during the period of an investment, the compounding formula must be amended slightly to $V = X(1+r_1)^y(1 + r_2)^{n-y}$

- The final value (or terminal value), S, of an investment to which equal annual amounts will be added is found using the formula $S = A(R^n - 1)/(R - 1)$ (the formula for a geometric progression).

- An effective annual rate of interest is the corresponding annual rate when interest is compounded at intervals shorter than a year.

- A nominal rate of interest is an interest rate expressed as a per annum figure although the interest is compounded over a period of less than one year. The corresponding effective rate of interest shortened to one decimal place is the annual percentage rate (APR).

- The basic compound interest formula can be used to calculate the net book value of an asset depreciated using the reducing balance method of depreciation by using a negative rate of 'interest'.

- The annual repayment (A) under a repayment mortgage can be calculated as

  $Sr(1 + r)^n / ((1 + r)^n - 1)$

- A sinking fund is an investment into which equal annual instalments are paid in order to earn interest, so that by the end of a given number of years, the investment is large enough to pay off a known commitment at that time. Commitments include the replacement of an asset and the repayment of a mortgage

  $S = A[((1 + r)^n - 1)/r]$ where   S = the required value of the fund at the end of n years
  A = the annual payment into the fund
  r = the rate of interest as a proportion.

- An annuity is a constant sum of money received or paid each year for a given number of years.

Test your knowledge

1   If a sum X is invested earning a simple annual interest rate of r, how much will the investor have after n years? (see para 1.2)

2   If a sum X is invested earning a compound annual interest rate of r, how much will the investor have after n years? (2.3)

3   How should withdrawals of money be dealt with in compound interest calculations? (2.6, 2.7)

4   How should changes in the rate of interest be dealt with in compound interest calculations? (2.8)

5   If an amount £X is added to an investment over n years and interest is earned at a rate of r% per annum, what will be the terminal value of the investment? (3.4)

6   What is meant by an effective annual rate of interest? (4.1)

7   What is a nominal rate of interest? (4.4)

8   What is the formula for the annual repayment of a repayment mortgage? (5.9)

Now try illustrative question 26 at the end of the Study Text

Chapter 26

DISCOUNTING

Introduction

Discounting is the reverse of compounding, the topic of the previous chapter. Its major application in business is in the evaluation of investments, to decide whether they offer a satisfactory return to the investor. We will be looking at two methods of using discounting to appraise investments, the net present value (NPV) method and the internal rate of return (IRR) method.

Discounting was examined in the May 95 exam and, according to the examiner, most candidates 'demonstrated a lack of understanding of discounting...'. Not only must you master the technique now, you must be completely sure of the basics since the topic appears at *every* stage of your future CIMA studies.

1 THE CONCEPT OF DISCOUNTING   5/97

The basic principles of discounting

1.1   The basic principle of compounding is that if we invest £X now for n years at r% interest per annum, we should obtain £X $(1 + r)^n$ in n years time.

1.2   Thus if we invest £10,000 now for four years at 10% interest per annum, we will have a total investment worth £10,000 $\times 1.10^4$ = £14,641 at the end of four years (that is, at year 4 if it is now year 0).

1.3   The basic principle of discounting is that if we wish to have £V in n years' time, we need to invest a certain sum *now* (year 0) at an interest rate of r% in order to obtain the required sum of money in the future.

1.4   For example, if we wish to have £14,641 in four years time, how much money would we need to invest now at 10% interest per annum? This is the reverse of the situation described in Paragraph 1.2.

Let X be the amount of money invested now.

$$£14,641 = X \times 1.10^4$$

$$X = £14,641 \times \frac{1}{1.10^4} = £10,000$$

1.5   £10,000 now, with the capacity to earn a return of 10% per annum, is the equivalent in value of £14,641 after four years. We can therefore say that £10,000 is the present value of £14,641 at year 4, at an interest rate of 10%.

Present value

1.6   The term 'present value' simply means the amount of money which must be invested now for n years at an interest rate of r%, to earn a given future sum of money at the time it will be due.

The formula for discounting

1.7   The discounting formula is

$$X = V \times \frac{1}{(1+r)^n}$$

where   V   is the sum to be received after n time periods
         X   is the present value (PV) of that sum
         r   is the rate of return, expressed as a proportion
         n   is the number of time periods (usually years).

The rate r is sometimes called a cost of capital.

Example: discounting

1.8   (a)   Calculate the present value of £60,000 at year 6, if a return of 15% per annum is obtainable.

       (b)   Calculate the present value of £100,000 at year 5, if a return of 6% per annum is obtainable.

       (c)   How much would a person need to invest now at 12% to earn £4,000 at year 2 and £4,000 at year 3?

Solution

1.9   (a)   PV $= 60,000 \times \dfrac{1}{1.15^6}$
                     $= 60,000 \times 0.432$
                     $= £25,920$

       (b)   PV $= 100,000 \times \dfrac{1}{1.06^5}$
                     $= 100,000 \times 0.747$
                     $= £74,700$

       (c)   PV $= (4,000 \times \dfrac{1}{1.12^2}) + (4,000 \times \dfrac{1}{1.12^3})$
                     $= 4,000 \times (0.797 + 0.712)$
                     $= £6,036$

       This calculation can be checked as follows.

	£
Year 0	6,036.00
Interest for the first year (12%)	724.32
	6,760.32
Interest for the second year (12%)	811.24
	7,571.56
Less withdrawal	(4,000.00)
	3,571.56
Interest for the third year (12%)	428.59
	4,000.15
Less withdrawal	(4,000.00)
Rounding error	0.15

Exercise 1

What is the present value at 7% interest of £16,000 at year 12?

Solution

$$PV = £16,000 \times \frac{1}{1.07^{12}} = £7,104$$

Capital expenditure appraisal

1.10 Discounted cash flow techniques can be used to evaluate capital expenditure proposals (investments).

1.11 Discounted cash flow (DCF) involves the application of discounting arithmetic to the estimated future cash flows (receipts and expenditures) from a project in order to decide whether the project is expected to earn a satisfactory rate of return.

There are two methods of using DCF techniques.

(a) The net present value (NPV) method
(b) The internal rate of return (IRR) method

2   THE NET PRESENT VALUE (NPV) METHOD   5/95, 5/96

2.1 The net present value (NPV) method works out the present values of all items of income and expenditure related to an investment at a given rate of return, and then works out a net total. If it is positive, the investment is considered to be acceptable. If it is negative, the investment is considered to be unacceptable.

Example: the net present value of a project

2.2 Dog Ltd is considering whether to spend £5,000 on an item of equipment. The 'cash profits', the excess of income over cash expenditure, from the project would be £3,000 in the first year and £4,000 in the second year.

The company will not invest in any project unless it offers a return in excess of 15% per annum.

Required

Assess whether the investment is worthwhile, or 'viable'.

Solution

2.3 In this example, an outlay of £5,000 now promises a return of £3,000 *during* the first year and £4,000 *during* the second year. It is a convention in DCF, however, that cash flows spread over a year are assumed to occur *at the end of the year*, so that the cash flows of the project are as follows.

	£
Year 0 (now)	(5,000)
Year 1 (at the end of the year)	3,000
Year 2 (at the end of the year)	4,000

2.4 The NPV method takes the following approach.

(a) The project offers £3,000 at year 1 and £4,000 at year 2, for an outlay of £5,000 now.

(b) The company might invest elsewhere to earn a return of 15% per annum.

(c) If the company did invest at exactly 15% per annum, how much would it need to invest now, at 15%, to earn £3,000 at the end of year 1 plus £4,000 at the end of year 2?

(d)   Is it cheaper to invest £5,000 in the project, or to invest elsewhere at 15%, in order to obtain these future cash flows?

2.5   If the company did invest elsewhere at 15% per annum, the amount required to earn £3,000 in year 1 and £4,000 in year 2 would be as follows.

Year	Cash flow £	Discount factor 15%	Present value £
1	3,000	$\dfrac{1}{1.15} = 0.870$	2,610
2	4,000	$\dfrac{1}{(1.15)^2} = 0.756$	3,024
			5,634

2.6   The choice is to invest £5,000 in the project, or £5,634 elsewhere at 15%, in order to obtain these future cash flows. We can therefore reach the following conclusion.

(a)   It is cheaper to invest in the project, by £634.
(b)   The project offers a return of over 15% per annum.

2.7   The net present value is the difference between the present value of cash inflows from the project (£5,634) and the present value of future cash outflows (in this example, £5,000 × $1/1.15^0$ = £5,000).

2.8   An NPV statement could be drawn up as follows.

Year	Cash flow £	Discount factor 15%	Present value £
0	(5,000)	1.000	(5,000)
1	3,000	$\dfrac{1}{1.15} = 0.870$	2,610
2	4,000	$\dfrac{1}{(1.15)^2} = 0.756$	3,024
		Net present value	+634

The project has a positive net present value, so it is acceptable.

Exercise 2

A company is wondering whether to spend £18,000 on an item of equipment, in order to obtain cash profits as follows.

Year	£
1	6,000
2	8,000
3	5,000
4	1,000

The company requires a return of 10% per annum.

Required

Use the NPV method to assess whether the project is viable.

Solution

	Cash flow £	Discount factor 10%	Present value £
0	(18,000)	1.000	(18,000)
1	6,000	$\dfrac{1}{1.10} = 0.909$	5,454
2	8,000	$\dfrac{1}{1.10^2} = 0.826$	6,608
3	5,000	$\dfrac{1}{1.10^3} = 0.751$	3,755
4	1,000	$\dfrac{1}{1.10^4} = 0.683$	683
		Net present value	(1,500)

The NPV is negative. We can therefore draw the following conclusions.

(a) It is cheaper to invest elsewhere at 10% than to invest in the project.
(b) The project would earn a return of less than 10%.
(c) The project is not viable (since the PV of the costs is greater than the PV of the benefits).

Discount tables

2.9 Assuming that money earns, say, 10% per annum:

(a) the PV (present value) of £1 at year 1 is $£1 \times \dfrac{1}{1.10}$ $= £1 \times 0.909$;

(b) similarly, the PV of £1 at year 2 is $£1 \times \dfrac{1}{(1.10)^2}$ $= £1 \times 0.826$;

(c) the PV of £1 at year 3 is $£1 \times \dfrac{1}{(1.10)^3}$ $= £1 \times 0.751$.

Discount tables show the value of $1/(1 + r)^n$ for different values of r and n. The 10% discount factors of 0.909, 0.826 and 0.751 are shown in the discount tables at the end of this Study Text in the column for 10%. (You will be given discount tables in your examination.)

Exercise 3

Daisy Ltd is considering whether to make an investment costing £28,000 which would earn £8,000 cash per annum for five years. The company expects to make a return of at least 11% per annum.

Required

Assess whether the project is viable.

Solution

Year	Cash flow £	Discount factor 11%	Present value £
0	(28,000)	1.000	(28,000)
1	8,000	0.901	7,208
2	8,000	0.812	6,496
3	8,000	0.731	5,848
4	8,000	0.659	5,272
5	8,000	0.593	4,744
		NPV	1,568

The NPV is positive, therefore the project is viable because it earns more than 11% per annum.

Project comparison

2.10 The NPV method can also be used to compare two or more investment options. For example, suppose that Daisy Ltd can choose between the investment outlined in Exercise 3 above *or* a second investment, which also costs £28,000 but which would earn £6,500 in the first year, £7,500 in the second, £8,500 in the third, £9,500 in the fourth and £10,500 in the fifth. Which one should Daisy Ltd choose?

2.11 The decision rule is to choose the option with the highest NPV. We therefore need to calculate the NPV of the second option.

Year	Cash flow £	Discount factor 11%	Present value £
0	(28,000)	1.000	(28,000)
1	6,500	0.901	5,857
2	7,500	0.812	6,090
3	8,500	0.731	6,214
4	9,500	0.659	6,261
5	10,500	0.593	6,227
		NPV =	2,649

Daisy Ltd should therefore invest in the second option since it has the higher NPV.

Expected values and discounting

2.12 Future cash flows cannot be predicted with complete accuracy. To take account of this uncertainty an *expected net present value* can be calculated which is a weighted average net present value based on the probabilities of different sets of circumstances occurring. Let us have a look at an example.

Example: expected net present value

2.13 An organisation with a cost of capital of 5% is contemplating investing £340,000 in a project which has a 25% chance of being a big success and producing cash inflows of £210,000 after one and two years. There is, however, a 75% change of the project not being quite so successful, in which case the cash inflows will be £162,000 after one year and £174,000 after two years.

Required

Calculate an NPV and hence advise the organisation.

Solution

2.14

Year	Discount factor 5%	Success Cash flow £'000	Success PV £'000	Failure Cash flow £'000	Failure PV £'000
0	1.000	(340)	(340.00)	(340)	(340.000)
1	0.952	210	199.92	162	154.224
2	0.907	210	190.47	174	157.818
			50.39		(27.958)

$$NPV = (25\% \times 50.39) + (75\% \times -27.958) = -8.371$$

The NPV is – £8,371 and hence the organisation should not invest in the project.

3 ANNUITIES *5/95*

3.1 As you know from Chapter 25, an annuity is a constant sum of money each year for a given number of years.

In Exercise 3, there was a constant annual cash flow of £8,000 for five years, years 1 to 5.

The arithmetic in the solution could have been simplified, as follows.

	8,000	×	0.901		
plus	8,000	×	0.812		
plus	8,000	×	0.731		
plus	8,000	×	0.659		
plus	8,000	×	0.593		£
equals	8,000	×	3.696	=	29,568
Less PV of costs					28,000
NPV					1,568

Annuity tables

3.2 To calculate the present value of a constant annual cash flow, or annuity, we can multiply the annual cash flows by the sum of the discount factors for the relevant years. These total factors are known as cumulative present value factors or annuity factors. As with 'present value factors of £1 in year n', there are tables for annuity factors, which are also shown at the end of this text. (For example, the cumulative present value factor of £1 per annum for five years at 11% per annum is in the column for 11% and the year 5 row, and is 3.696).

Example: annuities

3.3 (a) The PV of £1,000 earned each year from years 1 to 10 when the required return on investment is 11% per annum is £1,000 × 5.889 = £5,889.

(b) The PV of £100 earned each year from years 3 to 6 when the required return is 5% per annum is found as follows.

PV of £1 per annum for years 1 to 6 at 5%	5.076
Less PV of £1 per annum for years 1 to 2 at 5%	1.859
PV of £1 per annum for years 3 to 6 at 5%	3.217

£100 × 3.217 = £321.70

(c) Blob Ltd is considering a project which would cost £14,000 now and earn £3,000 per annum in years 1 to 4 and £2,000 per annum in years 5 to 10. The cost of capital is 12%. Is the project viable?

PV of £1 per annum at 12%, years 1 to 10	5.650
Less PV of £1 per annum at 12%, years 1 to 4	3.037
PV of £1 per annum at 12%, years 5 to 10	2.613

Years	*Cash flow*	*Discount factor*	*Present value*
	£	12%	£
0	(14,000)	1.000	(14,000)
1 - 4	3,000	3.037	9,111
5 - 10	2,000	2.613	5,226
		Net present value	+337

The project has a positive NPV and is therefore viable because it will earn more than 12% per annum.

The formula for the present value of an annuity

3.4 You may be expected to use the following formula to calculate the present value of an annuity of *£1* per period for t years (with the first payment at the end of period 1, rather than *now*)

$$PV = \frac{1}{r} - \frac{1}{r(1+r)^t}$$

3.5   The formula is provided in the exam. It is a development of the formula for the sum of a geometric progression but its derivation is outside the scope of your syllabus. Note that it is the PV of an annuity of *£1* and so you need to multiply it by the actual value of the annuity.

Exercise 4

What is the present value of £4,000 per annum for years 1 to 4, at a discount rate of 10% per annum?

Solution

$$PV = 4{,}000 \times \left(\frac{1}{0.1} - \frac{1}{0.1 \times 1.1^4} \right)$$

$$= 4{,}000 \times 3.170 = £12{,}680$$

This can be checked from the annuity tables: the PV for years 1 to 4 is £4,000 × 3.170 = £12,680.

Calculating a required annuity

3.6   If PV of £1 $= \dfrac{1}{r} - \dfrac{1}{r(1+r)^t}$, then PV of £a $= a \left(\dfrac{1}{r} - \dfrac{1}{r(1+r)^t} \right)$

$$\therefore a = \frac{PV \text{ of } £a}{\left(\dfrac{1}{r} - \dfrac{1}{r(1+r)^t} \right)}$$

This enables us to calculate the annuity required to yield a given rate of return (r) on a given investment (P).

Example: required annuity

3.7   The present value of a ten-year annuity receivable which begins in one year's time at 7% per annum compound is £3,000. What is the annual amount of the annuity?

Solution

3.8 $a = \dfrac{3{,}000}{\left(\dfrac{1}{0.07} - \dfrac{1}{0.07(1.07)^{10}} \right)}$

$$= \frac{£3{,}000}{7.024} = 427.11$$

The use of annuity tables to calculate a required annuity

3.9   Just as the formula can be used to calculate an annuity, so too can the tables. Since the present value of an annuity is PV = a × annuity factor from the tables, we have

$$a = \frac{PV}{\text{annuity factor}}$$

3.10   In the previous example, the annual annuity would be

$$\frac{£3{,}000}{\text{PV factor of £1 per annum at 7\% for 10 years}}$$

$$= \quad \frac{£3,000}{7.024}$$

$$= \quad £427.11$$

Annualised equivalents

3.11 An annualised equivalent is the equivalent constant cash flow (that is, annuity) in present value terms of a series of irregular cash flows. Their main use is in comparing the net present values of projects with different durations.

3.12 For example, a company (which has a cost of capital of 15%) may be deciding whether to replace company cars after a three-, four- or five-year cycle. The relevant cash flows might be as follows.

	Year	Three-year cycle £	Four-year cycle £	Five-year cycle £
Capital cost	0	(6,000)	(6,000)	(6,000)
Running costs	1	(280)	(280)	(280)
Running costs	2	(1,090)	(1,090)	(1,090)
Running costs	3	(1,120)	(1,120)	(1,120)
Trade in value	3	1,000	-	-
Running costs	4		(1,590)	(1,590)
Trade in value	4		700	-
Running costs	5			(1,260)
Trade in value	5			300
NPV at 15%*		(7,147)	(8,314)	(9,191)

* The workings are not shown, but as an exercise you could check the NPV calculations yourself.

3.13 These NPVs cannot be compared directly because they each relate to a different number of years. In order to make a comparison we must convert each NPV to an annualised equivalent cost. We do this by using cumulative discount factors as follows.

	Three-year cycle	Four-year cycle	Five-year cycle
NPV at 15%	£(7,147)	£(8,314)	£(9,191)
Cumulative 15% discount factor	÷ 2.283	÷ 2.855	÷ 3.352
Annualised equivalent cost	£3,131	£2,912	£2,742

3.14 The lowest annualised equivalent cost results from a five-year cycle and so the company should replace its cars every five years.

Perpetuities

3.15 A *perpetuity* is an annuity which lasts for ever, instead of stopping after n years.

3.16 The present value of a perpetuity is $PV = a/r$ where r is the cost of capital as a proportion.

Example: a perpetuity

3.17 Mostly Ltd is considering a project which would cost £50,000 now and yield £9,000 per annum every year in perpetuity, starting a year from now. The cost of capital is 15%.

Required

Assess whether the project is viable.

Solution

	Year	Cash flow	Discount factor	Present value
3.18		£	15%	£
	0	(50,000)	1.0	(50,000)
	1 - ∞	9,000	1/0.15	60,000
			NPV	10,000

The project is viable because it has a positive net present value when discounted at 15%.

The timing of cash flows

3.19 Note that both annuity tables and the formulae assume that the first payment or receipt is a year from now. Always check examination questions for when the first payment falls.

For example, if there are five equal payments starting now, and the interest rate is 8%, we should use a factor of 1 (for today's payment) + 3.312 (for the other four payments) = 4.312.

4   THE INTERNAL RATE OF RETURN (IRR) METHOD   5/96

4.1 The internal rate of return (IRR) method of evaluating investments is an alternative to the NPV method.

4.2 The NPV method of discounted cash flow determines whether an investment earns a positive or a negative NPV when discounted at a given rate of interest. If the NPV is zero (that is, the present values of costs and benefits are equal) the return from the project would be exactly the rate used for discounting.

4.3 The IRR method of discounted cash flow is to determine the rate of interest (the internal rate of return) at which the NPV is 0. The internal rate of return is therefore the rate of return on an investment.

4.4 The IRR method will indicate that a project is viable if the IRR exceeds the minimum acceptable rate of return. Thus if the company expects a minimum return of, say, 15%, a project would be viable if its IRR is more than 15%.

Example: the IRR method over one year

4.5 If £500 is invested today and generates £600 in one year's time, the internal rate of return (r) can be calculated as follows.

$$\text{PV of cost} = \text{PV of benefits}$$

$$500 = \frac{600}{(1+r)}$$

$$500\,(1+r) = 600$$

$$1+r = \frac{600}{500} = 1.2$$

$$r = 0.2 = 20\%$$

4.6 The arithmetic for calculating the IRR is more complicated for investments and cash flows extending over a period of time longer than one year. A technique known as the interpolation method can be used to calculate an approximate IRR.

Example: interpolation

4.7   A project costing £800 in year 0 is expected to earn £400 in year 1, £300 in year 2 and £200 in year 3.

Required

Calculate the internal rate of return.

Solution

4.8   The IRR is calculated by first of all finding the NPV at each of two interest rates. Ideally, one interest rate should give a small positive NPV and the other a small negative NPV. The IRR would then be somewhere between these two interest rates: above the rate where the NPV is positive, but below the rate where the NPV is negative.

4.9   A very rough guideline for estimating at what interest rate the NPV might be close to zero, is to take

$$\frac{2}{3} \times \left(\frac{\text{profit}}{\text{cost of the project}} \right)$$

In our example, the total profit over three years is £(400 + 300 + 200 – 800) = £100. An approximate IRR is therefore calculated as:

$$\frac{2}{3} \times \frac{100}{800} = 0.08 \text{ approx.}$$

A starting point is to try 8%.

(a)   Try 8%

Year	Cash flow	Discount factor	Present value
	£	8%	£
0	(800)	1.000	(800.0)
1	400	0.926	370.4
2	300	0.857	257.1
3	200	0.794	158.8
		NPV	(13.7)

The NPV is negative, therefore the project fails to earn 8% and the IRR must be less than 8%.

(b)   Try 6%

Year		Cash flow	Discount factor	Present value
	6%	£	6%	£
0		(800)	1.000	(800.0)
1		400	0.943	377.2
2		300	0.890	267.0
3		200	0.840	168.0
			NPV	12.2

The NPV is positive, therefore the project earns more than 6% and less than 8%.

4.10   The IRR is now calculated by interpolation. The result will not be exact, but it will be a close approximation. Interpolation assumes that the NPV falls in a straight line from +12.2 at 6% to –13.7 at 8%.

Graph to show IRR calculation by interpolation

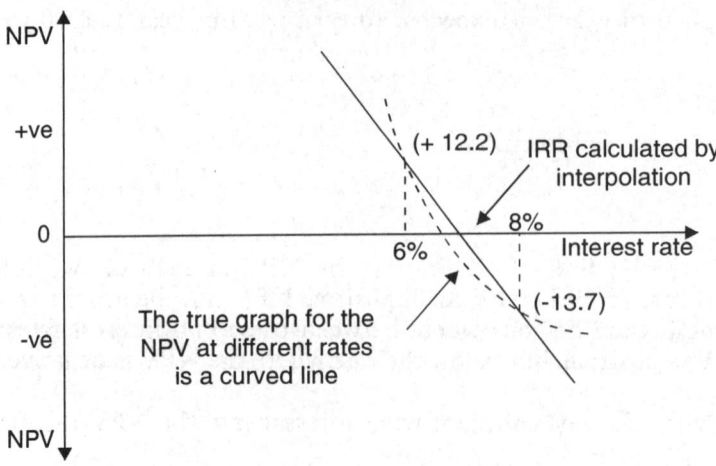

4.11 The IRR, where the NPV is zero, can be calculated as:

$$a\% + [\frac{A}{A - B} \times (b - a)]\% \text{ where}$$

a is one interest rate
b is the other interest rate
A is the NPV at rate a
B is the NPV at rate b

$$
\begin{aligned}
\text{IRR} &= 6\% + \left[\frac{12.2}{(12.2 + 13.7)} \times (8 - 6)\right]\% \\
&= 6\% + 0.942\% \\
&= 6.942\% \text{ approx}
\end{aligned}
$$

4.12 The answer is only an approximation because the NPV falls in a slightly curved line and not a straight line between +12.2 and −13.7. Provided that NPVs close to zero are used, the linear assumption used in the interpolation method is nevertheless fairly accurate.

4.13 Note that the formula will still work if A and B are both positive, or both negative, and even if a and b are a long way from the true IRR, but the results will be less accurate.

Chapter roundup

- Discounting is the reverse of compounding. The discounting formula is $X = V \times 1/(1+r)^n$.

- The concept of present value can be thought of in two ways.

  It is the value today of an amount to be received some time in the future.

  It is the amount which would have to be invested today to produce a given amount at some future date.

- Discounted cash flow techniques can be used to evaluate capital expenditure projects. There are two methods: the NPV method and the IRR method.

- The NPV method works out the present values of all items of income and expenditure related to an investment at a given rate of return, and then works out a net total. If it is positive, the investment is considered to be acceptable. If it is negative, the investment is considered to be unacceptable.

- An annuity is a constant sum of money each year for a given number of years.

- A perpetuity is an annuity which lasts forever, instead of stopping after n years.

- The IRR method is to determine the rate of interest (the IRR) at which the NPV is 0. Interpolation, using the following formula, is often necessary. The project is viable if the IRR exceeds the minimum acceptable return.

$$IRR = a\% + \left[\frac{A}{A-B} \times (b-a) \right]\%$$

- Ensure that you are aware of all of the points above and can use the formulae correctly.

Test your knowledge

1   What is the meaning of the term 'present value'? (see para 1.6)

2   What are the two usual methods of capital expenditure appraisal using DCF techniques? (1.11)

3   What is an annuity? (3.1)

4   What is the formula for the present value of an annuity? (3.4)

5   What is a perpetuity? (3.15)

6   What is the formula for a present value of a perpetuity? (3.16)

7   What is the internal rate of return of an investment? (4.3)

8   How would you determine the internal rate of return of a series of cash flows using interpolation? (4.8 - 4.11)

Now try illustrative question 27 at the end of the Study Text

Part H
Introduction to forecasting

Chapter 27

TIME SERIES ANALYSIS

This chapter covers the following topics.

		Syllabus reference	Ability required
1	The components of time series	2(h)	Skill
2	Finding the trend	2(h)	Skill
3	Finding the seasonal variations	2(h)	Skill
4	Forecasting and time series analysis	2(h)	Skill

Introduction

At last we come to the final topic in the Study Text: forecasting. We looked at various non-statistical ways in which costs can be estimated for budgeting purposes in Chapter 13. This being the quantitative methods sections of the Study Text, however, in this chapter and the next we are going to examine two *mathematical* forecasting methods, both of which can also be used to estimate costs and revenues for inclusion in budgets.

In this chapter we will be looking at a technique called time series analysis. With this forecasting method we look at past data about the variable which we want to forecast (such as sales levels) to see if there are any patterns. We then assume that these patterns will continue into the future. We are then able to forecast what we believe will be the value of a variable at some particular point of time in the future.

We will begin the chapter by looking at what makes up a time series and then, in Sections 2 and 3, we will see how to analyse a time series. Finally Section 4 explains how we use the analysed time series to actually do some forecasting.

In Chapter 28 we will be looking at the related techniques of correlation and regression.

1 THE COMPONENTS OF TIME SERIES

1.1 A time series is a series of figures or values recorded over time. The following are examples of time series.

(a) Output at a factory each day for the last month
(b) Monthly sales over the last two years
(c) Total annual costs for the last ten years
(d) The Retail Prices Index each month for the last ten years
(e) The number of people employed by a company each year for the last 20 years

1.2 As we saw in Chapter 19, a graph of a time series is called a historigram.

1.3 There are several features of a time series which it may be necessary to identify.

(a) A trend

(b) Seasonal variations or fluctuations

(c) Cycles, or cyclical variations

(d) Non-recurring, random variations. These may be caused by unforeseen circumstances, such as a change in the government of the country, a war, the collapse of a company, technological change or a fire.

The trend

1.4   The trend is the underlying long-term movement over time in the values of the data recorded. In the following examples of time series, there are three types of trend.

	Output per labour hour Units	Cost per unit £	Number of employees
19X4	30	1.00	100
19X5	24	1.08	103
19X6	26	1.20	96
19X7	22	1.15	102
19X8	21	1.18	103
19X9	17	1.25	98
	(A)	(B)	(C)

(a)   In time series (A) there is a downward trend in the output per labour hour. Output per labour hour did not fall every year, because it went up between 19X5 and 19X6, but the long-term movement is clearly a downward one.

(b)   In time series (B) there is an upward trend in the cost per unit. Although unit costs went down in 19X7 from a higher level in 19X6, the basic movement over time is one of rising costs.

(c)   In time series (C) there is no clear movement up or down, and the number of employees remained fairly constant around 100. The trend is therefore a static, or level one.

Seasonal variations

1.5   Seasonal variations are short-term fluctuations in recorded values, due to different circumstances which affect results at different times of the year, on different days of the week, at different times of day, or whatever. Here are some examples.

(a)   Sales of ice cream will be higher in summer than in winter, and sales of overcoats will be higher in autumn than in spring.

(b)   Shops might expect higher sales shortly before Christmas, or in their winter and summer sales.

(c)   Sales might be higher on Friday and Saturday than on Monday.

(d)   The telephone network may be heavily used at certain times of the day (such as mid-morning and mid-afternoon) and much less used at other times (such as in the middle of the night).

1.6   'Seasonal' is a term which may appear to refer to the seasons of the year, but its meaning in time series analysis is somewhat broader, as the examples given above show.

Example: a trend and seasonal variations

1.7   The number of customers served by a company of travel agents over the past four years is shown in the following historigram.

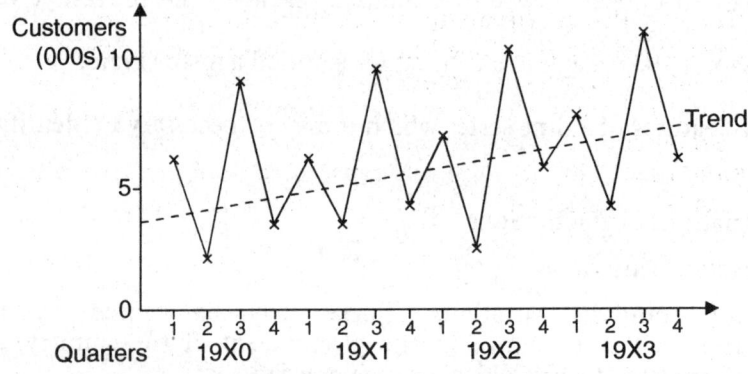

In this example, there would appear to be large seasonal fluctuations in demand, but there is also a basic upward trend.

Exercise 1

What seasonal variations would you expect to see in sales of video recorders?

Solution

Sales of video recorders might peak at Christmas and also before major sporting events such as Wimbledon.

Cyclical variations

1.8   Cyclical variations are medium-term changes in results caused by circumstances which repeat in cycles. In business, cyclical variations are commonly associated with economic cycles, successive booms and slumps in the economy. Economic cycles may last a few years. Cyclical variations are longer term than seasonal variations.

Summarising the components

1.9   In practice a time series could incorporate all four features and, to make reasonably accurate forecasts, the four features often have to be isolated. We can begin the process of isolating each feature by summarising the components of a time series by the following equation

$$Y = T + S + C + I$$

where Y = the actual time series
T = the trend series
S = the seasonal component
C = the cyclical component
I = the random or irregular component

1.10   Though you should be aware of the cyclical component, you will not be expected to carry out any calculation connected with isolating it. The mathematical model which we will use, the *additive model*, therefore excludes any reference to C and is

$$Y = T + S + I$$

1.11   We will begin by isolating the trend.

2   FINDING THE TREND   11/96

2.1   The main problem we are concerned with in time series analysis is how to identify the trend and seasonal variations.

2.2   There are three principal methods of finding a trend. The trend line can be *drawn by eye* on a graph in such a way that it appears to lie evenly between the recorded points, that is, a line of best fit is drawn by eye. (The line on the historigram in Paragraph 1.7 is an example.) Alternatively, a statistical technique known as *linear regression by the least squares method* can be used to calculate a line of best fit. Both of these methods are examined in the next chapter. In this chapter we will concern ourselves with a technique known as *moving averages*. This method attempts to remove seasonal variations from actual data by a process of averaging in order to produce trend values.

Finding the trend by moving averages

2.3   A moving average is an average of the results of a fixed number of periods. Since it is an average of several time periods, it is related to the mid-point of the overall period.

Example: moving averages

2.4

Year	Sales
	Units
19X0	390
19X1	380
19X2	460
19X3	450
19X4	470
19X5	440
19X6	500

Required

Take a moving average of the annual sales over a period of three years.

Solution

2.5   (a)   Average sales in the three year period 19X0 – 19X2 were

$$\left(\frac{390 + 380 + 460}{3}\right) = \frac{1,230}{3} = 410$$

This average relates to the middle year of the period, 19X1.

(b)   Similarly, average sales in the three year period 19X1 – 19X3 were

$$\left(\frac{380 + 460 + 450}{3}\right) = \frac{1,290}{3} = 430$$

This average relates to the middle year of the period, 19X2.

(c)   The average sales can also be found for the periods 19X2 - 19X4, 19X3 - 19X5 and 19X4 - 19X6, to give the following.

Year	Sales	Moving total of 3 years' sales	Moving average of 3 years' sales (÷ 3)
19X0	390		
19X1	380	1,230	410
19X2	460	1,290	430
19X3	450	1,380	460
19X4	470	1,360	453
19X5	440	1,410	470
19X6	500		

Note the following points.

(i)   The moving average series has five figures relating to the years from 19X1 to 19X5. The original series had seven figures for the years from 19X0 to 19X6.

(ii)   There is an upward trend in sales, which is more noticeable from the series of moving averages than from the original series of actual sales each year.

2.6   The above example averaged over a three-year period. Over what period should a moving average be taken? The answer to this question is that the moving average which is most appropriate will depend on the circumstances and the nature of the time series. Note the following points.

(a)   A moving average which takes an average of the results in many time periods will represent results over a longer term than a moving average of two or three periods.

(b) On the other hand, with a moving average of results in many time periods, the last figure in the series will be out of date by several periods. In our example, the most recent average related to 19X5. With a moving average of five years' results, the final figure in the series would relate to 19X4.

(c) When there is a known cycle over which seasonal variations occur, such as all the days in the week or all the seasons in the year, the most suitable moving average would be one which covers one full cycle.

Exercise 2

Using the following data, what is the three-month moving average for April?

Month	No of new houses finished
January	500
February	450
March	700
April	900
May	1,250
June	1,000

Solution

$$\frac{700 + 900 + 1,250}{3} = 950$$

Moving averages of an even number of results

2.7 In the previous example, moving averages were taken of the results in an *odd* number of time periods, and the average then related to the mid-point of the overall period. If a moving average were taken of results in an even number of time periods, the basic technique would be the same, but the mid-point of the overall period would not relate to a single period. For example, suppose an average were taken of the following four results.

Spring	120	
Summer	90	average 115
Autumn	180	
Winter	70	

The average would relate to the mid-point of the period, between summer and autumn. The trend line average figures need to relate to a particular time period; otherwise, seasonal variations cannot be calculated. To overcome this difficulty, we take a moving average of the moving average. An example will illustrate this technique.

Example: moving averages over an even number of periods

2.8 Calculate a moving average trend line of the following results.

Year	Quarter	Volume of sales '000 units
19X5	1	600
	2	840
	3	420
	4	720
19X6	1	640
	2	860
	3	420
	4	740
19X7	1	670
	2	900
	3	130
	4	760

Solution

2.9 A moving average of four will be used, since the volume of sales would appear to depend on the season of the year, and each year has four quarterly results.

The moving average of four does not relate to any specific period of time; therefore a second moving average of two will be calculated on the first moving average trend line.

Year	Quarter	Actual volume of sales '000 units (A)	Moving total of 4 quarters' sales '000 units (B)	Moving average of 4 quarters' sales '000 units (B ÷ 4)	Mid-point of 2 moving averages Trend line '000 units (C)
19X5	1	600			
	2	840			
	3	420	2,580	645.0	650.00
	4	720	2,620	655.0	657.50
19X6	1	640	2,640	660.0	660.00
	2	860	2,640	660.0	662.50
	3	420	2,660	665.0	668.75
	4	740	2,690	672.5	677.50
19X7	1	670	2,730	682.5	683.75
	2	900	2,740	685.0	687.50
	3	430	2,760	690.0	
	4	760			

2.10 By taking a mid point (a moving average of two) of the original moving averages, we can relate the results to specific quarters (from the third quarter of 19X5 to the second quarter of 19X7).

3 FINDING THE SEASONAL VARIATIONS   *11/96*

3.1 Once a trend has been established, by whatever method, we can find the seasonal variations.

3.2 The additive model for time series analysis is $Y = T + S + I$. We can therefore write $Y - T = S + I$. In other words, if we deduct the trend series from the actual series, we will be left with the seasonal and residual components of the time series. If we assume that the irregular movements component is relatively small, and hence negligible, the seasonal component can be found as $S = Y - T$, the de-trended series.

Example: the trend and seasonal variations

3.3 Output at a factory appears to vary with the day of the week. Output over the last three weeks has been as follows.

	Week 1 '000 units	Week 2 '000 units	Week 3 '000 units
Monday	80	82	84
Tuesday	104	110	116
Wednesday	94	97	100
Thursday	120	125	130
Friday	62	64	66

Required

Find the seasonal variation for each of the 15 days, and the average seasonal variation for each day of the week using the moving averages method.

Solution

3.4 Actual results fluctuate up and down according to the day of the week and so a moving average of five will be used. The difference between the actual result on any one day (Y) and the trend figure for that day (T) will be the seasonal variation (S) for the day.

3.5 The seasonal variations for the 15 days are as follows.

		Actual (Y)	Moving total of five days' output	Trend (T)	Seasonal variation (Y–T)
Week 1	Monday	80			
	Tuesday	104			
	Wednesday	94	460	92.0	+2.0
	Thursday	120	462	92.4	+27.6
	Friday	62	468	93.6	–31.6
Week 2	Monday	82	471	94.2	–12.2
	Tuesday	110	476	95.2	+14.8
	Wednesday	97	478	95.6	+1.4
	Thursday	125	480	96.0	+29.0
	Friday	64	486	97.2	–33.2
Week 3	Monday	84	489	97.8	–13.8
	Tuesday	116	494	98.8	+17.2
	Wednesday	100	496	99.2	+0.8
	Thursday	130			
	Friday	66			

3.6 You will notice that the variation between the actual results on any one particular day and the trend line average is not the same from week to week. This is because Y – T contains not only seasonal variations but random variations (residuals), but an average of these variations can be taken.

	Monday	Tuesday	Wednesday	Thursday	Friday
Week 1			+2.0	+27.6	–31.6
Week 2	–12.2	+14.8	+1.4	+29.0	–33.2
Week 3	–13.8	+17.2	+0.8		
Average	–13.0	+16.0	+1.4	+28.3	–32.4

3.7 Our estimate of the 'seasonal' or daily variation is almost complete, but there is one more important step to take. Variations around the basic trend line should cancel each other out, and add up to 0. At the moment they do not. The average seasonal estimates must therefore be corrected so that they add up to zero and so we spread the total of the daily variations (0.30) across the five days (0.3 ÷ 5) so that the final total of the daily variations goes to zero.

	Monday	Tuesday	Wednesday	Thursday	Friday	Total
Estimated average daily variation	–13.00	+16.00	+1.40	+28.30	–32.40	0.30
Adjustment to reduce total variation to 0	–0.06	–0.06	–0.06	–0.06	–0.06	–0.30
Final estimate of average daily variation	–13.06	+15.94	+1.34	+28.24	–32.46	0.00

These might be rounded up or down as follows.

Monday –13; Tuesday +16; Wednesday +1; Thursday +28; Friday –32; Total 0.

Exercise 3

Calculate a four-quarter moving average trend centred on actual quarters and then find seasonal variations from the following.

	Sales in £'000			
	Spring	Summer	Autumn	Winter
19X7	200	120	160	280
19X8	220	140	140	300
19X9	200	120	180	320

Solution

		Sales (Y)	4-quarter total	8-quarter total	Moving average (T)	Seasonal variation (Y-T)
19X7	Spring	200				
	Summer	120				
			760			
	Autumn	160		1,540	192.5	−32.5
			780			
	Winter	280		1,580	197.5	+82.5
			800			
19X8	Spring	220		1,580	197.5	+22.5
			780			
	Summer	140		1,580	197.5	−57.5
			800			
	Autumn	140		1,580	197.5	−57.5
			780			
	Winter	300		1,540	192.5	+107.5
			760			
19X9	Spring	200		1,560	195.0	+5.0
			800			
	Summer	120		1,620	202.5	−82.5
			820			
	Autumn	180				
	Winter	320				

We can now average the seasonal variations.

	Spring	Summer	Autumn	Winter	Total
19X7			−32.5	+82.5	
19X8	+22.5	−57.5	−57.5	+107.5	
19X9	+5.0	−82.5			
	+27.5	−140.0	−90.0	+190.0	
Average variations (in £'000)	+13.75	−70.00	−45.00	+95.00	−6.25
Adjustment so sum is zero	+1.5625	+1.5625	+1.5625	+1.5625	+6.25
Adjusted average variations	+15.3125	−68.4375	−43.4375	+96.5625	0

These might be rounded up or down to:

Spring £15,000, Summer −£68,000, Autumn −£43,000, Winter £96,000

Seasonal variations using the multiplicative model

3.8   The method of estimating the seasonal variations in the above example was to use the differences between the trend and actual data. This is called the *additive mode*. This model assumes that the components of the series are independent of each other, an increasing trend not affecting the seasonal variations for example.

The alternative is to use the *multiplicative model* whereby each actual figure is expressed as a proportion of the trend. Sometimes this method is called the *proportional model*. The model summarises a time series as $Y = T \times S \times I$. Note that the trend component will be the same whichever model is used but the values of the seasonal and residual components will vary according to the model being applied. You must be able to use both methods but the question will specify which is to be used.

3.9   The example in Paragraph 3.3 can be reworked on this alternative basis. The trend is calculated in exactly the same way as before but we need a different approach for the seasonal variations.

The multiplicative model is $Y = T \times S \times I$ and, just as we calculated $S = Y - T$ for the additive model (Paragraph 3.2) we can calculate $Y/T = S$ for the multiplicative model.

		Actual (Y)	*Trend* (T)	*Seasonal variation* (Y/T)
Week 1	Monday	80		
	Tuesday	104		
	Wednesday	94	92.0	1.022
	Thursday	120	92.4	1.299
	Friday	62	93.6	0.662
Week 2	Monday	82	94.2	0.870
	Tuesday	110	95.2	1.155
	Wednesday	97	95.6	1.015
	Thursday	125	96.0	1.302
	Friday	64	97.2	0.658
Week 3	Monday	84	97.8	0.859
	Tuesday	116	98.8	1.174
	Wednesday	100	99.2	1.008
	Thursday	130		
	Friday	66		

3.10   The summary of the seasonal variations expressed in proportional terms is as follows.

	Monday	*Tuesday*	*Wednesday*	*Thursday*	*Friday*
Week 1			1.022	1.299	0.662
Week 2	0.870	1.155	1.015	1.302	0.658
Week 3	0.859	1.174	1.008		
Total	1.729	2.329	3.045	2.601	1.320
Average	0.8645	1.1645	1.0150	1.3005	0.6600

Instead of summing to zero, as with the absolute approach, these should sum (in this case) to 5 (an average of 1).

They actually sum to 5.0045 so 0.0009 has to be deducted from each one. This is too small to make a difference to the figures above, so we should deduct 0.002 and 0.0025 to each of two seasonal variations. We could arbitrarily decrease Monday's variation to 0.8625 and Tuesday's to 1.162.

3.11   Note that the multiplicative model is better than the additive model for forecasting when the trend is increasing or decreasing over time. In such circumstances, seasonal variations are likely to be increasing or decreasing too. The additive model simply adds absolute and unchanging seasonal variations to the trend figures whereas the multiplicative model, by multiplying increasing or decreasing trend values by a constant seasonal variation factor, takes account of changing seasonal variations.

Exercise 4

Find the average seasonal variations for the sales data in Exercise 3 using the multiplicative model.

Solution

	Spring	Summer	Autumn	Winter	Total
19X7			0.83	1.42	
19X8	1.11	0.71	0.71	1.56	
19X9	1.03	0.59			
	2.14	1.30	1.54	2.98	

	Spring	Summer	Autumn	Winter	Total
Average variations	1.070	0.650	0.770	1.490	3.980
Adjustment to sum to 4	+ 0.005	+ 0.005	+ 0.005	+ 0.005	0.020
Adjusted average variations	1.075	0.655	0.775	1.495	4.000

4   FORECASTING AND TIME SERIES ANALYSIS

Making a forecast

4.1   Forecasts can be made using time series analysis data as follows.

(a)   Find a trend line either by finding a line of best fit (covered in the next chapter) or by moving averages. If the moving averages method is used the calculated trend line values have to be plotted on a graph.

(b)   Extend the trend line so that readings for points in time outside the span of time covered by the original data can be taken. Extending a trend line outside the range of known data, in this case forecasting the future from a trend line based on historical data, is known as *extrapolation*.

(c)   Adjust the readings found using the extrapolated trend line by the average seasonal variation applicable to the future period to determine the forecast for that period.

     (i)   With the additive model, add the variation to (or, for a negative variation, subtract it from) the extrapolated trend line reading.

     (ii)   With the multiplicative model, multiply the reading by the variation.

Example: forecasting

4.2   Use the trend values and the estimates of seasonal variations calculated in Paragraph 3.5 to 3.7 to forecast sales in week 4.

Solution

4.3   We begin by plotting the trend values on a graph and extrapolating the trend line.

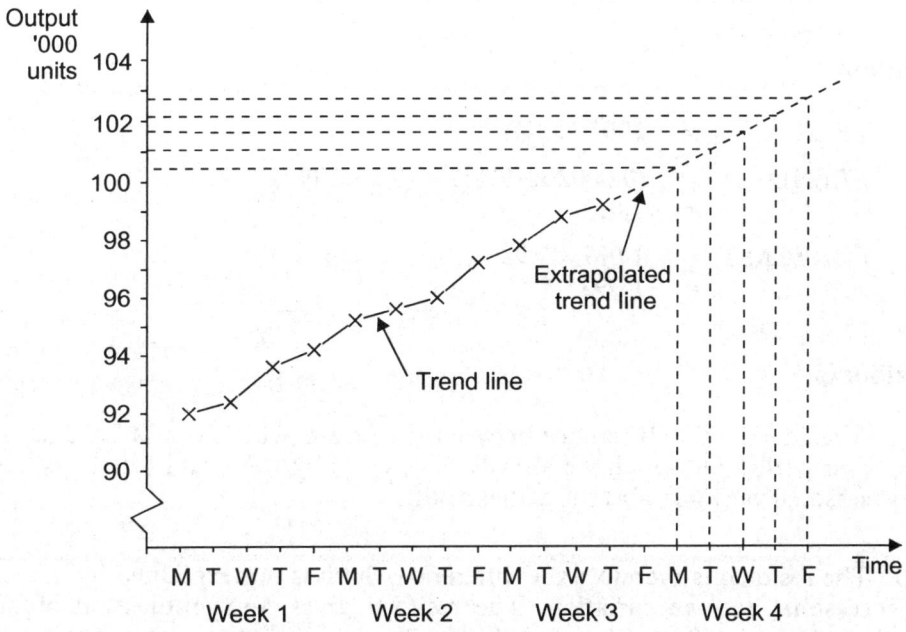

From the extrapolated trend line we can take the following readings and adjust them by the seasonal variations.

Week 4	*Trend line readings*	*Seasonal variations*	*Forecast*
Monday	100.5	−13	87.5
Tuesday	101.5	+16	117.1
Wednesday	101.7	+1	102.7
Thursday	102.2	+28	130.2
Friday	102.8	−32	70.8

4.4   If we had been using the multiplicative model the forecast for Tuesday, for example, would be $101.1 \times 1.1645 = 117.7$ (from Paragraph 3.10).

4.5   All forecasts are subject to error, but the likely errors vary from case to case.

(a)   The further into the future the forecast is for, the more unreliable it is likely to be.

(b)   The less data available on which to base the forecast, the less reliable the forecast.

(c)   The pattern of trend and seasonal variations cannot be guaranteed to continue in the future.

(d)   There is always the danger of random variations upsetting the pattern of trend and seasonal variation.

(e)   The extrapolation of the trend line is done by judgement and can introduce error.

4.6   You may be asked to forecast sales of a particular product in a given year by using an equation which calculates the trend.

Example: forecasting using an equation to calculate the trend

4.7   In a time series analysis, the trend equation for product Z is given by

$$\text{TREND} = 0.0002 \times \text{YEAR}^2 + 0.1 \times \text{YEAR} + 40.1$$

Due to the cyclical factor, it is estimated that the forecast sales for 1997 is estimated at 1.92 times trend. Calculate the forecast sales for 1997.

Solution

4.8 YEAR   = 1997

TREND   = $(0.0002 \times 1997^2) + (0.1 \times 1997) + 40.1$

= 1,037

FORECAST = $1,037 \times 1.92$

= 1,992

Residuals

4.9 A residual is the difference between the results which would have been predicted (for a past period for which we already have data) by the trend line adjusted for the average seasonal variation and the actual results.

4.10 The residual is therefore the difference which is not explained by the trend line and the seasonal average variation. The residual gives some indication of how much actual results were affected by other factors. Large residuals suggest that any forecast is likely to be unreliable.

4.11 In the example in Paragraph 3.5 to 3.7, the 'prediction' for Wednesday of week 2 would have been $95.6 + 1 = 96.6$. As the actual value was 97, the residual was only $97 - 96.6 = 0.4$.

Chapter roundup

- A time series is a series of figures or values recorded over time.

- A graph of a time series is called a historigram.

- There are four components of a time series: trend, seasonal variations, cyclical variations and random variations.

- The trend is the underlying long-term movement over time in the values of the data recorded. Seasonal variations are short-term fluctuations due to different circumstances which affect results at different points in time. Cyclical variations are medium-term changes in results caused by circumstances which repeat in cycles.

- One method of finding the trend is by the use of moving averages.

- Remember that when finding the moving average of an even number of results, a second moving average has to be calculated so that trend values can relate to specific actual figures.

- Seasonal variations are the difference between actual and trend figures. An average of the seasonal variations for each time period within the cycle must be determined and then adjusted so that the total of the seasonal variations sums to zero.

- Seasonal variations can be estimated using the additive model ($Y = T + S + I$, with seasonal variations = $Y - T$) or the proportional (multiplicative) model ($Y = T \times S \times I$, with seasonal variations = Y/T).

- Forecasts can be made by extrapolating the trend and adjusting for seasonal variations. Remember, however, that all forecasts are subject to error. Ensure that you can discuss when a forecast might be unreliable.

- We will look at forecasting using regression analysis in more detail in the next chapter.

Test your knowledge

1 What is the definition of a time series? (see para 1.1)

2 What are the four components that combine to form a time series? (1.3)

3 How can trend lines be found? (2.2)

4 How are trend values calculated when moving averages of an even number of results are taken? (2.9, 2.10)

5 Why are average seasonal variations adjusted to sum to zero? (3.7)

6 Distinguish between the additive model and the multiplicative model of time series. (3.8).

7 In what circumstances should the proportional model rather than the additive model be used? (3.11)

8 Describe how forecasts are made using time series analysis data. (4.1)

9 What is extrapolation? (4.1))

10 What is the term for the difference which is not explained by the trend line and the average seasonal variation? (4.10)

Now try illustrative question 28 at the end of the Study Text

Chapter 28

CORRELATION AND REGRESSION

This chapter covers the following topics.

		Syllabus reference	Ability required
1	Correlation	2(h)	Skill
2	The correlation coefficient and the coefficient of determination	2(h)	Skill
3	Spearman's rank correlation coefficient	2(h)	Skill
4	Lines of best fit	2(h)	Skill
5	The scattergraph method	2(h)	Skill
6	Least squares method of linear regression analysis	2(h)	Skill
7	The reliability of regression analysis forecasts	2(h)	Skill

Introduction

We looked at one mathematical forecasting technique in Chapter 27 and, you guessed it, we are going to look at the second in this, the final chapter of the Study Text. This chapter actually covers two related topics. The first three sections deal with correlation, which is concerned with assessing the strength of the relationship between two variables. Production costs and the level of production output for example, are likely to be correlated whereas there is likely to be very little correlation between the number of televisions sold and the number of pets taken to vets on a particular day.

We then turn our attention to forecasting. We will see how, if we assume that there is a linear relationship between two variables (such as selling costs and sales volume) we can determine the equation of a straight line to represent the relationship between the variables and use that equation to make forecasts or predictions. The equation can be derived and the predictions made using one of two methods, the scattergraph method or linear regression analysis, both of which are covered in this chapter.

In Chapter 27, we mentioned that linear regression analysis can be linked with time series analysis for forecasting purposes and we will be examining this in greater detail in this chapter.

Questions on correlation and regression *often* involve preparing diagrams (question 7 of the May 95 exam is an example). Be warned. The examiner is *not* impressed by scrappy and untidy diagrams. But not all questions require diagrams. The examiner commented that a common error in candidates' attempts at question 6 of the November 95 paper was to use scatter diagrams instead of calculations as required.

Once you get to the end of this chapter give yourself a pat on the back - you've made it to the end. But can you remember what we looked at in Chapter 1?.

1 CORRELATION

1.1 If a change in the value of one variable is accompanied by a change in the value of another variable, the two variables are said to be correlated.

1.2 Examples of variables which might be correlated are as follows.

(a) A person's height and weight

(b) The distance of a journey and the time it takes to make it

1.3   One way of showing the correlation between two related variables is on a scattergraph or scatter diagram, plotting a number of pairs of data on the graph. For example, a scattergraph showing monthly selling costs against the volume of sales for a 12-month period might be as follows.

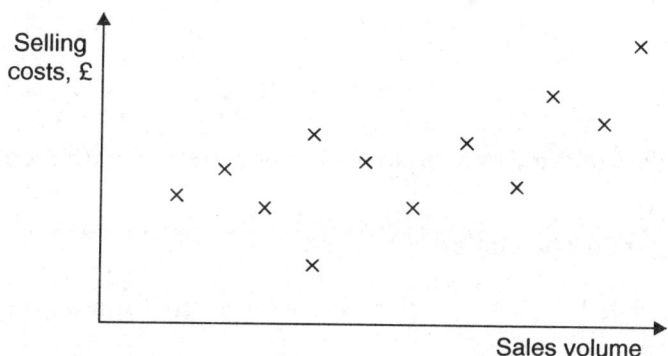

This scattergraph suggests that there is some correlation between selling costs and sales volume, so that as sales volume rises, selling costs tend to rise as well.

Degrees of correlation

1.4   Two variables can be one of the following.

   (a)   Perfectly correlated
   (b)   Partly correlated
   (c)   Uncorrelated

These differing degrees of correlation can be illustrated by scatter diagrams.

   (a)   Perfect correlation

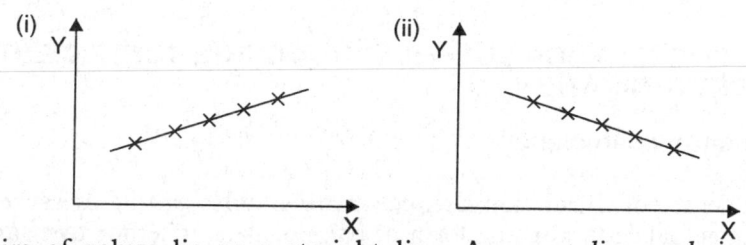

All the pairs of values lie on a straight line. An exact *linear relationship* exists between the two variables.

   (b)   Partial correlation

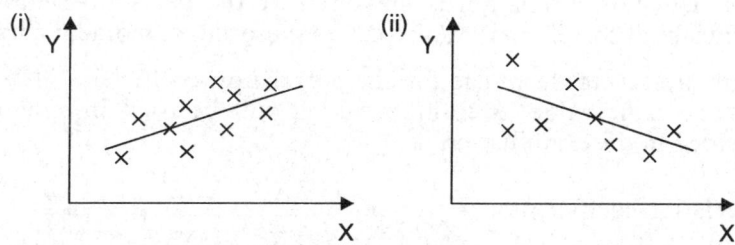

In (i), although there is no exact relationship, low values of X tend to be associated with low values of Y, and high values of X with high values of Y.

In (ii) again, there is no exact relationship, but low values of X tend to be associated with high values of Y and vice versa.

(c) *No correlation*

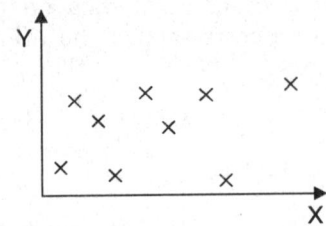

The values of these two variables are not correlated with each other.

Positive and negative correlation

1.5 Correlation, whether perfect or partial, can be positive or negative.

1.6 Positive correlation means that low values of one variable are associated with low values of the other, and high values of one variable are associated with high values of the other.

Negative correlation means that low values of one variable are associated with high values of the other, and high values of one variable with low values of the other.

Exercise 1

Which of the diagrams in Paragraph 1.4 demonstrate negative correlation?

Solution

Diagrams in (a)(ii) and (b)(ii)

---

2   THE CORRELATION COEFFICIENT AND THE COEFFICIENT OF DETERMINATION

S/95

The correlation coefficient

2.1 The degree of correlation between two variables can be measured, and we can decide, using actual results in the form of pairs of data, whether two variables are perfectly or partially correlated, and if they are partially correlated, whether there is a high or low degree of partial correlation.

2.2 This degree of correlation is measured by the Pearsonian correlation coefficient (the coefficient of correlation), r (also called the 'product moment correlation coefficient').

There are several formulae for the correlation coefficient, although each formula will give the same value. A formula which will be used in subsequent examples and is provided in the examination is:

$$\text{Correlation coefficient, } r = \frac{n\Sigma XY - \Sigma X\Sigma Y}{\sqrt{[n\Sigma X^2 - (\Sigma X)^2][n\Sigma Y^2 - (\Sigma Y)^2]}}$$

where X and Y represent pairs of data for two variables X and Y, and n is the number of pairs of data used in the analysis.

2.3 r must always fall between –1 and +1. If you get a value outside this range you have made a mistake.

r = +1   means that the variables are *perfectly positively correlated*
r = –1   means that the variables are *perfectly negatively correlated*
r = 0   means that the variables are *uncorrelated*

Example: the correlation coefficient

2.4   The cost of output at a factory is thought to depend on the number of units produced. Data have been collected for the number of units produced each month in the last six months, and the associated costs, as follows.

Month	Output '000s of units X	Cost £'000 Y
1	2	9
2	3	11
3	1	7
4	4	13
5	3	11
6	5	15

Required

Assess whether there is there any correlation between output and cost.

Solution

2.5 $r = \dfrac{n\Sigma XY - \Sigma X \Sigma Y}{\sqrt{[n\Sigma X^2 - (\Sigma X)^2][n\Sigma Y^2 - (\Sigma Y)^2]}}$

We need to find the values for the following.

(a) ΣXY Multiply each value of X by its corresponding Y value, so that there are six values for XY. Add up the six values to get the total.

(b) ΣX Add up the six values of X to get a total. $(\Sigma X)^2$ will be the square of this total.

(c) ΣY Add up the six values of Y to get a total. $(\Sigma Y)^2$ will be the square of this total.

(d) ΣX^2 Find the square of each value of X, so that there are six values for X^2. Add up these values to get a total.

(e) ΣY^2 Find the square of each value of Y, so that there are six values for Y^2. Add up these values to get a total.

Workings

X	Y	XY	X^2	Y^2
2	9	18	4	81
3	11	33	9	121
1	7	7	1	49
4	13	52	16	169
3	11	33	9	121
5	15	75	25	225
$\Sigma X = $ 18	$\Sigma Y = $ 66	$\Sigma XY = $ 218	$\Sigma X^2 = $ 64	$\Sigma Y^2 = $ 766

$(\Sigma X)^2 = 18^2 = 324$ $(\Sigma Y)^2 = 66^2 = 4{,}356$

$n = 6$

$r = \dfrac{(6 \times 218) - (18 \times 66)}{\sqrt{(6 \times 64 - 324) \times (6 \times 766 - 4{,}356)}}$

$= \dfrac{1{,}308 - 1{,}188}{\sqrt{(384 - 324) \times (4{,}596 - 4{,}356)}}$

$= \dfrac{120}{\sqrt{60 \times 240}} = \dfrac{120}{\sqrt{14{,}400}} = \dfrac{120}{120} = 1$

2.6   There is perfect positive correlation between the volume of output at the factory and costs which means that there is a perfect linear relationship between output and costs.

Correlation in a time series

2.7   Correlation exists in a time series if there is a relationship between the period of time and the recorded value for that period of time. The correlation coefficient is calculated with time as the X variable although it is convenient to use simplified values for X instead of year numbers.

For example, instead of having a series of years 1987 to 1991, we could have values for X from 0 (1987) to 4 (1991).

Note that whatever starting value you use for X (be it 0, 1, 2 ... 721, ... 953), the value of r will always be the same.

Exercise 2

Sales of product A between 19X7 and 19Y1 were as follows.

Year	Units sold ('000s)
19X7	20
19X8	18
19X9	15
19Y0	14
19Y1	11

Required

Determine whether there is a trend in sales. In other words, decide whether there is any correlation between the year and the number of units sold.

Solution

Workings

Let 19X7 to 19Y1 be years 0 to 4.

	X		Y		XY		X^2		Y^2
	0		20		0		0		400
	1		18		18		1		324
	2		15		30		4		225
	3		14		42		9		196
	4		11		44		16		121
$\Sigma X =$	10	$\Sigma Y =$	78	$\Sigma XY =$	134	$\Sigma X^2 =$	30	$\Sigma Y^2 =$	1,266

$(\Sigma X)^2 = 100 \qquad\qquad (\Sigma Y)^2 = 6,084$

$n = 5$

$$r = \frac{(5 \times 134) - (10 \times 78)}{\sqrt{(5 \times 30 - 100) \times (5 \times 1,266 - 6,084)}}$$

$$= \frac{670 - 780}{\sqrt{(150 - 100) \times (6,330 - 6,084)}} = \frac{-110}{\sqrt{50 \times 246}}$$

$$= \frac{-110}{\sqrt{12,300}} = \frac{-110}{110.90537} = -0.992$$

There is partial negative correlation between the year of sale and units sold. The value of r is close to −1, therefore a high degree of correlation exists, although it is not quite perfect correlation. This means that there is a clear downward trend in sales.

The coefficient of determination, r^2

2.8   Unless the correlation coefficient r is exactly or very nearly +1, −1 or 0, its meaning or significance is a little unclear. For example, if the correlation coefficient for two variables is +0.8, this would tell us that the variables are positively correlated, but the correlation is not perfect. It would not really tell us much else. A more meaningful analysis is available from the square of the correlation coefficient, r^2, which is called the coefficient of determination. r^2

2.9 r^2 (alternatively R^2) measures the proportion of the total variation in the value of one variable that can be explained by variations in the value of the other variable. In the exercise above, $r = -0.992$, therefore $r^2 = 0.984$. This means that over 98% of variations in sales can be explained by the passage of time, leaving 0.016 (less than 2%) of variations to be explained by other factors.

2.10   Similarly, if the correlation coefficient between a company's output volume and maintenance costs was 0.9, r^2 would be 0.81, meaning that 81% of variations in maintenance costs could be explained by variations in output volume, leaving only 19% of variations to be explained by other factors (such as the age of the equipment).

2.11   Note, however, that if $r^2 = 0.81$, we would say that 81% of the variations in y can be explained by variations in x. We do not necessarily conclude that 81% of variations in y are *caused* by the variations in x. We must beware of reading too much significance into our statistical analysis.

Correlation and causation

2.12   If two variables are well correlated, either positively or negatively, this may be due to pure chance or there may be a reason for it. The larger the number of pairs of data collected, the less likely it is that the correlation is due to chance, though that possibility should never be ignored entirely.

2.13   If there is a reason, it may not be causal. For example, monthly net income is well correlated with monthly credit to a person's bank account, for the logical (rather than causal) reason that for most people the one equals the other.

2.14   Even if there is a causal explanation for a correlation, it does not follow that variations in the value of one variable cause variations in the value of the other. For example, sales of ice cream and of sunglasses are well correlated, not because of a direct causal link but because the weather influences both variables.

2.15   Having said this, it is of course possible that where two variables are correlated, there is a direct causal link to be found.

3   SPEARMAN'S RANK CORRELATION COEFFICIENT

3.1   In the examples considered above, the data were given in terms of the values of the relevant variables, such as the number of hours. Sometimes however, they are given in terms of order or rank rather than actual values. When this occurs, a correlation coefficient known as Spearman's rank correlation coefficient, R should be calculated using the following formula.

Coefficient of rank correlation $R = 1 - \left[\dfrac{6\Sigma d^2}{n(n^2 - 1)} \right]$

where   n = number of pairs of data
        d = the difference between the rankings in each set of data.

The coefficient of rank correlation can be interpreted in exactly the same way as the ordinary correlation coefficient. Its value can range from -1 to $+1$.

Example: the rank correlation coefficient

3.2 The examination placings of seven students were as follows.

Student	Statistics placing	Economics placing
A	2	1
B	1	3
C	4	7
D	6	5
E	5	6
F	3	2
G	7	4

Required

Judge whether the placings of the students in statistics correlate with their placings in economics.

Solution

3.3 Correlation must be measured by Spearman's coefficient because we are given the placings of students, and not their actual marks.

$$R = 1 - \frac{6\Sigma d^2}{n(n^2 - 1)}$$

where d is the difference between the rank in statistics and the rank in economics for each student.

Student	Rank Statistics	Rank Economics	d	d^2
A	2	1	1	1
B	1	3	2	4
C	4	7	3	9
D	6	5	1	1
E	5	6	1	1
F	3	2	1	1
G	7	4	3	9
			$\Sigma d^2 =$	26

$$R = 1 - \frac{6 \times 26}{7 \times (49 - 1)} = 1 - \frac{156}{336} = 0.536$$

The correlation is positive, 0.536, but the correlation is not strong.

Tied ranks

3.4 If in a problem some of the items tie for a particular ranking, these must be given an average place before the coefficient of rank correlation is calculated. Here is an example.

Position of students in examination			Express as
A	1 =	average of 1 and 2	1.5
B	1 =		1.5
C	3		3
D	4		4
E	5 =		6
F	5 =	average of 5, 6 and 7	6
G	5 =		6
H	8		8

Exercise 3

Five artists were placed in order of merit by two different judges as follows.

Artist	Judge P Rank	Judge Q Rank
A	1	4 =
B	2 =	1
C	4	3
D	5	2
E	2 =	4 =

Required

Assess how the two sets of rankings are correlated.

Solution

	Judge P Rank	Judge Q Rank	d	d^2
A	1.0	4.5	3.5	12.25
B	2.5	1.0	1.5	2.25
C	4.0	3.0	1.0	1.00
D	5.0	2.0	3.0	9.00
E	2.5	4.5	2.0	4.00
				28.50

$$R = 1 - \frac{6 \times 28.5}{5 \times (25 - 1)} = -0.425$$

There is a slight negative correlation between the rankings.

4   LINES OF BEST FIT   *5/95*

4.1   Correlation enables us to determine the strength of any relationship between two variables but it does not offer us any method of forecasting values for one variable, Y, given values of another variable, X.

4.2   If we assume that there is a linear relationship between the two variables, however, and we determine the equation of a straight line (Y = a + bX) which is a good fit for the available data plotted on a scattergraph, we can use the equation for forecasting: we can substitute values for X into the equation and derive values for Y.

4.3   There are a number of techniques for estimating the equation of a line of best fit. We will be looking at the scattergraph method and simple linear regression analysis. Both provide a technique for estimating values for a and b in the equation

Y = a + bX

where   X and Y are the related variables and

a and b are estimated using pairs of data for X and Y.

5   THE SCATTERGRAPH METHOD   *5/95*

5.1   The scattergraph method is to plot pairs of data for two related variables on a graph, to produce a scattergraph, and then to *use judgement* to draw what seems to be a line of best fit through the data.

5.2   For example suppose we have the following pairs of data about output and costs.

Month	Output '000 units	Costs £'000
1	20	82
2	16	70
3	24	90
4	22	85
5	18	73

These pairs of data can be plotted on a scattergraph (the horizontal axis representing the independent variable and the vertical axis the dependent) and a line of best fit might be judged as the one shown below. It is drawn to pass through the middle of the data points, thereby having as many data points below the line as above it.

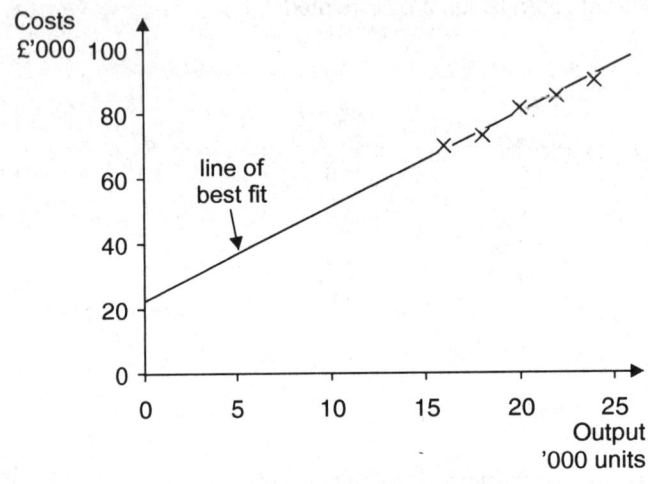

5.3   A formula for the line of best fit can be found. In our example, suppose that we read the following data from the graph.

(a)   When X = 0, Y = 22,000. This must be the value of a in the formula Y = a + bX.

(b)   When X = 20,000, Y = 81,000. Since Y = a + bX, and a = 22,000, this gives us a value for b of

$$\frac{81,000 - 22,000}{20,000} = 2.95$$

5.4   In this example the estimated equation from the scattergraph is Y = 22,000 + 2.95X.

Predictions and scattergraphs

5.5   If the company to which the data in Paragraph 5.2 relates wanted to predict costs at a certain level of output (say 13,000 units), the value of 13,000 could be substituted into the equation Y = 22,000 + 2.95X and an estimate of costs made.

If X = 13, Y = 22,000 + (2.95 × 13,000)

∴   Y = £60,350

5.6   Of course, predictions can be made directly from the scattergraph on the following page.

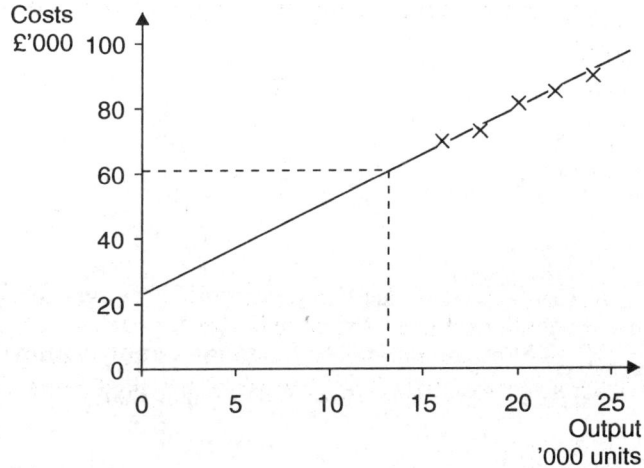

The prediction of the cost of producing 13,000 units from the scattergraph is £61,000.

6   LEAST SQUARES METHOD OF LINEAR REGRESSION ANALYSIS   *11/95*

6.1   This method involves using the following formulae for a and b in Y = a + bX.

$$b = \frac{n\Sigma XY - \Sigma X \Sigma Y}{n\Sigma X^2 - (\Sigma X)^2}$$

$$a = \overline{Y} - b\overline{X}$$

where   n is the number of pairs of data
$\overline{X}$ is the average X value of all the pairs of data
$\overline{Y}$ is the average Y value of all the pairs of data

6.2   There are some points to note about these formulae.

(a)   The line of best fit that is derived represents the *regression of Y upon X*.

A different line of best fit could be obtained by interchange in X and Y in the formulae. This would then represent the *regression of X upon Y* (X = a + bY) and it would have a slightly different slope. For examination purposes, always use the regression of Y upon X, where X is the independent variable, and Y is the dependent variable whose value we wish to forecast for given values of X. In a time series, X will represent time.

(b)   Since $a = \overline{Y} - b\overline{X}$, it follows that the line of best fit must *always* pass through the point ($\overline{X}$, $\overline{Y}$).

(c)   If you look at the formula for b and compare it with the first formula we gave for the correlation coefficient (Paragraph 2.2) you should see some similarities between the two formulae.

Example: the least squares method

6.3   (a)   Given that there is a fairly high degree of correlation between the output and the costs detailed in Paragraph 5.2 (so that a linear relationship can be assumed), calculate an equation to determine the expected level of costs, for any given volume of output, using the least squares method.

(b)   Prepare a budget for total costs if output is 22,000 units.

(c)   Confirm that the degree of correlation between output and costs is high by calculating the correlation coefficient.

Solution

6.4   (a)   *Workings*

X	Y	XY	X^2	Y^2
20	82	1,640	400	6,724
16	70	1,120	256	4,900
24	90	2,160	576	8,100
22	85	1,870	484	7,225
18	73	1,314	324	5,329
$\Sigma X = $ 100	$\Sigma Y = $ 400	$\Sigma XY = $ 8,104	$\Sigma X^2 = $ 2,040	$\Sigma Y^2 = $ 32,278

$n = 5$ (There are five pairs of data for x and y values)

$$b = \frac{n\Sigma XY - \Sigma X \Sigma Y}{n\Sigma X^2 - (\Sigma X)^2} = \frac{(5 \times 8,104) - (100 \times 400)}{(5 \times 2,040) - 100^2}$$

$$= \frac{40,520 - 40,000}{10,200 - 10,000} = \frac{520}{200} = 2.6$$

$$a = \overline{Y} - b\overline{X} = \frac{400}{5} - 2.6 \times \left(\frac{100}{5}\right) = 28$$

$$Y = 28 + 2.6X$$

where   Y = total cost, in thousands of pounds
        X = output, in thousands of units.

Compare this equation to that determined in Paragraph 5.4.

Note that the fixed costs are £28,000 (when X = 0 costs are £28,000) and the variable cost per unit is £2.60.

(b)   If the output is 22,000 units, we would expect costs to be

$28 + 2.6 \times 22 = 85.2 = £85,200$.

(c) $$r = \frac{520}{\sqrt{200 \times \left(5 \times 32,278 - 400^2\right)}} = \frac{520}{\sqrt{200 \times 1,390}} = \frac{520}{527.3} = +0.99$$

Regression lines and time series

6.5   The same technique can be applied to calculate a regression line (a trend line) for a time series. This is particularly useful for purposes of forecasting. As with correlation, years can be numbered from 0 upwards.

Exercise 4

Using the data in Exercise 2, calculate the trend line of sales and forecast sales in 19Y2 and 19Y3.

Solution

Using workings from Exercise 2:

$$b = \frac{(5 \times 134) - (10 \times 78)}{(5 \times 30) - (10)^2} = \frac{670 - 780}{150 - 100} = -2.2$$

$$a = \overline{Y} + b\overline{X} = \frac{78}{5} - \frac{(-2.2 \times 10)}{5} = 20$$

∴ Y = 20 – 2.2X where X = 0 in 19X7, X = 1 in 19X8 and so on.

Using the trend line, predicted sales in 19Y2 (year 5) would be:

20 – (2.2 × 5) = 9 ie 9,000 units

and predicated sales in 19Y3 (year 6) would be:

20 – (2.2 × 6) = 6.8 ie 6,800 units.

6.6 In some instances you may have to adjust your regression line forecasts by seasonal variations.

Exercise 5

Suppose that a trend line, found using linear regression analysis, is $Y = 300 - 4.7X$ where X is time (in quarters) and Y = sales level in thousands of units. Given that $X = 0$ represents 19X0 quarter 1 and that the seasonal variations are as set out below forecast the sales level for 19X5 quarter 4.

	Q_1	Q_2	Q_3	Q_4
Seasonal variations ('000 units)	−20	−8	+4	+15

Solution

$X = 0$ corresponds to 19X0 quarter 1

∴ $X = 23$ corresponds to 19X5 quarter 4

Trend sales level = $300 - (4.7 \times 23) = 191.9$ ie 191,900 units

Seasonally-adjusted sales level = $191.9 + 15 = 206.9$ ie 206,900 units

---

7 THE RELIABILITY OF REGRESSION ANALYSIS FORECASTS   *11/95*

7.1 As with all forecasting techniques, the results from regression analysis will not be wholly reliable. There are a number of factors which affect the reliability of forecasts made using regression analysis.

(a) It assumes a linear relationship between the two variables (since linear regression analysis produces an equation in the linear format) whereas a non-linear relationship might exist.

(b) The technique assumes that the value of one variable, Y, can be predicted or estimated from the value of one other variable, X. In reality the value of Y might depend on several other variables, not just X.

(c) When it is used for forecasting, it assumes that what has happened in the past will provide a reliable guide to the future. For example, if a line is calculated for total costs of production, based on historical data, the estimate could be used to budget for future costs. However, if there has been cost inflation, a productivity agreement with the workforce, a move to new premises, the dismissal of large numbers of office staff and the introduction of new equipment, future costs of production might bear no relation to costs in the past.

(d) When calculating a line of best fit, there will be a range of values for X. In the example in Paragraph 6.3 and 6.4, the line $Y = 28 + 2.6X$ was predicted from data with output values ranging from $X = 16$ to $X = 24$. Depending on the degree of correlation between X and Y, we might safely use the estimated line of best fit to predict values for Y in the future, provided that the value of X remains within the range 16 to 24. We would be on less safe ground if we used the formula to predict a value for Y when $X = 10$, or 30, or any other value outside the range 16 to 24, because we would have to assume that the trend line applies outside the range of X values used to establish the line in the first place.

(i) Interpolation means using a line of best fit to predict a value within the two extreme points of the observed range.

(ii) Extrapolation means using a line of best fit to predict a value outside the two extreme points.

When linear regression analysis is used for forecasting a time series (when the X values represent time) we have to assume that the trend line can be extrapolated into the future. This might not necessarily be a good assumption to make.

(e) As with any forecasting process, the amount of data available is very important. Even if correlation is high, if we have fewer than about ten pairs of values, we must regard any forecast as being somewhat unreliable. (It is likely to provide more reliable forecasts than the scattergraph method, however, since it uses all of the available data.)

7.2   A check on the reliability of the estimated line $Y = 28 + 2.6X$ can be made, however, by calculating the coefficient of correlation. From Paragraph 6.4, we know that $r = 0.99$. This is a high positive correlation, and $r^2 = 0.9801$, indicating that 98.01% of the variation in cost can be explained by the variation in volume. This would suggest that a fairly large degree of reliance can probably be placed on estimates .

7.3   If there is a perfect linear relationship between X and Y ($r = \pm 1$) then we can predict Y from any given value of X with great confidence.

7.4   If correlation is high (for example $r = 0.9$) the actual values will all lie quite close to the regression line and so predictions should not be far out. If correlation is below about 0.7, predictions will only give a very rough guide as to the likely value of Y.

Chapter roundup

- When the value of one variable is related to the value of another, they are said to be correlated.

- Two variables might be perfectly correlated, partly correlated or uncorrelated. Correlation can be positive or negative.

- The degree of correlation between two variables is measured by the Pearsonian (product moment) correlation coefficient, r. The nearer r is to +1 or -1, the stronger the relationship.

- The coefficient of determination, r^2, measures the proportion of the total variation in the value of one variable that can be explained by the variation in the value of the other variable.

- Spearman's rank correlation coefficient is used when data is given in terms of order or rank rather than actual values.

- The scattergraph method involves the use of judgement to draw what seems to be a line of best fit through plotted data.

- Linear regression analysis (the least squares method) is one technique for estimating a line of best fit. Ensure that you know how to use the formulae to calculate a and b in $Y = a + bX$.

- Once an equation for a line of best fit has been determined, forecasts can be made.

- Correlation and regression analysis do not indicate cause and effect. Even if $r = 1$, the correlation could still be spurious, both variables being influenced by a third.

Test your knowledge

1   Give some examples of variables which might be correlated. (see para 1.2)

2   Distinguish between positive and negative correlation. (1.6)

3   What range of values can the Pearsonian correlation coefficient take? (2.3)

4   How should the coefficient of determination be interpreted? (2.9-2.11)

5   When should Spearman's rank correlation coefficient be used? (3.1)

6   What is the scattergraph method for finding a line of best fit? (5.1)

7   When using the least squares method of linear regression, does it matter which variable is chosen as X? (6.2)

8   What are the factors which affect the reliability of forecasts made using the least squares method of linear regression? (7.1)

Now try illustrative question 29 at the end of the Study Text

Appendix
Mathematical tables

LOGARITHMS

	0	1	2	3	4	5	6	7	8	9	1	2	3	4	5	6	7	8	9
10	0000	0043	0086	0128	0170						4	9	13	17	21	26	30	34	38
						0212	0253	0294	0334	0374	4	8	12	16	20	24	28	32	37
11	0414	0453	0492	0531	0569						4	8	12	15	19	23	27	31	35
						0607	0645	0682	0719	0755	4	7	11	15	19	22	26	30	33
12	0792	0828	0864	0899	0934	0969					3	7	11	14	18	21	25	28	32
							1004	1038	1072	1106	3	7	10	14	17	20	24	27	31
13	1139	1173	1206	1239	1271						3	7	10	13	16	20	23	26	30
						1303	1335	1367	1399	1430	3	7	10	12	16	19	22	25	29
14	1461	1492	1523	1553							3	6	9	12	15	18	21	24	28
					1584	1614	1644	1673	1703	1732	3	6	9	12	15	17	20	23	26
15	1761	1790	1818	1847	1875	1903					3	6	9	11	14	17	20	23	26
							1931	1959	1987	2014	3	5	8	11	14	16	19	22	25
16	2041	2068	2095	2122	2148						3	5	8	11	14	16	19	22	24
						2175	2201	2227	2253	2279	3	5	8	10	13	15	18	21	23
17	2304	2330	2355	2380	2405	2430					3	5	8	10	13	15	18	20	23
							2455	2480	2504	2529	2	5	7	10	12	15	17	19	22
18	2553	2577	2601	2625	2648						2	5	7	9	12	14	16	19	21
						2672	2695	2718	2742	2765	2	5	7	9	11	14	16	18	21
19	2788	2810	2833	2856	2878						2	4	7	9	11	13	16	18	20
						2900	2923	2945	2967	2989	2	4	6	8	11	13	15	17	19
20	3010	3032	3054	3075	3096	3118	3139	3160	3181	3201	2	4	6	8	11	13	15	17	19
21	3222	3243	3263	3284	3304	3324	3345	3365	3385	3404	2	4	6	8	10	12	14	16	18
22	3424	3444	3464	3483	3502	3522	3541	3560	3579	3598	2	4	6	8	10	12	14	15	17
23	3617	3636	3655	3674	3692	3711	3729	3747	3766	3784	2	4	6	7	9	11	13	15	17
24	3802	3820	3838	3856	3874	3892	3909	3927	3945	3962	2	4	5	7	9	11	12	14	16
25	3979	3997	4014	4031	4048	4065	4082	4099	4116	4133	2	3	5	7	9	10	12	14	15
26	4150	4166	4183	4200	4216	4232	4249	4265	4281	4298	2	3	5	7	8	10	11	13	15
27	4314	4330	4346	4362	4378	4393	4409	4425	4440	4456	2	3	5	6	8	9	11	13	14
28	4472	4487	4502	4518	4533	4548	4564	4579	4594	4609	2	3	5	6	8	9	11	12	14
29	4624	4639	4654	4669	4683	4698	4713	4728	4742	4757	1	3	4	6	7	9	10	12	13
30	4771	4786	4800	4814	4829	4843	4857	4871	4886	4900	1	3	4	6	7	9	10	11	13
31	4914	4928	4942	4955	4969	4983	4997	5011	5024	5038	1	3	4	6	7	8	10	11	12
32	5051	5065	5079	5092	5105	5119	5132	5145	5159	5172	1	3	4	5	7	8	9	11	12
33	5185	5198	5211	5224	5237	5250	5263	5276	5289	5302	1	3	4	5	6	8	9	10	12
34	5315	5328	5340	5353	5366	5378	5391	5403	5416	5428	1	3	4	5	6	8	9	10	11
35	5441	5453	5465	5478	5490	5502	5514	5527	5539	5551	1	2	4	5	6	7	9	10	11
36	5563	5575	5587	5599	5611	5623	5635	5647	5658	5670	1	2	4	5	6	7	8	10	11
37	5682	5694	5705	5717	5729	5740	5752	5763	5775	5786	1	2	3	5	6	7	8	9	10
38	5798	5809	5821	5832	5843	5855	5866	5877	5888	5899	1	2	3	5	6	7	8	9	10
39	5911	5922	5933	5944	5955	5966	5977	5988	5999	6010	1	2	3	4	5	7	8	9	10
40	6021	6031	6042	6053	6064	6075	6085	6096	6107	6117	1	2	3	4	5	6	8	9	10
41	6128	6138	6149	6160	6170	6180	6191	6201	6212	6222	1	2	3	4	5	6	7	8	9
42	6232	6243	6253	6263	6274	6284	6294	6304	6314	6325	1	2	3	4	5	6	7	8	9
43	6335	6345	6355	6365	6375	6385	6395	6405	6415	6425	1	2	3	4	5	6	7	8	9
44	6435	6444	6454	6464	6474	6484	6493	6503	6513	6522	1	2	3	4	5	6	7	8	9
45	6532	6542	6551	6561	6571	6580	6590	6599	6609	6618	1	2	3	4	5	6	7	8	9
46	6628	6637	6646	6656	6665	6675	6684	6693	6702	6712	1	2	3	4	5	6	7	7	8
47	6721	6730	6739	6749	6758	6767	6776	6785	6794	6803	1	2	3	4	5	5	6	7	8
48	6812	6821	6830	6839	6848	6857	6866	6875	6884	6893	1	2	3	4	4	5	6	7	8
49	6902	6911	6920	6928	6937	6946	6955	6964	6972	6981	1	2	3	4	4	5	6	7	8

LOGARITHMS

	0	1	2	3	4	5	6	7	8	9	1	2	3	4	5	6	7	8
50	6990	6998	7007	7016	7024	7033	7042	7050	7059	7067	1	2	3	3	4	5	6	7
51	7076	7084	7093	7101	7110	7118	7126	7135	7143	7152	1	2	3	3	4	5	6	7
52	7160	7168	7177	7185	7193	7202	7210	7218	7226	7235	1	2	2	3	4	5	6	7
53	7243	7251	7259	7267	7275	7284	7292	7300	7308	7316	1	2	2	3	4	5	6	6
54	7324	7332	7340	7348	7356	7364	7372	7380	7388	7396	1	2	2	3	4	5	6	6
55	7404	7412	7419	7427	7435	7443	7451	7459	7466	7474	1	2	2	3	4	5	5	6
56	7482	7490	7497	7505	7513	7520	7528	7536	7543	7551	1	2	2	3	4	5	5	6
57	7559	7566	7574	7582	7589	7597	7604	7612	7619	7627	1	2	2	3	4	5	5	6
58	7634	7642	7649	7657	7664	7672	7679	7686	7694	7701	1	1	2	3	4	4	5	6
59	7709	7716	7723	7731	7738	7745	7752	7760	7767	7774	1	1	2	3	4	4	5	6
60	7782	7789	7796	7803	7810	7818	7825	7832	7839	7846	1	1	2	3	4	4	5	6
61	7853	7860	7868	7875	7882	7889	7896	7903	7910	7917	1	1	2	3	4	4	5	6
62	7924	7931	7938	7945	7952	7959	7966	7973	7980	7987	1	1	2	3	3	4	5	6
63	7993	8000	8007	8014	8021	8028	8035	8041	8048	8055	1	1	2	3	3	4	5	5
64	8062	8069	8075	8082	8089	8096	8102	8109	8116	8122	1	1	2	3	3	4	5	5
65	8129	8136	8142	8149	8156	8162	8169	8176	8182	8189	1	1	2	3	3	4	5	5
66	8195	8202	8209	8215	8222	8228	8235	8241	8248	8254	1	1	2	3	3	4	5	5
67	8261	8267	8274	8280	8287	8293	8299	8306	8312	8319	1	1	2	3	3	4	5	5
68	8325	8331	8338	8344	8351	8357	8363	8370	8376	8382	1	1	2	3	3	4	4	5
69	8388	8395	8401	8407	8414	8420	8426	8432	8439	8445	1	1	2	2	3	4	4	5
70	8451	8457	8463	8470	8476	8482	8488	8494	8500	8506	1	1	2	2	3	4	4	5
71	8513	8519	8525	8531	8537	8543	8549	8555	8561	8567	1	1	2	2	3	4	4	5
72	8573	8579	8585	8591	8597	8603	8609	8615	8621	8627	1	1	2	2	3	4	4	5
73	8633	8639	8645	8651	8657	8663	8669	8675	8681	8686	1	1	2	2	3	4	4	5
74	8692	8698	8704	8710	8716	8722	8727	8733	8739	8745	1	1	2	2	3	4	4	5
75	8751	8756	8762	8768	8774	8779	8785	8791	8797	8802	1	1	2	2	3	3	4	5
76	8808	8814	8820	8825	8831	8837	8842	8848	8854	8859	1	1	2	2	3	3	4	5
77	8865	8871	8876	8882	8887	8893	8899	8904	8910	8915	1	1	2	2	3	3	4	4
78	8921	8927	8932	8938	8943	8949	8954	8960	8965	8971	1	1	2	2	3	3	4	4
79	8976	8982	8987	8993	8998	9004	9009	9015	9020	9025	1	1	2	2	3	3	4	4
80	9031	9036	9042	9047	9053	9058	9063	9069	9074	9079	1	1	2	2	3	3	4	4
81	9085	9090	9096	9101	9106	9112	9117	9122	9128	9133	1	1	2	2	3	3	4	4
82	9138	9143	9149	9154	9159	9165	9170	9175	9180	9186	1	1	2	2	3	3	4	4
83	9191	9196	9201	9206	9212	9217	9222	9227	9232	9238	1	1	2	2	3	3	4	4
84	9243	9248	9253	9258	9263	9269	9274	9279	9284	9289	1	1	2	2	3	3	4	4
85	9294	9299	9304	9309	9315	9320	9325	9330	9335	9340	1	1	2	2	3	3	4	4
86	9345	9350	9355	9360	9365	9370	9375	9380	9385	9390	1	1	2	2	3	3	4	4
87	9395	9400	9405	9410	9415	9420	9425	9430	9435	9440	0	1	1	2	2	3	3	4
88	9445	9450	9455	9460	9465	9469	9474	9479	9484	9489	0	1	1	2	2	3	3	4
89	9494	9499	9504	9509	9513	9518	9523	9528	9533	9538	0	1	1	2	2	3	3	4
90	9542	9547	9552	9557	9562	9566	9571	9576	9581	9586	0	1	1	2	2	3	3	4
91	9590	9595	9600	9605	9609	9614	9619	9624	9628	9633	0	1	1	2	2	3	3	4
92	9638	9643	9647	9652	9657	9661	9666	9671	9675	9680	0	1	1	2	2	3	3	4
93	9685	9689	9694	9699	9703	9708	9713	9717	9722	9727	0	1	1	2	2	3	3	4
94	9731	9736	9741	9745	9750	9754	9759	9763	9768	9773	0	1	1	2	2	3	3	4
95	9777	9782	9786	9791	9795	9800	9805	9809	9814	9818	0	1	1	2	2	3	3	4
96	9823	9827	9832	9836	9841	9845	9850	9854	9859	9863	0	1	1	2	2	3	3	4
97	9868	9872	9877	9881	9886	9890	9894	9899	9903	9908	0	1	1	2	2	3	3	4
98	9912	9917	9921	9926	9930	9934	9939	9943	9948	9952	0	1	1	2	2	3	3	4
99	9956	9961	9965	9969	9974	9978	9983	9987	9991	9996	0	1	1	2	2	3	3	3

AREA UNDER THE NORMAL CURVE

This table gives the area under the normal curve between the mean and the point Z standard deviations above the mean. The corresponding area for deviations below the mean can be found by symmetry.

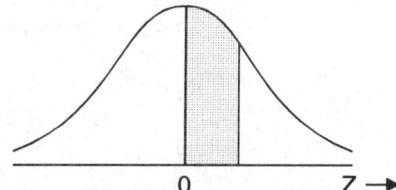

$Z = \frac{(x-\mu)}{\sigma}$	0.00	0.01	0.02	0.03	0.04	0.05	0.06	0.07	0.08	0.09
0.0	.0000	.0040	.0080	.0120	.0160	.0199	.0239	.0279	.0319	.0359
0.1	.0398	.0438	.0478	.0517	.0557	.0596	.0636	.0675	.0714	.0753
0.2	.0793	.0832	.0871	.0910	.0948	.0987	.1026	.1064	.1103	.1141
0.3	.1179	.1217	.1255	.1293	.1331	.1368	.1406	.1443	.1480	.1517
0.4	.1554	.1591	.1628	.1664	.1700	.1736	.1772	.1808	.1844	.1879
0.5	.1915	.1950	.1985	.2019	.2054	.2088	.2123	.2157	.2190	.2224
0.6	.2257	.2291	.2324	.2357	.2389	.2422	.2454	.2486	.2517	.2549
0.7	.2580	.2611	.2642	.2673	.2704	.2734	.2764	.2794	.2823	.2852
0.8	.2881	.2910	.2939	.2967	.2995	.3023	.3051	.3078	.3106	.3133
0.9	.3159	.3186	.3212	.3238	.3264	.3289	.3315	.3340	.3365	.3389
1.0	.3413	.3438	.3461	.3485	.3508	.3531	.3554	.3577	.3599	.3621
1.1	.3643	.3665	.3686	.3708	.3729	.3749	.3770	.3790	.3810	.3830
1.2	.3849	.3869	.3888	.3907	.3925	.3944	.3962	.3980	.3997	.4015
1.3	.4032	.4049	.4066	.4082	.4099	.4115	.4131	.4147	.4162	.4177
1.4	.4192	.4207	.4222	.4236	.4251	.4265	.4279	.4292	.4306	.4319
1.5	.4332	.4345	.4357	.4370	.4382	.4394	.4406	.4418	.4429	.4441
1.6	.4452	.4463	.4474	.4484	.4495	.4505	.4515	.4525	.4535	.4545
1.7	.4554	.4564	.4573	.4582	.4591	.4599	.4608	.4616	.4625	.4633
1.8	.4641	.4649	.4656	.4664	.4671	.4678	.4686	.4693	.4699	.4706
1.9	.4713	.4719	.4726	.4732	.4738	.4744	.4750	.4756	.4761	.4767
2.0	.4772	.4778	.4783	.4788	.4793	.4798	.4803	.4808	.4812	.4817
2.1	.4821	.4826	.4830	.4834	.4838	.4842	.4846	.4850	.4854	.4857
2.2	.4861	.4864	.4868	.4871	.4875	.4878	.4881	.4884	.4887	.4890
2.3	.4893	.4896	.4898	.4901	.4904	.4906	.4909	.4911	.4913	.4916
2.4	.4918	.4920	.4922	.4925	.4927	.4929	.4931	.4932	.4934	.4936
2.5	.4938	.4940	.4941	.4943	.4945	.4946	.4948	.4949	.4951	.4952
2.6	.4953	.4955	.4956	.4957	.4959	.4960	.4961	.4962	.4963	.4964
2.7	.4965	.4966	.4967	.4968	.4969	.4970	.4971	.4972	.4973	.4974
2.8	.4974	.4975	.4976	.4977	.4977	.4978	.4979	.4979	.4980	.4981
2.9	.4981	.4982	.4982	.4983	.4984	.4984	.4985	.4985	.4986	.4986
3.0	.49865	.4987	.4987	.4988	.4988	.4989	.4989	.4989	.4990	.4990
3.1	.49903	.4991	.4991	.4991	.4992	.4992	.4992	.4992	.4993	.4993
3.2	.49931	.4993	.4994	.4994	.4994	.4994	.4994	.4995	.4995	.4995
3.3	.49952	.4995	.4995	.4996	.4996	.4996	.4996	.4996	.4996	.4997
3.4	.49966	.4997	.4997	.4997	.4997	.4997	.4997	.4997	.4997	.4998
3.5	.49977									

PRESENT VALUE TABLE

Present value of $1 = (1+r)^{-n}$ where r = discount rate, n = number of periods until payment

This table shows the present value of £1 per annum, receivable or payable at the end of *n* years.

Periods	Discount rates (r)									
(n)	1%	2%	3%	4%	5%	6%	7%	8%	9%	10%
1	0.990	0.980	0.971	0.962	0.952	0.943	0.935	0.926	0.917	0.909
2	0.980	0.961	0.943	0.925	0.907	0.890	0.873	0.857	0.842	0.826
3	0.971	0.942	0.915	0.889	0.864	0.840	0.816	0.794	0.772	0.751
4	0.961	0.924	0.888	0.855	0.823	0.792	0.763	0.735	0.708	0.683
5	0.951	0.906	0.863	0.822	0.784	0.747	0.713	0.681	0.650	0.621
6	0.942	0.888	0.837	0.790	0.746	0.705	0.666	0.630	0.596	0.564
7	0.933	0.871	0.813	0.760	0.711	0.665	0.623	0.583	0.547	0.513
8	0.923	0.853	0.789	0.731	0.677	0.627	0.582	0.540	0.502	0.467
9	0.914	0.837	0.766	0.703	0.645	0.592	0.544	0.500	0.460	0.424
10	0.905	0.820	0.744	0.676	0.614	0.558	0.508	0.463	0.422	0.386
11	0.896	0.804	0.722	0.650	0.585	0.527	0.475	0.429	0.388	0.350
12	0.887	0.788	0.701	0.625	0.557	0.497	0.444	0.397	0.356	0.319
13	0.879	0.773	0.681	0.601	0.530	0.469	0.415	0.368	0.326	0.290
14	0.870	0.758	0.661	0.577	0.505	0.442	0.388	0.340	0.299	0.263
15	0.861	0.743	0.642	0.555	0.481	0.417	0.362	0.315	0.275	0.239

Periods	Discount rates (r)									
(n)	11%	12%	13%	14%	15%	16%	17%	18%	19%	20%
1	0.901	0.893	0.885	0.877	0.870	0.862	0.855	0.847	0.840	0.833
2	0.812	0.797	0.783	0.769	0.756	0.743	0.731	0.718	0.706	0.694
3	0.731	0.712	0.693	0.675	0.658	0.641	0.624	0.609	0.593	0.579
4	0.659	0.636	0.613	0.592	0.572	0.552	0.534	0.516	0.499	0.482
5	0.593	0.567	0.543	0.519	0.497	0.476	0.456	0.437	0.419	0.402
6	0.535	0.507	0.480	0.456	0.432	0.410	0.390	0.370	0.352	0.335
7	0.482	0.452	0.425	0.400	0.376	0.354	0.333	0.314	0.296	0.279
8	0.434	0.404	0.376	0.351	0.327	0.305	0.285	0.266	0.249	0.233
9	0.391	0.361	0.333	0.308	0.284	0.263	0.243	0.225	0.209	0.194
10	0.352	0.322	0.295	0.270	0.247	0.227	0.208	0.191	0.176	0.162
11	0.317	0.287	0.261	0.237	0.215	0.195	0.178	0.162	0.148	0.135
12	0.286	0.257	0.231	0.208	0.187	0.168	0.152	0.137	0.124	0.112
13	0.258	0.229	0.204	0.182	0.163	0.145	0.130	0.116	0.104	0.093
14	0.232	0.205	0.181	0.160	0.141	0.125	0.111	0.099	0.088	0.078
15	0.209	0.183	0.160	0.140	0.123	0.108	0.095	0.084	0.074	0.065

CUMULATIVE PRESENT VALUE TABLE

This table shows the present value of £1 per annum, receivable or payable at the end of each year for *n* years.

Periods					Discount rates (r)					
(n)	1%	2%	3%	4%	5%	6%	7%	8%	9%	10%
1	0.990	0.980	0.971	0.962	0.952	0.943	0.935	0.926	0.917	0.909
2	1.970	1.942	1.913	1.886	1.859	1.833	1.808	1.783	1.759	1.736
3	2.941	2.884	2.829	2.775	2.723	2.673	2.624	2.577	2.531	2.487
4	3.902	3.808	3.717	3.630	3.546	3.465	3.387	3.312	3.240	3.170
5	4.853	4.713	4.580	4.452	4.329	4.212	4.100	3.993	3.890	3.791
6	5.795	5.601	5.417	5.242	5.076	4.917	4.767	4.623	4.486	4.355
7	6.728	6.472	6.230	6.002	5.786	5.582	5.389	5.206	5.033	4.868
8	7.652	7.325	7.020	6.733	6.463	6.210	5.971	5.747	5.535	5.335
9	8.566	8.162	7.786	7.435	7.108	6.802	6.515	6.247	5.995	5.759
10	9.471	8.983	8.530	8.111	7.722	7.360	7.024	6.710	6.418	6.145
11	10.368	9.787	9.253	8.760	8.306	7.887	7.499	7.139	6.805	6.495
12	11.255	10.575	9.954	9.385	8.863	8.384	7.943	7.536	7.161	6.814
13	12.134	11.348	10.635	9.986	9.394	8.853	8.358	7.904	7.487	7.103
14	13.004	12.106	11.296	10.563	9.899	9.295	8.745	8.244	7.786	7.367
15	13.865	12.849	11.938	11.118	10.380	9.712	9.108	8.559	8.061	7.606

Periods					Discount rates (r)					
(n)	11%	12%	13%	14%	15%	16%	17%	18%	19%	20%
1	0.901	0.893	0.885	0.877	0.870	0.862	0.855	0.847	0.840	0.833
2	1.713	1.690	1.668	1.647	1.626	1.605	1.585	1.566	1.547	1.528
3	2.444	2.402	2.361	2.322	2.283	2.246	2.210	2.174	2.140	2.106
4	3.102	3.037	2.974	2.914	2.855	2.798	2.743	2.690	2.639	2.589
5	3.696	3.605	3.517	3.433	3.352	3.274	3.199	3.127	3.058	2.991
6	4.231	4.111	3.998	3.889	3.784	3.685	3.589	3.498	3.410	3.326
7	4.712	4.564	4.423	4.288	4.160	4.039	3.922	3.812	3.706	3.605
8	5.146	4.968	4.799	4.639	4.487	4.344	4.207	4.078	3.954	3.837
9	5.537	5.328	5.132	4.946	4.772	4.607	4.451	4.303	4.163	4.031
10	5.889	5.650	5.426	5.216	5.019	4.833	4.659	4.494	4.339	4.192
11	6.207	5.938	5.687	5.453	5.234	5.029	4.836	4.656	4.486	4.327
12	6.492	6.194	5.918	5.660	5.421	5.197	4.988	4.793	4.611	4.439
13	6.750	6.424	6.122	5.842	5.583	5.342	5.118	4.910	4.715	4.533
14	6.982	6.628	6.302	6.002	5.724	5.468	5.229	5.008	4.802	4.611
15	7.191	6.811	6.462	6.142	5.847	5.575	5.324	5.092	4.876	4.675

FORMULAE AND SYMBOLS

General section

$\pm$	plus *or* minus; positive *or* negative
$\neq$	not equal
$\triangleq$ or $\doteqdot$	approximately equal
$>$	greater than
$<$	less than
$a > b > c, c < b < a$	value of middle term lies between outer values
$\geq$	greater than or equal to
$\log_e N$	natural logarithm of N. Note that if $e^x = N$, $\log_e N = x$
$\log N$	$\log_{10} N$ common (Briggsian) logarithm of N. Note that if $10^x = N$, $\log N = x$

$$e^x = 1 + \frac{x}{1!} + \frac{x^2}{2!} + \ldots$$

xy or x.y	product of x and y; x multiplied by y; $(x)(y) = xy$
$\star$	multiplied by
$A \star B$	A times B
$y = f(x)$	y is a function of x
dy/dx or f'(x)	differential coefficient of $y = f(x)$; 1st derivative
d^2y/dx^2 or f''(x)	2nd derivative
x/y or $x \div y$	x divided by y
x^n	x to power n; the product xx ... to n factors; nth power of x
$\sqrt{x} = x^{1/2}$	square root of x
$\sqrt[n]{x} = x^{1/n}$	nth root of x
$x^{-n} = \dfrac{1}{x^n}$	reciprocal of nth power of x
$\lvert x \rvert$	absolute value of x (sign ignored)
Σx	summed values of variable x
$\displaystyle\sum_{i=1}^{n} x_i$	summed values of variable x over range x_1 to x_n inclusive
x!	factorial x; the product 1, 2, 3 ... x
$P(n,x)$ $_nP_x$	number of permutations of x things from n
$C(n,x)$ $_nC_x$ ^nC_x	number of combinations of x things from n
101_2	subscript $_2$ indicates binary number system
534_n	subscript n indicates number system based on n
$\int f(x)dx$	indefinite integral of f(x)
$\displaystyle\int_a^b f(x)dx$	definite integral of f(x) between limits $x = a$, $x = b$

Sets and probability

A=B	set A equals set B
ε	is an element of
⊂	inclusion; A⊂B means set A is included in set B
∩(cap)	conjunction, intersection; A∩B defines all elements included in *both* A and B
∪(cup)	Union; A∪B defines all elements in A *plus* all elements in B, no element being counted twice
A' or $\overline{A}$	negation the set of all elements *not* in A
n(A)	number of elements in set A
U	universe of discourse, sample space; note that for any set A+A'=U=1
φ( )	null or empty set
p(A)	probability of event A
p(A|B)	probability of event A, given B

General rules

$$P(A\cup B) = P(A) + P(B) - P(A\cap B)$$

$$P(A\cap B) = P(A).\, P(B|A) = P(B).\, P(A|B)$$

Statistics and Quantitative methods

μ	population mean
$\overline{x}$	sample mean
$Q_1 ... Q_n$	first ... nth quantile
cum x	cumulative total of variable x
d.f.	degrees of freedom
χ^2	chi-squared
F	*F* ratio
t	Student's t-statistic
n	number in the sample
N	population size
s	sample standard deviation
s^2	sample variance
σ	population standard deviation
σ^2	population variance
$s / \overline{x}$	coefficient of variation
r	coefficient of correlation
r^2(or R^2)	coefficient of determination
E(X)	expectation of X = probability ⋆ pay off
$p(X=x_1)$	probability that X equals x_1

Distributions

Binominal distribution

$$Pr(x) = {}^nC_x . p^x . q^{n-x}$$

$$^nC_x = \frac{n!}{(n-x)!(x)!}$$

$$Mean = n.p$$

$$Standard\ deviation = \sqrt{n.p.q}$$

Normal distribution

$$Z = \frac{x - \mu}{\sigma}$$

Poisson distribution

$$Pr(x) = \frac{e^{-m}.m^x}{x!}$$

where   e = exponential constant

          m = mean rate of occurrence

             = variance

Descriptive statistics

Arithmetic mean

$$\bar{x} = \frac{\sum x}{n}\ or\ \bar{x} = \frac{\sum fx}{\sum f}$$

Standard deviation

$$SD = \sqrt{\frac{\sum(x - \bar{x})^2}{n-1}}\ \ or\ \sqrt{\frac{\sum(x - \bar{x})^2}{n}}\ \ if\ n\ is\ 'large'$$

$$SD = \sqrt{\frac{\sum fx^2}{\sum f} - \bar{x}^2}\ \ (frequency\ distribution)$$

Index numbers

Laspeyres quantity	$100 \times \dfrac{\sum Q_1 P_0}{\sum Q_0 P_0}$
Paasche quantity	$100 \times \dfrac{\sum Q_1 P_1}{\sum Q_0 P_1}$
Laspeyres price	$100 \times \dfrac{\sum Q_0 P_1}{\sum Q_0 P_0}$
Paasche price	$100 \times \dfrac{\sum Q_1 P_1}{\sum Q_1 P_0}$

Time series

Additive model: Series = Trend + Seasonal + Random

Multiplicative model: Series = Trend * Seasonal * Random

Statistical inference

Estimated Standard Errors -

Sample mean: $\dfrac{s}{\sqrt{n}}$

Sample proportion: $\sqrt{\dfrac{pq}{n}}$

$\bar{x}_1 - \bar{x}_2 : \sqrt{\dfrac{s_1^2}{n_1} + \dfrac{s_2^2}{n_2}}$

Chi squared (χ^2)

$$\chi^2 = \sum \frac{(O - E)^2}{E}$$

Regression analysis

The linear regression equation of Y on X is given by:

Y $= a + bX$ *or*

$Y - \bar{Y} = b(X - \bar{X})$, where

$b = \dfrac{\text{Covariance (XY)}}{\text{Variance (X)}} = \dfrac{n\sum XY - (\sum X)(\sum Y)}{n\sum X^2 - (\sum X)^2}$

and a $= \bar{Y} - b\bar{X}$,

or solve $\sum Y = na + b\sum X$

$\sum XY = a\sum X + b\sum X^2$

Exponential $Y = ab^x$

Geometric $Y = aX^b$

Coefficient of correlation (r)

$r = \dfrac{\text{Covariance (XY)}}{\sqrt{\text{VAR(X)} . \text{VAR(Y)}}}$

$= \dfrac{n\sum XY - (\sum X)(\sum Y)}{\sqrt{\left\{n\sum X^2 - (\sum X)^2\right\}\left\{n\sum Y^2 - (\sum Y)^2\right\}}}$

Exponential smoothing

New Forecast   = Old Forecast + A(Old Actual Sales – Old Forecast)

or   = A(Old Sales) + (1 – A). Old Forecast

Queueing Theory - Simple Queues

Average time spent in *system* (ie both queueing and in the service point)

$$\frac{1}{\mu - \lambda} = \frac{1}{1 - \rho}\left(\frac{1}{\mu}\right)$$

Average number in the *system* (both queueing and in the service point)

$$\frac{\lambda}{\mu - \lambda} = \frac{\rho}{1 - \rho}$$

Average time spent in the queue

$$\frac{\rho}{\mu - \lambda} = \frac{\lambda}{\mu(\mu - \lambda)} = \frac{1}{\mu}\left(\frac{\rho}{1 - \rho}\right)$$

Average numbers in the queue

$$\frac{\rho\lambda}{\mu - \lambda}$$

Quality control

AQL = acceptable quality level

LTPD = lot(batch) tolerance proportion defective

α (alpha) = producer's risk

β (beta) = consumer's risk

OC = operating characteristic curve

Statistical process control

UCL = upper control limit ($\bar{x}$ + 3 Standard Errors)

LCL = lower control limit ($\bar{x}$ – 3 Standard Errors)

UWL = upper warning limit ($\bar{x}$ + 1.96 Standard Errors)

LWL = lower warning limit ($\bar{x}$ – 1.96 Standard Errors)

Inventory Control

EOQ basic model $\sqrt{\dfrac{2CoD}{Ch}}$

EBQ (gradual replenishment) $\sqrt{\dfrac{2CoD}{Ch(1 - \dfrac{D}{R})}}$

FINANCIAL MATHEMATICS

BPP note. You only need to be aware of the following formulae from the Financial Mathematics section of the CIMA *Mathematical Tables* for Paper 2. These formulae all appear in the first column of the first page of the Financial Mathematics section.

General

Annuity

The value of annuity of £1 per period for *t* years (*t*-year annuity factor) is:

$$PV = \frac{1}{r} - \frac{1}{r(1+r)^t}$$

Perpetuity

The value of a perpetuity of £1 per year is:

$$PV = \frac{1}{r}$$

Values and Sums

The value, V, attained by a single sum X, after n periods at r% is $V = X(1+r)^n$

The sum, S, of a geometric series of n terms, with first term A and common ratio R, is

$$S = A + AR + AR^2 + AR^3 + ... + AR^{n-1}$$

$$S = A\frac{(R^n - 1)}{R - 1}$$

Multiple choice questions and suggested solutions

Questions 1-30 are on cost accounting topics and questions 31-60 are on quantitative methods topics.

The following data are to be used for questions 1 and 2 below:

Dotsum Dashes Ltd manufactures a product in a process operation. Normal loss is 5% of input and is not costed. Loss is assumed to occur at the end of processing.

Data for May are as follows.

Opening stock of WIP	Nil
Input materials	6,000 units, cost £13,060
Direct labour	£5,000
Production overhead	300% of direct labour cost
Closing stock of WIP	Nil
Output to finished goods	5,800 units

1   What was the full cost of output to finished goods in May?

    A   £28,060
    B   £31,958
    C   £33,060
    D   £33,640

2   What would be the appropriate double entry in the cost accounts to record the abnormal loss or gain in May?

A	Debit	Process account	£570
	Credit	Abnormal loss/gain account	£570
B	Debit	Abnormal loss/gain account	£570
	Credit	Process account	£570
C	Debit	Process account	£580
	Credit	Abnormal loss/gain account	£580
D	Debit	Abnormal loss/gain account	£580
	Credit	Process account	£580

The following data are to be used for questions 3 to 6 below:

A manufacturing company, Leyton Friday Ltd, has three production departments X, Y and Z. A predetermined overhead absorption rate is established for each department on the basis of machine hours at normal capacity. The overheads of each department consist of the directly allocated costs of each department plus a share of a service department's overhead costs, apportioned in the ratio 5:2:3 to departments X, Y and Z respectively. All overheads are fixed costs.

The following incomplete information is available, relating to the period just ended.

	Production department		
	X	Y	Z
Budgeted directly allocated overhead expenses	£74,000	£44,000	£61,500
Budgeted service department apportionment	(?)	(?)	£42,000
Normal machine capacity (hours)	(?)	6,000 hrs	(?)
Predetermined absorption rate per machine hour	£7.20	(?)	(?)
Actual machine utilisation (hours)	21,200 hours	(?)	10,000 hrs
Over/(under) absorption of overhead	(?)	£(6,720)	£(11,500)

Actual overhead expenditure incurred in each department was as per budget.

3   The absorption rate per machine hour in Department Y is

    A   £7.33
    B   £11.20
    C   £12.00
    D   £19.00

4   Actual machine hours worked in Department Y were

    A   5,400 hrs
    B   5,440 hrs
    C   6,560 hrs
    D   6,600 hrs

5   Normal capacity and the over- or under-absorbed overhead in Department X were

	Normal capacity	*Overhead over-/(under-) absorbed*
A	20,000 hours	£8,640
B	20,000 hours	£(8,640)
C	22,400 hours	£8,640
D	22,400 hours	£(8,640)

6   Normal capacity and the absorption rate per hour in Department Z were

	Normal capacity	*Absorption rate per hour*
A	11,111 hours	£10.35
B	11,111 hours	£9.20
C	11,250 hours	£10.35
D	11,250 hours	£9.20

The following data are to be used for questions 7 and 8 below:

Receipts and issues of part number 6288 for the month of August are as follows.

	Receipts Units	*Total value* £	*Issues* Units
3 August	2,000	6,000	
7 August	3,000	9,900	
11 August	2,000	8,000	
16 August			4,000
24 August	3,000	10,500	
30 August			5,000

Opening stocks of part number 6288 were 1,000 units, valued at £2,800.

7   Using a FIFO method of stock valuation, the cost of the issued parts in the month was

    A   £30,200
    B   £30,400
    C   £30,900
    D   £31,100

8   Using a LIFO method of stock valuation, the cost of the issued parts in the month was

    A   £30,900
    B   £31,100
    C   £31,400
    D   £33,100

9 Which one of the following would NOT help to explain a favourable direct materials usage variance?

    A   Using a higher quality of materials than specified in the standard
    B   Achieving a lower output volume than budgeted
    C   A reduction in quality control checking standards
    D   A reduction in materials wastage rates

The following data are to be used for questions 10 to 12 below:

Budgeted information relating to two departments in Rydons Tables Ltd for the next period is as follows:

Department	Production overhead £	Direct material cost £	Direct labour cost £	Direct labour hours	Machine hours
1	27,000	67,500	13,500	2,700	45,000
2	18,000	36,000	100,000	25,000	300

Individual direct labour workers within each department earn differing rates of pay, according to their skills, grade and experience.

10 What is the most appropriate production overhead absorption rate for Department 1?

    A   40% of direct material cost
    B   200% of direct labour cost
    C   £10 per direct labour hour
    D   £0.60 per machine hour

11 What is the most appropriate production overhead absorption rate for Department 2?

    A   50% of direct material cost
    B   18% of direct labour cost
    C   £0.72 per direct labour hour
    D   £60 per machine hour

12 During the period, job number 9287 is carried out by Rydons Tables Ltd. Production data is as follows.

Direct material cost		£40
Direct labour	- department 1	4 hours at £5 per hour
	- department 2	9 hours at £4 per hour
Machine hours	- department 1	65 hours
	- department 2	1 hour

What is the total production cost of job 9287 using overhead absorption rates based on your selection in questions **10** and **11**?

    A   £141.48
    B   £142.48
    C   £195.00
    D   £201.48

13 The following data relates to the stores ledger control account of Duckboard Ltd, a manufacturing company, for the month of October 19X2.

	£
Opening stock	18,500
Closing stock	16,100
Deliveries from suppliers	142,000
Returns to suppliers	2,300
Cost of indirect materials issued	25,200

The issue of direct materials would have been recorded in the cost accounts as

A	Debit	Stores ledger control account	£112,100
	Credit	Work in progress control account	£112,100

B	Debit	Work in progress control account	£112,100
	Credit	Stores ledger control account	£112,100

C	Debit	Stores ledger control account	£116,900
	Credit	Work in progress control account	£116,900

D	Debit	Work in progress control account	£116,900
	Credit	Stores ledger control account	£116,900

14 Hump Ltd manufactures a single product, which had the following sales and production results over two operating periods.

	Period 1	Period 2
Sales (units)	50,000	60,000
Production (units)	70,000	50,000

The sales price is £10 per unit. Direct materials and direct labour costs are £5 per unit. All manufacturing overheads are absorbed into product costs at a predetermined rate of output, based on normal output of 60,000 units per period. Any under- or over-absorbed overhead is transferred to the P&L account at the end of each period. Budgeted manufacturing overhead is £180,000 per period for fixed costs and £1 per unit of variable overhead.

Assuming that actual costs were as expected, what was the profit reported in period 2 using the absorption costing method described, and what would the profit have been if marginal costing techniques had been used instead?

	Absorption costing profit	Marginal costing profit
A	£30,000	£60,000
B	£30,000	£70,000
C	£40,000	£60,000
D	£50,000	£70,000

15 What is the name given to a standard that can be achieved, allowing for normal shrinkage, wastage and machine breakdowns, if a standard unit of work is performed efficiently, a machine is properly operated or materials are properly used?

A   Attainable standard
B   Basic standard
C   Current standard
D   Ideal standard

16 The following information relates to job 2468, which is being carried out by Soxon Feet Ltd to meet a customer's order.

	Department A	Department B
Direct materials consumed	£5,000	£3,000
Direct labour hours	400 hrs	200 hrs
Direct labour rate per hour	£4	£5
Production overhead per direct labour hour	£4	£4
Administration and other overhead	20% of full production cost	
Profit margin	25% of sales price	

What is the selling price to the customer for job 2468?

A   £16,250
B   £17,333
C   £19,500
D   £20,800

17   Crack Tribb Ltd manufactures a single product and has drawn up the following flexed budget for the year.

	Level of activity		
	70%	80%	90%
	£	£	£
Direct materials	31,990	36,560	41,130
Direct labour	58,100	66,400	74,700
Production overhead	75,600	77,400	79,200
Other overhead	60,000	60,000	60,000
Total cost	225,690	240,360	255,030

What would be the total cost in a budget that is flexed at the 55% level of activity?

A   £179,185
B   £189,015
C   £190,185
D   £203,685

18   Each unit of product Alpha requires 3 kgs of raw material. Next month's production budget for product Alpha is as follows.

Opening stocks:	
raw materials	15,000 kg
finished units of Alpha	2,000 units
Budgeted sales of Alpha	60,000 units
Planned closing stocks:	
raw materials	7,000 kg
finished units of Alpha	3,000 units

The number of kilograms of raw materials that should be purchased next month is:

A   172,000
B   175,000
C   183,000
D   191,000

19   Patacake Ltd produces a certain food item in a manufacturing process. On 1 November, there was no opening stock of work in process. During November, 500 units of material were input to the process, with a cost of £9,000. Direct labour costs in November were £3,840. Production overhead is absorbed at the rate of 200% of direct labour costs. Closing stock on 30 November consisted of 100 units which were 100% complete as to materials and 80% complete as to labour and overhead. There was no loss in process.

The full production cost of completed units during November was

A   £10,400
B   £13,600
C   £16,416
D   £16,800

The following data are to be used for questions 20 to 22 below:

Actual sales of a retail company, Markup Ltd, for November and December 19X1, together with budgeted monthly sales for January-June 19X2, are shown below.

		Sales £	
19X1	November	160,000	(actual)
	December	210,000	(actual)
19X2	January	80,000	
	February	60,000	
	March	100,000	
	April	90,000	
	May	120,000	
	June	150,000	

The company sells food products with a very short shelf life, and so it carries no stocks of goods beyond the end of any day. All goods purchased on any day are resold during the day.

The purchase price of the goods for Markup Ltd is 75% of their retail price. Purchases are on $1^1/2$ months' credit. Sales are 50% for cash and 50% on credit. One half of credit customers pay after 1 month and the other half pay after 2 months.

There are no bad debts. Sales and purchases occur at an even rate throughout each month.

20 What are the budgeted cash receipts in February 19X2?

    A   £77,500
    B   £102,500
    C   £132,500
    D   £175,000

21 What are the budgeted cash receipts in the six month period January - June 19X2?

    A   £600,000
    B   £615,000
    C   £625,000
    D   £640,000

22 What are the budgeted cash payments to suppliers in the six month period January - June 19X2?

    A   £450,000
    B   £495,000
    C   £510,000
    D   £680,000

23 The following information relates to job 3579, which is being carried out by Mittenson Hands Ltd to meet a customer's order.

Materials issued to job 3579	£5,000
Materials transferred to job 2456	£400

Grade X labour (direct labour): 200 hours at £3 per hour basic rate. 100 of these hours were worked in overtime, at the request of the customer, in order to complete the job earlier.

Overtime premium is £1 per hour.
Production overhead is £5 per direct labour hour.

A supervisor, Wat Chover, recorded on his job sheet that 20 hours of his time was spent on this job. He is paid £5 per hour, and the cost of his time is treated as a direct labour cost in the company's cost accounts.

What is the full production cost of job 3579?

A   £6,300
B   £6,400
C   £6,500
D   £6,900

24   Brixon Morter Ltd is a manufacturing company, which is based in a single factory location. In its cost accounts, it uses an absorption costing system. 70% of the building is taken up by the production divisions, with the remainder of the space taken up by general administration (20%) and marketing (10%). The rental cost for the premises in the year just ended was £40,000.

Which one of the following bookkeeping entries would have been recorded in the company's integrated cost/financial accounts for the period?

A	Debit	Rent account	£28,000
	Credit	Production overhead control account	£28,000
B	Debit	Cash	£40,000
	Credit	Rent account	£40,000
C	Debit	Production overhead control account	£28,000
	Credit	Rent account	£28,000
D	Debit	Production overhead control account	£40,000
	Credit	Rent account	£40,000

25   Barbarama Ltd purchases and re-sells a single item of product. Opening stock on 1 March was 400 units, valued at £1.80 each. Further receipts and sales during the month were as follows.

		Units	£ per unit
8 March	Receipts	600	2.10
14 March	Receipts	500	?
25 March	Sales	1,250	4.00

The company uses the FIFO method of stock valuation. Gross trading profit for March was £2,500. What was the cost per unit of the 500 units received on 14 March?

A   £1.94
B   £2.00
C   £2.04
D   £2.08

26   The following cost behaviour pattern has been observed for maintenance costs at various levels of production

Volume	Maintenance cost
Hours	£
14,000	26,800
9,800	21,760
10,560	22,672
15,400	28,480

What will be the likely maintenance cost for a volume of 12,000 hours?

A   £22,192
B   £22,971
C   £24,400
D   £26,645

27   Rypoll Dage Ltd has recorded the following wages costs for direct production workers in the month of November 19X1.

	Direct workers	
	£	
Basic pay	63,000	
Overtime premium	2,000	- overtime not worked for any specific job
Holiday pay	500	
	65,500	
Income tax	(12,000)	
Employees' National Insurance	(4,000)	
Cash wages	49,500	
Employer's National Insurance	7,800	

The accounting entries for these wages costs would be

A	Debit	Wages control account	£49,500
	Credit	Work in progress control account	£47,000
	Credit	Production overhead control account	£2,500
B	Credit	Wages control account	£57,300
	Debit	Work in progress control account	£54,800
	Debit	Production overhead control account	£2,500
C	Credit	Wages control account	£65,500
	Debit	Work in progress control account	£63,000
	Debit	Production overhead control account	£2,500
D	Credit	Wages control account	£73,300
	Debit	Work in progress control account	£70,800
	Debit	Production overhead control account	£2,500

*The following data are to be used for questions **28** to **30** below:*

Saber Fencing has already incurred research and development costs of £100,000 on a contract, and expects to incur £150,000 more in costs before the R & D project is completed in one year's time. The estimated future costs are as follows.

	Expected future costs
	£
Materials	60,000
Staff costs	50,000
Overheads	40,000
	150,000

The expected sales value of the completed research is just £60,000.

Materials. Contracts have already been exchanged for the purchase of the remaining £60,000 of materials needed. If not used, the materials must be disposed of at a cost of £2,500.

Staff costs. The expected future staff costs represent the annual salaries of Ray Peer and Chris Swords, who each earn £20,000 per annum, and an allocation of £10,000 of the salary of their supervisor A Pay, who is in overall charge of several research projects. If this project is abandoned, Ray and Chris will be made redundant, each receiving £9,000 in compensation.

Overheads. Future overhead costs represent depreciation of £20,000 on plant and machinery and an allocation of the general fixed overheads incurred by the business. The plant and equipment was bought for the project and has no other use. Its current disposal value is £18,000 and in one year's time will be £11,000.

The company is considering whether or not to continue with the research project.

28 What are the materials costs that are relevant to the decision about whether to continue with the project or not?

A Nil
B £2,500
C £60,000
D £62,500

29 What are the staff costs that are relevant to the decision about whether to continue with the project or not?

A £18,000
B £22,000
C £28,000
D £40,000

30 Ignoring interest costs, what are the costs of the plant and machinery, plus the costs of general overheads, that are relevant to the decision about whether to continue with the project or not?

A £7,000
B £18,000
C £27,000
D £38,000

31 A chart drawn in such a way that the number of items in each class is represented by the area of the bar is called

A an ogive
B a histogram
C a line chart
D a Gantt chart

32 In the general equation for a straight line y = a + bx the number a represents

A the gradient
B the intercept on the x axis
C the intercept on the y axis
D the value of x when y = 0

33 The mean of numbers 2, x, 4 ,-x, 9 is

A 3
B 4
C 5
D impossible to calculate

34 When the mean purchase price of 100 units at £50, 100 units at £70 and 200 units at £x is £80, the value of x is:

A £40
B £60
C £80
D £100

35 Invoices have an average value of £200 and a standard deviation of £40 and are normally distributed. The probability that an invoice selected at random has a value of less than £240 is approximately

A 0.1587
B 0.3413
C 0.6587
D 0.8413

36   A business buys two components, the A and the B. In 19X1 each A cost £5, each B cost £8 and the numbers of each used were 2,000 of A and 3,000 of B. By 19X5 the prices were £6 and £10 and the numbers used 2,200 and 2,500. A Paasche price index for 19X5 based on 19X1 will be

    A   120
    B   122.5
    C   123.23
    D   123.53

37   A scatter diagram of y against x appears as follows.

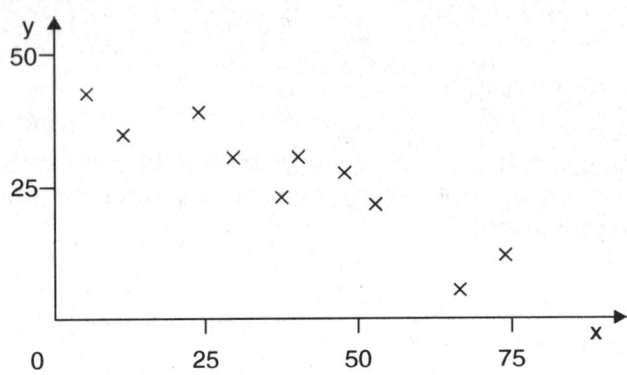

The correlation coefficient of y against x is approximately

    A   −0.9
    B   −0.2
    C   0
    D   0.2

38   The regression coefficient b for y on x for the diagram in question 37 is approximately

    A   −0.7
    B   −0.2
    C   0
    D   0.2

39   The expression $\dfrac{\left(p^4\right)^7}{p^2}$ equals

    A $p^{5/2}$
    B p^{26}
    C p^9
    D p^{12}

40   The net present value of a project involving an outlay of £10,000 at time 0 and receipts of £2,000 at each of times 2 to 7 discounted at a discount rate of 10% is

    A   £2,080
    B   £(268)
    C   £(2,082)
    D   None of these

41   The mean price of 11 objects is £17, and 16 objects £14. What is the mean price of all 27 objects to the nearest penny?

A   £11.48
B   £22.15
C   £16.00
D   £15.22

42     $ax^2 - 3x + 20$ equals zero when x is –4 or +2.5. The value of a is

A   –2
B   –1.5
C   1
D   1.5

43   A sample of 260 students sit a mock exam having finished studying their text. Their average mark is 65 with a standard deviation of 4 marks. 95% confidence limits for the average score of all students who finish the text are

A 65 ± 48.6
B 65 ± 4.86
C 65 ± 0.486
D 65 ± 0.0486

44   A job carries a monthly salary of £1,000, payable in arrears. The net present value now of next year's salary, assuming an annual rate of interest of 12% is:

A   £8,900
B   £9,470
C   £10,370
D   £11,260

45   There are two quantities, X and Y. X = –1 and Y = –2.

Therefore:

A $2X^2 > Y^2 < 0$
B $2X^2 < Y^2 < 0$
C $2X^2 < Y^2 > 0$
D $2X^2 > Y^2 > 0$

46   The following formula is used in the calculation of loan repayments.

R = 2PC/B(N + 1)

Rearranging the terms, it follows that

A   N = (2PC – R)/B
B   N = (2PC – 1)/BR
C   N = 2PC/B(R + 1)
D   N = (2PC/BR) – 1

47   The correlation coefficient between X and Y for 20 pairs of values is r = –0.5. Read the following statements.

I   On the average, X increases twice as fast as Y decreases.
II   50% of the variation in Y can be explained by changes in X.
III   25% of the variation in X can be explained by changes in Y.

Which is true?

A   I only
B   I and II only
C   II only
D   III only

48   A wholesaler spends an equal amount on each of five different types of stock. The unit prices of the stock are £4, £8, £10, £16 and £20 respectively.

The mean price per unit (to two decimal places) is

A   £8.51
B   £10.00
C   £11.60
D   Impossible to calculate without further information.

49   An accountant is given three identical-looking, unlabelled floppy disks, each containing two programs. One disk contains two perfect programs, one disk contains two faulty programs, and one disk contains one perfect and one faulty program. After selecting a disk at random the accountant randomly selects one of the two programs. If the program selected is perfect, the probability the other program on this disk is also perfect is

A   1/4
B   1/3
C   1/2
D   2/3

50   A standard normal distribution, not drawn to scale, is shown below. The shaded section represents one-third of the total area under the curve.

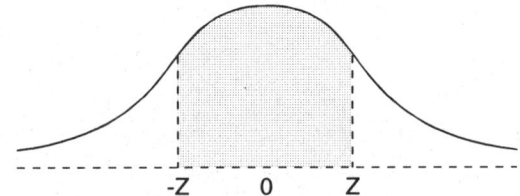

The value of |Z| (to two decimal places) is

A   0.07
B   0.13
C   0.25
D   0.43

51   The percentage of rejects in a quality control check is as follows.

   1   1   5   7   2   8   3   5   5   3

The difference between the arithmetic mean and the median percentage of rejects is:

A   0
B   1
C   2
D   3

52   A company has weekly fixed costs of £5,000 and variable costs per unit of production of £10. The equation of the straight line relating production (P) to costs (C) is therefore

A   C = 5,000P + 10
B   P = 5,000 + 10C
C   C = 5,000 + 10/P
D   C = 5,000 + 10P

53 $\sqrt{Y} = X^2 - 2X + 1$

If $X = -8$, Y equals

A   9
B   49
C   81
D   6,561

54   The present value of £50,000 receivable three years from now, assuming a rate of interest of 9%, is (to the nearest pound)

A   £38,600
B   £42,000
C   £63,500
D   £64,935

55   Which of the following is/are required for an accountant to select a stratified random sample of invoices?

I   Each invoice must be given an equal chance of being picked.
II   A record of all invoices is necessary.
III   The number of invoices in each stratum must be known.

A   I only
B   II only
C   III only
D   II and III only

56   A simple random sample of 250 invoices reveals that the mean value is £105 with a standard deviation of £25. 90% confidence limits for the whole (large) batch of invoices are given by the statement £105 ± X, where X is measured to the nearest pound. X equals

A   £6
B   £12
C   £3
D   £4

57   A company's sales figures for January 19X5 (month 0) to December 19X5 (month 11) have been analysed into a trend and percentage seasonal variations using regression analysis. The regression line is y = 520 + 17x, where x is the month number and y is the sales in £'000. The average seasonal variation for September is 97%. Sales in September 19X5 are forecast as (to the nearest £'000)

A   £656,000
B   £520,000
C   £636,000
D   £504,000

58   Monthly demand for a product is approximately normally distributed with a mean of 10,000 units and a standard deviation of 2,000 units. The probability of monthly demand being less than 6,000 units is:

A   0.0013
B   0.0228
C   0.0475
D   0.2257

59   What sum of money receivable three years from now will have a present value of £5,000 if r = 10%?

    A   £3,755
    B   £5,000
    C   £6,658
    D   £7,194

60 Two management accountants rank the credit-worthiness of seven companies as follows.

	H	I	J	K	L	M	N
MA 1	Second	Fourth	Sixth	First	Fifth	Third	Seventh
MA 2	Fourth	Third	Fifth	Second	Sixth	First	Seventh

Spearman's coefficient of rank correlation

$$R \text{ (rank)} = 1 - [6\Sigma d^2/n(n^2 - 1)]$$

will be closest to

    A   −0.79
    B   −0.14
    C   0
    D   0.79

1   D

	Units
Input	6,000
Normal loss (5%)	300
Expected output	5,700
Actual output	5,800
Abnormal gain	100

Cost per unit	Total costs	£(13,060 + 5,000 + 15,000) = £33,060
	Expected output	5,700 units
	Cost per unit	£5.80

Full cost of output = £5.80 × 5,800 = £33,640

2   C   Here is the process account in full.

	Units	£		Units	£
Direct materials	6,000	13,060	Finished goods	5,800	33,640
Direct labour		5,000	Normal loss	300	0
Production overhead		15,000			
	6,000	33,060			
Abnormal gain	100	580			
	6,100	33,640		6,100	33,640

Value of abnormal gain = £5.80 × 100 = £580.

3   C   *Apportionment of service department costs*

	Ratio	£
Dept Z	3	42,000 (given)
Dept X	5	70,000
Dept Y	2	28,000
		140,000

Absorption rate, Dept Y	£
Allocated overheads	44,000
Apportioned service dept costs	28,000
	72,000

Normal capacity	6,000 hrs
Absorption rate	£12 per machine hour

4   B

Under-absorbed overhead, Dept Y	6,720
Absorption rate per hour	£12 per hr
Difference between actual hours and normal hours	560 hrs

Under-absorbed overhead, given actual expenditure equal to budget, means actual hours less than normal hours.

	Hours
Normal machine capacity, Dept Y	6,000
Difference	560
Actual machine hours	5,440

5   A

Department X budgeted and actual overheads	£
Allocated	74,000
Apportioned service dept costs	70,000
	144,000

Absorption rate per hr (given)	£7.20
Normal capacity (machine hours)(144,000 ÷ £7.20)	20,000 hrs

	£
Absorbed overheads (21,200 hrs × £7.20)	152,640
Actual overheads	144,000
Over-absorbed overhead	8,640

6   D

	£
Actual overhead expenditure (same as budget, £61,500 + £42,000)	103,500
Under-absorbed overhead	(11,500)
Overhead actually absorbed into production costs	92,000

Actual machine hours	10,000 hrs
Absorption rate per hour	£9.20

$$\text{Normal capacity} = \frac{\text{Budgeted overheads}}{\text{Absorption rate}} = \frac{£103,500}{£9.20 \text{ per hour}} = 11,250 \text{ hrs}$$

7   A   The unit price of parts received was

3 August	£3.00
7 August	£3.30
11 August	£4.00
24 August	£3.50

Value of parts issued, using FIFO

		£	£
16 August	1,000 at £2.80 each (o/stock)	2,800	
	2,000 at £3.00 each	6,000	
	1,000 at £3.30 each	3,300	
			12,100
30 August	2,000 at £3.30 each	6,600	
	2,000 at £4.00 each	8,000	
	1,000 at £3.50 each	3,500	
			18,100
Total value of parts issued			30,200

8   C   Value of parts issued, using LIFO

		£	£
16 August	2,000 at £4.00	8,000	
	2,000 at £3.30	6,600	
			14,600
30 August	3,000 at £3.50	10,500	
	1,000 at £3.30	3,300	
	1,000 at £3.00	3,000	
			16,800
Total value of parts issued			31,400

9   B   Variations in output volume (item B) should not affect usage of materials per unit produced. A high quality of material (item A) might reduce wastage or scrap levels (item D) which would in turn improve the materials usage rate. With lower quality control standards (item C), there should be fewer rejected items, a higher proportion of successfully-completed items, and so an improvement in materials usage.

10   D   All of the suggested overhead absorption rates could be acceptable. However, a time-based method should be used whenever possible because most items of overhead expenditure tend to increase with time. A direct labour cost percentage is to an extent time based, but if differential wage rates exist this can lead to inequitable overhead absorption. Since Department 1 appears to be primarily for machine work, a machine hour rate should be used.

11 **C** For the same reasons as for question 10, a time-based method should be used. Since Department 2 appears to be labour intensive, a direct labour hour rate is the most appropriate.

12 **A** The overhead absorption rates from questions 10 and 11 are (£27,000 ÷ 45,000 =) £0.60 per machine hour in department 1 and (£18,000 ÷ 25,000 =) £0.72 per direct labour in department 2. The total production cost can be calculated as follows:

	£
Direct material	40.00
Direct labour	
- department 1 4 hours × £5	20.00
- department 2 9 hours × £4	36.00
Overhead	
- department 1 65 machine hours × £0.60	39.00
- department 2 9 labour hours × £0.72	6.48
	141.48

13 **D**

STORES LEDGER CONTROL ACCOUNT

	£		£
Opening stock b/f	18,500	Creditors (returns)	2,300
Creditors/cash (deliveries)	142,000	Overhead accounts	
		(indirect materials)	25,200
		WIP (balancing figure)	116,900
		Closing stock c/f	16,100
	160,500		160,500

14 **A** *Absorption costing*   Fixed cost per unit = £180,000 ÷ 60,000 = £3
Total cost per unit = £(5 + 3 + 1) = £9

	£	£
Opening stock (20,000 × £9)		180,000
Costs of production (50,000 × £9)		450,000
		630,000
Less Closing stock (10,000 × £9)		(90,000)
Cost of sales		540,000
Sales (60,000 × £10)		600,000
Gross profit		60,000
Overhead absorbed (50,000 × £3)	150,000	
Overhead incurred	180,000	
Under-absorbed overhead		(30,000)
Net profit		30,000

Marginal costing

	£
Sales (60,000 × £10)	600,000
Less variable costs of sales (60,000 × £(5 + 1) per unit)	360,000
Contribution	240,000
Fixed costs	180,000
Profit	60,000

Note. The difference in profit, £30,000, is the difference between the value of the reduction in stocks (by 10,000 units) during the period. In absorption costing, stock is reduced in value by £90,000 and in marginal costing (cost £6 per unit) the stock reduction would be only £60,000. Since these stock reductions become a cost of sales in the period, the marginal costing profit is higher by £30,000.

15 **A** An attainable standard represents future performance and objectives that are reasonably attainable. It will be more 'demanding' than a current standard (which is a short-term standard reflecting current conditions, possibly developed from a longer-term basic standard). It will be less demanding than an 'ideal' standard, which makes no allowance for spoilage, wastage and machine breakdowns, and assumes ideal operating conditions.

16   D

	Dept A	Dept B	Total
	£	£	£
Direct materials	5,000	3,000	8,000
Direct labour	1,600	1,000	2,600
Production overhead	1,600	800	2,400
Full production cost			13,000
Other overheads (20%)			2,600
Cost of the job			15,600
Profit (25% of sales = $33^1/_3$ % of cost)			5,200
Sales price			20,800

17   D

	55% level of activity
	£
Direct materials	25,135
Direct labour	45,650
Production overhead (part fixed (£63,000), part variable (£0.18/unit))	72,900
Other overhead	60,000
	203,685

18   B

	Units
Increase in finished goods stock required	1,000
Budgeted sales of product Alpha	60,000
Production required	61,000

	Kg
Raw materials usage budget ($\times$ 3 kg)	183,000
Decrease in raw materials stock budgeted	8,000
Raw materials purchase budget	175,000

19   D

		Equivalent units	
	Total units	*Materials*	*Labour/ overhead*
Finished units	400	400	400
Closing stock	100	100	80
	500	500	480
Cost		£9,000	£11,520
			(£3,840 $\times$ 300%)
Cost per equivalent unit		£18	£24

Cost of completed units = 400 $\times$ £(18 + 24) = £16,800.

20   B

	£
50% of sales in February (cash sales)	30,000
25% of sales in January	20,000
25% of sales in December	52,500
	102,500

21   D   The quickest method of calculation is to take opening debtors plus sales minus closing debtors.

	£'000
Debtors at 1 January 19X1 (25% of 160 + 50% of 210)	145
Sales in January - June (80 + 60 + 100 + 90 + 120 + 150)	600
	745
Debtors at 30 June 19X2 (25% of 120 + 50% of 150)	105
Cash receipts in January - June	640

22   **C**   There are no stocks, and so purchases in any period will relate to sales in the same period. Since 1¹/₂ months' credit is taken, the payments in the January - June period will be for the following purchases.

¹/₂ of November 19X1 purchases
Purchases in December - April
¹/₂ of May 19X2 purchases

This is (in £'000) 75% (80 + 210 + 80 + 60 + 100 + 90 + 60) = 510

23   **C**

	£
Materials issued less transfers	4,600
Grade X labour (200 hours × £3)	600
Overtime premium (direct cost of job 3579)	100
Supervisor (direct labour) (20 hrs × £5)	100
Production overhead (220 hrs × £5)	1,100
Job cost	6,500

24   **C**

RENT ACCOUNT

	£		£
Cash	40,000	Production overhead	28,000
		Admin overhead	8,000
		Marketing overhead	4,000
	40,000		40,000

Answer C is therefore correct.

25   **D**

	£
Sales (1,250 x £4)	5,000
Gross profit	2,500
Material cost of sales	2,500

Cost of units sold:	£
1st 400 units (x £1.80)	720
Next 600 units (x £2.10)	1,260
	1,980
Total cost of 1,250 units sold	2,500
Balance: cost of last 250 units sold	520

Cost per unit (£520 ÷ 250) =   £2.08

26   **C**   Dividing each cost by the corresponding volume does not produce a constant figure and therefore this is not a linear variable cost. Using the high-low method to separate the fixed and variable costs:

	Hours	£
Low	9,800	21,760
High	15,400	28,480
Difference	5,600	6,720

Therefore, variable cost per hour = $\dfrac{£6,720}{5,600}$ = £1.20

Fixed cost = £21,760 – (9,800 × £1.20) = £10,000
Total maintenance cost for 12,000 hours

	£
Fixed cost	10,000
Variable cost (1.20 × 12,000)	14,400
	24,400

27   **D**

WAGES CONTROL ACCOUNT

	£		£
Cost ledger control a/c (or income tax a/c, cash a/c, employees' Nat Ins, employer's Nat Ins) (65,500 + 7,800)	73,300	Work in progress control a/c (direct wages)	70,800
		Production overhead control a/c (indirect wages)	2,500
	73,300		73,300

28   **B**   All past costs and committed costs are irrelevant to the decision. Relevant costs are just the disposal costs of £2,500 that would be incurred if the project were abandoned.

29   **B**   The full salary of A Pay is a cost that will be incurred whether or not the project goes ahead, and so the relevant cost of his allocated salary cost is nil. Relevant staff costs are as follows.

	£
Salaries of Ray Peer and Chris Swords (incurred if the project goes ahead)	40,000
less Redundancy payments (incurred if the project is abandoned)	18,000
Net relevant costs	22,000

30   **A**   The allocation of general fixed overheads is not a relevant cost for the decision. Depreciation is a notional (non-cash) cost and should be ignored. The only relevant cost is the loss of disposal value on the plant and machinery.

	£
Revenue if plant is sold now	18,000
Revenue if plant is sold in 1 year's time	11,000
Relevant cost of using plant for 1 year	7,000

31   **B**   This is the definition of a histogram.

32   **C**

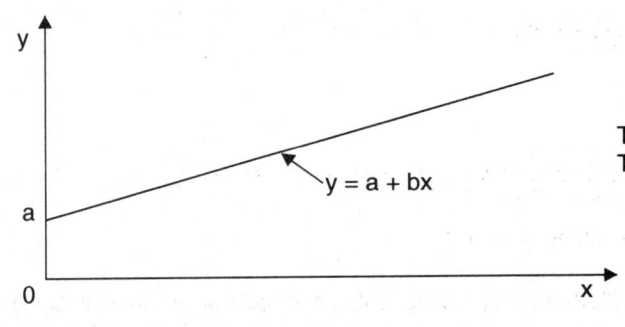

The gradient is b.
The intercept on the y axis is a.

33   **A** $\text{Mean} = \dfrac{\Sigma x}{n} = \dfrac{2 + x + 4 - x + 9}{5} = 3$

34   **D** $80 = \dfrac{(100 \times 50) + (100 \times 70) + (200 \times x)}{100 + 100 + 200}$

∴ $80 \times 400 = 5{,}000 + 7{,}000 + 200x$
$32{,}000 - 12{,}000 = 200x$
$20{,}000 = 200x$
∴ $x = 100$

35   **D**

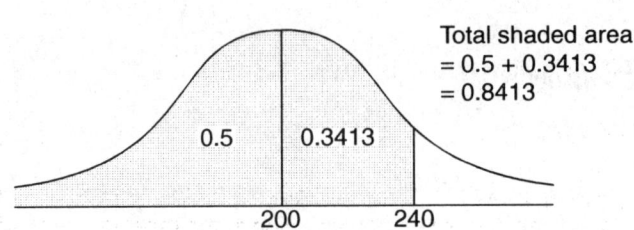

Total shaded area
= 0.5 + 0.3413
= 0.8413

36   C   Paasche price index number $= 100 \times \dfrac{\Sigma Q_1 P_1}{\Sigma Q_1 P_0}$

	P_0	P_1	Q_1	$Q_1 P_0$	$Q_1 P_1$
A	5	6	2,200	11,000	13,200
B	8	10	2,500	20,000	25,000
				31,000	38,200

Index for 19X5 on 19X1 $= \dfrac{38,200}{31,000} \times 100$

$= 123.23$

37   A   We have significant negative correlation.

38   A   The best straight line is approximately a line joining (0, 50) to (75, 0) which has a gradient of −0.67. This gradient is the same as the regression coefficient b.

39   B $\dfrac{\left(p^4\right)^7}{p^2} = p^{4 \times 7 - 2} = p^{26}$

40   C

Time	Flow £	Discount Factor 10%	NPV £
0	(10,000)	1.000	(10,000)
2 - 7	2,000	*3.959	7,918
			(2,082)

* 4.868 − 0.909

41   D   Mean $= \dfrac{\text{Sum of values of items}}{\text{number of items}}$

$= \dfrac{\left(11 \times \pounds 17\right) + \left(16 \times \pounds 14\right)}{27}$

$= \pounds 15.22$

42   A   By trial and error, the option satisfying the expression is a = −2.

43   C   95% confidence limits will be given by

$\bar{x} \pm 1.96 \dfrac{\sigma}{\sqrt{n}}$ $= \bar{x} \pm 1.96 \dfrac{s}{\sqrt{n}}$

$= 65 \pm 1.96 \dfrac{4}{\sqrt{260}}$

$= 65 \pm 0.486$

44   D   Monthly rate of interest $= (1.12)^{1/12} - 1 = 0.0095 = 1\%$

Using cumulative present value tables for 1% and for 12 instalments the present value is £1,000 × 11.26 = £11,260.

45   C $2X^2 = 2$, $Y^2 = 4$, $2 < 4$, $4 > 0$.

46   D   R   =   2PC/B(N+1)
N+1   =   2PC/BR
N   =   (2PC/BR) - 1

47   D   I confuses the correlation coefficient with the equation of the regression line. The proportion of the variation in one variable explained by variation in the other is $r^2 = (-0.5)^2 = 0.25 = 25\%$.

48 A Assume that £100 is spent in total.

Unit price £			Units bought
4	20/4	=	5.00
8	20/8	=	2.50
10	20/10	=	2.00
16	20/16	=	1.25
20	20/20	=	1.00
			11.75

Mean price = £100/11.75 = £8.51

49 D *Disk   Programs*

D1   P1, P2 (both perfect)
D2   P3 (perfect), P4 (faulty)
D3   P5, P6 (both faulty)

The first program inspected was one of P1, P2 and P3, with equal probability. In two out of these three possibilities (P1 and P2), the other program on the disk will be perfect, so the required probability is 2/3.

50 D

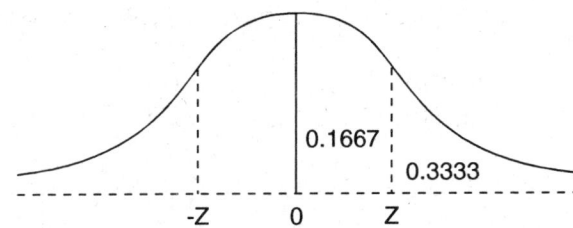

The area under the normal curve between the mean and 0.43 standard deviations above the mean is (from tables) 0.1664.

51 A Arithmetic mean = (1 + 1 + 5 + 7 + 2 + 8 + 3 + 5 + 5 + 3)/10 = 40/10 = 4

Percentages in order: 1 1 2 3 3 5 5 5 7 8

Median = (3 + 5)/2 = 4

Difference = 4 – 4 = 0

52 D

53 D $\sqrt{Y}$ = (–8)^2 – 2 (–8) + 1 = 64 + 16 + 1 = 81

Y = 81^2 = 6,561

54 A From tables, present value = £50,000 × 0.772 = £38,600

55 D

56 C X = 1.65 × £25/$\sqrt{250}$ = £2.61

57 C September: x = 8

∴ Sales in £'000 = (520 + (17 × 8)) × 97% = 656 × 97% = £636,320

58 B 6,000 units is $\dfrac{10,000 - 6,000}{2,000}$ = 2 standard deviations below the mean.

From tables, the required probability is 0.5 – 0.4772 = 0.0228.

59 C From tables, the present value of £1 in three years time at 10% is £0.751.

The sum of money receivable in three years with a present value of £5,000 is therefore £5,000/0.751 = £6,658.

60   D   The rankings are as follows.

		2	4	6	1	5	3	7	
		4	3	5	2	6	1	7	
$\lvert d\rvert$	=	2	1	1	1	1	2	0	
d^2	=	4	1	1	1	1	4	0	$\Sigma d^2 = 12$

$$R\ (\text{rank}) = 1 - \left(\frac{6 \times 12}{7(49 - 1)} \right)$$
$$= 1 - 0.21$$
$$= 0.79$$

Illustrative questions and suggested solutions

Examination standard questions are indicated by marks and time allocations.

1. DISHWASHERS

The costs listed below have been estimated for the forthcoming year for a company which makes dishwashers.

	£'000
Energy costs and water (heating and general)	20
Electricity for machines	14
Rent and rates	180
Repairs and maintenance: machinery	25
buildings	10
Raw materials	750
Maintenance of patterns and jigs	45
Direct wages	1,040
Direct wages related costs	115
Foremen's wages	83
Indirect wages related costs	10
Production management salaries	133
Depreciation of machinery	150
Security	10
Inspection and commissioning (production)	60
Carriage on raw materials	49
Carriage outwards	88
Salesmen's salaries and commissions	100
Salesmen's expenses	50
Design and estimating related to sales function	75
General management and administration	32
Advertising	40
Accounts	100

REQUIREMENT:

Identify which of these costs are production overheads, which are selling and distribution overheads, which are administration overheads and which overheads are shared between the three categories and calculate the total for each category and for shared costs.

2. COST BEHAVIOUR

Show, by means of a sketch, a separate graph of cost behaviour patterns for each of the listed items of expense. You should label the axes of each graph clearly.

(a) Electricity bill: a standing charge for each period plus a charge for each unit of electricity consumed.

(b) Supervisory labour.

(c) Production bonus, which is payable when output in a period exceeds 10,000 units. The bonus amounts in total to £20,000 plus £50 per unit for additional output above 10,000 units.

(d) Sales commission, which amounts to 2% of sales turnover.

(e) Machine rental costs of a single item of equipment. The rental agreement is that £10 should be paid for every machine hour worked each month, subject to a maximum monthly charge of £480.

3. **EFFECTIVE STOCK CONTROL**

Describe the essential requirements of an effective material stock control system.

4. **STOCK ITEM - CODE NUMBER 988988**

The bin card for stock item code no 988988 in a small company's stores contains the following information for the month of June 19X1.

Opening stock 1 June: 60 units, value £360.

Date	Receipts Units	Supplier's invoice price per unit £	Issues Units
5 June	120	5.90	
10 June			80
14 June	40	6.05	
17 June			80
20 June	20	6.20	
24 June			80
25 June	100	6.30	

The current average market price per unit was £6 on 1 June, rising to £6.20 on 10 June, £6.25 on 15 June and £6.40 on 30 June.

The following methods of stock pricing are being considered.

(a) FIFO
(b) LIFO
(c) Periodic weighted average
(d) Cumulative weighted average
(e) Standard cost
(f) Replacement cost

REQUIREMENT:

Use each of these methods to show the following.

(a) The cost of each batch of materials issued to production
(b) The value of closing stock at 30 June

For the standard cost method of evaluation you should assume that the standard cost per unit of Item No 988988 is £6.

5. **COMPONENTS A, B AND C**

A factory manufactures three components A, B and C.

During week 26, the following was recorded.

Labour grade	Number of employees	Rate per hour £	Individual hours worked
I	6	4.00	40
II	18	3.20	42
III	4	2.80	40
IV	1	1.60	44

Output and standard times during the same week were as follows.

Component	Output	Standard minutes (each)
A	444	30
B	900	54
C	480	66

The normal working week is 38 hours. Overtime is paid at a premium of 50% of the normal hourly rate.

A group incentive scheme is in operation. The time saved is expressed as a percentage of hours worked and is shared between the group as a proportion of the hours worked by each grade.

The rate paid is 75% of the normal hourly rate.

REQUIREMENT:

Calculate the total payroll showing the basic pay, overtime premium and bonus pay as separate totals for each grade of labour.

6. ABSORPTION RATES

Outline the procedures and information required in order to establish a set of predetermined production overhead absorption rates for a company manufacturing a range of different products in a factory containing a number of production departments and several service departments.

7. MARGINAL AND ABSORPTION   *27 mins*

X Ltd commenced business on 1 March making one product only, the standard cost of which is as follows.

	£
Direct labour	5
Direct material	8
Variable production overhead	2
Fixed production overhead	5
Standard production cost	20

The fixed production overhead figure has been calculated on the basis of a budgeted normal output of 36,000 units per annum.

You are to assume that all the budgeted fixed expenses are incurred evenly over the year. March and April are to be taken as equal period months.

Selling, distribution and administration expenses are as follows.

Fixed	£120,000 per annum
Variable	15% of the sales value

The selling price per unit is £35 and the number of units produced and sold was as follows.

	March Units	*April* Units
Production	2,000	3,200
Sales	1,500	3,000

REQUIREMENTS:

(a) Prepare profit statements for each of the months of March and April using the following.

    (i)   Marginal costing

    (ii)   Absorption costing   **10 Marks**

(b) Present a reconciliation of the profit or loss figure given in your answers to (a) (i) and (a) (ii) accompanied by a brief explanation.   **5 Marks**

Total Marks = 15

8. MAKE OR BUY DECISION   *27 mins*

A company manufactures and sells three components, but has requested its purchasing manager to investigate the prices of an overseas producer. The following costs and prices are made available.

Component	X	Y	Z
Production (units)	20,000	40,000	80,000
	£	£	£
Direct material cost, per unit	0.80	1.00	0.40
Direct labour cost, per unit	1.60	1.80	0.80
Direct expense cost, per unit	0.40	0.60	0.20
Fixed cost per unit	0.80	1.00	0.40
Selling price each	4.00	5.00	2.00
Imported price	2.75	4.20	2.00

REQUIREMENTS:

(a) Produce recommendations to management as to whether any component should be purchased on the basis of cost only.   **4 Marks**

(b) Calculate the profit the company will make by producing all the components itself.   **3 Marks**

(c) State if your recommendation in (a) above is likely to affect the profit and by how much.

3 Marks

(d) Assuming management proposes to go ahead and import some of the components, describe matters that you would bring to their attention.**5 Marks**

Total Marks = 15

9. **BAKED POTATO LTD**

The following balances were extracted from the cost accounts of Baked Potato Ltd in November 19X1.

	1st November £	30th November £
Raw materials stock	62,659	77,312
Work in progress: materials	9,288	7,677
Work in progress: labour	5,003	4,684
Work in progress: production overhead	1,251	1,561
Finished goods stock	12,729	14,133

During the month, purchases of raw materials amounted to £96,237 and the total payroll cost to £73,455.

The payroll cost could be analysed as follows.

	£
Direct labour	48,680
Indirect production labour	12,806
Administration labour	4,060
Selling and distribution labour	7,909
	73,455

Included in the issues of raw materials were the following items.

Items valued at £11,355 for factory maintenance
Items valued at £3,978 for office supplies
Items valued at £2,167 for distribution operations

Factory overhead was budgeted at £15,000 and budgeted direct labour cost was £45,000. The absorption rate is based on direct labour cost.

REQUIREMENT:

From the information given, prepare the following accounts for November 19X1.

(a) Raw materials stocks
(b) Wages and salaries cost
(c) Work in progress
(d) Finished goods stock

10. JOB COSTING   *27 mins*

A specialist manufacturer of purpose-built plant engaged in three separate jobs in May 19X3. The following costs were incurred.

	Job A	Job B	Job C
Direct materials purchased	£524	£671	£382
Direct labour			
Skilled (hours)	158	170	16
Semi-skilled (hours)	316	190	30
Site expenses	£118	£170	£25
Selling price of job	£3,318	£2,750	£1,950
Completed at 31 May 19X3	100%	80%	25%

The following information is available.

Direct materials for the completion of the jobs have been recorded.

Direct labour rates: skilled £5 per hour; semi-skilled £4 per hour.

Site expenses tend to vary with output.

Administration expenses total £440 per month and are to be allocated to the jobs on a labour hour basis.

On completion of the work the practice of the manufacturer is to divide the calculated profit on each job 20% to site staff as a bonus, 80% to the company. Calculated losses are absorbed by the company in total.

REQUIREMENTS:

(a) Calculate the profit or loss made by the company on Job A.   **3 Marks**

(b) Project the profit or loss made by the company on Jobs B and C.   **8 Marks**

(c) Comment on any matters you think relevant to management as a result of your calculations.   **4 Marks**

Total Marks = 15

11. PROCESS X   *27 mins*

Bonto Ltd produces a simple product in two processes, process R and process X. The following information relates to process X for period 4.

Work in progress at start of period - nil.
Material transferred from process R during the period - 2,500 kgs valued at £7,145.
Wages paid - 234½ hours at £4 per hour.
Other direct costs allocated - £463.
Normal waste during processing - 5% of process R input. This has a scrap value of 16p per kg and is credited to the process account.
At the end of period 4 there were 2,100 kgs transferred to finished stock, and 150 kgs remained in work in progress.
The work in progress is 100% complete so far as materials are concerned, but only 80% of labour costs and 60% of other direct costs have been incurred.

REQUIREMENT:

Construct the process X account, showing your workings clearly.   **15 Marks**

12. TWO HOSPITALS   *27 mins*

The following information relates to two hospitals for the year ended 31 December 19X5.

	St Matthew's	St Mark's
Number of in-patients	15,400	710
Average stay per in-patient	10 days	156 days
Total number of out-patient attendances	130,000	3,500
Number of available beds	510	320
Average number of beds occupied	402	307

Cost analysis	*In-patients* £	*Out-patients* £	*In-patients* £	*Out-patients* £
Patient care services				
Direct treatment services and supplies (eg nursing staff)	6,213,900	1,076,400	1,793,204	70,490
Medical supporting services:				
Diagnostic (eg pathology)	480,480	312,000	22,152	20,650
Other services (eg occupational therapy)	237,160	288,600	77,532	27,790
General services				
Patient related (eg catering)	634,480	15,600	399,843	7,700
General (eg administration)	2,196,760	947,700	1,412,900	56,700

Note. In-patients are those who receive treatment whilst remaining in hospital. Out-patients visit hospital during the day to receive treatment.

REQUIREMENTS:

(a) Prepare a statement showing the following for each hospital for each cost heading.

 (i) Cost per in-patient day, in £ to two decimal places

 (ii) Cost per out-patient attendance, in £ to two decimal places   **8 Marks**

(b) Calculate for each hospital the bed-occupation percentage.   **2 Marks**

(c) Comment briefly on your findings.   **5 Marks**

Total Marks = 15

13. MASTER BUDGET

Outline the organisation required for the preparation of a master budget.

14. TWO THINGS

(a) Describe briefly the benefits to cash budgeting from the use of a particular type of software package.

(b) Give three reasons why the reported profit figure for a period does not normally represent the amount of cash generated in that period.

15. DOODLE LTD   *27 mins*

Doodle Ltd manufactures and sells a range of products, one of which is the squiggle.

The following data relates to the expected costs of production and sale of the squiggle.

Budgeted production for the year	11,400 units
Standard details for one unit:	
direct materials	30 metres at £6.10 per metre
direct wages	
Department P	40 hours at £2.20 per hour
Department Q	36 hours at £2.50 per hour

Budgeted costs and hours per annum
Variable production overhead (factory total)

Department P	£525,000 : 700,000 hours
Department Q	£300,000 : 600,000 hours

Fixed overheads to be absorbed by the squiggle

Production	£1,083,000 (absorbed on a direct labour hour basis)
Administration	£125,400 (absorbed on a unit basis)
Marketing	£285,000 (absorbed on a unit basis)

REQUIREMENTS:

(a) Prepare a standard cost sheet for the squiggle, to include the following.

    (i)   Standard total direct cost
    (ii) Standard variable production cost
    (iii) Standard production cost
    (iv) Standard full cost of sale   **13 Marks**

(b) Calculate the standard sales price per unit which allows for a standard profit of 10% on the sales price.   **2 Marks**

                                                            Total Marks = 15

16. SUMMARY PRODUCTION BUDGET   *27 mins*

A four-week summary production budget for LB Ltd, an organisation which produces a single product, is as follows.

Production quantity	240,000 units
Production costs	
Material	336,000 kg at £4.10 per kg
Direct labour	216,000 hours at £4.50 per hour
Overheads	£1,920,000

Overheads are absorbed at a predetermined direct labour hour rate.

During the four-week period the actual production was 220,000 units which incurred the following costs.

Material	313,060 kg costing £1,245,980
Direct labour	194,920 hours costing £886,886
Overheads	£1,934,940

REQUIREMENTS:

(a) Calculate the cost variances for the period.   **12 Marks**

(b) Give reasons why the direct labour efficiency variance may have arisen.
                                                                        3 Marks

                                                            Total Marks = 15

17. BEATLES

The following spreadsheet is designed to process monthly payroll deductions for four employees, John, Paul, George and Ringo. They pay income tax at 25% and national insurance at 10%. The necessary formulae have not yet been input.

	A	B	C	D	E
1		*John*	*Paul*	*George*	*Ringo*
2	Gross pay	1,500	1,200	1,400	1,300
3					
4	Income tax				
5	National Insurance				
6	Total deductions				
7					
8	Net Pay				
9					
10					

REQUIREMENT:

Devise suitable formulae for the following cells.

(a) Cell B4
(b) Cell C5
(c) Cell D6
(d) Cell E8

18.   RODEO ROUND-UP LTD

Rodeo Round-up Ltd is a company of circus performers which tours the country. Box office takings for the recent month have been as follows.

Venue	*Box office receipts*
	£
Clapham	3,480
West Riding	5,278
Weston-super-Mare	1,356
Badminton	2,542
Huntingdon	3,174
Epsom	2,603
Ascot	1,539
Wincanton	4,562
Reading	4,328

REQUIREMENTS:

(a) Approximate the above data to the nearest £100.

(b) Estimate the absolute and relative maximum errors in the total of your rounded data.

(c) State the actual error in your total.

19.   SAMPLING METHODS   27 *mins*

(a) Sampling methods are frequently used for the collection of data. Explain the terms simple random sampling, stratified random sampling and sampling frame.   **6 Marks**

(b) Suggest a suitable sampling frame for each of the following in which statistical data will be collected.

   (i)   An investigation into the reactions of workers in a large factory to new proposals for shift working.   **1 Mark**

   (ii)   A survey of students at a college about the relevance and quality of the teaching for their professional examinations.   **1 Mark**

   (iii) An enquiry into the use of home computers by school children in a large city.   **1 Mark**

(c) Explain briefly, with reasons, the type of sampling method you would recommend in each of the three situations given above.   **6 Marks**

Total Marks = 15

20.   PARROTS LTD

Illustrate the following data by means of a histogram and an ogive.

The distribution of average weekly wages paid to direct labour employees at the factory of Parrots Ltd is as follows.

Weekly average wage	Number of employees
£	
51 and < 56	5
56 and < 61	8
61 and < 66	12
66 and < 71	16
71 and < 76	21
76 and < 81	25
81 and < 86	20
86 and < 91	14
91 and < 96	6
96 and < 101	3

21.   JOURNEY TIMES   *27 mins*

(a) Set out the advantages and disadvantages of the mean, median, and mode as measures of central tendency.   **3 Marks**

(b) Journey times to work of employees of a company were as follows.

Time Minutes	No of employees
less than 10	14
10 but " " 20	26
20 " " " 30	64
30 " " " 40	46
40 " " " 50	28
50 " " " 60	16
60 " " " 80	8
80 " " " 100	4

REQUIREMENTS:

(i)   Obtain the mean, median and mode of travel time to work.   **10 Marks**

(ii)   Negotiations are under consideration for payment for average travelling time to work. State, giving reasons, which measure of central tendency you would use if you are (1) the employer, and (2) a trade union representing the employees.   **2 Marks**

Total Marks = 15

22.   TITE FIST LTD

Tite Fist Ltd's payroll for one week in 19X5 was as follows.

Weekly earnings	Number of employees
£	
30 and < 40	6
40 and < 50	11
50 and < 60	32
60 and < 70	40
70 and < 80	45
80 and < 90	23
90 and < 100	3

REQUIREMENTS:

(a) Calculate the coefficient of variation.

(b) Explain the meaning of the coefficient of variation in this example.

23. LA PASSION SPARES LTD *27 mins*

La Passion Spares Ltd has been in business for ten years, and now has four independent divisions operating in four different product markets. Results for the ten years have been as follows.

	Division A		Division B		Division C		Division D	
	Sales volume '000 units	Value £m	Sales volume '000 units	Value £m	Sales volume '000 units	Value £m	Sales volume '000 units	Value £m
19X0	3.0	0.30	-	-	-	-	-	-
19X1	3.2	0.32	-	-	-	-	-	-
19X2	3.5	0.37	1.0	0.20	-	-	-	-
19X3	3.6	0.40	1.4	0.29	-	-	-	-
19X4	3.8	0.44	1.5	0.32	0.8	0.08	-	-
19X5	3.9	0.47	1.8	0.43	1.0	0.11	4.0	0.25
19X6	4.0	0.52	2.1	0.51	1.2	0.14	4.3	0.30
19X7	4.2	0.57	2.2	0.55	1.3	0.16	4.2	0.32
19X8	4.0	0.56	2.4	0.67	1.5	0.20	4.4	0.35
19X9	3.0	0.33	2.5	0.75	1.0	0.14	4.6	0.41

The company wishes to establish an index to measure changes in the volume of the business. 19X5 is to be the base year.

REQUIREMENTS:

(a) Calculate the index figure for 19X9 using:

  (i) the Laspeyre method;
  (ii) the Paasche method. **10 Marks**

  Note that you should first calculate unit selling prices.

(b) Explain why 19X5, and not 19X0 (the year the company began operations) was chosen as the base year. **2 Marks**

(c) Explain why the Paasche index might be preferable to the Laspeyre index in this example. **3 Marks**

Total Marks = 15

24. ACE

Calculate the following probabilities.

(a) Drawing two aces from a pack of 52 playing cards in two successive draws (with and without replacement).

(b) Drawing the ace of hearts and the ace of spades in that order (assuming replacement).

(c) Selecting from a list of respondents to a questionnaire used in a sample survey from which it was found that 50% owned their own homes, 60% owned a car and 90% had a television set, a respondent who owned:

  (i) his home and a car;
  (ii) all three of the above assets;
  (iii) none of the above assets.

25. BATTERIES

A company produces batteries whose lifetimes are normally distributed with a mean of 100 hours. It is known that 96% of the batteries last at least 40 hours.

(a) Estimate the standard deviation lifetime.

(b) Calculate the percentage of batteries that will last less than 57 hours

26. HOUND CAMPING LTD

(a) The treasurer of Hound Camping Ltd had to invest some surplus cash. He decided on the following investments.

   (i) £8,000 was placed in a bank deposit account for three years. The expected annual rate of interest is 11%, calculated yearly.

   (ii) £15,000 was placed in a savings account for five years, with interest added yearly at 14%.

   (iii) £6,000 was placed in an account for four years where the annual interest rate is expected to be 10% for the first two years and 15% in years 3 and 4, with interest added at the end of each year.

How much interest will be earned in total from the three investments?

(b) The treasurer is also aware of three other investments.

   (i) Investment A would last for three years, and pay interest at a nominal rate of 10.5%. Interest would be added every half year, compound.

   (ii) Investment B would last for five years, with a nominal interest rate of 12%, payable monthly.

   (iii) Investment C would last for four years, with a nominal interest rate of 12%, payable quarterly.

Compare investments A, B and C with the investments in (a)(i), (a)(ii) and (a)(iii) respectively, and decide which is the better investment, A or (a)(i), B or (a)(ii), and C or (a)(iii).

27. DAISY HOOF LTD

Daisy Hoof Ltd is considering a project to purchase some equipment which would have the following cash flows.

Year	Cash flow £
0	(50,000)
1	18,000
2	25,000
3	15,000
4	10,000

The estimated trade-in value of the equipment, which is £2,000, has not been included in the cash flows above.

The company has a cost of capital of 16%.

REQUIREMENTS:

Calculate the following.

(a) The NPV of the project

(b) The IRR of the project

28. HOPWOOD TRENDS LTD

The quarterly sales of Hopwood Trends Ltd in recent years have been as follows.

Quarter	1 Units	2 Units	3 Units	4 Units
19X2	200	110	320	240
19X3	214	118	334	260
19X4	220	124	340	278

REQUIREMENTS:

(a) Calculate a moving average of quarterly sales.
(b) Calculate the average seasonal variations.

29.   SMALL COMPANY   *27 mins*

A small company has recorded the following data on volumes and costs of production for the last ten months.

Production ('000 units)	10	4	6	9	10	8	5	7	11	12
Costs (£'000)	15	11	12	19	22	20	16	13	24	20

	Production	*Costs*
Sums	82	172
Sums of squares	736	3,136

REQUIREMENTS:

(a) Find the appropriate least-squares regression line so that costs may be predicted from the level of production.   **6 Marks**

(b) State the fixed costs of the factory.   **1 Mark**

(c) Plot a scatter diagram of the data, including the regression line.   **5 Marks**

(d) By the method you consider most appropriate, predict the costs of production for next month when output is scheduled to be 10,000 units and assess the likely reliability of your prediction.   **3 Marks**

Total Marks = 15

1   DISHWASHERS

	Total £'000	Production £'000	Selling and distribution £'000	Administration £'000	Shared costs £'000
Energy costs and water (heating and general)	20				20
Electricity for machines	14	14			
Rent and rates	180				180
Repairs and maintenance:					
machinery	25	25			
buildings	10				10
Maintenance of patterns and jigs	45	45			
Direct wages related costs	115	115			
Foremen's wages	83	83			
Indirect wages related costs	10	10			
Production management salaries	133	133			
Depreciation of machinery	150	150			
Security	10				10
Inspection and commissioning	60	60			
Carriage outwards	88		88		
Salesmen's salaries and commissions	100		100		
Salesmen's expenses	50		50		
Design and estimating related to sales function	75		75		
General management and administration	32			32	
Advertising	40		40		
Accounts	100			100	
	1,340	635	353	132	220

2   COST BEHAVIOUR

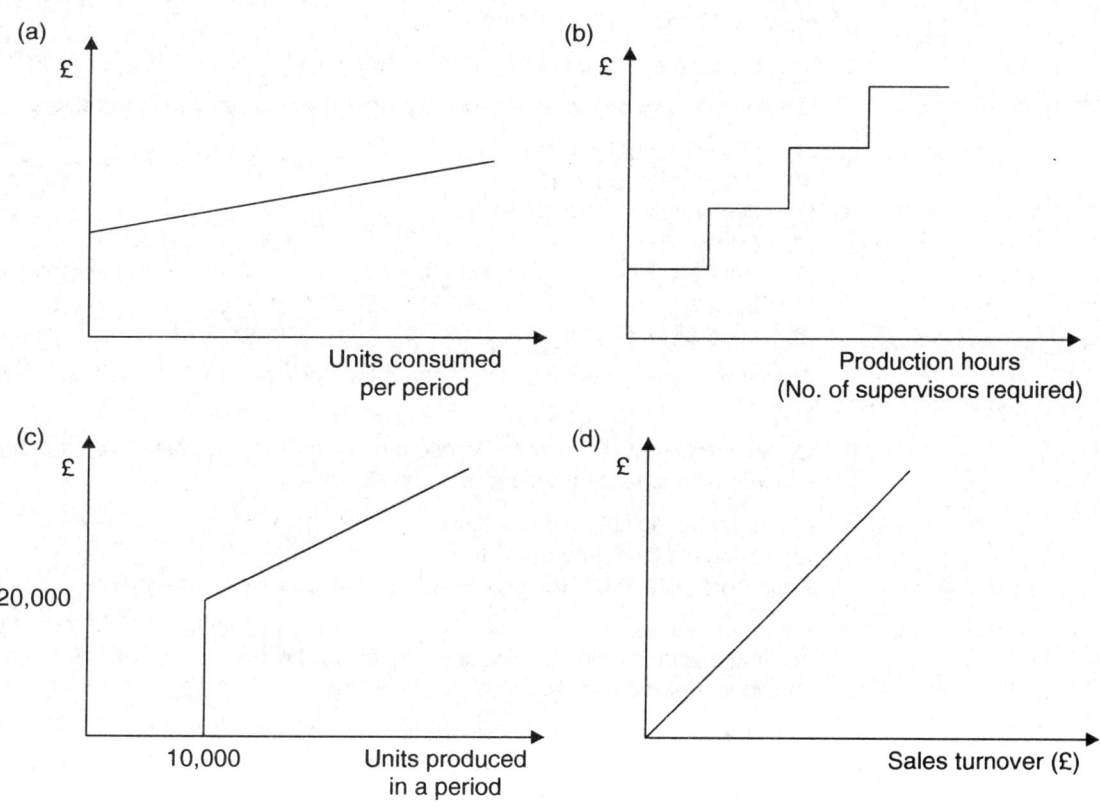

(e)

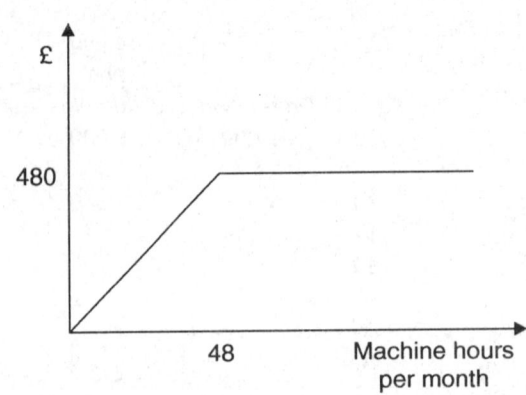

3   **EFFECTIVE STOCK CONTROL**

The requirements of an effective material stock control system may be considered under the headings of physical control, clerical control and stock checks.

(a)   *Physical control*

(i)   Goods should be kept in a secure place (restricted access, separately identifiable and so on).

(ii)   They should be kept in a place where they do not deteriorate too quickly.

(iii)   Different types of goods should be kept separately.

(iv)   The location of the goods should be clearly labelled.

(v)   A maximum stock level for each item should be established; its level should not rise above this.

(vi)   A reorder level should be established; when the level is reached, more of the item should be ordered.

(vii)   As goods are received into stock, they should be counted and checked for quality.

(b)   *Clerical control*

(i)   All movements of stock (in and out) should be immediately recorded (this is the essence of good clerical control).

(ii)   Usually, such a record is maintained in two ways.

On stores ledger accounts. These give the following detailed information.

(1)   Quantity received into stores
(2)   Description (such as part numbers)
(3)   Date received into stores
(4)   Price paid
(5)   Reference (so that the corresponding record in the accounting system may be traced)
(6)   Details (1), (2), (3) and (5) for issues from stores

The combination of details (1)-(6) gives the balance of stock still held at any moment in time.

On bin cards (not mandatory). These are normally kept at the location of the item. At a minimum the details on these would be as follows.

(1)   Date of receipt, and quantity
(2)   Date of issue, and quantity
(3)   From (1) and (2), the number of units of the item remaining

Either stores ledger accounts or bin cards would also contain information about maximum and reorder levels; comparison of the balance of physical stock to these should trigger the necessary course of action.

(iii)   Replacement goods should only be ordered on proper authority; this would normally involve purchase requisition forms signed by a senior manager.

(iv)   Replacement goods should only be received into stock once their quality and quantity have been checked; these checks would normally be evidenced by the stores manager's signature on the goods received note.

(v)   Goods should only be issued from stores into production on proper authority; such authority should be properly evidenced.

(c)   *Stock checks*

The efficacy of both physical and clerical controls is considerably enhanced if the stock is physically counted on a regular basis and this amount is then compared to the quantity on the stores ledger accounts.

Four further points should also be made.

(i)   A physical stocktake should occur at least annually (it is often useful to have it coincide with the business year end).

(ii)   However, some firms organise their stocktakes on a cyclical basis: at regular intervals throughout the year a proportion of the items of stock are counted, so that by the end of the year, all elements of stock have been considered. This method of stocktaking is described as continuous.

(iii)   Once the physical quantity of stock has been established, the clerical records should immediately be amended if necessary to reflect reality.

(iv)   The reason for the difference between physical and book stock should be established; if it represents a control failure steps should be taken to ensure that such an occurrence does not happen again.

4   STOCK ITEM-CODE NUMBER 988988

The purchase costs in June were as follows.

5 June	120	units at £5.90	708
14 June	40	units at £6.05	242
20 June	20	units at £6.20	124
25 June	100	units at £6.30	630
	280	units	1,704
Value of opening stock	60	units at £6.00	360
	340		2,064

(a)   *FIFO*

			Value
Issues		*Workings*	£
10 June		60 units at £6.00	
	plus	20 units at £5.90	478
17 June		80 units at £5.90	472
24 June		20 units at £5.90	
	plus	40 units at £6.05	
	plus	20 units at £6.20	484
Cost of issues			1,434
Closing stock		100 units at £6.30	630
			2,064

The cost of materials issued plus the value of closing stock are exactly equal to purchase costs plus opening stock (£2,064).

(b)   *LIFO*

			Value
Issues		*Workings*	£
10 June		80 units at £5.90	472
17 June		40 units at £6.05	
	plus	40 units at £5.90	478
24 June		20 units at £6.20	
	plus	60 units at £6.00	484
Cost of issues			1,434
Closing stock		100 units at £6.30	630
			2,064

Once again, the cost of issues plus the value of closing stock equals £2,064.

(c) *Periodic weighted average*

Cost of receipts in the period (June) + cost of opening stock	£(1,704 + 360)
Number of units received in the period + units in opening stock	280 + 60

Cost per unit issued in the period   £6.0706   per unit

		£	£
Value of opening stock			360
Value of purchases in June			1,704
			2,064
Cost of issues:			
10 June	80 × £6.0706	486	
17 June	80 × £6.0706	486	
24 June	80 × £6.0706	486	
			1,458
Value of closing stock (balancing figure)			606

There is no discrepancy between the cost of purchases and opening stock and the combined value of materials issued and closing stock.

(d) *Cumulative weighted average*

	Units	Value £	Unit price £
Opening stock	60	360	6.0000
5 June receipts	120	708	5.9000
Average price	180	1,068	5.9333
10 June issues	80	475	5.9333
	100	593	5.9333
14 June receipts	40	242	6.0500
New average price	140	835	5.9643
17 June issues	80	477	5.9643
	60	358	5.9643
20 June receipts	20	124	6.2000
New average price	80	482	6.0250
24 June issues	80	482	6.0250
	0	0	0
25 June receipts	100	630	6.3000

	£
Value of issues	
10 June	475
17 June	477
24 June	482
	1,434
Closing stock value	630
	2,064

There is no discrepancy between the combined value of closing stocks plus materials issued, and the costs of purchases.

(e) *Standard cost*

		£
Issue costs		
10 June	80 × £6	480
17 June	80 × £6	480
24 June	80 × £6	480
		1,440
Value of closing stock	100 × £6	600
		2,040

(f)   *Replacement cost*
       Issue costs

			£
10 June	80 × £6.20		496
17 June	80 × £6.25		500
24 June	80 × £6.25		500
			1,496
Closing stock, 30 June	100 × £6.40		640
Value of materials plus closing stock			2,136

5   COMPONENTS A, B AND C

Calculation of overtime premium

Grade	Overtime premium (50% of basic rate) £/hour (a)	Overtime hours payable (b)	Overtime premium £ ((a) × (b))
I	2.00	2 hrs × 6 = 12	24.00
II	1.60	4 hrs × 18 = 72	115.20
III	1.40	2 hrs × 4 = 8	11.20
IV	0.80	6	4.80

Calculation of standard hours produced

Component		Standard hours
A	$444 \times \dfrac{30}{60}$ hours	222
B	$900 \times \dfrac{54}{60}$ hours	810
C	$480 \times \dfrac{66}{60}$ hours	528
		1,560

Actual time taken

Grade		Hours
I	6 × 40 hrs	240
II	18 × 42 hrs	756
III	4 × 40 hrs	160
IV	1 × 44 hrs	44
		1,200

∴ Time saved = (1,560 − 1,200) hrs = 360 hrs

Time saved as a percentage of hours worked = $\dfrac{360}{1,200} \times 100\% = 30\%$

Calculation of bonus payable

Grade	Bonus hours		75% basic rate £	Bonus payable £
I	240 × 30%	= 72.0	× 3.00	216.00
II	756 × 30%	= 226.8	× 2.40	544.32
III	160 × 30%	= 48.0	× 2.10	100.80
IV	44 × 30%	= 13.2	× 1.20	15.84
				876.96

Calculation of total payroll

Grade	Basic pay		£	Overtime premium £	Bonus £	Total £
I	240 × £4.00	=	960.00	24.00	216.00	1,200.00
II	756 × £3.20	=	2,419.20	115.20	544.32	3,078.72
III	160 × £2.80	=	448.00	11.20	100.80	560.00
IV	44 × £1.60	=	70.40	4.80	15.84	91.04
			3,897.60	155.20	876.96	4,929.76

6   ABSORPTION RATES

The first step is to divide the company into cost centres. These usually take the form of direct production cost centres concerned with manufacturing the products. Usually a multi-product firm would have one department (cost centre) for each product and a number of more general production cost centres, such as machining, drilling and so on, acting as a back-up.

In addition to these, the administrative and service facilities should be divided conveniently into 'service' cost centres. The overall objective of the absorption system is to ensure all overhead costs are allocated or apportioned to the final units of production, so that a unit cost can be used subsequently for stock valuations and pricing purposes. The basic cost data should come from the budget for the coming period. In formulating the cost budgets, therefore, regard should be had to the requirements of the absorption costing system. The two are clearly inter-linked and should not be regarded as completely separate systems.

Having achieved this, the service department costs must be reapportioned to production cost centres in as fair a basis as possible. Regard should be had for the use made by each production cost centre of the facilities of that service centre. Very often, reciprocal arrangements between service centres make this process difficult. The maintenance department often have to carry out work in other service departments such as the canteen, but the canteen also provides a service to maintenance. Methods and procedures must be chosen which are not unnecessarily complicated or costly to apply, but which at the same time are fair.

Having arrived at an apportioned overhead cost for each production cost centre, the final stage is to determine an absorption rate for overheads which may be added to direct costs in arriving at unit cost.

Two factors are important here. Firstly determining the basis of absorption (per unit, labour hour, or machine hour and so on) and secondly, the level of activity used (for example budgeted, normal, maximum). Data must therefore be available for each possibility and again the budgets should provide the majority of the information needed.

7   MARGINAL AND ABSORPTION

(a) (i)   PROFIT STATEMENTS FOR MARCH AND APRIL
            (Marginal costing basis)

	March £	March £	April £	April £
Sales		52,500		105,000
Opening stock (at £15 per unit)	-		7,500	
Variable costs of production	30,000		48,000	
	30,000		55,500	
Closing stock	7,500		10,500	
		22,500		45,000
		30,000		60,000
Variable selling, distribution and administration costs		7,875		15,750
Contribution		22,125		44,250
Fixed costs				
Production				
(£5 × 36,000 × 1/12)	15,000		15,000	
Selling, distribution and administration	10,000		10,000	
		25,000		25,000
Net (loss)/profit		(2,875)		19,250

(ii)   PROFIT STATEMENTS FOR MARCH AND APRIL
        (Absorption costing basis)

	March £	March £	April £	April £
Sales		52,500		105,000
Opening stock (at £20 per unit)	-		10,000	
Standard cost of production	40,000		64,000	
	40,000		74,000	
Closing stock	10,000		14,000	
	30,000		60,000	
Under-/(over-) absorbed production overhead (1,000 × £5; 200 × £5)	5,000		(1,000)	
		35,000		59,000
Gross profit		17,500		46,000
Selling, distribution and administration expenses				
Fixed	10,000		10,000	
Variable	7,875		15,750	
		17,875		25,750
Net (loss)/profit		(375)		20,250

(b)   PROFIT RECONCILIATION STATEMENT

	March £	April £
Marginal costing (loss)/profit	(2,875)	19,250
Fixed production overheads b/f in opening stock valuation		(2,500)
Fixed production overhead c/f in closing stock valuation	2,500	3,500
Absorption costing (loss)/profit	(375)	20,250

Under absorption costing, the profit for March is increased because £2,500 of the total fixed production costs incurred is carried forward in the closing stock valuation. This £2,500 results in a corresponding reduction in the April absorption costing profit, but it is outweighed by the £3,500 fixed production costs carried forward in the closing stock valuation.

8   MAKE OR BUY DECISION

(a)

	X £	Y £	Z £
Unit variable costs:			
direct material	0.80	1.00	0.40
direct labour	1.60	1.80	0.80
direct expense	0.40	0.60	0.20
Total variable cost	2.80	3.40	1.40
Imported price	2.75	4.20	2.00
Saving/(increased cost) of purchasing	0.05	(0.80)	(0.60)

On the basis of cost only, component X should be purchased.

(b)

	X £'000	Y £'000	Z £'000	Total £'000
Sales value	80	200	160	440
Variable costs	56	136	112	304
Contribution	24	64	48	136
Fixed costs	16	40	32	88
Profit	8	24	16	48

(c)   The recommendation in (a) will increase profit because of the saving of £0.05 per unit of component X.

∴ Increased profit = £0.05 × 20,000 = £1,000
∴ Total profit will be £49,000

(d)   Matters which managers should consider are as follows.

  (i)   Will the quality be maintained by the overseas producer?

  (ii)   Will continuity of supply be guaranteed?

  (iii) How long is the quoted price fixed for? Will exchange rates cause fluctuations in prices?

  (iv)   Can any profits be earned from the available capacity not used to produce component X?

  (v)   What will be the effect on labour morale of importing requirements of component X?

9   BAKED POTATO LTD

The overhead absorption rate is $33^1/_3$ % of direct labour cost, calculated as follows.

$$\frac{\text{Budgeted overhead}}{\text{Budgeted labour cost}} = \frac{£15,000}{£45,000} = 33^1/_3\text{ \%}$$

(a)

RAW MATERIALS STOCKS

	£		£
Opening stock b/d	62,659	Production overhead	11,355
Purchases (creditors)	96,237	Administration overhead	3,978
		Sales and distribution overhead	2,167
		Work in progress *	64,084
		Closing stock c/d	77,312
	158,896		158,896

* Balancing item

(b)

WAGES AND SALARIES COST

	£		£
Cash and other sundry accounts	73,455	Work in progress	48,680
		Production overhead	12,806
		Administration overhead	4,060
		Sales and distribution overhead	7,909
	73,455		73,455

(c)

WORK IN PROGRESS

	£	£		£	£
Opening stock b/d			Finished goods stock		130,611
Materials	9,288		(balancing item)		
Labour	5,003		Closing stock c/d		
Production overhead	1,251		Materials	7,677	
		15,542	Labour	4,684	
Raw materials stock		64,084	Production overhead	1,561	
Wages and salaries					13,922
(direct labour)		48,680			
Production overhead					
($33^1/_3$% of labour)		16,227			
		144,533			144,533

(d)

FINISHED GOODS STOCK

	£		£
Opening stock b/d	12,729	Cost of sales (balancing item)	129,207
Work in progress	130,611	Closing stock c/d	14,133
	143,340		143,340

10   JOB COSTING

(a)   *Job A*

		£	£
Direct materials			524
Direct labour			
Skilled (158 hours at £5)		790	
Semi-skilled (316 hours at £4)		1,264	
			2,054
Site expenses			118
Administrative expenses			
(474 hours at £0.50 (W))			237
			2,933
Selling price			3,318
Calculated profit			385
Divided: staff bonus 20%			77
profit for company 80%			308
			385

Working

$$\text{Administration expenses absorption rate} = \frac{£440}{880} \text{ per direct labour hour}$$

$$= £0.50 \text{ per direct labour hour}$$

(b)   It is assumed that direct labour costs, site expenses and administration expenses will increase in proportion to the total labour hours required to complete jobs B and C. There will be no further material costs to complete the jobs.

	Job B			*Job C*		
		£	£		£	£
Direct materials			671			382.00
Direct labour						
Skilled	170 hrs at £5.00	850		16 hrs at £5.00	80	
Semi-skilled	190 hrs at £4.00	760		30 hrs at £4.00	120	
Site expenses		170			25	
Administration						
expenses	360 hrs at £0.50	180		46 hrs at £0.50	23	
		1,960			248	
Costs to completion	20/80 × £1,960	490		75/25 × £248	744	
			2,450			992.00
Total costs			3,121			1,374.00
Selling price			2,750			1,950.00
Calculated (loss)/profit			(371)			576.00
Divided: staff bonus (20%)			0			115.20
(Loss)/profit for company			(371)			460.80

(c)   Job B is projected to result in a loss, and management should investigate this and negotiate an increase in the selling price if possible. In particular, the relative costs should be examined. It is possible that all of the skilled work has already been carried out and only unskilled labour is required to complete the job. Job B has a higher proportion of skilled labour than jobs A and C, and management should investigate whether this was allowed for in the estimate.

The reasons for the loss should be established.

(i)   If it is the result of inadequate estimating, the estimation procedure should be reviewed to prevent recurrence.

(ii)   If it is the result of a lack of control over costs, appropriate action should be taken to exercise control in future.

11   **PROCESS X**

Workings

Loss in process	2,500 kgs – (2,100 + 150)kg	= 250 kg
Normal loss	5% × 2,500 kg	= 125 kg
∴ Abnormal loss		= 125 kg

STATEMENT OF EQUIVALENT UNITS OF PRODUCTION

	Total		Equivalent units				
		Materials		Labour		Other direct costs	
	Units	Units	%	Units	%	Units	%
Normal loss	125	0		0		0	
Abnormal loss	125	125	100	125	100	125	100
Finished stock	2,100	2,100	100	2,100	100	2,100	100
Work in progress	150	150	100	120	80	90	60
	2,500	2,375		2,345		2,315	
Costs		*£7,125		£938		£463	
Cost per equivalent unit	£3.60	£3.00		£0.40		£0.20	

* £7,145 less scrap value of normal loss £20 = £7,125.

STATEMENT OF EVALUATION OF WORK IN PROGRESS

	Materials	Labour	Other direct costs	Total
Equivalent units	150	120	90	
Cost per equivalent unit	£3	£0.40	£0.20	
Total value	£450	£48	£18	£516

PROCESS B ACCOUNT

	kg	£		kg	£
Process R	2,500	7,145	Finished stock	2,100	7,560
Wages paid		938	Normal loss - scrap	125	20
Other direct costs		463	Abnormal loss	125	450
			Work in progress	150	516
	2,500	8,546		2,500	8,546

12   **TWO HOSPITALS**

(a) (i) and (ii)

	St Matthew's		St Mark's	
	Cost per in-patient day	Cost per out-patient attendance	Cost per in-patient day	Cost per out-patient attendance
	£	£	£	£
Number of in-patient days *	154,000	-	110,760	-
Number of out-patient attendances	-	130,000	-	3,500
	£	£	£	£
Patient care services				
Direct treatment	40.35	8.28	16.19	20.14
Medical support				
Diagnostic	3.12	2.40	0.20	5.90
Other services	1.54	2.22	0.70	7.94
General services				
Patient related	4.12	0.12	3.61	2.20
General	14.26	7.29	12.76	16.20
Total cost	63.39	20.31	33.46	52.38

* Number of in-patient days = number of in-patients × average stay.

St Matthew's	= 15,400 × 10 days	= 154,000
St Mark's	= 710 × 156 days	= 110,760

(b)   *Bed-occupation percentages*

St Matthew's $= \dfrac{402}{510} \times 100\% = 78.8\%$

St Mark's $= \dfrac{307}{320} \times 100\% = 95.9\%$

(c)   *Cost per in-patient day*

St Mark's has a lower cost than St Matthew's. This is partly due to the fact that St Mark's has a higher bed-occupation percentage, which indicates that this hospital is making more efficient use of the available resources. A higher bed-occupation will mean that the fixed costs are spread over more cost units, thus reducing the unit cost.

Cost per out-patient attendance

St Matthew's has a lower cost in this case, probably owing to the large volume of patients. It is likely that more efficient systems are in operation to cope with the higher activity.

Overview

It is evident from the figures that the two hospitals care for very different types of patient. St Mark's deals with long stays and does not attend to many out-patients. St Matthew's in-patients stay for a short time and are far fewer in number than the out-patients. Despite the use of comparable cost units, caution is therefore necessary before reaching any firm conclusions regarding the relative costs.

13   MASTER BUDGET

(a)   There should be a budget manual. This is a written manual of instructions setting out the responsibilities of individuals, and the procedures and forms and records relating to the preparation of the master budget. The budget manual will also indicate the following.

(i)   The timescale for preparing each part of the budget
(ii)   The individual departmental, operational or functional budgets to be prepared

(b)   Where the business uses a system of standard costing, there should be an organisation/responsibilities for reviewing the standards annually.

(c)   There should be a budget committee, possibly chaired by the chief executive, with members (senior managers) representing every department or operation in the organisation. This committee should have the authority to make decisions about the budget and give instructions accordingly to departmental management.

(d)   There should be a budget officer, possibly a management accountant, to act as secretary to the budget committee, issue committee meeting minutes, chase up late departmental budgets, bring together the master budget into a P & L statement and budgeted balance sheet and so on.

(e)   The departmental/operational budgets required to produce the master budget must be clearly defined and stated in sequence of preparation - for example sales budget, finished goods stock budget, production budget, machine utilisation budget, direct labour budget, materials usage budget, overhead cost centre budgets, cash budget and so on.

Budgeted costs and revenues are built up on the basis of cost centres. There must be a structure of such centres, and managers responsible for the budget of each individual centre.

(f)   In large organisations with subsidiary companies, the budget organisation for the group must provide for budgeting at subsidiary level, followed by budgeting at group level.

(g)   For control purposes, the budget period should be divided up into control periods, and the budgeted revenues, costs and cash flows also divided accordingly.

Budget cost allowances can thus be produced. A budget cost allowance is the cost which a budget centre is expected to incur in a control period.

(h)   A system should exist for reviewing the fixed assets expenditure budget within the framework of the preparation of the annual master budget.

14   TWO THINGS

(a)   The use of a spreadsheet package (such as Supercalc or Lotus 1-2-3) considerably simplifies cash budgeting. A budget can be set up using the usual format, and can then be altered at will, so that the preparer can see the effects of, for instance, increased sales, different debt collection periods and so on. Time is saved, accuracy is improved, and amendments can be made very speedily and easily.

(b)   The principal reasons why profit will not equal cash flow are as follows.

(i)   The 'matching concept' means that costs and revenues do not equal payments and receipts. Revenue is recognised in the profit statement when goods are sold, and any revenue not received recorded as a debtor. Similarly, costs are incurred when a resource is acquired or subsequently used, not when it happens to be paid for.

(ii)   Some items appearing in the profit statement do not affect cash flow. For example, depreciation is a 'non-cash' deduction in arriving at profit.

(iii)   Similarly, items may effect cash flow but not profit. Capital expenditure decisions (apart from depreciation) and stock level adjustments are prime examples.

15   DOODLE LTD

Workings

The budgeted direct labour hours = 11,400 × (40 + 36) = 866,400 direct labour hours.

The fixed production overhead absorption rate = £1.25 per hour (£1,083,000 ÷ 866,400 hours).

The variable production overhead rate (both for costs incurred and absorbed) is:

department P :   75 pence per hour
department Q :   50 pence per hour

STANDARD COST SHEET - THE SQUIGGLE

	£	£
Direct materials: 30 metres at £6.10		183
Direct wages		
Department P: 40 hours at £2.20	88	
Department Q: 36 hours at £2.50	90	
		178
(a) (i) Standard total direct cost		361
Variable production overhead		
Department P: 40 hours at £0.75	30	
Department Q: 36 hours at £0.50	18	
		48
(ii) Standard variable production cost		409
Fixed production overhead: 76 hours at £1.25		95
(iii) Standard production cost		504
Administration overhead (note 1)		11
Marketing overhead (note 2)		25
(iv) Standard cost of sale		540
Standard profit (10% of sales price)		60
(b) Standard sales price		600

Notes

1   £125,400 ÷ 11,400

2   £285,000 ÷ 11,400

16   SUMMARY PRODUCTION BUDGET

(a)   We need to begin by calculating a standard unit cost.

		£
Materials:	1.4 kg (ie 336,000 kg/240,000) × £4.10	5.74
Direct labour:	0.9 hrs (ie 216,000 hrs/240,000) × £4.50	4.05
Overheads:	0.9 hrs × £8 (ie £1,920,000/240,000)	7.20
		16.99

Variances

Material

	£
313,060 kg should have cost (× £4.10)	1,283,546
but did cost	1,245,980
Material price variance	37,566 (F)

220,000 units should have used (× 1.4 kg)	308,000 kg
but did use	313,060 kg
Variance in kgs	5,060 kg (A)
× standard cost per kg	× £4.10
Material usage variance in £	£20,746 (A)

Direct labour

	£
194,920 hrs should have cost (× £4.50)	877,140
but did cost	886,886
Direct labour rate variance	9,746 (A)

220,000 units should have taken (× 0.9 hrs)	198,000 hrs
but did take	194,920 hrs
Variance in hours	3,080 hrs (F)
× standard rate per hour	× £4.50
Direct labour efficiency variance in £	£13,860 (F)

Overheads

	£
Standard overhead absorbed (220,000 × 0.9 × £8)	1,584,000
Actual cost	1,934,940
Overhead variance	350,940 (A)

(b) The favourable *direct labour efficiency variance* may have arisen for one of the following reasons.

   (i)   Better quality material used than anticipated when standard set.

   (ii)   Better quality equipment used than anticipated when standard set

   (iii)   Errors in recording labour time (that is, not all labour time recorded)

   (iv)   Standard too easy to attain

   (v)   Fewer production delays than anticipated

   (vi)   More care with material taken than anticipated, resulting in less material loss than included in standard

   (vii)   Worker motivation

   (viii) Use of more skilled labour than anticipated when standard set

17   BEATLES

(a)   B4 = + B2 * 0.25

(b)   C5 = + C2 *0.10

(c)   D6 = + D4 + D5

(d)   E8 = + E2 – E6

18   RODEO ROUND-UP LTD

(a)

Venue	Receipts, rounded to the nearest £100
	£
Clapham	3,500
West Riding	5,300
Weston-Super-Mare	1,400
Badminton	2,500
Huntingdon	3,200
Epsom	2,600
Ascot	1,500
Wincanton	4,600
Reading	4,300
	28,900

(b)   The maximum error in the rounding for each venue is $\pm £50$. There are nine venues.

(i)   The maximum absolute error is $9 \times \pm £50 =$ $\pm £450$

(ii)   The maximum relative error is $\dfrac{\pm £450}{£28,900} \times 100\% =$ $\pm 1.56\%$

(c)   The actual error is the difference between the actual receipts and the rounded value.

	£
Actual total receipts	28,862
Rounded value of receipts	28,900
Actual error	+38

19   SAMPLING METHODS

(a)   With simple random sampling, the sample is selected in such a way that every item in the population has an equal chance of being included.

A random sample can be selected from the sampling frame by two main methods.

(i)   The lottery method amounts to picking numbered pieces of paper out of a box.

(ii)   Random number tables can be used. This method is to be preferred as it makes bias very unlikely.

In many practical situations it is convenient to use a computer to generate the random numbers to select the items, especially where a large sample is required.

Stratification is in many situations the best method of choosing a sample when the population can be divided into strata. With a random sample there is a small probability that all the items selected will come from one stratum. For example, if seeking a random sample of CIMA students it is possible that the sample selected will consist solely of students for Stage 1. Stratified sampling removes this possibility, as first the population is stratified (divided up into its components, in our example Stage 1 students, Stage 2 students and so on) and then random samples are taken from each stratum. At least some items will therefore be selected from each stratum.

A sampling frame is a list of all the items in a population. An example would be the membership list of the Chartered Institute of Management Accountants, if we wished to estimate the average pay of a member.

(b)   (i)   The sampling frame should be a list of all workers who will be affected by the new proposals. The personnel department should be able to provide such a list.

(ii)   The college registration department should be able to provide a list of all students attending courses which prepare them for their professional examinations.

(iii)   The Education department of the local authority should be able to provide a list of all schoolchildren in the city, or a list of schools which could supply lists of their pupils. These lists of pupils could then be combined to form the sampling frame.

(c)   In the large factory, the recommended type of sampling method would depend on whether the workers affected by the new proposals were homogeneous and in one department, or whether they logically fitted into separate levels of seniority, different departments and so on.

In the former case, simple random sampling would be appropriate. In the latter case, stratified random sampling would be appropriate.

In the college it is likely that the different years of each course would be given separate tuition which was more or less relevant to the professional examinations. Stratified random sampling should therefore be performed, taking as the strata each year of each course.

In the large city, both simple random sampling and stratified random sampling would be prohibitively expensive to carry out. A system such as multi-stage sampling would be more appropriate. A random sample would be taken from each school in a random selection of schools from throughout the city.

20   PARROTS LTD

The total number of employees is 130.

Since every class interval is the same width, £5, no adjustments are necessary in drawing the histogram.

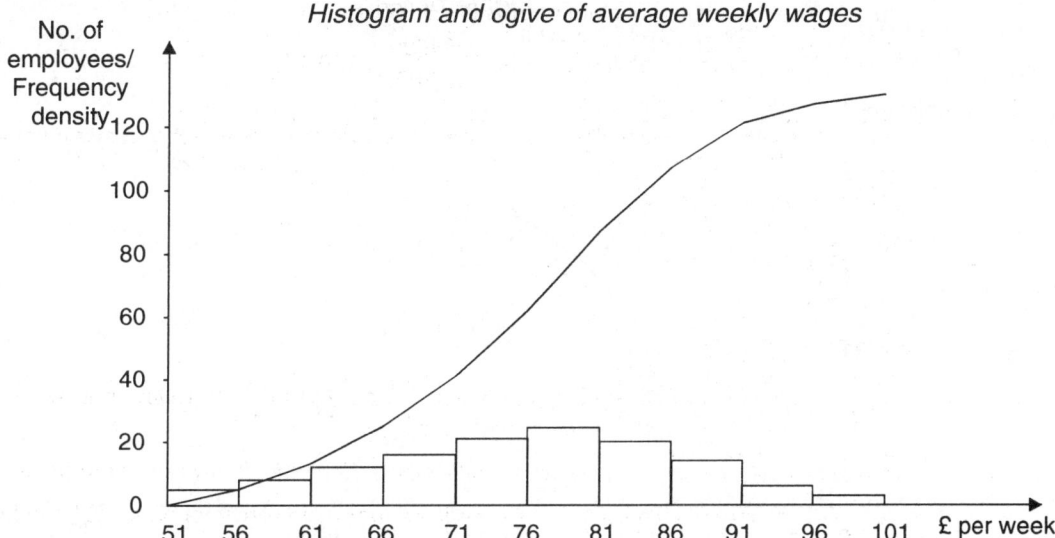

Histogram and ogive of average weekly wages

21   JOURNEY TIMES

(a)   (i)   *The mean*

The mean has the following advantages.

(1)   It is widely understood.
(2)   It uses every value in its computation.
(3)   It gives a unique value.

It does, however, have two major disadvantages.

(1)   It may give an impossible value (eg 2.2 children).
(2)   It may be distorted by extremely high/low values.

(ii)   *The mode*

Advantages of the mode are as follows.

(1)   It is an actual value.
(2)   It is not distorted by extreme values.

It has the following disadvantages.

(1)   It may not be unique.
(2)   It ignores dispersion about the modal value.
(3)   It does not take every value into account.

(iii)   *The median*

The median has the advantage that it is not distorted by extreme values but there is a disadvantage to the median. It does not take every value into account.

(b)   (i)

Times	Midpoint x	Frequency f	fx	Cumulative frequency	Height of histogram bar
0 - 10	5	14	70	14	14
10 - 20	15	26	390	40	26
20 - 30	25	64	1,600	104	64
30 - 40	35	46	1,610	150	46
40 - 50	45	28	1,260	178	28
50 - 60	55	16	880	194	16
60 - 80	70	8	560	202	4(8÷2)
80 - 100	90	4	360	206	2(4÷2)
		206	6,730		

$$\text{Mean } \bar{x} = \frac{\Sigma fx}{\Sigma f} = \frac{6,730}{206} = 32.67 \text{ minutes}$$

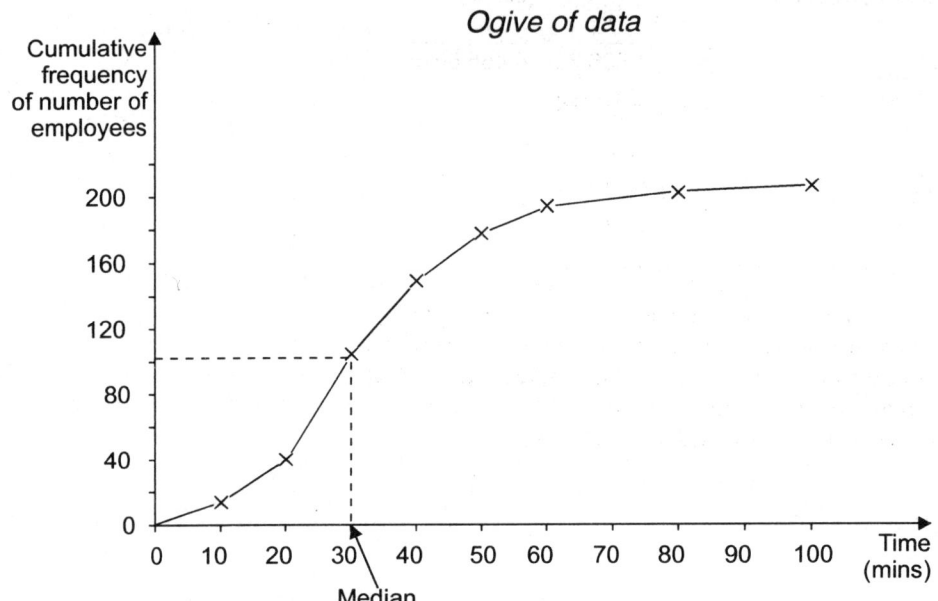

Ogive of data

Median = 30, approximately

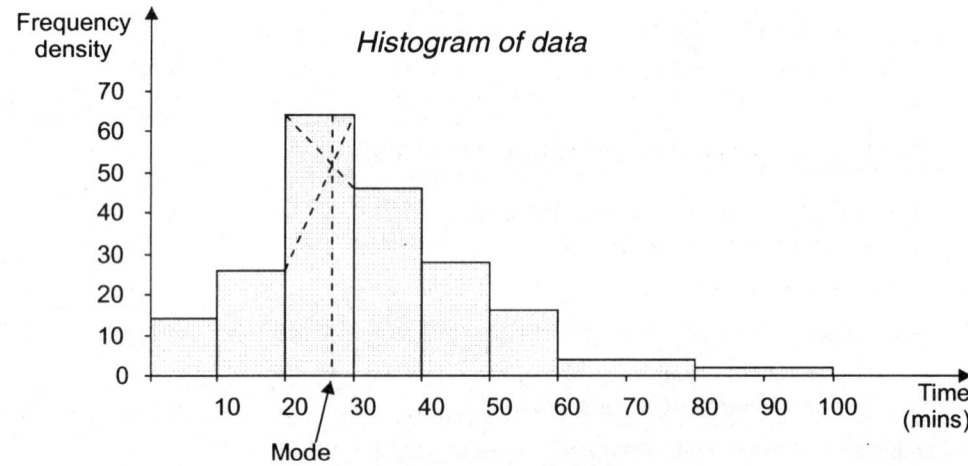

Histogram of data

Mode = 27, approximately

(ii)   (1)   The employer would seek to minimise the amount paid for travelling time. He should therefore choose the mode, perhaps arguing that the modal time is the most representative because the largest number of employees take that long to come to work.

        (2)   The trade union would seek to maximise the amount paid for travelling time. It should therefore choose the mean, perhaps arguing that the mean time is the only average which takes into account the travelling times of *all* employees.

22 TITE FIST LTD

(a) *Mid-point*

x	f	fx	fx²
£			
35	6	210	7,350
45	11	495	22,275
55	32	1,760	96,800
65	40	2,600	169,000
75	45	3,375	253,125
85	23	1,955	166,175
95	3	285	27,075
	160	10,680	741,800

$$\text{Mean} = \frac{10,680}{160} = £66.75$$

$$
\begin{aligned}
\text{Standard deviation} &= \sqrt{\frac{741,800}{160} - (66.75)^2} \\
&= \sqrt{4,636.25 - 4,455.5625} \\
&= \sqrt{180.6875} \\
&= £13.44
\end{aligned}
$$

$$\frac{\text{Standard deviation}}{\text{Mean}} = \frac{£13.44}{£66.75} = 0.20$$

Coefficient of variation = 0.20

(b) The coefficient of variation is a measure of dispersion, being the ratio of the standard deviation to the mean. A coefficient is useful for comparing the relative dispersion of two different distributions. For example, it could be used to compare the dispersion of earnings around the mean in week 1 and the mean in week 2 to see if there is any noticeable change in the variability of earnings among the workforce.

23 LA PASSION SPARES LTD

(a)

	19X5		19X9					
	P_0	Q_0	P_1	Q_1	$Q_1 P_0$	$Q_0 P_0$	$Q_1 P_1$	$Q_0 P_1$
	£	'000s	£	'000s				
A	120.51	3.9	110.00	3.0	361.53	469.99	330.00	429.00
B	238.89	1.8	300.00	2.5	597.22	430.00	750.00	540.00
C	110.00	1.0	140.00	1.0	110.00	110.00	140.00	140.00
D	62.50	4.0	89.13	4.6	287.50	250.00	410.00	356.52
					1,356.25	1,259.99	1,630.00	1,465.52

(i) The Laspeyre volume index for 19X9 based on 19X5 =

$$100 \times \frac{\Sigma Q_1 P_0}{\Sigma Q_0 P_0} = 100 \times \frac{1,356.25}{1,259.99} = 107.64$$

(ii) The Paasche volume index for 19X9 based on 19X5 =

$$100 \times \frac{\Sigma Q_1 P_1}{\Sigma Q_0 P_1} = 100 \times \frac{1,630.00}{1,465.52} = 111.22$$

(b) 19X5 was chosen as the base year because it was the first year in which all divisions were operating. An earlier year would therefore have been an unrepresentative base for an index.

(c) There was a substantial fall in sales volume in division A between 19X5 and 19X9, so an index based on 19X5 quantities will not properly reflect current sales. The Paasche index, using 19X9 volumes, is likely to be preferable in this case to a Laspeyre index because it reflects the new distribution of sales between the divisions.

24   ACE

(a)   *Assuming replacement*

P(Ace) = 4/52 = 1/13

P(Ace on second draw) = 1/13

P(Ace followed by Ace with replacement) = (1/13) × (1/13) = 1/169 .

Without replacement

P(Ace) = 1/13

P(Ace on second draw) = 3/51 = 1/17

P(Ace followed by Ace without replacement) = (1/13) × (1/17) = 1/221

(b)   P(Drawing ace of Hearts) = 1/52

P(Drawing ace of Spades) = 1/52 (if replacement is assumed)

P(Ace of hearts followed by ace of Spades) = (1/52) × (1/52) = 1/2,704

(c)   P(Own Home) = P(H)   = 0.5

P(Own Car) = P(C)   = 0.6

P(Own TV) = P(TV)   = 0.9

(i)   P(Home and Car)   =   P(Home) × P(Car)

=   0.3

(ii)   P(all three owned)   =   P(Home) × P(car) × P(TV)

=   0.27

(iii)   P(None owned)   =   (1 − P(H)) (1 − P(C)) (1 − P(TV))

=   0.5 × 0.4 × 0.1

=   0.02

25   BATTERIES

(a)   96% of batteries have a life exceeding 40 hours. From normal distribution tables, we can ascertain that 96% of the area under the normal curve lies to the right of 1.75 standard deviations below the mean.

Therefore 100 hours − 40 hours = 1.75 standard deviations

$$\text{Standard deviation} = \frac{60 \text{ hours}}{1.75} = 34.3 \text{ hours}$$

(b)   The probability of a battery's life being less than 57 hours is represented by the area to the left of (100 − 57)/34.3 = 1.25 standard deviations below the mean, which is (0.5 − 0.3944). 10.56% of batteries will last less than 57 hours.

26   HOUND CAMPING LTD

(a)   The total value of each investment will be calculated. After deducting the original principal, the interest earned will be found.

		£
(i)	Value at the end of three years = £8,000 × 1.11^3	10,941.0
(ii)	Value at the end of five years = £15,000 × 1.14^5	28,881.2
(iii)	Value at the end of four years = £6,000 × 1.1^2 × 1.15^2	9,601.4
		49,423.6
Less principal (8,000 + 15,000 + 6,000)		29,000.0
Interest earned, in total		20,423.6

(b)   (i)   The effective annual rate of interest of investment A is

$1.0525^2 − 1 = 0.1078 = 10.78\%$

This is a lower return than investment (a)(i), which is therefore preferable.

(ii)   The effective annual rate of interest of investment B is

$1.01^{12} − 1 = 0.1268 = 12.68\%.$

This is less than the return from investment (a)(ii), which is therefore preferable.

(iii)   If investment C were £6,000, it would earn

£6,000 × 1.03^{16} by the end of year 4 = £6,000 × 1.6047= £9,628.20

This would be a slightly better return than that from investment (a)(iii).

27   DAISY HOOF LTD

(a)

Year	Cash flow £	Discount factor 16%	Present value £
0	(50,000)	1.000	(50,000)
1	18,000	0.862	15,516
2	25,000	0.743	18,575
3	15,000	0.641	9,615
4	12,000	0.552	6,624
		NPV	330

(b)   The IRR is a little above 16%. Try 18%.

Year	Cash flow £	Discount factor 18%	Present value £
0	(50,000)	1.000	(50,000)
1	18,000	0.847	15,246
2	25,000	0.718	17,950
3	15,000	0.609	9,135
4	12,000	0.516	6,192
		NPV	(1,477)

Using interpolation, the IRR approximately equals

$$16\% + \left[\frac{330}{330 + 1,477} \times (18 - 16) \right]\% = 16.37\%.$$

28   HOPWOOD TRENDS LTD

(a)

Year	Quarter	Sales	Moving total of 4 quarters' sales	Moving average of 4 quarters' sales	Mid point of moving averages (÷8)	Variation
19X2	1	200				
	2	110				
			870	217.5		
	3	320			219	+101
			884	221.0		
	4	240			222	+18
			892	223.0		
19X3	1	214			225	-11
			906	226.5		
	2	118			229	-111
			926	231.5		
	3	334			232	+102
			932	233.0		
	4	260			234	+26
			938	234.5		
19X4	1	220			235	-15
			944	236.0		
	2	124			238	-114
			962	240.5		
	3	340				
	4	278				

(b)

Year	Quarter	1	2	3	4	Total
19X2				+101	+18	
19X3		−11	−111	+102	+26	
19X4		−15	−114			
		−26	−225	+203	+44	− 4
Unadjusted average		−13.0	−112.5	+101.5	+22.0	−2
Adjustment		+0.5	+0.5	+0.5	+0.5	+2
Adjusted average		−12.5	−112.0	+102.0	+22.5	0

29   SMALL COMPANY

The dependent variable, Y, is cost. The independent variable, X, is production.

$$\Sigma X = 82 \qquad\qquad \Sigma Y = 172$$

$$\Sigma X^2 = 736 \qquad\qquad \Sigma Y^2 = 3{,}136$$

$$\Sigma XY = 10 \times 15 + 4 \times 11 + 6 \times 12 + 9 \times 19 + 10 \times 22 + 8 \times 20 + 5 \times 16 + 7 \times 13 + 11 \times 24 + 12 \times 20 = 1{,}492$$

(a) The regression line is $Y = a + bX$, where $\quad b = \dfrac{n\Sigma XY - \Sigma X\Sigma Y}{n\Sigma X^2 - (\Sigma X)^2}$

$$a = \overline{Y} - b\overline{X}$$

$$b = \frac{10 \times 1{,}492 - 82 \times 172}{10 \times 736 - 82^2} = 1.2830$$

$$a = 17.2 - 1.283 \times 8.2 = 6.68$$

Thus $Y = 6.68 + 1.283X$ (£'000).

(b) When there is no production, X = 0 and Y = 6.68. That is, fixed costs are £6,680.

(c)

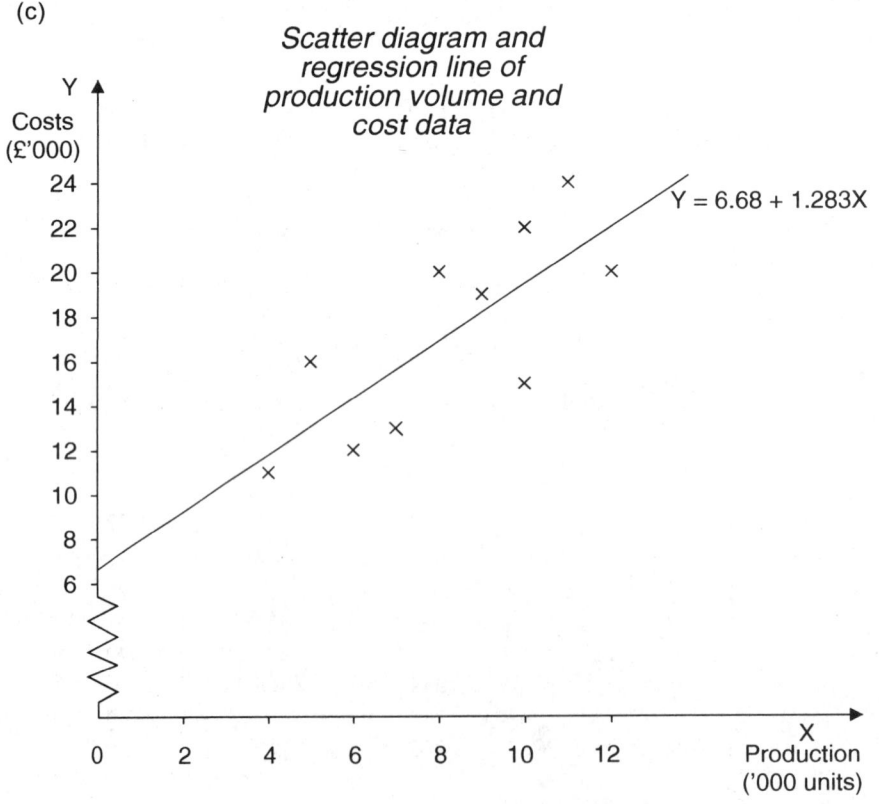

Scatter diagram and regression line of production volume and cost data

(d) If production is 10,000 units, then

$$X = 10$$
$$Y = 6.68 + 1.283 \times 10$$
$$= 19.51$$

That is, costs will be £19,510.

As we observed values of x both above and below ten, we are interpolating so we may have reasonable confidence in this forecast. It should be noted, however, that on the two previous occasions when output was 10,000 units, costs were £15,000 and £22,000 respectively. This suggests that costs can fluctuate considerably, so one should not place too much reliance on the exact prediction.

Class questions

1. SM (15 marks)   *27 mins*

SM Limited makes two products, Exe and Wye. For product costing purposes a single cost centre overhead rate of £3.40 per hour is used based on budgeted production overhead of £680,000 and 200,000 budgeted hours as shown below.

	Budgeted overhead £	Budgeted hours
Department 1	480,000	100,000
Department 2	200,000	100,000
	680,000	200,000

The number of hours required to manufacture each of the products is as follows.

	Exe	Wye
Department 1	8	4
Department 2	2	6
	10	10

There were no work in progress or finished goods stocks at the beginning of the period of operations but at the end of the period 10,000 finished units of Exe and 5,000 finished units of Wye were in stock. There was no closing work in progress.

The prime cost per unit of Exe is £30. The pricing policy is to add 50% to the production cost to cover administration, selling and distribution costs and to provide what is thought to be a reasonable profit.

REQUIREMENTS:

(a) Calculate what the effect is on the company's profit for the period, by using a single cost centre overhead rate compared with using departmental overhead rates.   **9 Marks**

(b) Show by means of a comparative statement what the price of Exe would be using:

(i)   a single cost centre overhead rate; and
(ii) departmental overhead rates.   **6 Marks**

Total Marks = 15

2. M VERSUS A

What are the most important features which distinguish marginal costing from absorption costing?

3. TOMMY RUMBLER FOODS LTD

One of the products sold by Tommy Rumbler Foods Ltd is manufactured in process NZ55.

Information for the week ended 18 August was as follows.

Process NZ55

Input: material X	18,000 kg at £1 per kilogram
material Y	12,000 kg at £2 per kilogram
Labour	1,720 hours at £3 per hour
Normal loss	5% of input
Sale price of scrap	£0.32 per kilogram
Output	27,600 kilograms

There was no opening or closing work in progress in process NZ55.

REQUIREMENT:

Prepare the process NZ55 account for the week ended 18 August.

4. **HAROLD GODWINSSON LTD** *27 mins*

Harold Godwinsson Ltd makes two products, the Viking and the Norman, and is preparing an annual budget for 19X3.

The following information is available.

STANDARD DATA PER UNIT OF PRODUCT

Direct material	*Standard price per kilo* £	*Viking* kg	*Norman* kg
Athelstan	1.50	8	4
Halfdan	4.00	5	10

Direct wages	*Standard rate per hour* £	Hours	Hours
Thames	3.50	6	12
Serfs	1.00	10	6

Fixed production overhead is absorbed on a direct labour hour basis. There is no variable overhead. Administration, selling and distribution costs are absorbed on a budgeted basis of $16^2/3\%$ of production cost.

Gross profit on production cost is budgeted at 25% of selling price.

BUDGETED DATA: SALES FOR THE YEAR

	Viking £'000	*Norman* £'000
Division		
Danelaw	1,808	1,280
Wessex	600	1,600
Mercia	900	2,600
Kent	500	800

Finished goods stock, valued at standard production cost

1 January 19X3	238	628
31 December 19X3	595	1,413

	Athelstan £'000	*Halfdan* £'000
Direct material stocks, valued at standard prices		
1 January 19X3	120	160
31 December 19X3	40	180

Fixed production overhead, per annum = £3,717,000
Direct labour hours, per annum = 1,062,000 hours

It is expected that there will be no work in progress at the beginning or end of the year.

REQUIREMENT:

Using the information given above, prepare the following.

(a) Production budget
(b) Direct materials cost budget
(c) Purchases budget
(d) Direct wages budget

15 Marks

5. **CASH BUDGET** *27 mins*

A redundant manager who received compensation of £80,000 decides to commence business on 4 January 19X8, manufacturing a product for which he knows there is a ready market. He intends to employ some of his former workers who were also made redundant but they will not all commence on 4 January. Suitable premises have been found to rent and second-hand machinery costing £60,000 has been bought out of the £80,000. This machinery has an estimated life of five years from January 19X8 and no residual value.

Other data

(a) Production will begin on 4 January and 25% of the following month's sales will be manufactured in January. Each month thereafter the production will consist of 75% of the current month's sales and 25% of the following month's sales.

(b) Estimated sales are

	Units	£
January	Nil	Nil
February	3,200	80,000
March	3,600	90,000
April	4,000	100,000
May	4,000	100,000

(c) Variable production cost per unit

	£
Direct materials	7
Direct wages	6
Variable overhead	2
	15

(d) Raw material stocks costing £10,000 have been purchased (out of the manager's £80,000) to enable production to commence and it is intended to buy, each month, 50% of the materials required for the following month's production requirements. The other 50% will be purchased in the month of production. Payment will be made 30 days after purchase.

(e) Direct workers have agreed to have their wages paid into bank accounts on the seventh working day of each month in respect of the previous month's earnings.

(f) Variable production overhead: 60% is to be paid in the month following the month it was incurred and 40% is to be paid one month later.

(g) Fixed overheads are £4,000 per month. One quarter of this is paid in the month incurred, one-half in the following month, and the remainder represents depreciation on the second-hand machinery.

(h) Amounts receivable: a 5% cash discount is allowed for payment in the current month and 20% of each month's sales qualify for this discount. 50% of each month's sales are received in the following month, 20% in the third month and 8% in the fourth month. The balance of 2% represents anticipated bad debts.

REQUIREMENT:

Prepare a cash budget for each of the first four months of 19X8, assuming that overdraft facilities will be available.

15 Marks

6. **E LTD**   *27 mins*

(a) Show by journal entries (narrations are not required) how the following transactions would be accounted for within the integrated accounting system of E Ltd which uses standard prices for materials. The price variance is isolated on purchase.

October

1   E Ltd bought and received 1,000 kilogrammes of raw material AB from D Ltd for £5,500. The standard price of material AB was £5 per kilogramme.

3   400 kilogrammes of material AB were issued to production.

6   20 kilogrammes of material AB were accidentally knocked off a shelf in the stores. The spilled contents were unusable and had no scrap value.

8   200 of the 400 kilogrammes issued to production on 3 October were found to be sub-standard and returned to the stores with a material returns note. These 200 kilogrammes were immediately returned to D Ltd. Replacements were issued to production with additional requirements against a requisition note for 300 kilogrammes.   **10 Marks**

(b) 'An integrated accounting system is superior to a non-integrated system.'

You are required to comment on the above statement, demonstrating that you understand the difference between the two systems, and explain two advantages and two limitations of an integrated system.   **5 Marks**

Total Marks = 15

7.   FORMULA

Consider the following formula.

$$K = \frac{J}{R - 2(M + R)}$$

(a) If $K = 8$, $R = 1$ and $M = \frac{1}{2}$, what is the value of J?

(b) Using the same value for K, what is:

$$K^2 + \sqrt{\frac{K}{2}}$$

8.   MIST HOOK LTD

Mist Hook Ltd has estimated that next year's sales in each of its four sales regions will be as follows.

Region	Estimated sales £
North	740,000
South	920,000
East	1,010,000
West	1,150,000

The estimates are correct to the nearest £10,000.

REQUIREMENTS:

(a) Calculate the maximum absolute error in the sales estimates.

(b) Calculate the maximum relative error.

(c) Calculate the profit, stating the limits of possible errors, if the cost of producing the goods to meet the sales demand is estimated to be as follows.

	£	Maximum relative error
Labour costs	1,200,000	± 5%
Material costs	1,400,000	± 6%
Other expenses	900,000	± 3%

9.   DISTRIBUTION OF WEALTH

The following figures relate to the distribution of wealth in Utopia in the years 19X0 and 19X9.

| Net wealth per household | | 19X0 | | 19X9 | |
Over Dollars	Not over Dollars	No. of households '000	Total wealth of households '000m dollars	No. of households '000	Total wealth of households '000m dollars
-	1,000	5,200	2.6	3,500	2.0
1,000	3,000	5,400	8.6	4,900	7.4
3,000	5,000	3,100	14.0	2,900	13.1
5,000	8,000	2,200	14.3	3,800	24.9
8,000	12,000	1,200	11.8	1,500	14.7
12,000	16,000	600	8.4	700	9.9
16,000	25,000	300	6.0	500	11.2
25,000	50,000	100	3.8	200	7.4
50,000	100,000	100	7.5	100	7.5
100,000	-	100	1.5	0	0.0
		18,300	78.5	18,100	98.1

REQUIREMENT:

Present the information in the form of a Lorenz curve and comment on the results.

---

10. **WORK SCHEDULES 15 marks**   *27 mins*

On the Monday morning of each week, a supervisor gives her 14 employees their work schedules for the next five days. She speaks to each employee separately, and goes over any points of detail which may need to be cleared up and answers any questions about the individual's schedule.

The time required to deal with each employee varies. As soon as she has finished with one employee, the supervisor is free to see the next. There are periods when employees are queuing to see her, and there are periods when she is free.

The following data are for the interview times on one Monday morning.

Employee No.	Arrival time Starts interview	Completion time Ends interview
1	9.00	9.03
2	9.03	9.07
3	9.07	9.09
4	9.11	9.16
5	9.16	9.19
6	9.22	9.24
7	9.24	9.27
8	9.27	9.28
9	9.30	9.34
10	9.34	9.36
11	9.36	9.40
12	9.42	9.45
13	9.45	9.50
14	9.50	9.52

REQUIREMENTS:

(a) Illustrate the variability of interview times by preparing a frequency distribution. Calculate the mean interview time for this distribution. **5 Marks**

(b) Calculate the standard deviation of the interview times for this distribution.
                                                                    5 Marks

(c) Each employee is given a certain number of tasks for the week. Over a year, the mean weekly number of tasks for one employee is 27, with a standard deviation of 4.2 tasks. Calculate the mean and standard deviation for the number of tasks performed by that employee over a six-week period. State any assumption you make.   **5 Marks**

Total Marks = 15

11.   NINE TERMS

27 mins

Samples of invoices from two suppliers are being compared. A computer program has been used to simplify this work. An analysis of the amounts shown on the invoices (in pounds) is given below.

Supplier	N	Mean	Median	Standard deviation	Standard error of mean
X	30	522.50	489.50	138.70	25.32
Z	30	507.60	488.00	86.90	15.87

Supplier	Minimum	Maximum	First quartile	Third quartile
X	289.00	877.00	426.00	615.00
Z	332.00	805.00	463.50	541.50

(a) Explain each of the nine statistical terms in the table so that a non-technical manager could understand.   **10 Marks**

(b) Assuming the data to be simple random samples, find 95% confidence limits for the unknown population mean of invoices from supplier X.   **5 Marks**

Total Marks = 15

12.   WILFRED AND MABEL

(a) Your rich Uncle Wilfred dies and leaves you £5,000 invested in unit trusts. Your accountant advises you that the value of your investment can be expected to grow by 8% per annum compound. Estimate the value of the investment after six years.

(b) You now decide to increase the value of the investment, and instruct your bank manager to invest £1,000 annually in unit trusts. If the first purchase is made 12 months after the death of your uncle, estimate the total value of your investment six years after his death.

(c) Your Aunt Mabel has also decided to invest some money on your behalf. She has made an initial investment (at year 0) of £2,000 and will add a further £1,500 each year until the end of year 5 (starting a year from now), when the entire investment will be handed over to you. What will it be worth at this time if interest is earned at 10% per annum?

(d) Aunt Mabel has an investment of £300,000. The investment is expected to earn interest of 10% per annum for two more years, and 8% per annum for the two years after that. She expects to withdraw £40,000 from the investment at the end of each year, beginning at the year 1. (It is now year 0.) What will be the value of her investment at year 4?

13.   EARTHWORM GARDEN CENTRE

The cash sales of the Earthworm Garden Centre for the four weeks of February 19X3 were as follows.

	Week 1 £	Week 2 £	Week 3 £	Week 4 £
Wednesday	510	500	540	550
Thursday	360	380	390	410
Friday	570	580	580	600
Saturday	800	820	830	850
Sunday	850	840	870	900

The centre is closed on Mondays and Tuesdays.

REQUIREMENT:

From these data, calculate the trend, the average 'seasonal' (daily) variations and the residuals.

Glossary
and Index

Abnormal gain The gain resulting when actual loss is less than the normal or expected loss.

Abnormal loss The loss resulting when actual loss is greater than normal or expected loss.

Absorption costing A method of costing, that, in addition to direct costs, assigns all, or a proportion of, production overhead costs to cost units by means of one or a number of *overhead absorption rates*. (CIMA *Official Terminology*)

Absorption rate A means of attributing overhead to a product or service, based for example on direct labour hours, direct labour cost or machine hours. (CIMA *Official Terminology*)

Account-classification/engineering method A simple cost estimation technique involving the classification of costs as fixed, variable or semi-variable.

Activity based costing (ABC) An approach to the costing and monitoring of activities which involves tracing resource consumption and costing final outputs. Resources are assigned to activities and activities to cost objects based on consumption estimates. The latter utilise cost drivers to attach activity costs to outputs. (CIMA *Official Terminology*)

Attributable fixed cost Cost which, although fixed within a relevant range of activity level or regarded as fixed because management has set a budgeted expenditure level, would either increase if certain extra activities were undertaken or decrease/be eliminated if the business either reduced the scale of operations or shut them down.

Basis of apportionment A physical or financial unit used to apportion costs equitably to cost centres. (CIMA *Official Terminology*)

Bin card A record of receipts, issues and balances of the quantity of an item of stock handled by a store. (CIMA *Official Terminology*)

Budget A quantitative statement, for a defined period of time, which may include planned revenues, expenses, assets, liabilities and cash flows. (CIMA *Official Terminology*)

Budget committee Ideally comprises representatives from every part of the organisation and oversees the budgeting process by coordinating and allocating responsibility for budget preparation, timetabling, providing information to assist in budget preparation and monitoring the budgeting and planning process by comparing actual and budgeted results.

Budgetary control The practice of establishing budgets which identify areas of responsibility for individual managers and of regularly comparing actual results against expected results.

Budgeted capacity Standard hours planned for the period, taking into account budgeted sales, supplies, workforce availability and efficiency expected. (CIMA *Official Terminology*)

By-product Output of some value produced incidentally in manufacturing something else (main product). (CIMA *Official Terminology*)

Cash budget A statement in which estimated future cash receipts and payments are tabulated in such a way as to show the forecast cash balance of a business at defined intervals.

Clock card A document for recording an employee's starting and finishing times.

Committed cost A future cash outflow that will be incurred regardless of whatever decision is taken now about alternative opportunities.

Continuous stocktaking The process of counting and valuing selected items at different times on a rotating basis. (CIMA *Official Terminology*)

Continuous operation costing See process costing.

Contribution Sales value less variable cost of sales. (CIMA *Official Terminology*)

Control account An account recording total costs.

Cost accounting An internal reporting system for an organisation's own management

Cost behaviour The variability of input costs with activity undertaken. (CIMA *Official Terminology*)

Cost centre A production or service location, function, activity or item of equipment for which costs are accumulated. (CIMA *Official Terminology*)

Cost department The department responsible for keeping cost accounting records.

Cost driver Any factor which causes a change in the cost of an activity. (CIMA *Official Terminology*)

Cost estimation The measurement of historical costs to predict future costs.

Cost plus pricing Method of arriving at a selling price by adding a desired profit margin to total cost.

Cost pool A group of all costs that are associated with the same activity or cost driver.

Cost unit A unit of product or service in relation to which costs are ascertained. (CIMA *Official Terminology*)

Cumulative weighted average pricing A pricing method which calculates a weighted average price for all units in stock. Issues are priced at this average cost and the balance of stock remaining would have the same unit valuation.

Delivery note A document containing details of the quantity and specifications of accompanying goods; may also be referred to as a despatch note, a carrier's note or a consignment note. (CIMA *Official Terminology*)

Departmental/functional budget See functional budget.

Differential/incremental cost The difference in total cost between alternatives; calculated to assist decision-making. (CIMA *Official Terminology*)

Differential piecework scheme Payment method offering an incentive to employers to increase their output by paying higher rates for increased levels of production.

Direct cost Expenditure which can be economically identified with and specifically measured in respect to a relevant cost object. (CIMA *Official Terminology*)

Economic order quantity (EOQ) The most economic stock replenishment order size, which minimises the sum of stock ordering costs and stockholding costs. (CIMA *Official Terminology*)

Engineering method See account-classification method.

Equivalent units Notional whole units representing uncompleted work. Used to apportion costs between work in progress and completed output, and in performance assessment. (CIMA *Official Terminology*)

First in, first out (FIFO) The principle that the oldest items or costs are the first to be used. (CIMA *Official Terminology*)

Fixed budget A budget which does not include any provision for the event that actual volumes of production may differ from those budgeted.

Fixed cost A cost which is incurred for an accounting period, and which, within certain output or turnover limits, tends to be unaffected by fluctuations in the levels of activity (output or turnover). (CIMA *Official Terminology*)

Flexible budget A budget which, by recognising different cost behaviour patterns, is designed to change as volume of activity changes. (CIMA *Official Terminology*)

Free stock The stock balance representing what is really available for future use.

Full capacity Output (expressed in standard hours) that could be achieved if sales orders, supplies and workforce were available for all installed workplaces. (CIMA *Official Terminology*)

Full costing Another name for absorption costing.

Function costing See service costing.

Functional/departmental budget A budget of income and/or expenditure applicable to a particular function.

Functional classification A group of costs that were all incurred for the same basic purpose.

Goods received note A record of goods at the point of receipt. (CIMA *Official Terminology*)

Group bonus scheme Incentive scheme related to the output performance of an entire group of workers, a department or even the whole factory.

High day-rate system Incentive scheme whereby employees are paid a high hourly wage rate in the expectation that they will work more efficiently than similar employees on a lower hourly rate.

High/low method A technique for determining the fixed and variable components of a total cost that uses actual observations of total cost at the highest and lowest levels of activity and calculates the change in both activity and cost.

Idle time The period for which a workstation is available for production but is not used due to, eg a shortage of tooling, material or operators. (CIMA *Official Terminology*)

Incremental cost See differential cost.

Indirect cost/overhead Expenditure on labour, materials or services which cannot be economically identified with a specific saleable cost unit. (CIMA *Official Terminology*)

Individual bonus scheme Incentive scheme whereby individual employees qualify for a bonus on top of their basic wage, with each person's bonus being calculated separately.

Integrated accounts A set of accounting records which provides both financial and cost accounts using a common input of data for all accounting purposes. (CIMA *Official Terminology*)

Interlocking accounts / non-integrated accounts A system in which the cost accounts are distinct from the financial accounts, the two sets of accounts being kept continuously in agreement by the use of control accounts or reconciled by other means. (CIMA *Official Terminology*)

Job A customer order or task of relatively short duration. (CIMA *Official Terminology*)

Job cost sheet A detailed record of the amount, and cost, of the labour, material and overhead charged to a specific job. (CIMA *Official Terminology*)

Job costing A form of specific order costing in which costs are attributed to individual jobs. (CIMA *Official Terminology*)

Joint products Two or more products separated in processing, each having a sufficiently high saleable value to merit recognition as a main product. (CIMA *Official Terminology*)

Just-in-time (JIT) A system whose objective is to produce or to procure products or components as they are required by a customer or for use, rather than for stock. (CIMA *Official Terminology*)

Labour turnover A measure of the number of employees leaving/being recruited in a period of time expressed as a percentage of the total labour force.

Last in, first out (LIFO) A little-used method of pricing the issue of material using the purchase price of the latest unit in stock. (CIMA *Official Terminology*)

Marginal cost The part of the cost of one unit of product or service which would be avoided if that unit were not produced, or which would increase if one extra unit were produced. (CIMA *Official Terminology*)

Marginal costing The accounting system in which variable costs are charged to cost units and fixed costs of the period are written off in full against the aggregate contribution. Its special value is in recognising cost behaviour, and hence assisting in decision-making. (CIMA *Official Terminology*)

Master budget The set of budgeted profit and loss account, budgeted balance sheet and cash budget.

Materials/stores requisition A document which authorises the issue from store of a specified quantity of materials. (CIMA *Official Terminology*)

Materials returned note A record of the return to stores of unused material. (CIMA *Official Terminology*)

Materials transfer note A record of any transfers of material between stores, cost centres, or cost units. (CIMA *Official Terminology*)

Mixed cost See semi-variable cost.

Normal loss The loss expected during the normal course of operations for unavoidable reasons.

Operation card/piecework ticket Card recording the total number of items (or pieces) produced by a pieceworker and the number of pieces rejected.

Opportunity cost The value of the benefit sacrificed when one course of action is chosen, in preference to an alternative. (CIMA *Official Terminology*)

Over-absorbed overhead See under-absorbed overhead.

Overhead See indirect cost.

Overhead absorption rate A means of attributing overhead to a product or service, based for example, on direct labour hours, direct labour cost or machine hours. (CIMA *Official Terminology*)

Period cost See fixed cost.

Periodic stocktaking A process whereby all stock items are physically counted and then valued. (CIMA *Official Terminology*)

Periodic weighted average pricing A pricing method whereby a retrospective average price is calculated for all materials issued during the period.

Perpetual inventory The recording as they occur of receipts, issues, and the resulting balances of individual items of stock in either quantity or quantity and value. (CIMA *Official Terminology*)

Personnel department The department responsible for engaging employees, their discharge, transfer, classification and method of remuneration.

Piecework scheme Remuneration method whereby workers are paid for each unit produced.

Piecework ticket See operation card.

Practical capacity Full capacity less an allowance for known unavoidable volume losses. (CIMA *Official Terminology*)

Preventative cost Cost incurred in trying to keep employees in their jobs.

Process/continuous operation costing The costing method applicable where goods or services result from a sequence of continuous or repetitive operations or processes. Costs are averaged over the units produced during the period, being initially charged to the operation or process. (CIMA *Official Terminology*)

Product cost The cost of a finished product built up from its cost elements. (CIMA *Official Terminology*)

Purchase order A written order for goods or services specifying quantities, prices, delivery dates and contract terms. (CIMA *Official Terminology*)

Purchase requisition An internal instruction to a buying office to purchase goods or services, stating their quantity and description and generating a purchase order. (CIMA *Official Terminology*)

Rectification cost Cost incurred in rectifying sub-standard output.

Relevant costs Costs appropriate to a specific management decision. (CIMA *Official Terminology*)

Remuneration method Basis on which employee is paid.

Reorder level Level at which action should be taken to replenish stocks.

Reorder quantity Quantity of stock ordered when stock reaches reorder level.

Replacement cost Cost incurred as a result of hiring new employee(s).

Replacement cost pricing A method of pricing materials issues and valuing stock at the current replacement cost of material.

Scrap Discarded material having some value. (CIMA *Official Terminology*)

Semi-fixed cost See semi-variable cost.

Semi-variable cost/semi-fixed cost/mixed cost A cost containing both fixed and variable components and which is thus partly affected by a change in the level of activity. (CIMA *Official Terminology*)

Service/function costing Cost accounting for services or functions, eg canteens, maintenance, personnel. These may be referred to as service centres, departments or functions. (CIMA *Official Terminology*)

Spreadsheet A term for a microcomputer modelling package, being loosely derived from the likeness to a spreadsheet of paper divided into rows and columns.

Standard A benchmark measurement of resource usage, set in defined conditions. Standards may also be set at attainable levels which assume efficient levels of operation, but which include allowances for normal loss, waste and machine downtime, or at ideal levels, which make no allowance for the above losses, and are only attainable under the most favourable conditions. (CIMA *Official Terminology*)

Standard cost The planned unit cost of the products, components or services produced in a period. The main uses of standard costs are in performance measurement, control, stock valuation and in the establishment of selling prices. (CIMA *Official Terminology*)

Standard cost pricing A materials issues pricing method whereby all issues are at a predetermined standard price.

Standard costing A control technique which compares standard costs and revenues with actual results to obtain variances which are used to stimulate improved performance. (CIMA *Official Terminology*)

Step cost A cost which is fixed in nature but only within certain levels of activity.

Stock control The systematic regulation of stock levels. (CIMA *Official Terminology*)

Stocktaking / physical inventory See continuous stocktaking and periodic stocktaking.

Stores requisition See materials requisition.

Sunk cost A past cost not directly relevant in decision-making. (CIMA *Official Terminology*)

Timekeeping department The department responsible for accurately recording time spent in the factory by each worker (attendance time) and time spent by each worker on each job or operation (job time).

Timesheet A record of how a person's time has been spent. Used to calculate pay, to assess the efficient use of time or to charge for work done. (CIMA *Official Terminology*)

Under- / over-absorbed overhead The difference between overhead incurred and overhead absorbed, using an estimated rate, in a given period. (CIMA *Official Terminology*)

Value added Sales value less the cost of purchased materials and services. This represents the worth of an alternation in form, location or availability of a product or service. (CIMA *Official Terminology*)

Variable cost A cost which varies with the measure of activity. (CIMA *Official Terminology*)

Variance The difference between a planned, budgeted or standard cost, and the actual cost incurred. The same comparisons may be made for revenues. (CIMA *Official Terminology*)

Variance analysis The evaluation of performance by means of variances, whose timely reporting should maximise the opportunity for managerial action. (CIMA *Official Terminology*)

Absolute error The difference between a recorded value and an absolute value .

Additive model A method of estimating seasonal variations using the absolute differences between trend and actual data.

Annual percentage rate (APR) A rate of interest, calculated annually, which is equivalent to a given rate of interest.

Annuity A series of constant cash flows received over a period of years.

Arithmetic mean An average.

Array A list of items in order of value.

Attribute A property which an object has either got or not got which cannot be measured, for example the sex of a person.

Average A representative figure that is used to give some impression of all the items in a population.

Bar chart A method of presenting data in which quantities are shown in the form of bars on a chart, the length of the bars being proportional to the quantities.

Base period The point in time given the value of 100 in an index.

Census Enumeration of an entire population.

Central limit theorem The statistical rule that a sampling distribution of sample means is normally distributed.

Chain base method A method of indexing in which changes are taken as percentages of values in the period immediately before

Chart A method of visual display of data.

Class interval A subdivision within a frequency distribution.

Cluster sampling A cheap sampling method which can be used when no satisfactory sampling frame exists. It is similar to multistage sampling in that it involves the random selection of a number of small areas from the population but every item in the small areas is then examined.

Coefficient of determination A measure of the proportion of the change in the value of one variable that can be explained by variations in the value of the other variable.

Coefficient of variation A relative measure of dispersion which compares the dispersion of two distributions.

Complementary event A term used in probability when determining the probability of an event *not* occurring.

Component bar chart A bar chart that gives the breakdown of each total into its components (by splitting each bar into sections).

Compound annual rate of interest (CAR) Another name for the APR .

Compound bar chart A bar chart in which two or more separate bars are used to present components of each total.

Compound interest Interest accrued on the principal plus the reinvested interest.

Conditional probability The probability of an event occurring, conditional on another event having occurred.

Confidence interval A range of values between which a predetermined percentage of sample statistics will fall.

Continuous variable A variable which can (theoretically) take on any value between two given values (eg height).

Correlation The degree to which change in one variable is related to change in another. The interdependence between variables.

Correlation coefficient A measure of the degree of correlation between two variables.

Cumulative frequency curve An ogive drawn as a curve.

Cumulative frequency distribution Shows the total number of times a value above or below a certain amount occurs.

Cumulative frequency polygon An ogive drawn with straight lines.

Cyclical variations Medium-term changes in result caused by circumstances which repeat in cycles.

Data Scientific term for facts, figures and measurements which are available or have been collected, usually for some form of statistical analysis.

Decile The value of each dividing point when a population is divided into ten equal groups.

Dependent variable A variable whose value is influenced by the value of another variable.

Depreciation An accounting technique whereby the cost of a capital asset is spread over a number of different accounting periods as a charge against profit in each of the periods.

Discounted cash flow A cash flow represented in present value terms.

Discrete variable A variable that can only take a finite or countable number of values within a given range.

Effective annual rate of interest The equivalent annual rate of interest when interest is calculated at intervals shorter than annually.

Error Mistake in recording/observing data, for example as a result of rounding.

Expected value A weighted average value based on probabilities.

Extrapolation Process of predicting a value outside a range of known data.

First quartile See lower quartile.

Frequency distribution The distribution of the number of times the value of a particular variable occurs.

Frequency distribution curve A frequency polygon of a grouped frequency distribution, the class intervals being very small.

Frequency polygon A chart, derived from a histogram, which makes the assumption that the frequency of occurrence of data items is not evenly spread.

Graph A form of visual display showing, by means of a straight line or curve, the relationship between two variables.

Grouped frequency distribution The distribution of the number of times values within ranges of particular variables occur.

Histogram A data presentation method for (usually) grouped data of a continuous variable. Visually similar to a bar chart but frequencies are represented by areas covered by the bar rather than by their height.

Historigram The graph of a time series.

Independent variable A variable whose value affects the value of another variable.

Index numbers Numbers which measure the magnitude of change (usually of prices or of quantities) over a period of time.

Integer A whole number.

Internal rate of return The rate of return at which the net present value of an investment is zero.

Interpolation Process of finding a value within a range of known data.

Interquartile range The difference between the lower and upper quartiles.

Laspeyre index An index using prices or quantities from the base year as weights.

Least squares method Method of finding the line of best fit.

Line of best fit Represents the best linear relationship between two variables.

Line of uniform distribution Straight line on a Lorenz curve joining the points (0%, 0%) to (100%, 100%).

Log-linear graph See semi-logarithmic graph.

Lower quartile The value of the item below which 25% of the population falls.

Mean deviation Measure of the average amount by which values in a distribution differ from the arithmetic mean.

Median The value of the middle member of an array or distribution

Mode An average, being the most frequently occurring value.

Moving averages A technique involving the calculation of consecutive averages over time to establish the trend of a time series.

Multiple bar chart See compound bar chart.

Multiplicative model A method of estimating seasonal variations whereby each actual figure is expressed as a percentage of the trend.

Multistage sampling A sampling method involving (usually) the division of a geographical area into a number of small areas, the selection of a small sample of these, the division of the small areas into even smaller areas and again a random selection of these areas. The process is repeated until a random sample of the smallest units is taken.

Mutually exclusive outcomes Outcomes such that the occurrence of one excludes the possibility of the other occurring.

Negative correlation Relationship such that low values of one variable are associated with high values of the other, and high values of one variable are associated with low values of the other.

Net present value method A capital expenditure appraisal method which works out the present value of all items of income and expenditure related to an investment at a given rate of return and then works out a net total. If the total is positive the investment is acceptable but if negative it is not.

Nominal rate of interest An annual rate of interest quoted when interest is compounded over periods of less than one year.

Normal distribution A probability distribution most often applied to continuous variables.

Ogive A graph which shows the cumulative number of items with a value less than or equal to, or alternatively greater than or equal to, a certain amount.

Paasche index An index using prices/quantities from the current year as weights.

Payoff table A decision making aid showing the results of different actions under various circumstances.

Percentage component bar chart A component bar chart in which the length of each bar is equal but the length of the sections of the bar vary according to the relative size of the components of the total.

Percentile The value of each dividing part when a population is divided into 100 equal groups.

Perfect correlation An exact linear relationship existing between two variables.

Perpetuity An annuity which lasts for ever.

Pie chart Shows pictorially the relative sizes of the component elements of a total.

Population Any finite or infinite collection of individuals, measurements etc, defined by some characteristic common to those individuals, measurements etc.

Positive correlation Relationship such that low values of one variable are associated with low values of the other, and high values of one variable are associated with high values of the other.

Present value The amount of money which must be invested now for n years at an interest rate of r% to earn a given future sum of money at the time it will be due.

Primary data Data collected specifically for a current purpose.

Power The nth power of a number is a value which when divided by that number $(n-1)$ times equals that original number.

Principal Original investment before interest added.

Probability A measure of likelihood.

Probability distribution An analysis of the proportion of times each particular value occurs in a set of items.

Proportional model See multiplicative model.

Quantiles Collective name for the dividing points used to analyse a population.

Quartile The value of each dividing point when a population is divided into four equal groups.

Quartile deviation Half the difference between the lower and upper quartiles.

Quota sampling Commonly used by market researchers, this sampling method involves stratifying the population and restricting the sample to a fixed number in each strata. The interviewer controls the choice of sample respondents.

Range Difference between highest observation and lowest observation.

Raw data Primary data which have not been processed.

Reciprocal The reciprocal of a number is one divided by that number.

Reducing balance method A depreciation method whereby the annual depreciation charge is a constant percentage of the net asset value at the beginning of the period.

Regression A method of predicting values of one variable given values for another variable.

Residual The difference between the result that would have been predicted by a trend line adjusted for the average seasonal variation and the actual result.

Root The nth root of a number is a value which, when multiplied by itself $(n-1)$ times equals that original number.

Sample A collection of information (ideally representative of the population from which it is taken).

Sampling distribution of the mean A frequency distribution of the mean of a large number of samples.

Sampling distribution of a proportion A frequency distribution of the required proportion in a large number of samples.

Sampling frame Numbered list of all items in a population.

Seasonal variations Short-term fluctuations in recorded values, due to different circumstances which affect results at different times of the year, month or whatever.

Secondary data Data which are already in existence that are used, adapted or adopted for a current purpose.

Semi-interquartile range See entry for quartile deviation.

Semi-logarithmic graph A graph in which the logarithm of the dependent variable is plotted against the value of the independent variable.

Simple interest Interest earned in equal amounts very year (or month) and which is a given proportion of the original investment.

Simple random sample Sample selected in such a way that every item in the population has an equal chance of being included.

Sinking fund An investment into which equal annual instalments are paid in order to earn interest, so that by the end of a given number of years, the investment is large enough to pay off a known commitment at that time.

Skewness The asymmetry of a frequency distribution curve.

Spearman's rank correlation coefficient A measure of the degree of correlation between two variables when the data are given in terms of order or rank rather than actual values.

Standard deviation Square root of the variance.

Standard error Standard deviation of a sampling distribution.

Stratified sampling A sampling method whereby the population is divided into strata or categories and random samples are taken from each strata.

Systematic sampling A sampling method which selects every nth item after a random start.

Table A matrix of data in rows and columns, the rows and columns having titles.

Tally marks A simple way of presenting data, each tally mark reflecting the occurrence of an event, value etc once.

Terminal value The value of an investment at the end of an investment period.

Third quartile See upper quartile.

Time series A series of figures or values recorded over time.

Trend The underlying long-term movement over time in the values of data recorded.

Upper quartile The value of the item above which 25% of the population falls.

Variable Something that can be measured.

Variance Average of the squared mean deviation for each value in a distribution.

Z chart A data presentation method which shows the value of a variable plotted against time over a period, the cumulative sum of values for that variable over the period to date and the period moving total for that variable.

ORDER FORM

For further question practice on Stage 1 *Cost Accounting and Quantitative Methods*, BPP publish a companion Practice & Revision Kit (January 1997). This contains a bank of questions, mostly drawn from past examinations, plus a full test paper. Fully worked suggested solutions are provided for all questions, including the test paper. The new edition will be published in January 1998.

You may also wish to make use of our innovative revision product, CIMA Passcards. Published in February 1997 they are designed to act as last-minute revision notes and memory prompters. A new edition will be available in February 1998.

To order your Practice & Revision Kit and Passcards ring our credit card hotline on 0181-740 2211. Alternatively, send this page to our Freepost address or fax it to us on 0181-740 1184.

To: BPP Publishing Ltd, FREEPOST, London W12 8BR   **Tel: 0181-740 2211**
                                                         Fax: 0181-740 1184

Forenames (Mr / Ms): _____

Surname: _____

Address: _____

_____

Post code: _____   Date of exam (month/year):_____

Please send me the following books:	Price £	Quantity	Total £
CIMA Stage 1 *Cost Accounting and Quantitative Methods* Kit	8.95	....	....
CIMA Stage 1 *Cost Accounting and Quantitative Methods* Passcards	4.95	....	....

Postage and packaging:

UK: £2.00 for first plus £1.00 for each extra   ....

Europe (inc ROI): £2.50 for first plus £1.00 for each extra   ....

Rest of the World: £5.00 for first plus £3.00 for each extra   ....

We guarantee delivery to all UK addresses inside 3 working days. Orders to all EU addresses should be received within 4 working days. All other orders to overseas addresses should be received within 12 working days.

I enclose a cheque for £ _____ or charge to Access/Visa/Switch

Card number | | | | | | | | | | | | | | | | | | |

Start date (Switch only) _____   **Expiry date** _____   **Issue no. (Switch only)**_____

Signature _____

Data correct at time of publication

To order any further titles in the CIMA range, please use the form overleaf.

ORDER FORM

To order your CIMA books, ring our credit card hotline on 0181-740 2211. Alternatively, send this page to our Freepost address or fax it to us on 0181-740 1184.

To: BPP Publishing Ltd, FREEPOST, London W12 8BR   **Tel: 0181-740 2211**
                                                           Fax: 0181-740 1184

Forenames (Mr / Ms): _____

Surname: _____

Address: _____

_____

Post code: _____   Date of exam (month/year):_____

Please send me the following books:

	6/97 Text £	1/97 Kit £	2/97 Passcards £	Text	Kit	Passcards	£
Stage 1							
Financial Accounting Fundamentals	17.95	8.95	4.95	....	....	....	....
Cost Accounting and Quantitative Methods	17.95	8.95	4.95	....	....	....	....
Economic Environment	17.95	8.95	4.95	....	....	....	....
Business Environment and Information Technology	17.95	8.95	4.95	....	....	....	....
Stage 2							
Financial Accounting	17.95	8.95	4.95	....	....	....	....
Operational Cost Accounting	17.95	8.95	4.95	....	....	....	....
Management Science Applications	17.95	8.95	4.95	....	....	....	....
Business and Company Law	17.95	8.95	4.95	....	....	....	....
Stage 3							
Financial Reporting	18.95	9.95	5.95	....	....	....	....
Management Accounting Applications	18.95	9.95	5.95	....	....	....	....
Organisational Management and Development	18.95	9.95	5.95	....	....	....	....
Business Taxation (FA 97 Con) (6/97 Text, 6/97 P/c, 9/97 Kit)	18.95	9.95	5.95	....	....	....	....
Business Taxation (FA 97 Lab)	18.95	9.95	5.95	....	....	....	....
Stage 4							
Strategic Financial Management	18.95	9.95	5.95	....	....	....	....
Strategic Management Accountancy and Marketing	18.95	9.95	5.95	....	....	....	....
Information Management	18.95	9.95	5.95	....	....	....	....
Management Accounting Control Systems	18.95	9.95	5.95	....	....	....	....

Postage and packaging:

UK: Texts £3.00 for first plus £2.00 for each extra ....
Kits and Passcards £2.00 for first plus £1.00 for each extra ....

Europe (inc ROI): Texts £5.00 for first plus £4.00 for each extra ....
Kits and Passcards £2.50 for first plus £1.00 for each extra ....

Rest of the World: Texts £8.00 for first plus £6.00 for each extra ....
Kits and Passcards £5.00 for first plus £3.00 for each extra ....

_____

=======

We guarantee delivery to all UK addresses inside 3 working days. Orders to all EU addresses should be received within 4 working days. All other orders to overseas addresses should be received within 12 working days.

I enclose a cheque for £ _____ **or charge to Access/Visa/Switch**

Card number | | | | | | | | | | | | | | | | | |

Start date (Switch only) _____ **Expiry date** _____ **Issue no. (Switch only)**___

Signature _____

REVIEW FORM & FREE PRIZE DRAW

All original review forms from the entire BPP range, completed with genuine comments, will be entered into one of two draws on 31 January 1998 and 31 July 1998. The names on the first four forms picked out on each occasion will be sent a cheque for £50.

Name: _____   Address: _____

_____

_____

How have you used this Text?
(Tick one box only)

☐ Home study (book only)

☐ On a course: college _____

☐ With 'correspondence' package

☐ Other _____

Why did you decide to purchase this Text?
(Tick one box only)

☐ Have used companion Kit

☐ Have used BPP Texts in the past

☐ Recommendation by friend/colleague

☐ Recommendation by a lecturer at college

☐ Saw advertising

☐ Other _____

During the past six months do you recall seeing/receiving any of the following?
(Tick as many boxes as are relevant)

☐ Our advertisement in the *CIMA Student*

☐ Our advertisement in *Management Accounting*

☐ Our advertisement in *Pass*

☐ Our brochure with a letter through the post

Which (if any) aspects of our advertising do you find useful?
(Tick as many boxes as are relevant)

☐ Prices and publication dates of new editions

☐ Information on text content

☐ Facility to order books off-the-page

☐ None of the above

Have you used the companion Practice & Revision Kit for this subject?   ☐ Yes   ☐ No

Your ratings, comments and suggestions would be appreciated on the following areas.

	Very useful	*Useful*	*Not useful*
Introductory section (Syllabus, Guidance notes, etc)	☐	☐	☐
Introductions to chapters	☐	☐	☐
Main text	☐	☐	☐
Exercises and examples	☐	☐	☐
Chapter roundups	☐	☐	☐
Quizzes	☐	☐	☐
Illustrative questions	☐	☐	☐
Content of suggested solutions	☐	☐	☐
Glossary and index	☐	☐	☐
Structure and presentation	☐	☐	☐

	Excellent	*Good*	*Adequate*	*Poor*
Overall opinion of this Text	☐	☐	☐	☐

Do you intend to continue using BPP Study Texts/Kits?   ☐ Yes   ☐ No

Please note any further comments and suggestions/errors on the reverse of this page.

Please return to: Neil Biddlecombe, BPP Publishing Ltd, FREEPOST, London, W12 8BR

REVIEW FORM & FREE PRIZE DRAW (continued)

Please note any further comments and suggestions/errors below.

FREE PRIZE DRAW RULES

1   Closing date for 31 January 1998 draw is 31 December 1997. Closing date for 31 July 1998 draw is 30 June 1998.

2   Restricted to entries with UK and Eire addresses only. BPP employees, their families and business associates are excluded.

3   No purchase necessary. Entry forms are available upon request from BPP Publishing. No more than one entry per title, per person. Draw restricted to persons aged 16 and over.

4   Winners will be notified by post and receive their cheques not later than 6 weeks after the relevant draw date. Lists of winners will be published in BPP's *focus* newsletter following the relevant draw.

5   The decision of the promoter in all matters is final and binding. No correspondence will be entered into.